SO-AKR-588

AT ISSUE

Politics in the World Arena

SIXTH EDITION

Steven L. Spiegel

University of California, Los Angeles

ST. MARTIN'S PRESS
New York

Senior editor: Don Reisman
Project management: Butler Udell Design
Cover design: Ben Santora

Library of Congress Catalog Card Number: 89-63941
Copyright © 1991 by St. Martin's Press, Inc.
All rights reserved. No part of this book may be reproduced, stored in a retrieval
system, or transmitted by any form or by any means, electronic, mechanical,
photocopying, recording, or otherwise, except as may be expressly permitted by
applicable copyright statutes or in writing by the Publisher.
Manufactured in the United States of America.
5432
fedcbi

For information, write:
St. Martin's Press, Inc.
175 Fifth Avenue
New York, NY 10010

ISBN: 0-312-03721-X

Preface

The changes that have taken place in world politics since 1988 have been so remarkable and sweeping that not a single article in this text has appeared in previous editions of *At Issue*. The articles presented here were chosen from more than 500 essays examined in an extensive investigation of the major journals and periodicals covering international affairs. In making the final selection, I gave serious consideration to the preferences and reactions of my students. Among the criteria for inclusion were readability, the variety and range of both the problems addressed and the ideological and national views represented, and the likelihood of continuing relevance in the face of probable changes in events.

This sixth edition of *At Issue*, like the previous five, seeks to present the most useful and interesting articles on the major political, economic, and social issues in current international affairs—among them, the apparent end of the cold war, the convulsions in Eastern Europe and the Soviet Union, racial and ethnic conflict, the balance of power, the possibility of world order, and the emerging economic competition in both the Atlantic and Pacific Rims. My aim is to give students a general sense of the complexities and dynamics of present-day world politics while providing background information on specific issues. Although my concern does not focus exclusively on the problems encountered by Americans in formulating and conducting foreign policy, this volume is generally oriented toward the international problems that affect the United States. The book is designed for use in American foreign policy courses, as well as courses in world politics.

In preparing this edition, I was confronted with a special problem: the unusually fast-paced changes that were occurring in world politics in late 1989 and early 1990. In one week, as the final table of contents was being prepared, President Gorbachev succeeded in gaining the end to communist monopoly of power in the Soviet Union, agreed to talks on German unity, and accepted President Bush's proposals for conventional troop withdrawals in Europe. Meanwhile, the South African government released Nelson Mandela, the most revered black leader in the country, after twenty-seven and one-half years of incarceration. Because no volume can keep up with a world in which such momentous changes are occurring in quick succession, we selected articles that we believe can be used over an extended period of time even if particular details are overtaken by events. Students should weigh the material, bearing in mind that concepts and intellectual directions count far more than individual developments. It is also useful for students to consider whether developments that took place after an article's publication refute theories presented in particular articles.

I am grateful to many people who have given me advice and assistance in preparing this sixth edition. I am especially indebted to dozens of colleagues around the country who have used the first five editions and have generously taken the time to make suggestions for improving the book. From its beginning, this volume has been a collaborative effort with my students in world politics and American foreign policy courses at UCLA. Their encouragement and vigorous participation have made the project an exciting one.

In preparing this edition, I was fortunate indeed to have the assistance of an extraordinary group of student volunteers. Many critics claim that today's undergraduate and graduate students are interested solely in career and personal gain. This has certainly not been the case with the team of enterprising young scholars who assisted me with this project. Beginning in the summer of 1989 and extending through early 1990, these students spent hours and even days searching and reexamining library shelves to fill gaps in a partially completed manuscript. They endured with me the frustration of repeatedly selecting a particularly exciting article, only to have it become unalterably outdated by a new turn of events.

David Pervin coordinated the whirl of student researchers, stoically and efficiently seeking to weave some order out of the chaos of twenty people all working on their own schedules and with specific topics or journals. He conducted part or all of our weekly meetings when I was unable to attend. Naomi Renek assisted him, particularly assuming responsibility for keeping track of who was reading which articles. She also maintained contact with all journals regarding permissions to reprint articles. She pursued these thankless tasks with devotion and good cheer.

At the end of the summer, when the group was seemingly over-whelmed by the pressures generated by the need to reorganize the volume in the light of recent events, Gitty A. Cannon and David A. Plotkin undertook the task of preparing a sample table of contents, which guided our activity for the next several months. David also served as summer coordinator. Jacqueline Fernandez was especially helpful in assisting in the preparation of introductions to particular sections. I am grateful for her willingness to devote extra time to this project, especially as an active volunteer after her graduation. In addition, Gitty A. Cannon, Jill Cannon, William Kysella, James Paskell, and Sumi Sousa all worked from beginning to end, reviewing articles, attending meetings, and offering opinions. I am indebted to them for their loyalty, their steadfastness, and their important contributions to the completed volume. Kira Burt, Nicole Goldner, Matthew Haskins, Bryan King, Scott B. Lasensky, Benjamin J. Lloyd, Philip H. Lo, Shirin Lowfigh, Melisa McCoy, Michael Minden, Thomas Grant Neusom, Harriet Newman, Val D. Philips, Kevin M. Razban, Samira Sadeghi, John Siegler, Jr., Kathleen Urbanic, Kelly Wachowicz, Heather White, James Wong, and Jinah Yun all worked for shorter periods, and their contributions were significant and appreciated. Gitty A. Cannon, Mathew Haskins, Michael J. Law-rence, James Paskell, Sumi Sousa, and Heather White all assumed espe-cially heavy burdens along the way, particularly when we had to make difficult choices among competing articles.

As always, my wife Fredi provided invaluable consultation and inspi-ration. When the multitude of articles seemed beyond comprehension, she offered the encouragement that made it possible to conclude the task in an expeditious and orderly manner. I again wish to thank Mira, Nina, and Avi for keeping out of the piles of papers and heaps of magazines that cluttered the house while this edition was being pre-pared.

I would also like to thank the following reviewers, who supplied me with useful information to help guide my revisions: Lewis Brownstein, State University of New York, College at New Paltz; Michael Doyle, Princeton University; Jack Fruchtman, Jr., Towson State University; Kevin J. Latham, U.S. Naval Academy; Charles G. MacDonald, Florida International University; Thomas W. Mullen, Dalton College; and Robert Weiner, University of Massachusetts/Boston.

The subjects discussed in this volume represent some of the most important questions facing the world's leaders today, and many of the articles present grim alternatives and disturbing analyses. Yet the major breakthroughs of the recent past have led to widespread satisfaction in the West that the democratic victory in the cold war enhances prospects for peace, security, and democracy. Even in the likely event that new tensions and issues will emerge to replace problems that have been solved, these developments should give us reason for solace and optimism. Meanwhile, I trust this volume will place the confusing kaleidoscope of recent events in perspective. Above all, I hope that the reader's experience with this book will help create a study of international politics which is both stimulating and intellectually rewarding.

Steven L. Spiegel

Contents

Prologue   1

Part One   THE BURDEN OF THE STRONG   5

The Global Balance of Power: Can the Great Powers
Rule the World?   11

1   **The Springtime of Nations** *Michael Howard*   11
2   **After the Cold War** *George F. Kennan*   25
3   **Beyond the Cold War** *Jeane J. Kirkpatrick*   35
4   **The Erosion of the Superpowers: The Military
    Consequences of Economic Distress** *Walter Goldstein*   48

Arms: The Crisis Imposed by Technology   62

5   **Security, Arms, and Arms Control** *Raymond L. Garthoff*   62
6   **Arms Control after the Cold War** *Joseph S. Nye, Jr.*   73
7   **The End of Arms Control** *Charles Krauthammer*   92

Competitors and Allies: Pas de Deux   102

The Atlantic Rim

8   **Redefining Europe and the Atlantic Link** *Robert D.
    Hormats*   102
9   **America's Economic Dependence** *Felix Rohatyn*   119

The Pacific Rim

10 International Politics in the Pacific Rim Area *Robert Gilpin* 130
11 Japan: Their Behavior, Our Policy *Chalmers Johnson* 143
12 America's High-Tech Decline *Charles H. Ferguson* 157
13 China after Tiananmen: The Failure of American Policy
    Marie Gottschalk 173

Part Two   THE CONFLICT OF PEOPLES 189

Imperialism and Intervention: Dynamism of the Strong 195

14 What Should We Do in the World? *Stanley Hoffmann* 195
15 Coping with the '90s *Charles William Maynes* 212

Religious and Ethnic Nationalism 227

16 Post-Communist Nationalism *Zbigniew Brzezinski* 227
17 The Coming of Africa's Second Independence *Colin
    Legum* 240

Haves and Have-Nots: Upheaval between North and South 254

18 South–North Dangers *Ivan L. Head* 254
19 Slaying the Drug Hydra *Scott B. MacDonald* 268
20 The Political Economy of the Andean Cocaine Industry
    Rensselaer W. Lee III 272
21 Robbin' Hoods: How the Big Banks Spell Debt Relief
    Jeffrey Sachs 293

Revolution: The Weak Respond 300

22 Eastern Europe: The Year of Truth *Timothy Garton Ash* 300
23 Can South Africa Change? *George M. Fredrickson* 317
24 The Impact of the Intifada *Bishara A. Bahbah* 337
25 The Perils of a Palestinian State *Steven L. Spiegel* 343
26 Terrorism: A Balance Sheet *Shireen T. Hunter* 350

Part Three   THE CRISIS OF INSTITUTIONS 367

The Crisis of International Institutions 371

27 Exploiting the Recent Revival of the United Nations
    Frederick Lister 371

28 Influence, Marginality, and Centrality in the
    International Legal System *Louis Henkin*   396

The Crisis of National Institutions   412

29 After the Cold War *Richard J. Barnet*   412
30 The End of America's Postwar Ethos *Michael Vlahos*   434
31 Linking Gorbachev's Domestic and Foreign Policy
    Agendas *George W. Breslauer*   449
32 To the Stalin Mausoleum *Z*   466

Part Four   THE PROBLEMS OF A CHANGING WORLD:
            WILL THE WORLD AS WE KNOW IT SURVIVE?   485

The Environment   487

33 Redefining Security *Jessica Tuchman Mathews*   487

The Economy   501

34 The Coming Global Boom *Charles R. Morris*   501

Contributors   516

Prologue

The purpose of this volume is threefold: to gain an improved understanding of the dynamics of current world politics; to identify the crucial
developments in international politics with which American foreign policy must deal; and to explore the major issues that will require careful
and painful decisions on the part of policymakers in the years ahead.
The readings in *At Issue* are designed to provide material for discussion
and debate in the hope that they might contribute to a new American
approach toward the rest of the world. Such an approach should be
devoted less to ideological abstractions and simple contrasts between
weakness and strength or between internationalism and isolationism.
Instead, it should be inclined more toward a recognition and respect of
the distinct cultures in which the peoples of the world exist.

The book is divided into four parts. The first part, "The Burden of the
Strong," concentrates on the relations between the major powers, especially in light of the declining cold war and the revolutions in Eastern
Europe. We assess the prospects for future relations between the United
States and the Soviet Union; the effect of China and its domestic politics
on the global balance of power; the role of the Western European states
and Japan as allies and as economic competitors of the United States;
and the future of great-power relations within Europe and Asia. We also
consider the role of armaments—especially nuclear weapons—in the
balance of power between the United States and the Soviet Union and
between less powerful nations that are members of the international
system. We explore the prospects for arms control and the implications
of the spread of chemical, nuclear, and biological weapons and long-
range ballistic missiles—especially to many Third World countries.

The second part, "The Conflict of Peoples," examines the nature and
causes of current conflicts between great and small nations and between
the satisfied and dissatisfied. We analyze current great-power intervention policies. Although we stress the role of religious and ethnic differences in conflict, we also consider the effects of economic gaps between
rich and poor nations and of conflicting great-power aims. We also
examine the turmoil in the Third World, which has led to a growing
crisis between North and South and to a diverse set of responses to the
affluent West by parties that feel disadvantaged. These responses range
from revolution, to reliance on the drug trade, to the strategy of terror-

1

ism, to economic challenges raised by countries that are dependent on the export of a single commodity.

The third party, "The Crisis of Institutions," deals with the problems that plague political institutions on all levels of global society. Here we consider the role of the United Nations and the present and future significance of international law in world politics. Will the United Nations continue to revive and assume an effective place in an increasingly complex international environment? If conflict between the great powers decreases, will the function of international law be enhanced? Or will the antagonism of many Third World countries to western concepts of universal procedures and norms increase? The third part also focuses on the nation-state, paying special attention to the United States and the Soviet Union. We explore conflicting philosophies about the content of foreign policy and about organizational constraints and bureaucratic procedures that some claim cause governments to act in seemingly irrational ways.

Finally, in the fourth part, "The Problems of a Changing World: Will the World as We Know It Survive?" we focus on developments in world economic patterns, population growth, the food supply, the greenhouse effect, the environment, and new areas of high technology. We examine the possible effects of these issues on rich and poor nations alike. New technologies have enabled people of different cultures to come into closer contact through faster means of travel and communications, with both constructive and destructive results. The transistor radio has become a means of whipping the masses into frenzied hatred, the jet airplane an instrument of destruction and a tool of terrorists, the oil well a symbol of exploitation and blackmail, and the computer a source of international competition and conflict. Thus, we want to ask ourselves whether interdependence will become a source of enhanced cooperation in world politics or whether increased contacts between peoples will facilitate hostilities.

Some have argued that the end of the cold war means the end of history as we know it, with the ultimate triumph of liberal democracy. Others see only the dawning of a new era—replete with continual conflicts and dissension. It is ironic indeed that at a time when the superpowers have reached a nuclear standoff and when accommodation is prevalent, the number of people killed in local upheavals has increased at an accelerating rate. The atomic bombs dropped on Hiroshima and Nagasaki killed or wounded approximately 220,000 Japanese; but as many as 3 million people were killed in the 1971 war for independence in Bangladesh, more than 2 million died in the unsuccessful effort to establish an independent state in Biafra, 4 to 5 million people perished in Indochina during the prolonged and continuing civil strife in that area, and the Iran–Iraq war in the 1980s produced over a million casualties. On the one hand, the nuclear balance of terror and growing economic and social pressures have made the great powers cautious. On the other hand, weaker states and groups have improved their capacity to engage in traditional but increasingly destructive types of conflict.

It is evident that future challenges to American foreign policy will be profound, and debates over how to deal with the problems raised by recent changes in world politics will become more heated. There are many who believe that the emergence of a united Germany, the weakening of the USSR, and the revolutions in Eastern Europe are central to American foreign policy concerns. How far should we go in aiding Mr. Gorbachev, and how can we help Europe adjust to a new era in which Germany plays a stronger role and Eastern Europe at last has the option of being free? Others believe that the locus of power in world politics is already moving to Asia: the so-called Pacific Rim, with its huge population and its advances in high technology will be the center of world politics in the twenty-first century, and the Europeans and Americans will be forced to adjust accordingly. Yet others believe that the destruction of the environment, with its threat to the continuation of life as we know it, necessitates a reevaluation of the very meaning of national security. What better time to develop a truly planetary definition of global politics than at the transition point into the post–cold war era? Still others believe that the relations between the industrial and Third World states, between the "haves" and "have nots," are critical to world politics.

With regard to all these issues, many ongoing debates are likely to emerge in new form as the cold war ends. There are debates in the United States about how to handle producer–consumer relations of the type epitomized by OPEC and the oil-importing nations. There are divergent perspectives about the future role of high technology and about whether America should lean toward protectionism or toward free trade policies. There are disputes about the proper approach to the Soviet Union on such issues as arms control and technical and economic assistance to a reformist Soviet government, uncertainty over the future of nuclear weapons, arguments about future policy directions in Western Europe, deep and bitter conflicts over the strategic and moral factors at the heart of alternatives in Central America and South Africa, and debates about proper policy approaches toward the Middle East on such issues as Islamic fundamentalism and the Palestinian question. There are those who would redefine the needs of national security and transfer expenditures from defense to the domestic arena, whereas at the same time others believe that defense spending must be maintained to assure the Soviet threat is permanently thwarted. There are those who believe that a viable future can emerge only through increasing interdependence, whereas others assert that only military deterrence can provide the basic structure for a balance of world power. As international politics becomes increasingly complex and unpredictable, the diversity of methods for dealing with specific problems increases. The observer is often perplexed by the resulting multitude of analyses and prescribed solutions.

In this edition we focus on these debates in an effort to comprehend both the dilemmas raised by current international conditions in their transitory state and the range of solutions that has been offered to deal with them. No single explanation or answer can be all-encompassing. Yet an examination of particular points of view can begin to lead us toward unraveling the political complexities of the modern world and provide a guide for judging the successes and failures of any government that may be in power as we move toward a new world politics in the twenty-first century.

PART ONE

The Burden of the Strong

One of the great transformations in world politics in recent decades occurred in the late 1980s, a transformation so profound that its implications are as yet unclear. In the Soviet Union the monopoly of power for the Communist party has ended, and a multiparty system is potentially evolving. At the same time, regional, ethnic, and political conflicts in the USSR, revolutions in every East European country except Albania, and emerging German unity confirm that we are truly entering a new period of world history. In the wake of world-changing events and the accompanying euphoria, it is difficult to recall that as recently as 1983, in a speech to the National Association of Evangelicals in Orlando, Florida, President Reagan declared (clearly referring to the Soviet Union):

> Let us pray for the salvation of all those who live in that totalitarian darkness—pray they will discover the joy of knowing God. But until they do, let us be aware that while they preach the supremacy of the state, declare its omnipotence over individual man and predict its eventual domination of all peoples on the Earth—they are the focus of evil in the modern world.

In our opening section on the role of the great powers, we present four essays that attempt to assess the significance of these dramatic changes in world politics. The first, "The Springtime of Nations" by Michael Howard, focuses on the significance of the revolutions of 1989 in Eastern Europe. Although he does not ignore the tragic massacre of Chinese students in Tiananmen Square, which ended China's democratic movement at least temporarily, Howard concentrates on the truly electrifying events in Europe in 1989, a year that history books will make famous, and the developments that may well change a generation's perceptions about world politics.

With these events placed in perspective by Michael Howard, we turn to "After the Cold War" by George F. Kennan. Kennan, of course, is the famous American diplomat, historian, and analyst who, in the late 1940s, conceived the containment doctrine, a plan to limit the expansion of Soviet power. In his broad overview of relations between the United States and the Soviet Union, Kennan—writing at the outset of the Bush administration—attempts to place changes in the USSR in historical context and to analyze how Americans should adjust to these remarkable developments.

Our third author, Jeane J. Kirkpatrick, writes from a more conservative perspective in "Beyond the Cold War." Although she and Kennan agree that the cold war is ending, they interpret the situation differently. To Kennan, America and the Soviet Union shared responsibility for the evolution of the Soviet-American post–World War II conflict, as we know it. To Kirkpatrick, however, Gorbachev is attempting to change the world because the Soviets caused the conflict in the first place. Kirkpatrick is also less willing than Kennan to accept the complete conclusion of the cold war. She argues that the conflict "will be over when the Soviet Union removes its troops from all East European countries that request it to do so (as the United States once removed forces and abandoned bases in France)." Yet by acknowledging the potential of these developments, Kirkpatrick begins to anticipate the day when American burdens in Europe may be diminished.

A persistent question in postwar world politics, as reflected in the subtitle of this section, is: Can the Great Powers Rule the World? Walter Goldstein addresses this question directly in "The Erosion of the Superpowers: The Military Consequences of Economic Distress." Both superpowers have suffered heavy burdens in their worldwide responsibilities throughout the post–1945 period. The economic consequences of these burdens have caught up with the United States and, more visibly, with the Soviet Union. Goldstein deals with these implications in an enlightening essay comparing the serious problems that both countries face.

We move next to examining the implications of the profound changes in Soviet-American relations for the balance of nuclear power and the process of arms control. Raymond L. Garthoff in "Security, Arms, and Arms Control" discusses the concept of deterrence, an idea that has dominated the balance of terror in the nuclear era, and reviews the history of arms control efforts. In the new period toward which we are moving, we can expect an agreement to reduce the number of nuclear weapons as well as further progress regarding troop reductions in Europe. Garthoff, like Kennan, believes that the new Soviet thinking on these issues opens new opportunities for conflict amelioration and even for cooperation.

The developments Garthoff discusses lead us to the broader panorama of arms control in "Arms Control after the Cold War," an article by Joseph S. Nye, Jr. Nye deals with a full palette of issues that are already emerging on a long list of state concerns. In addition to the question of arms reduction and control in the superpower nuclear arsenals, Nye covers other matters such as the control of nuclear proliferation, the problems of chemical and biological weapons, and the emerging concerns over the spread of ballistic missile technology around the world. The Iran–Iraq War of the 1980s graphically demonstrated that many of these nonnuclear weapons constitute clear and present dangers, because they are far more likely to be used than nuclear arms. Therefore, if Soviet and American cooperation is to increase, these types of issues must be addressed. Nye provides a guide to anyone concerned about these troubling problems.

In "The End of Arms Control," Charles Krauthammer presents a more conservative and unusual analysis. Krauthammer believes that arms control actually increases the risk of nuclear war. Because the public sees arms control as progress toward reducing the threat of war, leaders are encouraged to move in this direction. In contrast to popular perceptions, Krauthammer believes that clashing interests and ideology are the real bases of war; we should therefore, he states, place greater importance on reducing political frictions rather than the number of missiles. This controversial position should allow much room for discussion and reexamination in the light of ongoing events.

Next we examine relations among all the great powers, with an emphasis on economic factors. We subdivided the section on competitors and allies to deal separately with the Atlantic and Pacific Rims, a division appropriate to emerging world conditions. In the Atlantic Rim section, we present two articles that deal with America's economic problems and with developing changes in Europe.

First, Robert D. Hormats, in "Redefining Europe and the Atlantic Link," addresses the implications of the projected economic unity of the European Economic Community, in which all internal barriers to "the movement of goods, capital, people and services" will be ended by 1992. This dramatic undertaking encompasses twelve countries: the United Kingdom, Ireland, France, the Federal Republic of Germany, Italy, Belgium, the Netherlands, Luxembourg, Denmark, Greece, Spain, and Portugal. Although political unity is not part of the plan, the European Community is bound to have a greater voice in world politics, especially with the imminence of German unification. Hormats deals with the wide implications of this development for the Europeans themselves and their relations with the United States, the Soviet Union, and Eastern Europe. This comprehensive article discusses the political, economic, and military changes Europe will undergo in the 1990s.

Second, "America's Economic Dependence," by Felix Rohatyn, deals with the United States' economic deficiencies: the trade imbalance, the awesome national debt, and the heavy foreign investment in the United States. Rohatyn also addresses the problems of Third World debt and declining American competitiveness vis-à-vis both Japan and Europe. For this author, any solutions to America's current economic problems must begin with changes in the domestic economy.

From this analysis of the European arena, we turn to Robert Gilpin's thorough examination, "International Politics in the Pacific Rim Area." Gilpin points out that in the history of international relations, economic, technological, and demographic developments have caused the center of economic and political activities to shift from one location to another. To Gilpin, all the changes that are occurring in world politics enhance the importance of the Pacific Rim. Most of these countries lack the burden of immense military establishments and can therefore devote more funds to research and development and to the technical application of scientific discoveries. Moreover, increasing economic globalization favors many Pacific Rim countries because they have developed strategies designed to take advantage of expanding interdependence. Whether the growing importance of Pacific Rim countries is largely economic, or will also assume military dimensions, will constitute one of the great questions of the next era of world politics.

In the wake of Gilpin's far-reaching analysis, we move to explore the concept of East Asian politics and the nature of emerging competition in this area. In "Japan: Their Behavior, Our Policy," Chalmers Johnson is critical of both Japan's policies and America's reaction to them. Johnson first reviews the changes in world politics which have accelerated Japan's importance in the world political system. He then explains the issues Japan faces, including its potential political role as a leader in Asia. In his conclusion, he evaluates the unstable relationship between Japan and the United States. Johnson believes that the United States must "recognize that Japan has replaced the USSR as America's most important foreign policy problem," and he calls on Americans to take the issue seriously. Without leadership in both Tokyo and Washington, he predicts continued tensions.

If this warning is not sufficient to engage the reader, then I suggest he or she move on to "America's High-Tech Decline" by Charles H. Ferguson. Ferguson reiterates the message of several articles in this section that Japan is eclipsing the United States economically and technologically. Although Japan is a political and military ally, it is also an economic adversary. Ferguson calls on the United States to attempt internal reforms in order to manage the emerging technological competition with Japan. In pulsating tones he invokes a series of steps that he believes the United States must take to salvage its position in world affairs. These steps have important implications for both American political influence and living standards at home.

From the relationship between the United States and Japan, we move to the relationship with China, where Marie Gottschalk, in "China after Tiananmen: The Failure of American Policy," is highly critical of America's dealings with the Chinese. She believes that since the 1972 renewal of close contacts between Beijing and Washington, the United States has been hesitant and unwilling to challenge China's human rights violations for fear of moving that country closer to the Soviet Union. Gottschalk calls for a reevaluation of this approach, which she believes to be obsolete and misguided. Whether or not we agree with Gottschalk's analysis, it is difficult to ignore the depth and complexity of her analysis regarding both relations among East Asian states and China's foreign policy.

THE GLOBAL BALANCE OF POWER: CAN THE GREAT POWERS RULE THE WORLD?

1

The Springtime of Nations

MICHAEL HOWARD

I

In 1989, while the nations of Western Europe celebrated the bicentenary of the French Revolution, the nations of Eastern Europe reenacted it.

The similarities were striking. In every major country east of the Iron Curtain, *anciens régimes* that had lost all ideological credibility had been brought by corrupt and incompetent leadership to the point of economic collapse. As in eighteenth-century France, economic crisis precipitated mass popular discontent, led by intellectuals who had long been harassed by a censorship severe enough to infuriate but not sufficiently brutal to crush them. In some cases—the Soviet Union and Poland—the governments themselves took the initiative (as had the ministers of Louis XVI of France in summoning the Estates General) by opening consultations with opposition elements they had long tried to ignore or destroy. In others—East Germany, Czechoslovakia, Bulgaria and Romania—the regimes simply crumbled (like the French monarchy between 1789 and 1791) before repeated and implacable mass demonstrations.

The process reached a climax on the afternoon of November 9, 1989, when the Berlin Wall, a symbol of oppression at least as gruesome as the

Reprinted by permission of *Foreign Affairs, America and the World, 1990.* Copyright 1990 by the Council on Foreign Relations, Inc.

Note: It is a violation of the law to reproduce this selection by any means whatsoever without the written permission of the copyright holder.

Bastille, was pierced by crowds who poured into West Berlin, dancing, singing and weeping for joy. Unlike the events of 1789 all this happened, Romania alone excepted, without the loss of a single life.

We can well understand the feelings of William Wordsworth when he wrote:

> Bliss was it in that dawn to be alive
> But to be young was very Heaven!

The parellel is not altogether a comfortable one. Wordsworth lived to regret his youthful enthusiasm. The fall of the Bastille in 1789 was followed by events so terrible that many Frenchmen still wonder whether the revolution deserves to be celebrated at all.

II

There are other analogies yet more disquieting. The French Revolution did not set off an immediate chain reaction throughout Europe, unlike the revolutions of 1848 when, fired by the example of Paris, crowds in Brussels, Vienna, Budapest, Milan and Warsaw poured onto the streets. Barricades were erected, governments collapsed like ninepins, leaving a power vacuum into which moved eloquent but inexperienced leaders, faced with the task of translating into reality the ideals they had been preaching in opposition. They fumbled and fought among themselves. Liberals and radicals found they had as little in common as either had with the old order. The forces of reaction, scotched but not killed, bided their time and struck back. By the end of 1849 order had been restored, the revolutionary leaders were in exile, and tougher if more pragmatic gendarmes had taken charge of the European continent. That Springtime of Nations was over almost before it had begun.

Argument by analogy is an activity that professional historians properly mistrust. For one thing, the events we recall occurred in a context so richly different from our own that we are liable to misunderstand their significance. For another, the memory of those past events is itself a historical determinant. The men and women of 1848 would not have acted as they did had they not remembered the course taken by events in Paris after 1789. Lenin might not have acted as he did in 1917 had he not drawn from the events of both 1789 and 1848 the idea of establishing a "dictatorship of the proletariat" before free elections could bring moderates to power. President Mikhail Gorbachev does not need the expertise of the West to remind him of the fate of the tsar liberator, Alexander II of Russia.

The lesson of 1789 and 1848 is not that events repeat themselves in some Thucydidean fashion. It is that during long periods of peace such as those which Europe enjoyed from 1763 to 1789, 1815 to 1848 and 1945 to 1989, economic and social development engenders a political dynamic of its own. If governments are not responsive to that force, they will sooner or later be swept away. Paradoxically, the man who discerned and explained this process most clearly was Karl Marx himself—a great European philosopher whose works appear to have been as little studied in the Soviet Union as they are in the United States.

In the Soviet Union since 1945 that process was slow but nonetheless inexorable. After a generation of wars and civil wars, the iron framework imposed on the Soviet peoples by Stalin and maintained in its essentials by his successors at least provided a measure of stability and order that made possible the gradual modernization of Soviet society. For Soviet citizens who remembered the early years of the twentieth century, the system was no worse than what had gone before, and there were good indicators in the economy of the 1950s that life was improving. The Western record of boom and slump, unemployment and pockets of Fascism certainly looked increasingly unattractive. Khrushchev cannot have been alone among his fellow-countrymen with his confident prediction to the West, "We will bury you."

By the 1970s, however, it was clear that the Soviets could do nothing of the kind. The socialist system was not, after all, delivering on its promise of rewards in this world—a promise that distinguished it from earlier ideologies whose consolation for human misery in this life was the promise of felicity in the next. Agreed, the early paradise had to be deferred. The Soviet peoples had to accept deprivation so that future generations could reap the rewards of their labor. But the Soviet cohorts growing up in the 1970s and 1980s *were* the future generation. They had no collective memory of tsarist oppression, invasion or civil wars. Increasingly literate, intelligent, urbanized, and bourgeois in their inclinations if not in their occupations, they wanted their inheritance now. The aging Soviet leaders relapsed into immobilism and corruption like the cardinals of a decadent church. Only the presence of a few enthusiastic acolytes in the Third World and the continuing military confrontation with the West continued to provide the leadership and its ideology with a raison d'être.

Gorbachev was thus no fortuitous *deus ex machina*. He was exceptional in his talents rather than in his perceptions; talents first appreciated by Yuri Andropov, who as chief of the KGB had recognized the worsening predicament of his country, and who, before his premature death, managed to maneuver Gorbachev into the line of succession. Not even Andropov, however, could have foreseen the skill with which Gorbachev would consolidate and maintain his internal authority and the boldness with which he would unleash the forces of revolutionary change. For five years the world watched astounded as, like an expert skier, Gorbachev used the very steepness of the slopes down which he hurled himself to maintain his balance and momentum. It watched also with apprehension, fearful that at any moment he would come crashing to the ground.

Last year revealed the huge dimensions of the task confronting Gorbachev. The Soviet economic situation worsened. The coal miners, on whose cooperation economic recovery heavily depended, went on strike. Nationalist and ethnic disorders broke out in Georgia, Azerbaijan, Armenia and Uzbekistan. The three Baltic republics mounted demonstrations demanding independence that were impressive for their dignity and restraint. They provoked Gorbachev's ire, but there was no backlash of repression.

The Soviet leader was calm in his handling of the March elections to the Congress of People's Deputies, when Communist Party candidates were defeated even in cases when no alternative candidates offered themselves. Meetings of the congress were televised live, and the scathing criticisms of the regime voiced by the new deputies only strengthened Gorbachev's hand in disposing of the old guard. Predictably he found himself attacked from both sides, radicals who thought he was doing too little and conservatives who thought he was doing too much. When in May he was elected president with greatly enhanced powers by a suspiciously large majority of 95.6 percent, and when a few months later he summoned his chief newspaper critics and berated them for an hour and a half, right-wing critics in the West were able to argue that nothing had really changed; the old authoritarianism was there under a new guise. Anyhow, they gloated, he was clearly bound to fail.

III

The people who watched Gorbachev's discomfiture with the greatest satisfaction, however, were the leaders of the People's Republic of China. They had realized, almost two decades earlier than had the Soviets, that the modernization promised by Marxism would never be achieved without some concessions to a market economy and massive borrowing of capital and technology from abroad. They realized also that such a process could be immensely disruptive unless it was controlled with an iron hand from above. Once an entrepreneurial society had developed, they explained to sympathetic Western visitors, political reform would automatically follow; to introduce it prematurely would be to place their whole future in hazard. The troubles unleashed by Gorbachev's policies in the Soviet Union seemed to indicate that the Chinese leaders were correct.

But the People's Republic could no longer be so insulated from the world that modernization could occur under ideal laboratory conditions. Scores of thousands of young Chinese had now visited the West to be trained in the skills needed for China's development, and they now knew what they were missing. For them and their generation, events in the Soviet Union provided a model to be followed rather than an example to be shunned. An announcement by Chinese Premier Li Peng on April 3, 1989, that his government would not initiate any Soviet-style reforms, followed by the death of pro-reform leader Hu Yaobang on April 15, sparked off student demonstrations, which by the end of the month had coalesced into a huge and continuous mass meeting in Tiananmen Square in the center of Beijing.

Perhaps more skillful leadership on both sides, combined with more sophisticated riot-control techniques, might have avoided the bloodshed that followed on the night of June 3–4, when army tanks moved in and crushed the protesters under the eyes of the world's television cameras. Perhaps the hard-liners in the Chinese leadership were determined anyhow to use the occasion as they did, simultaneously to destroy the protest movement nationwide and to purge the party of its more moderate members under Chairman Zhao Ziyang. In any case, an example was set that horrified the world.

The repression, in the short run at least, proved effective. There did not yet exist in China, as in the communist countries farther west, a Marxist-type "revolutionary situation" in which a developed middle class and a powerful industrial proletariat had been fused by their frustration into a serious political force capable of finishing what the students had begun. Like the Europeans in 1848, the Chinese masses in a still overwhelmingly agrarian society remained quiescent and the army loyal. But like the governments of 1848, the Chinese authorities have gained only a breathing space. The more successfully they press on with modernization, the more their power will be eroded. Unless they imitate Gorbachev's courage in embracing the future, the Chinese leaders will be faced, sooner or later, with other Tiananmen Squares.

The June 1989 massacre of Chinese students and their supporters, however, showed the East European leaders of communist regimes that if they wanted to stifle protests in their own countries, that kind of bloodshed was the price they would have to pay. Gorbachev made it clear that he would not do it for them, and only Romania's despot, Nicolae Ceauşescu, had the nerve to do it on his own—at the cost of his and his wife's lives and the slaughter of thousands of his countrymen. In any case, both Hungary and Poland had already passed the point of no return. In Budapest an already liberalized Communist Party bought peace by granting freedom of political association and allowing multiparty elections; the new leaders stopped calling themselves "communists" and dropped the title "Workers' Republic" from the name of the state. More important, Hungary opened its frontier with Austria, permitting a stream of emigration to the West from East Germany that by the autumn had turned into a flood.

In Poland Solidarity, a unique body that was more than a trade union but less than an organized political party, had already established an unassailable position, with the support of the Catholic Church, as the legitimate voice of the Polish people. In January Solidarity was again legalized by the Polish communist regime; in February it was brought into formal consultation; in April it approved a new representative constitution; in June it swept the board in free elections; and in August Solidarity became the senior partner in a coalition government headed by its own man, Tadeusz Mazowiecki. Poland's communist leaders were as reluctant to concede power to the independent labor union as Solidarity was to take it. When Mazowiecki assumed office he confronted an economic nightmare. But Gorbachev forced through a shotgun marriage, no doubt calculating quite correctly that once Solidarity was in power the burden of sustaining Poland's economy would be shifted from the shoulders of the Soviet Union to those of the sympathetic and wealthy West.

Even the most optimistic Western observers did not expect the hard-line communist states of Czechoslovakia and East Germany to fall so easily. For one thing their economies were comparatively successful; their standard of living was respectable even by Western standards. For another, Czechoslovakia and East Germany constituted the frontier provinces of the communist world; it was assumed that military considerations alone would prevent the Soviet Union from allowing them the freedom of action possible for their more sheltered neighbors farther east.

But in the autumn the regimes of East Germany and Czechoslovakia collapsed as well. In August tens of thousands of East Germans went on holiday in Hungary and did not come back. Passing through the newly opened Austro-Hungarian border, or directly from Czechoslovakia, the East Germans traveled to West Germany where they knew they could obtain automatic rights of citizenship. By November their number was approaching 200,000, an emigration on the scale that had forced the East German government 28 years earlier to erect the Berlin Wall.

The hemorrhage began, as it had then, to drain the East German economy. In October, mass demonstrations in Leipzig and East Berlin forced the resignation of Erich Honecker and his government. Honecker's successor, Egon Krenz, tried to control the situation by dismantling the Berlin Wall and promising free elections, before he also was swept from power at the beginning of December.

As for Czechoslovakia, a combination of firm warnings from Moscow and increasingly bold street demonstrations toppled the administration of Miloš Jakeš on November 17 and set that country back on the path to democracy from which it had been so cruelly diverted half-a-century earlier. The Balkan satrapy of Bulgaria had already fallen into line, and on December 22 Ceauşescu was bloodily deprived of power.

By the end of the year the communist era in Eastern Europe was only an evil memory.

IV

Even to chronicle the events of 1989 leaves one breathless, and it is still too soon to appreciate their full significance for the future of East–West relations. One thing, however, is clear. The liberation of Eastern Europe occurred not in face of objections from Moscow, but with positive Soviet support. Gorbachev advised the communist leaders in Poland to co-opt Solidarity. He warned both Honecker and Jakeš of the consequences of resisting the stream of history; he kept Soviet troops in their barracks; and (so far as we know) it was he who also advised Krenz to demolish the Berlin Wall. By the beginning of December the Soviet Union and its allies in the Warsaw Pact had explicitly renounced the Brezhnev Doctrine, as the West had been demanding they should for the past twenty years.

The course of those events could only signify a deliberate decision by the Soviet leadership to withdraw from the affairs of Eastern Europe. Soviet troops remained, but they were now on alien if not hostile territory. Events had undoubtedly moved far faster and further than Gorbachev had expected, but still, he must have believed that any loss in military security would be outweighed by the abandonment of a huge political liability.

Gorbachev no doubt further calculated that the West would be compelled by public opinion to respond with some dismantling of its own military structure. Skeptics in the West maintained that this had been the Soviet objective all along—that behind the Soviets' pacific professions there lay the Machiavellian intention of dividing the United States from its European allies. Others accepted Gorbachev's assurances at face value. It seemed quite logical that he should want to end a confrontation as unnecessary as it was counterproductive, and rejoin the world from which the Soviet Union had turned away seventy years before. Whatever Gorbachev's intentions, by the end of 1989, Eastern Europe was free and seemed likely to remain so. If this produced problems within the Western alliance, it did not seem an excessive price to pay.

V

How was the West to respond to all this? In the United States a new president had taken office at the beginning of the year. In spite of his long familiarity with affairs of state, George Bush was an unknown quantity: an affable and apparently rather weak man who needed to reassure his party's hard-liners that he was "hard-nosed" and "tough." His presidential term began badly. Bush arrived in the White House after an electoral campaign whose combination of triviality and personal abuse had been watched by overseas friends of the United States with amazement and by intelligent Americans with shame. He was initially surrounded by advisers who seemed to see little difference between the conduct of American foreign policy and that of an election campaign. For them, Gorbachev simply replaced the Democrat Michael Dukakis as an adversary who had to be upstaged. Gorbachev's policy initiatives were seen as ploys to be countered, and his regrettable skill at seizing the headlines needed to be met by comparable Madison Avenue techniques.

From the American media, as usual, came insistent demands for dynamic leadership and policy initiatives—sweeping arms control proposals, spectacular budget cuts. Congress equally demanded budget cuts but insisted that the United States should not let down its guard. Hardline conservatives, who had been losing power even in the final months of the Reagan Administration, warned that even if Gorbachev was "for real" he was atypical and would be swept away by stronger forces that would reestablish the traditional Soviet threat. What kind of policy would Bush fashion out of all this?

Fortunately the president's learning curve was steep. The advice of the foreign policy and intelligence communities, the views of his European allies and the rapport established between Secretary of State James A. Baker and Soviet Foreign Minister Eduard Shevardnadze all combined to convince Bush that Gorbachev was indeed "for real," a responsible colleague in the reshaping of the world order rather than (in the unfortunate phrase of presidential spokesman Marlin Fitzwater) "a drugstore cowboy."

During the spring the Soviet Union initiated the unilateral reduction of its forces in Eastern Europe, which Gorbachev had promised at the United Nations in December 1988. In May 1989 both the United States and Soviet Union submitted proposals for conventional arms reductions in Europe within negotiable reach of each other. In the light of these reductions, President Bush was able quite skillfully to defuse the wrangling among his European allies over whether new land-based tactical missiles should be installed in West Germany to replace those removed under the Intermediate-range Nuclear Forces Treaty in 1988. Strategic Arms Reduction Talks were resumed in Geneva in June, albeit without any evident sign of progress. The United States still refused either to abandon the Strategic Defense Initiative or to submit its naval forces to any kind of arms control. But both leaders made it clear that they now expected results from arms control negotiations. Congress, facing the consequences of the gigantic deficit run up by the Reagan Administration, began to expect them as well.

When Presidents Bush and Gorbachev met for an unscripted discussion at sea off the island of Malta in December (a choice of venue that starkly illustrated how little either knew about the Mediterranean and its winter climate) all, except the barometer, seemed set fair. Bush laid out a program of economic cooperation to ease, however marginally, Soviet domestic problems. He and Gorbachev agreed to press on with arms reductions at a rate that left some U.S. officials shaking their heads. Both leaders confirmed their conviction that the peoples of Eastern Europe should be allowed to find their own way to freedom, without intervention by the superpowers. And they took their first look at a totally unexpected possibility that, whether they welcomed it or not, lay beyond the power of either to prevent: the reunification of Germany.

The assumption by the overwhelming majority of Western observers (including the present writer) that East Germany was the most stable and successful of the Soviet satellites had inhibited any serious speculation, let alone planning, about what would happen if the regime there collapsed. The best expected was some liberalization that would make possible a greater degree of *Annäherung* (rapprochement) with the Federal Republic of Germany. The initial October Demonstrations in East Germany against Honecker had indicated no popular demand for German reunification, and the emerging opposition groups were explicitly set against it. Professing socialists as they all were, absorption by their wealthy capitalistic cousins was not the destiny they preferred for their country.

By the end of November, however, the cry *Deutschland einig Vaterland* was being bellowed out by the crowds of Leipzig. That response may have been a gut reaction against not only the detested regime but also the entire state apparatus that it had created. It may have been a simple desire to share as quickly as possible in the West's material advantages of which they had been deprived for so long. It may have been atavistic nationalism of a kind highly unwelcome to their Polish neighbor, to name only one. But it meant that, however sincere Western leaders like Margaret Thatcher were in saying that German reunification was "not on the agenda," they were badly mistaken. Reunification was very much on the agenda for the Germans themselves. Chancellor Helmut Kohl surprised and discomfited his allies but delighted the deputies of the Bundestag when he announced on November 28, without prior consultation, a program by which he hoped to achieve it.

By its constitution's Basic Law the Federal Republic was pledged to seek German reunification. Its allies had equally pledged themselves to support this goal. But the entire postwar structure of Europe had been created on the basis of two distinct and independent German states. Their reunification would involve radical change of a kind less welcome to Germany's neighbors than their political leaders liked to admit. There was little fear that a reunited Germany would revert to the hideous policies of the Third Reich, but its East European neighbors, much as they might enjoy German economic aid and investment, looked with no enthusiasm on the revival of German political power. As for the European Community, the prospect of so large an increment to the population and economic potential of the Federal Republic created problems of balance of an all too familiar kind—one that evoked historical sensitivities especially in France.

Given the strong economic, political and military links established between the Federal Republic and its Western neighbors, and given also the virtual dissolution of the Warsaw Pact, a neutral Germany was almost unthinkable and not seriously discussed. But would a reunited Germany embedded in the West be tolerable to a Soviet Union whose security interests the United States had tacitly undertaken to observe? If the alliance structures remained, would the presence of Soviet forces in the eastern territory of a reunited Germany be compatible with German sovereignty? If Soviet troops were withdrawn, would the presence of American forces be seen as necessary, either by the Germans or the United States?

Those were some of the huge questions that confronted statesmen of both East and West at the end of the year. Barring a total reversal of Soviet policy, which became less likely with every passing day, it was clear that the answers lay neither in Washington nor in Moscow but in Europe itself, and that the superpowers would have to adjust to whatever decisions the Europeans made about ordering their own continent. Never had the cries for American leadership, which continued to emanate from Congress and the media, sounded so archaic. The low-key style favored by President Bush may have irritated Americans who looked for drama and headlines, but the qualities on which he prided himself—prudence, caution, concern for allied susceptibilities and a thorough understanding of the issues—were as appropriate to the new conditions in Europe as President Truman's rugged courage had been forty years earlier.

George Bush reassured the allies that American troops would remain in Europe for as long as they were wanted. He reassured President Gorbachev that the United States would not exploit the situation to the Soviet disadvantage. Given the extraordinary concatenation of events, Europe was as fortunate to have Bush in the White House as they were to have Gorbachev in the Kremlin.

VI

For the nations of the European Community these new problems could hardly have presented themselves at a less convenient moment. They were already deeply at odds with one another. Under the urging of the extreme centralist president of the European commission, Jacques Delors, with the backing of his countryman François Mitterrand, the Community was being driven toward the target date of 1992, by which time an entirely free market was due to be created, at a speed that alarmed the British—or at least their idiosyncratic leader Margaret Thatcher. The further steps of creating a single convertible currency, a central bank and homogenization of labor regulations were ones that she refused even to visualize, and at European summit meetings she repeatedly found herself in a minority of one.

For the British, the sudden emergence of the new German question— together with the not improbable eventuality of the countries of Eastern Europe demanding associate membership—seemed a good opportunity to pause and take stock. For the French it seemed even more important than ever to lock the Federal Republic into an indissoluble West European system before Bonn began to develop independent yearnings toward the East. At the final European summit in Strasbourg in December Chancellor Kohl, anxious to show that his government's commitment to reunification did not affect its commitment to the West, again sided with the French. President Bush gave clear support for the rapid achievement of European unity. Domestic developments in Britain strongly indicated that Mrs. Thatcher was not politically immortal. In spite of her resistance the development of a strong, centralized European Community, capable of absorbing East Germany and acting independently on the political scene, seemed by the end of the year to be more probable rather than less.

"The German question," as Kohl himself stressed, could only be solved within a European context. It was not only the frontier of Germany that would be moved east if reunification took place, but that of Europe as a whole. President Gorbachev spoke movingly of the creation of "a Common European House." Whether there would be room in such a house for the Soviet Union was problematic, but the establishment of democratic regimes in Poland, Hungary, Czechoslovakia, East Germany and even Romania, all economically dependent on the West, meant that it would certainly stretch "from Brest to Brest," and that Germany would be at the heart of it. Within that framework it was not too difficult to visualize links between the two Germanys developing from the financial and the administrative to the political, leading to a confederal structure as close or as loose as circumstances demanded. There were plenty of models to choose from in Germany's past. Whether the German Democratic Republic would be able to maintain any separate identity, however, remained to be seen.

It is also shared opinion between East and West that the two alliances should remain in being, to ensure stability during a transitional period likely to be turbulent. It will not now be easy, however, for the military of either side to get anyone to take seriously their demands for modernization. Military planning and updating to meet the traditional "threat" will seem increasingly unreal. Conventional arms reductions indeed may well outrun formal agreements.

As for the situation at the end of this transitional period, it remains undefined. Events in Europe have moved too fast for anyone, East or West, to clarify their new strategic objectives. But two developments must be reckoned with.

First, a reunified Germany, whenever and however it comes about, would mean a reunified German army, with all that it implied in the enhancement of West European military potential. Second, the political withdrawal of the Soviet Union from Eastern Europe would mean the withdrawal, sooner or later, of Soviet military forces. The Finlandization of the area—the creation of a neutral belt over which the Soviet Union would have a *droit de regard*—would be the appropriate result. Under these circumstances the American troop presence could be reduced to the maintenance of base installations for mobile and predominantly maritime forces. All these options now seem to be open, and it is hardly premature to begin thinking of them. Prudent statesmanship would suggest a transitional period extending over at least ten years, but events have a habit of running ahead of prudent statesmen.

VII

1989 was indeed "the Year of Europe," in a far more profound sense than that announced with such Olympian condescension by Henry Kissinger 16 years ago. Events on so seismic a scale have occurred nowhere else in the world. But disturbing long-term processes have continued that may force their way to the front of tomorrow's agenda. Conflicts in the Middle East and Central America remain unresolved and apparently unresolvable. Racial confrontation continues in Southern Africa together with starvation and civil war elsewhere on the continent. Sophisticated weapons still proliferate to unstable Third World countries; and among Islamic fundamentalists there remains a sullen and inextinguishable hatred of the West and all its values.

More disquieting has been the continuing inability of Third World countries to absorb their rapidly multiplying populations, and the magnetic attraction of those wealthy Western societies that cannot prevent their poorer neighbors from crossing their borders and eking out a living; thereby creating internal social and political tensions of a deeply alarming kind. For the nations of southern Europe, Spain, Italy and France, the Mediterranean rather than the Elbe has for long been emerging as the real front line, as has the Rio Grande for the United States and perhaps the interface between European and Asiatic Russia in the Soviet

Union. One can become too apocalyptic about the future. The world is not about to become engulfed in a global race war. But the end of the ideological cold war will only reveal the vast dimensions of the problems still confronting us. History will go on and it will be far from boring.

The end of ideological confrontation, however, should have one far-reaching consequence for the affairs of the world. The Soviet Union (barring its total disintegration) will remain a great power and will continue to pursue its interests throughout the world; but those interests will be as likely to lie in cooperating with the West as in opposing it. The Soviets may no longer see it to be in their national interest to support every revolutionary movement in the Third World that, professing Marxism-Leninism, turns to Moscow for help.

Conversely Washington may no longer feel it necessary to support any regime, however brutal, corrupt and arbitrary, that opposes communism. The emergence of an agreed settlement over Namibia is almost as hopeful a portent of such cooperation as events in Eastern Europe. The Soviet Union may find it as hard to control the policies of Cuba as does the United States those of Israel, but Moscow is bound to realize the profound unwisdom of even appearing to countenance revolutionary regimes in Central America. Then the United States may abandon its neurotic obsession with that unhappy region and cease picking at it like a scab, by its constant interventions creating the very wounds it is trying to heal. The United States might also come to appreciate that an Afghanistan stabilized under Soviet influence might suit U.S. interests better than one controlled by Muslim fundamentalists. Ideologues nourish one another, and the eclipse of those in Moscow should at least erode the passions of their *doppelgänger* in Washington.

What, finally, of our disquieting historical analogies? Will liberation inevitably be followed by anarchy, reaction and renewed repression as in the earlier Springtime of Nations? The exact pattern of events is unlikely to repeat itself for the reasons already given, but no one can be under the illusion that the next ten years in either the Soviet Union or in Eastern Europe will be happy or easy ones. To free oneself, as André Gide once remarked, is only the beginning. The real problem is to live in freedom.

But there is another analogy perhaps even more pertinent than those of 1789 and 1848. In 1919 President Woodrow Wilson visited Europe and was hailed by ecstatic crowds in London, Rome and Paris as a peacemaker, a statesman whose vision and wisdom had ended a terrible war and now promised perpetual peace. No less well-deserved enthusiasm has greeted Mikhail Gorbachev on his visits to the West; but as with Wilson, support for him at home is muted and his domestic problems accumulate. The question insistently presents itself: Whatever his own transcendent abilities and undeniable goodwill, can Gorbachev bring his own country with him? Or will the new European order he is trying to build collapse as did Woodrow Wilson's, for lack of the essential support that his own country alone can provide?

To this question 1990 will no doubt provide the answer. There may indeed be a backlash, bringing to power a tough, authoritarian regime that will put an end to both glasnost and perestroika. But authoritarian regimes, as Jeane Kirkpatrick has so frequently reminded us, are not totalitarian regimes. However brutal, a new regime could not restore the exploded ideology of Marxist-Leninism. Any future Soviet leader would still have to solve the same problems that brought Gorbachev into power and to recognize, like Gorbachev, that the solution lies in good relations with the West, a reduction in military expenditure and a renunciation of global ambitions. As for the reimposition of Soviet rule on an Eastern Europe from which every shred of communist legitimacy has now disappeared, it is hard to see what benefits Moscow would hope to set against the enormous and calculable costs. A post–Gorbachev Soviet Union, like the post–Wilsonian United States, might relapse for a time into self-absorbed isolation within its own borders. The West could live with that outcome. Our relations with the Soviet Union would be no worse (if no better) than those with the People's Republic of China. But that is the worst outcome that can plausibly be visualized: not agreeable, certainly, but considerably more tolerable than anything that has gone on before.

Whatever happens, the structure of world politics has been changed, and changed irrevocably. The problems that those changes present to our statesmen are urgent and complex, but never has there been a better opportunity—not in 1945, not even in 1918—to construct a new order that will finally defuse Europe as a focus of world conflict and allow it to reemerge, after nearly a century of pain and horror, as a dynamic and stable center of prosperity and peace. However inadequately those opportunities are grasped, 1989 is likely to be seen as a historic turning point, one ending the catastrophic era that began in 1914. It has been an *annus mirabilis:* a truly wonderful year.

2

After the Cold War

GEORGE F. KENNAN

Is the cold war over? And, if so, what does this mean for American policy toward the Soviet Union? . . .

It might be worth recalling that, traditionally, Russia was never seen by Americans as an enemy of the United States. The czarist autocracy, to be sure, was distasteful to most Americans as a form of government. But we were prepared to take it as it was, to maintain normal relations with it, and to make the best of these relations so long as Russia posed no threat to our national security.

All this changed with the Russian Revolution in 1917. There seems to be a widespread impression in this country that the cold war, as something signifying a state of sharp conflict and tension between the two governments, began only in 1945, after World War II. The impression is erroneous.

Never were American relations with Russia at a lower ebb than in the first 16 years after the Bolshevik seizure of power in 1917. Americans were deeply shocked by the violence of the revolution, by the fanaticism and cruelty of the new rulers, by their refusal to recognize the debts and claims arising out of the recent war, and above all by the brazen world-revolutionary propaganda they put out and the efforts they mounted to promote Communist seizures of power in other countries.

Over all those 16 years, as many of us can today recall, we had no official relations whatsoever with the Soviet regime. Even after the exchange of diplomatic relations at the end of 1933, the relationship remained during the rest of the 1930's, a distant and troubled one. The Stalinist tyranny was after all not a form of government with which it was easy for anybody to coexist. And the cynicism of Stalin's pact with Hitler, at the outset of World War II, did nothing to improve the attitudes of most Americans toward the Soviet regime.

From 1941 to 1945, when both the Soviet Union and the United States were at war with Germany, the mutual antagonism of the two political systems was muted in the interests of their military collaboration. But this outwardly professed friendship never went very deep on either

Copyright 1989 by The New York Times Company. Reprinted by permission of The New York Times Company, and Harriet Wasserman Literary Agency, Inc., as agents for the author.

Note: It is a violation of the law to reproduce this selection by any means whatsoever without the written permission of the copyright holder.

side; and no sooner were hostilities over than new and serious sources of friction began to emerge.

The war, after all, had wrought fundamental changes in the entire background of the relationship. The interest in world revolution, which had long been fading even before the war, had almost totally disappeared as a feature of Soviet policy and rhetoric. But new sources of difficulty had arisen to replace it.

The outcome of the hostilities had placed the Soviet Union in military and political control of most of the eastern half of the European continent. This constituted a major displacement of the balance of power in Europe. Alone, this was bound to be disturbing for the Western allies. But the seriousness of the change was magnified by several other factors. One was the failure of the Soviet Government to match, by any extensive demobilization of its own forces in Europe, the extensive demobilizations promptly carried out there by the Western powers. Another was the cruel suppression at the hands of Soviet police and party authorities of every trace of independent democratic government in the countries of Eastern and Central Europe the Soviet forces had overrun.

On top of this, it soon became evident that the Soviet leaders were trying to take advantage of the war-shocked, exhausted, and confused state of several of the Western European peoples with a view to fastening upon them Communist minority regimes similar to those Moscow was already busy installing in the part of Europe under its authority.

And finally, there was injected into all of this a new and highly confusing factor—a factor without precedent in human history, overthrowing all traditional military concepts and inflaming all military fears and ambitions: the nuclear weapon and its introduction into the arsenals of the United States and the Soviet Union.

It was out of this witches' brew that the cold war emerged, as the symbolic expression of a new, highly antagonistic Soviet-American relationship. It represented, at the outset, a curious realization of Trotsky's famous formula of "no war, no peace." Diplomatic relations were to be continued, to be sure; and the guns, including the nuclear ones, were for the moment to remain silent.

But the threshold of actual hostilities was, at that time, never remote. Many people, including Stalin himself, thought it likely, if not inevitable, that this threshold would soon be passed. On both sides, great military establishments began to be trained, and taught to think, as though war, or some form of military showdown, was the way the conflict was bound ultimately to end. In many ways, in everything except the silence of the weapons, war already became a reality in the minds of millions of men, military and civilian.

Although there were to be successive later crises, the high point of the cold war was probably reached during the Korean War. And we all know the further course of events. Fortunately, for all of us, war between the United States and the Soviet Union did not break out. The crisis was surmounted.

And in the ensuing four decades, down to the middle of the 1980's, each of these components of the cold war, while often retaining its initial validity in the perceptions of people in both countries, diminished in sharpness, and often in reality. The peoples of Western Europe soon recovered their political balance, their prosperity, and their self-confidence. After the success of the Marshall Plan, there could no longer be any question of dangerous Communist penetration in that region.

Both sides, furthermore, soon began to learn to live, after a fashion, with the nuclear weapon, at least in the sense that they came to recognize that this was a suicidal weapon that must never be used—that any attempt to use it would lead only to a disaster in which all concepts of victory or defeat would become meaningless. And as for the relationship of conventional military forces in Europe: not only did the development of the NATO alliance restore an approximate military balance in the heart of the European continent, but—more important still—it became increasingly clear with the passage of the years that neither side had either the incentive or the desire to unleash even a conventional war, much less a nuclear one, in that region.

One might have thought that in the light of these changes, the highly militarized view of East–West relations that the term "cold war" signified might have faded. But military preparations and weapons races are stubborn things. They engender their own patterns of habit and suspicion. These ride along on their own intrinsic vitality even when the original reasons for them have largely faded.

So in this sense the cold war lived on in the minds of many people through the 1960's, and 70's, even after most of the justification for it had faded. And it was only in the middle of the 1980's, with the emergence of a Russian leader intelligent enough to recognize that the rationale of the cold war was largely unreal, and bold enough to declare this publicly and to act accordingly, that the world was brought to realize that one epoch—the epoch of recovery from the enormous dislocation of World War II—had passed; and that a new one was beginning—an age that would, to be sure, create new problems, as all great changes in international life are bound to do, but would at the same time also present new possibilities.

This is the point at which we now find ourselves. The initial sources of contention between the two governments—the prewar ones, that is—no longer have serious significance. The ones flowing from the outcome of World War II have been extensively moderated and Mikhail S. Gorbachev, the Soviet leader, has shown every evidence of an intention to see them substantially eliminated. Where do we go from here?

The Russia we confront today is in many respects like nothing we have known before. The last vestiges of the unique and nightmarish system of rule known as Stalinism are now disappearing. What we have before us is in many respects the freest period Russia has ever known, except perhaps for the few years of feverish change that just preceded the outbreak of World War I in 1914.

But we must be careful when we use this term "freedom." This does not mean that Russia is becoming like us. This it is not doing, could not do, and should not be expected to do. Forms of government and the habits of governments tend over the long run to reflect the understandings and expectations of their peoples. The Russian people, like a number of other peoples of the Soviet Union, have never known democracy as we understand it. They have experienced next to nothing of the centuries-long development of the discipline of self-government out of which our own political culture has evolved. If you presented them tomorrow with our political system, most of them would not know what to do with it; and what they did do might be far from our expectations.

It is clear, then, that whatever happens, and whatever may be the fate of Gorbachev's efforts at the restructuring of Soviet society, Russia is, and is going to remain, a country very different from our own. We should not look for this difference to be overcome in any short space of time.

Beyond which, Russia, as a great modern country in a unique geographic position, and the heir to extensive involvements flowing from that position, is bound to have political interests quite different from our own. These are, fortunately, for the most part, not ones that conflict seriously with ours. Such differences as remain are not ones that should preclude a normal relationship, particularly when leadership on the Russian side is in the hands of a man such as Gorbachev. But this disparity does mean that one should not look, over the long term, for quite the same sort of political intimacy with Russian regimes that we might expect from a country that had inherited more of our own legacy of political outlooks and institutions.

All that being said, we are faced with the fact that Gorbachev has given every evidence, for his part, of an intention to remove as many as possible of the factors that have hampered Soviet-American relations in the past; and a number of bold steps he has taken in that direction do testimony to the sincerity of his effort. To the extent he is able to carry these efforts to conclusion (and that depends to some extent on the response from our side), they present the most favorable opportunity the United States has had in the last 70 years to develop a normal, constructive and hopeful relationship with the Soviet Union.

Gorbachev's position is obviously an extremely difficult one. The burdens he has assumed are almost superhuman. His efforts at internal economic reform have served, thus far, mainly to reveal that the damages done to Soviet society, economically, socially and spiritually, by 50 years of Stalinist terror and Brezhnevist corruption and stagnation are greater than any of us had supposed. It is going to take longer than anyone had realized to repair those damages and build a healthy society.

Whether Gorbachev will be given the time to do this, no one can say. His difficulties are heightened by the fact that his reforms have had the unintended and unexpected effect of inflaming nationalistic feelings in several of the non-Russian ethnic communities of the Soviet Union, thus rendering acute a political problem—namely, the relations of the non-Russian periphery to the Russian center—which many of us had thought was only a problem of the more distant future. Particularly in the case of the three Baltic countries this has led to a situation of great potential instability; for what goes on in those parts of the Soviet Union interacts with what goes on in the so-called "satellite" countries of Eastern and Central Europe, farther afield; and if things get farther out of hand in this entire region, situations could be produced that would appear to threaten not just the political but also the strictly defensive military interests of the Soviet Union, which could have serious consequences.

How long Gorbachev will be able, or permitted by his colleagues, to bear these burdens, no one can say. His position has important elements of strength: his great reputation as a statesman, plus the fact that whoever might succeed to his powers would also have to succeed to his problems, something of which all his opponents must be painfully aware. The pressures, on the other hand, are cruel.

It is equally impossible to make predictions about what, were Gorbachev to be removed, would follow. That conditions could not revert to what they were before he took power is one of the few things on which almost everyone agrees. The intellectuals have been given their head; and it is unthinkable that this generation of them should ever again be bottled up as they were before. Not only that, but the Gorbachev economic reforms, unproductive as they may have been to date, have been formally accepted by the highest bodies of party and government; and this stamp of approval is not apt to be withdrawn until and unless someone can come up with a better alternative, which no one, as yet, has shown any sign of doing.

One must suppose, therefore, that whoever might replace Gorbachev would have to follow extensively in his footsteps, though possibly at a slower speed and without his boldness of leadership.

Particularly is this true in the field of foreign policy, which should be of greatest interest to us. Within Russia, this has been the least controversial of Gorbachev's fields of activity. Hard-liners, military and civilian, might like to retract, if they could, some of the more conciliatory steps he has taken in the area of arms control; but they would soon find that they faced the same financial stringencies he has been attempting to master, and they would presumably have little room, here too, to maneuver.

One must suppose, therefore, that a good portion of what Gorbachev represents would survive him, even if he were to be removed at an early date. Meanwhile, to our good fortune, he hangs on, suspended precariously in midair, to be sure, supported mainly by his incomparable qualities of insight, imagination and courage, and by the relative mediocrity and intellectual poverty of most of his opponents.

To American policymakers, the Russian scene of this particular moment presents, then, a series of tremendous uncertainties—uncertainties greater than Russia has ever known since the fateful year of 1917. If one were to be asked, What is it that is most likely to happen in the coming period, one could say only—the unexpected.

These uncertainties are unquestionably reasons for great alertness, caution and prudence in American policy toward that country. They are not, however, reasons for neglecting the opportunities offered by Gorbachev's policies for the easing of military tensions and for improving the atmosphere of East–West relations generally. If realistic and solid agreements are made now, while the iron is hot; if these agreements, as is to be expected, are seen in Moscow as being in Soviet interest; if they are, as they should be, inherently self-enforcing; if, as is to be expected, they are sealed in formal undertakings—then they are not apt to be undone simply by changes in the Soviet leadership.

What, then, should be the objectives of American policy toward the sort of international partner Gorbachev is trying to make out of Russia? What could we, from our side, do to promote the normalization of this relationship and to shape its future in a manner commensurate with its positive possibilities?

It would seem obvious, to this writer at least, that our first concern should be to remove, insofar as it lies within our power to do so, those features of American policy and practice that have their origins and their continuing rationale in outdated cold war assumptions and lack serious current justification.

To some extent, this has already been done. Cultural exchanges and people-to-people contacts are proceeding briskly, no longer seriously impeded from either side. The same may be said of scholarly exchanges. In all these areas, the initiative has normally and properly to come from private parties. The government's task is primarily not to stand in the way, but to lend its support wherever this is really needed. That things have gone as well as they recently have in these forms of contact is encouraging testimony to the private demand for them and to their usefulness as components of normal relations between two great peoples.

In the commercial field, too, progress has been made; but here obstacles remain—obstacles for which there is no present justification and the removal of which should present no problems.

One hears a certain amount of discussion about whether we should not give aid to Gorbachev. The entire question is misconceived. One must bear in mind the difference between trade and aid. Gorbachev has not asked us for anything in the nature of loans or special credits or other abnormal forms of assistance; he is most unlikely to do so, and we would be ill advised to give it even if he did.

What the Russians are asking for, and deserve to be given, are only the normal facilities for trade, facilities that include of course the extension of the usual commercial credits by both parties in specific business deals. Here, two needless obstructions persist, both dating from the 1970's, in the form of the Jackson–Vanik and Stevenson amendments to the 1974 Trade Act, which in effect deny to the Soviet Union normal customs treatment and restrict the facilities for commercial credit. For these restrictions, which proved to be of little or no benefit to anyone at the time, there is no longer any justification at all; and the sooner Congress removes them, the better.

For the rest, once minimum security precautions have been observed, let Soviet-American trade proceed as it will. The prospects for it are not open-ended. The Soviet side has at this time little to offer in export items, and has sharply limited amounts of foreign exchange available for imports. But these prospects are also not insignificant; and they should not be curtailed by unnecessary official restrictions.

The most serious of the factors weighing on the Soviet-American relationship is unquestionably the problem of arms control, including the continuing competition in the development of strategic nuclear weapons and the standoff in conventional forces in Central Europe. This exorbitant confrontation of military strength, out of all reasonable proportion to the political differences that are supposed to justify it, constitutes an inexhaustible source of mistrust and suspicion between the two parties, distracts public opinion from more serious aspects of the relationship, and pre-empts vast quantities of resources that could well be used for more creative purposes.

What can be done about it?

Obviously, not everything depends on us. It takes two, at every point, to perform this tango. But since Gorbachev has given impressive signs of his intention to do his best in this respect, and has taken a number of conciliatory and even unilateral steps in that direction, this would be a good time for us to review our own record and to see whether it could not be improved.

We have, of course, had one significant success in recent years: the so-called I.N.F. (Intermediate Nuclear Force) agreement, eliminating intermediate-range nuclear weapons from the forces of both sides stationed in Central Europe. This success was made possible by the willingness of both Mr. Reagan and Mr. Gorbachev to override all the intricacies of negotiation at the technical-military level and to take the bold steps, each giving reasonable credit to the good faith of the other side. But it has carried us only a small distance along the path of general arms reduction. For the rest, our record may well stand questioning.

We could certainly have had by this time, had we wished to have it, a comprehensive nuclear test ban; and nothing, surely, could have gone farther to assure extensive, if gradual, reductions in nuclear weaponry. We do not have it.

We could in all probability have had by this time, had we wanted to, the 50 percent reduction in long-range nuclear missiles which both Mr. Reagan and Mr. Gorbachev recognized as desirable and which, once achieved, would presumably have changed the whole climate of the arms control problem. We do not have it. We chose to give higher priority to the Strategic Defense Initiative, and to the modernization and consequent buildup of our strategic nuclear arsenals.

The maintenance of the present American conventional deployments in West Germany absorbs, we are told, some 40 percent of our great military budget. Nothing within the realm of practical possibility could have contributed more directly and importantly to the reduction of the Federal budget than a significant reduction in these expenditures. For years we have been toying timidly with negotiations over the possible reductions of these forces, and have gotten nowhere. These negotiations having now been moved to a much wider forum (that of the Atlantic-to-Urals talks in Vienna, embracing a greatly expanded number of participants), the prospects for any success in the coming period would seem to have been diminished rather than improved.

Gorbachev, in the meantime, has announced important changes in Soviet doctrine affecting the mission and the composition of the Soviet forces in this region, changes envisaging in particular the removal from the forward positions of forms of weaponry that would lend themselves to employment for sudden aggressive purposes. This change of doctrine has been accompanied by a number of specific suggestions from the Soviet or Warsaw Pact side for confidence-building measures of one sort or another, and by extensive unilateral Soviet measures of restraint.

The responses by which these initiatives have been met on our side have been, for the most part, reluctant, embarrassed, and occasionally even surly. These responses have caused a great many people elsewhere in the world to wonder whether we really have any serious interest in arms control at all.

Can we not do better than that?

The hesitations that have underlain these unenthusiastic responses seem to have been largely connected with the impression, so frequently propounded and supported in official American circles, that there has been an "overwhelming" Soviet superiority in conventional forces in the Central European theater and that this situation would continue to prevail even after completion of the unilateral Soviet withdrawals Gorbachev has announced. There are many of us who would strongly dispute that thesis, and dispute it on the basis of statistics fully available to, and even recognized by, official Washington circles.

The confusion seems to arise from several more fundamental miscalculations. There has been the use of unrealistic and seriously misleading NATO-versus-Warsaw Pact comparisons for measuring Soviet and American forces in Central Europe. There has been the persistent assumption that the American tactical and short-range nuclear weapons in West Germany are an essential element of "deterrence," without which there would be serious danger of a Soviet attack in that region. Finally, and in close connection with this assumption of aggressive Soviet designs, there has been the insistence of our military authorities that the extent of the "threat" presented to us by any foreign power must be measured solely by our estimate of that power's capabilities, ignoring its interests and intentions.

A new administration in Washington owes it to itself to re-examine these assumptions, and others like them, and to ask itself whether, considering both the dangers and the expense of the maintenance by both parties of these enormous and inordinate arsenals, we could not find more realistic means of measuring the problem and more hopeful ways of promoting its solution.

If, in this way, some of the more obvious and extensive impediments to a better relationship with the Soviet Union could be overcome, the greater part of what needs to be done would have been accomplished. Bilateral relations between sovereign governments are not the area in which greater positive things are to be achieved, rather a way in which conflicts of interest are to be composed and negative things are to be avoided. If we succeeded in doing no more than to eliminate the greatest sources of conflict prevailing between these two governments, this alone would have been a great accomplishment.

But this would not be the end of the story. There are limited possibilities for useful collaboration even between governments so different in traditional and in ideological inspiration as the Soviet and American ones. These possibilities relate to a number of fields; but the greatest and most important of these, without question, is that of environmental protection and improvement on the planetary scale.

The dangers now beginning to overshadow us all in this respect are confirmed for us not only by many of the findings of the scientists but in some instances by our own perceptions. The greater part of what we could and should be doing to ward off this disaster has to be done within the national framework; and here both the Russians and ourselves have a great deal to catch up on before we can say that we have done all that lay within our power to do. But environment recognizes no national boundaries, and to achieve their maximum effectiveness the national efforts have to be supplemented by international ones. This fact is now coming to be widely recognized in Russia as well as here; and environmental movements are springing up all over the Soviet Union.

There are no two countries that could, if they wanted to, contribute more by joint effort in this field than the United States and the Soviet Union. The same applies to the area of space research. If we could get over the idea that outer space is there primarily to be exploited by us for our military advantage, there would clearly be important possibilities for collaboration with the Soviet Union in the whole great field of space research.

All this collaboration would be justified if only by the direct effects it was designed to achieve. But the probability ought to be recognized that to the extent the two countries could join their efforts in this manner, the remaining impediments to a firm and useful relationship between them would be the more easily overcome; because in the very process of collaboration in a necessary and peaceful process, useful to all humanity, the neurotic impulses of military and political rivalry would be bound to be overshadowed; and the peoples might find, in the intermingling of their own creative efforts, a firmness of association which no other intergovernmental relationships could ever assure.

What we are seeing today is, in effect, the final overcoming of the Russian Revolution of 1917. The present Soviet leaders are the first of that sort who, in trying to shape the society of their country, will have to relate themselves not just to the post-1917 revolutionary period but to the entire span of Russian history. What they are creating, and what we must now face, is another Russia, entirely identifiable neither with the revolutionary period nor with the centuries of czarist power that preceded it.

Just as the designing of this new Russia calls for innovation on the part of those in Moscow who are responsible for it, so it calls for innovation on the part of an American government that, more importantly perhaps than in the case of any other of the world's governments, has to relate to it.

3

Beyond the Cold War

JEANE J. KIRKPATRICK

I

The postwar era collapsed in 1989. When the year began, relations among countries were essentially what they had been for forty years: a divided Europe, a Soviet Union that maintained an East European empire by force, and an America that assumed "superpower" responsibilities vis-à-vis its allies in NATO and in Asia. By the year's end the countries of Eastern Europe seem to have been liberated from the pressures of the Brezhnev Doctrine (though Soviet troops remained). Communist governments put in place and held there by force had collapsed. The division of Europe had been overcome symbolically with the collapse of the Berlin Wall, and literally with the progressive opening of borders between Hungary and Austria, Czechoslovakia and Austria, East Germany and West Germany. More than 700,000 Soviet troops were still stationed throughout Eastern Europe, but the will to empire had apparently been replaced by a will to modernization.

Meanwhile the relative decline in U.S. economic power, the rising pressure of budget and trade deficits and the apparently declining Soviet military threat made defense costs and the "superpower" responsibilities of the United States seem less necessary to the defense of Europe and more difficult to justify or to finance. The cold war is over—nearly. The postwar era is finished—absolutely.

The structures through which international affairs have been conducted for the past forty years have been shaken to their foundations. Now comes the time of rebuilding. An American administration with an avowed aversion to "big think" (as one administration official called it) will likely be confronted with the most sweeping reorientation of U.S. foreign policy since 1947.

By 1989 four major processes of change were at work reshaping what had come to be called East–West relations: liberalization and reform inside the Soviet Union; the democratization of Eastern Europe; the determined move toward economic integration in Western Europe; and

Reprinted by permission of *Foreign Affairs, America and the World, 1990*. Copyright 1990 by the Council on Foreign Relations, Inc.

Note: It is a violation of the law to reproduce this selection by any means whatsoever without the written permission of the copyright holder.

a new, apparently irresistible drive toward unification of East and West Germany. The conjunction and the cumulative impact of these ongoing changes promised to transform Europe—and the U.S. role in Europe.

All these changes were important, but the most important was change within the Soviet Union. It is, above all, Mikhail Gorbachev who is changing the world.

II

Mikhail Gorbachev is what Sidney Hook called an "event-making man": a man whose actions transform the historical context in which he acts. He has already loosened the reins that have tightly controlled Soviet society since the Bolshevik Revolution—largely eliminating censorship, largely freeing emigration, permitting religious freedom not enjoyed in the Soviet Union since 1917, overhauling the structures of government, and providing elections with competition, discussion of public issues and a degree of choice. Gorbachev has not brought democracy to the Soviet Union—yet—but he has sponsored a new tolerance of diversity and restraint in the use of force that have had a profoundly liberating effect. Civil society is being liberated from the suffocating embrace of the state. The consequence is an outpouring of ethnic, religious, political and economic demands and analyses, a mushrooming of political groups formed around new causes. So far economic reforms have disrupted the Soviet economy without increasing production. But all this activity and diversity, all this openness and restructuring, are transforming the Soviet Union, Europe and East–West relations.

Obviously Gorbachev is not the only source of change in the world, in the West or in the Soviet Union. Alexander Solzhenitsyn, the late Andrei Sakharov, Anatoly Sharansky, the refuseniks and generations of dissidents have articulated alternatives to the stifling official Soviet prescription and have provided models of courage and honesty. Ronald Reagan and the Reagan Administration dramatized the need for change and made the case for freedom. The democracies of Western Europe provided nearby examples of the benefits of freedom.

The Information Age, the Strategic Defense Initiative, cocom, the decision to deploy Pershing missiles in Europe and the promise of the European Community (EC) doubtless also contributed to the Soviet motivation to change. Stagnation and the worsening economic situation were an important spur to change. The fact that the Soviet Union is the only industrial nation in the world with rising infant mortality rates and declining life expectancy statistics as well as worsening living standards contributed to the felt need for change.

But it was Gorbachev who, from the apex of the Soviet system, acted. The laws of history to the contrary, the Soviet Union was founded on the decisions of a single man and is being reshaped by the decisions of another. As Lenin thought he could jump over stages of history, Gorbachev apparently believes he can move the Soviet polity "backward" in Marx's historical trajectory from "socialism" to a stage of "pluralism" that the Bolshevik Revolution "skipped" on its way to the end of history.

Gorbachev's sweeping program of political, cultural and economic reform marks the end of totalitarianism in the Soviet Union. And with the dream of total power inside the country has apparently gone the dream of total power in the world.

Political reforms have already substantially altered the framework within which decisions are made on economic, military and foreign policy. Gorbachev seems to have understood the importance of changing the political method. The new Soviet method is a kind of imperfect parliamentarianism—which moves a giant step from government by force to government at least partly representative and responsible.

The method involves significant restraint in the use of force, internally and externally—whether toward striking Soviet miners, the Baltic republics' demands for autonomy or East European protest demonstrations. Gorbachev's restraint in the use of force has transformed the situation in Eastern Europe, opened the way for a democratic revolution and altered relations with the United States and Western Europe.

The importance of these events for the world can be understood only when it is also understood that ever since World War II the Soviet Union has shaped relations among major powers in the West—absorbing some countries, provoking others to defend themselves. The opinions of revisionists to the contrary notwithstanding, the Truman Doctrine, the Marshall Plan, NATO, containment policy, the Reagan Doctrine and large American defense budgets were elements of the American and West European response to the stimulus of Soviet expansion and force.

The East European empire and the Brezhnev Doctrine symbolized the Soviet Union's will to conquest, its contempt for democratic self-determination and self-government, and its reliance on force as an ordinary instrument of foreign policy. The Soviet threat mobilized the West.

But shortly after becoming general secretary, Gorbachev said that each Warsaw Pact member could choose its own way. He said the Soviet use of force against fellow socialists or fellow Europeans was "unthinkable." Nikita Khrushchev, Leonid Brezhnev and even Joseph Stalin had made such declarations; the difference lay in what they did, not in what they said. Gorbachev accepted and even encouraged dramatic moves toward self-government by Hungary, Poland, East Germany, Czechoslovakia, Bulgaria, Romania. 1989 was the year during which Gorbachev demonstrated that—at the very least—there were new, much broader parameters around which the people of Eastern Europe were free to act.

The cold war was grounded in the Soviet Union's will to empire and its use of force—symbolized by the tanks that subjugated Budapest in 1956 and Prague in 1968. The abandonment of the Brezhnev Doctrine and of the effort to control Eastern Europe by force marks the end of the cold war.

We are nearly there, despite the Soviet troops in Eastern Europe, for there is powerful evidence that the will to conquest is gone, at least under this Soviet government.

III

These momentous, unanticipated changes will not only liberate Eastern Europe. If completed, they will liberate the United States and Western Europe from the constraints of the sustained global military preparedness imposed by the cold war.

The United States confronts these dramatic events with a new president and new administration that are cautious by instinct. The Bush Administration took longer than many wished in "reviewing" East–West relations, leading some observers to worry aloud that the United States by its slowness would "discourage" change in the East bloc. Obviously this was an unnecessary concern.

The most pressing issue confronting the Bush Administration was not how to encourage change but how to react to the changes that developed. The administration reacted carefully; the president not only declined to "dance on the Berlin Wall," as one congressional leader suggested he do, he has deliberately refrained from "gloating" about the manifest failure of communism and has offered repeated assurances that he will not seek to "exploit" the upheavals in the East. President Bush was carefully nonprovocative during his trip to Poland and Hungary in July. He indicated a desire to be helpful in the process of reform and made clear his own strong feelings about the importance of liberalization or democratization of East European dictatorships. But he has not sought to become a principal actor. He stands ready to help.

The question "Should we help Gorbachev?" should be rephrased as "What can we do to help Gorbachev?" and "What should we help Gorbachev do?":

- Gorbachev has pursued a rather large number of conflicting policies in the years that he has governed the Soviet Union. He is still engaged in a concerted effort to develop some very high-tech weapons. We do not want to help this Soviet effort.
- He is still spending billions supplying governments that deprive their citizens of self-determination and self-government and their societies of pluralism, for example Cuba and Afghanistan. We do not want to help him do this either.

· He is still resisting the introduction into the Soviet economy of private property and profit-making. We do not want to reinforce such reticence, if for no other reason than that it will cripple reform.

We want to help the Soviet people and Gorbachev as he moves his society toward pluralism, democracy and economic progress as we once helped countries of Western Europe.

The idea of a "Marshall Plan" for the Soviet Union, however, is particularly ill-conceived. It overlooks the fact that France, Britain, the Benelux countries and the other West European Marshall Plan recipients were modern industrial societies before they were devastated by war. Their people had the beliefs and habits of modern men and women. The Soviet Union is not a modern industrial society. It is rather, as *The Times* of London has noted, a Third World country with First World weapons. Its structures and traditions do not encourage development.

In the years since President Truman offered technical assistance to less-developed countries, aid programs aimed at economic development have been undertaken by most countries in Western Europe and North America. The world has learned a good deal about how one country can and cannot help another to economic modernization.

Whatever one may think of alternative ways of organizing society and economies, it remains a fact that command economies, in which centralized bureaucracies direct things, do not produce economic growth. This strategy of development leads to stagnation. Moreover, the ill effects of this mode of economic organization cannot be overcome by resource transfers. It is like pouring water into the Sahara.

The development of Korea, Taiwan, Chile and a dozen other successes was based on respect for market forces and on individual initiative. Their experience shows that full democratic freedoms are not necessary to make market economies work, but some profit incentives and free movement of labor are. The Soviet system still features public ownership of almost everything, little freedom of movement for workers and few opportunities to profit.

Almost everything in Soviet society discourages and inhibits movement toward a more dynamic, market-oriented economy. To increase production, efficiency and growth, material incentives are needed but still lacking. To produce the goods that will serve as incentives to produce more, enterprise, flexibility and decentralization are needed—yet centralization, rigidity, and uncertainty prevail. As economist Padma Desai has emphasized, the Soviets began reform with an inadequate understanding of how a market system works, and with "overwhelming state ownership of the means of production and a one-party state." Both are extremely unhelpful.

Not only that, but as societies develop, it is not just modes of production that change. People must change. Attitudes toward time, toward achievement, toward authority, toward one's self and one's future are all associated with modernization. People must believe that their situation can get better before they will work to make it better. These human correlates of modernization drive economic development.

It is not clear that modernization can be achieved under conditions of socialism. The economic actor who drives the market system is an individual who makes decisions for himself about what is best for him to do—where to work, what to work at. The explosion of the individual into history created the energy that powered the modernization process. But socialism is proudly, confidently based on opposite conceptions. It focuses on collectives—on classes above all—and subordinates the individual to collectivity. It makes calculations in terms of the impact of policy on a collectivity. The collective rewards it offers are probably less than effective in stimulating individual effort, as intangible rewards are usually less effective than tangible incentives. A society in which rewards are collective but discipline is individual can probably neither achieve nor establish and sustain genuine growth. No socialist system has.

There is another very basic obstacle to Soviet economic growth. Socialism of any kind requires decision-makers who—at least in principle—make decisions that will be good for the whole, not "merely" for the decision-maker himself. More important, the decision-maker does not feel any direct economic consequences of his decision. He does not grow rich if he makes a good decision nor go without if he makes a bad decision. In a socialist system the one responsible for economic decisions does not enjoy economic benefits nor suffer the economic consequences.

In a system of centralized socialist planning, the decision-maker is more remote from his decision, is likely to be less informed about it and less directly affected by its consequences. A socialist system does not eliminate the self-interest of the decision-maker, but it changes the nature of his interest. The socialist planner's success depends on good interpersonal bureaucratic relations. In a market system success depends on the goods produced and the profit achieved. The socialist system tends, by its very nature, to transform economic decisions into political decisions.

How then is it possible to stimulate production? How can the hierarchical, centralized, one-party state be persuaded to forgo comprehensive control over the economy—especially if those in power do not really want to do so? How can market incentives become an effective stimulus when the centralized planners tax away the lion's share of the resulting profits? How can supply respond to demand in the context of centralized bureaucratic planning? How can workers be expected to work harder if there are no rewards for enterprise? What does it matter if, in any case, there is nothing to buy with money earned?

In this situation it seems clear that resource transfers to the Soviet Union should be avoided. Economic assistance should be tied fairly directly to programs that encourage and reinforce the development of new incentives and new modes of production—not because we want to control Soviet affairs or exploit Soviet difficulties but because we want the economy to succeed.

Moreover, it is essential that in trying to help Gorbachev the United States and other Western governments seek forms of aid that will help create and strengthen structures of freedom and promote trade that ties the Soviet Union and Eastern Europe into the business activities (not the bureaucracies) of the world, through which they can make money and, as Lenin admonished, learn to trade. What is true in the Soviet Union is also true in Eastern Europe—in both places state monopolies and entrenched bureaucracies work quietly against reform.

IV

Mikhail Gorbachev came to the general secretary's office in 1985 with a complex global agenda on which he had already begun to act. Repair of the Soviet relationship with China was a high priority. Overcoming the division of Europe to create a "Common European House" was another. Diminishing Soviet vulnerability to U.S. missiles drove an arms control agenda that also emphasized denuclearization of Europe.

He has made great progress toward all these foreign policy goals. He visited China, charmed Europe and weakened NATO. He secured withdrawal of U.S. intermediate-range missiles from Europe. But his greatest concern has been to construct a new European order from the Atlantic to the Urals.

Gorbachev has written and spoken frankly about his conception of Europe, in which the Soviet Union is to be an integral factor. He has visited Europe's capitals and courted its leaders. What does Gorbachev want for the Soviet Union in Europe? Respect, influence, perhaps hegemony in the "great European family." He has said repeatedly that he wants to put an end to the view that his country is aggressive and threatening. There is no Soviet threat, he has insisted. But what is the Soviet Union if it is not a threat?

Here we come to the Soviet problem. The Soviet Union is a military, not an economic, power. Gorbachev would like to maintain the Soviet status as a great power, as a country whose views are taken into account.

He does not want the Soviet Union to be odd man out in a united Europe. He does not want the Soviet Union to be isolated. If the Warsaw Pact countries lunge Westward—joining the EC or the European Free Trade Association, withdrawing from the Warsaw Pact, as several clearly long to do, orienting their policies to the West—the Soviet Union stands to lose its status as a major power.

The best way for the Soviet Union to remain a great power is to be the leader of a bloc. But the Soviets can only be the head of the Eastern bloc if the Eastern bloc survives. Its viability is not certain, but one other thing is: Communist governments can only survive if they are protected by Soviet troops. Preserving the bloc requires preserving East Germany, which is the Western bulwark of the Warsaw Pact. Preserving Soviet influence requires preserving the Warsaw Pact itself, because it is the foundation of a Soviet position in Europe.

From the Soviet point of view, the disposition of Germany thus becomes part of the larger question: How can the Soviet Union prevent itself from being isolated in the new Europe? If all or most of the countries of the East opt for a multiparty system, free elections and free market policies, they will orient themselves toward the West. They will depart the Council for Mutual Economic Assistance and the Warsaw Pact.

Germany is a special problem that cannot be deferred. The disposition of "the German question" has enormous importance for the future of NATO and the EC, and for the balance of forces in Europe.

The question of German unification burst onto the European agenda last fall after the dramatic, unanticipated push of Germans west through the hole in the Hungarian border and then through West German embassies in Warsaw and Prague. Protest rallies against the government rapidly turned into demonstrations in favor of unification. "We are one people!" they shouted. West German generosity and hospitality seemed to say the same. The world was suddenly reminded that the existence of East Germany depended on the division of Europe into communist and democratic blocs, and vice versa. A separate democratic East German state makes no sense. One of the first acts of a Germany that enjoyed self-government and self-determination would be to vote for national unification.

Suddenly other countries remembered that there were two divisions of Germany undertaken for two quite different reasons: the first division, carved out by the Allies, was designed to render Germany less dangerous; the second, carved out by Stalin, was designed to consolidate forever Soviet power in one part of Germany. Now the fear of a powerful, reunited Germany remains—even when the Soviet appetite lessens.

The very question of unification creates problems: To oppose it risks alienating the Germans forever; to support it means opposing Gorbachev and helping make Germany the most powerful state in the EC.

Gorbachev has made no proposal for the elimination of NATO and the Warsaw Pact, or for a unified, neutral Germany, or a unified Germany of any kind—doubtless because East Germany is an important chip in the high-stakes poker game Gorbachev is still playing.

If East Germany joins West Germany in the EC it would enhance the power of the West and contribute to the isolation of the Soviet Union. As long as the East German state exists, it serves as a bridge between East and West over which Gorbachev can walk on his way to play an important role in the "great European family." Both Germanys still remain dependent on the Soviet Union for progress toward the dream of a single Germany. And as long as Germany is divided the Soviets need not worry about re-creation of a major central European power.

The Soviet government faces two alternatives in Europe. It can try to maintain the status quo, preserve Communist parties and governments (under some guise) and keep Soviet troops and the Warsaw Pact in place. This option requires preserving an East German state and accepting the continued presence of American troops and NATO to protect the continent from Soviet hegemony.

Or the U.S.S.R. could sacrifice the East German state for a unified but neutral Germany, with the expectation that a neutral Germany would mean the end of NATO and of the U.S. military presence in Europe. This option would also re-create a major power—Germany—in the center of Europe.

After the Malta summit in December, the Soviets and the East German government (which is still wholly responsive to Soviet policy) came out squarely against unification. "We say no to reunification," read banners at one demonstration attended by the new East German Communist Party chief Gregor Gysi, the new president, Manfred Gerlach, and the Soviet ambassador to East Germany. But, as I write, word has arrived that Gysi has proposed the withdrawal of all foreign troops from Germany, and the reduction of German forces—tantamount to a neutral Germany. Bonn has indicated some interest.

Obviously the United States has a major stake in this. NATO without Germany is not viable, especially since France is not a fully integrated member. An American military presence in Europe outside the NATO framework is not likely to be acceptable either in Europe or the United States. A good many Americans—especially American officials—are as keen to remain in Europe as they are to "help" Gorbachev. . . .

Both the United States and the Soviet Union may be said to have a kind of objective vested interest in the continued division of Europe. The United States has in common with the Soviet Union the prospect of a significantly reduced future role in Europe. For four decades, in a divided Europe in which the Soviet Union maintained control of Eastern Europe, Western Europe needed U.S. help to defend against Soviet forces in a forward position. American military power was viewed as essential to the security of Western Europe, either because West European states were unable to defend themselves or because they (and we) had grown accustomed to the United States shouldering the burden.

If the cold war is over, the United States loses the related economic burdens and also its "superpower" status. It loses a good deal of the influence in Europe and Asia to which many Americans have become attached and accustomed.

NATO is not the only institution that is crucially affected by the question of German unification; so is the EC. Germany outside the Community is unthinkable. But a unified Germany inside the EC would alter the balance of power among the 12, and quite possibly leave Britain and even France more open to adding new members from the East—despite what European Commission President Jacques Delors had said about not admitting new members before 1992. Hungary has already applied for and been granted observer status in the European Parliament. Poland has manifested interest in a close relationship with the EC, and it seems very likely that one or more of the East European countries will apply for formal membership. How that application looks to the 12—when and if it comes—will be influenced by what happens on German unification.

V

The cold war was a direct result of successive Soviet governments' policy of using force to extend and preserve power in Eastern Europe. It will be over when the Soviet Union removes its troops from all East European countries that request it to do so (as the United States once removed forces and abandoned bases in France).

A withdrawal of Soviet forces is prerequisite to the full self-determination and self-government of Eastern Europe. Even though Soviet forces in the region have not been used to preserve entrenched governments, they could be; and there is no guarantee of the policy of Gorbachev's successor. No one can be certain of the Soviet Union's future, and therefore the maximum efforts should be made to make the world safer during the period that the Soviet Union is governed by men ready to reduce force and forces.

Obviously the United States should not agree to treating NATO and Warsaw Pact forces equally. NATO forces are present with the full consent of the host countries. Those countries participate in NATO voluntarily. When the countries of Eastern Europe have chosen their new governments, their decisions about membership in the Warsaw Pact will have a validity comparable to those of NATO members. The withdrawal of Soviet troops from Eastern Europe should be—in the first instance—a matter between East European governments and the Soviet Union, when the East European peoples have elected governments that can make legitimate decisions in their behalf.

Meanwhile, just as the principal goal in Conventional Forces in Europe talks should be deep reductions, the primary goal of arms talks should be arms reductions and destruction, not arms limitations: START, not SALT. The Bush Administration should seek the greatest mutual verifiable reductions compatible with protecting the United States against attack from the missiles of the dozen other countries with the capacity to produce and deliver nuclear and other unconventional weapons of mass destruction.

If troop withdrawal and the destruction of weapons are to come, it will be because the Soviet Union has lost its will to empire and is focused on international development. It will not be because we have devised a perfect agreement.

Americans have a well-known tendency to attempt to settle international disputes by contract. Hans Morgenthau, George Kennan, Henry Kissinger and others have noted an American tendency to legalism in the conduct of foreign affairs. We have attempted to outlaw war by contract, to guarantee human rights by contract, to eliminate categories of weapons by contract. The Covenant of the League of Nations was one elaborate contract authored by Americans. The Charter of the United Nations is another, of which Americans were the principal architects. Arms control agreements are the most common contemporary example of a contractual approach to international affairs.

But such contracts achieve their goals only when they serve the interests and reflect the power relations of the signatories. There is no supranational referee to enforce international contracts, no supranational police to ensure compliance; if there were one, it would be as politicized by interested parties as the United Nations has become.

Contracts are not needed to prevent nonaggressive nations from engaging in aggression, and they do not bind aggressors. No arms agreement is needed to protect us from the nuclear missiles of France and Britain and no arms agreement alone can be relied upon to protect us from potential adversaries. Arms agreements have never succeeded in containing, or even slowing, an arms race—though they have occasionally diverted weapons development onto another track.

However, the destruction of weapons is helpful, especially when it occurs in conjunction with a refocusing of national attention and resources. It is reasonable to hope that sweeping international reform will bring such refocusing.

The basic problem between the U.S.S.R. and the United States is Soviet expansion and empire. That is the problem in Europe and in so-called regional conflicts. The difficulties will only be resolved as the Soviet appetite for expansion ends, as it seems to be doing. When it does end, the Soviet Union will be willing to halt its heavy flow of arms to

Afghanistan and permit the Afghan people self-determination. When it ends the Soviet government will stop organizing and channeling huge arms shipments to Cuba, Nicaragua and Syria. It will cease equipping terrorist groups. It will become part of the solution to these problems.

Until then the United States can attempt to negotiate an agreement that may—or may not—expand areas of peace. But like arms agreements, these will prove unreliable and only marginally helpful. (For example, the United States did not negotiate Soviet withdrawal from Afghanistan. They decided to withdraw and we negotiated an agreement about what would follow—an agreement that did not work well.)

VI

The end of the cold war—when it comes—will inevitably reduce the importance of the U.S. role in Europe. The Soviet threat made NATO and U.S. military power vitally important to Western Europe. NATO is, and from the viewpoint of Europeans always has been, about the defense of Europe. This is its raison d'être. NATO is the framework through which Americans were integrated into the task of deterring and, if necessary, defending Western Europe against attack. Regular communication and cooperation in this common task strengthened the bonds between the United States and other NATO members. Gorbachev and his colleagues are quite right in believing that removing the Soviet threat removes the reason for large numbers of U.S. forces in Europe.

Is it time to dismantle NATO? The Bush Administration has already begun to scramble to find other functions for the alliance. The central theme—and title—of Secretary Baker's speech at the Berlin Press Club in December was "America in Europe After the Cold War." At about the same time that President Bush, seeking to reinforce NATO, declared that "the United States is and will remain a European power," Baker in Berlin asserted, "NATO will remain North America's primary link with Europe," and proposed new functions for the organization.

Baker's vision of a "New Europe on the basis of a New Atlanticism," with NATO as its central institution, reflects the familiar American view of NATO as a multipurpose alliance of democracies, a view Europeans have always resisted and are likely to continue to resist.

Baker proposed four new functions for NATO in the "new security structure for Europe." France objected to the first—a NATO arms control verification staff—even before Baker articulated it in Berlin. The second—a larger NATO role in dealing with regional conflicts and unconventional weapons—has been successfully resisted by Europe throughout the cold war because almost all NATO countries pursue their own national interests in Asia, Africa, the Middle East and Latin America. This is why it proved impossible to get an effective antiterrorist policy among NATO countries, why France did not permit overflight of U.S. planes en route to a bombing mission in Libya, why Italy has sometimes limited the right of U.S. planes to land at NATO airbases, and why Germany's foreign office resisted cooperation on sales to the Middle East of the essential elements of a chemical weapon plant. It is why this or that European state has declined to help "resistance movements" in Afghanistan, Angola, Cambodia and Nicaragua. It is extremely unlikely that significant joint planning to deal with these matters can be developed, regardless of what happens in Eastern Europe.

The United States' NATO partners are also not likely to be enthusiastic about Baker's third suggestion: that the West work through the Helsinki Conference on Security and Cooperation in Europe to develop measures to promote human rights and democratic institution-building in the East. West European governments have endorsed Gorbachev's proposal for reconvening the 35 members of the CSCE. They see the CSCE as a place for cooperation and bridge-building to the East and will resist East–West polarization—which in any case will not develop if Poland, Hungary, Czechoslovakia and East Germany complete the transition to democracy.

Finally, American leaders need to face the fact that while most NATO members feel friendly and even grateful to the United States for its help through the long period of Europe's vulnerability, they do not regard the United States as a European power. They have not invited the United States to join the EC and are not about to do so. They are not enthusiastic about declarations like Baker's that we will create a new Europe on the basis of a new Atlanticism. Europeans are already engaged in creating a new Europe on the basis of the EC. They do not see the United States as a "partner" in this process. Americans need to understand this.

Willingness to withdraw U.S. troops also entails risks for Europe. It will leave the Soviet Union the strongest power on the continent. In a relationship between neighbors, one of whom is very strong and one much weaker, the independence and security of the weaker depend simply on the restraint of the stronger. Western Europeans know this. It is not likely that they will seek mutual withdrawal of U.S. and Soviet troops as an acceptable security arrangement. It is also not likely that American taxpayers will accept a prolonged U.S. presence in Europe in the absence of a persuasive Soviet threat.

If things develop in Eastern Europe as expected, Europeans will have new burdens to assume. Americans will have old burdens to relinquish. We will need to learn to be a power, not a superpower. We should prepare psychologically and economically for reversion to the status of a normal nation, still seeking to encourage democratic institutions, strengthen the rule of law and advance American interests.

4

The Erosion of the Superpowers: The Military Consequences of Economic Distress

WALTER GOLDSTEIN

Conventional wisdom suggests that the nuclear condominium exercised by the United States and the Soviet Union will survive the century. But there is an element of doubt. The relative economic power of both superpowers has been reduced in recent years as their own allies and trade rivals surpassed their sluggish gross national product (GNP) growth rates. Both powers now face some measures of economic distress. Nevertheless, it is assumed that their strategic nuclear duopoly will remain unchallenged. Equipped with 25,000 strategic and tactical nuclear warheads apiece, and with armed forces several million strong, the two countries stand alone as the prime users of coercion in the international order.

When the two world leaders met at the summit conclaves of the late 1980s, they enjoyed a lordly sense of preeminence. The level of confidences exchanged between President Gorbachev and Presidents Bush or Reagan required no third party or *interlocutor valable*. The chieftains spoke boldly for their own collective security alliances as they talked about changing the strategic balance and disbanding theater nuclear forces in central Europe. Each made a formal show of consulting loyal allies after their private feasts concluded, more to display good manners than to acknowledge collegial obligation.

The immediate purpose of the 1987 and 1988 summits was to remove intermediate-range nuclear forces (INF) from central Europe, to negotiate longer term proposals for the strategic arms reduction talks (START), and to promote a range of détente understandings between the superpower leaders. The ulterior motives of the summit duo were less visible. Both needed to strengthen their power standoff against their own allies and against the other's global probing. More important, neither could afford to maintain current obligations. It was becoming too expensive to maintain (1) the forces needed to police their worldwide spheres of

Revised and reprinted by permission of the *SAIS Review*, Vol. 8, No. 2, 1988. Copyright 1988 by Johns Hopkins Foreign Policy Institute, SAIS.

Note: It is a violation of the law to reproduce this selection by any means whatsoever without the written permission of the copyright holder.

influence; (2) the nuclear arsenals to guarantee an extended and assured deterrence; and (3) the commitments to preserve hegemony in key areas of the Third World. Their own allies in Europe were divided, if not unhelpful, about paying for the modernization of conventional forces. And the two leaders themselves had already had to back down from expensive engagements in Afghanistan and the Persian Gulf, from their endless involvements in the Middle East and in the tropical jungles of Central America, and from the national liberation wars of Southeast Asia and sub-Saharan Africa. As a riptide of political charge and anti-Communist revolution swept across Europe, the emperors discovered that they were covered with fewer and fewer clothes; they questioned if they should now collaborate and restore their ascendancy.

Historians will probably argue in future years about which factor was most instrumental in forcing the superpowers to modify their global positions in the 1980s. One school of historians will surely insist that the chief factor prompting change was the vast expenditures incurred by the escalation of the arms race. President Reagan championed this explanation. He emphasized that his administrations spent more than $2 trillion on military programs, including a costly plan to develop a space-based defense system, the Strategic Defense Initiative (SDI), which forced the Kremlin "to their knees." A second school will argue that more of the credit is due to Mikhail Gorbachev; he seized power from the hidebound cadres in Eastern Europe and in the Kremlin, at considerable risk, to proffer arms control and regional settlements that even President Reagan's stalwart cold warriors could not refuse. A third school is likely to suggest that domestic weariness turned both societies in the 1980s. The rhetoric of ideological confrontation and cold war enthusiasm had begun to lose its saliency as payments for the arms race multiplied beyond control. Strenuous demands were raised by constituencies ranging from youth and women's groups to angry ethnic minorities and antinuclear activists. Critics questioned the call by bemedalled generals to buy ever more expensive weapons and battle systems for outer space. Instead, they talked about the economic insecurity created by excessive military commitments. They advocated a "new phase" in the superpowers' dialogue as they tuned out the doctrinal appeals of Leninist *apparatchiki* or Pentagon "freedom fighters" and focused on GNP growth problems instead.

Unfortunately, the mass media used its colorful glamor to attribute the superpowers' newfound amity to the personalities of Reagan and Gorbachev. As the oldest president of the United States and the youngest in the USSR, they were committed to overturn the political power hierarchies and the cold war doctrines that had brought each of them to power. The irony of their personal repudiation of "confrontation politics" was not lost to the world. Both had risen through the power institutions of the warfare state, insisting that frequent tests of strength should be made in military confrontation. It was a notable achievement for each leader to accomplish such a historic reversal. Of course, they attributed their ideological conversion to realistic calculations rather than to sentimental responses. The suspicion grew, however, that they had begun to worry about the rate of inflation and deficit financing in their ailing domestic economies; and that they listened more attentively to their economic forecasters and planners than to the weapons advice of their Joint Chiefs of Staff. Both had felt threatened by the crash of the stock markets and the turndown in world trade in 1987–88. They apparently agreed that military threat levels had receded and that the correction of economic drift and decline claimed a more urgent priority. Following the upheavals in the Soviet Union and Eastern Europe at the close of the 1980s, it was obvious that strategies of confrontation simply had to be abandoned.

THE COURSE OF ECONOMIC DECLINE

There were two ways to measure the astronomical costs paid in the 1980's by the superpowers to maintain their global strength of conventional forces and to modernize their nuclear arsenals. Both approaches were by definition imprecise. The first calculated the percentage of GNP and central government expenditures on the armed services, weapons procurement, military research and development (R and D), overseas garrisons, pensions, and veterans' benefits. The figure cited for each superpower, in dollar equivalent terms, was roughly $300 billion a year. This amounted to roughly 6.7 percent of the GNP of the United States and more than 15 percent for the USSR. The figures were generally accepted in the West, but the Soviet calculations were contested by angry conservatives in both countries.[1]

Unfortunately, every gauge of military spending is distorted by definitional and denominational ambiguities. Soviet weapons and support costs are usually concealed within other categories of government expenditure, and the numbers of troops or weapons given are not reliable. In the United States and Europe there is no uniform accounting for veterans' pensions, for overseas transfer costs, or for the military portion of the interest payments incurred in carrying the national debt. The conversion of rubles or yen into dollar denominations has been even more misleading, since the dollar's value fluctuated sharply on most currency exchanges in the last few years. It gained nearly 50 percent after 1982, then declined 50 percent after 1985, and rose 15 percent in 1989.

The second measure involves the economic opportunity costs incurred by defense spending. This approach tries to estimate the potential benefits sacrificed in order to build military might, and it tries to assess the value of the resources deflected from productive industries to satisfy the manpower and high-technology needs of the armed services. This gauge is subjective, at best, since no estimate of potential benefits or opportunity costs can ever be accurate. Only one example need be cited. The cost to the United States of financing eight years of Mr. Reagan's military buildup came to roughly $2 trillion; in comparison, the U.S. national debt was $1 trillion when he entered office in 1981 and $3 trillion when he left in 1989. It would be difficult to demonstrate that the military outlays were excessive or that the $2 trillion defense budget would actually have been invested more wisely in export industries or social welfare priorities, since no major war took place.

When evaluating opportunity costs it is useful to compare the advantages gained by industrial nations that rigorously restricted their military expenditures with those that did not. For a start, most European members of NATO devoted less than half of the 6.7 percent of GNP that had been allocated in the U.S. Japan spent only 1 percent, compared with the Soviets' contribution of 15 percent to its military machine, and the Soviets' economic growth consequently lagged badly. In prior eras, when rearmament drives were labor-intensive, it was held that a valuable boost to the economy could be gained by war spending. This notion no longer holds. Nations that spend heavily on armaments, such as the United States and United Kingdom, forfeited valuable gains in industrial productivity and economic growth. By contrast, their more pacific neighbors invested resources in high-technology industries, R and D, social infrastructure, and capital expansion. West Germany and Japan built powerful export industries to advance their international security. The nations which spent 5 percent or more of GNP on military purposes faced a relentless loss of markets and in their currency's value.

The superpowers forfeited additional benefits overseas by taxing themselves strenuously to rearm. In two years (1983–85) the U.S. capital position switched from that of the leading creditor to leading debtor. By 1990 its foreign debts exceeded $600 billion, and within a decade the deficit on external account could reach $1 trillion. At that point the cost of annual service payments could equal net export revenues, leaving the U.S. financial position in the permanent debtor position of a Third World nation. In its own way, the Soviet Union dropped further behind in the race for economic "competitiveness" and solvency. It has recorded a negative rate of GNP growth since 1980, it had to devalue the ruble by 90 percent, and it has suffered an extremely high degree of inflation. Today the Soviets depend significantly on high-technology imports to support their standard of living, but their exports have failed to capture a significant share of world markets and their indebtedness is now mounting. Although it remains an impressive *military* giant, the Soviet Union has seen its economic prowess surpassed by Japan and the European Community. It has been stridently challenged by its former allies in Eastern Europe and its own ethnic minorities, and the great shortcomings of the Russian economy have been exposed in Mr. Gorbachev's *glasnost* campaign to face home truths.

THE HIGH COSTS OF BUYING MILITARY STATUS

The question of opportunity costs can be rephrased in light of the superpowers' poor economic performance: What is the economic utility of creating expensive military capabilities? Is it cost-effective today to invest in additional military might when there has been a steady diminution in industrial prowess? Caution must be used in framing an answer. Comparative costs are formulated in dollar units, but they are difficult to evaluate accurately because the dollar fluctuates wildly on the money markets. For example, when the yen soared against the dollar it appeared that Japan, the least martial of America's allies, had suddenly become the biggest military spender. Though a limit of 1 percent of GNP had been placed on Japan's total military spending, its outlays (including military pensions) exceeded $40 billion. When denominated in current dollars, Japan's defense cost more than the budgeted appropriations of France, the United Kingdom, or West Germany, each of which allocated anywhere from 3 to 5.5 percent of GNP to the armed services. If the U.S. or each of its NATO allies had cut military spending to 1 percent of GNP, they too could have eliminated the deficits in their domestic *and* external accounts.[2]

Considerable damage would be done to U.S. defense industries if Japan were to produce all of its own aircraft in the 1990s, rather than contracting with the United States, or if it cut back on its offset payments for the 145,000 U.S. forces stationed in East Asia. It is already a matter of dispute that the United States pays heavily for Japan's defense while suffering a trade deficit with Japan of momentous proportions. Both nations fear the trade war tensions that might erupt if the bases were closed or turned over to a Japanese lend-lease agreement, and both have chosen not to fret. A similar problem has emerged over funding the 325,000 U.S. troops stationed in Europe. Should the United States tax itself to preserve its regional hegemony and maintain the outposts of its Atlantic and Pacific empires indefinitely? Or should it threaten to quit unless the Europeans at last consent to pay for the majority of NATO's expenditures? Strikingly, the Soviets faced a comparable set of difficulties in Afghanistan. The costs distorted the budget priorities of the Soviet economy and the Red Army. No material assistance was offered by Warsaw Treaty allies. If the Kremlin ever published national account figures, it would appear that the burdens of military action in Afghanistan, Angola, and of offering support to Cuba, Libya, and Syria had helped ruin the Soviet Union's balance of payments and its industrial strength.

A revealing study of the economic burdens of empire, *The Rise and Fall of the Great Powers,* has recently been published by a Yale historian, Paul Kennedy. As the subtitle indicates, his work focuses on "Economic Change and Military Conflict from 1500 to 2000."[3] Kennedy suggested that every majestic empire of Europe, from the Hapsburgs in the seventeenth century to the Victorian zenith of the United Kingdom, repeated the mistakes of "imperial overstretch." After each had conquered its colonies through war, the European empires inevitably slipped into a course of economic decline. Since 1945, America has repeated the cycle. Kennedy related the decline in U.S. manufacturing leadership and in its balance of payments position to the "imperial overstretch" in its military aspirations. The decline has been masked by the preeminent status of the United States' economic and military capabilities and by its success in expanding the international influence of its capitalist market and culture. For nearly fifty years the United States remained the leading power center of the Western world; its military might, political weight, and cultural influence were not challenged by China, Japan, or the European Economic Community. When necessary, the United States managed to share its imperial costs either by charging offset expenses against its reluctant allies or by devaluing its currency and forcing European central banks to support the dollar. But the strategies of enforced burden-sharing have come to an end. Most of the allies today condemn the relentless piling up of deficits on the domestic and external accounts, and they have called for a radical restructuring of public finances in the U.S. imperium.

The astronomical expense of maintaining the U.S. military supremacy and its "spheres of influence" has swollen to the size of its national debt. Each year the servicing of the debt becomes more expensive. Industrial investments at home and overseas have been squandered to finance wars of peripheral significance or weapons of dubious utility. The security that should have been bought with investment in armaments has been imperilled by the excessive strains placed on the U.S. economy. Kennedy could have drawn the comparison between Philip the Second, who ruined Spain's national treasury to build the Great Armada, and Ronald Reagan, who doubled the national debt "on his watch" and who dreamed of creating an SDI astrodome—an endeavor that would have doubled the deficit yet again. The historian suggested an epitaph that may be fitting: "Rome fell; Babylon fell; Scarsdale's turn will come."

Mr. Gorbachev faced a greater threat from the military and bureaucratic factions in the Kremlin as he fought for his campaign of *perestroika.* If his restructuring campaign fails, the Soviet Union will never compete economically with the West, or even with its richer allies in Eastern Europe. It cannot support exhausting military programs if it is to modernize the low-productivity agriculture and low-technology industries of the Soviet economy. And what benefits could it ever reap if its military power were based on the feeble finances of a Third World economy?

Nevertheless, Professor Kennedy believes that the United States is unique: it is still able to resolve its imperial dilemma, if it chooses, by changing its priorities. While empires of the past were governed by rigid dogma and elite cadres, the political and economic systems of the United States are pluralist in structure and flexible in function. The capacity of each system to change course and shift its values is somewhat unique. It cannot be matched either by today's authoritarian regimes or by the class-bound societies of past empires. The prediction is often made that the United States will emulate the long and painful course of decline set by the United Kingdom, but there is no compelling reason why this must occur. The United States still towers over its allies as the preeminent nuclear and military power, as does the Soviet Union in Eastern Europe. Their bloc leadership may be challenged in the 1990s, but it will not be replaced. There is no single nation or regional federation of nations that can usurp the global role and influence exercised by the superpowers.

As the twentieth century comes to a close, a novel vision has been glimpsed: the arms race cannot be funded at increasing levels, or even at present rates, for an indefinite future. It simply must slow down and eventually grind toward a halt. Though embittered ideologues in both camps dissent, they cannot block further progress on the INF treaties, the START negotiations, or the reunification of the two Germanys. It is obvious that the resources to intensify or even to sustain the nuclear arms race are no longer available, and that they could not be restored, even if major social subsidies and welfare programs were to be canceled.

A comparison with the relatively unburdened economies of their own neighbors and allies has shocked both the Soviet Union and the United States. The superpowers have paid too high a price to act as the world's policemen. It is no longer reasonable to build a first-rate military power base and a second-rate industrial economy. Instead of funding all of the military's outlays, it has become imperative to invest in high-technology industries, capital formation, good educational and health facilities, and means to lighten debt-servicing payments. High defense spending drains away the growth resources needed by a dynamic society. But after forty years of cold war it is apparent in Washington and in Moscow that there is a strong resistance to cutting defense appropriations. Conservative groups have insisted on keeping military outlays intact, and neither government has dared to find a "peace dividend" by changing its foreign policy priorities.

THE FINITE USES OF FORCE

The attitudes of both superpower leaders toward nuclear war and deterrence have been severely modified in fact, if not in financing. Neither assumes that nuclear war is likely, let alone inevitable, or that the rapid modernization of arsenals must be achieved at all costs to secure a stable

deterrence posture. Mr. Gorbachev, for his part, has revised the dogmatic principles of "scientific socialism." He no longer argues that class
strife and the logic of capitalist destruction will lead to global confrontation. The change in U.S. beliefs followed a similar direction. A report
issued by a top-level policy group in the Pentagon concluded in 1987
that strategies based on massive nuclear retaliation were neither credible
nor cost-effective and should be replaced with a new doctrine of "discriminate deterrence."[4]

Recent summit meetings reflected this switch from ideological passion to economic calculation. Neither side chose to accelerate payments
for new strategic or conventional weapons. Both argued heatedly about
"Star Wars" defense systems and European deployments, but their exercises in diplomatic bluffing were not impressive. Neither could afford
to augment defense spending by 10 percent—and certainly not by 15
percent—when their deficit spending is clearly excessive. Military expenditures for both superpowers have been frozen for the last four years
at roughly $300 billion each, and neither side has dared to increase—or
decrease—the rate of military authorizations.

Current rates of military expenditures can be analyzed from another
perspective. The real gross world product (GWP) increased at a rate of
62 percent per capita between 1960 and 1987; by contrast, inflation-
adjusted military outlays grew by 146 percent. During this twenty-
seven-year period, worldwide military spending mounted to a total of
$13.8 trillion (in 1983 dollars), but the increment added to GWP grew by
only $8.6 trillion.[5] Annual GWP between 1980 and 1985 rose at a rate of
2.4 percent while military spending rose at 3.2 percent, thus absorbing
more than the total dividend of GWP growth.[6]

Specific data for the Soviet Union is still unreliable, but it is likely to
follow the patterns recorded by Western countries: the continuing
growth of gross domestic product (GDP) is inversely correlated with
spending on national security. In the United Kingdom and the United
States military outlays were particularly generous and GDP growth was
stunted during the 1960s and 1970s. By 1985 the United States' wealth
was 47.5 percent of the total economic product of the NATO countries
plus Japan, but its defense spending accounted for 70 percent of their
total military outlays; moreover, with only one-third of the combined
population of its allies, the United States contributed 40 percent of all
military and civilian defense personnel.[7]

A further set of comparative data can help advance the argument.

· *Public health and education expenditures* in both the United States and
  the USSR amount to only half of military appropriations. Interestingly, the superpowers rank poorly in all measures of public
  health and education, and the consequences could be serious if
  their workforces fail to compete in skill, productivity, and good

health with the trading societies which now threaten to overtake
them in aggregate and per capita wealth.

· *Total military expenditures* on research and development exceeds $75
billion a year, most of it paid for by the superpowers. SDI and other
weapons projects were supposed to generate valuable spill-over
benefits for civilian R and D, but they have failed to boost the
modernizing of vital export industries. Productivity gains in what
were once competitive industries have not materialized, while
economies with only small defense burdens have raced ahead in
science-based and capital-intensive pursuits.

· *Both nuclear leaders are net debtors* on the world trade and money
markets. Their balance of payments positions have deteriorated,
their investments in infrastructure appear to have declined, and
their currencies have lost value. Their merchandise trade balances
pile up larger deficits, and an inflow of foreign currency payments
is needed to finance their investment and security commitments.
No reversal of these crippling trends is likely to occur in either
country for years to come.

Defense spending has become known as "Keynesianism on ste-
roids." It is stimulating in the short run, highly addictive and ruinous
in the long run. Though the spree of military spending might have moved
the superpowers toward détente during the 1980s, neither can ignore
the punishing side effects: deficits have become terrifyingly expensive to
service every year, interest payments now cost more than investments
in infrastructure and industrial modernization, and inflationary pressures have climbed while the purchasing power of each defense dollar
has shrunk. A budget of $300 billion buys less and less each year while
the tax burden of financing grows heavier. The escalation trend could
not continue and the spending curves will simply have to flatten. In the
first years of the Reagan administration (between 1980 and 1985) defense
appropriations increased 55.3 percent; now the rate of annual increment
has been decisively halted. Outlays have stuck at roughly $300 billion for
five consecutive years, and they have flattened out in the Soviet Union
as well. If allowance is made for the cumulative effects of inflation, the
real purchasing by defense agencies has fallen by 10 to 15 percent.[8]

It is obvious that current and pending arms control agreements will
not depress further defense spending. Even if conventional forces in
Europe (CFE) and START reductions were quickly effected, budget
levels would be scaled down by less than 5 percent, since the major
share of appropriations still goes to personnel and conventional force
commitments. Moreover, the "bow wave" created by procurement contracts in the last few years has yet to crest. Due to a time lag in actual
contract payments, there could even be an increase in military outlays
before any significant retrenchment appears. It is estimated that the

backlog of appropriated but unexpended funds still waiting in the pipeline equals a full year's budget. The budgets of the 1980s clearly favored weapons modernization and defense industry investments rather than military readiness and personnel; they imposed many budget reductions on the latter in order to protect procurement and research categories.[9]

THE ECONOMIC DISTRESS OF THE SUPERPOWERS

There is a danger of exaggerating the economic difficulties facing the leadership elites in the United States and USSR. Neither country's industrial structure is bankrupt, nor is its economy nearing the point of collapse. But both systems are seriously overextended. They no longer command the resources needed to fulfill the global security roles to which they had once committed themselves. For entirely differing reasons, both have overdrawn their investment capital and their overseas accounts, and both have failed to match the competitive spirit of their successful allies and trade rivals. At home they face urgent demands to raise consumption standards and capital funds, but they cannot hope to do so while a major portion of GDP and of central government expenditure is siphoned away for military purposes.

Despite the sharp differences between their political systems, there are two choices that the superpowers can pursue as they try to resolve their common dilemma of "imperial overstretch." Depending on their success in improving their bilateral relations and a range of confidence-building arrangements between Moscow and Washington, they can move toward one of two long-term goals:

1. To phase out nuclear and conventional defense commitments in central Europe and to lower tension levels in troubled Third World regions while still maintaining their duopoly of police powers; or
2. To create a global management system which would build upon multilateral forms of economic and financial stability, and anchoring the security or deterrence concerns of the alliance blocs within regional or treaty partnerships.

There is no simple dichotomy between these two choices. Any course of action will involve both unilateral and multilateral decisions. But the options can be usefully categorized, first in terms of the levels of economic or military cooperation required; and, second, by the degree to which the superpowers will have to rely on their allies, adversaries, and outsiders.

A set of basic choices will have to be made in the near future; they cannot be evaded or once again postponed. For nearly half a century the two bloc leaders were able to buy peace and to preserve a relatively

stable hegemonic order at a cheap price. Except in a few cases, their
bipolar concentration of power went largely unchallenged. They were
able to mask the signs of economic deterioration that were slowly crack-
ing open the foundations of their military ascendancy. Now the mas-
querade is over. Neither has an extra \$1 or \$2 trillion to modernize its
nuclear deterrent, or to strengthen its conventional capabilities, and
certainly not to do both together. Their intercontinental and sea-
launched ballistic missile squadrons are still formidable symbols of
power, but the industrial expansion that both societies need is truly in
peril. They cannot afford under present conditions to sustain global
deterrence postures or a war-fighting capability in central Europe—or
anywhere else, for that matter.[10]

The option of negotiating a cutback of force structures and deployments is the more practical of the two and is therefore, ironically, the
most resisted of the solutions presently available. Soviet leaders had to
walk out of Afghanistan, Kampuchea, and the inconclusive wars in
Africa, and to drag themselves into negotiating an end to the nuclear
arms race. For their part, the Reagan and Bush regimes were equally
reluctant to scale back military commitments in the Persian Gulf or
Nicaragua, or in the awesome cost of maintaining 300,000 troops in
Germany. Various proposals have been advanced to economize in these
high-priced ventures but they eventually fell by the wayside. In most
cases they required a unilateral force withdrawal, or a risky cutback in
strategic deterrence, or a diplomatic loss of face that no superpower
could easily accept. The principle of bloc leadership helped preserve
nuclear stability and bipolar order as well as the amour propre of the
leaders. Each superpower guaranteed the security of its allies and pro-
tectorates; in return, the dependents acknowledged political preeminence and the global leadership of their protector. In retrospect, the
condominium of the superpowers was built on both threat and exchange relationships that proved to be remarkably durable and inexpen-
sive to the hegemonic powers.[11]

On the U.S. side it is clear that the military power-equations of the
Cold War period must soon change. Japan and European allies are worried that the failing dollar will affect their own currency reserves and
monetary policy. If the U.S. defense budget and the federal deficit
should grow, inflation will spread worldwide. They fear that the U.S.
will bring home some of its garrisons stationed in Europe or Asia in the
1990s; or that Congress will be so irritated by their "free rider" refusal to
pick up the defense burdens of a collective security alliance that it will
resort to trade sanctions or policy reprisals.[12] Unofficial suggestions to
lighten U.S. costs in Europe, or to "decouple" U.S. strategic forces from
European tactical forces, prompted nervous responses from European
parties both on the Left and the Right. In the last resort, neither wants to
disrupt the hegemonic balance. Most Europeans prefer to cooperate

with the arms control deals that were negotiated over their heads in the summit meetings than to oppose them, and they have also volunteered to support the exchange value of the dollar. But at some point they will demand that the post–Reagan regime should either restore a vigorous bloc leadership in NATO, or, alternatively, correct its overstretched positions in order to strengthen its economic power base.

The second choice available to the superpowers is more ambiguous and challenging. It also requires a departure from established principles of conflict and "containment" behavior. The status ascendancy of the bloc leaders would be opened up to challenge; their nuclear duopoly and political dominance would also be diminished as nations turned increasingly toward multilateral action and away from bipolar hierarchies. It is not certain whether the military security pacts would survive if greater concern were invested in building institutions for global management. As the next century opens it may be necessary for security arrangements to correspond to economic forms of pluralism rather than thermonuclear duopolies of power.

The chief obstacle to change will probably come from the superpowers themselves. Their pretences of power and invulnerability will have to be considerably trimmed. The USSR will fall to third and soon to fourth or fifth place in the world order if it is ranked by national wealth or industrial product rather than by military firepower. The standing of the U.S. economy will also be impaired. It accounted for more than half of the world's wealth in manufacturing product in 1945, but its share had fallen to 31.5 percent by 1980 and it is likely to decline to 20 percent by the end of the century.[13] More important, U.S. financial assets and industrial investments overseas had once been the dominant factor in world trade and credit flows. Today the United States owes so much to foreign holders of dollar securities that its external account is in disrepair and it is increasingly vulnerable to threats by foreign lenders to liquidate their dollar holdings. Unless it can manage to slash its consumption standards or its defense budget, which President Bush refuses to do, it will be sensitive to every tremor in the Eurodollar market or in the Pacific rim market. The current trade-off requires the allies in Europe and Asia to lend the United States sufficient money to pay for most of their own defense. This paradoxical arrangement will come apart if the U.S. trade balance deteriorates or if its credit rating should weaken. At that point, the United States might have to threaten to withdraw the 400,000 troops deployed overseas. That threat could create powerful tensions among allied governments on both sides of the moldering "iron curtain" which had once divided the world.

The conclusion remains that the great power game cannot survive for long in its current form, and neither can the bipolar division of strategic power. Not even the dramatic changes that toppled six communist regions in Eastern Europe in 1989 were able to shatter the Warsaw Pact built by Moscow. It is reasonable to predict that both superpowers will now have to shed the illusions and expenses of empire, though for entirely differing reasons. They will both discover that the purchase of hegemony "on the cheap" is no longer within their grasp. The days of the American Century or of the Communists' Commonwealth are finished. The superpowers' economic distress must deny them the range of diplomatic coercion, military initiative, and nuclear contingency planning that they once commanded. It was the United Kingdom's fate to lose an empire and its world role. It may be the turn now for the Pax Atomica to come apart, not because new challengers emerge to unseat the old but simply because the two hegemonical powers have become too debilitated to cut their losses and change their strategic posture.[14]

The gradual loss of coercive status by the superpowers will surely benefit the middle-sized and newly industrialized countries in the world economy. This slow but radical movement could lead to two bold, system-wide innovations. First, contemporary modes of interstate threats and sanctions will eventually give place to a more rational and plural form of exchange behavior. After all, preparing for war is a costly alternative to trading in peace. Second, ideological enmities and nuclear anxieties will tend to change as economic relationships proliferate. Tensions between the two Germanys and their neighbors, between the rich and poor nations, between socialists and capitalists, will not dissolve; however, they might become subject to more rational control procedures. There is no certainty that plural forms of management can be peacefully negotiated or that economic rivalry will replace military violence. There is one factor that could speed the process of transformation, however, and that is the constant decline in the autonomy of the superpowers. How the Soviet Union and the United States choose to negotiate the decline is critical. If they bitterly resist the trend and reject the opportunities now dawning to change the system, they might have to use their nuclear strength—against each other or their allies—to preserve their dominant influence. Alternatively, they might recognize that economic power is at least as vital as nuclear coercion, and that in the international economic order their preeminence will not escape the process of erosion that is now undermining their position of leadership.

NOTES

1. Most of the comparative data on military personnel, weapons spending, GNP growth rates, productivity gains, and capital investment ratios cited in these pages were drawn from *The Military Balance 1987–1988* (London: International Institute for Strategic Studies, 1987) and from the *Budget of the U.S. Government, FY 1989* (Washington, D.C.: Government Printing Office, 1988). Also see Hugh Mosley, *The Arms Race: Economic and Social Consequences* (Lexington, Mass.: Lexington, 1985); and Lloyd J. Dumas, *The Overburdened Economy* (Berkeley, Calif.: University of California, 1986).

2. See "Capitalism in Conflict" by Shafiqul Islam, in *Foreign Affairs*, vol. 69, no. 1 (1989–90): 172–82, for a comparison of U.S. and Japanese growth data.

3. Paul Kennedy, *The Rise and Fall of the Great Powers: Economic Change and Military Conflict from 1500 to 2000* (New York: Random House, 1987).

4. See Mikhail Gorbachev, *Perestroika: New Thinking for Our Country and the World* (New York: Harper & Row, 1987); and the U.S. Department of Defense, *Discriminate Deterrence* (Washington, D.C.: Government Printing Office, 1988).

5. Economic data on GDP levels, defense budgets, and dollar conversions were drawn from Ruth Leger Sivard, *Survey of World Military and Social Expenditures* (Leesburg, Va.: World Priorities, 1987); and the *SIPRI Yearbook 1986: World Armaments and Disarmament* (New York: Oxford University Press, 1986).

6. *SIPRI Yearbook 1986*, 210.

7. See Caspar Weinberger, *Report on Allied Contributions to the Common Defense* (Washington, D.C.: Department of Defense, 1987), 5.

8. Useful data are compiled in the *Statistical Abstract of the United States 1988* (Washington, D.C.: Department of Commerce, 1987); on Soviet spending, see *The Military Balance 1987–1988*, 27–33. The FY91 budget proposed by the Bush administration eliminated all hope of a "peace dividend." Defense appropriations actually increased by 2 percent to $306 billion, though real purchasing power fell by another 5 percent. Following a stormy debate in the U.S. Congress, the Bush priority of keeping up the Pentagon budget was widely endorsed.

9. On the "bow wave" spending of backlogged funding, and also for an expert analysis of the FY 1989 budget request, see Stephen Cain, *The FY 1989 Defense Budget* (Washington, D.C.: Center on Budget and Policy Priorities, 1988).

10. See the conservative analysis of William W. Kaufmann, *A Reasonable Defense* (Washington, D.C.: The Brookings Institution, 1986), 9–12. He quotes from Churchill's memory of a cabinet meeting before World War I. Churchill had asked for six new dreadnoughts, but Lloyd George insisted on limiting expenditure to four, so the Asquith Cabinet compromised at eight.

11. On the cheap cost of securing hegemonic authority over its allies, see David P. Calleo, *Beyond American Hegemony: The Future of the Western Alliance* (New York: Basic Books, 1987).

12. See Robert E. Osgood, "Europe's Dependence on American Protection," in Walter Goldstein, ed., *Clash in the North: Polar Summitry and NATO's Northern Flank* (Washington, D.C.: Pergamon-Brassey's, 1988).

13. Paul Kennedy, "The First World War and the International Power System," *International Security*, vol. 9, no. 2 (1984): 36–39. A sharp criticism of Professor Kennedy and others who forecast the decline of U.S. hegemony appears in Samuel P. Huntington, "The U.S.: Decline or Renewal?," *Foreign Affairs*, vol. 67, no. 2 (1988–89): 76–96.

14. Calleo, in *Beyond American Hegemony* (see footnote 11), writes an excellent theoretical chapter on the loss of hegemonic authority. He examines the historical record of the United Kingdom and then the United States before asking why they lost power. Was it the hegemon that weakened its political and economic clout, or was it the hegemonic order that was transformed from a unilateral to a plural structure? The author concludes on a prophetic note (see page 126): "[W]hereas Soviet expansionism is reasonably contained, American fiscal and monetary disorder is not. . . . [The U.S. roles of] containing Soviet military power and maintaining a viable world economy seems increasingly incompatible."

ARMS: THE CRISIS IMPOSED BY TECHNOLOGY

5

Security, Arms, and Arms Control

RAYMOND L. GARTHOFF

. . . [T]here is today *potential* for a real turning point of historical significance in American and world politics and security relationships. "Arms control" is not, of course, an end in itself. Neither is "deterrence" or "defense." All are categories of possible means to achieve security, and the choice of a mix of specific policies and measures can enhance—or degrade—security.

The United States is, overall, the most powerful nation in the world. Our security in the nuclear age is nonetheless irretrievably bound up with that of other nations in many ways. Most dramatically, our security and indeed our very survival is dependent on our geopolitical rival and putative adversary, the Soviet Union—as of course their survival is dependent upon the United States. The choice of the share of reliance each places on unilateral defense policy, or on collaborative negotiated arms control and reduction, is similarly bounded not only by what the other side does in its defense programs but also by the limits of what it is prepared to agree to in terms of negotiated constraints.

DETERRENCE

The security predicament of the two powers is not new. Ever since the burgeoning tensions of the early postwar period generated the cold war, and especially after the Soviet Union too acquired nuclear weapons, the

Reprinted by permission of the *Harvard International Review* and Dr. Raymond L. Garthoff. Copyright 1989, International Relations Council, Inc.

Note: It is a violation of the law to reproduce this selection by any means whatsoever without the written permission of the copyright holder.

United States has depended on a defense policy resting on two foundations: unilateral nuclear deterrence, and collective Western (NATO) alliance deterrence, of Soviet aggression. There is an overlap that has been called "extended deterrence," an extension of the unilateral American strategic nuclear capability to defend Western Europe as well as North America. Alliance defense forces in Europe are regarded as an essential concomitant to, but not a substitute for, the extended umbrella of the American nuclear deterrent.

Deterrence has become such a fixed foundation of American and Western European security thinking that its new role, and its limitations, have scarcely been recognized. Deterrence is an instrument (or a strategy) of policy, rather than an objective. Our objective is the prevention of war, above all the prevention of nuclear war, but also the prevention of a conventional war of aggression against the West (in practical terms, a conventional attack against the whole or any part of NATO Europe). But deterrence is predicated on influencing calculations of a potential attacker; deterrence, if successful, prevents only deliberate initiation of war by a potential attacker who would otherwise expect to gain from such an attack. Deterrence cannot, by its very nature, prevent war generated by accident, or miscalculation, or inadequately controlled escalation from a crisis, or preemption by an adversary who believes his opponent is already irretrievably committed and imminently launching an attack. Decisions and actions should be consonant with the prevention of war rising from any cause, not only deterrence of aggressive and acquisitive war. Measures designed to enhance deterrence, for example, should not increase risks of war by lowering the threshold of preemption or risking less feasible control of escalation in a crisis, including possible spillover into limited hostilities.

Deterrence is so firmly accepted that it is invoked to justify virtually any proposed increase in military capability. Since almost any accretion of military power is widely assumed to add something to deterrence, and everyone supports deterrence, it is not hard to see why the claim is advanced. Rarely is a rigorous challenge advanced in terms of questioning requirements for deterrence, with one exception. Military-technical considerations of relative invulnerability or survivability, and less convincing arguments for a hard-target kill capability for strategic retaliatory forces, are qualities presumed to enhance deterrence. Unfortunately, in many cases they also contribute to disarming first-strike capability. Moreover, we focus exclusively on protecting the survival of *our* deterrent, while continuing to develop more effective threats against that of our adversary. Hardly ever do criteria for enhancing strategic stability include reducing the threat perception of the other side.

Deterrence and the prevention of war may not, in fact, require many of the forces dedicated to that purpose. Requirements of deterrence, however, while logically geared to the rational calculation of a putative adversary, in practice are often really geared to the impressions of Western publics and governments. Thus while much (conceivably, even all) of what is described and even conceived as a policy and a force posture to sustain deterrence of the Soviet Union is probably redundant to that purpose, it may be necessary to provide reassurance to Western (including American) public and even official opinion. It is sometimes argued that one can't have too much insurance (although none of us would apply that argument in our personal budgets). A much greater danger than underinsurance is failure to recognize that some measures intended to contribute to deterrence of attack, apart from redundancy, may actually stimulate other risks of war.

There is also the too little considered question of just what it is we seek to deter. Do we seek to deter actions *short* of an attack on the United States or its allies? The most reasonable expansion of the object of deterrence would be deterrence of any *threat* to use military power, for example, an ultimatum to surrender some sovereign asset. A threat of such a nature, although in practice quite unlikely, can be deterred or countered by a counterthreat, in extension of the defensive purpose of deterrence.

Deterrence should not, however, be stretched to include what Thomas Schelling long ago described as "compellence." For example, a few years ago I heard an enthusiastic senior American military official assert in a public forum that new strategies for deep attack on Soviet forces in Eastern Europe would give us greater capabilities for deterrence—for example to prevent Soviet intervention in Poland or Czechoslovakia to maintain communist rule. That would not be deterrence, but compellence, and any attempt to apply that conception of deterrence would, apart from all other risks and dangers, quickly cause a crisis in NATO, which is not an alliance constructed for the purpose of furthering the political liberation of Eastern Europe by military or any means.

The existence of two counterposed alliances in Europe has become a settled fact of political life. This is not to say that it is immutable or permanent. But both sides have long ago come to terms with accepting it as a political reality not justifying the risks of any attempts at forcible change, thus reinforcing (or, perhaps, rendering moot) deterrence of an attack.

Military power has never been used directly by either superpower against the other or its core allies, and rarely even against countries closely associated with the other superpower. Nonetheless it has been an ever-present factor, and a few close calculations (as over Berlin) or miscalculations (as in the Cuban missile crisis), or independent actions of associates (as in several Near Eastern wars) have posed crises. Nonetheless, security of both has been maintained principally by political restraint reinforced to an uncertain but evidently adequate degree by military deterrence. In addition, the two countries have gradually experimented with arms negotiations, occasionally even with limited arms agreements.

ARMS CONTROL

The first burst of limited accords came in the mid-1960's, in the wake of the Cuban missile crisis and dramatically perceived risks of war. Still, the measures then agreed on were modest and peripheral: the "hot line" for crisis communication to dispel misconceptions that could seriously exacerbate risks: the limited nuclear test ban, that disposed of a common and global risk from radioactive contamination but did not—and was not intended to—curtail weapons development; and an agreement not to place nuclear weapons into outer space. The two powers, after overcoming possible political problems with allies, agreed on arms control for *others*, in particular nuclear weapons nonproliferation, or for themselves in areas of no military promise (in Antarctica and on the seabed).

Serious efforts at limiting the arms of the two superpowers became possible only in the 1970's, when two conditions had come to prevail. First was the amassing of such large arsenals of nuclear weapons that it was becoming evident that an agreed quantitative cap would be in the interests of both, and even more important, when a rough essential parity in strategic nuclear forces had been reached. This was the basis that made possible first a freeze on the number of strategic missile launchers in SALT I early in the decade, and on an equal number of strategic missile launchers and bombers (with certain permissive but comparable limits on warheads as well) in SALT II by the close of the decade. While these constraints were better than none, they were too little and too late to make any real contribution to stability and security. This permitted opponents of such accords to argue against the value of arms control.

What had failed, however, was not arms control, but the willingness of the two powers to give arms control a chance to contribute meaningfully to security. Neither the United States nor the Soviet Union was prepared to accept equitable serious constraints on its own military programs. The SALT I and II agreements limiting strategic offensive arms were therefore, while of some political value, only modest steps in arms control, and arguably even of negative effect on arms control by placing its value in question.

The one notable exception was the ABM Treaty. It, too, was acceptable to both sides only because it cut off what then were expensive and ineffective ballistic missile defenses. But it was potentially a real breakthrough in arms control because it was undertaken for unlimited duration, and with serious constraints (though not a complete ban) on development and testing as well as deployment of future ballistic missile defense technologies. By neutralizing the ballistic missile defense side of the offense–defense strategic equation, it made possible far more limited strategic offensive forces. This was not, however, more than a possibility, and the rush to MIRV (multiple-independently targeted reentry vehicles) despite the agreement to ban a major ABM defense—which MIRV had initially been designed to overcome. Too much has been laid at the door of the Soviet Union for not agreeing to strategic reductions in the 1970's—we never proposed reductions that would seriously or comparably curtail American as well as Soviet strategic forces. Nonetheless, the Soviet Union, too, was excessively cautious and conservative in its position. Both sides preferred to agree to minimal limitations that, while improving the predictability of the strategic balance, did not significantly curb either existing or even planned strategic forces.

THE STRATEGIC DEFENSE INITIATIVE

The ABM Treaty, while not halting the existing competition in strategic offensive arms, did curtail its escalation and contribute to strategic stability. Since March 1983, however, its future has been under a dark cloud. The idea of pursuing an active research and development program with the aim of deploying a nationwide ballistic missile defense had not been seriously considered within the United States government. Nonetheless, President Ronald Reagan personally seized upon the idea and decided to launch a surprise initiative. He publicly championed his hasty decision to commit the United States to a strategic defense initiative (SDI) as a political fait accompli. The idea of unleashing American technological genius to provide a total defense appealed to a nostalgic, anachronistic, even atavistic deep desire to see America again invulnerable, independent, and self-reliant, freed from the shackles of interdependence, with its fate no longer tied to mutual vulnerability through mutual deterrence. President Reagan's image was indeed, as he proclaimed then and often thereafter, even when only he still believed it, that his SDI would make nuclear weapons impotent and obsolete. His commitment was not based on science, but on faith, so scientific-technical and military-technical arguments were irrelevant and his vision unchangeable. The vision was a mirage.

The SDI was not intended, at least by President Reagan, to give the United States strategic domination of nuclear mutual deterrence. After the summit meetings in Geneva and Reykjavik, General Secretary Mikhail Gorbachev came to recognize this personal entrancement of the president but could not break its thrall. It became a cruel irony of fate that President Reagan's own desire to banish the nuclear specter on the one hand opened up the prospect for real nuclear disarmament, while foreclosing it with the other through stubborn dedication to the quixotic pursuit of his SDI illusion. Reagan's insistence on negotiating nuclear arms reductions, rather than more limitations, a cynical slogan of his associates in the early 1980's, suddenly came to life in his personal encounter of another kind of Reykjavik. While the prospect of agreement on eliminating all strategic nuclear weapons, or even all nuclear weapons, came within reach at Reykjavik, it could not be grasped because he still held tight to the beguiling image of self-attained strategic independence through the SDI. Nonetheless, owing to the conjunction of Reagan's and Gorbachev's parallel determination to move toward reducing the role of nuclear weapons, another ploy intended by its authors in the Reagan Administration as a fail-safe propaganda coup in 1981 as the "zero option" became an accord "eliminating an entire class of nuclear weapons" in the intermediate-range nuclear forces (INF) treaty of December 1987. And major elements of a strategic arms reduction treaty (START) were far advanced—though still stymied over recommitment to the ABM Treaty—by the time the Reagan administration left office.

An ill-conceived "reinterpretation" of the ABM Treaty provisions banning the testing and development of mobile, air, and space-based ABM systems and components was adopted by the Reagan Administration in October 1985 without either appropriate foundation or due consideration. This has created a serious new obstacle to any agreement. The US Congress has refused to permit the leeway for wider SDI testing that the reinterpretation was intended to provide, but the Reagan Administration refused to abandon it and the Soviet Union will not accept it.

REAGAN'S LEGACY

The legacy of the Reagan Administration in the field of defense, arms control, and security—more generally—is more complex than it may at first appear. Reagan, who truly sought to overcome big government and fiscal irresponsibility, added another cabinet department and left the United States standing tall—on a mountain of debt, twice what had been accumulated by *all* his thirty-nine presidential predecessors. No small contribution to that debt was a defense "policy" that measured strength by a unique form of supply-side faith: how much we spent on defense, rather than what we got for those massive outlays. And we did spend plenty, over 2 *trillion* dollars since 1981. Yet except for a larger navy than we can now afford to man there is little to show for that increase. The "window of vulnerability" so frighteningly depicted in 1980 was closed not by enhanced defense capabilities but by the sober realism of the Scowcroft Commission. While we have added more than 2,000 improved strategic warheads to our force (all land-based missiles still in silos), the Soviets have added over 3,000 more accurate warheads to their force (with two mobile land-based ICBM systems operational). In fact, if the nominal fifty-percent reduction in strategic forces postulated in the present draft START agreement is agreed upon and implemented, the actual forces of the two sides will be back to about the 1980 level. (The technical reasons for this are complex, but derive from counting rules generous to American bomber-carried weapons, and our insistence on excluding weapons such as nuclear-armed sea-launched cruise missiles [SLCM's].) The military strategic relationship remains basically stable, but is not very different. We were not so weak as we were pictured in 1980, nor so much stronger now; what has changed is the official rhetoric and the public impression.

Reagan, whose gut attitude toward international arms control in 1981 was not very different from his negative sentiment toward domestic gun control, ended up championing the INF Treaty and the process of strategic arms reduction. Reagan lashed out at the rulers of an Evil Empire and called for a new Crusade, not only arming "Freedom Fighters" on three continents but christening them the moral equivalent of our Founding Fathers. Yet this same man became the first president ever to meet four times with the Soviet leader. The same Soviet Union which has been repeatedly charged with multiple violations of existing arms agreements (at least most of which are embarrassingly contrived), is now accepted as the partner for new agreements.

In sum, the legacy of the Reagan administration is to bequeath a public confidence in "again" being militarily (if not fiscally) solvent and standing tall, yet also negotiating for arms reductions. The slogan of the Reagan Administration, "strength, realism, negotiation," is after all common sense. Yet it remains to be seen whether even a direct successor Republican administration led by a less charismatic leader can keep the support of both bipartisan centrists and conservatives and neoconservatives who have chafed under Reagan but have not been converted to the virtues of arms control. The false impression of a pattern of Soviet violation of past arms agreements may come back to haunt a less unchallengeable president as he seeks approval for future agreements.

FROM BREZHNEV TO GORBACHEV

Let us turn now to the other essential ingredient in the rebirth of arms control. Successive Soviet leaders from 1980 to 1985 had difficulty in adjusting to the American defection from détente and arms control. Moreover the harsh rhetoric, the enormous American investment in seeking military superiority (as they saw it), and the utter failure of their own efforts to generate international opposition to the INF deployment, led by the end of 1983 to an exasperated walkout from the INF and START negotiations. This decision also reflected their recognition that the START and INF negotiations were deadlocked. While public opinion in Europe had compelled the United States to begin the INF talks by late 1981 (in order to maintain support for continuing INF deployment), and opinion in the United States itself favoring a nuclear freeze had led to START a few months later, this public sentiment could not make the American leadership adopt positions that were compatible with Soviet as well as American interests, as seen by the Soviet leadership. Their own approach was a linear development of the incremental, gradual approach of SALT talks. In the 1970's, the US administrations had wanted to reach agreements, and conservative minimalist accords could be reached. The American administration in the first half of the 1980's had continued to seek minimal constraints on American forces, but had insisted on drastic one-sided Soviet reductions as a quid pro quo. So leaving the START and INF talks was no loss, and they hoped this break-off of strategic arms talks for the first time in fifteen years would jolt Western publics, and governments, into being more reasonable. But this was a bad misjudgment. The only effect (predictably enough) was to put the blame on the Soviet Union for walking out, while the United States and NATO governments needed only piously to reaffirm readiness to resume talks at any time.

The Soviet leadership recognized this error and prepared to redress it even before Gorbachev came to power. But the fact that Gorbachev and his key advisors and associates brought what they called a "new thinking" to the whole range of security issues would have crucial importance in leading to a new era in Soviet-American relations and arms negotiations. While the change of the 1985–88 period could not have occurred without Reagan's acquiescence, the key motivating factor in readiness to take bold new departures, and make major concessions, was Gorbachev's new thinking.

GORBACHEV'S NEW THINKING ON SECURITY

The new Soviet leadership under Gorbachev has been revising the Soviet approach to international affairs with breathtaking speed and scope. While policy takes time to formulate and implement, and much will depend on what we do, Gorbachev and his colleagues have already made radical changes in traditionally ingrained political, military, and ideological conceptual assumptions. The first major public and authoritative pronouncements were made at the 27th Party Congress in February 1986, and the Soviet political establishment and leadership—not without differences and even sharp controversy—have continued to build a new conceptual framework and to move in new policy directions. At the Party Congress, Gorbachev advanced a new assessment of the world. For the first time in such an authoritative forum, he advanced the concept of one interdependent world and interests of humankind *transcending* class interests and class struggle and the contention of two ideological systems or worlds.

The central focus and theme of his report to the Congress on Soviet foreign policy was on security, couched in an unprecedented way. Preventing nuclear war, and promoting disarmament and peaceful coexistence, have long been prominent avowed Soviet aims, but now they were said to be "the main line of the party's activity in the world arena," and were given a new context. The heart of Gorbachev's argument was the conclusion that *no* nation can any longer find security in military power, either in defense or deterrence. "The character of contemporary weapons," he said, "does not leave *any* state hope of protecting itself by military-technical means alone, for example by creating even the most powerful defense." And, while mutual deterrence is more effective than defense, "security cannot indefinitely be based on fear of retaliation, that is on doctrines of 'deterrence' or 'intimidation.' " Rather, "the task of insuring security increasingly is a political task, and can be resolved only by political means." Moreover, security cannot be absolute for any country, and can only be mutual, specifically for the Soviet Union *and* the United States, and "if one takes international relations as a whole, it can only be universal." Finally, building on the earlier discussion of global interdependence, he concluded by calling for the "creation of a comprehensive system of international security"—military, political, economic, and humanitarian.

The new thinking on security directly affects military doctrine and defense policy, and arms control policy, as well as a myriad of aspects of Soviet foreign policy. In military policy, not only are concepts of reasonable sufficiency and strategic stability being developed, but military doctrine is—with some difficulty—being recast in more defensive terms. The very definition of military doctrine has been changed to expand it from concepts of preparing for and waging war to include as its highest aim the prevention of war. Deterrence, based on parity in a strategic balance, is Soviet as well as American policy. The Soviets are now, however, looking beyond that to seek more effective long-term ways to prevent war.

What counts, ultimately, is change in policy and action, but conceptual change lays the foundation. Soviet foreign policy in the security area has already changed in many observable ways: the withdrawal from Afghanistan, the new support for United Nations peacekeeping forces, the active efforts to resolve the regional conflicts in Angola and Kampuchea, a new openness in many spheres, including military affairs. The arms control sphere has seen credible proposals for whatever extent of nuclear arms reduction the West will accept, down to the elimination of all nuclear weapons; acceptance of extensive and intensive verification, including on-site inspection; acceptance in the INF Treaty of asymmetrical reductions larger on the Soviet side; readiness to accept non-symmetrical reductions of half of the Soviet SS-18 ICBM's in an initial START agreement; proposals for verified detailed data exchange, and asymmetrical reductions in European conventional arms talks; acceptance of monitored constraints and advance scheduling of military exercises; and many more.

To be sure, Gorbachev has not unilaterally dismantled the Soviet military machine, and will not. Some unilateral measures well beyond the two-year nuclear-testing moratorium may come, including reductions. Moreover, many other important actions in the military security sphere may be taken unilaterally. But most potential measures with respect to cutting back substantially on military power will undoubtedly depend upon reciprocal Western action and probably on negotiated arms reduction agreements. There are, from the Soviet side, vastly increased possibilities for such agreements.

NEW THINKING IN WASHINGTON?

As President Reagan once quipped in challenging the Soviet leaders to engage seriously in arms negotiation, "it takes two to tango." Quite so. President Gorbachev has now invited us to join in a ball.

Many Americans are now hopeful that the Soviet Union may be prepared to reduce tensions, arms, and ambitions. Yet many of these same people are also skeptical and wary. Again to quote President Reagan, in a closely related context, *"Doceriai, no proveriai"*—"Trust, but verify." That is not a bad platform. The United States need not, and should not, take steps that would make security hostage to unproven Soviet performance. What we can do, and should do, is to demonstrate our readiness to take even far-reaching steps that would be in the mutual security interest of both sides if the Soviet Union is prepared to do the same. And we should be responsive to Soviet initiatives advanced with the same objective. Hard negotiation will undoubtedly still be necessary. Not all proposals, Soviet or American, will prove negotiable. Our allies must be a constant active partner, directly in negotiations that directly concern their forces and territory, and indirectly in our decision-making in all negotiations that affect their security.

American and alliance defense and arms control policy should be integrated more closely than ever. Not only must arms control positions and defense policy be compatible, but both should serve security objectives.

While often not interchangeable, in some cases they may be. For example, the best solution to reduce ICBM silo vulnerability remains de-MIRVing of the threatening force of the other side. No longer should conservative assumptions be made as to what arms reductions may be negotiable; the Soviets might well agree to eliminating all SS-18 and SS-24 missiles if in exchange the United States agreed to eliminate all MX and Trident II missiles. This could obviate the requirement for either MX or Midgetman.

The impasse over ballistic missile defense and other space-based weapons must be broken. The best way would be a recommitment to the ABM Treaty, as signed, with mutual commitment to good faith mutual consultation on its interpretation and application *and* negotiation on proposed amendments to loosen, or tighten, various provisions.

Existing nuclear testing constraints could be given formal status by ratification of the treaties signed in 1974 and 1976, now accompanied by additional measures to assure confidence in verification. Beyond that it would be highly desirable to reduce the existing 150 kiloton threshold. A very conservative approach could reduce it by as little as ten percent per annum for seven years, or as much as twenty percent per annum for four years, to be followed by a conference to consider whether a comprehensive ban was by then considered acceptable. The course of strategic arms reductions during the four- to seven-year period would be one important consideration.

President Bush indicated in his election campaign his interest in achieving a complete ban on chemical weapons. This is also a Soviet aim, and the chief problems are third country chemical warfare programs and capabilities and the very great limitations on complete verification. The aim of as complete an elimination of such weapons as is practical should be pursued.

The most complex and difficult negotiations will concern conventional arms in Europe. Progress is likely to be slow, but we can begin with the Warsaw Pact offer to exchange data in detail, and to verify that data through necessary means including on-site inspection, followed by asymmetrical reductions to remove asymmetrical advantages of one or the other side. The process of balancing security while reducing and restructuring forces into more defensive postures will be very difficult, but it offers promise for enhanced security for both sides.

The most important aspect of new thinking needed everywhere is a readiness for realistic steps to curtail reliance on military means. No doubt military power will remain a major background factor in national power and international relations. But it should remain only an ultimate and potential recourse, and the use of military means should no longer be based on traditional terms of expediency based on calculations of cost and risk.

The new Soviet conception of security, or at least Soviet positions on issues, may be self-serving, as are those of all powers. The new Soviet thinking, however, opens up greatly expanded areas for possible agreement based on the security and other interests of the United States and other countries as well as of the Soviet Union. Security *has* become indivisible in the important sense that neither superpower can itself become secure by making the other insecure. Security can only be achieved by a balance of interests. The challenge we face is not to fend off the new Soviet flexibility and readiness to negotiate, but to meet it with flexibility on our own part in order to reach, where possible, accords based on the interests of both or all parties, thereby creating greater security for all.

6

Arms Control after the Cold War

Joseph S. Nye, Jr.

I

For the past 30 years, arms control has been central to the U.S.-Soviet relationship. Now, if the cold war is over, what will be the role of arms control? On the one hand, the relaxed political climate improves the prospects for reaching and ratifying agreements. On the other, improved U.S.-Soviet relations also reduce anxiety about nuclear weapons and urgency about arms control initiatives. Polls show that Americans are now more worried about the state of the U.S. economy and drugs than about the Soviet Union and threat of nuclear weapons.

Geopolitical analysts warn about the diffusion of power in world politics; the spread of chemical and ballistic missile technologies to some 20 nations in the next decade will pose a new type of security threat. Some critics assail the Bush Administration for moving too slowly on the traditional bipolar strategic arms control agenda; others call for giving a

Reprinted by permission of *Foreign Affairs*, Winter 1989–1990. Copyright 1989 by the Council on Foreign Relations, Inc.

Note: It is a violation of the law to reproduce this selection by any means whatsoever without the written permission of the copyright holder.

higher priority to proliferation and multilateral measures. Still others continue to warn that all arms control agreements are a snare and a delusion. The new twist for the time ahead is that the United States and the Soviet Union, though remaining antagonists on the traditional agenda, will find themselves to be partners in some of the emerging problems of arms control.

II

The 1980s began with a sharp debate about the merits of arms control. Many officials in the Reagan Administration contended that arms control was more of a problem than a solution; it lulled public opinion in Western democracies into accepting Soviet strategic superiority. While the pressure of public opinion brought the administration back to arms control negotiations within its first year, little was accomplished until 1986. Then, in its last two years, the Reagan Administration signed an Intermediate-range Nuclear Forces (INF) agreement, causing consternation among many of the president's most ardent supporters. In addition, the administration made substantial progress toward a treaty in the Strategic Arms Reduction Talks (START).

Some conservatives were outraged by Ronald Reagan's new views: Howard Phillips called him a speech-reader for appeasers.[1] But other conservatives base their skepticism on a more general critique of arms control. Irving Kristol, for example, has recently reiterated his charge that arms control agreements do not lead to enduring settlements of conflicts but instead

> tend to be slow, tedious and conducted in an atmosphere of skepticism and suspicion. As a result, agreements are likely to have limited scope. Moreover, technological innovations in weaponry, to say nothing of changes in national leadership, will always make an arms control treaty vulnerable to conflicting interpretations or outright indifference.[2]

Some aspects of this case against arms control have merit. Weapons are symptoms rather than basic causes of hostility. The legalistic approach to seeking compliance with treaties can lead to disproportionate responses in a period of extreme distrust. Arms control negotiations may sometimes slow the process of change. For example, over the past decade NATO has reduced short-range nuclear weapons based in the front lines of Europe. It is quite plausible that efforts to negotiate these reductions in the context of formal arms control agreements would have hindered this stabilizing change. Similarly, some Soviets say that Mikhail Gorbachev announced a unilateral reduction of conventional forces in 1988 at the United Nations rather than at the bargaining table for fear that negotiations would slow the process.

Even some of the founding fathers of modern arms control, such as Thomas Schelling, have expressed skepticism about too much reliance on formal agreements.[3] Many strategists believe that types of weapons, their vulnerability and their susceptibility to central control are more important than their numbers. Reductions are not good per se, but must be judged in light of these characteristics. At low numbers, deceptive practices, hidden weapons and breakouts from treaty constraints could have a greater impact on security than at higher levels. However, given the high levels of existing arsenals, reductions would have to be much deeper than currently foreseen before such factors become a serious security problem.

A careful study of the U.S.-Soviet arms control record in the pre-Gorbachev era concluded that critics' fears that arms control agreements would lull the public and weaken the defenses of democracies have not been borne out. On the other hand, the hopes of proponents that arms control would save money and lead to dramatic reductions were not borne out either.

> What emerges above all is the modesty of what arms control has wrought. Expectations, for better or worse, for the most part have not been realized. The stridency of the debate, however, provides little clue to this modest reality. . . . If the history reveals anything, it is that arms control has proven neither as promising as some had hoped nor as dangerous as others had feared.[4]

In the past three decades, arms control agreements were concluded only when neither side had an appreciable advantage: agreements were not reached when either side had a strong preference for development of a new weapon. Based on this modest record, critics argue that arms control contributes little to international stability.

Critics, however, miss the point: arms control is part of a political process. Too often the experts judge arms control proposals on their technical details rather than on their political significance. For example, the INF agreement was militarily insignificant. In fact one could argue that, in terms of stability, by first removing longer-range nuclear missiles from Europe rather than starting with the short-range artillery, the INF agreement seized the wrong end of the stick concerning command and control of weapons during crises. But the political significance of the INF agreement—the improvement in the U.S.-Soviet relationship in the second half of the Reagan Administration—far outweighed the technical problems related to the details of military doctrine.

Arms control reassures the publics in Western democracies. The process is an inevitable and important part of the political bargaining over defense budgets and modernization. Whatever the strategists may say, the public cares about reductions in numbers because it is difficult to grasp other measurements or present them in clear political terms.

Numbers matter because they are a readily perceived index. Since a major benefit of arms control is domestic political reassurance, general ceilings or reductions can make important contributions to security and force planning even if the number of weapons alone is a poor measure of the risk of nuclear war.

Arms control also provides reassurances to adversaries. In a sense, all of arms control is a confidence- and security-building measure. By increasing transparency and communication among adversaries, worst case analyses are limited and security dilemmas are alleviated. It may be that the most important aspects of the two Strategic Arms Limitation Talks (SALT) agreements were the provisions on open skies for satellite reconnaissance, the agreed counting rules for various types of weapons and the establishment of a Standing Consultative Commission to discuss alleged violations and misunderstandings. In that sense, informal operational arms control and formally negotiated reductions are not exclusive alternatives; they can complement one another.

The agreements on incidents at sea, crisis centers, confidence- and security-building measures in Europe and the recent agreement on the Prevention of Dangerous Military Activities have been scorned by some experts as the "junk food" of arms control. But the classical distinctions between reductions in arms and measures to build confidence and security have begun to blur. Both structural and operational arms control are parts of a larger process of political reassurance among adversaries.

Skeptics might reply that despite the past political role of arms control, the current climate of U.S.-Soviet relations makes further arms control unnecessary because the public and the Soviets no longer need such reassurance in the Gorbachev era. But such a reply fails to understand the institutional role of arms control agreements. As arms control agreements become accepted, political leaders and bureaucratic planners on both sides are less likely to base their strategy upon far-fetched worst case scenarios. Arms control and defense plans tend to reinforce each other. Despite its rhetoric in the early 1980s, the Reagan Administration was better off staying within the framework of the two SALT agreements because they constrained the Soviets and there was little that the United States could build in the short run. To take a different example, in November 1983 the Soviets walked out of INF negotiations with the United States to protest new NATO deployments, yet they still continued to meet with the United States to discuss nonproliferation via institutions that had been established when relations were easier.[5]

In the 1950s the early theorists of modern arms control aimed to reduce the risk and damage of war and save resources. Since those goals are not very different from the objectives of defense policy, it is natural for defense and arms control measures to interact as complementary means to the same ends. As a pattern of reciprocity develops, both sides begin to redefine their interests. Even in the pre-Gorbachev era, as dour a figure as Andrei Gromyko reportedly lobbied to include rising young

Soviet officers in SALT delegations on the grounds that "the more contact they have with the Americans, the easier it will be to turn our soldiers into something more than just martinets."[6]

The opportunities presented by the current political climate and the possibility of a return to cold war relations reinforce the argument for reaching good agreements now: their institutional effects will linger and ameliorate our security problems if relations deteriorate in the future between the United States and the Soviet Union. While Gorbachev's glasnost may have increased transparency and communications beyond the arms control process, both formal reductions (such as the asymmetrical reductions in conventional forces in Europe) and informal agreements that provide access to information (such as exchanges among military officers and visits to Soviet facilities) can help lock in gains for Western security.

Skeptics also neglect a further political role of arms control: the establishment of international security regimes. By treating the military relations among states as a problem of common security, arms control agreements help legitimize some activities and discourage others. These international regimes cannot be kept in separate watertight compartments. For example, the long-term management of nuclear proliferation would be impossible in the context of a totally unconstrained U.S.-Soviet nuclear arms race. Similarly, it is difficult to imagine the United States and Soviet Union managing the diffusion of chemical and biological weapons technology if these two countries were engaged in unconstrained developments in those fields.

Skeptics point out that most states develop nuclear and chemical weapons because of security problems with their neighbors, not because the United States or the Soviet Union promise to disarm. This argument is largely correct. The existence of Article Six of the Nonproliferation Treaty (NPT), in which the superpowers promise to reduce their arsenals, did not deter Pakistan, South Africa or Israel in their nuclear policies. On the other hand, a renewal of the NPT in 1995 will be harder if it must take place in the context of a sharp U.S.-Soviet nuclear arms competition. As one looks further down the road and contemplates the diffusion of destructive power and technology to poor countries and transnational groups, bilateral U.S.-Soviet arms control cannot be divorced from the multilateral arms control problem. On the contrary, the management of international security in the future is likely to require more, not less, attention to the political role of arms control.

III

If measured in terms of numbers of strategic warheads, Soviet missile accuracy and the vulnerability of U.S. intercontinental ballistic missiles (ICBMS), the strategic balance actually worsened during the Reagan years. So why the striking changes in the American arms control policy in the 1980s? Reagan's military budgets, his rhetoric about the Strategic Defense Initiative and the INF deployment in Europe all played a role, but the primary answer is Mikhail Gorbachev. Immediately after coming to power in 1985, Gorbachev altered the Soviet stance in strategic talks by conceding the validity of U.S. concerns about the vulnerability of fixed land-based missiles. In 1986, he permitted intrusive on-site inspections related to confidence- and security-building measures in Europe. In 1987 Gorbachev agreed to an INF agreement largely on Western terms, and in December 1988 he announced unilateral cuts in Soviet conventional forces. Most recently in 1989 he proposed deep asymmetrical cuts in conventional forces in Europe.

Behind President Gorbachev's various proposals, however, lies a deeper Soviet problem. Ironically, at about the same time that Reagan and Defense Secretary Caspar Weinberger were declaring the Soviets to be in a superior position, a younger generation of Soviet economists and officials began to realize the seriousness of their country's economic problems. With a five percent economic growth rate in the 1960s, the Soviet Union was able to finance Leonid Brezhnev's massive nuclear and conventional force buildup. But real Soviet economic growth slackened and in the early 1980s dropped to zero, according to Abel Aganbegyan, one of Gorbachev's economic advisers. The large military expenditures were one cause, and they began to bite.

In addition, the Soviet Union's overly centralized economic system was having difficulty coping with the third Industrial Revolution, i.e., the creation of an information-based economy by the application of computers and telecommunications. By their own accounts, the Soviets lagged ten years behind the West in computer technology, and according to Soviet economist Nikolai Shmelyev, only eight percent of Soviet industry met world standards.[7] These conditions and failures in Soviet foreign policy compelled Gorbachev's ambitious reform program of economic restructuring, domestic liberalization and new thinking in foreign policy.

The new thinking has downgraded the concept of class struggle as the basis for all international affairs and has stressed universal human values; in military affairs, it has introduced the standard of "reasonable sufficiency" of forces in place of superiority or parity. Arms control has become a central concept in Gorbachev's approach to international affairs and helped him to justify reductions in the secrecy that previously cloaked all military matters in the Soviet Union. Adopting the slogan "common security" has allowed much greater transparency in Soviet military activities. The evolution of Soviet arms control proposals reflects and reinforces these new dimensions of Soviet thinking.

Ironically, the Gorbachev phenomenon has had two contrary effects on arms control. The new Soviet attitudes and proposals make arms control easier, but they also reduce the public sense of urgency about strategic arms. Gorbachev has moved a long distance in the direction of the West, but issues of verification and trust have also become somewhat easier to handle in the current climate. The Soviet Union has become more open, even permitting Western delegations to visit and photograph sites at close hand, which Americans had previously photographed only from many miles away in space.

The diminished sense of threat may ease some of the deep dilemmas of verification. Verification issues played a modest part in the arms control debates of the 1960s and early 1970s, but they dominated the American arms control debate in the late 1970s and the 1980s. The political demands for verification began to outstrip what was technically feasible. Many things that the United States could monitor quite adequately for intelligence purposes were not absolutely verifiable. Single instances of alleged violations were used to attack broader Soviet intentions. Ambiguous events and minor transgressions of formal treaties were blown out of proportion; the politics of verification became more stringent than the politics of military security. But in the era of glasnost, although the verification requirements remain formidable, distrust is somewhat eased.

In the early 1980s, when the Western publics feared a considerable likelihood of stumbling into nuclear war, rallies for a nuclear arms freeze filled the streets and public parks. Arms control seemed an urgent part of the process of avoiding nuclear war. Now, however, that sense of urgency has diminished with the shift in Soviet rhetoric and behavior. By lowering the sense of threat among the Western publics, Gorbachev unintentionally reduced public pressure for rapid progress in arms control. This permissive climate may help explain the slow progress on START at the beginning of the Bush Administration.

When Reagan left office, the broad outlines of a START agreement were discernible. Within a limit of 6,000 accountable weapons on 1,600 delivery vehicles, no more than 4,900 could be deployed on ballistic missiles. The Soviets would halve the number of their heavy ICBMs and thus their overall missile throwweight. In addition, all the bombs (although not the air-launched cruise missiles) that could be carried by a bomber would count as one weapon. This undercounting of bombs meant that the overall U.S. strategic nuclear arsenal would be cut by some 30 percent—to 8,000–9,000 weapons—while the Soviet arsenal would be cut by nearly 40 percent—to 7,000–8,000 weapons.

Three large issues remained: (1) how to deal with mobile missiles; (2) whether to follow a strict interpretation of the Antiballistic Missile (ABM) Treaty of 1972; (3) and how to verify limits on sea-launched cruise missiles. The eleventh round of START negotiations in the summer of 1989 made little progress on these issues, but when Foreign Minister Eduard Shevardnadze and Secretary of State James Baker met in September at Jackson Hole, Wyoming, the Soviets suggested a way to finesse two of them.

They dropped their demand for a guarantee that the United States would not withdraw from the ABM treaty, but reserved their right to withdraw from any new START agreement limiting offensive weapons if the United States violated the terms of the ABM treaty "as signed." They also offered to dismantle the large radar under construction at Krasnoyarsk, which Shevardnadze now publicly concedes was an open violation of the ABM treaty. On sea-launched cruise missiles, the Soviets offered to move the issue outside of START if the United States would include it in broader discussions on naval arms control. In turn, the United States dropped its demand for a ban on all mobile missiles, which would have required the Soviets to destroy their SS-24 and SS-25 ICBMs, the equivalents of U.S. proposed rail-mobile and road-mobile missiles. (In any case, the really tough negotiations on this issue are not with the Soviets but rather within the administration, and between the administration and Congress.)

Progress was also made on verification measures and after the Jackson Hole meeting, President Bush declared "a good likelihood" of a START agreement being ready to sign at a summit in Washington in 1990. Baker and Shevardnadze also announced progress on procedures for verification of nuclear tests, of chemical weapons stockpile reductions and on which aircraft were to be included in an agreement on conventional forces in Europe.

Without seeking any direct linkage between the negotiations, the administration had earlier been happy to see priorities shift from strategic negotiations to conventional force talks (CFE) in Europe. The administration had been slow to respond to the dramatic new proposals Shevardnadze put on the table in Vienna in March 1989, but the action quickened after Chancellor Helmut Kohl, responding to German domestic politics, sought arms control negotiations related to the short-range nuclear forces on German territory. The ensuing NATO crisis led to a spurt of creative energy in the Bush Administration in May, resulting in the president's proposal to negotiate cuts in the conventional forces in Europe by 30 percent within a year. Difficulties in defining boundaries, zones and types of aircraft remain, but many observers are optimistic about the outcome.

Behind both negotiations, however, lurks uncertainty about the future of Gorbachev and his reforms. Skeptics in the Defense Department and elsewhere in the administration argue that the United States should not let down its guard. They point to the reversal of Khrushchev's reforms two decades ago and warn that Gorbachev's reforms are similarly reversible. They urge an attitude of "wait and see." Others argue that the possibility of reversal makes it all the more urgent to seize this opportunity to reach favorable agreements in an approach that can be characterized as "locking in gains." On balance, however, uncertainties about the permanence of the Gorbachev phenomenon tend to slow progress in arms control.

IV

While debate continues on a prudent response in the bilateral relationship, other analysts argue for more attention to a different aspect of the current era, the diffusion of power in world politics. So long as an intense superpower hostility blanketed world politics, the gradual diffusion of power in world politics was not readily noticeable. With the diminished Soviet threat in the Gorbachev era and Soviet withdrawal from some of its Third World positions, other changes in the nature of world politics have become more visible.

Some, such as Yale historian Paul Kennedy, portray such changes as a decline of American hegemony, but the concept of decline is a misleading way to portray the situation.[8] The United States is not in decline in relation to such powers as the Soviet Union, the European Community or China. Nor is it accurate to refer to the emerging situation as "multipolar," if that means returning to a balance among a number of nations with roughly equal power resources, analogous to the period before 1945.

The word "polycentrism" comes closer to describing the current diffusion of power. As world politics becomes more complex, all major states are less able to achieve their purposes. Although the United States has leverage over particular countries, it has far less leverage over the complex system as a whole. But it is not alone in this situation. All great powers today are less able to use traditional power resources to achieve their purposes because private actors and smaller states have become more important in many issues.

While several trends contributing to the diffusion of power are economic, at least three are related to the use of force. One trend is the process of modernization in developing countries. Increased social awareness and nationalism make military intervention and external rule more costly. In 1953 the United States restored the shah of Iran to his throne with a minor covert action. It is hard to imagine, however, how many troops would have been needed to restore the shah in the socially mobilized and nationalistic Iran of 1979. Similarly, the defeats of the United States in Vietnam and of the Soviet Union in Afghanistan were less the result of the increased power of a weak state than the increased cost for outsiders of ruling socially mobilized and nationalistic populations.

Another trend in the diffusion of power is the spread of technology, which enhances the capabilities of less developed states. While the superpowers maintain a large lead in military technology, the forces that many Third World states will be able to deploy in the 1990s will make regional superpower intervention more costly than it was in the 1950s. In addition, at least a dozen Third World states have developed a significant capability to export arms, and more countries are acquiring sophisticated weapons capabilities. Twenty countries could now make chemical weapons and 15 Third World nations could be producing their own ballistic missiles in the 1990s. In addition to the five states that had the bomb when the NPT was signed in 1968, India, Pakistan, Israel and South Africa now have a nuclear capability and others may follow. Although a small nuclear capability does not make these states contenders for global power, it does increase the potential cost of regional intervention by larger powers. Technology also enhances the power of private groups. For instance, handheld antiaircraft missiles helped guerrillas in Afghanistan and new plastic explosives are effective tools for terrorists.

Finally, the changing nature of the issues in world politics is diminishing the ability of great powers to control their environment. An increasing number of issues do not simply pit one state against another; in some issues, all states try to control private, transnational non-state actors. The solutions to many issues of transnational interdependence will require collective action and cooperation among states. Areas for global action include ecological changes such as acid rain and global warming, health epidemics such as AIDS, and illicit trade in drugs and control of terrorists. While force may sometimes play a role, traditional instruments of power are rarely sufficient in dealing with such issues. New power resources, such as effective communication and use of multilateral institutions, may prove more relevant.

Moreover, the superpowers will need the cooperation of small weak states, which often cannot manage their own problems alone. For example, it may do no good for the United States to use its military or economic power resources to press Colombia to curtail the production of cocaine if a weak Colombian government cannot control private gangs of drug dealers. Such situations give rise to the "power of the weak." The ability of the great powers to control their environment and get what they want in the 1990s is likely to be less than traditional indicators of military power would suggest.

Some political scientists have gone so far as to argue that war has become obsolete and will follow the practices of dueling, slavery and colonialism in history.[9] An alternative view is that the increased cost of using military force will restrict large countries more than small countries, and that the net effect will be an erosion of the traditional hierarchy of world politics. War remains prevalent in the poor areas of the globe. The Middle East, for instance, resembles more the classic security dilemma described by Thucydides than the modern transnational interdependence that exists among developed countries.[10] And private transnational terrorist groups readily use force and have increasing capacity to do so.

If this portrait of current trends is even partially correct, the bipolar focus of the past will not be sufficient. Americans will need to think more broadly about the role of arms control in world politics. In fact, on many of these issues, the United States and the Soviet Union will find themselves on the same side.

V

Concern over the proliferation of technology is not new. The NPT has been in force for two decades, and in 1995 the majority of the states party to the treaty must vote on extending its duration. What is new, however, are the interactions between nuclear, chemical, biological and ballistic missile technology, the increase in the number of states involved and the new threats posed for national security. A critical question is what role the arms control process can play in coping with these new threats.

Technology spreads with time, and many technologies of mass destruction have a long duration. Modern chemical weaponry, for example, is a 75-year-old technology. Nuclear technology is now half-a-century old and intercontinental ballistic missiles have been with us for some three decades. Nonetheless, one should not be fatalistic about the spread of technology. Policy can make a difference in the rate and conditions under which it spreads. For example, in 1963 President Kennedy foresaw a world in the 1970s with some 25 nuclear states; today the number is only a third of what he predicted.[11]

In a world in which self-defense is a recognized right of states, it is remarkable that some 140 states have signed a treaty by which they deny themselves access to the most destructive weaponry. The broad nonproliferation regime—the NPT, the International Atomic Energy Agency (IAEA), the nuclear suppliers' guidelines and various bilateral agreements—has not solved the problem of nuclear proliferation but it has alleviated it by placing added burdens on the proliferator. Clever bureaucrats and military officers find obstacles in their way. Political leaders must face the fact that developing nuclear weaponry may have too great a political cost. While some countries have not adhered to the treaty, the regime has so far constrained the problem of nuclear proliferation to a handful of problem countries.[12]

The very success of the nonproliferation regime, however, has driven potential proliferators underground into covert actions. The important new developments in nuclear proliferation are the existence of the four covert or de facto nuclear states—Israel, India, Pakistan and South Africa—and the prevalence of efforts to use clandestine facilities dedicated to military purposes rather than the misuse of commercial nuclear energy sources, the major problem in the 1970s.

This transformation of how nations "go nuclear" has made the monitoring of proliferation more difficult and raised concerns about the gradual erosion of the nuclear threshold. By the early 1970s, Israel and India became de facto nuclear powers in addition to the five designated in the NPT. In the 1980s, South Africa and Pakistan joined the "covert proliferators." Three more states may attain that status in the 1990s: Argentina, Brazil and North Korea. A North Korean nuclear weapon would enormously complicate the strategic situation in that region, as both South Korea and Japan might feel the pressure to reverse their current policies of restraint and develop their latent nuclear capabilities.

In addition, secondary nuclear suppliers such as Argentina, Brazil and India may make controlling nuclear exports more difficult in the future. In the past, once a nation developed a nuclear weapon, it soon realized the value of denying others the same capability—but before that realization, it often made mistakes. For example, France helped Israel, and the Soviet Union helped China who in turn helped Pakistan.

In a complicated world of covert proliferation, the danger of mistakes grows. Since many of the states acquiring new nuclear capabilities lack the political and technological capacity to control nuclear weaponry, the risk of leakages to terrorist groups or of unauthorized use during political turmoil will also increase.

The question of chemical weapons proliferation differs from nuclear proliferation in several ways. First, there are more countries—20 is a frequently cited number—suspected of having or trying to develop chemical weapons. In addition, the technology is relatively simple and it lacks the difficulties of control and monitoring associated with radiation. The dual uses of chemical technologies for fertilizers, pesticides and herbicides as well as weapons is even closer than the overlap between commercial and military nuclear facilities.[13] Thus far, the proliferation of chemical weaponry has not seriously infected Latin America or Africa, but in the Middle East and Southeast Asia it has involved some of the world's poorest countries. In that sense, the aphorism that chemical weaponry is the poor country's atom bomb has some justification. What is more, in the Middle East the taboo against use of chemical weapons has been broken in the Iran-Iraq War: Iraq even used chemicals against its own Kurdish population.

After World War I, the 1925 Geneva Protocol prohibited the first use of chemical weapons but permitted their production and stockpiling. The Geneva Protocol remains the principal international constraint, although it has been supplemented in recent years by an informal institution, the "Australia group." Nineteen chemical suppliers met under Australian auspices in 1985 to discuss tougher export controls on chemicals that are precursors to the manufacture of weapons. The group has agreed to require formal licenses on eight specific chemicals and has a warning list for 30 more in hopes that industry will voluntarily alert national governments to any suspicious foreign interest in those substances.

In addition, since 1980, the U.N. Conference on Disarmament has been engaged in negotiations on a chemical weapons convention (cwc) that would place a complete and total ban on chemical weapons in all states. The ban would prohibit the production or stockpiling of chemical weapons and would require the destruction of all existing chemical weapons stocks.

Verification remains the most difficult issue. A small chemical weapons plant could be hidden within a larger industrial infrastructure or built in a remote area. These verification problems might be addressed (though not fully solved) through ad hoc inspections of non-declared facilities. In addition, commercial chemicals that could be used in the manufacturing of weapons must be monitored at both the production and consumption end points. The burden of monitoring will fall upon a proposed international authority, which will send out inspection teams. The cost of visiting all declared production and consumption facilities for the first ten years is projected to be in the range of $150 million to $300 million per year. In comparison, the IAEA spends only $25 million a year on its inspection of civilian nuclear plants.

The chemical weapons convention started out in the early 1980s with a strong emphasis on curtailing Soviet capabilities in Europe, but it has now evolved into a situation in which the U.S.-Soviet component seems less important than the proliferation dimension. In effect, it is now more of a nonproliferation instrument than a U.S.-Soviet bilateral arms control treaty.

Critics of the convention argue that the United States should not sign such a treaty because it would not be verifiable and universal.[14] These are the same classic arguments, now made in the context of the diffusion of power, that have often bedeviled arms control in the bilateral U.S.-Soviet relationship. They must be answered in terms of comparative risks—verification will not be perfect and membership will not be total. The question is whether the risks to American security are greater in the absence of any global ban on chemical weapons than with an admittedly imperfect treaty. A treaty provides a basis for stronger export control legislation among our allies and others who adhere to it. It would also help reinforce the norm against chemical weapons. In that sense, an imperfect cwc would have some of the same benefits and problems as the NPT.

Biological weapons are of slightly less immediate concern than chemical weapons. According to American government officials, there are about ten countries with current or developing capabilities to employ living organisms (such as anthrax, lassa fever or typhus, as opposed to inert toxins).[15] Biological weapons, however, have limited military utility since their dispersal mechanisms are difficult to manage; a change of wind can make them as lethal to the attacker as they are to the defender. Moreover, it is difficult to sustain the living organisms in biological weapons in hot climates for long periods. For these reasons, biological weapons are better suited for mass destruction than as precise military instruments. This lack of military utility may have thus far slowed their development.

In addition, since 1972, a biological weapons convention has banned the use or possession of these weapons. Research continues, however, since the convention allows the development of antidotes against biological weaponry. Suspicions have arisen that the loopholes in the treaty have permitted some countries, including the Soviet Union, to develop more than a minimal weapons capability. Unlike the draft CWC, the biological weapons convention is a brief document without provisions for verification. Many experts believe that one of the key challenges in this area will be to develop a protocol outlining detailed procedures for verification.

The Iran-Iraq War put the problem of ballistic missile proliferation, as well as of chemical weapons, high on the agenda of security concerns. The war in the Persian Gulf highlighted the dangers posed by the spread of ballistic missiles. In addition, China sold missiles with a range of 2,000 miles to Saudi Arabia in 1989, and Israel used an indigenously developed missile, the Jericho II, as a basis for a satellite-launching rocket. This, in turn, raised the possibility that Israel might soon have a theoretical capability to strike the region of Moscow with nuclear weapons. In 1989 India tested its Agni missile with a range of 1,500 miles.

Altogether, 14 less developed countries now possess ballistic missiles.[16] A dozen of them are also suspected of chemical weapon capabilities. Half of these countries' missiles have ranges under 200 miles and most rely on imported technical capability. Israel's and India's accomplishments in developing indigenous medium-range missile capability are thus far the exceptions rather than the rule. Many of the ballistic missiles in the Third World are derivatives of Soviet Frog 7s or Scud Bs with ranges of 40 to 90 miles. But a number of countries now have the expertise to modify and upgrade their imported missiles significantly. For example, Iraq has produced two upgraded versions of the Scud B, with ranges of 385 to 565 miles.

Looming ahead is the prospect that what has been done for range can also be done for accuracy. Until now, most of the short-range ballistic missiles in the Third World have been relatively inaccurate. The Scud-B has a circular error probability of about 1,000 yards at a range of 190 miles, thus restricting its use to large soft targets. By adapting the inertial navigational systems built for commercial and military aircraft, however, it may become possible to reduce the CEP to 40 yards at such ranges. With this accuracy, missiles would become a weapon against military targets capable of being effectively coupled with nuclear, chemical or high-explosive warheads.

Such capabilities would place American efforts at power projection under greater stress and they might jeopardize regional crisis stability. The capability to strike quickly and to overcome air defenses might add to the inherent pressure to preempt in moments of crisis. The erosion of crisis stability in regions such as the Middle East would make U.S. involvement more dangerous. Many of the nations with advanced ballistic missile programs are also interested in acquiring nuclear, chemical and biological weapons.

In 1987, a missile technology control regime was created by the United States, Britain, Canada, France, Germany, Italy, and Japan. Like the NPT, the MTCR is an inherently discriminatory regime that divides states into two classes: those states with missiles with a range of at least 190 miles and a payload of at least 1,000 pounds, and those states without such missiles. However, unlike the Nonproliferation Treaty, the MTCR is not a treaty among 140 nations, but an export control understanding between the United States and its six allies. Moreover, there is no international organization to monitor missile-related exports, and each national government is expected to regulate its own exports. In some ways, the MTCR is akin to the 1978 nuclear suppliers' guidelines, similarly based on a list of sensitive items that require some form of export control.

In favor of the MTCR is the fact that missile technology is still quite complex. A modern missile requires thousands of precision-crafted moving parts that must function perfectly. Thus missile programs in the developing world are vulnerable to supplier disruption. The MTCR helped to slow down the Condor-II program, an Argentine missile that was being developed in concert with Egypt, Iraq, and Saudi Arabia. On the other hand, the MTCR has three major problems. First, some member governments have applied export restrictions in a rather loose manner in order not to shut off profitable commercial deals. Second and more important, membership remains at just seven countries. As long as many states remain outside the MTCR, the importing countries will have access to a robust black market as well as to supplies from other governments.

A third problem related to MTCR effectiveness is the question of legitimacy. Unlike nuclear and chemical weaponry, there is no taboo against ballistic missiles. President Reagan argued that fast flyers are a greater threat to crisis stability than slow flyers, but this distinction has not been recognized in international politics. There is no moral stigma attached to ballistic missiles. This leaves open the question of how effective a regime will be if its membership remains sparse and the weapon it is trying to discourage is not generally perceived as illegitimate.

VI

What can be done about the diffusion of military power and the proliferation of the technologies of mass destruction?

The first step is to be realistic about goals. Stemming proliferation is only one aspect of foreign policy. There will always be trade-offs between efforts to slow the spread of dangerous technology and other foreign policy objectives—witness the vacillating U.S. performance in trying to slow Pakistan's nuclear weapons development in the 1980s, when Pakistan provided the critical supply route for American assistance to the Afghan resistance. Moreover, we have to think about what steps to take after technology has spread. Clichés about horses being out of the barn are misleading; it makes a difference how many horses remain in the barn and how quickly they are fleeing. Our goal should be to slow the rate of spread of dangerous technologies in order to better manage their destabilizing effects. With this goal we buy time, but we also need to use that time to seek political settlements. Multilateral arms control agreements will be an important part of the mix of policy instruments but they cannot stand alone.

In the area of nuclear nonproliferation, we need to deal with the covert proliferators without weakening our efforts to discourage further proliferation. The greatest danger to our security is that one of these covert proliferators may lose control of its nuclear weapons because of inadequate technical safeguards or domestic political turmoil. Once a nation can build nuclear weapons, we should try to persuade it to freeze or halt the level of its development, rather than proceeding to produce and even to deploy a large nuclear arsenal. While we may not be happy about countries that have bombs in their basements, a bomb in the basement is less dangerous than bombs spread all over the front lines where they are susceptible to military revolt, theft or leakage into terrorist hands.

We need to supplement our traditional support for the NPT, the IAEA and the nuclear suppliers' agreement, with regional efforts to encourage greater confidence among threatening neighbors. Inspection agreements and high-level visits between Indians and Pakistanis, for example, or between Argentines and Brazilians, could contribute to reducing the pressures for development of war-fighting arsenals in those regions. In the Middle East, on the other hand, it is hard to imagine effective arms control agreements without progress in the Middle East peace process. Moreover, progress in limiting chemical weapons in the region may also be linked with both the nuclear and general peace issues.

Halting or slowing chemical, biological and missile technology will also require the use of multiple instruments. Even an imperfect chemical weapons convention strengthens barriers against the possession and use of chemical weapons. It could reinforce export controls and legitimate the use of force in self-defense against chemical threats by reaffirming the stigma against chemical weapons. Finally, good intelligence collection and early warning will be an important part of the package of policy instruments. The official inspection scheme will complement rather than replace national intelligence efforts in this area. In the area of biological weaponry, negotiation of a protocol relating to verification would help to reinforce the existing stigma against biological weapons and would serve as a basis for the other instruments such as export controls, sanctions and intelligence.

In containing missile technology, the next step should be to broaden the acceptance of an export control regime. This may require renegotiation because of Soviet and Chinese concern about not being included in the early stages of the development of the current MTCR. Once again, however, the agreement must be developed in the context of other instruments, including intelligence collection.

In all of these issues related to the diffusion of power, U.S. and Soviet involvement will be quite different from their relationship in bilateral strategic arms control. The United States and the Soviet Union will be, in effect, on the same side of the table. In many cases, the United States may find it more difficult to agree with its allies than with the Soviets on cooperation and export controls. The United States, however, will have to consider the prospect of sharing more intelligence regarding chemical, nuclear and biological terrorism with the Soviets. And the degree of cooperation in coping with the diffusion of technology will vary with the ups and downs of the overall U.S.-Soviet political relationship. If the diffusion of power continues, it is all the more important for the two superpowers to use the current opportunity to construct multilateral regimes that remain useful even if the power of the founders wanes or the political climate between them changes.

VII

In the post–cold war era, arms control may lead to major reductions in the forces of the superpowers. Even in this new era, however, military forces will still be needed because of the normal course of great power politics and because of the new diffusion of destructive power. Moreover, there is always the prospect that the changes in the Soviet Union could be reversed.

The United States can protect itself against reversal in three ways. First, it should seek those reductions that not only enhance U.S. security, but that take time for a new Soviet leadership to restore. Second, the United States should seek verification and inspection procedures that, if violated by a new Soviet leader, set off clear alarms. Third, it should seek procedures for informal visits and consultations that reinforce groups dedicated to glasnost in the Soviet political and military leadership. Thus, careful attention to detail is needed to make sure that dismantling the military edifices of the cold war does not create technical instabilities that would reduce or threaten U.S. security in the future. At the same time, technical details should not blind Americans to the larger political roles of arms control.

It has become fashionable to speak of the recent end of the cold war and even of the "end of history." When the cold war ended may well be a matter of semantics: strictly defined, as a period of intense hostility and little communication, it probably ended in the 1960s. The "little cold war" of the early 1980s was mostly rhetorical. More important is the fact that the cold war and the division of Europe produced four decades of relative stability, albeit at a high price for East Europeans.

Rather than the end of history, we are now seeing the return of history in Europe with its ethnic tensions and the unsolved problem of Germany's role, which Bismarck put on the international agenda in 1870. The peaceful evolution of new arrangements in Europe will make reassurance more necessary than ever. Arms control can play a large part in that reassurance by reducing and restructuring force levels in the conventional arms negotiations and by establishing a variety of confidence-building measures in the Conference on Security and Cooperation in Europe. Negotiating gradual changes in the overall European security framework can help to alleviate the anxieties and overreactions that would otherwise derail economic evolution and integration of the continent.

The United States can use this period to accumulate security gains, banking them against a possible future downturn or reversal in U.S.-Soviet relations. Because the institutional effects of arms control tend to continue, an important goal now for the United States is to lock in the benefits of the Gorbachev era: force reductions in START and CFE, as well as verification and consultation procedures that build transparency and regularized communication. In turn, this broad process may help to reinforce the changing security concepts in the Soviet Union. Agreements create domestic effects there as well as in this country.

Finally, the current period of improved bilateral relations provides an important opportunity for the United States and the Soviet Union to work together with other countries to reinforce and establish regimes for dealing with the diffusion of power. Here too there are gains to be locked in. Such multilateral arms control regimes will have to be considered in a broader context of security. For example, the superpowers have already rediscovered the value of U.N. peacekeeping forces, itself a confidence- and security-building measure. They may also rediscover the wisdom of the early postwar architects of the U.N. Charter and particularly of the U.N. Security Council. In an era when the great powers are reducing their involvement in the Third World, other countries may develop greater interest in measures for the regional constraint of force. There are signs that some of the less developed countries have begun to understand that their traditional litany of complaints are somewhat beside the point. As one U.N. diplomat put it to me privately, "What are we going to do when we don't have the great powers to kick around any more?"

There are several implications for U.S. policy about the new role of arms control in a post–cold war period. The United States will have to pay more attention to the multilateral dimensions of arms control, and more attention to the relationship between bilateral and multilateral arms control. It will have to pay more attention to the relationship of arms control to regional political processes. And the United States will have to pay more attention to how arms control relates to other instruments and other goals in U.S. foreign policy.

Arms control will never provide all the answers to national security. In some cases, it might even do more harm than good. In all cases, it will have to be integrated with other dimensions of policy and other policy instruments. But the changing nature of world politics suggests both new roles and new importance for arms control. If an arms control process did not exist, we would assuredly have to invent it.

NOTES

1. Quoted in "The Treaty: Another Sellout," *The New York Times*, Dec. 11, 1987.

2. Irving Kristol, "Forget Arms Control," *The New York Times*, Sept. 12, 1989.

3. Thomas Schelling, "What Went Wrong With Arms Control?" *Foreign Affairs*, Winter 1985/86.

4. Albert Carnesale and Richard Haass, eds., *Superpower Arms Control: Setting the Record Straight*, Cambridge: Ballinger Books, 1987, p. 355.

5. See Alexander George, Philip Farley and Alexander Dallin, eds., *U.S.-Soviet Security Cooperation: Achievements, Failures, Lessons*, New York: Oxford University Press, 1988.

6. Arkady Shevchenko, *Breaking with Moscow*, New York: Ballantine, 1985, p. 270.

7. Quoted in the author's book *Bound to Lead: The Changing Nature of American Power*. New York: Basic Books, (forthcoming), Chapter 4.

8. Paul M. Kennedy, *The Rise and Fall of the Great Powers: Economic Change and Military Conflict from 1500 to 2000*, New York: Random House, 1987. This section draws upon Chapter 6 of the author's *Bound to Lead*.

9. John Mueller, *Retreat from Doomsday: The Obsolescence of Major War*, New York: Basic Books, 1988.

10. In the fifth century B.C., "the Spartans proposed that not only should Athens refrain from building her own fortifications, but that she should join them in pulling down all the fortifications which still existed." Thucydides reported that while the Athenians sent a delegate to negotiate with Sparta, they simultaneously "built their fortifications high enough to be able to be defended." *The Peloponnesian War*, New York: Penguin Books, 1972, p. 88.

11. John Kennedy, quoted in Albert Carnesale, *et al.*, *Living with Nuclear Weapons*. A Report by the Harvard Nuclear Study Group. Cambridge: Harvard University Press, 1983.

12. The following discussion of proliferation is based on the discussions of the Aspen Strategy Group summer meeting. See Bobby R. Inman, Joseph S. Nye, Jr., William Perry and Roger Smith. *Responding to the Proliferation of Nuclear, Chemical, and Ballistic Missile Capabilities*. New York: University Press of America (forthcoming).

13. Lewis Dunn, "Chemical Weapons Arms Control," *Survival*, May–June 1989, pp. 209–225.

14. Amoretta Hoeber and Douglas Feith, "Poisoned Gas, Poisoned Treaties," *The New York Times*, Dec. 6, 1988; Frank Gaffney, "Chemical Warfare: Beware of Bush's Perilous Delusions," *The Wall Street Journal*, Oct. 3, 1989.

15. Michael Gordon, "U.S. Seeks Curbs on Biological Weapons," *The New York Times*, July 27, 1989.

16. These assessments are based on presentations to the Aspen Strategy Group by Albert Wheelon, Janne Nolan and Kent Kresa. See Inman, *et al.*, *op. cit.*

7

The End of Arms Control

CHARLES KRAUTHAMMER

In the 1970s, the conservative opposition to arms control was based as much on psychology as on strategy. Whatever the strategic effects, argued opponents, arms control had disastrous psychological effects. It lulled the West into a false sense of security about Soviet intentions, encouraged passivity to the Soviet threat, and led to a weakening of Western resolve and defenses.

There is some truth to this argument, but not much. Arms control alone should not bear the full weight of blame for the silly euphoria about the Soviets that swept the West in the '70s. The euphoria was part of the general atmosphere of détente that was created by frequent and chummy summitry, by increased trade and other cooperative ventures (like the absurd Soyuz–Apollo lovefest), and by the (Western) assumption that all geopolitical competition and conflicts would be newly subjected to mutual restraint. Arms control was but a small part of the story.

Moreover, even if arms control does lull, some lulls are worse than others. The 1970s lull turned out to be rather unilateral. While the West rested, the Soviets vigorously expanded both their overseas empire and their nuclear advantage. (Hence Harold Brown's immortal definition of the arms race: "When we build, they build. When we cut, they build.") The coming decade, however, will be quite the reverse. Having bitten off too much, the Soviets are in a period of at least temporary consolidation. Even if the worst of the charges laid at arms control are true, some

Reprinted by permission of *The New Republic*, copyright © 1988, The New Republic, Inc.

Note: It is a violation of the law to reproduce this selection by any means whatsoever without the written permission of the copyright holder.

Western relaxation in a period of Soviet relaxation is not a mortal danger. The costs might well be worth bearing, assuming there are other benefits to arms control.

Finally, before rejecting arms control for its negative psychological effects, consider its positive psychological effects. Any agreement, no matter how bad, shores up at least temporarily Western belief in deterrence. "The more compelling arguments for reducing nuclear weapons tend to be political," writes Joseph Nye. "The marginal effects such cuts may have on strategic stability are far less important than ensuring a broad base of public support for nuclear deterrence." Recent history has borne this out dramatically. The early '80s saw a vast mobilization against nuclear weapons and deterrence. With the resumption of arms talks, the agreement on INF, and the prospect of a START treaty, the movement fizzled. If arms control helps keep the West committed to deterrence, at the cost of some lulling, then perhaps it is worth the bargain.

But what if these "political," i.e., psychological, effects are based on illusion? Arms control is reassuring because Western publics believe that nuclear treaties reduce the chances of nuclear war and thus make the world safer. What if this belief is false? If nuclear reductions, such as the 50 percent reduction contemplated in the coming START treaty, actually leave us less safe, should we be signing treaties merely to satisfy irrational, if popular, beliefs?'

Thomas Schelling, one of the first and most acute of this country's thinkers about nuclear weapons, several years ago asked the emperor's new clothes question about arms control: "Who needs arms control if economical and reliable retaliatory weapons are available that are neither susceptible to pre-emption nor capable of pre-emption?" It is the kind of question only a child, a neophyte, or a sage with the benefit of 30 years of nuclear jesuitics behind him could ask. "On the 'arms control' interest in reducing numbers [of nuclear weapons]," writes Schelling, "nobody ever offers a convincing reason for preferring smaller numbers." No one does, and yet the enthusiasm for the 50 percent reductions envisioned in the START treaty (if the bugs, such as verification, can be worked out) is nearly universal. As we begin the ostentatious dismantling of INF missiles and anticipate the dawning of the START era, it is time to pause and return to Schelling's question: Why exactly are we embarked on this enterprise?

The popular faith in arms control—the belief that cutting numbers is in itself a good thing—rests on three assumptions.

1. *Arms control saves money.* If arms control saves money, the sums are negligible. Generally speaking, however, it may increase defense expenditures. This is because treaties like START decrease stability (the survivability of one's deterrent force) by eliminating redundancy. In

order to regain the *pre-existing* level of nuclear stability, the United States will be forced under START to overhaul, reconfigure, and redesign drastically its strategic nuclear arsenal in order to make it a survivable and reliable retaliatory force. START will create such pressure to cut the number of America's best retaliatory weapons—ICBMs, SLBMs (submarine-launched ballistic missiles), and ALCMs (air-launched cruise missiles)—that a myriad of proposals are already on the table for redesigning the U.S. strategic deterrent to maintain its survivability. At sea, this may mean a new fleet of smaller submarines, so our reduced SLBM force is spread over more boats. In the air, it may mean a heavy reliance on manned bombers, which are extremely expensive but practically unregulated under START "counting rules." On land, it may mean redesigning old or inventing new systems that are mobile, superhardened, or otherwise protected (by some version of SDI, for example) to compensate for the loss of safety in numbers. All that costs money.

But even if START led to no increase in nuclear expenditures, it would certainly lead to an overall increase in defense expenditures. That is because nuclear arms control puts more of a burden for deterrence on conventional defense. The most ardent arms control advocates not only recognize this fact, they celebrate it. Michael Dukakis, for example, opposes almost all nuclear modernization but wants still to appear tough on defense. He therefore goes to extraordinary lengths to advocate bolstering conventional defenses. In a speech to the Atlantic Council in June, Dukakis went so far as to declare the goal of developing the ability "of fighting—and winning—a conventional war" in Europe, something the Europeans, who have experienced two conventional wars this century on their soil, are no doubt delighted to hear. Conventional deterrence may or may not be as effective as nuclear deterrence in preventing war (again: the history of this century is hardly an argument for conventional deterrence), but one thing is certain: it is far more expensive. The same bang will require many more bucks.

2. *Arms control prevents accidents.* Another illusion. As Nye points out, "The sheer number of weapons is not the major factor governing the odds of accidental war." The crucial factor is the technical sophistication of the nuclear weapons and their trigger mechanisms. And this improves as new systems are introduced. If your life depended on its reliability and accuracy, would you rather trust in a vacuum-tubed Univac computer circa 1958 or in five hand-held Sharp calculators circa 1988? The key to reducing the chances of accidental war is nuclear modernization, not numbers reduction.

3. *Arms control reduces the risk of nuclear war.* Our intuition tells us that the fewer nuclear weapons in this world, the less our chances of getting killed by one. That intuition does not stand up to the most elementary analysis. Schelling dispatches it quite succinctly: "For the most part, people simply think that smaller numbers are better than bigger ones.

Those who believe we already have ten times what we need never explain why having merely five times as many should look better." The nuclear hysteria of the early '80s was generated by the repeated reminder that we had constructed for ourselves a world in which Armageddon could occur at any minute. But what can arms control do to prevent this? You either reduce the number of weapons below the level that can bring Armageddon, or you don't. If you do, then you have abolished deterrence and ushered in a period of nuclear insecurity and instability unknown since the earliest days of the nuclear age (when bomb shelter drills were not the silly exercises they appear to us today). And if you don't reduce nuclear arsenals below the point at which you can destroy the other side once over, then what's the point of arms control? The balance of terror persists. The nuclear nightmare is in no way abolished.

There is only one circumstance under which reducing numbers, say a 50 percent cut, makes sense: as a way station to zero. But except for President Reagan and a few other nuclear naïfs, no one thinks that zero nuclear weapons is either achievable or desirable. In a world of total disarmament, the premium on cheating, hiding, and secret rearmament would be extraordinary. Lacking a retaliatory threat, every country would be at risk from nuclear breakout and blackmail by every other country. In a world of Qaddafis and Khomeinis and Saddam Husseins, ignoring for the moment the Soviets, there could not be a more unstable nuclear regime. Not even Hobbes could have imagined a world of such perpetual danger and universal insecurity.

In the absence of world government (a nightmare of a different sort), we will have to rely on deterrence for safety against nuclear (and chemical and biological) attack for generations. Safety depends on deterrence, and, all things being equal, there is safety in numbers. The more nuclear weapons you have, scattered in more places, delivered in more ways (to complicate defenses), using a greater variety of physical principles (ballistic missiles, cruise missiles, gravity bombs), the less the chance that any adversary would ever consider a pre-emptive nuclear attack on you—i.e., the less the chance of nuclear war. There is safety in redundancy. Arms control, if taken seriously, aims to reduce that redundancy.

Now, all things are not always equal. Some kinds of nuclear weapons are more destabilizing to the nuclear balance than others. Arms control that specifically reduced or eliminated these destabilizing weapons might be worthwhile. The House Armed Services Committee report on START sets out clearly the criterion for evaluating any arms control regime. The chief purpose of arms control, it argues, is "to improve what is called crisis stability and thereby reduce the possibility of nuclear war. Stability is achieved when it is unlikely that either side will strike pre-emptively in a time of international crisis. Reductions and limits may or may not promote crisis stability. Those that do are worthwhile." And those that don't are not. The arms control that we are engaged in now—quantitative arms control, number reduction—does not.

Why not?

Nuclear weapons don't launch themselves. People launch them. But there is a sense in which nuclear weapons—or more precisely, their force structure, meaning the way in which they are arranged and protected—can, during a crisis, incline the leaders of one side or the other to launch. If a leader thinks that his military power is in danger of being pre-emptively destroyed, he may, if he reaches a point where he thinks war is inevitable, be tempted to launch his own weapons pre-emptively. If his weapons had not been structured so that his choice in a crisis was only "use 'em or lose 'em," he would have no such temptation.

If arms control is to have any point, other than to salve consciousness or appease public opinion, it must increase nuclear stability. One has to ask, therefore, what any agreement does to force structure. How will the nature of the nuclear arsenals on the two sides be changed by an arms control agreement? And will that change make pre-emption (a first strike) more or less likely in a crisis?

Absolute numbers tell you very little about crisis stability (except for the rule that the more launches you have and the more dispersed they are, the better). What counts for crisis stability is a ratio: the ratio of A's accurate warheads to B's targets, such as missile silos. If A has many more warheads than B has targets, then A could in a crisis launch (or better: threaten to launch) a fraction of its arsenal in a pre-emptive attack, wipe out B's retaliatory force, and still have enough warheads left over to force B to capitulate. If, on the other hand, the ratio of warheads to targets is 1, then there is no incentive for and thus no threat of pre-emptive attack. War may one day come, but the configuration of the superpowers' arsenals will in no way have contributed to it.

What does the 50 percent reduction of START do to the crucial warhead/target ratio? "All experts agree," writes Henry Kissinger, "that if existing U.S. strategic forces are cut by 50 percent, the vulnerability of the land-based and submarine-based strategic forces will increase immediately and mount progressively as the accuracy of Soviet missiles and the effectiveness of Soviet anti-submarine forces grow." Kissinger does the calculation for you: "Today the Soviet Union has 3,080 SS-18 warheads aimed at 1,000 U.S. silos. After START, assuming the United States retains its most effective weapons, the Soviets would have 1,540 warheads aimed at 364 silos, thereby raising the ratio of warheads to silos from 3.08:1 to 4.2:1. It is hard to argue that such a result would be a contribution to 'stability.'"

James Woolsey, former undersecretary of the Navy under President Carter, points to another source of increasing vulnerability of the

U.S. nuclear arsenal. The 1983 Scowcroft Commission Report, which Woolsey helped write, argued that the ICBM leg of the triad was not yet in danger of pre-emption because of the difficulty the Soviets would have in launching a simultaneous attack on both American bomber bases and ICBM silos. "That was a position that was described by some of media at the time"—TNR included—"as doing away with the window of vulnerability," argues Woolsey. "It was no such thing—it was saying that we had more time to shut the window of vulnerability than some people had been suggesting." Now, argues Woolsey, that time is running out. The Soviets are about to open the window wide with their new fleet of quiet Delta 4 and Typhoon submarines, whose new SSN-20 and SSN-23 missiles could be drawn up close to American shores and simultaneously attack the land and air-based leg of the American nuclear arsenal in the 1990s.

"Arms control is not creating these problems," writes Woolsey. "What is creating the problem is not having a survivable ICBM force. But this type of pressure, under a deep reductions regime for arms control, can, at the margin, make the problem harder." What makes it harder is that under a 50 percent cut, it makes sense to cut the oldest, least reliable, least accurate weapons, such as the silo-based, single-warhead Minuteman II, of which the United States has 450. That would leave the United States its most accurate, most modern weapons. But they are highly MIRved, i.e., they carry many warheads per missile. That means fewer targets for the Soviets to think of pre-empting in a crisis. And that means more, not less, nuclear instability.

Now, to avoid this obvious consequence of START, there are schemes for creating more baskets for our nuclear eggs. But they are costly and complicated. Minuteman II, for example, could be redesigned to make it more safe and accurate. There are schemes for building a new fleet of smaller subs so as to disperse our submarine deterrent. Or for plugging up some of the missile tubes on existing Trident subs and thus enabling us to deploy more subs without breaking START limits on SLBMs. It is possible that after chopping up subs and sealing missile tubes, after restricting or destroying some of our most modern nuclear weapons, after rebuilding and redesigning our ICBM and bomber forces and perhaps building a whole new submarine fleet, we might return to the level of nuclear stability that we enjoy right now. The question is: What's the purpose of this enormous, expensive, uncertain Rube Goldberg exercise?

The only point is to reduce absolute numbers. But the goal of any defense policy should be nuclear stability. Absolute numbers, in themselves, are irrelevant.

Indeed, reduced numbers can easily become the enemy of stability. How? One essential requirement for arms control is verifiability. If you can't verify and confirm what weapons the other side has, the whole arms control enterprise collapses. Which leads to the paradox. Small, concealable weapons are bad for arms control because they are hard to verify. But they are good for stability, because they are hard to target. Both effects stem from the same cause: these weapons are hard to find. And if you can't find a weapon, that means that you can't count it for arms control purposes, but it also means that you can't target it for first-strike purposes. Which means it is always there for retaliation.

Because of the verification problem, the United States took the position at the START talks that mobile missiles should be banned or severely restricted. And the Soviets took the same position vis-à-vis sea-launched cruise missiles. (The argument over SLCMs and the mobiles shows how the arms control is less a search for nuclear stability than it is a struggle for unilateral advantage. Both SLCMs and mobiles pose severe verification problems. But the United States wants to cripple only mobiles and the U.S.S.R. wants to do the same only to SLCMs. Why? Because the Soviets have a big lead in mobiles and the United States has a big lead in SLCMs.) If arms control is your objective, then it makes sense to ban these weapons. But if strategic stability is your objective, then you would want as many of these running around as possible since they are virtually invulnerable.

"Almost all experts agree," writes Kissinger, "that mobile missiles are to all practical purposes unverifiable in the vast expanse of the Soviet Union." Senator Al Gore disputes this and has come up with an elaborate scheme for corralling missiles in various locations and in effect chaining them to fixed missile silos during peacetime. That way they can be counted. But, of course, that way they can be targeted. And suddenly unchaining and dispersing them in a time of crisis would be a disastrous impetus toward nuclear war, comparable to the European mobilizations of August 1914 that set in train World War I. The Air Force has a similar idea of chaining the small mobile ICBM to existing Minuteman silos in the northern states. Brent Scowcroft, John Deutch, and Woolsey point out that this would leave the missiles vulnerable to "rather straight-forward Soviet efforts to put them at risk—e.g., depressing the trajectory of Soviet submarine-launched missiles, thus enabling them to catch the northern-deployed mobile ICBMs before they could get far enough from their known parking spots."

Gore recognizes these difficulties and argues for a very elaborate scheme whereby a certain percentage of mobile missiles would be allowed to roam free and exercise in peacetime. But the problem recurs: the fewer mobiles that are allowed to roam around, the more vulnerable the ICBM force becomes to pre-emptive attack. And the more mobiles that are allowed to roam around, the more unverifiable becomes any treaty.

But who cares about verifiability? What's the point of restricting mobiles with arms control? Single warhead mobiles, such as the Soviet SS-25 and the U.S. Midgetman, are so stabilizing that the more deployed on both sides the better. "If the United States had a survivable mobile ICBM," writes Scowcroft, Deutch, and Woolsey, "the Soviets would need so much throwweight to attack it (it would require a massive barrage attack) that any cheating they could do by covertly deploying mobile ICBMs themselves would be strategically insignificant."

The verification problem is even worse with another very stabilizing nuclear system, the SLCM, easy to hide and too slow for use as a preemptive weapon. It is the perfect retaliatory weapon. But there is no known way to verify SLCMs, which is why the United States wants them left out of any START treaty. If that happens, it might be the best thing to be said about START.

There is another way in which verifiability becomes an enemy of stability. It involves what are called "counting rules." There is no way to know how many warheads one side actually puts on a missile. In the past, therefore, each side had to count the maximum number of warheads that *could* be put on a missile against its arms control ceiling, regardless of how many it *actually* put on the missile. For example, if the American D-5 SLBM was tested with ten warheads, each missile would count as ten regardless of how many the United States actually put on the D-5. This approach is a service to verifiability, since no verification of warhead numbers is required. But this approach is destabilizing because it pushes each side to pack as many warheads onto a missile as possible. It thus increases the ratio of warheads to targets. If you are being counted for the maximum number of warheads, you might as well pack them on. But packing multiple warheads onto missiles is one of the chief sources of nuclear instability today.

The Washington summit came up with a solution for START. Henceforth counting rules would be negotiated. The D-5 missile is now agreed, arbitrarily, to be carrying eight warheads even though it can carry ten. Similarly, the Soviet SSN-23 will be counted as carrying four missiles, even though it has been tested to carry eight to ten. What these artificially low counting rules do is allow each side to spread its deterrent force over more missiles, which makes for more redundancy, which makes for more stability. Fine. But what happened to verifiability? Under arbitrary counting rules, the number of warheads each side thinks the other has becomes utterly unverifiable and thus can be significantly underestimated. There is no way to know whether the Soviets have four or ten warheads on the SSN-23. The antagonism between verifiability and stability is insoluble. The best that can be said for the new counting rules is that, given the choice, they sacrifice the requirements of arms control to the requirements of stability. That's more than can be said for the proposals to ban or limit mobiles and SLCMs.

Dramatic quantitative arms control is a threat to stability for yet another reason. Large numbers promote stability because they provide each side with a cushion in case it miscalculates the size of the other side's threat or in case the other side suddenly increases its threat by means of a technological breakthrough or cheating. If one side makes a technological breakthrough, say in anti-submarine or in anti-ballistic missile warfare, that could put the other side's deterrent in jeopardy. The more redundancy that side has both in that threatened system and in others, the less such a technological breakthrough matters—and the more stable the nuclear balance.

Numerical arms control works the other way. The more the number of weapons is reduced, the more the premium on technological breakthrough or cheating. Suppose both sides have 10,000 warheads and one side conceals 1,000. In strategic terms, that means nothing. But suppose both sides, thanks to arms control, have only 500 warheads and one side is hiding 1,000. It has achieved clear nuclear superiority and the capacity—and the incentive—for pre-emptive attack in a crisis. The more deeply nuclear arsenals are cut, the more cheating matters, the more the safety of the world comes to depend on airtight verification. But why depend on inherently imperfect verification regimes? Schelling's question returns: "Who needs arms control if economical and reliable retaliatory weapons are available?"

At the beginning of the 1980s, agitation over the nuclear issue reached its peak, when it became an axiom that nuclear arms control was the most important issue of the day. In fact, the lessons of 40 years show that arms control between the great powers may be the least important issue of the day. Great powers do not use nuclear weapons. Both superpowers have now lost very costly and painful wars against very weak Third World adversaries that have no nuclear weapons. Neither superpower came close to exercising its unilateral nuclear advantage. In the very early years of the nuclear era, it was still possible to think of a great power using nuclear weapons. Hiroshima did, after all, occur. But Hiroshima drew its model from World War II strategic bombing. "Little Boy" was conceived by the United States as a way to concentrate a whole bomber fleet's weapons into one package. But thanks to the vast numbers of nuclear devices on both sides and the dazzling variety of systems for delivering them, the great powers have come to recognize that their nuclear arsenals are useless as actual instruments of war.

Not all countries have come to that recognition, however. The real threat for the future will come from tiny arsenals in the hands of unstable powers. There the Hiroshima model still applies. Iraq used poison gas against Iran and might very well have used nuclear weapons had it not been stymied by Israel's uniquely energetic non-proliferation policy. All the more reason for the great powers to retain overwhelming arsenals as a deterrent against attack by unstable and demonstrably barbaric states.

Superpower arms control has concerned itself almost exclusively with capping or reducing numbers. This exercise has always been a bit of a charade. The one exception is the ABM Treaty, a rare example of qualitative arms control that banned not only a class of weapons (so did INF, to little effect) but an entire concept of nuclear warfare, namely nuclear defense. Apart from ABM, most arms control has accomplished very little. The offensive weapons caps of SALT I and SALT II did little to change the likelihood of war. To the extent that force structure can promote or undermine crisis stability, they might have marginally increased the likelihood of war because they created incentives for MIRVing. But in the end, the real determinant of war is the degree to which the interest and values of the superpowers conflict and the degree to which either side is prepared to risk war to advance those interests and values. Nuclear force structure has a marginal effect. The absolute number of nuclear weapons has none.

The great gestures and ostentatious treaties capping these numbers are public events conducted largely for political reasons, i.e., to satisfy the popular faith that numerical cuts make a real difference in reducing the risk of nuclear war. In fact, these weapons make convenient bargaining counters precisely because they are so unusable. They are like poker chips with no bank behind them. That is why they served as the subject of choice for superpower negotiations during the first forty years of the cold war, when the superpowers were so antagonistic that there was nothing else to talk about. Nuclear arms control created the illusion of agreement and provided a choreography of conciliation without really changing anything on the ground. The main purpose of arms control was to symbolize the lessening of tension between the superpowers. It could do that well because the agreements concerned something abstract and airless. Arms control worked best when—and because—it was useless.

Arms control is thus a legacy of the infancy of the cold war. It gave the illusion of reducing the threat of war. But the real issue, the real potential cause of war is decidedly non-nuclear: it is the conflict of interests and ideology that plays itself out in geopolitical competition and regional conflicts around the world. If, as many are saying, the Soviet Union is preparing to enter a new era of relations with the West, then it is time for us both to turn to the real war and peace issues of this world and give up our comfortable, distracting arms control obsession.

COMPETITORS AND ALLIES: PAS DE DEUX

THE ATLANTIC RIM

8

Redefining Europe and the Atlantic Link

ROBERT D. HORMATS

I

The postwar division of Europe is slowly eroding. This is partly a consequence of the thaw in relations between Washington and Moscow. But it would not be possible without the powerful influence of a resurgent and increasingly self-confident European Community. The West Europeans themselves have become the engineers and chief architects reshaping Europe, with economic forces driving the process. The growing unity and prosperity of the EC exert a magnetic force on Eastern Europe, setting in train a process by which the two halves of the continent are steadily reducing barriers to the movement of goods, ideas and people—and largely on terms that support Western values and interests.

The future shape of Europe will depend heavily on whether the Community can achieve sufficient cohesion and prosperity in the next decade to accomplish two tasks: first, to generate centrifugal forces in Eastern Europe strong enough to draw reform-minded nations there more closely into its economic and political orbit, but without threatening Moscow to the point that it intervenes to reverse the process; second, to create centripetal forces in Western Europe strong enough that the West Germans will see any future association between their country

Reprinted by permission of *Foreign Affairs*, Fall 1989. Copyright 1989 by the Council on Foreign Relations, Inc.

Note: It is a violation of the law to reproduce this selection by any means whatsoever without the written permission of the copyright holder.

and East Germany as taking place in a Community context. If it can achieve these objectives, the EC, by virtue of its moral, political and social—as well as economic—strength, will be well positioned to form the centerpiece around which any future "common European home" will be built, and become the chief arbiter of its rules.

Inevitably, U.S.-European relations will be altered as the West Europeans seek to reduce their political dependence on Washington, as tensions with the Soviets ease and as progress is made in rolling back the division of the continent. For much of the postwar period the perception of a major Soviet threat served as the cementing force for NATO and as a basis to rally popular support in the West for large expenditures on sophisticated weaponry. That same threat also constituted a compelling argument for reaching compromises between the United States and Western Europe on potentially divisive trade and monetary issues in order to preserve alliance unity.

In the years ahead, Western Europe can be expected to explore actively what it sees as dramatic new political possibilities in Eastern Europe and the U.S.S.R. that were unavailable in the past due to its own lack of coherence and Soviet intransigence. Western Europe will also assert more boldly its international commercial interests and demonstrate its independence of the United States on a number of foreign policy issues. NATO relationships are bound to come under greater scrutiny. Already Western Europe insists on a stronger voice in allied security affairs, and it will continue to do so in the future.

Washington will be increasingly uncomfortable with the challenges that Western Europe's more independent posture poses to its leadership. But in the final analysis the Community's growing unity can be an enormous asset for the United States if a new basis for cooperation between America and Europe on economic and defense matters can be found. The future shape of Atlantic relations will depend heavily on whether the United States can accommodate Western Europe's desire for greater independence of economic and political action and for significant progress in reducing East–West tension on the continent. It will equally depend on whether Western Europe can accommodate America's desire for Western Europe to assume a greater portion of responsibility for its own defense and more actively promote the well-being of the global economy. Under such a formula the United States would still be the indispensable leader of the West, but would have to find ways to build consensus rather than force it, and be willing to accept power-sharing as the natural handmaiden of burden-sharing.

The current environment of progress and optimism in Europe is, however, vulnerable to three potential threats. The first is a major blowup in Eastern Europe or one of the Baltic states, ignited by an outburst of nationalism or intense dissatisfaction with economic conditions. That could thwart arms control negotiations, cause an abrupt hardening of Soviet attitudes toward normalization with the West and undermine both glasnost and perestroika. Internal developments in the Soviet Union, similar to those in China this year which challenged the very authority of the Communist Party itself, could have similar effects, leading to a reversal of President Mikhail Gorbachev's policies or causing his removal.

The second threat is a turn toward protectionism by either the European Community or the United States; that would severely weaken Western economic cooperation and strengthen pressures for unilateral action on economic and political, as well as security, matters.

The third is a global recession, which could prompt weaker West European companies to seek a slowdown or halt in the removal of internal barriers associated with achieving the 1992 goal of a single market. A world recession would also deal a serious blow to exports of socialist nations, whose economies are already in a precarious situation, further jeopardizing their stability.

In this period of dramatic change, West Europeans and Americans will constantly need to remind themselves that, although their policies are likely to diverge increasingly on a greater number of issues, a fundamental and durable source of their international economic and political influence—and certainly of their security in what is still a highly uncertain, if improving, global environment—is their close relationship with one another. Societies on both sides of the Atlantic will need to keep that point in sharp focus lest the forces of change obscure it.

II

Western Europe is now challenged by its own postwar success. It is moving energetically to tear down, by the end of 1992, internal barriers to the movement of goods, people, capital and services—a process that many regard as establishing the basis for greater West European political unity and a more clearly defined European voice in international affairs.

Europe's course of action over the next decade will be significantly influenced by its international economic possibilities. European prosperity is inextricably intertwined with that of the United States and other major trading nations outside Europe. Expanding trade within the European Community will clearly be the most important stimulus to European growth. Trade will also grow with the nations of the European Free Trade Association (EFTA)—Finland, Sweden, Norway, Switzerland, Austria and Iceland—which together form what is by far the EC's largest trading partner. And there will doubtless be benefits in expanding trade with Eastern Europe, as part of the political and economic normalization process now under way with that region. The United States, however, will remain the most important offshore commercial and financial partner of Western Europe. And the Far East will be both a formidable competitor and a growing market for European goods. Alliances with American, Asian and other European companies will grow as these firms invest heavily in the EC in anticipation of 1992, and as EC firms seek to team up with them to build economies of scale, engage in cooperative research to share costs and position themselves quickly to deliver newly developed products to global markets.

Thus, while Western Europe strengthens its internal economic unity, the importance of its links with the rest of the world will limit any tendency to turn inward. The ultimate test of the Community's economic reforms will be their success in helping its companies to better meet foreign competition in an open global economy—not to insulate them from it—and in putting those companies in a position to negotiate alliances with large foreign firms on an equal footing.

Another constraint on Europe's future is internal. A unified West European economy will require a strong intra-European political consensus. It cannot sweep aside the need for bargains among its independent sovereign states; in that regard, the analogy of a "United States of Europe" is flawed. The 13 original American states did not embody distinctly separate nationalities with ancient languages, cultures, histories and institutions. The nations of Europe do. Such distinctions remain important, although they have not stood in the way of progress and need not inhibit it in the future. But further progress in tearing down internal economic impediments will depend more on how credible the process seems to the electorates of individual nations than on whether the idea conforms to a particular economic or bureaucratic model, however ideal.

A broad political consensus will be required to sustain the momentum of integration, particularly if those interests that are adversely affected by additional internal competition or increased mobility of labor try to derail or slow the process. Technicians can take the process only so far, but political support can no longer be bought by subsidies or protection. Membership in the Community means that each nation has agreed to take a broader vision of its interests and to relinquish the use of these tools in relations with its neighbors. Years of attempting to preserve fragmented, protected and highly regulated national economies have led to competitive weakness and high unemployment in Europe, while Canada, Japan and the United States have surged technologically and succeeded in generating millions of new jobs.

Virtually all else that Western Europe hopes to accomplish over the rest of this century at home and abroad will depend on its success in building a unified and more efficient single market that generates new jobs, accelerates social progress, and enables Europeans to engage more fully in the global technological revolution. This would also establish a stronger basis for Western Europe to assume a greater role in its own defense and to aid reform in Eastern Europe. This process will be partic-ularly important to retain and enhance the tight integration of West Germany with the rest of Western Europe.

For all these reasons, the cohesion that Western Europe seeks also serves America's interests—a point underscored by President Bush when, on his visit to Leiden in mid-July, he stated that "a stronger Europe, a more united Europe, is good for my country. And it is a development to be welcomed, a natural evolution within an alliance, the product of true partnership, 40 years in the making."

III

Establishing a well-functioning single internal market by 1992 will hardly be a smooth process. But whether it is achieved by then or not until the year 2000 is not a crucial issue. The process of tearing down internal barriers is well and wisely under way; it may slow from time to time in coming years, but it can only be reversed at great cost. By the end of this century, if all goes reasonably according to plan, Western Europe will be a far more efficient economic entity than it is today—with a larger number of world-class companies capable of going head-to-head with competitors abroad. These companies will not necessarily be exclu-sively European in ownership or location, but the European compo-nents are likely to be in a stronger position in global corporate alliances owing to the single market.

Within Europe it is inevitable that more power and influence will shift from national capitals to European Community institutions. This will involve a transfer of a measure of sovereignty, but world economic conditions—specifically, the rapid rise in global economic interdepen-dence and an even higher degree of interdependence within Western Europe—already imply a diminution of sovereignty. Governments can-not hope to promote prosperity at home in isolation. The fundamental economic goals of West European nations now must be attained by pooling their efforts in the context of the Community. Specific or short-term national objectives will need to be suppressed to accomplish longer-term objectives of scale, efficiency and stable growth.

Over time the European Commission will assume a greater regulatory role on issues relating to mergers, the environment, government sub-sidies and so forth. But as it does, it will come under greater scrutiny by the Council of Ministers, composed of ministers of national govern-ments, and the European Parliament, directly elected by voters in mem-ber nations. The council and parliament will, like national governments, constantly debate whether Western Europe should structure its inte-grated economy along socialist, social democratic, liberal, or conserva-tive lines. But the worst examples of government regulation at the national level—which were enacted when heavy regulation was fashionable and have survived through inertia even as their costs have become increasingly burdensome—are not likely to be replicated as Europe creates new rules from a fresh start. Political leaders, with Prime Minister Margaret Thatcher in the lead, are likely to ensure that as the commission assumes more power it does not replicate the mistakes of national governments, and indeed the commission itself generally shows no signs of doing this. But the Community will probably put in place regulations that provide generous minimum benefits for workers, implement strong environmental standards and actively protect consumers. Although measures in these areas are likely to be less market-oriented than those in the United States, they will reflect social considerations deemed by many Europeans to be important dimensions of the new Europe.

One particularly controversial idea is that of creating a European central bank. It is favored by those who see it as further tying Europe together economically and believe that the decision to eliminate capital controls by all members of the Community by 1992 requires a central bank to manage monetary policy. They also assert that over time a common currency, under a European central bank, will be required to avoid trade distortions that result from exchange rate fluctuations to which Western Europe would be vulnerable if it retained separate currencies.

Creating a central bank and a common currency will be difficult, however. One frequently cited model is the U.S. Federal Reserve. But the Federal Reserve makes decisions based on inputs from regional governors, who have considerable influence, and is responsive (although not beholden to) a nationwide political and financial constituency. In Europe today, monetary policy and the European Monetary System are heavily influenced by, and indeed borrow credibility from, the highly regarded anti-inflationary policy of the German Bundesbank—with other nations following along to varying degrees. To be successful a new system will have to retain a similar level of credibility, while also commanding legitimacy in all 12 EC nations, most of which are unaccustomed to their central bank's having the same degree of power as does the Bundesbank and maintaining a similarly rigorous monetary policy. Unless it enjoys market credibility and popular support from Dublin to Rome—as well as in Frankfurt—a European central bank would find it difficult to operate without excessive intervention by political forces.

In the next decade it is likely that the European Community will create a central bank roughly equivalent in structure to the U.S. Federal Reserve System, but with more limited powers. EC Commission President Jacques Delors has put forward a creative and comprehensive blueprint for a new European monetary system. Whether his propositions are adopted in whole or in part, intensified monetary cooperation within Europe is likely. At the Madrid summit of the EC leaders in June, significant steps were taken to this end. Over time the European Currency Unit will be utilized more extensively for denominating commercial transactions and financing governments, private corporations and entities such as the European Development Fund. The ECU will at a minimum become a parallel currency within the Community, although by 2000 it probably will not have displaced national currencies.

Nevertheless, as the ECU's role in global financial and monetary affairs becomes more prevalent and substantial, it will have profound effects on the international monetary system, thereby requiring the United States and other countries in the Group of Seven to consider whether changes in that system are required. Indeed, it would be wise to begin studying possible reforms of the international monetary system in parallel with the EC's exercise to reform its internal system. Future reforms in the international monetary system will need to reflect changes in the European Monetary System.

By design and by the sheer magnetism of its economic pull, the Community—in its own right and as the result of a panoply of new trade arrangements that it is likely to negotiate (as described in the next section)—will become an increasingly formidable trading force in the remainder of the century, and will be able to use access to its market as a powerful lever to obtain access for its products to other world markets.

Up to a point, utilizing economic strength to obtain trading advantages is a legitimate tactic. But used in excess, it would lead to conflict between Western Europe and its key trading partners—particularly the United States. That in turn could weaken NATO security ties if Americans—alarmed by threats to their commercial interests—insist that Washington threaten to withdraw troops from Western Europe in retaliation or to force concessions from the Community.

The current Uruguay round of multilateral trade negotiations is, in this respect, of critical importance. An earlier negotiating round, the Kennedy Round, was launched at the beginning of the 1960s to reduce tariffs around the world, largely to keep the newly formed European Economic Community from turning inward. The current round can do likewise if its major players—the United States, Japan, the EC, Canada, Australia, and a number of major Third World nations—are willing collectively to commit themselves to reduce myriad nontariff barriers now distorting international commerce.

For the EC this means negotiating agreements that open more of its industries to competition from outside (in return, of course, for similar measures by its trading partners), just as those industries also are being exposed to intensified competition from within Europe, due to a lowering of internal barriers in the 1992 process. Those EC industries accustomed to high levels of protection or government subsidy will likely resist. EC governments might be tempted to respond to pleas for help from industries being hurt by increased competition from within Europe by declining to open further to non-EC competition, e.g., resisting pressure to liberalize access to their government procurement markets, or by shielding industries temporarily from imports of non-European goods through tight transition measures.

If Europe is perceived by Americans as resisting progress in the Uruguay Round or creating new barriers to outside competition, Washington will find itself besieged by domestic pressures to take trade measures against Europe—even if for broader political or security reasons it wishes not to do so. Perception of a "bloc mentality" emerging in the Community would also give impetus to the creation of competing trading blocs—in the western hemisphere or among nations on the Pacific rim. Even though such units would probably be less formally organized than the Community, they could constrain Western Europe's global trading opportunities.

A similar type of danger would result from the overly aggressive use by Washington of provisions of the 1988 Omnibus Trade Act. That could drive the Community to impose new restrictions of its own in retaliation, and generate pressures for the EC to utilize its growing economic cohesion to counter American pressure. The net result could be that trade disputes would drive a wedge between Europe and America on political and security matters. It is likely, however, that during the 1990s Europe and the United States will reach understandings that put most major trade differences behind them or at least permit them to be resolved in an orderly fashion.

IV

In coming years the Community, which already has trade agreements with many of its neighbors, is likely to negotiate new agreements with a broader range of countries. While the Community is putting in place the directives and rules that together form the basis for the single market, it will not accept new members. After that, pressures on it to do so will grow; certainly Austria and Turkey will push hard. The risk perceived in the Community, however, is that the entrance of new members in the next several years could overburden the EC apparatus. There is resistance in some EC members to admission of low-wage countries on grounds that this would give unfettered access to low-cost goods, thereby costing them jobs and profits, and flood their economies with cheap labor.

There is also concern that applications for membership would force the Community to confront the question of whether inclusion of nations neutral by treaty or by long-standing policy would prevent the Community from ever becoming a political and security union as envisaged by the Treaty of Rome. Alternatively, the EC would have to work out arrangements so that neutrals such as Austria could join and cooperate fully on economic matters, while remaining outside of EC political and security collaboration.

By the end of this century there will probably not be many new full members in the Community. Far more numerous will be nations associated by bilateral arrangements of various types. Agreements are likely to be negotiated establishing free trade ties with EFTA neutrals such as Switzerland and Finland, as well as Austria if it is not permitted to join, and with Mediterranean countries such as Cyprus and Malta. These accords can also permit greater cooperation in areas such as investment, setting common product standards and adopting similar types of labor benefits. Still other arrangements—for instance, with East European nations and possibly the U.S.S.R.—could lead to trade expansion and liberalization on a more limited scale. The net result will be a widening map of trade and economic ties in Europe, centered on the Community.

It might be possible to envisage by the end of this century a Europe of concentric economic circles: (1) the EC at the core; (2) several neutrals, and other nations in the Mediterranean, enjoying particularly close economic relations with, or associate membership in, the EC, along with frequent consultations with the Council of Ministers and European Parliament on a range of economic and political matters; (3) some East European nations, and perhaps even the U.S.S.R., having arrangements with the EC that permit substantially increased two-way trade, along with investment treaties to encourage new and joint ventures. Associate membership might also be possible for those whose reforms over time lead their economies to operate largely on the basis of market forces. This structure could form the basic architecture of the "common European home."

East–West trade is likely to remain a small percentage of total West European trade, even if new trade agreements are reached, but it can play an important role in supporting economic reforms in the Soviet bloc and reducing the dependence of a number of COMECON countries on the Soviet Union. For several years Western Europe will find it difficult to increase or even maintain its net exports to the United States, as the latter attempts to reduce its enormous trade deficit. Thus, increased exports to the East will be attractive for some EC industries, even if large-scale trade financing is required to support them.

In recent years America and Europe have frequently differed over the pace and character of improvements in economic relations with the Soviet Union. Effective Western management of East–West economic relations is likely to be especially important for harmony in the alliance in the decade ahead.

As the effort to normalize economic relations with socialist economies proceeds, the West must consider a pivotal question: On whose terms should that normalization take place? Because the West's approach to economic policy has succeeded and the East's has failed, arrangements that simply "split the difference" would be counterproductive. Extending large-scale credits to socialist nations, or allowing them to participate in global economic institutions, without evidence of significant reform on their part would be self-defeating.

The West's goal should be to draw the Soviets and the East Europeans over time into the network of international, market-oriented economic relationships in support of, and in parallel with, domestic economic reforms in those nations. And it should maintain a strong consensus on ways to avoid—through the COCOM group of Western nations constituted to control technology transfer—sales of technology that could potentially benefit the Soviet military. In a similar spirit it should agree to avoid the provision of subsidized credits to socialist nations.

Both President Bush and President Gorbachev have supported the goal of bringing the Soviet Union into the international economic system. Gorbachev dramatized this point in a letter to the Paris economic summit in July that stressed: "Our perestroika is inseparable from a policy aiming at our full participation in the world economy." Soviet membership in global institutions such as the General Agreement on Tariffs and Trade (GATT) and the World Bank/International Monetary Fund is inappropriate at the moment, largely because of the still heavy hand of government on, and virtual absence of effective market forces in, the Soviet economy. But there are various ways in which these institutions and Moscow might actively exchange information on developments in the Soviet economy and the global economy as well. This exchange could permit Soviet officials to understand better the practical consequences of normalizing economic and trade relations with the rest of the world and help the Western nations and others to understand better how the Soviets would perform as members or observers in international institutions.

Observer status in the GATT for the Soviet Union should be considered, but only after the conclusion of the Uruguay Round. Addressing this now would divert attention from the round's urgent negotiating goals. Consideration of Soviet observership, of course, assumes that the USSR's internal reforms continue. Granting observership need not imply a commitment to ultimate full membership, which should be decided separately. In the meantime an active and systematic exchange of information and an organized set of consultations should take place between GATT and Soviet trade experts. This would aim at helping the Soviets design a tariff and pricing system consistent with the process of normalizing trade relations with market economies, and at giving the Kremlin a chance to dispel fears in the West that it would use GATT membership or observer status to politicize the organization, as it has done with respect to trade issues in the United Nations.

The World Bank and the International Monetary Fund do not have the equivalent of GATT's observer status. But systematic consultations among their experts and those of the U.S.S.R. could permit those institutions to obtain more information on the Soviet economy and its financing needs, and enable Soviet reformers to avail themselves of these institutions' expertise on exchange rates, pricing, banking and credit issues. In both cases, closer contacts will help Soviet officials to determine how to adjust their policies and practices to participate more effectively in the world economy.

Western Europe can utilize its particular economic strengths and historical ties to draw individual nations of Eastern Europe gradually closer (recognizing the differences in their approach to economic reform) and away from economic dependence on Moscow, without threatening Soviet security relationships. Indeed, the Kremlin might find closer economic ties between Eastern and Western Europe to be a face-saving and practical way of reducing its own costly commitments and avoiding a blowup in the region due to economic dissatisfaction.

The Community's unique advantage in this respect was recognized at the Paris economic summit. Both West German Chancellor Kohl and President Bush supported giving the EC Commission the lead in coordinating efforts to assist reform in Eastern Europe and provide food aid to Poland. This action helped to "depoliticize" the aid from Moscow's standpoint, and made it easier for East Europeans to accept the help without appearing to the Kremlin to be slipping into America's clutches. It also enabled West Germany to play a key role in Eastern Europe within the context of the EC, countering concerns elsewhere that it might be tempted to take unilateral initiatives in the region, and reinforcing in the minds of West Germans the idea that improving ties with the East could be done in a Community framework.

On another front, member nations of the Community are gradually linking loans to, and trade with, their socialist neighbors to efforts to lower tensions and support reforms. Most West European trade and credits are not tied to political conditions, but some links have been made. In 1987 West German loans to Hungary were provided on the condition that liberal reforms continue and cultural contacts be permitted to grow. In 1988 the French government announced its intention to link its roughly $2 billion in new credits to the Soviet Union to progress in reducing conventional arms in Europe. Such conditions avoid the inconsistency of providing the Soviets large amounts of money while Moscow continues to maintain massive conventional forces that require offsetting Western defense spending. Also in 1988 the Community and COMECON signed a declaration of "mutual recognition." The Community insisted on and obtained two conditions—that West Berlin be treated as part of the EC, and that future trade agreements be with individual COMECON nations, not with the Moscow-dominated COMECON organization itself.

The latter condition was a step toward loosening Moscow's economic grip on Eastern Europe. Soon after, the Community reached a trade agreement with Hungary, thus rewarding Eastern Europe's most reform-minded and market-oriented economy; the EC promised to phase out most of its quotas against Hungary, which agreed to provide easier access for Community businesses. A more limited agreement was reached later with Czechoslovakia. The U.S.S.R., Poland and Bulgaria are seeking similar arrangements, but they are unlikely to receive as favorable treatment because their governments have tightly controlled prices. Without credible, market-oriented price mechanisms there is a greater chance that these nations will dump or heavily subsidize exports to the Community.

Thus, the Community approach to COMECON nations is dual track. It aims at helping individual nations of Eastern Europe regain their historical position as an integrated part of Europe in terms of trade, human rights, freedom of movement and democratic reforms. But they would not yet be included as members in the EC because their economies are not able to integrate fully with those of Western Europe and they do not adhere to market principles. Moreover, these countries are of course still members of the Warsaw Pact.

Over time, Poland, Hungary and Czechoslovakia should be able to resume, to the extent geopolitics will allow, their positions as integral parts of Europe. By culture, religion, and history they can in no way be considered a logical part of the Soviet sphere of influence, much less of its empire. Ties between Paris and Warsaw, Vienna and Budapest, Prague and Berlin are as much a part of the common European background as are the Renaissance, the Reformation, Chopin, Voltaire, and Beethoven. Thus, trying to bring the two parts of Europe closer together responds to a historical urge that both sides feel. The historical basis of a "whole Europe" or "common home," after all, goes back to the empire of Charlemagne, and then the Holy Roman Empire, and should at a minimum encompass the territories of those empires; both were culturally and geographically primarily West European.

V

There is an emerging debate in Europe over how it might assume more responsibility for its own security. One school of thought—advanced, among others, by members of the Social Democratic Party in West Germany and the Labour Party in Britain—holds that the Soviet Union and Western Europe can reconcile most of their ideological and political differences very quickly. This line opposes new expenditures for nuclear weaponry and supports significantly intensified East–West trade and financial relations. It argues that improved East–West ties will make it possible to achieve Charles de Gaulle's dream of a Europe from the Atlantic to the Urals, or at a minimum to tear down barriers to the movement of people and dramatically reduce tensions. Western Europe, the argument continues, should loosen its military and political links to the United States—which are seen as an abnormal legacy of the cold war—and "Europeanize" Western Europe's security. An extreme version of this argument holds that Western Europe should quickly denuclearize and distance itself from Washington on security matters in order to hasten the process of intra-European normalization.

Another, more centrist, school advances a very different vision. It is one of a Western Europe that, while asserting more control over its own economic and political future and pursuing closer economic and political ties with the East, as well as freer movement of people to and from its socialist neighbors, remains firmly a part of the Atlantic alliance and militarily well prepared, with a credible nuclear deterrent. This vision is based on the view that NATO's unity and its defense capability must be preserved even as relations with the Soviets improve, that Western strength and NATO cohesion are in fact a prerequisite for success in future arms reduction talks with Moscow, and that they are in any case needed because the long-term outlook for Soviet policy is still unclear. Moreover, the argument continues, the alliance provides Western Europe the protection that enables it to concentrate on strengthening its internal economic cohesion.

The concept of Europe that will emerge will not be the product of an American vision but of forces within Europe itself. Yet the stakes for the United States are high. America's international power and influence are heavily dependent on its alliances with Western Europe as well as Japan. But American policy cannot be predicated on the assumption that the postwar status quo will last indefinitely, that Western Europe will accept permanent animosity with the U.S.S.R. or permanent barriers with Eastern Europe, or that America's allies will not increasingly seek to assert their self-identity and moral independence in international affairs—often in ways that differentiate them from the United States.

Nonetheless, global stability continues to depend heavily on the United States. Washington and its allies must find the proper balance between America's efforts to reduce its costly global role, while still being able to lead the alliance effectively, and Western Europe's efforts to play a more independent global role, while continuing to rely on U.S. ground forces and its nuclear deterrent. On both sides of the Atlantic leaders recognize that no country today possesses America's combination of military power, wealth and political authority; none can play the role of "replacement power" should America's global influence weaken significantly, as America did when Britain's power declined earlier in this century.

Western Europe's strategic options are limited by global power relationships. Western Europe confronts a military superpower to its east. As long as Europe is not a military superpower (even if it is an economic one), it must depend on the world's other superpower, its ally the United States, to counter Soviet influence and Soviet bloc armies. Some Soviet threat will remain, notwithstanding Gorbachev's encouraging announcements of unilateral force cuts in Eastern Europe and his willingness to negotiate substantial additional cuts, as long as Soviet military forces remain large and offensively postured and Moscow's political and military domination continues in Eastern Europe. As long as there is a potential threat of Soviet intimidation, America's defense commitment and its military presence will remain vital to Western Europe's security and to its ability to resist pressures from Moscow.

Nevertheless, a new political consensus will be required to underpin Western security relationships. NATO has long had to live with the facts of democratic life: when relations with the Soviets improve, citizens of NATO nations become reluctant to support military expenditures and question the need for the alliance to possess major deterrent capabilities. It is difficult to rally people around a pastel banner. Increasingly NATO governments will have to ensure that public support for the organization depends on more than the perception of an imminent Soviet threat. They will need both to underscore the need for NATO as insurance against a reversal of Soviet policy and to expand the range of issues on which NATO engages the common efforts of the European and North American democracies—from student exchanges, to fighting the drug trade, to resisting terrorism, to countering threats to the environment. All of these will take on greater importance in the 1990s. By moving effectively in at least a few of these areas, NATO can increase its relevance to younger generations, to whom the importance of support for NATO is not as obvious as it is to those whose political views were formed at the height of the cold war.

As fear of the Soviets has declined, so has popular support for NATO and for maintaining current nuclear arsenals. Antinuclear sentiment is particularly strong in West Germany. Much of Gorbachev's public relations campaign is an effort to loosen the Federal Republic's ties to the alliance (although not necessarily to encourage it to leave NATO, since that would intensify pressure on East Germany to leave the Warsaw Pact). Without strong Federal Republic support, NATO's conventional defense and nuclear deterrent would be ineffective—and Moscow fully understands this.

West Germany's role as a NATO ally is particularly vital to the balance of power on the European continent and to the West's ability to exert influence in central Europe. Therefore, the United States and its allies will have to address the deeply felt unease in the Federal Republic regarding Germany's status as a divided nation and the increasing discomfort of West Germans at being constrained from pursuing social, political and economic objectives in areas of Eastern Europe where they have historically been influential. . . .

For the Community the major goal will be to strengthen its interlocking trade and financial ties with West Germany—leading to greater political and security cohesion—to anchor the Federal Republic firmly to the West, countering any tendency for it to seek a Bismarckian "middle ground" in central Europe. Prosperity in the EC, in contrast to the failures of socialism in Eastern Europe, should serve as a reminder to both Germanys that their brightest future together lies in East Germany's moving gradually toward West Germany, where prosperity and social progress are enhanced by membership in the EC.

France is especially cognizant of the need for close links with Germany, and between Germany and the rest of Western Europe. The need for close cooperation between Paris and Bonn, dramatized in the public reconciliation between France and Germany ratified by President de Gaulle and Chancellor Konrad Adenauer in 1962 at Reims Cathedral, has been carried on enthusiastically by the present French and German leaders; the two countries are still the driving force for reducing internal barriers in the Community, creating a common monetary system and forging closer military ties. France, having translated its passionate sense of national destiny into an almost equally passionate sense of European destiny, is the spiritual leader of the new Europe while West Germany is the economic leader.

VI

Differences in the approach of Western Europe and the United States concerning the improvement of economic ties with Eastern Europe are to be expected, and indeed are in many respects appropriate due to circumstances of history and geography; but any change in security relationships between East and West will require a clear agreement within NATO. Strategic stability on the continent cannot be attained if Americans and West Europeans pursue separate strategies.

Here as in economics, the central question is: On whose terms? Some Europeans argue that greater accommodation with Moscow is prudent "hedging" policy. Still others argue on moral grounds for unilaterally moving toward a nuclear-free Western Europe. But these notions, if broadly embraced, risk acceptance of the idea that more normal relations in Europe must be achieved to a substantial degree on Moscow's terms. The opposite proposition is more accurate. Western democracies will be in a powerful position vis-à-vis Moscow for years to come. The Soviet Union and its allies need a respite from international tensions in order to achieve domestic economic priorities.

President Bush made the most of these circumstances by taking the initiative at the 1989 NATO summit to offer proposals aimed at lowering

Warsaw Pact and NATO force levels. In many respects the summit was a watershed, for it took the United States and its allies off the defensive in the "initiative competition" with Gorbachev, and demonstrated NATO's resolve to link large conventional cuts to cuts in short-range nuclear weapons. It also, temporarily at least, diffused pressure in the U.S. Congress for unilateral conventional force cuts in Europe.

One particular area in which the allies will need to coordinate more actively is arms control. Europeans are apprehensive not only when America becomes too belligerent toward Moscow, but also when it appears too eager to reach agreement. Toughness stirs up apprehensions about nuclear war and gives ammunition to antinuclear groups; arms reduction negotiations raise apprehensions over possible decoupling of the U.S. defense commitment from Europe. America's allies, including Japan, need to be brought into a NATO-centered process of consultations on arms control strategy—which in coming years will involve negotiations on strategic, conventional and perhaps short-range nuclear arms—both to minimize misunderstandings that breed apprehensions and to ensure that progress on one side of the Eurasian landmass does not add to problems on the other.

The West's primary negotiating goal now should be to press Gorbachev to make good on his own concepts of "reasonable sufficiency" and "defensive" military doctrine. It should seek a dismantling of a large portion of Soviet conventional forces and equipment that are forward-deployed in Eastern Europe and western military districts of the Soviet Union. Asymmetrical cuts in conventional forces should, as the United States has suggested, be a prerequisite for cuts in short-range nuclear weapons. The latter weapons would then not be required in such great abundance by NATO because conventional cuts would make the Warsaw Pact far less able to launch a surprise attack and engage in massive offensive operations. If that goal can be attained, and if effective verification procedures can be established, the end of the century could see a dramatic reduction of tensions and lower-cost security in Europe.

Assuming a reduction of East–West tensions and asymmetrical conventional force cuts, fewer American divisions will be required on the continent—and therefore one or two of the five U.S. divisions there could be withdrawn as the result of an intra-NATO agreement, with little risk to West European security or NATO cohesion. It is also likely that the nuclear deterrent capabilities of Britain and France will be enhanced by that time—a possibility that neither the United States nor Western Europe should negotiate away. There is likely to be closer nuclear cooperation between Britain and France, as well as expanded coordination between their nuclear force planners and the commanders of conventional forces in West Germany. Over time this should give the Germans greater confidence in the credibility of these deterrents as a supplement to those of the United States. Improvements in intra-West European military cooperation will also demonstrate to Americans that Europeans are doing more for themselves. But at the end of this century there will still be no alternative to an American nuclear guarantee and troop presence in Europe.

If conventional troop negotiations achieve satisfactory results, and economic relations between the EC and its eastern neighbors improve as expected, the United States and its European allies should be prepared to go further: to explore opportunities for new security arrangements with the Soviet Union that will permit governments to come to power in Eastern Europe whose legitimacy is based on genuine voter support and which are closely associated with the Community (the second concentric circle around the EC core, described earlier), although they could remain in COMECON as well. A zone of this sort on its western border might become an increasingly attractive prospect for Moscow. But the United States and its European allies will have to reach a consensus on these issues before approaching the U.S.S.R. and the East Europeans. Community leadership of the dialogue with the East Europeans, and even with the U.S.S.R.—consistent with the approach set at the Paris summit on economic aid to Eastern Europe—might provide greater reassurance to both than if the United States were to seem to dominate the process. It would also alleviate any concerns about a "Yalta II" agreement made over the heads of the Europeans. The Community should be one of the guarantors of the integrity of the agreement, though in the end the role of the United States will be decisive for Moscow.

One caveat must be noted. A backlash in the U.S.S.R. is still possible that could significantly retard or even reverse the process of glasnost and perestroika. If this occurs, Moscow's more relaxed attitude toward both economic and political reform in Eastern Europe could suffer. The West will need to be alert to such contingencies, even though optimism now reigns. Division within Western Europe, or between it and America, over how to react to abrupt and adverse change in the U.S.S.R. can be limited by anticipating such developments, at least as possibilities, and consulting closely about how they might be coped with.

VII

In these and other areas, the United States will need to work not only with individual West European nations as it has, but also with the European Community—which will likely be the forum for its members to harmonize foreign policy on an ever larger range of issues. More frequent discussion between the U.S. secretary of state and foreign ministers of a representative group of EC members (perhaps the foreign minister of the nation holding the EC presidency, plus the foreign ministers of the countries preceding and succeeding in the EC presidency) might be useful—and relations with Eastern Europe and the U.S.S.R. are an apt subject for such discussion. The Europeans will want these consultations to represent something more than a symbolic act; they will want to be listened to and to feel confident that America's position gives their collective views appropriate weight. And, as in the case of economic support for Eastern Europe, they will insist on being in the lead on important subjects.

In the era of John F. Kennedy there was an expectation on both sides of the Atlantic that NATO could become a partnership of equals. This was also a vision of Jean Monnet and Paul Henri Spaak—two fathers of today's Europe. This goal is not likely to be realized by 2000, but a far greater parity is. Western Europe will not over this period become a military superpower or possess a fully credible nuclear deterrent, nor will it be prepared to exercise a global political role of a scope similar to America's. But it can and will be a powerful global economic force. It will also have forged a more distinctly European set of policies and attitudes on global political issues.

The character of the Atlantic relationship will depend heavily on whether America and Europe together can find the right formula for accommodating Europe's desire for greater autonomy and influence on global and alliance issues, along with America's desire for Europe to assume greater responsibility for its defense and for global economic stability. If such an accommodation can be reached, the process of normalization between Western and Eastern Europe can proceed without weakening Western security, and the Community's growing unity will provide the most powerful boost to the fortunes of the West and to democratic values in this century. By the year 2000 the continent should be a safer and more prosperous place.

9

America's Economic Dependence

FELIX ROHATYN

I

The coming decade will set the stage for the world of the 21st century. Will that world be chaotic or orderly? Will there be growth or stagna-

Reprinted by permission of *Foreign Affairs*, Winter 1988–1989. Copyright 1988 by the Council on Foreign Relations, Inc.

Note: It is a violation of the law to reproduce this selection by any means whatsoever without the written permission of the copyright holder.

tion? Will the United States be able to play the preeminent role that it played in this century? This is the context in which we must examine the present.

The ideological walls are crumbling all over the world. The basic national objectives in both the communist and the free worlds consist of sustained economic growth, greater competitiveness, and higher standards of living. The global divisions that continue to exist, and that will become more and more serious, will be between haves and have-nots, rich and poor, competitive and inadequate. Such distinctions, however, will no longer be primarily ideological in source.

The most important event since the end of World War II is the recognition by the leaders of both the U.S.S.R. and China that communism is not a viable system. While Soviet and Chinese reforms have been so far mostly limited to economics, they will inevitably spread to the political sphere. The Soviets and the Chinese have embarked on reform because their economies were collapsing, their citizens wanted a higher standard of living and their military wanted up-to-date technology and educated armed forces. But the underlying cause was that their system, in addition to being philosophically unacceptable, is inefficient and noncompetitive in the modern world. Until the end of this century and later, U.S.S.R. and China will be dealing with their internal economic and social problems.

The evolution of Western Europe toward a unified market by 1992 is driven by similar broad objectives. President François Mitterrand's attempt to govern France with a classical socialist program came to a painful end in 1983. His successful reelection this past year was due, in good part, to his adoption of a moderate social democratic program geared to a market economy and aimed at global competitiveness. The same is true of left-wing governments in Spain and Italy, as well as conservative governments in the United Kingdom and West Germany. All of these European countries seek higher standards of living, better education and lower unemployment, with varying levels of government involvement in economies driven primarily by the private sector. It is interesting to note, parenthetically, that all of these countries have more extensive social safety nets than the United States and higher levels of government spending as a percentage of GNP (between 40 and 50 percent as compared to about 35 percent for the United States).

In the less-developed parts of the world, the objectives are also the same, but the ability to achieve them is problematic. Mexico, Brazil, Argentina, the Philippines—all are crushed by a combination of debt service, corruption, high birth rates, and stagnating or decreasing standards of living. The threat to political stability arising from this economic inadequacy is very great. The political fate of these countries will depend on their economic success or failure, and not vice versa.

II

Issues of global economic development cut across both domestic and foreign policy, and will require major efforts in both areas. The level of industrial capacity built up all over the world, and the ability to transfer technology from developed to less-developed countries, requires increased worldwide demand. This can only come from healthier economies in the less-developed countries—including, one can hope, increased demand from within the Soviet bloc and, ultimately, from India and China, together with strong, continued growth in the West.

Massive investment by the private and public sectors also will be required. This investment can best be financed by worldwide reductions in defense spending. Over the long run, it is likely that more and more countries will conclude that priority should be given to economic growth over military spending. Mikhail Gorbachev's proposal for unilateral Soviet conventional force reductions, delivered before the U.N. General Assembly in December, is a reflection of that reality. Moreover, communication and information technology, financial deregulation and worldwide capital markets have eliminated the traditional borders of our financial and economic system. The world has become totally interdependent.

As for the United States, the policies of the Reagan Administration have contributed not only to our economy's interdependence with the rest of the world, which is perfectly healthy, but to its *dependence* on outsiders, which is not. The necessity to finance part of the U.S. budget deficit with foreign capital; the necessity, over the last two years, for foreign central banks to acquire more than 150 billion dollars to support our currency; our trade deficit and growing foreign debt; the steep increase in domestic assets sold abroad to finance our deficits—all of these factors, and more, have created a dependence on the policies of other sovereign governments and private interests that affect every U.S. domestic issue.

Even though this phenomenon was briefly recognized during the 1970s, as a result of the energy crisis and the rapid accumulation of "petrodollars" by the member-states of the Organization of Petroleum Exporting Countries, the subsequent collapse of oil prices and the careless "recycling" of petrodollars to the Third World by the Western banking system obscured the situation. Now, however, recognition of the truth is inescapable: *no* meaningful domestic government decision is free of international consequences, in view of our financial situation as the world's greatest debtor.

These factors all argue for the proposition that "domestic policy" is an outmoded expression and an obsolete concept. It is obvious that government policies, with respect to education, taxes, infrastructure, entitlements, and so on, affect mostly our own citizens. However, those policies can only be formulated within the framework of an economic policy that is global in nature and concept—partly because of the new world we live in, but especially because of our huge indebtedness.

A similar argument can be made with respect to national security affairs, though somewhat in reverse. Just as economic policy inevitably transcends our borders, questions of national security have become woven into the fabric of our domestic policy. The two—economic policy and national security policy—are related to each other, depend on each other, and must be considered as worldwide in their scope. Thus, the next president's vision of the world will be crucial in determining how we treat these matters.

III

Several aspects of U.S. economic policy have significant impact on foreign policy. Our annual trade deficit ranges somewhere between $130 billion and $150 billion. In addition, net financial outflows as a result of our increasing foreign debt are about $20 billion each year, and they are likely to go higher. It is critical to bring this deficit down for several reasons.

First, the growing foreign debt created by our trade deficit requires continued willingness on the part of our foreign partners to finance the deficit at reasonable rates. They may not always remain so willing— market forces may not leave them any choice. Second, the increasing transfer of U.S. wealth abroad, resulting from the ever-increasing interest we must pay on our foreign debt, will create consistent downward pressure on the American standard of living. Third, the inability to achieve at least rough balance in our trade accounts will perpetuate a loss of competitiveness this country cannot afford.

Achieving a positive outcome will be a daunting challenge. To bring our balance-of-payments deficit to zero by, say, 1994, will require an improvement in the trade balance of about $200 billion per annum in order to make up for increasing interest costs and other financial outflows (such as dividends and interest paid out to foreign-owned companies and rent on foreign-owned real estate). Our net foreign debt by 1994 will be about $1 trillion, and the interest thereon will approach a level somewhere between $50 billion and $60 billion per annum, at a minimum.

A $200-billion annual savings in trade would be a tremendous achievement, and may not be feasible. In order to have a chance to achieve a healthy trade balance (other than by a collapse of the U.S. import market as the result of a deep recession) the purchasing power of Third World countries must be reflated, and the dollar cannot be allowed to collapse. Clearly, this effort will involve policy and national security issues.

In 1982 the Third World debt problem moved to the forefront of economic policymaking concern when Mexico announced it was unable to service its debt. Brazil, Argentina, the Philippines, and other developing countries were not far behind. Neither were Poland and other Eastern European countries. The total Third World debt was then about $800 billion.

The debt-relief program that was started then involved programs of austerity imposed by the International Monetary Fund, just enough in new credits to service the old debts, and stretch-outs of existing loans. The result is that the debt now approaches $1.2 trillion; developing countries are paying out a net of between $20 billion and $30 billion every year to developed countries. As a result of their rapidly growing populations, the standard of living in these countries is eroding rapidly. In this connection, it will be ironic if two of the most conservative institutions in the West—the commercial banks and the Catholic Church—rescue communism from the brink of defeat in the developing world by, in the one case, demanding the repayment of debts that cannot be repaid, and, in the other, refusing to recognize that the control of population growth is an absolute necessity.

The United States should play the leading role in beginning to reverse this process, not only because we need world growth for our own benefit, but, more specifically, because the political and economic stability of many of these countries, especially Mexico, is vital to us. The reasons are too obvious to require much elaboration: the threat to the security of our borders, high levels of illegal immigration, potential unrest in large Hispanic communities in the United States, the financial exposure of our banks. To play such a leading role, however, we would have to lower interest rates by reducing our own borrowing needs, commit major new capital to the World Bank to enable it to play its required role, and provide our banks and financial institutions with enough capital and stability to provide future financing. None of this is possible today, because our continuing budget deficits require constant borrowing and high interest rates; our banks are too weak vis-à-vis their Japanese and European counterparts to play their required role; and increasingly negative political reactions to foreign influence in this country make support of the World Bank and other multinational institutions ever more difficult. . . .

IV

It is most unfortunate that, at a time when the economic and political systems of the United States are the envy of the world, our failure to deal with domestic budgetary issues will create serious impediments to our ability to influence events in the rest of the world, and may create an isolationist backlash in this country. Our basic weakness is due to excessive levels of debt, both in the government and private sectors. This affects every aspect of our policies.

For example, in order for Soviet President Gorbachev's perestroika to have any chance for success, sooner or later a number of events will have to take place: large-scale Western credits will have to be extended to the Soviet Union to buy consumer goods; imports of Western technology and capital goods must be permitted for longer-term development; and some degree of geopolitical agreement will have to be reached regarding Eastern Europe.

The first of these processes has already started; in the last year private British, German, French and Italian banks have committed a total of over $12 billion to the Soviet Union. In most of these cases, government guarantees are provided to the banks. The United States may well be shut out of this process, not only because American banks lack the capacity to participate, but mostly because we have no concerted business–government strategy or structures to deal with such issues. We have wasted huge amounts of money in Eastern Europe, for instance; our commercial banks are exposed for almost $10 billion in Poland alone, with no prospect for repayment and little, if any, for political benefit.

The ability of the Federal Reserve Bank (or the Export-Import Bank) to guarantee certain types of credits to communist-bloc countries would be a useful tool in a geopolitical strategy vis-à-vis the Soviet Union and Eastern Europe, if such credits could be linked to other agreements such as one providing for a reduction of forces in Europe. Such a capability would also be useful as part of a possible Middle East settlement. It is likely that any such settlement, if it ever happens, would include massive economic assistance.

There is at present, however, no structure that would permit such a coordinated strategy; neither in the State Department nor in the Treasury Department nor in the Federal Reserve does such authority reside. Nor do we, as a country, have the surplus capital to implement this kind of strategy, even if we could manage it.

At a time when both superpowers have implicitly recognized the irrelevance of nuclear weapons (except as a deterrent), the real power in the world is coming to consist of surplus capital combined with national self-discipline, advanced technology and superior education. The leading nations of tomorrow, by those standards, are likely to be Japan and post-1992 Western Europe. The United States, once the unquestioned leader of the West, falls short in every one of these categories. The main reason for our failure is our addiction to debt, which affects every one of these areas.

This addiction to debt, fueled in the 1980s by financial deregulation, supply-side economics and stock market speculation, has occurred in the government sector as well as in the private sector; it covers both our external debt and our domestic debt. Domestic government debt has soared from about $1 trillion in 1980 to about $2.7 trillion currently, as a result of a series of annual budget deficits ranging from $140 to $220 billion. The national debt will be over $3 trillion by 1992. Our foreign debt is now about $500 billion (compared to a positive balance of about $150 billion in 1980) and will reach about $1 trillion in 1992. During this same period, the debt of U.S. non-financial companies has grown dramatically in relation to their equity. Almost $200-billion-worth of high-yield "junk bonds" have been issued, often in connection with acquisitions, leveraged buyouts, or other corporate restructurings. As a result of these and similar transactions, the equity capital of American non-financial corporations has been reduced by more than $400 billion over the last five years.

The perverse linkage of our deficits and our international economic posture was evident throughout the past decade. Sky-high interest rates in the early 1980s, driven by the Federal Reserve's fight against inflation, pushed the dollar up by fifty percent and caused a recession. The resulting budget deficit, caused by tax cuts and high defense spending, resulted in a typical "Keynesian" recovery which, because of the high dollar, sucked in huge amounts of imports, creating an ever larger trade deficit. The latter was used to finance our budget deficit but, simultaneously, destroyed large sectors of U.S. manufacturing.

When the Reagan Administration's long-standing policy of "benign neglect" of the dollar was reversed in 1985, and the value of the dollar was sharply driven down, these deficits continued. But the foreign investment needed to finance the deficits shifted significantly from portfolio investment to direct investment in U.S. property and businesses. Commercial real estate and U.S. corporations were acquired by Japanese and European interests at an accelerating rate—and this trend will inevitably continue. The outcome of the recent presidential election gives no hope of a fundamental change in either the economic policy or the policymaking structure of our government. This may make it very difficult for the United States to maintain its leadership role in the world of the 1990s. As long as the United States is a huge importer of capital, and as long as it is not capable of making the domestic improvements necessary to be competitive in export markets, it will abdicate its leading role more and more to Japan and Europe.

V

Another area of growing importance and sensitivity is the foreign ownership of U.S. business. By the end of 1987 foreign claims on U.S. assets had reached $1.5 trillion. This figure includes ownership of government bonds, stocks, companies, real estate and so forth.

Back in 1980 the figure was one-third its present level. Direct investment, namely the full ownership of companies, stood at $263 billion last year, as opposed to $83 billion in 1980. Increases in the amount of U.S. dollars held abroad because of our trade deficit and the likely continued weakness of the dollar (assuming nothing is done about our budget deficit) will accelerate this trend. It is worth noting that the value of all companies listed on the New York Stock Exchange is about $2 trillion; the total current U.S. foreign debt of about $500 billion represents about 25 percent of that amount. The $1-trillion foreign debt level forecast for 1992–93 will most probably represent a significantly higher proportion (unless the level of the stock market doubles during this period), and the level of direct investment is likely to increase materially. If the securities markets and the dollar both go lower, it is sure that much of this $1 trillion will be invested in permanent assets (companies, real estate, etc.) instead of government bonds. Thus we will be forced to accelerate the process of selling long-term, productive businesses to finance short-term budget and trade deficits. That is unsound.

Of the major industrial powers in the world, only the United States allows the purchase of controlling interest in key companies without some type of government review, or without giving domestic purchasers some type of preference. Japan, Germany, Switzerland, France and Italy all have such safeguards. Even Great Britain recently stopped Kuwait from acquiring more than twenty percent of British Petroleum, on grounds of national interest review requirements. Insofar as acquisitions are concerned, American companies are at a considerable economic disadvantage vis-à-vis their foreign competitors, because of accounting and tax treatment—the economic differential can be as much as 25 percent. This is an important area, in which corrective action should be considered, since it will become a larger issue in the near future.

For the present, the fundamental economic issues are the budget and trade deficits. But the control issue should not be ignored—if the current economic policies that tacitly encourage the sale of American assets to finance our deficits continue. In the long run, foreign control of a larger proportion of American business, coupled with our failing educational system, will have significant implications for innovation, product development and research, in addition to increasing the level of financial transfers abroad. Those are the real determinants of America's future economic independence and the legacy of the 1980s.

There are two different ways of looking at foreign direct investment. The first, and currently dominant view, is that direct investment (such as the foreign purchase of a company) is permanent and desirable, and preferable to portfolio investment such as the purchase of government bonds which can be sold easily and thus may create significant market volatility. The alternative view is that the sale of a permanent asset (e.g., a manufacturing company or a bank) in order to pay for net imports of foreign goods is not necessarily advantageous either from a financial point of view or, ultimately, from the point of view of overall policy.

For example, if the United States sells $1 billion in 10-year U.S. bonds to pay for $1 billion of imports, we can ultimately repay the bonds for $1 billion plus interest; on the other hand, if a U.S. company is bought by foreign interests to pay for the same $1 billion of imports, the result is very different. That same company, 10 years from now, may be worth $5 billion or $10 billion; it is creating permanent and growing remittances of profits, dividends and technology abroad. The cost in terms of national wealth is ultimately much greater.

Selling permanent assets is an easy solution at this time and it relieves the U.S. government from having to sell equivalent amounts of government bonds, possibly at higher rates of interest to finance its deficits. But it creates a permanent claim on our economy, as opposed to the temporary claim represented by borrowing. It thereby reduces the pressure of the most important market discipline motivating the Congress and the administration to deal with the deficits: higher interest rates and/or a lower dollar.

The control of large business units has more serious implications now than ten years ago. This is a result of the emergence of a global economy, as well as of the revolution in communications and data-processing technology. Many industries which were then discrete and separate now overlap. The control of a large enterprise carries with it the ability to make decisions determining questions of worldwide plant-site selection, worldwide supplier selection, product design, R&D siting and control and management development. These can have an important national impact, as more and more companies are bought by foreign interests. And in the case of large financial institutions, the control of credit policy is obviously very important, especially in times of financial stress.

Technological and regulatory changes are additional factors. In the United States, in one form or another, there have been historical restrictions or limitations on the foreign ownership of sensitive defense industries, banks and certain media, such as network TV. No effort, however, has been made to define, or redefine, these categories for the current era. An adequate defense industry does not consist solely of the capacity to manufacture weapons; it includes the production of all kinds of sophisticated electronics, communications, special materials and many other types of high technology. Should restrictions be applied in any of these areas? Banking has also changed: with the expected lifting of the Glass-Steagall Act, the dividing line between commercial banking and the securities industry will be eliminated. Should restrictions on foreign ownership be extended to the securities industry, or, alternatively, eliminated from banks? The same quandary applies to the media. The major networks have seen their market share eroded from almost 100 percent of the television audience to nearly 60 percent by the advent of cable television, video cassettes, etc. Should restrictions applicable to network TV be extended to the cable industry, or alternatively, eliminated from networks?

Foreign control of American businesses, especially in light of the scale on which it is likely to take place, is a valid issue of national interest. Control of financial institutions involves our international posture. Control of the media (practically all of book publishing is now foreign-owned) can affect public opinion and our political system. Control of manufacturing will affect the know-how and technology around which much of future growth will be created.

It may be that a searching, sophisticated debate of this issue will lead to the conclusion that the United States, alone among all developed Western industrial powers, should allow practically unlimited foreign control of domestic business institutions. Such a decision would be attributed to American faith in the market system and unwillingness to interfere with free flows of capital. In reality, however, it will be a decision based on our overdependence on foreign capital and our fear of frightening that capital away.

National policies should never be based on fear, either in security matters or in economic matters. The issue of foreign control is a complicated and emotional issue. It does not lend itself to clear-cut answers and should be approached with extreme care. It is an issue to be discussed with our trading partners, and there are many subsidiary issues which should be examined: reciprocal rights of ownership; equal rules of the game for acquisition in areas such as accounting and taxes; equal regulation and sharing of financial responsibility in areas such as banking and securities; and many more. But the issue will not go away. It should be examined dispassionately before political pressure to find drastic remedies becomes too severe.

VI

The United States once claimed the twentieth century as its own; yet the "American Century" ended up lasting little more than twenty years. Nevertheless, the United States can help shape the 21st century, but only if it changes the way it manages its domestic economic affairs. The world may not exist in fifty years because of a scientific or military catastrophe—but if it does it will be under the major influence of those powers that can export capital, that can harness and develop technology in large manufacturing enterprises, that have dominant financial institutions, that have superior educational systems, and that can finance their military requirements at whatever level their national security requires. These are likely to be Japan and a more unified Western Europe.

This is not the course on which the United States is embarked today; that course, however, cannot be avoided.

It would not require enormous national sacrifice to bring our current $150-billion budget deficit into rough balance over the next four years. It would require a firm, long-range plan acceptable to the administration and Congress; such a plan could be elaborated by the National Economic Commission.

The deficit-reduction package should consist of equal amounts of new taxes and expenditure cuts. Our energy prices are the lowest in the world. Increasing gasoline taxes by 25 to 50 cents per gallon would provide $25 billion-$50 billion per annum in new revenues and still leave U.S. gasoline prices at a level significantly below European prices. It would also conserve energy and reduce imports by a significant amount. A surcharge on personal income, raising the top effective rate to 33 percent or 35 percent would still leave tax rates significantly below their pre-1981 levels and provide significant revenue and fairer distribution. Insofar as entitlements such as social security, Medicare and Medicaid are concerned, limiting cost-of-living allowances (COLAS) to one or two percentage points below the inflation rate, or taxing the benefits of higher-income recipients, would have significant impact on the budget and still pass the test of equity. National defense is essentially frozen at present levels that the country can well afford.

The United States is a great and wealthy nation with enormous natural assets as well as a vital and free political system. However, as everyone knows, balance sheets consist of both assets and liabilities, and our liabilities are growing at fearsome rates. They can be visible (such as our domestic and external debts); they can be camouflaged (such as our $70 billion-$100 billion in contingent liabilities to the savings and loan industry or the questionable credits of our banking system); or they can be hidden, as are the failures of our educational system and the lack of public and private investment. But if those liabilities, created by our failure to deal with domestic economic policy, are not dealt with in the near future, they will cost the United States its preeminent role as a world power.

A long-term plan to deal with our economic problems, if brought forward with a strong bipartisan commitment from the White House and Congress, would generate a strong positive response from the financial markets. It should deal with our budget deficit. It should deal with our trade deficit and the Third World debt. It should deal with new domestic investment and our competitive posture in the world. It would propel us forward into the next century and would enable the United States to fulfill its necessary role as the leader of the Western world. It is an absolute necessity.

THE PACIFIC RIM

10

International Politics in the Pacific Rim Era

ROBERT GILPIN

On 25 September in the year 1513, the Spanish explorer Vasco Núñez de Balboa discovered what was for Western civilization a new ocean. He called this body of water, seemingly more tranquil than the turbulent waters of the Atlantic, the "Pacific Ocean." The name was appropriate with respect to more than its seemingly tranquil waters. For most of the next half millennium, the Pacific Ocean and its peripheral societies became relatively passive objects of European and North American powers. Western conquest, imperialism, and exploitation have been the fate of the Asian peoples of the immense Pacific Rim, who were economically and technologically behind the West.

During the past half century or more, however, this condition of passivity and dependence has begun to change dramatically and at an accelerating pace. In 1904–5, the Japanese delivered a devastating defeat to the Russian empire that rocked the foundations of this encroaching giant; a rising Asian power had shown that Western nations were not invincible. Then in 1931, the Japanese began their own career of imperial expansion, intended to drive the West out of Asia and to create their own empire in East Asia. The Chinese people began to stir in the middle of the nineteenth century and by the turn of the century they had revolted against the domination of both their Manchu conquerors and Western imperialists.

In the post–World War II era, the demand of Asians to be masters of their own destiny has intensified. Following a century of turmoil and weakness, Mao Zedong liberated China and established a unified, cen-

Reprinted from *Annals AAPSS* 505 (September 1989), copyright by *Annals AAPSS*. Reprinted by permission of Sage Publications, Inc., copyright (1989) American Academy of Political and Social Science. Reprinted by permission of Sage Publications.

Note: It is a violation of the law to reproduce this selection by any means whatsoever without the written permission of the copyright holder.

tralized state. From the ashes of colonial rebellions and international conflicts, other independent states have arisen in Indonesia, Korea, and elsewhere around the Pacific Rim. Balboa's Pacific is no longer tranquil or merely subordinate to the ambitions of external powers. As the twentieth century draws to a close, the Pacific is rapidly emerging as the world's most dynamic arena, and its peoples are driving forces of global economics and international politics.

In the history of international relations, economic, technological, and demographic developments have, over the centuries, caused the center of economic and political activities to shift from one locus to another. The modern world's history can best be understood as a process of historical change that began in the Mediterranean and subsequently diffused north to Atlantic seaboard states and then spread both westward across the Atlantic and eastward across the Eurasian continent. These forces of change swept across both the North American continent and what geographer Halford J. Mackinder called "the heartland of the Eurasian continent" in eastern Europe and European Russia.[1] Today, these historical movements of economic, political, and technological forces are converging on the Pacific.

In his massive and multivolume history of this movement of the global political economy, the French historian Fernand Braudel has told this story graphically in terms of the rise and decline of great and dominant urban centers. As one national city has replaced another, the shifts in the international distribution of power and wealth

> interrupt the calm flow of history. . . . When Amsterdam replaced Antwerp, when London took over from Amsterdam, or when in about 1929, New York overtook London, it always meant a massive historical shift of forces, revealing the precariousness of the previous equilibrium and the strengths of the one which was replacing it. The whole circle of the world-economy was affected by such changes and the repercussions were never exclusively economic, as the reader will probably already suspect.[2]

Today, the "precarious equilibrium," to use Braudel's expression, of the contemporary international system is being upset with the emergence of Tokyo, Beijing, and, in Latin America, São Paulo as global centers of accumulating material wealth and national power. The ongoing shift in the international distribution of power toward the Pacific and toward the Southern Hemisphere has placed the dominant centers in Europe and North America on the defensive. The "calm flow of history" is being disrupted, at least for most Europeans and North Americans, who have enjoyed in the postwar era both unprecedented prosperity and, with the exceptions of the Korean and Vietnam wars, what the historian John Lewis Gaddis has rightly called "the long peace."[3]

The postwar international system is changing with a rapidity unknown in human history. The spectacular rise of Japan and of other economic competitors in East Asia and elsewhere in the so-called Third World is transforming the world economy. The repercussions of this shift in the global division of labor are not exclusively economic, as Braudel suggests, but are beginning to spill over into the realm of international politics. China, which began to industrialize earlier in this century, has already become a major regional power armed with nuclear weapons and is fast becoming a global rival to the superpowers. Because of its large economy, Japan's expenditure of only a little more than 1 percent of its gross national product on national defense has moved that country to third place after the United States and the Soviet Union in funding of the military. Of equal significance, the Japanese are increasingly allocating these resources in order to create a high-technology defense industry. The economic, technological, and demographic forces at work in these two major powers and throughout the Pacific Rim have unleashed a profound and far-reaching process of political change.

EXPLAINING POLITICAL CHANGE

If we had an adequate theory of economic and political change, it would be possible to explain these historic transformations and to predict their long-term political effects. Alas, the social sciences do not and probably never will have anything like a comprehensive understanding of these matters. As the Nobel laureate and pioneer of development economics, W. Arthur Lewis, has sardonically characterized the situation, "The process of social change is much the same today as it was 2,000 years ago. . . . We can tell what change will occur if it occurs, what we cannot foresee is what change is going to occur" and, one should add, what its effects will be.[4] The best we can do is to identify what is being changed, analyze the forces producing the change, and extrapolate on the basis of past experience the likely consequences.

The explanation of international political change requires an understanding and integration of three factors that lead to major changes in international politics as they are altered and interact with one another. The first is the structure and functioning of the international system, that is, the distribution of power among the dominant states in the international system and the political relationships among the most powerful states and other states in the system. The second is what I shall call, for lack of a better term, the environmental setting of the international system, such as economic, technological, and cultural influences on economic and political behavior. The third is the nature of the domestic regimes of the actors or societies, especially those aspects that affect the ability of a country to adapt to changes in the economic and technological environment of international relations. These three factors and changes in these factors help explain the dynamics of international relations both in the past and in the present.

The primary determinant of the structure of the international system is what the French sociologist Raymond Aron called a "hegemonic war." In the words of Aron, a hegemonic war

> is characterized less by its immediate causes or its explicit purposes than by the extent and the stakes involved. It affect[s] all the political units inside one system of relations between sovereign states. Let us call it, for want of a better term, a war of hegemony, hegemony being if not the conscious motive, at any rate the inevitable consequence of the victory of at least one of the states or groups.[5]

In short, what is at issue in a hegemonic war, as opposed to lesser types of wars, is the leadership and the overall structure of the existing international system. It was such a hegemonic conflict, World War II, that created the era that is now coming to an end.

Other developments, such as the entry of new states into an international system or the decline of dominant ones, can also alter the structure of an international system. The emergence of China, Japan, and Brazil as major industrial and potentially great military powers is a contemporary example. The relative decline of the United States and the Soviet Union, both of which rose to global preeminence as a consequence of World War II, illustrates the latter type of development. In the past, such major shifts in the distribution of power among the states in an international system have led to hegemonic war. Our own age, because of the restraining force of nuclear and other weapons of mass destruction, may be the first in which a transformation of the international system occurs that is not the result of hegemonic war. As I have written in another context, the task of ensuring peaceful rather than violent change is the greatest test of statesmanship in our era.[6]

Every international system exists in an environment composed of economic, technological, and cultural factors. Although most of these components of the environment are, of course, the conscious creation of human beings, once a new idea or technology comes into existence it assumes over time a life of its own. Its influence spreads throughout the international system and affects human behavior. Thus the rise of market economies, the industrial revolution, and the enterprising spirit of capitalism transformed European society in the early modern period. Although these developments initially took place in particular European societies, they spread rapidly throughout Western Europe and enabled European civilization to advance to a dominant global position. Almost all aspects of international relations were profoundly transformed as a consequence of these developments. By the same token, significant changes in the economic and technological environment, which took place in the latter decades of the nineteenth century, brought this European-centered age to a close and ushered in by midcentury the era of the American and Soviet superpowers. Today environmental changes are once again transforming the contours of the international economic and political system.

Whether a particular society is able to take advantage of the changed environment and the opportunities that it provides to increase national wealth and power is primarily a function of the third factor causing historic change, namely, the society's economic, political, and social system as well as, one might add, good fortune. Some domestic structures are more conducive than others to adaptation to economic or technological change. For example, as Nathan Rosenberg and L. E. Birdzell, Jr., argue in their book *How the West Grew Rich*—and, one should add, "powerful"—the rise of the industrial great powers of Western Europe and North America was a consequence of their pluralistic and fluid social and political systems. In contrast to the rigid cultures of Asia and elsewhere, the flexibility of European societies facilitated institutional and technological innovation that led to economic growth and industrial supremacy. What may promote economic growth in one environmental setting, however, may fetter it in another, thereby enabling other, more suitably adapted societies to take the lead. Great Britain, which in the seventeenth century was the pioneer in the first industrial revolution, which was based on the exploitation of coal, iron, and steam power, could not adapt easily to the second industrial revolution, which occurred in the late nineteenth century and was based on the exploitation of modern science.[7] As a result, it forfeited the economic and technological lead to Germany and the United States, which were better adapted to the requirements of economic success. Today these two nations as well as other industrial powers are being challenged by Japan and other Pacific Rim countries that appear more adept at exploiting contemporary scientific and technological developments.

With this simple model of political change in mind, I examine in the rest of this article the rise of the Pacific Rim and the significance of this historic development for contemporary international relations. The discussion begins with a consideration of the postwar international system and then turns to those environmental and other developments that are transforming this postwar system and elevating the Pacific Rim nations to a greatly enhanced role in the global system. These emergent Asian and Third World nations thus far appear to be better adapted than are the United States and European nations, including Eastern Europe and the Soviet Union, to take advantage of contemporary economic and technological developments. Although it is much too soon to know whether this is the case, what is certainly true is that the competition for position in the global system is intensifying.

THE POSTWAR SYSTEM

The postwar system and what we have come to call the cold war were a direct outgrowth of World War II. The conflict between the United States and the Soviet Union originated in the unwillingness of the two former allies to accept the consequences of the war and in the inability of each side to accept the other's conception of the postwar international order. Subsequently, what had originally been a geographically restricted conflict of political interest centered almost exclusively on Western Europe expanded into a global conflict between two hostile ideologies. This interest and ideological struggle quickly escalated into a power struggle and an unprecedented arms race between two military alliances and political blocs.

The American Bloc

The American bloc has had two basic components: the American relationship with Western Europe and American ties with Japan. Although these two quite separate alliances have certain common features, they also have several differences that have become more significant with the increasing importance of the Pacific Rim components of the bloc.

As relations with the Soviet Union deteriorated after 1945, the United States realized that there were fundamental problems related to Western Europe that required solution. The most pressing need was to assist the revival of the West European economy while also finding a way to guarantee the military security of the West Europeans against the threat from the Soviet Union. To achieve an American commitment to the pursuit of these goals, the American people had to be linked psychologically to Western Europe. A retreat into isolationism like that which had followed World War I and contributed to the outbreak of World War II had to be prevented.

The Marshall Plan, which encouraged intra-European cooperation, and the formation of the European Economic Community (EEC), or Common Market, were regarded as the solution to the economic problem of a devastated and fragmented Europe. The creation of a huge market in Western Europe would give the West Europeans the strength to resist native Communist parties and the blandishments of the Soviet Union. Although the Common Market represented a violation of the American ideal of a multilateral world and entailed discrimination against American exports, American policymakers assumed that the Common Market with its external tariff and protective Common Agricultural Policy was a necessary stepping stone to an eventual multilateral system rather than an end in itself. It was expected that once Western Europe had regained its economic strength and confidence, it would lower its external barriers and participate in the open world economy envisioned by the United States at Bretton Woods in 1944. In the meantime, the United States required an economic quid pro quo in the form of access to the EEC for American multinational corporations. Thus the United States tolerated what it assumed would be temporary discrimination against American exports in order to rebuild Western Europe and thwart Soviet expansionist designs.

The North Atlantic Treaty Organization (NATO) was formed in 1949 to link the two sides of the Atlantic and bring Western Europe under the American nuclear umbrella. Through the strategy of extended deterrence the United States communicated to the Soviet Union that an attack on Western Europe would be tantamount to an attack on the United States itself. The stationing of American troops on European soil has been a visible sign of this commitment. The North Atlantic Treaty identified and legitimated for Americans and West Europeans alike the linking of their security.

In Asia, the United States also found itself facing a political, economic, and strategic challenge, because World War II and its aftermath had strengthened the position of the Soviet Union in East Asia. The Red Army had gained advanced positions in the region, the Japanese economy had been even more devastated than had initially been appreciated, and North Korea and China had become Communist and part of the Soviet bloc. With the traditional markets of Japan now in hostile hands, there was an intense concern that the forces of economic gravity would pull Japan toward the Soviet Union and its Chinese ally. Today it is difficult to understand that 35 years ago American officials despaired over the problem of ensuring Japanese economic survival.

The United States wanted to integrate Japan into a larger framework of economic relationships and thereby remove the attractiveness of the Communist-dominated Asian market. There were, however, no large neighboring non-Communist economies to which the Japanese economy could be attached. In order to overcome this problem of an isolated and vulnerable Japan, the United States took several initiatives. One was to expedite the decolonization of Southeast Asia; after all, one cause of the Pacific War had been that European colonizers had closed these economies to the Japanese. The United States also sponsored Japanese membership in the so-called Western Club. Despite strong West European resistance based on intense fear of Japanese economic competition, the United States secured Japanese participation in the International Monetary Fund, the World Bank, and other international economic organizations. In addition, the United States gave Japan relatively free access to the American market and American technology without an economic quid pro quo, although it did require strategic concessions—air and naval bases—from the Japanese.

In order to guarantee Japanese security, the United States also spread its nuclear umbrella over Japan. The American-Japanese Mutual Security Treaty (MST), however, differs fundamentally from the NATO alliance. Under the North Atlantic Treaty, an external attack on any member obliges the others to consider measures of mutual defense. In the MST, the United States agrees to defend Japan if it is attacked, but the Japanese are not obligated to defend the United States. Also, whereas the NATO agreement applies only to the territory of its members, the MST refers to the outbreak of hostilities in the entire Pacific region. Through this agreement the United States obtained the right to use air and naval bases in Japan to defend and secure its position in the western Pacific. The Japanese were given access to the American market in exchange for the right to anchor on Japan the American strategic position in East Asia.

The Soviet Bloc

Naturally, much less is known about the structure and functioning of the Soviet bloc than about the American bloc. At the core of the bloc, of course, stands the Soviet Union. Its relations with its allies, however, are vastly different from those of the United States with its allies. Whereas the United States has operated largely as *primus inter pares*, the Soviet Union has behaved as a traditional imperial power. The Soviet Union has found it very difficult to treat its allies as equals. In place of consultation, it has fashioned a number of policies and institutions to maintain what the Chinese call its "hegemonic" position over the other socialist countries.

The principal instruments of Soviet domination have been the Red Army and the Warsaw Pact. In contrast to the NATO alliance and the MST, the Warsaw Pact has a twofold mission. The purpose of stationing Soviet troops in Eastern Europe, except for Bulgaria and Romania, is not only to protect the bloc against external attack but also to prevent any popular uprisings and potential defections from the Soviet system such as have occurred in every member of the Pact except Bulgaria and Romania. This military presence has been reinforced by the institutionalization of Stalinism in all of the Eastern European countries. Stalinist measures include the "leading role" of the Communist Party in political affairs, the organization of command economies based on central planning, and the linking of these economies through the state trading mechanisms of the Council for Mutual Economic Assistance.[8] The Soviet secret police (KGB) keeps Moscow well informed on the offical deliberations of bloc governments. At the diplomatic level, the nations of the Warsaw Pact and the overseas socialist countries such as Cuba and Vietnam have been linked to the Soviet Union through a series of friendship treaties. Last, but not least, overarching the system is the Brezhnev Doctrine, by which the Soviet Union claims the right to intervene in socialist countries to prevent their defection from the socialist international system.

The rigidity of these instruments of Soviet domination, however, has contributed considerably to the political fragility and economic inefficiencies of the socialist system. Soviet hegemony was a major cause of the Chinese decision in the early 1960s to break from the system, to increase economic ties with the West, and to play an independent role in the global system. Of more contemporary relevance, the traditional political instruments of Soviet policy are poorly adapted for a political world whose center of gravity is shifting toward Asia and the Pacific. The failure of the Red Army and the Brezhnev Doctrine in Afghanistan has constituted a serious setback. In Vietnam, Africa, and elsewhere, the Soviet Union finds itself with costly commitments that produce few economic or political benefits. Its traditional policies have only generated opposition and cooperation among its potential enemies. For example, the United States, China, and Japan have found common cause in resisting Soviet expansionism in East Asia.

In the economic sphere, the command economies of the Soviet bloc and the system of barter exchange connecting the socialist countries may have been well suited for the leading industries of the earlier postwar period based on heavy industry and mass production. The command economies promoted rapid reconstruction and industrialization and reduced the economic vulnerability to what Eastern-bloc leaders regarded as a threat from the West. These methods of economic organization and international trade are poorly devised, however, to take advantage of the economic revolution associated with the computer and other rapidly developing technologies.

The Soviet Union has gained relatively little in economic benefits and in fact has paid a high economic price for the security benefits provided by its system. This is not to deny the massive achievements of the Soviet Union in transforming itself from a devastated and backward country at the end of World War II to a superpower. But these achievements are rapidly eroding. Japan has aleady displaced it as the world's second-largest economy. In both the political and economic realms, the Stalinist legacy and its associated institutions constitute a major impediment to the capacity of the Soviet Union and other socialist countries to adapt to the changing global economic and political system.

The transformation of the world's economic and political systems associated with the increasing importance of the Pacific Basin has begun to change the Soviet perception of its long-term interests. Secretary Mikhail Gorbachev's celebrated speech on 28 July 1986 at Vladivostok, which called for a rapprochement with China and recognized the growing economic importance of Japan and the other Pacific Rim countries, reflected this new attitude. The Soviets cannot afford to alienate a militarily significant China and a Japan flush with capital and advanced technology for export. The Soviet disengagement from Afghanistan, moves toward a settlement in Southeast Asia, and a scaling-down of its provocative naval buildup in the region are elements of a Soviet attempt to improve its position in the Pacific.

THE TRANSFORMATION OF WORLD POLITICS

The continuing transformation of world politics is due to three major changes in the environment of international relations. These technological, economic, and related changes have enhanced the role and importance of the Pacific in the international economic and political system. As in the past, the shift in the global locus of economic and military power is altering fundamental relationships.

The first environmental change is the impact of the nuclear revolution. Both the United States and the Soviet Union have realized that their political and ideological conflict cannot be resolved through military means. The contest between the superpowers has in effect resulted in a draw. The focus of this struggle in central Europe is characterized by a stalemate. The efforts of both sides to translate nuclear or conventional military power into political advantage have not succeeded. Nor have the attempts of the superpowers to break this stalemate through gaining advantage in the so-called Third World proven to be successful. This failure on the military and political planes is shifting the struggle for power in the international system to the economic realm and has dramatically increased the number of significant players. As Mackinder postulated early in this century, the increasing destructiveness of armed conflict and the decreasing utility of military force, at least between industrialized countries, appears to be causing nations to concentrate on "the struggle for relative efficiency."[9]

In the postwar era of superpower military and political rivalry, the Pacific Rim nations were at a disadvantage. Not only were they militarily inferior, but geography and recent historical experience made them dependent upon one or another of the superpowers. But in a world where the superpowers are increasingly inhibited from attempting to translate military might into political gains, the Pacific Rim nations have much greater room for maneuver and actually have certain advantages. Lacking the burden of immense military establishments, except for South Korea, and with dynamic economies, they are very well positioned to engage in the global intensification of economic competition.

The second major change in the environment of international relations is closely related. As in the latter decades of the eighteenth century and again in the late nineteenth century, the world is entering a new phase of the ongoing industrial revolution that will have equally important results. The immense scale of contemporary research and development in many countries, the decreased lead time between scientific discovery and technical application, and the pervasive influence of the computer revolution are transforming all aspects of industrial society. This technological development will be profound for the structure and functioning of the international political economy.

Since the end of the nineteenth century, the industrial economies of the world have been based on the materials and technologies of the second phase of the industrial revolution, such as steel, petroleum, and the internal-combustion engine. These technologies gave rise to the mass production and heavy industries that led to the economic, military, and political predominance of the United States and the Soviet Union. Today these industrial technologies, or what Christopher Freeman has called Fordism, are decreasingly relevant for the economic growth and competitiveness of the superpowers as well as many other advanced economies.[10] As comparative advantage in these industries shifts to the rapidly developing economies in Asia and Latin America, the developed economies must create new industrial structures based on the emergent high technologies associated with bioengineering, the computer revolution, and other science-based technologies. This situation has led to an intensified competition between the advanced countries for technological and economic leadership. As northeast Asia has become not only the most economically dynamic region on the globe but also its electronics capital, it is rapidly taking the lead in the contemporary technological revolution.

The third major environmental change is the globalization of the world economy. The liberalization of trade, the integration of financial markets, and the role of the multinational corporation in the internationalization of production have created a truly interdependent world economy. In trade, finance, and production, economic interdependence among national economies has expanded rapidly over the past several decades. The economies of such countries as Japan and the East Asian newly industrializing countries that have taken the greatest advantage of this expanding interdependence have surpassed those socialist and less developed economies that have emphasized economic autarky. As the Soviet Union under Gorbachev has acknowledged, unless an economy participates in this global interdependence, it cannot possibly develop its full potential.

This process of economic globalization and increasing interdependence, however, is not a linear one leading to the disappearance of economic and political boundaries. On the contrary, the major centers of the world economy—the United States, the Soviet Union, Western Europe, Japan, and the newly industrializing countries of East Asia, Latin America, and elsewhere—are adopting trade, industrial, and investment policies in order to strengthen their competitive position. The American Omnibus Trade Bill of 1988, Gorbachev's efforts to restructure the Soviet economy, the increased Japanese emphasis on an economic strategy based on domestic growth and overseas investment by its corporations, the decision of the EEC to create a vast internal market beginning in 1992, and the aggressive export-oriented strategies of the newly industrializing countries are all responses to what former West German Chancellor Helmut Schmidt has called "the struggle for the world product."[11] In this gathering contest, the Pacific Rim countries will play an increasingly important role and will set the pace for the rest of the world.

THE GLOBAL SIGNIFICANCE OF THE TRANSFORMATION

A comparison of the main features of the postwar international system with those of the emergent system indicate the significance of the transformation taking place. In the former, there were sharp lines of political division between the two blocs in Western Europe; in the Pacific, the political situation is more fluid and the dividing lines are blurred. Despite the efforts of the superpowers to divide Asia into exclusive spheres of influence, the diversity and geography of the region have prevented such a development. In this region, the nations are not split by two hostile alliance systems. With the exception of the Association of Southeast Asian Nations, whose influence is very limited, the political relations are bilateral and continually in flux. Both superpowers have to adjust their cold-war policies and learn how to live with a more pluralistic international system.

The United States and the Soviet Union have also tended to subordinate the Pacific to the Atlantic. Events in the Pacific Basin have been analyzed and interpreted from a European-centered perspective rather than as important in their own right. Americans saw Korea as the beginnings of a Soviet assault on the West, and the Soviets have been slow to appreciate the indigenous dynamism of East Asia. The strategic stalemate in central Europe and the increasing significance of the Pacific Rim are forcing both superpowers to appreciate that this region must be approached on its own special terms.

Not only the political-military system but the postwar economic system was also Atlantic centered. In every aspect of economic affairs the Pacific was subordinated to the Atlantic. For example, it is interesting to note that the subtitle of Richard Cooper's 1968 path-breaking analysis of the world economy was *Economic Policy in the Atlantic Community*.[12] The institutions of the international economy conceived at Bretten Woods in 1944 and discussed by Cooper were designed principally with Western-style economies in mind. The emphasis on the liberal economic principles of most favored nation, unconditional reciprocity, and national treatment as the means by which to liberalize world trade and create interdependencies between national economies were derived from Western experience and conceptions of economic behavior. The question, therefore, arises whether or not these rules governing global economic relations are suitable for a world economy composed of strong, non-Western economies with a much greater commitment to state intervention in the economy.

Another potential implication of the global transformation of international affairs is the decreasing relevance of traditional ideologies. The postwar system has witnessed the competition between Western liberalism and Soviet Marxism for global supremacy. The former is identified with an emphasis on the market, individualism, and democracy. The latter is characterized by a commitment to state planning, collectivism, and authoritarianism. Whatever the merits of these doctrines, they are both Western and have little relevance for East Asia; as a result they are in retreat as guiding principles of political and economic affairs. In the Confucian-influenced cultures of China, Japan, and northeast Asia as well as elsewhere in the Pacific, the antipodes of market versus state, individual versus collectivity, or democracy versus authoritarianism are formulated differently.[13] The dynamism of these Asian economies and the demographic scale of these societies suggest that their conceptions of the way to organize economic, social, and political affairs will weigh heavily in the emergent global system.

CONCLUSION

The increasing importance of the Pacific poses a major challenge to the rest of the world. It is a challenge that is global in extent and, for the moment, almost entirely on the plane of economic competition. If historical experience still has any relevance, however, this situation could change and military rivalries could result as China, Japan, and other Pacific Rim nations become more powerful. In this transformed global environment, the clash between the American and Soviet blocs, which largely determined the nature of the postwar bipolar international order, has decreased in significance. In its place, a more pluralistic and far more complex system of independent and interdependent states is rapidly coming into existence. How these many and differing players will interact and together shape the global economic and political order has yet to be determined.

NOTES

1. Halford J. Mackinder, *Democratic Ideals and Reality* (New York: Norton, 1962).
2. Fernand Braudel, *The Perspective of the World-Civilization*, vol. 3, *15th–18th Century* (New York: Harper & Row, 1979), p. 32.

3. John Lewis Gaddis, *The Long Peace: Inquiries into the History of the Cold War* (New York: Oxford University Press, 1987).

4. W. Arthur Lewis, *Theory of Economic Growth* (New York: Harper & Row, 1970), pp. 17–18.

5. Raymond Aron, "War and Industrial Society," in *War Studies from Psychology, Sociology, Anthropology*, eds. Leon Branason and George W. Goethals (New York: Basic Books, 1964), pp. 197–98.

6. Robert Gilpin, *War and Change in World Politics* (New York: Cambridge University Press, 1981).

7. W. Arthur Lewis, *Growth and Fluctuation, 1870–1913* (London: George Allen & Unwin, 1978), p. 133.

8. For a discussion of these Stalinist features of Soviet societies, see Seweryn Bialer, *The Soviet Paradox: External Expansion, Internal Decline* (New York: Knopf, 1986).

9. Halford J. Mackinder, "The Geographical Pivot of History," in *Democratic Ideals and Reality*, by Mackinder, p. 242 (first published in 1904).

10. Christopher Freeman, *Technology Policy and Economic Performance: Lessons from Japan* (New York: Pinter, 1987).

11. Helmut Schmidt, "Struggle for the World Product," *Foreign Affairs*, 52:437–51 (Apr. 1974).

12. Richard Cooper, *The Economics of Interdependence: Economic Policy in the Atlantic Community* (New York: McGraw-Hill, 1968).

13. Roy Hofheinz, Jr., and Kent E. Calder, *The Eastasia Edge* (New York: Basic Books, 1982).

11

Japan: Their Behavior, Our Policy

CHALMERS JOHNSON

My thesis is a controversial one, and you have every reason to be skeptical of it. I will argue that the structure of world politics, including international economic relations, is at a genuine turning point. Skepticism is justified because the oldest and most shopworn gambit of all experts, pundits, and consultants is that he or she sees a new turning point, a major crossroads, or a situation that demands cardinal choices. In fact, genuine change is not nearly as common as our sensation-driven mass media and overworked but undereducated journalists would have us believe.

All of us who work in the field of modern Japan have files of articles from the past forty years claiming that "Japan is at the crossroads," when all that Japan actually did was look at the crossroads but not

Reprinted with permission of *National Interest*, Fall 1989. Copyright © 1989 National Affairs, Inc.

Note: It is a violation of the law to reproduce this selection by any means whatsoever without the written permission of the copyright holder.

choose a new direction. Similarly, thirty years ago all of us read small libraries about "the uniting of Europe" that proved to be illusory because of de Gaulle's intransigence, and about how the Canadians would never risk the loss of their national identity in a free trade agreement with the Americans. But today Europe *is* uniting and the Canadians *have* ratified an agreement that ties their economy closely to that of the United States. Clearly, something is changing. I contend that it is the structure of international relations.

By structure I mean two things. First, I refer to those aspects of reality that can only be changed over a long term—such things as, for example, the fact that Japan is today the world's richest nation in terms of per capita income. The second meaning of structure is the set of ideas, or paradigm, through which human beings view reality and decide which events are of great importance and which are lower down on the list of priorities. The postwar view of an irreconcilable conflict between communist and capitalist versions of international order is an example of a structural paradigm. It seems to me that the postwar world's "structure," in both senses of the word, is starting to change. New realities demand new policies, and the old paradigm of a nuclear-armed bipolar world is losing its authority to set the priorities of nations. We are today in a period of transition in which nations are groping for new conceptual foundations for world order. This new idea of reality has not yet emerged, but we can begin to identify some of the trends and developments that have made the old paradigm obsolete.

It seems to me that there are six major trends changing the structure of global affairs and, interestingly enough, it is the sixth one that is decisively affecting the first five. The *first* trend is the American recognition that the United States is no longer a hegemonic power. *Second* is the growing awareness both within and outside the Communist bloc that the Soviet Union has become seriously decrepit. *Third* is the growing tendency of the Western allies to link issues of economics and security in light of the declining Soviet threat. *Fourth* is the scheduled uniting of Europe in 1992. *Fifth* is the dawning realization that the world's trade imbalances can never be corrected through so-called free trade alone. And *sixth* is a growing understanding that the economic dynamism of Japan and its emulators in East Asia cannot be explained away as due to temporary or contingent factors or as a result of culture, but must be explained in its own right and dealt with as a matter of specific strategy. I shall discuss briefly the first five of these trends in relationship to the sixth before addressing the problem of Japan itself.

THE END OF HEGEMONY

The United States enters the 1990s in a strange position compared to the 1980s. On the one hand, it is beset by serious macroeconomic imbalances—a national debt around $3 trillion, large fiscal deficits, huge trade imbalances, a Third World debt totalling over $1.2 trillion, and a domestic savings rate that is at an all-time low. These kinds of problems are caused by America's commitments around the world—its "imperial overreach" to use Paul Kennedy's concept in *The Rise and Fall of the Great Powers*—and by a combination of mismanagement and infatuation with economic nostrums that promise easy and painless solutions.

There is growing evidence that the American people are prepared to sacrifice in order to deal with these problems. American public opinion polls are starting to tell a consistent story. Concerns about the future are making Americans less internationalist, more willing to cut the military budget, and much more wary and suspicious of Japan as an ally. In an *American Insight* poll of January 1989 Samuel Popkin concludes that "business leaders and government policy-makers are in a position to whip up public support for a major drive toward economic revitalization." Similarly, a Gallup Poll published in the March 13th, 1989 *New York Times* found some 79 percent of Americans believing that tensions among the superpowers had moderated and, as a result, they advocated balancing the national budget by cutting defense expenditures, governmental pensions, and foreign aid. Gallup also notes, "An inward-looking America is overwhelmingly opposed to increased foreign investment in the U.S. and sees Japan as supplanting the United States as the world's leading economic power."

As these polls suggest, Americans are slowly becoming aware that their economic problem with Japan is not entirely American-made and that living with a super-rich Japan will require specific measures that go beyond general support of the global trading system. According to a high-level report delivered to the new American administration's trade representative and supervised by the chief executives of American Express and Corning Glass, bilateral American trade with Japan reveals the following characteristics:

- The trade deficit with Japan is 40 percent of the overall United States trade deficit and is declining at a substantially lower rate than for the global deficit, despite a 60 percent appreciation of the value of the yen against the dollar since 1985.
- Japan's imports, particularly of manufactured goods, are between 25 and 45 percent below what would be expected of a country with Japan's economic attributes.
- Total liberalization of Japanese agriculture would result in an increase of crop imports by over 90 percent and livestock by over 40 percent.

It seems probable that the United States will deal with these problems through some form of managed trade, or what is today being called a "results-oriented trade policy," using the Omnibus Trade and Competitiveness Act of 1988 as a club to enforce it. I shall return to this subject in the discussion of my fifth trend—the shift away from free trade in order to deal with global trade imbalances.

Any discussion of the decline of American hegemonism must include the issue of American military commitments. It has begun to dawn on some Americans that the single most effective way to regain American competitiveness vis-à-vis Japan would be to cut American defense expenditures to Japanese levels—around 1.5 percent of GNP. If the Americans did that they could balance their governmental budget and still have approximately $100 billion left over for productive investments. At the present time there are some 325,000 American service personnel stationed in Europe and another 144,000 afloat in the Pacific or based in Guam, Japan, the Philippines, and South Korea. Expenditures directly related to European defense consume about 60 percent of the annual $300 billion U.S. defense budget.

COMMUNIST DECREPITUDE AND THE PACIFIC

It is of course the second main trend, the suddenly revealed decrepitude of the USSR, that makes it possible and even probable that the Yankees will finally start to go home. In May of this year the world witnessed the first summit meeting between the Soviet Union and China since Khrushchev met Mao in Peking in October 1959. Even a decade ago renewed friendly relations between Russia and China would have been seen as an unmitigated disaster. Sino-Soviet hostility was viewed as necessary to guarantee that Russian armies would not be aimed at the West and Chinese armies not aimed at Southeast Asia. Today, a Sino-Soviet summit seems not to threaten anyone, and, in fact, Western nations are wishing at least the USSR well in its efforts to emerge from the straightjacket of discredited economic doctrine.

China is another story. The reactionary rule of Deng Xiaoping and his bloody repression of the Chinese people's aspirations for some degree of democracy and governmental accountability seem to have set back China's belated efforts to join the world's most rapidly developing economic area. Without doubt the reassertion of Communist party despotism in China will cripple China's next generation of leaders and managers, cause a flight of investment capital from the Chinese mainland, and accelerate the refugee flow from Hong Kong. It also underscores the correctness of Taiwan's developmental policies both economically and politically—something that the nations who have read Taiwan out of virtually every international organization will have to ponder. But an inward-looking Chinese mainland is unlikely to be a security threat to anyone—except those unlucky enough to live there, who will of course try to get out. The paradox of modern China is that all Chinese outside of China are among the world's richest and most productive people, whereas those inside China are among the world's poorest and least productive. The events of June 1989 have ensured that this will continue to be more or less true for the immediate future.

Nonetheless, Mikhail Gorbachev's efforts at perestroika do not automatically mean that it is safe for the United States to find the savings it needs by cutting defense spending radically. And this is not just because Gorbachev might fail. Even if he did fail, or if the Chinese became a renewed threat to Southeast Asia, the United States would not necessarily feel responsible for countering this threat. It is clear that Americans increasingly expect their allies in Europe and Asia to assume at least their own conventional defense. This is one of the secondary reasons for the movement toward a united Europe by 1992—to provide the economic foundations through which Europe can supply more of its own defense. Whether one regards the United States as being in decline or as having succeeded magnificently in its postwar policies of rebuilding Europe and Japan, or perhaps a combination of both, a situation has developed that calls for a new division of labor in providing for the common defense. And the end of superpower hegemony should mean that both the U.S. and the USSR can turn some of their resources toward rebuilding their economic infrastructures.

However, in the short run Americans probably will not cut their defense expenditures drastically because their ability to project power remains a major source of leverage in the world, particularly in the Pacific. Differing from Europe, the nations of the Pacific do not have a common enemy—the Japanese fear the USSR, the South Korean enemy is North Korea, the Vietnamese distrust China, the Thai and Cambodian enemy is Vietnam, the Taiwanese oppose mainland China, and the Indonesians also still fear China. (For the Australians, it may be all or none of the above; and for New Zealand the chief enemy seems to be the U.S.) Under these circumstances the United States has a role to play as a power broker in the Pacific region. To what extent it actually can or will play this role is still an open question, depending on such things as the renegotiation of the treaty for the Philippine bases and the development of anti-Americanism in South Korea.

Meanwhile it seems likely that both the U.S. and the USSR will react to their changing environments by husbanding their resources and attempting to develop a sophisticated diplomacy of maneuver and balance. As the world shifts increasingly back to a situation in which economic performance is the primary index of national power, as it was in the late nineteenth century, military capability will become less important as an end in itself and resume its place as a means to an end.

Japan has contributed mightily to these trends. In the postwar dispensation Japan was understood to have strategic but not economic importance for the Free World. This was the reason why Japan was allowed to maintain an undervalued currency and to protect its domestic market so much longer after the war than any other advanced industrial democracy. But all that has changed. Without question the death this past year of the Showa Emperor marked the end of an era for Japan. Retrospectives, obituaries, and documentaries laid to rest not only him but also the image of Japan as a war-stricken, defeated country. Japan now stands revealed for what it is today: the world's richest big nation in terms of per capita income, the major source of long-term capital on earth today, the financier of America's budgetary and trade deficits, the leader of a campaign of foreign direct investment in North America and Western Europe that is unprecedented in scope and velocity, and the master of many new areas of technology such as telecommunications, semiconductors, robotics, nuclear power generation, and new materials. Nowhere do Americans see greater need for a new division of labor than in their relations with the Japanese.

THE TRADE-DEFENSE LINKAGE

One reason why current arrangements between Japan and the U.S. stand revealed as inadequate and outdated is that the issues of trade and defense have become linked in people's minds. This third trend is one that in the past both the Japanese and American governments have sought strenuously to avoid. With regard to Japan, three major events have helped to forge this linkage. The first was the 1987 revelation that the Toshiba Machine Company had illegally shipped machine tools to the USSR that significantly enhanced the ability of Soviet submarines to escape detection at sea by the U.S. The Americans were not pleased to see their costs of maintaining deterrence raised, particularly when the Japanese make no contribution to that deterrence.

The second event was the failure of Japan during the Iran–Iraq war to join the United States and Western Europe in their efforts to keep the Persian Gulf open to shipping. Even though Japan is more dependent on Mideast oil for its energy supply than any other advanced industrial democracy, its failure to participate in the Gulf operation also freed it from such difficult political issues as the attack on the USS Stark and the shooting down by a U.S. naval vessel of an Iranian airliner. The U.S. does not advocate full Japanese rearmament, but it does advocate pricing such things as oil for Japan somewhat closer to their true cost.

The third event has been Japan's refusal to buy American (or for that matter European) fighter aircraft for its so-called self-defense forces, even though it has large trade surpluses with both regions and foreign aircraft are superior in terms of quality and price. Japan's protestations of pacifism have been undermined by its decision to produce its own fighter aircraft using domestic taxpayers' funds.

EUROPE AND JAPAN

The fourth trend, towards a united Europe, is also related to Japan's emergence as an economic power. The uniting of Europe is arguably the most important development in current international politics and the single most significant reaction thus far to Pacific economic dynamism. As Roy Jenkins recently observed in the London *Times*, "Previously in Europe the politicians led reluctant businessmen and hesitant economies toward the promised land of a more integrated market. Now it is the other way around." Economic necessity (or self-interest) is the primary reason for the European decision to integrate—as well as for the Canadians to enter into a free trade agreement with the United States. The Europeans, Canadians, and Americans are developing a united front in order to compete effectively with Japan and the other capitalist developmental states of East Asia. In an important sense both the Canadian-American and the European developments constitute a de facto shift to Japanese economic rules—such as a greater reliance on cartels—even though the Japanese do not like to be emulated in this way.

The Japanese have reacted sharply against both the Canadian-American agreement and the European 1992 proposal. The Canadian agreement is less threatening to them because they are already heavily involved in manufacturing and other forms of investment in both the United States and Canada. Moreover, the United States remains the easiest place on earth for foreigners to acquire assets or go into business without even having to report their activities to the U.S. government. As of 1988 Japanese direct investment was distributed roughly two-fifths in North America, a fifth each in Southeast Asia and Latin America, and only 15 percent in Europe. Until quite recently many Japanese looked on Europe with disdain and took pride in their immunity to "Eurosclerosis" or the "English disease" (*Eikokubyo*), meaning the rigidities, labor disputes, and lagging growth rates associated with the 1970s. *PHP Intersect*, a Japanese magazine, recently reported that "Many Japanese still have an outdated view of individual European states, tending to regard them as cultural museums—Beefeaters, cathedrals, Leonardo da Vinci, and so on." That view is changing fast. The numbers of Japanese manufacturers in Europe jumped from 280 subsidiaries or joint ventures in 1987 to around 400 by the end of 1988.

Is it accurate to regard "Europe, Inc." as a specific answer to Japan, Inc.? It would seem so. On March 19th of this year the *Washington Post* reported, "European officials indicate privately that any European Community trade barriers after 1992 are likely to be aimed at Japan." And in Tokyo, even one of the few relatively successful European exporters, the head of BMW Japan, told *PHP Intersect* in March that after 1992 the European Community will require reciprocity from Japan in the sense that "Japanese automakers will be permitted a 10 percent share of the European market only if their European counterparts receive a similar share in Japan." This insistence on reciprocity is virtually certain to be required in financial services, which are not at the present time covered by GATT. Japanese banks control some 10 percent of all deposits in European banks, but European banks control only 0.35 percent of all deposits in Japanese banks.

TOWARDS ADVERSARIAL TRADE

Of course, the Canadian-American agreement and the uniting of Europe might also mean an end to the era of free trade and a shift to economic blocs that offer free trade to insiders but protectionism to outsiders. As of now this seems to be the predominant trend. The movement away from multilateralism, the fifth of the major trends altering the structure of international relations, is occurring primarily because of the peculiar pattern exhibited by Japan in the global economy and the inability thus far to cause Japan to alter its behavior through normal commercial influences (e.g., better prices and equal quality of foreign products compared with domestically manufactured goods). It is not true that at present the Canadian-American or European movements are intended primarily to replace the multilateral trading system or to slow the advance of the Pacific economies. But they could easily turn in that direction if Japan continues to practice what Peter Drucker has called "adversarial trade." Adversarial trade means that a country tends not to import any of the products that it exports. This stands in contrast to "competitive trade," in which firms and consumers in a country manufacture, sell, and purchase a wide range of goods from all over the world depending only on their preferences and comparative shopping.

Japan of course denies that it practices adversarial trade. In a recent interview for the *Journal of Japanese Trade and Industry* (March–April 1989), Katsuo Seiki, director of the West Europe Division of MITI's International Trade Policy Bureau, said, "We like to think . . . that there are already fewer institutional barriers—tariffs, quotas, and what have you—in Japan than in Europe and the United States. What are the remaining problems?" The Japanese explain the anomalies in their trade—the low import penetration into Japan of manufacturers, the complete lack of change in U.S. semiconductor sales in Japan between 1973 and 1986, Japan's insensitivity to changes in the macroeconomic environment—as a result of a lack of effort, cultural barriers, an overly short-term perspective on the part of foreign salesmen, and poor quality. This is not the whole story, however, and Mr. Seiki deserves an answer to his question.

Let us take the easy items first. Japan's barrier against free trade in rice is one of the most blatantly illegal trade practices in the industrialized world and in clear violation of article XI of the GATT treaty. It was one thing to tolerate protectionism in this sector when Japan was still recovering from the effects of World War II; it is quite another thing, some two Asian wars later, for Japan to force its households to spend more than a third of their income on food. Similarly, even where Japan has agreed to end quotas and special levies on such products as imported beef, it still erects tariff walls that begin at 70 percent and decline slowly to a mere 50 percent. Why should Japanese consumers pay a 50 percent higher price for a common food item when the rest of the world accepts Japanese cars, cassettes, and cameras on the basis of free trade? Equally to the point, Japan's distribution system has evolved into a non-tariff barrier that artifically restricts the choices of Japanese consumers—an unusual burden to bear for the nation with the largest trade surplus as a share of GNP in human history.

But these cases are only the obvious and best-known Japanese exceptions to the rules. Three other Japanese institutions are not non-tariff barriers to trade at all, but they create competitive conditions within Japan that consistently discriminate against foreigners. The Japanese understandably reject foreign proposals that they should remodel their society to make it work like other nations party to the GATT treaty. But they should understand that their rejection leaves their trading partners with only two options: either to remodel their own societies in the Japanese direction or to find some way of pricing Japan's exports so that Japan bears the costs of its peculiar national institutions.

The three institutions I have in mind are administrative guidance, industrial groups (*keiretsu*), and Japan's organization of research and development. Administrative guidance refers to the discretionary authority entrusted to Japan's governmental officials to find tailor-made solutions to problems or to implement policies that do not have a legal basis (for example, Japan's prohibition against the import of refined petroleum products). Because of administrative guidance, a foreigner can *never* master the rules of doing business in Japan. The rules change with the bureaucrats put in charge of implementing them, and the legal system does not function to ensure that government officials enforce the law in a predictable manner. Administrative guidance was a powerful tool for Japan's rapid economic development, but it makes trying to do business in Japan as difficult as it is in a communist country.

Keiretsu, or what before the war were called *zaibatsu*, are Japan's famous industrial conglomerates. They are held together by cross shareholding (with a portion of the shares never traded regardless of price in order to prevent foreign or domestic takeovers), interlocking directorates, intragroup financial commitments, and overlapping memberships in the councils and presidents' clubs of each group. *Keiretsu* activities include putting together complex economic ventures at home and abroad, sharing of technology, employment of redundant personnel from member firms, and research and development. The benefits to members include preferential service from a group's bank and trading company, relative insulation from business cycles, and the ability to devote more resources to expanding productive capacity and market share.[1] The *keiretsu* form of industrial organization is one of Japan's most important contributions to modern capitalism. At the same time it clearly violates Western conceptions of anti-trust and makes a mockery of much of the economic theory that is predicated on the workings of "market forces." Western nations have yet to come up with a competitive march for the Japanese *keiretsu*, and the problem is becoming acute as *keiretsu* relationships are extended to North America and Western Europe through direct investment by Japan. *Keiretsu* are institutions uniquely suited to the protection of a domestic market while taking aggressive advantage of foreign markets where such arrangements are prevented by law.

My final case of a mismatch between Japan and the West is the way research and development is organized. Japan does its R&D in proprietary, company-owned research institutes, whereas the West does much of its research in universities and engineering schools that are open to all qualified students in accordance with the principle of academic freedom. The result is that the flow of technology still remains conspicuously in Japan's direction and not the other way around, even though Japan today spends almost as much on R&D as the United States and does not engage in military research. These problems are exacerbated by Japan's inadequate protection of intellectual property rights by international standards. As a consequence of these differences, there is today a marked trend toward the privatization of research as Western companies and universities try to compete with Japan.

The doctrine of free trade, together with related elements of classical economic theory such as comparative advantage and the ability of the price mechanism to correct imbalances in trade among nations, seems slowly to be losing ground in the face of these kinds of Japanese anomalies. Perhaps the best example of this is the American attempt from 1985 to the present to correct its disastrous trade deficit with Japan by lowering the value of the dollar against the yen. "Advocates of a lower dollar," writes Daniel Burstein in the February 19, 1989 *New York Times*, "base their case on econometric modeling showing how a weaker dollar makes American goods more competitive abroad and foreign goods less so at home. But several years of experience now make clear what should have been obvious from the beginning: the world we live in does not much resemble the model." To the extent that Japanese rules actually do become world rules, free trade will be replaced by such principles and practices as specific reciprocity, proprietary research, international cartels, orderly marketing agreements, and managed trade. It will not necessarily be a poorer world, economic theory notwithstanding, but it will be a different one.

PROBLEMS FOR JAPAN

What are Japan's likely courses of action in response to these five trends? Other than a slow process of ameliorative change after considerable foreign pressure, Japan's only initiative thus far is its cautious exploration of a cooperative relationship among Pacific nations. This follows Australian Prime Minister Bob Hawke's proposal of January 1989 in Seoul for a new Pacific economic cooperation body. Hawke argued that this proposed organization should be loosely modeled after the OECD (Organization for Economic Cooperation and Development) in Paris, and he insisted that he did not have a trading bloc such as Europe 1992 in mind. His proposal parallels earlier ideas advanced by former Japanese Prime Minister Nakasone for a Pacific Forum for Economic and Cultural Cooperation, by former U.S. Secretary of State Shultz for a Pacific intergovernmental forum, and by U.S. Senator Bill Bradley for a Pacific coalition on trade and economic development. On March 22, 1989, Japanese Prime Minister Takeshita ordered MITI to work out the details of an Asian-Pacific economic cooperation pact as soon as possible.

It seems probable that Japan is preparing the ground for a possible Pacific trading bloc in case the North American and European developments work against Japanese trade. In fact, Prime Minister Hawke's proposal may have been intended to preempt a yen bloc comparable to the Greater East Asia Co-prosperity Sphere of fifty years ago. In a press conference following his address in Seoul, Hawke acknowledged that in a worst-case, collapse-of-GATT type of situation, his proposed cooperative body might turn into a trading bloc.

There are obvious problems with all of these proposals. One of them is that economic relations among the Pacific nations have developed informally and any attempt to give them a formal structure tends to diminish these relationships. Thus, for example, both South Korea and Taiwan trade with mainland China, but none of them wants to talk about it. Two of the most powerful economies in the Pacific—Taiwan and Hong Kong—are not nation states, and one of them, Hong Kong, is scheduled to be turned over to the management of one of the most economically incompetent eight years from now. South Korea is already suspicious of a possible invitation to join the OECD because it fears that joining any group will blunt its economic efforts. In Southeast Asia, the members of ASEAN (Association of Southeast Asian Nations) said to MITI Minister Shigeo Muraoka that they were willing to discuss Japan's economic cooperation pact but they wanted to include the United States in it, which Hawke's original proposal failed to do. Except in the cases of China, Indonesia, and Malaysia, the United States remains the most important market for both the newly industrialized economies and the ASEAN nations.

The larger unspoken problem is Japanese leadership in Asia. Japan has yet to come to terms with its history of imperialism and militarism in East Asia or with the fact that its postwar position as a client of the United States to some extent protected it from the scrutiny of its fellow Asians. Historically, Japan posed the greatest threat to China of any of the imperialist powers, and the Chinese have certainly not forgotten this. Ding Xinghao of Shanghai's Institute of International Studies notes, "Japan's view is always a flying goose format with Japan as the head goose. Our memories are long, so we aren't about to fly in Japan's formation."[2] Similarly, despite Japan's recent neonationalist revisions of its role in World War II, Robert Wargo warns, "One of the most dangerous courses [for Japan] is to try to argue that the war was fought to liberate Greater Asia from the Americans and the Europeans. If Japan wanted to liberate Asia, why didn't it start with Korea?"[3] None of this is to say that Japan cannot offer leadership in Asia. It is rather to stress that Japan has not yet confronted the real problems in doing so.

I conclude (like a symphony) by reiterating my opening statement. The combination of an end of American hegemony, a decrepit Soviet Union, a linkage between trade and defense, Europe 1992, an end to free trade, and the emergence of Japan as the world's leading industrialized nation adds up to a change in the structure of international relations. Although these forces are making the old institutions and paradigms obsolete, indications concerning the shape of the institutions of the future are thus far only tentative and experimental. What does seem certain is that the new paradigm when it emerges will confound virtually all of our old categories. It may well be true that Japan is the most advanced capitalist nation today. But it may equally well prove true, as many foreign observers of the Japanese government-business relationship have concluded over the years, that "Japan is the only communist nation that works."

WHAT AMERICA SHOULD DO

In the meantime the situation that exists today between Japan and the United States is profoundly unstable. The year 1989 marks the twenty-first anniversary of bilateral American trade deficits with Japan, deficits that are so large they threaten the stability of the political relations between the two allies. There are only two ways to reduce these deficits: Japan must buy more from the United States, or the United States must stop buying so much from Japan. The latter could be achieved overnight through a new version of former President Nixon's import surcharge, this time applied only to Japanese products. The better, but harder, solution would be for Japan genuinely to enlarge domestic demand, as its own analysis of the world's economic imbalances (known as the Maekawa Report) recommended. This would require political leadership to open up land for new housing and to end the hammer lock of mom-and-pop stores (*kado-mise*) on Japanese retail sales. In the mid-1980s stores with four or fewer employees still accounted for an astonishing 56 percent of retail sales in Japan, compared with 3 percent in the United States and 5 percent in Western Europe. Japanese family stores require a vast apparatus of wholesalers to keep them stocked. These wholesalers have a vested interest in restricting retail outlets that compete primarily on the basis of price, as do those in the United States and other Western nations. One Japanese bank economist recently calculated that Japanese retail prices are 4.2 times higher than wholesale prices, whereas the analogous U.S. ratio is 1.8 to 1. Those who speak for Japan, including those who are on a Japanese retainer regardless of nationality, conveniently forget about these Japanese barriers to trade when they accuse the United States of protectionism. If the United States is protectionist, it is without question the most incompetent protectionist in history.

The United States has tried to force resolution of some of these issues through section 301 of the Trade Act of 1988. Despite loud and intemperate criticism of this action in such places as Japan and Australia, including personal attacks on Carla Hills, the United States Trade Representative, for implementing a law that she had no role in enacting, section 301 is actually an effective reminder of the time-table that exists on the world trading system. It takes between twelve and eighteen months to implement section 301, and the so-called Uruguay Round of negotiations to try to make the General Agreement on Tariffs and Trade (GATT) workable and relevant to the 1990s also has about twelve to eighteen months to run. All that section 301 does is to warn the world of what is waiting if the world's richest nations continue to stall on fixing the GATT treaty. This is a more realistic approach toward encouraging serious negotiations than the continuous invocation of the name of Saint Adam Smith by the vestal virgins of the economics profession.

But the Trade Act and Section 301 by themselves will not preserve the postwar system of international trade or halt the decline of the United States into the status of a second-class economic power (i.e., like the USSR). It will also be necessary for the Americans to do the following things:

- Start financing their own government and stop living off borrowings from Japanese savers.
- Recognize that Japan has replaced the USSR as America's most important foreign policy problem and that relations with Japan require specific, goal-oriented, closely monitored strategies.
- Create an American Department of International Trade and Industry (DITI) to coordinate American economic policy and end the situation in which Washington has become a (foreign and domestic) lobbyists' paradise.

· Adopt policies to get the United States back into consumer electronics and other industries of the future.
· Enact a foreign investor's disclosure law and demand specific reciprocity in foreign direct investment for both Americans and investors in America.
· Undertake reform of American economic institutions to build into them incentives that give managers a longer-term perspective.

Even if by some miracle the Americans should do all of these things, the need for which is well known to virtually all American business and political elites, the structure of international relations will still continue to change. It will just not change quite so obviously to the disadvantage of the United States.

The fundamental problems in Japanese-American relations are not in any sense conceptual but political. It is easy to envisage solutions to bilateral problems that preserve the most valuable transoceanic trading relationship that ever existed and that has made the parties to the relationship the richest people on earth. What threatens the relationship are entrenched interests in the preservation of the system of inequalities that characterized Japanese-American relations during the 1960s. For the Americans this means the interests of the defense establishment in the role of America as hegemon athwart the Pacific, of the diplomatic establishment in Cold War dualism, of the economic intellectuals in not having to recognize that they have been blind-sided by Japanese institutional inventiveness, and of the Atlanticists in not having to come to grips with problems for which they do not have the requisite skills. For the Japanese this means the interests of exporters over importers, of industrialists over consumers and environmentalists, of the ruling party in continuing to avoid the responsibilities of leadership, and of the cultural nationalists in their view of Japan as unique and not subject to the standards they routinely apply to foreigners. Given the insipid 1988 American electoral contest and the simultaneous Japanese discovery of "structural corruption" in the Recruit bribery case, the chances of political leadership to resolve Japanese-American differences are poor. Under these circumstances it seems that Pacific relationships will continue to deteriorate until crisis forces serious thinking in the countries that have the most to lose.

NOTES

1. Ulrike Wassman and Kozo Yamamura, "Do Japanese Firms Behave Differently? The Effects of *Keiretsu* in the United States," in Kozo Yamamura, ed., *Japanese Investments in the United States: Should We Be Concerned?* (Seattle: Society for Japanese Studies, 1989), pp. 119–147.

2. "Though Rich, Japan Is Poor in Many Elements of Global Leadership," *Wall Street Journal*, January 30, 1989. For a Japanese article that uses the concept of *ganko batten* (flying-goose-formation development), see Takashi Inoguchi, "90-nendai 'keizai taikoku' no konnan-na sentaku" (Difficult Choices in the 1990s for the 'Economic Superpower'), *Ekonomisuto*, December 6, 1988, pp. 70–75.

3. *PHP Intersect*, March 1989, p. 46.

12

America's High-Tech Decline

CHARLES H. FERGUSON

Technological revolutions often contribute to shifts in wealth and geopolitical influence by changing the sources of industrial and military success. In this respect, information technology is proving no exception. Advanced information technology is profoundly changing global competition, both commercial and military, in such fields as semiconductors, computers, fiberoptic communications, high-definition television, industrial control systems, robotics, office automation, globally integrated financial trading systems, military C^3I (command, control, communication, and intelligence), smart weapons, and electronic warfare.

As this transformation progresses, the United States is being gradually but pervasively eclipsed by Japan. In semiconductors, automated machine tools, advanced manufacturing, and mass-produced electronics products, America's problems are already severe. More significant, the long-term structural patterns of U.S.-Japanese interaction in finance and high technology imply a future of U.S. decline and dependence on Japan. Moreover, the behavior of the embryonic though rapidly advancing Japanese defense industry suggests that this prediction holds for military technology as well as for commercial activities. Although a strong U.S. response could soften this decline, the economic and political costs of effective remedial action make some further deterioration almost inevitable.

Although America's nuclear and other military resources assure that it will remain a superpower for some time, Japanese ascendancy will probably have major economic and geopolitical consequences. The combination of financial power and technological primacy could provide Japan not only higher living standards but also the potential for wide influence over international affairs, including U.S. policy, and for the development of Japanese military power. Conversely, these developments could place pressure on American living standards, thereby risking domestic social and political problems. They could also affect America's global posture through trade tensions, declining economic influence, pressure to reduce federal expenditures, and military

Reprinted with permission from *Foreign Policy* 74 (Spring 1989). Copyright by the Carnegie Endowment for International Peace.

Note: It is a violation of the law to reproduce this selection by any means whatsoever without the written permission of the copyright holder.

inefficiency. The U.S. economy might shift toward lower-technology activities in which competitiveness would be maintained through devaluation and wage reduction; industries dependent on high levels of investment, education, and technological progress would decline. Indeed, this process is already under way.

Of the many implications of these developments, two stand out as particularly important. First, U.S. technological decline in an era of globalized economic activity implies that foreign and national security policy now depends upon economic and technology policy to a degree not seen since the advent of nuclear weapons. The future economic and geopolitical security of the United States will be determined ever more heavily by the fundamental health of its technology-intensive industries. Many difficult adjustments—longer time horizons, lower capital costs, increased investment, improved education, reforms in defense and commercial technology policy, and greater cooperation between U.S. private and public institutions—will therefore be necessary.

Second, America's future will also depend on a more sophisticated and realistic approach toward U.S.-Japanese relations, Japanese industrial behavior, and Japanese economic policy. Given America's increasingly limited resources and the growing internationalization of high-technology competition, the United States must focus on those activities—technological, commercial, and military—in which future strength is both achievable and necessary, as opposed to those in which rivalry, Japanese control, or international cooperation is more appropriate. Moreover, while Japan is a military ally and has developed many goods and services that are valuable to the United States, American policy must recognize that Japan is also a closed, highly controlled, and systematically predatory actor in the international economy. The simultaneous need to preserve the military-diplomatic alliance while responding to Japan's technoeconomic Prussianism will therefore prove a critical challenge for U.S. policy. Thus far, Japan has viewed its economic, technological, and trade policies, including its negotiations with the United States, as a continuation of competition and predation by other means. Notwithstanding vague promises to the contrary, there is no evidence that this strategy has changed.

The decline of American high technology involves two distinct classes of forces, neither of which is likely to attenuate. The initial source of U.S. problems was domestic and took the form of shortsightedness and rigidity in U.S. government policies, industrial structure, and corporate strategy. These institutional rigidities included continued reliance upon tax and economic policies biased toward consumption; a fragmented political and economic structure that impeded long-term technological and strategic coordination; policies for basic research, higher education, trade, and military systems that allowed other countries to enjoy asymmetric access to U.S. technological resources; and the entrenchment of outdated techniques within American industry, even in high-technology sectors. Over the past quarter of a century these weaknesses have accumulated as American political and economic decision making has become increasingly shortsighted and the mismatch between U.S. conduct and international reality has grown progressively larger.

These problems long remained unnoticed because they arose during a period, roughly from 1945 to 1975, in which America dominated global high technology. During this period Japan restricted both American imports and direct investment while massively importing U.S. technology. The United States led in basic research, and its firms typically dominated world markets, except in Japan, for products such as semiconductors, computers, machine tools, and electronic instruments.

However, even before Asian competitors directly challenged U.S. high technology in world markets, U.S. savings rates, capital investment, productivity growth, and commercial technology generation began to decline relative to earlier periods and to other countries. For example, annual U.S. productivity growth declined from 3 per cent in the 1950s to 1 per cent by the early 1980s. Recently these problems have, if anything, worsened; America's underlying macroeconomic condition has deteriorated sharply in the 1980s. Living standards and geopolitical commitments have been temporarily maintained only through unsustainable levels of borrowing and disinvestment.

And now a second source of decline, namely external competitive pressure, has been added. Future U.S. behavior will be seriously constrained by the rapid internationalization of Japanese industry, the discipline of global financial markets, the pace of international technology transfer, the rise of foreign competition, the lower capital and engineering costs of other countries, and the diminishing importance of the U.S. market relative to total world demand. In both high technology and global finance, Japan will clearly be the largest source of these external pressures.

POSTWAR SYSTEMS

Following World War II, America evolved a set of technological and industrial systems that were liberal and open. Yet while U.S. policies promoted freer international economic activity, they were also often parochial in outlook and based upon a presumption of inherent and perpetual U.S. superiority.

Relationships between domestic policy and international competition were generally neglected. For example, Japan's aggressive economic behavior was overlooked, in part because economics and technology policy were thought secondary to military alliances. Similarly, the United States relied on domestic macroeconomic policies that effectively subsidized borrowing and consumer spending. When American demand was satisfied predominantly by domestic production and American industry itself was the globally preeminent user of U.S.-generated research and technology, such policies were tolerable, and possibly even in the U.S. interest. But in a global economy, such openness and consumption subsidies support foreign producers as much as, or more than, they benefit U.S. industry. Indeed, U.S. exports of technology have continued to grow even while the United States has become a huge net importer of electronics and other high-technology products. Likewise, the low savings and investment rates that accompanied policies based on consumption and borrowing were tolerable when the United States maintained technological superiority. But as investment requirements and foreign competition have increased, these policies have exacerbated the problem.

Similarly, the postwar U.S. industrial system was rooted in an earlier time when international trade was minor and technological change was slower. The system was characterized by arm's-length or antagonistic relations between business and government, between the financial and industrial systems, among management and labor, and even between large U.S. firms and their principal suppliers, customers, and competitors. The economy and its major firms were organized sectorally, with little interaction among major sectors. Moreover, firms could switch suppliers, and individuals could switch employers, with little difficulty. The system facilitated the continuous creation of small entrepreneurial firms but was much less successful at financing efforts needing large and risky long-term investments. Repeatedly U.S. firms would develop new technologies, only to find themselves defeated in market competition by the superior manufacturing and financial power of Japanese imitators or licensees.

American industry relies on techniques evolved from early experiences with routinized, mechanical mass production, such as Henry Ford's assembly lines. In high technology, American practice was also shaped by military demand for early production runs of expensive, advanced products. However, this production system is generally inappropriate today. Its reliance upon arm's-length, short-term relationships impedes coordination in complex environments. The system was built for slowly changing markets and mechanical systems rather than for rapidly changing, information-intensive technologies and differentiated, globally competitive markets. For example, design and engineering were managed separately from production and quality control, with resultant neglect for the effect of proper design upon manufacturability. Scale economies were exploited to the extreme, emphasizing long runs of identical products and conservative engineering tolerances. Producers thereby minimized their reliance on the skill and commitment of workers and on coordination with suppliers.

U.S. high-technology industries often employed a specific strategy for managing technology life cycles. They began with domestic low-volume handicraft production of expensive experimental products. As the technology matured, firms shifted toward traditional mass production of increasingly standardized products. Where fixed mechanical automation was impractical, low-wage offshore labor was used to cut production costs. When proprietary technical advantage in product design ceased to exist, U.S. firms tended to exit "mature" markets, ceding them to Asian producers.

Simultaneously with the evolution of this "Fordist" system, the military exercised wide influence over U.S. high technology, including information technologies. In fact, from the late 1940s through the mid-1970s, military research and development (R&D) usually led commercial technology in such sectors as radar systems, numerically controlled machine tools, robots, computers, digital networks, and microelectronics. But while defense R&D produced a great deal of innovation, Defense Department support may also have generated substantial problems for American firms facing a future of intense global competition.

Defense priorities reinforced U.S. industry's tendency to favor elaborate systems early in their life cycles, to emphasize product innovation over process improvement, and to regard product customization and mass production as mutually exclusive. Moreover, Defense Department operations and procurement procedures have gradually reduced the commercial benefits of defense R&D. For example, defense microelectronics has fallen far behind commercial markets in both technology and cost.

Through both adaptive evolution and strategic calculation, Japan evolved a set of political and industrial arrangements that presented a powerful strategic response to American hegemony. Its production system was superbly adapted to global competition in technology-intensive industries. Japan became a statist, strategically cohesive free rider in the world technology system. Its policies favored technology imports, savings, export-dependent growth, and protectionism in the service of domestic strategic economic planning and long-term competitive advantage. Conversely, Japanese policy discouraged expenditures—such as personal consumption, military spending, basic research, product imports, and capital outflows—that did not yield domestic benefits.

Government policy, as well as the structure of the Japanese financial and tax systems, favored industrial concentration, long time horizons, and domestic cooperation among competitors. Consequently, most Japanese financial and manufacturing activities were controlled by about a dozen enormous, vertically integrated industrial complexes. This structure facilitated domestic coordination of technological development and the control of foreign competition. It also gave Japanese corporations extraordinary control over their work forces. The lifetime employment system, for example, depends upon the fact that major Japanese employers do not hire each other's employees without permission. Since employees cannot change firms, personal welfare thus depends upon long-term performance within the company and, in turn, the company's long-term performance in the world economy.

Aided by these incentive structures and government policies, Japanese high-technology firms systematically excluded U.S. firms from Japanese markets; imported, copied, and stole U.S. technologies; and eventually launched export drives into the American market. But in addition, Japanese industry developed a unique production system oriented toward rapid product cycles, differentiated markets, continuous integration of new product and process technologies, and flexible—as opposed to rigidly standardized—mass production.

The operational components of this system include just-in-time manufacturing, which requires close coordination between suppliers and producers; continuous improvement of production processes; flexible, small-lot mass production; a design philosophy emphasizing workability, quality, and frequent, incremental redesign; and a highly skilled, relatively flexible work force. Strategically, the system involves exclusion of foreign competitors; systematic acquisition of external technology; rapid design cycles and short product life spans; a progression from technically mature, low-cost mass markets to advanced and differentiated high-technology markets; flexible mass production of related but customized products; and long-term links with other domestic industries and suppliers. It has proved an excellent system for highly integrated, computerized production processes and is especially well suited to high-technology industries, where competition takes place in global markets that are volatile and differentiated.

THE RISE OF INFORMATION TECHNOLOGY

Information technology is driving economic and military transformations likely to prove as fundamental as any past industrial revolution. In fact, the technological progress of the information sector is literally unprecedented in economic history. In the major digital information industries—communications, computers, control systems, microelectronics, and software—this growth and progress will continue for another 20 years or more, when information processing will probably be the industrialized world's largest economic activity. Further, information technology affects not only the producing industries themselves but also other areas: the automation of design, manufacturing, and other activities; industrial products ranging from numerically controlled machine tools to consumer electronics; and, finally, military power.

Already these effects are large. The world semiconductor industry, currently $40 billion, is expected to reach $150 billion by the next century. World computer production, now approximately $200 billion, will then exceed $500 billion. Computer software production, already 2 per cent of U.S. gross national product (GNP), will be even larger. Since these industries offer high wages and are heavily dependent on human capital, the direct benefits accruing to successful competitors will include higher GNP, living standards, and wealth. Even so, the indirect effects will most likely be greater. The computerization of design, information management, industrial process control, and manufacturing has yielded productivity gains in many industries and is considered the largest probable source of productivity growth in the industrialized economies over the next several decades. The same is true of product technologies. In a growing number of industries, most notably computers and telecommunications equipment, semiconductor technology has become a major determinant of competitive advantage.

The military implications of information technology are, if anything, larger. First, military operations have come to rely heavily on information systems infrastructure for C^3I, surveillance, and management. Second, computerization is at least as important to the design, production, and maintenance of weapons systems as it is to commercial industry. Finally, and analogously to the commercial world, information technology is by far the most important source of current and prospective growth in the capabilities of conventional and nuclear weapons.

The world defense electronics market, not counting military purchases of commercial computers, already exceeds $25 billion per year and is growing rapidly. The electronic content of combat aircraft in terms of cost, for example, may soon reach 50 per cent. Progress in information technology, primarily in electronics, increasingly determines the accuracy of weapons delivery systems, the capabilities of surveillance and warning systems, the development of precision-guided munitions, the combat survivability of aircraft and warships, and, increasingly, the cost of weapons systems. In many of these areas superior information technology is considered to be the principal advantage of U.S. systems relative to those of potential adversaries.

Some of the most significant factors in the global strategic balance derive not from nuclear weapons technology itself but rather from the technologies required for design, guidance, sensing, and control. With some major exceptions, such as gyroscopes and inertial guidance systems, these capabilities are driven by information technology. Examples include the terrain-following guidance systems of U.S. cruise missiles, the American advantage in antisubmarine warfare, the accuracy of new U.S. submarine-based ballistic missiles, the increasing accuracy of U.S. and Soviet intercontinental ballistic missiles and of satellite-based verification and early warning systems, and the survivability of command and control capabilities.

Clearly, then, the information technology revolution is broad. And although the United States retains leadership in research, in advanced systems design, and in some product markets, Japan must now be considered the world leader in electronics as a whole. Japan's electronics exports currently total about $65 billion and are eight times larger than its electronics imports. Conversely, the United States is now a large net importer of electronics worldwide and a net importer from Japan of advanced electronic materials, computer-controlled machine tools, computers, consumer electronics, robots, semiconductors, and telecommunications equipment.

Japanese efforts began 20 years ago with low-cost consumer electronics. Now Japan holds world leadership in innovation as well as in manufacturing; and consumer electronics has become a large, sophisticated sector with growing linkages to computers, semiconductors, and telecommunications. Moreover, Japanese electronics leadership is now far broader and includes critical industrial technologies.

In the past decade, Japan's share of the world semiconductor market has nearly doubled, to 49 per cent, while U.S. industry's share has declined from 55 per cent to 39 per cent. Japanese industry now has 90 per cent of the world market for the newest generation of semiconductor memories—1-megabit DRAMS (dynamic random access memory chips) that are critical to all computer systems. During the same decade, Japan's share of world computer production has also doubled, to 20 per cent, and exports have risen by a factor of 15. Similarly, between 1955 and 1985 the U.S. share of worldwide machine tool production declined from 40 per cent to 12 per cent, while Japan's rose from 1 per cent to 24 per cent; moreover, by 1984, 67 per cent of Japan's production was numerically controlled, compared with 40 per cent of U.S. production. Japanese firms also now lead in world markets for compact disc systems, computer displays, consumer video systems, digital audio tape, electronic cameras, facsimile systems, laser printers, personal copiers, and videocassette recorders.

A wide variety of evidence suggests that Japan has achieved parity with or even superiority over the United States in many information technologies. For example, between 1975 and 1982, Japanese shares of worldwide patenting activity in integrated circuits, lasers, robotics, and telecommunications grew rapidly while U.S. shares fell, sometimes dramatically.

Similarly, assessments by the U.S. Defense Science Board, the U.S. Japanese Technology Evaluation Program, and various private studies have concluded that although the United States still leads in some areas of R&D, leadership in engineering, production, and commercial technology has already passed to Japan.

The evidence clearly indicates that Japan's flexible, integrated production system is far more efficient and adaptable than conventional U.S. practices, even without automation. The rise of flexible automation in production further increases the Japanese advantage, and Japan leads the United States in the automation of manufacturing, even in high-technology industries.

These advantages are having a tremendous economic impact. Recently, worldwide studies of automobile assembly conducted at the Massachusetts Institute of Technology showed that Japanese firms averaged 20.3 worker-hours per vehicle in Japan and 19.6 worker-hours per vehicle when assembling in the United States. Conversely, U.S. producers averaged 25.8 worker-hours per vehicle, while European producers at home averaged 39.3 worker-hours per vehicle. Japanese plants averaged 53 defects per 100 vehicles, as opposed to 89 for American producers operating in the United States and 102 for Europeans.

These studies also confirmed several widely shared conclusions concerning automation. Japanese producers led not only in robotics investment but also in the effectiveness of its use. Japanese plants also handled a far more varied and complex production mix. U.S. and European plants appeared to be wasting the technology's potential for improving production mix complexity, product customization, and quality. Other recent automobile studies have concluded that Japan also holds a wide lead in design and engineering management, which allows Japanese firms to take a new car from conception to design to production in one-half the total effort and in two-thirds the elapsed time needed by American and European companies.

Nor is the automobile example exceptional. Japan's total installed base of machine tools is of newer vintage and more heavily computerized than America's. The Japanese manufacturing sector uses several times as many robots per unit of output as the U.S. manufacturing sector. And the Japanese economy uses more than twice as many semiconductors per unit of output as the U.S. economy. Perhaps the most striking evidence, however, involves flexible manufacturing systems (FMSs), which use integrated computer control of entire production lines. In the mid-1980s, one study by Ramchandran Jaikumar, a leading specialist in automated manufacturing, surveyed the Japanese and U.S. installed base of FMSs. More than 40 per cent of the world's FMSs were located in Japan; and because of superior training and management practice, Japanese systems vastly outperformed technically similar U.S. systems. Development time averaged more than 50 per cent longer in the United States, and Japanese systems handled an average of 22 new-part designs per year, compared with 1 for U.S. systems. Despite the fact that U.S. systems on average produced only 10 different parts simultaneously while Japanese systems produced 93, Japanese systems still had far higher total output (120 units per day as opposed to 88) and capacity utilization rates (84 per cent as opposed to 52 per cent). No U.S. systems operated unattended; 18 Japanese systems did. And although no comparably systematic study of semiconductor or computer manufacturing yet exists, the available evidence suggests that, with the possible exception of the International Business Machines Corporation (IBM), U.S. manufacturing performance in these sectors trails that of Japan.

JAPANESE GLOBALIZATION

A new phase of U.S.-Japanese competition based on the internationalization of Japanese industry began in the 1980s. Japanese economic success generated large currency reserves, exchange-rate shifts, and political pressures that have been forcing, but also permitting, Japanese firms to expand aggressively worldwide. Japanese high-technology consumers, such as the automobile, electronics, and financial sectors, have strengthened their positions in the U.S. market while continuing to purchase preferentially from Japanese producers. Additionally, Japanese high-technology producers are establishing ties to U.S. technology sources like universities, national laboratories, and start-up firms while generally continuing to discriminate against U.S. high-technology firms in Japan. In 1987, for example, Japanese firms purchased 20 times as many U.S. firms as U.S. concerns purchased Japanese ones. Strategic investments and technology licensing by Japanese firms in America are commonplace, while such investments by U.S. firms in Japan are rare. Ironically, Japanese firms such as Nippon Electric Company (NEC), the world leader in semiconductor sales, are beginning to locate low-skill assembly operations in the United States partly to circumvent trade controls.

The attributes of Japanese high-technology industries play an important role in their ability to expand overseas while continuing to block foreign penetration of Japanese markets. As is typical of most Japanese industries, these sectors are extremely concentrated. Six firms, all with annual revenues of more than $10 billion and with close links with other major Japanese industries, produce approximately 85 per cent of Japanese semiconductors, 80 per cent of Japanese computers, 80 per cent of Japanese telecommunications equipment, and 60 percent of Japanese consumer electronics. A single $2 billion firm, Fanuc (Fujitsu Automatic Numerical Control), controls 80 per cent of the domestic market and 40 per cent of the world market for machine tool electronic control systems. Fanuc is also the world's largest robot producer and is 40 per cent owned by Fujitsu, Japan's largest computer manufacturer. Likewise, the Japanese defense industry is dominated by four heavy industrial firms that often share contracts.

Moreover, the equity and debt of Japanese high-technology firms and many of their suppliers are closely held within the major industrial groups. These groups, which are led by the world's largest banks and trading companies, each comprise more than 100 companies with total revenues of $100 billion or more. For instance, the leading companies in the Sumitomo group own not only 19 per cent of NEC, whose corporate revenues total more than $15 billion, but also almost 10 per cent of Matsushita, a $40 billion electronics firm. Large manufacturers, in turn, control many subcontractors: Two firms, one of them 51 per cent owned by NEC and the other 22 per cent owned by Fujitsu, control 90 per cent of Japanese production of semiconductor test equipment.

The role of the Japanese financial industry, which is concentrated much like the industrial sector, may prove particularly important. The Japanese financial services sector now includes the world's 7 largest banks, 4 of the 10 largest securities firms, and also the largest insurance and trading companies. This sector is a major purchaser of computer systems; a major arbiter of trade flows; a major capital supplier to high-technology industries; and, increasingly, a major investor in foreign companies that produce or use high-technology goods.

As a result of Japan's industrial concentration and strong government industrial policy, the country's industrial behavior is subject to a degree of strategic control unthinkable in the United States or Western Europe. The protectionism, prevention of direct foreign investment, obstructionism in trade negotiations, unidirectional technology flows, and industrial targeting displayed by Japanese industry and government are not accidental or marginal. Rather, economic and technological nationalism is an enduring feature of the postwar Japanese system, an uncomfortable fact infrequently acknowledged in American policy deliberations concerning economic security.

This is not to say that Japan's behavior is static or inflexible. Several forces—ranging from the rise of the yen and the prospect of U.S. stagnation to competition from newly industrializing countries and a possible gradual resurgence of Japanese nationalism—are leading to several changes in Tokyo's policy. These include increasing the use of low-wage, offshore labor and stimulating the domestic Japanese market. Such policies serve as cosmetic actions to open Japanese markets, primarily for low-technology subassemblies and luxury consumer goods. These domestic forces also appear to be generating growth in the Japanese defense industry, which is dominated by the electronics and heavy industrial companies.

The growth of Japan's defense industry offers striking parallels to that of commercial electronics. Indeed, the director of procurement for the Japan Defense Agency was previously a Ministry of International Trade and Industry official responsible for policy toward the semiconductor and computer industries. Japan's defense industry strategy rests upon domestic protectionism, licensed technology, access to American technology and defense facilities, and the same systematic progression to advanced products witnessed in other sectors. While Japan's so-called Three Principles have in effect precluded weapons exports, there is much evidence that Japan is preparing to become a weapons exporter.

American policy facilitates Japanese production of U.S. weapons as a way of sustaining armament supplies during wartime, while U.S. weapons export procedures are unwieldy. The result is a massive technology transfer to Japanese firms, a trend supported by Japanese industry. U.S. defense firms find these licensing arrangements highly profitable, though some admit privately that they are creating future competitors. The Japanese defense industry already possesses licensing or coproduction arrangements covering F-15s, F-16s, P-3Cs, and other aircraft; commercial and military helicopters; missile systems; jet engines; and many military electronics systems. In addition, several Japanese electronics firms are supplying large dual-use subsystems, such as aircraft communications, to U.S. defense contractors.

In several cases, particularly missiles, radars, and electronics, the typical cycle of Japanese industrial development is well under way. Indeed, the quality of Japanese military technologies has led the U.S. Defense Department to seek access to them and to consider "renting" Japanese weapons. Japanese missiles have been tested in the United States, and mechanisms have been considered to facilitate the importation of Japanese weapons. Several Japanese antiaircraft, antitank, and antiship missiles are now considered equal or superior to those produced by U.S. defense firms.

Consequently, the commercial and military sectors appear to be developing along broadly similar lines. If these trends continue, Japanese industry will eliminate the collective technological superiority previously enjoyed by the United States. The United States will grow increasingly dependent on Japanese technology. The strategic concentration of the Japanese system will confer substantial advantages in bilateral negotiations and global rivalry. And U.S. firms, including defense contractors, will encounter more and more difficulty in obtaining access to Japanese markets, technology, intermediate products, and advanced capital equipment in areas whose "downstream" product markets are targeted by Japanese firms. Conversely, Japanese penetration of U.S. markets and technology sources will increase. These developments could have profound effects. Therefore, improving America's technological performance and coping with the effects of Japanese technological and industrial power should become a major part of U.S. policy.

A U.S. RESPONSE

The United States now faces a challenge more fundamental than any since the cold war: the simultaneous need for internal reform and for the management of a new strategic balance, namely its technological competition with Japan. If America fails it will encounter something approaching an economic crisis, including severe tradeoffs between its global commitments and its domestic living standards. America's goals should include a strong technological position, careful management of its interdependence with Japan, and channeling of Japanese strength into appropriate and stabilizing forms of geopolitical or military burden sharing.

An adequate U.S. response must therefore include three components. First, the United States must improve its own economic environment, productivity growth, and technological performance. Second, it must reform its military procurement system, defense industrial base, and posture toward technological security. And third, the United States must manage its relationships with Japan in a more realistic and sophisticated way.

This challenge derives not only from Japan, but also from America's own mismanagement. Unless the United States restores its own technological and economic vitality, no amount of strategic bargaining, protectionism, or military spending will ensure its future security. However, the United States must also respond to Japan's technoindustrial Prussianism—without xenophobia or hostility, but also without naiveté. Continued U.S. decline is more likely to provoke dangerous social pressures than would any strong but rational policy. In short, the United States must learn that these issues of high technology and Japanese industrial policy, not just Soviet warheads, will determine the future national security of the United States.

Given this challenge, how might the United States proceed? It must first bolster economywide productivity growth if it is to achieve other objectives. Otherwise the country will face a host of problems, from spending constraints and declining living standards to dependence on foreign credit and social tensions, that could preclude effective policy-making for high technology or anything else.

U.S. productivity policy must include measures to increase U.S. savings rates and capital investment and to shift resources toward real economic activity as opposed to distributional contention in legal, regulatory, and financial arenas. However, such generic policies should be supplemented with a policy for high-technology industries, as well as a policy for diffusing advanced technology throughout the economy. Four substantive measures seem particularly appropriate: changing the financial incentives seen by firms, managers, and employees in evaluating high-technology investments; ensuring better cooperation and coordination among industry, labor, and government; improving the quality of the U.S. work force; and investing aggressively in high-technology infrastructure and services for both government and the private sector.

Considerable leverage could be obtained through federal regulatory, procurement, and funding powers. Federal efforts could assist cooperative projects structured to lengthen firms' time horizons, reduce but not eliminate private risk in long-term investing, funnel benefits toward U.S. firms as opposed to foreign free riders, and provide a balanced combination of technical cooperation and market competition among companies.

Digital information technology has major implications for education, training, and the work force. Trends in microprocessor control, personal computing, and networking imply that large organizations, whether commercial, governmental, or military, will increasingly use information systems that are widely distributed. Improving performance through distributed information systems will therefore depend in large part upon the education and training of working-level personnel. So in the long run education, too, is national security. America will suffer if its educational system fails to provide basic linguistic, quantitative, and computing skills.

National laboratories, federal procurements, and infrastructure projects could serve as focuses for public and private efforts in process and product R&D. One goal might involve a nationwide digital communications and services system. Telephone companies could be permitted to include in their rate bases the costs of wiring the country for fiberoptic cable. Federal contracts to develop equipment standards and prototypes could facilitate American entry into markets such as digital, modular high-definition televisions. These federal contracts could be channeled through competing American consortia, each composed of an alliance of U.S. semiconductor, computer, telecommunications, and information services concerns. Later, foreign access to the network and to U.S. markets could be conditioned on proven, not promised, U.S. shares in foreign activities and markets.

To be sure, these are new matters to industry and government, and so far both have handled them poorly. U.S. semiconductor policy, for example, must at this point be considered a disaster. The United States has chronically underinvested in semiconductor technology, particularly in manufacturing, since the 1970s. The U.S. computer industry became heavily dependent upon DRAMS supplied by Japanese firms that dominate the Japanese computer industry and control more than 75 per cent of world production. A shortage of Japanese DRAM supplies cost the American computer industry more than $2 billion in 1988. Moreover, the U.S. share of the Japanese semiconductor market has declined despite a 1986 trade agreement mandating that it be doubled; yet the State Department wants minor U.S. sanctions lifted to avoid diplomatic tensions.

The American high-technology community contains many extremely gifted and imaginative people. With sufficient drive, incentive, and resources there is every reason to expect improvement in the U.S. system's collective management abilities. But the effectiveness of American policy will rest heavily on industrial cooperation, low-cost capital, and rationalization of federal policymaking and administration. Federal policy must support high technology, not control it. Wherever possible, incentive mechanisms should be chosen over direct federal administration.

The Defense Department and the U.S. defense industry are now technologically lagging participants in a global, predominantly commercial, high-technology industrial system. As American industry is painfully learning to manage its technology base, to shorten its product cycles, to scan global technology, and to reduce its bureaucratic overheads, so, too, must the defense sector. U.S. defense procurement should therefore shift toward commercial components, industry standard designs, and flexible automation to increase efficiency and also to support the commercial base upon which U.S. security ultimately depends. For where American technology decays, whether commercial or specifically military, the Pentagon will be forced to choose between inferior U.S. technology and whatever Japanese industry is willing to sell.

Thus while growing reliance on Japanese military technology, and even on Japanese weapons systems, is inevitable and possibly even desirable, the United States should manage its military technology relationships with Japan as carefully as its commercial relationships. The United States should consider an effort to integrate Japanese industrial techniques and commercial technology into the U.S. weapons design and production system—perhaps through consulting and services contracts with Japanese firms—as an attractive alternative to buying Japanese weapons. Where using Japanese military technology is deemed necessary, licensing to U.S. producers should be strongly preferred over direct product purchases from Japan.

And conversely, licensing U.S. weapons technology to Japanese firms should be strictly limited, particularly for high-technology conventional offensive systems, for those associated with power projection or land operations rather than sea-lane defense, and where control of a technology's availability to third countries is particularly important. Where combat sustainability goals merit producing U.S. weapons systems in Japan, direct foreign investment and wholly owned production subsidiaries operated by U.S. firms should be employed.

Strategic bargaining with Japan must therefore become a consideration of the first order in U.S. policy. If the U.S. decline in high technology continues, American economic performance, defense policy, and diplomacy will become more susceptible to Japanese influence. This dependence would take several forms. First, the technology levels of U.S. commercial and military systems would depend increasingly on access to Japanese industrial and technological supplies and resources. Second, Japan could become a significant exporter of high-technology weapons, with or without U.S. approval. Third, Japan could become a significant diplomatic or military power. And fourth, the United States would lose much of its remaining ability to employ technology denial as a tool of foreign policy, relative not only to Japan but to other countries as well.

So the most general, and perhaps the most important, point to be made on the strategic management of U.S.-Japanese interactions is that it requires much more intellectual power and care than are currently devoted to it. The United States must realize that Japanese national interests, technology strategy, and global industrial behavior deserve a serious, objective analysis, one unclouded by outdated ideologies or wishful thinking. The available evidence suggests that the U.S.-Japanese technology rivalry must be shaped by two guiding principles: the enforcement of reciprocity in economic and technological relations, and careful attention to both American interests and international stability.

These principles could be put in motion with several policy initiatives. The United States should establish an industry–government–university mechanism to monitor Japanese activities in the U.S. high-technology system and U.S. participation in the Japanese system. Washington should also establish a mechanism to review the Japanese defense industry, its relationship with U.S. and other national defense industries, and the relationship between its activities and Japanese military policy. The United States should announce and enforce a policy of punitive tariffs on carefully chosen Japanese high-technology products and services where persistent predation or closure is observed. Further, the United States should take steps to boost the intellectual and financial resources devoted to economic and trade policy and to Japanese affairs, both within the government and in the country at large. The mismatch in this realm is illustrated well by the fact that 18,000 Japanese are studying at American universities, many of whom are sent by Japanese corporations, while only 900 Americans are studying in Japan.

As Japan grows stronger, its domestic interactions will become increasingly important to the international system and to U.S. policy. The complacency that has led the United States into its current predicament is a luxury it can no longer afford.

13

China after Tiananmen: The Failure of American Policy

MARIE GOTTSCHALK

Henry Kissinger was right when he wrote in July that "China remains too important for America's national security to risk the relationship on the emotions of the moment."[1] Unfortunately, the "emotions of the moment" driving U.S. policy toward China today are the same ones that have shaped Sino-American relations for the past 15 years. Shared by Democratic and Republican administrations alike, they include a sentimental attachment to the Chinese leaders who normalized relations with the United States, an abiding faith in the notion that a strong and friendly China is needed as a counterweight to Soviet influence in Asia, and a reverence for China's potential as a billion-strong market for American products and investments. Moreover, the United States has had an unshaken belief that political liberalization will inevitably accompany economic liberalization in the case of China.

For nearly two decades now, these "emotions of the moment" have underpinned Washington's special relationship with Beijing. Because of the presumed centrality of that relationship to U.S. interests, Washington has applied a different set of standards and expectations to China than to most other nations. It has assumed that there is a natural convergence between Chinese and U.S. interests, and that U.S. support for human rights in China can only come at the expense of the long-term political and economic interests of the United States.

The Bush administration remains captive to these assumptions. Slow to condemn the June massacres of thousands of civilian demonstrators in the Chinese cities of Beijing and Chengdu, the administration has gone to great lengths to preserve the basis of its special relationships with China. Not only has President Bush opposed the package of sanctions passed nearly unanimously by Congress last summer, but he has not even adhered to the limited sanctions he himself announced following the military attack on Tiananmen Square. On June 5, the president declared that U.S. military sales to China would be suspended. Less than a month later, he approved the shipment of $48 million of military-

Reprinted by permission of *World Policy Journal*, vol. VI, no. 4, Fall 1989.

Note: It is a violation of the law to reproduce this selection by any means whatsoever without the written permission of the copyright holder.

equipped aircraft to the People's Republic. On June 20, Bush called for the suspension of high-level meetings between U.S. and Chinese officials. Weeks later, to the surprise and delight of the Chinese leadership, James Lilley, the U.S. ambassador to China, showed up at a banquet in the Chinese city of Tianjin held to celebrate the recent signing of a long-term contract between China and a U.S.-based company. Li Ruihuan, who was elevated to the Politburo's powerful Standing Committee in the political shake-up following the assault on Tiananmen, attended the banquet, and photographs of Li and Lilley were splashed over the front pages of Chinese newspapers.[2]

In short, the Bush administration has been quietly moving toward resuming business as usual with Beijing, even though the political situation in China has deteriorated in the months since the June massacres. The administration is thus following the path of its predecessors, acquiescing to actions by the Chinese leadership that it would find reprehensible and threatening to U.S. interests if committed by the leadership of most any other country.

The time for a reassessment of Sino-American relations is long overdue. China's domestic and international conditions have changed enormously since President Richard Nixon's visit in 1972. So has the nature of economic and strategic relations in much of the Pacific Rim. Yet U.S. policy has remained surprisingly constant, driven by outdated sentiments and questionable assumptions. By failing to rethink this approach, the so-called realists have pursued a surreal path in Sino-American relations that has not only hurt the cause of political reform and human rights in the People's Republic, but also America's long-term interests in the region.

Since the historic warming of Sino-American relations in 1972, the desire for a strong, stable, and friendly China to check Soviet influence in Asia has overshadowed all other considerations in U.S. policy toward the People's Republic. Presidents from Nixon onward, including Jimmy Carter, have ignored the issues of political reform and human rights in China, believing that to raise them with Chinese leaders would be counterproductive and undermine U.S. strategic and economic interests.[3] In response to the few critics who questioned whether China could remain a stable friend of the United States without undergoing significant political reforms, the architects of U.S. policy argued that as the People's Republic modernized and liberalized its economy, greater political freedom would inevitably follow.

At a press conference two days after thousands of unarmed civilians were wounded or killed by Chinese troops, President Bush stood by this policy. "Now is the time to look beyond the moment to important and enduring aspects of this vital relationship for the United States," he said. Bush went on to assert, "As people have commercial incentive, whether it's in China or in other totalitarian systems, the move to democracy becomes inexorable."[4] While the president was speaking of China's inevitable march to democracy, soldiers were randomly shooting terrified Chinese citizens in the aftermath of the massacre. And while Bush was reaffirming America's enduring relationship with Beijing, none of China's top leaders had been seen in public for 11 days, and U.S. officials had to admit they did not know who, if anyone, was in charge of the government.[5]

Bush's response highlights a persistent flaw in U.S. policy toward the People's Republic. In its quest and desire for a strong, "stable" China to serve as a counterweight to the Soviet Union, Washington has over the years aligned itself with a leadership and political system that are in fact highly unstable. U.S. officials considered China stable because Deng Xiaoping appeared to be in charge, because he appeared to have handpicked a successor (Hu Yaobang, then Zhao Ziyang), and because he appeared committed to economic liberalization. This understanding of stability, however, is narrow and undemocratic. The tendency to equate constancy of leadership at the top with stability, first with Mao Zedong, then Deng, caused the United States to underestimate or neglect the enormous pressures in China for change in the political system—pressures that have increased with the opening of the economy.

Washington satisfied itself that Deng was accommodating these pressures because of the American proclivity to believe liberalizing the market goes hand in hand with liberating the mind and the political system. Oddly, U.S. officials remain convinced of this despite numerous examples, including the Philippines under Ferdinand Marcos and Singapore under President Lee Kuan Yew, in which modernization did not necessarily lead to smoothly expanding political freedoms. Following the June 3–4 massacre, Bush went out of his way to praise Deng for moving China "towards openness, towards democracy, towards reform."[6] Even after Deng appeared on television four days later, commending the People's Liberation Army troops who carried out the massacre and expressing no remorse for the killings, the White House refrained from criticizing him directly. This continuing faith in Deng, the political reformer, is astounding in light of all the evidence to the contrary.

On political questions, Deng has a chilling record. As general secretary of the Chinese Communist Party in the 1950s, he was responsible for carrying out the Anti-Rightist Campaign, which sent hundreds of thousands of Chinese to labor camps, where most of them languished until the late 1970s. During the 1978–79 Democracy Wall movement, he encouraged protesters only long enough to solidify his position in the party leadership, then called for the arrest of many of its activists, including Wei Jingsheng, whose biggest crime was to call for adding a "fifth modernization" to Deng's four—democracy. Wei was sentenced to a 15-year jail term after a show trial and has since spent many years in solitary confinement. He is said to have lost his teeth and his mind. Yet

Deng was unmoved by calls earlier this year from Chinese intellectuals to release him and other political prisoners. The government has even refused to reveal which prison Wei is in, or to confirm that he is still alive.

Deng himself is the best icon of how unreformed and brittle China's political system remains. Although Deng has held no formal position in the government since giving up the title of vice premier in 1980, he is still the nation's paramount leader, and the biggest question looming over China's political future is who will succeed him. The enormity of this question cannot be overstated. Historically, succession has been traumatic in China. The Cultural Revolution, responsible for an estimated 1 million deaths and 100 million persecutions, was in part a battle over succession. Despite four decades in power, the Chinese Communist Party has found no institutionalized way of passing power among leaders.

The potential for traumatic succession is magnified by the fact that power in China is highly concentrated at the top, as there are few checks and balances in the political system. Moreover, the party has a monopoly not only on political life, but also on the nation's social, cultural, and economic life. As a result, any instability within the leadership produces tremors throughout the country. Chinese filmmaker Chen Kaige recently likened the Chinese political system to a giant magnet that orders the pattern of all the individual filings. When that magnet is gone, one good jolt can scatter the filings everywhere.[7]

In recent years, Chinese society has begun to chafe under the rigid control of that magnet. More and more, people have come to view the rule of Deng and his colleagues as illegitimate. As Liu Binyan, China's best-known journalist, put it, "Of the four factors that once gave the Communist Party the highest prestige of any rulers in Chinese history— Maoist ideology, clean government, party discipline, and military power—all but the last had evaporated."[8] The economic reforms of the past decade have created intense pressures for political reform as Chinese citizens have increasingly demanded government action to clean up corruption, curb inflation, and deal with the myriad of problems created by economic liberalization. The government's failure to respond to these demands or to grant its people greater political freedom has resulted in the collapse of the Communist Party's credibility and legitimacy. American leaders, however, have been inattentive to the profound domestic and international consequences of the party's sinking legitimacy, in part because the United States often pays scant attention to why people in other nations act politically.[9]

U.S. foreign policy toward China has always rested on conflicting propositions. A penchant for *realpolitik* has inclined repeated administrations to prefer "stability" and friendly leaders above all else. A deeply embedded liberalism, by contrast, has consistently argued that economic liberalization will create political liberalization, and that a liberal country will be a friendly country. An attachment to these conflicting propositions only partially explains why Sino-American relations have developed the way they have, however. The U.S. Congress and American public, both highly moralistic in the 1970s and 1980s about human rights violations in such countries as Chile, the Soviet Union, El Salvador, and South Africa, were generally silent about abuses in China. Some kept quiet because of guilt about America's 30-year estrangement from the People's Republic and a desire to see that the United States had buried the Cold War hatchet with at least one communist nation. Others refrained from criticizing the People's Republic because—viewed from afar—it seemed to be a socialist success story. Academics generally kept quiet for fear of losing their access to do research in China, and because many of them also bought the U.S. government's argument that to raise human-rights questions would jeopardize American interests.[10] Human-rights organizations, too, were slow to get involved with China, initially because of the difficulty of getting reliable information, and later because the enormous scale of the violations threatened to place too great a strain on their small staffs and limited resources.[11]

To justify their silence on human rights abuses in China over the past 15 years, some Americans have also argued that recent violations are tame in comparison with the Chinese Communist Party's earlier record. Nixon used this rationale in an article calling for a limited U.S. response to the June massacre. "They have done far worse before Tiananmen Square," he wrote, going on to cite hundreds of thousands—maybe millions—killed in the Cultural Revolution and 20 million dead in the famine that followed the Great Leap Forward.[12] By this reasoning, Americans should be satisfied with the state of civil rights in their country because at least blacks are not slaves anymore.

Until they saw millions of Chinese take to the streets last spring, many Americans also clung to the belief that political freedom and human rights are relatively unimportant to the Chinese people because they come from a 3,000-year political tradition of highly centralized, authoritarian rule, not one of respect for individual liberties. In fact, Confucianism, which stresses humanism, compassion for others, and the obligation to behave in a moral fashion, is compatible in many ways with modern-day ideas about human rights and political freedom.[13] "Humanism isn't the privilege of the West. It's quite an insult to think human rights don't matter as much in China," Liu Binyan said in an interview earlier this year.[14] The Chinese, many of whom have been brutally denied protections Americans take for granted, undoubtedly have a keener appreciation of the need for such rights. What else could explain their willingness to lie down in front of tanks and stand up to soldiers with live ammunition?

The lure of China's huge, relatively untapped market—which

spawned America's initial interest in the country as early as the 18th century—has also contributed to the U.S. tendency to ignore unsavory aspects of Chinese political life. Heady dreams of "selling a billion boxes of detergent" have given many Americans a wildly optimistic view of the potential of that market.[15] Overall, Americans have sold themselves on the notion that China is destined to be an economic and political giant in the 21st century. If U.S. policy-makers were consistent realists, however, they would worry about whether such a China would necessarily be an asset to the United States. Instead, the assumed link between a market economy and a friendly power has been pushed to the forefront while issues related to political rights and liberties have been ignored.

The United States has thus pursued a confused "realist" path in its relations with the People's Republic, based on the unrealistic assumption that China is likely to remain a stable friend even as it suppresses the demands of its citizens for greater political freedom. U.S. "realism" with respect to China has also been grounded in a second flawed assumption—that of the enduring convergence of U.S. and Chinese interests, especially in relation to the Soviet Union. In light of recent changes in Soviet foreign policy, the transformation of the Asian political landscape, and China's potentially destabilizing regional ambitions, the belief in such a convergence of interests seems increasingly hard to comprehend.

For nearly two decades, the United States has had a remarkably static, one-dimensional view of China's role in the region. Simply put, Washington has counted on China to thwart Soviet ambitions in the Pacific Rim and to be a friendly haven for U.S. traders and investors. To these ends, the United States has developed over the years a close military and strategic relationship with China. That relationship, initiated by Nixon and nurtured by the Ford and Carter administrations, came into full blossom during the Reagan years despite a rocky start because of a spat over U.S. missile sales to Taiwan. In the early years of the Reagan administration, China was reclassified as a "friendly nonally," and many restrictions on the sale of advanced military technology were lifted. Exchanges of high-level military personnel proliferated, as did U.S. arms sales to China. When the United States suspended military sales to China this summer, $600 million worth of arms deals were pending.[16]

Ironically, the United States has continued to deepen its strategic relationship with China even as enormous changes in the East Asian region have rendered such a relationship obsolete. Today there are scenes that were once unimaginable: Pyongyang feting South Korea's Hyundai group; the Soviet Union courting South Korean capital; Thailand making overtures to Vietnam to develop a trading zone in Indochina; and Hungary establishing the East bloc's first embassy in

Seoul. Alignments in the region have loosened as trade, investment, and economic growth have supplanted military security and ideology as the key interests in the region.[17] The Soviet Union has not been immune to these trends. Indeed, Moscow's strategy of downgrading its strategic interests in favor of integrating the Soviet Union into the dynamic East Asian economy is in large part responsible for the relaxation of tensions in the region.

Yet despite these changes, the outdated and overdrawn concept of the "strategic triangle" continues to exert a powerful influence over Sino-American relations. In his commentary on Tiananmen, Nixon raised the specter of rapidly thawing relations between Beijing and Moscow should the United States take too strong a stand against the massacre.[18] Henry Kissinger, who once remarked that the Soviets have a "neuralgic"[19] fear of the Chinese, warned in the days after the Tiananmen killings that the Soviet Union could get a "free ride" if the United States strongly condemned China. At a time when Moscow is unilaterally reducing its naval and military forces in the region and has embarked on an ambitious effort to increase its economic relations with Japan and South Korea, such warnings seem anachronistic in the extreme.

Even if one still regards the Soviet Union as a serious threat, it is hard to take seriously the worries about a reconstituted Sino-Soviet alliance. A cozy relationship between the People's Republic and the Soviet Union in the near future is improbable regardless of how the United States responds to recent events in China: the history of mistrust and bad blood between the Soviet Union and China simply runs too deep. China learned during the 1950s not to become excessively dependent on an outside power far more powerful and developed than itself.[20] It also seems unlikely that China's estrangement from the United States, should it come about, would induce the Soviet Union to rethink a strategy of détente with the West that it deems crucial to its own economic developments. In economic terms, what China and the Soviet Union have to offer each other is inconsequential relative to what both of them need from the West. China can provide labor and consumer products to the Soviet Union, which in turn can provide natural resources and refurbish old Soviet-designed factories within China. But neither nation can supply the other with the capital and high technology their economies desperately need in order to develop.

A closer relationship with the Soviet Union is an especially unwelcome proposition for the Chinese leadership on ideological grounds, given the very different political climates in Beijing and Moscow today. While Chinese citizens were decidedly lukewarm about Bush's visit in February, they were effusive about Mikhail Gorbachev's visit in May. Students greeted the Soviet leader with signs reading *gongkai*—the Chinese word for *glasnost*—and sought a meeting with him. Many of the speakers at student demonstrations in the spring explicitly referred to political reforms under way in the Soviet Union and Eastern Europe as possible models for China. Deng Xiaoping, in his June 9 speech analyzing the causes of the recent unrest, alluded to the influence that changes in the Soviet Union and Eastern Europe had had on recent events in China. "This storm had to come sooner or later," he said. "It was determined by both the international atmosphere and by China's own microclimatic conditions."[21] From China's point of view, greater exposure to the "flies and worms"[22] of *glasnost* may be just as undesirable as exposure to the "flies and worms" of Western bourgeois liberalism that have come through China's open door.

The White House seemed at one point to have recognized the extreme improbability of a revived Sino-Soviet alliance. Prior to the May Sino-Soviet summit—the first in 30 years—several administration officials indicated that they were unconcerned about the prospect of warmer relations between Beijing and Moscow. Bush went as far as to say the summit meeting was a "good thing, and it's nothing detrimental to the interests of the United States."[23] (Interestingly, the Chinese themselves tried to alleviate possible U.S. fears about the summit by letting Washington know that tensions between China and the Soviet Union would not be eased by a single visit.) The invocation of the "strategic triangle" since the massacre, then, seems to be mostly a tactical move on the part of certain U.S. officials who continue to exaggerate China's importance in order to justify their policy of containing the Soviet Union and their emotional attachment to America's special relationship with China.[24]

Yet this emotional attachment has not been without costs to U.S. interests and to the prospects for long-term peace and stability in the Pacific region. Preoccupied with its strategic relationship with China, the United States has tended to ignore areas where U.S. and Chinese interests diverge and to overlook actions on the part of China that could undermine regional and international stability. Washington has failed to consider seriously that China's strategic interests are driven by far more than just the dislike for the Soviet Union that it shares with the United States.

Because of China's size, resources, and long history of cultural and political domination in the region, the countries of Asia and the Pacific regard the People's Republic with far more ambivalence than does the United States.[25] One legacy of the century of "shame and humiliation" that characterized China's relations with the rest of the world from the mid-19th to the mid-20th century is an enormous desire to be both materially strong and politically respected in the world.[26] Deng's "four modernizations" are predicated on making China the equal of the other major powers, so as to avoid further humiliations of the sort suffered when foreign forces invaded China and carved it up into spheres of influence. Many Japanese analysts, however, fear that Beijing's program of economic modernization will transform China into a "powerful, assertive, and disruptive military and political force in Asia."[27] Others predict that China's economic program will eventually fail, causing great political, social, and economic turmoil in the People's Republic and in Asia as a whole.

Nations in the region tend to be suspicious and fearful of China in part because of the outstanding territorial disputes Beijing has with many of its 13 neighbors. They are also all too aware of China's history of funding and nurturing the communist insurgency movements of its neighbors, most notably in Malaysia and Indonesia in the 1960s. The People's Republic has, it is true, made some commendable overtures recently toward lessening tensions in the region: it has ceased for the most part supporting insurgencies in ASEAN nations; it hosted the first Sino-Indian summit in decades last December; and it has reduced its saber-rattling toward Taiwan and removed many of the restrictions on travel between that disputed island and the mainland. Nonetheless, on the whole China's record in the region remains unsettling, and there is ample reason to worry about the future course of Chinese policy.

While reductions in the size of the People's Liberation Army and in China's defense budget have received much favorable attention in the United States, potentially destabilizing changes in China's military force posture have gone overlooked. The People's Republic, which is the world's third-largest military power, has shifted from preparing for a large-scale defensive war against the Soviet Union to preparing for territorial disputes and local wars. To enable China to project power in the Pacific more effectively, Deng's military modernization program has favored the Chinese navy. China has built new naval bases and up-to-date warships and missiles, and is planning to build its first aircraft carrier. Beijing also intends to enhance its submarine fleet, already the third largest in the world. It has beefed up its capability for long-distance troop deployments, and conducted naval exercises further and further afield from China.[28]

While China's military posture has clearly changed, its overall strategic, economic, and diplomatic intentions in the Pacific region remain very unclear. Beijing has historically regarded its neighbors with a degree of condescension. A "candidate superpower,"[29] it has been far more oriented toward Western nations and the superpowers than toward its neighbors. As a result, it has relatively little experience in cooperating with other countries in the region. As academic Steven I. Levine put it, China is "a regional power without a regional policy."[30] It also has a propensity to engage in ignoble military gamesmanship, as evidenced by its active support of the Khmer Rouge in Cambodia and its periodic "gunboat diplomacy," most notably in the Spratly Islands, a strategic and reportedly oil-rich archipelago in the South China Sea claimed by Vietnam, the Philippines, Malaysia, Taiwan, and China. (In early 1988, for example, China appeared to be trying to provoke an incident with Vietnam when its warships landed Chinese troops on the archipelago.[31])

Despite considerable reason for concern about China's military intentions, the United States has continued to sell sophisticated weapons to China and to encourage its military modernization. At the same time, the U.S. government has done little to induce China to be militarily responsible. For years the United States has been silent as China armed the Khmer Rouge, practiced gunboat diplomacy, and rapidly expanded its arms sales to volatile regions outside of East Asia, most notably the Middle East and South Asia. In fact, China's emergence in this decade as one the world's leading arms dealers coincided—not so coincidentally—with the rapid growth of U.S. sales of high-technology weapons to Beijing. While the United States was selling increasingly sophisticated weaponry to China, China was gaining a reputation as a supplier of sophisticated arms at bargain-basement prices. Beijing has relied heavily on its arms sales to unstable parts of the world to support its own arms industry and military modernization program. It has, for example, sold Chinese-made Silkworm missiles to Iran and "East Wind" intermediate-range ballistic missiles to Saudi Arabia.[32] Chinese scientists have also helped Pakistan develop nuclear capability.

Chinese sales of highly sophisticated arms to explosive areas of the world exemplify Beijing's readiness to subordinate global responsibilities to its own desire to modernize. Although a Reagan administration official once lamented that "China appears as a rogue elephant on the arms market, ready to sell anything for money," the United States has remained reluctant to see the link between Chinese arms sales and U.S. technology transfers to China.[33] Nor has Washington been willing to antagonize the Chinese leaders by actively pressuring them to halt such sales.

This reluctance was clearly evident in Washington's relatively tolerant attitude toward Chinese arms sales to Iran during the Persian Gulf war, which tended to undermine U.S. and Soviet efforts to contain the conflict (although it should be recalled that the United States itself secretly sold weapons to Iran). Beijing consistently denied selling weapons to Iran, even after State Department officials confronted Chinese officials with aerial photographs of the missiles leaving China and arriving on the same ship at the Iranian port of Bandar Abbas. The Reagan administration finally responded to the irrefutable evidence in October 1987 by imposing curbs on the export of some high-technology products to China. But just five months later, the United States lifted the ban during a visit to Washington by then Foreign Minister Wu Xueqian. Moreover, it did so without getting any explicit assurance that China would refrain from future arms sales.[34]

By failing to condemn Chinese actions that are aggressive or destabilizing, the United States has only encouraged further irresponsible behavior on the part of China. Moreover, because of its close strategic identification with Beijing, the United States has been unwittingly implicated in China's geostrategic ambitions. The ambitions Beijing seems to harbor could, if left unchecked by political reform and democratization within China and by a less accommodating United States, have serious long-term consequences for peace in East Asia and the world. The prospect of a militarily confident and competent China might be what ultimately pushes Japan to undergo a massive buildup of its own. Rising Japanese militarism in turn could force the Soviet Union to abandon its current disarmament agenda and expand its Pacific military posture. The United States might then find itself in the middle of a dangerous, high stakes four-power (perhaps five-power if India joins in) balancing act in Asia and the Pacific.

In its relationship with China, the United States has behaved like a guest at a dinner party, refusing to raise sensitive subjects—be they arms sales or human rights—for fear of being ignored or, worse, being replaced at the head of the table by the Soviet Union. Consequently, Washington has contributed to the belief among the Chinese leadership that how Beijing treats its people and its neighbors is irrelevant to how Washington and the world treat China. In this way, the United States has reinforced China's view that it can become a strong, modernized, and respected nation without fundamentally changing its polity or its behavior. As Deng explained to other top Chinese leaders following the suppression of student demonstrations in 1986 and 1987, "A few years ago we punished some exponents of liberalization like Wei Jingsheng, who broke the law. We've arrested him and we're not going to let him go. Has this brought discredit to us? No, China's image was not damaged."[35]

Since assuming the presidency, George Bush, who was the U.S. envoy to China from 1974 to 1975, has continued this pattern of positive reinforcement for negative behavior. On his visit to China early this year, Bush failed to address the issue of human rights, even after a phalanx of 100 Chinese policemen trailed dissident Fang Lizhi to ensure he did not attend a Texas-style barbecue to which the United States had also invited Premier Li Peng and military strongman Yang Shangkun.[36] In the weeks leading up to the June crackdown, Washington again gave no indication that it cared how China chose to deal with domestic dissent. On May 19, the day martial law was declared, three U.S. naval ships went through with their planned courtesy call in Shanghai, the second visit by U.S. warships to China in 40 years. Two days later, when Bush finally made his first public comments about the demonstrations that had begun in mid-April, he refrained from directly criticizing the Chinese government or indicating that Sino-American relations would suffer should PLA troops attack the peaceful demonstrators. Instead, he merely encouraged the students to "continue to fight for what you believe in."[37]

The flaws in U.S. policy have become even more apparent in the aftermath of the military assault on Tiananmen. Millions have been chilled by a campaign of state terror that has resulted in the arrest of tens of thousands of Chinese and the secret executions and torture of an unknown number.[38] Rather than stiffen its response in light of this intensified repression, the Bush administration has backed away from the limited sanctions it announced in June. Instead of developing a new framework for Sino-American relations in the aftermath of Tiananmen, Washington has perpetuated its policy of indifference. Its response has amounted to little more than fleeting statements of condemnation and minimal sanctions applied halfheartedly at best as it has quietly moved to resume "business as usual" with Beijing.

The United States stands in need of a new China policy—one that lies somewhere between funding Chinese "freedom fighters" and making the Chinese economy scream, on the one hand, and, at the other extreme, quietly moving toward resuming the special relationship. The new framework needs to incorporate several new premises. First, U.S. policy must reflect the fact that Chinese and U.S. interests will only converge over the long term if China knows that its respect in the world is tied to what the United States and other nations think is respectable and legitimate behavior. This means that Washington has to put Beijing on notice that actions like its slaughter of unarmed demonstrators and its bullying of neighbors will come at great cost internationally.

The United States must also develop a less static view of East Asia and of China's role in the region. It needs to shift its focus from nurturing a strategic relationship with China to working with all the major powers in the region, including Japan, the Soviet Union, the People's Republic, and India, to create a secure, stable environment where none feels so threatened as to embark on a massive military buildup. It also should move away from the excessively bilateral nature of its dealings with China and should develop a coordinated response with other nations to continuing repression in the People's Republic.

Finally, the United States needs to discard the liberal faith that liberalized markets bring liberalized minds. In evaluating China's economic reformers, the United States must not once again be so mesmerized by China's phenomenal economic growth as to overlook indications of an unhealthy polity and unstable economy.

Sanctions should be an important element—though not the only element—of this new framework. While sanctions will not fundamentally alter China's political situation, if applied appropriately they could be extremely useful in making clear to Beijing that its international standing depends in part on its behavior at home. Sanctions can thus help to moderate the actions of the current regime and to impede its ability to consolidate power. As used so far, however, the sanctions approach is unlikely to be very effective for several reasons. In announcing his sanctions, Bush never publicly identified the steps China would have to take for sanctions to be lifted. Nor did he specify the measures the United States would take should the situation in China deteriorate further. Most seriously, Bush has backed down from the limited sanctions he announced in June, effectively rewarding China for its increasingly repressive behavior. The sanctions have also been undercut by the administration's failure to coordinate its actions with its allies so as to convince China that these reflect international, not just American, notions of legitimate behavior.

Sanctions have the potential to be quite effective with Beijing. There is no doubt that China is concerned about its international reputation. One legacy of China's century of "shame and humiliation" is its desire to be not only economically and militarily strong, but also politically respected in the world. This is evident from the extraordinary measure China took of summoning all of its ambassadors home in early July to determine how best to deal with worldwide criticism. Another reason why sanctions could be effective is that the current leadership has given every indication that it believes China's future economic health depends on continued access to foreign credit, technology, and markets. In speeches since the massacre, Deng Xiaoping and other Chinese leaders have repeatedly stressed their intent to keep China's door open to Western business, and China has been aggressively courting foreign businesspeople since June. It even tried to entice Volvo to open a plant in China by promising to supply cheap convict labor, an offer that Volvo executives at first took to be a hoax.[39] Deng is particularly sensitive to the impact that America's view of China has on foreign investors. In the late 1970s, Deng was anxious to normalize relations with the United States because he believed that this would give all foreign businessmen the confidence to make substantial investments in China.

One reason for the Bush administration's failure to view sanctions as a serious policy option is, no doubt, its concern about harming U.S. business interests. But sanctions, in the long run, can in fact help U.S. business interests. While the People's Republic has opened its door widely over the past decade to foreign trade and investment, the gatekeepers, for the most part, have been powerful, nepotistic ministries and trading companies, many of which, like the China International Trust and Investment Corporation, are controlled by the children of top Chinese officials. Consequently, access to the market depends on having access to relatives of the leadership. Businessmen like Henry Kissinger and Prescott Bush, the president's brother, have an enormous advantage in this semi-reformed, semi-feudal business environment, for their personal connections go a long way.[40] Political and economic reforms, if properly carried out, could break this hold by helping to decentralize the business environments. Smaller businesspeople, both in China and the United States, would then have a better shot at sharing the fruits of the market, for they would not have to hire the likes of Kissinger, Prescott Bush, or Alexander Haig, or bribe the offspring of Chinese officials, to walk through the "open" door. Greater political reform would also help ameliorate problems that have made many foreigners disenchanted with the China market—problems like rampant corruption, zigzagging economic policies, and social and political instability.

The Bush administration has done little to indicate that it seriously intends to use sanctions or other measures to distance itself from an unpopular, illegitimate regime that, because of enormous domestic problems, has neither the confidence nor the capability to be relied upon to play a constructive role in world affairs at present. As the Bush administration moves to restore the "special relationship" cultivated by its predecessors, however, it will increasingly find itself caught in a policy, rather than making policy, for it will have to contend with factors that preceding administrations have not had to deal with. The likelihood of a protracted, possibly violent succession struggle is great, thus the probability of future political, military, and economic turmoil is higher than it has been in years. Furthermore, the issue of human rights will become harder to ignore because the scale of the current round of repression is enormous and unlikely to abate soon. In particular, the plight of Fang Lizhi, the nation's leading dissident who is wanted on charges of "committing crimes of counterrevolutionary propaganda" and who remains in the U.S. Embassy where he sought refuge shortly after the Tiananmen killings, will be a constant reminder of the ongoing repression and a constant irritant in Sino-American relations.

The Bush administration must also be prepared to contend with a united, articulate lobby of Chinese students and scholars whose cause enjoys enormous support among Americans. There are now 40,000 Chinese students in the United States and many of them do not wish to return home when their visas, which Washington extended for a year, expire. A few years ago, China raised a storm over the U.S. decision to grant political asylum to a single Chinese, Hu Na, one of the nation's leading tennis players. A number of students have already asked U.S. officials to do something about the harassment they say they are experiencing by Chinese officials in this country.[41] Finally, as 1997 draws closer, the United States—and the world—may be faced with a mass emigration from Hong Kong and a collapse of Hong Kong's economy on the eve of its return to the Chinese mainland.

The current framework for Sino-American relations is completely inadequate to deal with these situations. For that reason, the United States may once again find itself reacting to events overseas rather than helping to shape events in a way that furthers the cause of freedom in China and the cause of stability in the Asian Pacific Rim. At the moment, the United States appears caught in an untenable policy that reminds one of Mao's famous dictum: "Everything under the heavens is in chaos and the situation is excellent."

NOTES

1. Henry Kissinger, "The Caricature of Deng as a Tyrant is Unfair," *Washington Post*, August 1, 1989.

2. See *China Daily*, August 11, 1989.

3. For a good, comprehensive account of how the United States has handled the human rights question, see Roberta Cohen, "People's Republic of China: The Human Rights Exception," *Human Rights Quarterly*, Vol. 9, No. 4 (November 1987), pp. 447–549; also, Susan Shirk, "Human Rights: What About China?" *Foreign Policy*, No. 29 (Winter 1977–78), pp. 109–127.

4. "Excerpts from Bush's News Session," *New York Times*, June 6, 1989, p. A15.

5. In a piece about the anticipated removal of Zhao Ziyang, Nicholas Kristof wonderfully captured the mystery of who, if anyone, was running China: "There was high drama and some farce in the spectacle of much of the world waiting in fascination for the results of a meeting that has not even been publicly announced, restoring power to a man whose job was never acknowledged to be in doubt, until his existence itself no longer could be reported in the local newspapers." See "Changes at Top Are Hinted As Leaders Meet in Beijing," *New York Times*, May 24, 1989.

6. *New York Times* (fn. 4).

7. Perry Link, "The Chinese Intellectuals and the Revolt," *New York Review of Books*, June 29, 1989, p. 40.

8. *New York Times*, May 4, 1989.

9. See David P. Forsythe, *Human Rights and U.S. Foreign Policy: Congress Reconsidered* (Gainsville, FL: Florida University Presses of Florida, 1988), pp. 152–174.

10. At a meeting of Chinese and American intellectuals last spring, Michael Oksenberg, a professor of political science at the University of Michigan and a key figure in the normalization of diplomatic ties with China a decade ago, asked the question, "What are U.S. national interests?" He then suggested that stability of the Chinese government was one of them, and that no foreign policy should be based on "sentiment," even if such "sentiment" favored democracy and human rights. See Link (fn. 7). Also illustrative of this point are the testimony of Oksenberg and Professor A. Doak Barnett of Johns Hopkins University before the House Subcommittee on Asian and Pacific Affairs on July 19, 1989.

11. Cohen (fn. 3). Amnesty International, and to a lesser extent other human rights groups, became actively involved in the late 1970s following the government's suppression of the Democracy Wall movement. Amnesty has produced some pathbreaking reports on human rights violations in China, beginning with *Political Imprisonment in the People's Republic of China* (London: Amnesty International Publications, 1978); and, most recently, "People's Republic of China: Preliminary Findings on Killings of Unarmed Civilians, Arbitrary Arrests, and Summary Executions Since June 3, 1989," released August 30, 1989.

12. Richard Nixon, "The Great Wall vs. The Fax," in *New Perspectives Quarterly*, Summer 1989, pp. 57–58.

13. See John F. Cooper, Franz Michael, and Yuan-li Wu, *Human Rights in Post-Mao China* (Boulder, CO: Westview Press, 1985); R. Randle Edwards, Louis Henkin, and Andrew J. Nathan. *Human Rights in Contemporary China* (New York: Columbia University Press, 1986); Yuan-li Wu et al., *Human Rights in the People's Republic of China* (Boulder, CO: Westview Press, 1988); Andrew J. Nathan, *Chinese Democracy* (New York: Alfred A. Knopf, 1985); and Merle Goldman, "Human Rights in the People's Republic of China," *Daedalus*, No. 112 (Fall 1983).

14. *New York Times*, "Week in Review" interviews, February 19, 1989.

15. Graeme Browning, *If Everybody Bought One Shoe* (New York: Hill & Wang, 1989).

16. In another reverse from the Carter administration, Reagan officials agreed soon after coming into office to begin selling police equipment, including computers and finger-printing machines, to China. At the time, China's police were in the midst of carrying out a crackdown on the remaining supporters of the Democracy Wall movement and were soon to embark on a massive anticrime campaign that resulted in thousands of executions, many of them for petty crimes.

17. Nayan Chanda, "A Dispersion of Power," *Far Eastern Economics Review* (hereafter *FEER*), March 30, 1989.

18. Nixon (fn. 12).

19. See Donald S. Zagoria, "The Moscow-Beijing Detente," *Foreign Affairs*, Vol. 61, No. 4 (Spring 1983), p. 861.

20. See Jonathan D. Pollack, "China and the Global Strategic Balance," in Harry Harding, ed., *China's Foreign Relations in the 1980s* (New Haven, CT: Yale University Press, 1984).

21. Robert Delfs, "Doddering Helmsman," *FEER*, June 29, 1989.

22. In announcing stricter regulations on study in the West, He Dongchang, China's vice minister in charge of the State Education Commission, said that China's open door needed "wire gauze screen" to keep the "flies and worms" out. See "Improvement on Sending Students Abroad Urged," *China Daily*, September 2, 1989.

23. Robert Pear, "U.S. Sees Summit as Positive Event," *New York Times*, May 15, 1989.

24. For a good discussion of this, see Steven I. Levine, "Chinese Foreign Policy in the Strategic Triangle," in June Teufel Dreyer, ed., *Chinese Defense and Foreign Policy* (New York: Paragon House, 1988).

25. Steven I. Levine, "China in Asia: The PRC as a Regional Power," in Harding (fn. 20).

26. Harry Harding, "China's Changing Roles in the Contemporary World," in Harding (fn. 20).

27. Harry Harding, *China and Northeast Asia: The Political Dimensions* (Lanham, MD: University Press of America, 1988), p. xvi.

28. Tai Ming Cheung, "Force Projection," *FEER*, July 27, 1989, pp. 19–20; also Tai Ming Cheung, "Command of the Seas," *FEER*, July 27, 1989, pp. 16–18.

29. This is the term coined by analyst Jonathan D. Pollack of the RAND Corporation.

30. Levine (fn. 25), p. 107.

31. Jerry Cushing, "Beached Again on Shoals," *FEER*, March 17, 1988, pp. 23–25.

32. Tai Ming Cheung, "China's Bargain Sale: Bangs for a Buck," *FEER*, June 2, 1988; Nayan Chanda, "The Third World Race for Ballistic Missiles," *FEER*, June 2, 1988; Tai Ming Cheung, "Proliferation is Good, and There's Money In It, Too," *FEER*, June 6, 1988.

33. Chanda (fn. 32).

34. Clyde H. Farnsworth, "U.S. Will Penalize China on Missiles," *New York Times*, October 23, 1987; Edward A. Gargan, "Beijing Faults U.S. High-Tech Curbs," *New York Times*, October 24, 1987; Nayan Chanda, "Much to Do About Nothing," *FEER*, March 24, 1988.

35. Geremie Barme, "Political Prisoners Hidden in the New Era," *FEER*, January 14, 1988, p. 41.

36. Orville Schell, "An Act of Defiance," *New York Times Magazine*, April 16, 1989.

37. Bernard Weinraub, "Bush Urges Protesters to 'Stand Up' for Beliefs," *New York Times*, May 22, 1989.

38. See Amnesty International (fn. 11).

39. Robert Taylor, "China's Convict Labour Lure for Western Investors," *Financial Times*, August 10, 1989.

40. John K. Fialka, "Mr. Kissinger Has Opinions on China—and Business Ties," *Wall Street Journal*, September 15, 1989, p. 1; Adi Ignatius, "Bush Brother, Other Americans Are Talking Business With China," *Wall Street Journal*, September 18, 1989, p. 12.

41. Constance L. Hays, "Chinese Students in U.S. Say Beijing Has Harassed Them," *New York Times*, July 22, 1989; Kinsey Wilson, "Intimidation on Campus," *Newsday*, June 15, 1989.

PART TWO

The Conflict of Peoples

The second part of this volume concentrates on conflicts between peoples: disputes between nations or groups in close proximity which are thrust into conflict by economic, ideological, social, or ethnic differences; and disputes between strong and weak powers over divergences in military strength and wealth. Each article focuses on deeply held attitudes that people have toward other people and, at the same time, each article offers a different perspective on the origins of international conflicts.

The opening section addresses the problem of great-power intervention in the affairs of weaker states. In this edition, I have selected two articles that struggle with defining the American role in the post–cold war world. Although the U.S. intervention into Panama in December 1989 to capture Manuel Noriega suggests that interventions may not be obsolete, their frequency nevertheless will be diminished and the role of the United States (as well as the Soviet Union) will be changed. In "What Should We Do in the World?" Stanley Hoffmann describes the changing role of the United States in world affairs in the wake of diminishing American power and altered world conditions. He emphasizes distinctions between military and economic instruments of power and attempts to dissect the reasons for this relative decline, exploring ways in which the United States can adjust by changing its goals, strategy, tactics, and policies.

According to Hoffmann, policies of containment and military intervention could be replaced by policies of cooperation and diplomatic intervention to solve regional conflicts. The United States could also devote itself to solving problems of injustice and inequity, such as Third World debt, apartheid in South Africa, and human rights. The acceptance of the increased importance of Europe and Japan in international affairs will thus lead to a diminished American role—a world where there are problems that "the United States can do nothing about." Hoffmann sees this development as a welcome one."

Charles William Maynes, in "Coping with the '90s," also struggles with implications of the diminished American role in the new world order. Maynes explains why he thinks the "American empire," which was based on "a deference of respect, not of fear," declined. Maynes does not believe that military intervention is a way to re-create this empire. Rather, he identifies four types of problems that the United States must address in the 1990s: economics, security, immigration, and a broad range of global issues, from AIDS to the environment to drugs. In dealing with these issues, he agrees with Hoffmann that military intervention is not the answer. Rather, the United States will have to develop a new international role, exhibiting greater skill and pursuing more complex policies.

In the second section of Part Two, we deal with the rise of indigenous religious and ethnic nationalism. In the modern world these forces have generated important political tensions both within and between states. Despite the seeming popularity of Marxist doctrine throughout the world, ethnicity and religious identification have actually been stronger bases for loyalty and political action than class. Thus, we are faced with a paradoxical situation in which recent technological improvements in communication and transportation—changes that could lead to "unification"—are coinciding with a period of "fragmentation" in which people tend to identify with entities different from, and often smaller than, their state. Instead of causing cooperative impulses, the new world "disorder" has frequently led to intensified conflict.

The two articles in this section deal with two prominent examples of widespread religious and ethnic nationalism, extending from Islamic fundamentalism to serious fissiparous tendencies in Eastern Europe and the Soviet Union. The latter question is addressed in Zbigniew Brzezinski's "Post-Communist Nationalism." As Brzezinski points out, the West has traditionally ignored the nationalities issue in the Soviet Union. However, ethnic tensions in the Soviet empire have risen to such a height that the issue can no longer be ignored. Brzezinski examines how nationalist conflicts have destroyed the illusion of communist cohesion in both Eastern Europe and the Soviet Union.

From the ethnic crisis in Eastern Europe, we move to Africa where Colin Legum, in "The Coming of Africa's Second Independence," introduces us to the depressing multitude of dire conditions on that continent. Facing gross population expansion, Africa is experiencing widespread starvation, malnutrition, disease, and death owing to an economic emergency that has grown out of hand. To most of the newly independent African countries, the crisis represents a failure in ideology and in government. Legum reports an incipient democratic tide, moving the continent away from the single-party state, which was distinctive of the early years of independence for many African states. Legum refutes the argument that single-party states were the most effective means of integrating the large variety of ethnic communities, which compose most African states. He also warns that in most countries of the continent's northern sector, Islamic fundamentalism may be an alternative if democracy is not implemented. Those of us who are concerned about the appalling suffering of Africa's masses in recent years can only hope that Legum is correct when he concludes, "Africa stands poised for its second period of liberation," which will be democratic.

Next, we examine the gap between "have" and "have-not" countries and the problems of exploitation, inequality, economic development, and perceived ethnic discrimination. Algeria's late president, Houari Boumedienne, voiced the complaint of most Third World countries in a speech he delivered to the United Nations General Assembly in April 1974: "The will to gain and cling to their position of dominance over world resources has been the guiding principle in the behavior of the major imperialist powers of the world."

The accuracy of Boumedienne's statement is examined in the first article of this section, "South–North Dangers," by Ivan L. Head. Head offers a view sympathetic to the Boumedienne position, arguing that the arrogance of the "haves" in relation to the "have-nots" will only result in harm to the North's security as well. The gap between the North and the South is growing, and, in his opinion, the North must bear the brunt of the blame. He addresses the issues of population, economics, and scientific and military disequilibrium, and in each case demonstrates how that disequilibrium has turned the South into an arena of abject wretchedness. Head concludes with a stirring cry for the North, in its own self-interest, to aid the South while it is still possible to administer foreign aid effectively.

An example of degradation in the South detrimentally affecting the North is the drug trade, which is the subject of the next two articles. Scott B. MacDonald reiterates the worldwide scope of the problem in "Slaying the Drug Hydra," whereas Rensselaer W. Lee III zeroes in on the question of the U.S. failure to stop the South American cocaine trade in "The Political Economy of the Andean Cocaine Industry." Lee provides a fascinating view of the drug trade which is seldom noted in the headlines. He points out that drug traffickers contribute to both political corruption and economic well-being in several South American countries. Therefore, combatting the drug trade is an extremely complex issue, made more difficult by the resentment of many South Americans at the tactics of the United States, which they see as an infringement on their national sovereignty. Lee argues that a change in the habits of drug users in the United States could offer the ultimate solution to the drug problem: without a demand, there will not be a supply.

The arena of Third World debt is another example of Ivan Head's warning that problems in the South come back to plague the North. "Robbin' Hoods": How the Big Banks Spell Debt 'Relief,' " by Jeffrey

Sachs, paints a grim picture of the U.S. banks' relief efforts in Central and South American countries. According to Sachs, the banks are concerned solely with making a profit, a goal that may or may not assist in debt reduction. Sachs argues that there is a huge difference between the banks' rhetoric and reality. Publicly, they pretend they are helping indebted countries; in reality, their efforts do not provide any relief at all. Sachs argues that the U.S. Treasury has been the banks' ally, preventing the International Monetary Fund from stepping in and acting as a "bankruptcy judge." Until real solutions are provided and banks share the burden of lowering debts, the American taxpayer will continue to pay for an irresponsible debt policy and impoverished Latin American countries will continue to suffer.

From this examination of the relationships between "haves" and "have-nots," we move on to a broader topic entitled "Revolution: The Weak Respond." This section deals with a wide variety of problems in world politics which are not analogous to each other. Timothy Garton Ash, in "Eastern Europe: The Year of Truth," describes the exhilaration of being an eyewitness to the revolutions of 1989. He tries to understand why these communist regimes, which once appeared impregnable, suddenly collapsed with a relative minimum of violence—with the exception of Romania. He argues that the yearning to build pluralist democracies among these peoples was accompanied by a deep respect for "civil society." "The year 1989 was the springtime of societies aspiring to be civil." These peoples want to join the European Community as fully, and as soon, as feasible. This development would help resolve outstanding ethnic, material, and economic problems. Yet, Ash discerns an "ethos of solidarity" that has developed in East European countries over the last decade, which he hopes will not be lost in the new era.

Our second article in this section, "Can South Africa Change?" by George M. Fredrickson, is in an unusual form for this volume: it is a book review of seven works that deal with political and economic conditions in South Africa. The article was written before the release of Nelson Mandela and the legalization of many previously outlawed organizations such as the African National Congress. Nonetheless, it does assess the fundamental problems South Africa faces and in doing so highlights the possible importance of the reforms instituted by President F. W. de Klerk. Fredrickson offers an opportunity to explore a variety of alternative solutions for South Africa's endemic conflict between races, ideologies, and classes. If South Africa is to move toward resolving the conflict in the near future, it will have to address the political and economic issues that Fredrickson reviews.

We continue with two articles that deal with a conflict that is often, and mistakenly, compared to the South African situation: the Arab-Israeli dispute. These articles deal from different perspectives with issues raised by the Intifada, the Palestinian uprising that began on December 9, 1987, in protest of Israeli occupation of the West Bank and Gaza Strip. In "The Impact of the Intifada," Bishara A. Bahbah argues that the Palestinians' strategy has evolved through several phases. The aim of destroying the state of Israel with the support of the Arab world gave way, when it failed, to the PLO's attempt to liberate Palestine through armed struggle. Bahbah argues that the current strategy, a consequence of the Palestinian uprising, is to gain acceptance of a Palestinian state alongside Israel. Bahbah maintains that, even though the Intifada was not planned, it has been more successful than either war or diplomacy in advancing Palestinian aspirations.

By contrast, in "The Perils of a Palestinian State" Steven L. Spiegel addresses the problems associated with the aim of creating a Palestinian state on the West Bank and the Gaza Strip. Spiegel discusses the economic, geopolitical, and security problems that would arise if such a state existed. He pays particular attention to the nature of the Palestinian polity which might emerge—democratic or authoritarian—and to the foreign policy such a state might pursue. Spiegel also details a variety of problems a Palestinian state might encounter, which would likely lead to conflicts with Israel, and he warns that Yassir Arafat's true intentions remain unclear. Only a declared Palestinian willingness for a grand alliance with Israel would have any chance of remaining stable. But Spiegel remains skeptical, cautioning that progress toward a settlement will be at a slow pace. Those who anticipate a quick resolution of the problem are bound to be sadly disillusioned.

We conclude the section on revolution with "Terrorism: A Balance Sheet" by Shireen T. Hunter. In this article Hunter contends that terrorism has not had any significant impact on the Middle East or on any Western country. Although terrorists have caused great personal tragedies and have gained enormous publicity in the media, she argues they have largely failed to accomplish their policy goals. Hunter discusses the policies of Iran, Syria, and Libya and concludes with an analysis and evaluation of potential efforts to combat the terrorism problem.

IMPERIALISM AND INTERVENTION: DYNAMISM OF THE STRONG

14

What Should We Do in the World?

STANLEY HOFFMANN

There are periods of history when profound changes occur all of a sudden, and the acceleration of events is such that much of what experts write is obsolete before it gets into print. We are now in one of those periods, which obliges the United States to rethink its role in the world, just as it was forced to do by the cataclysmic changes that followed the end of the Second World War.

For more than forty years American foreign policy has been dominated by the contest with the Soviet Union. The strategy of containment, defined by George F. Kennan in 1946–1947 and applied by all American administrations since, often in a manner that displeased Kennan, may not have been an adequate compass at all times. The Soviet Union found ways of leaping across the barriers that the United States tried to erect, with military alliances and bases, all around the Soviet empire. Moreover, the imperative of containment failed to provide clear guidance for dealing with a host of regional and internal conflicts, especially in developing areas. Nevertheless, containment proved to be an extraordinarily sturdy concept. It was flexible enough to serve such diverse policies as the original strategy of alliance-building and confrontation, the détente of the early 1970s (aimed at providing Moscow with incentives for self-containment), and occasional attempts at "rollback," including the Reagan doctrine. And while there were constant clashes

As originally appeared in *The Atlantic Monthly*, October 1989.

Note: It is a violation of the law to reproduce this selection by any means whatsoever without the written permission of the copyright holder.

over the Third World between "globalists," keen on interpreting the politics and conflicts of, say, the Middle East, Central America, and southern Africa strictly in terms of the Soviet-American contest, and "regionalists," who believed that we had to deal with the local sources of trouble, the two groups agreed that the main goal of American diplomacy was to prevent the expansion of Soviet influence. In the view of the globalists, this goal required reliance on friendly clients and stern opposition to the Soviet Union and its allies; in that of the regionalists, it required the avoidance of moves that could push local nationalists into the arms of Moscow. Similarly, in the 1970s there were those (led by Zbigniew Brzezinski) who wanted a Washington–Beijing anti-Soviet entente, and those (led by Henry Kissinger) who wanted a triangular game that would allow the United States to be closer to both Moscow and Beijing than the two were to each other. Still, containment of Moscow was the aim of both groups.

The momentous changes of the past three years have done more than any other trends or events since 1947 to deprive U.S. foreign policy of this overriding rationale. The détente of the early 1970s was a limited rapprochement between superpowers that were continuing to arm even while seeking to control jointly some parts of the arms race. It was a shaky convergence of contradictory calculations, in which the United States was trying to impose its version of stability and its own predominance on the Soviets, while the Soviets were hoping for condominium. Despite the defection of China, Moscow was still the center of a powerful empire. Today this empire is in serious trouble, China appears the more repressive and cruel of the two Communist giants, and Mikhail Gorbachev has gone far toward fulfilling the prophecy of Gyorgy Arbatov, the head of Moscow's Institute of USA and Canadian Affairs, who said that the new Soviet Union would deprive the United States of its main enemy.

As if stupefied by the pace of events, many members of the American foreign-policy establishment behave like the orphans of containment— clinging to the remains of an obsolete strategy and incapable of defining a new one. And yet this is the moment coolly to re-evaluate American interests in the world. For many years our perceptions (often mistaken) of the Soviet threat drove our policy and defined, or distorted, our interests. Any great power has fundamental concerns, such as survival, physical security, and access to essential sources of energy, raw materials, and markets. In addition it has what specialists in international relations call milieu goals: promoting its values abroad, or at least preserving chances for the flowering of those values, and shaping international agreements and institutions in such a way that the nation's fundamental objectives and values are served. These very general interests are translated into something that can be called the national interest—a more precise list of concerns that takes into account external factors, such as the distribution of power in specific areas between friends and foes, and internal ones, such as the imperatives and prohibitions set by domestic political and economic forces. In periods of extreme international tension, when there appears to be one global enemy, any move made by the adversary tends to be seen as a threat, creating a national interest in repelling it. A bipolar conflict thus serves as a Procrustean bed: each side's definition of its interests is dictated by the image of the enemy. Now that the enemy recedes, a redefinition of those interests becomes possible, and necessary.

In order to understand what the United States ought to do now, we have to begin by taking stock of where we are—of the main features of the international system in which we operate, and of the main perils it contains.

THE TWO WORLD SYSTEMS

The traditional theory of international relations which professors have taught their students, and which statesmen have practiced, treats international politics as if it were exclusively the strategic and diplomatic game of states as it was played in the days of Thucydides or in the eighteenth century. But the key reality of the post–1945 period is that states play in two arenas. The first is the traditional strategic and diplomatic one, in which there is no broad international consensus, and in which power tends to be used in the way it always has been, usually as a contest in which my gain is your loss. The second is the economic arena, in which a variety of games are played—about trade, finance, energy, raw materials, the environment, and so forth—and most countries, but not all of them, are closely linked; they are interdependent in the sense that even the more powerful and less vulnerable are affected by what happens elsewhere. Here states combine the usual attempts to gain relative advantages with an awareness that this is not a zero-sum game, and that every country has an interest in the prosperity of the global economy and of the other players. Here the logic of "anarchy"—the fragmentation of the world into sovereign states—is checked by the logic of and a broad consensus on, an open global economy. While international organizations are all fragile, and none of them has power over the major states, they are more numerous and effective in the second arena than in the first.

Each arena has its own distribution of power. In the strategic and diplomatic arena, we have been blessed or cursed, depending on one's point of view, by bipolarity—by the dominance of the United States and the Soviet Union. The economic arena, however, has been marked for a very long time by American hegemony. This is still largely the case, although increasingly important roles are, of course, being played by

West Germany and Japan. What's more, here there are major players that are not states but, rather, regional organizations and multinational corporations, banks, and speculators, whose capital movements, investments, and loans deeply affect the world economy and contradict the efforts of states to preserve, singly or jointly, some control.

Moreover, each arena has its own, unprecedented restraints upon it. In the strategic and diplomatic field restraint has been imposed by nuclear weapons. What is new here, as McGeorge Bundy has shown in his book, *Danger and Survival,* is that above a certain level of force, superiority does not make any difference, because there is nothing one can *do* with those weapons (as Robert McNamara has been telling us ever since he stopped being Secretary of Defense). Nuclear weapons have restrained the superpowers from all direct military confrontation, which is quite an unprecedented achievement. In addition, these weapons are largely unusable for political blackmail (for it is hard to wrest gains by brandishing weapons that one doesn't want to use), and the result is that on the very field that is dominated by two powers, they are often impotent. What we find, therefore, is a downgrading of the great powers, a relative pacification at the top, and a continuation of the traditional "state of war" among other powers at lower levels, because despite prophecies about the obsolescence of war, nuclear restraints certainly have not eliminated violence altogether.

In the economic arena the restraints are different but perhaps even more interesting: they are the shackles of economic interdependence. The economies of the main players have become so thoroughly intertwined that any state that tries to exert its power for competitive, immediate, or hostile gains risks creating formidable boomerang effects, as we have seen, for instance, in the case of OPEC, and may be seeing in the future with Japan. To be sure, there is a constant tension between the forces of protectionism—interest groups harmed by open borders and external competitors, bureaucracies trying to save their fiscal policy and other instruments of domestic control—and the imperatives of the open capitalist economy. But, paradoxically, the fact that the agenda for this arena is set by the demands of domestic consumers and producers tends to make those imperatives prevail over the occasional domestic backlash against interdependence or the occasional temptation of states to use their economic power belligerently. This is so because very few states, including the biggest ones, are capable of reaching their economic objectives by what has been the basic principle of international affairs: self-help.

Finally, the internationalization of production—the fact that when you buy a product these days it is hard to know what its nationality is—and the global nature of financial markets result in even more restraints on the manipulation of economic power by any given state. Because the use of force is irrelevant in this realm, its politics are, in fact, an unstable hybrid of international politics without war and domestic politics without central power.

THE DIFFUSION OF POWER

These features have been visible for a while. But some changes have taken place only in recent years. On the strategic and diplomatic front the most interesting trend has been the beginning of the end of the Cold War. Some of the reasons for this trend are external, or international, the main one being the extensive limitations on the effectiveness of force to which I have already alluded. In addition to the nuclear restraint, we must consider the increasing capacity for resistance among the victims of external force, especially if those victims get support from the outside, as usually happens, or if, like the Palestinians in the occupied territories, they fight at a level that makes successful repression difficult. Here recent experiences are telling. We have witnessed remarkably parallel American experiences in Vietnam and Soviet experiences in Afghanistan; the Israelis have been thwarted in Lebanon (which also gives Syria much trouble); the Vietnamese are calling it quits in Cambodia; and so on. Plainly there exists a wide inability to use force abroad for the control of a foreign people. These frustrations lead one to a conclusion once expressed by a former French Foreign Minister (a very shrewd man who liked to talk in apparent banalities): if you can't win a war, you might as well make peace. Thus the bizarre epidemic of peace in 1988. There is another external reason for the beginning of the end of the Cold War. Over time, inevitably, there had to be some loosening of the two blocs that have confronted each other; the compression of all the internal divergences and conflicts within them could not last forever. It was largely artificial: they were compressed as long as there was a cold-war condition, a kind of mimicked state of war; once it became clear that war was being postponed indefinitely, there was no reason for the blocs to remain as rigid as they once had been.

Of course the dominant reasons for the ending of the Cold War are internal. In the United States, apart from economic factors to which we will come, there is what is quite improperly called the Vietnam syndrome, which is simply the marked reluctance of the American public to become engaged in protracted, uncertain wars for unclear purposes in secondary parts of the world. After all, Ronald Reagan, a rather popular President, did not succeed in getting the U.S. public to support the contra war against Nicaragua, nor did the American public support the presence of the United States Marines in Lebanon, once the awful cost became visible. In the Soviet Union the internal situation is far more serious, and there is a rather desperate need for retrenchment because of the economic predicament.

In the realm of economic interdependence, the evolution of recent years has two main characteristics. One is that despite the considerable difficulties of the past two decades, the economic relations among the advanced countries have developed successfully. To be sure, there has been a creeping erosion of the international principles of free trade established after the Second World War. Nevertheless, a relatively open and growing international economy has been preserved despite the economic shocks of the 1970s—no mean achievement, especially if one compares this with the situation that prevailed between the wars. The second trend, which is much more disturbing, has occurred in North–South relations; there we have not been so successful. An increasing differentiation has taken place between the developing countries that have been able to join the industrial world, and whose economic take-off has been spectacular, and the many other countries that have failed, and have fallen more and more deeply into debt. Between the latter countries and the rest of the world the gap has grown ever wider.

Behind this evolution in both fields there is one very important trend, which concerns the distribution of power. The surface manifestation is a diffusion away from the superpowers. But we are not moving back to the traditional world in which *several* great powers had reasonably equal weight. In the strategic and diplomatic field we now find a coexistence of weakened global superpowers and regional balances of power, which are often unstable and where an important role is played by what are sometimes called regional influentials. In the arena of interdependence an increasing role is being played by a tightening European Community, by Japan, in some areas by Saudi Arabia. The aspect of this diffusion of power that is most significant for us here is the relative decline of the United States, to use the obligatory cliché of the past two years (after all, a cliché is simply a truth that too many people have uttered and that many resist). Many public officials and academics have wrapped themselves in the American flag in the long debate on decline. They keep saying, quite rightly, that—if one compares the United States in the world today with the United States in the world of 1945–1950—a major part of this decline is not only normal but has been planned by the United States. Since 1945, when, after all, the world situation was completely abnormal, the United States has done its best to help the economies of Western Europe, Japan, South Korea, and Taiwan; as a result the American share of world GNP was bound to decrease.

However, there is more to it than that. The United States has become a debtor nation that depends on the willingness of others to provide the funds necessary to finance its budget deficit; we are going to be burdened for a long time by that debt. The United States has also seen its competitiveness decline for reasons that are largely internal and that cannot simply be dismissed by referring to the inevitable growth of other countries. The phenomena of overconsumption and underinvestment; insufficient industrial productivity; rigidity, waste, and short-sightedness in industry; and the problems in American education, particularly technical education, which have been much discussed though not much has been done about them, are the main culprits here. As a result the United States is simply no longer the leader in a number of key sectors in the world economy. Granted, this is less significant than it would have been in past international systems, where declining in key sectors meant a dangerous advantage for a major new military challenger. In the current system the United States faces no military challenger that is in better shape than it is. Nevertheless, this decline means that the American capacity to mold the international system of the future is not what it used to be, insofar as technological predominance often leads to wide influence abroad, and technological decline reduces the dependence of others on American civilian and military goods.

BEYOND THE COLD WAR

Given these features and trends of the world of the late 1980s, what ought American foreign policy to be? The point of departure must be the recognition of a paradox. The United States remains the only "complete" great power, the possessor of the largest military arsenal and of the most powerful economy in the world. On the other hand, both the diffusion of power in recent years and the partial impotence of military and economic power because of the restraints on its uses make it much more difficult for the United States to impose its will on others and to shape outcomes according to its preferences. We can still lead, toward goals that have a reasonable chance of being deemed by others compatible with their own interests. But we can no longer rule. Games of skill must replace tests of will. Our waning power to command and control needs to be supplemented by the new kind of power that the international system requires: the power to convince and to deal. In order to be effective, we have to define our national interest in a way that has a chance both of preserving a national capacity for steering toward world order (not because we are wiser than other nations but because there is no other candidate for the job) and of persuading others that their long-term concerns and ours mesh.

We cannot replace a fading vision—that of containment—with mere short-term management and avoidance of trouble, because the present offers opportunities for a decisive change in direction, and because there are simply too many dangers ahead to allow us to stumble from issue to issue in a "pragmatic" way. Nor can we follow the advice of neo-isolationists who believe that the United States ought not only to reduce its commitments and its military presence abroad, now that the Cold War is ending, but also to transfer to other powers the responsibility for dealing with the world's perils. That a great deal of what some call "devolution" needs to take place is not in doubt, but there is a gap between devolution and abdication. The truth is that only our continuing involvement is likely to draw other powers into an effort for world order, precisely because our past predominance has led others to rely on our initiatives and has led us to hug political control even as we rhetorically deplore the costs and burdens that come with it.

We have to define first our goals, then our strategy. Our first goal ought to be the rearrangement of our relationship with the Soviet Union, away from both the old Cold War and the rather misleading exchange of misunderstandings that was the détente of the 1970s. This new relationship will inevitably be partly competitive, because our two nations will continue to have conflicting interests in many parts of the world, but it ought to be competitive without excessive militarization, and partly cooperative on issues in which there will be or already are converging interests.

A second goal ought to be to facilitate a transition to a world in which major new threats to world order will be neutralized. One is the threat of fragmentary violence resulting from sharp internal conflicts in many of the weak countries of the world—conflicts in which others will be tempted to intervene—and from the regional conflicts that still rage in many parts of the world. Some conflicts are likely to surface or to worsen once the discipline exerted on each camp by the Cold War is no longer there, once often centrifugal or nostalgic nationalisms (in Eastern Europe, for instance) replace artificial and defunct ideological solidarities. Another new threat is the threat of chaos in world economic relations, because of mismanagement by states (or the huge problem of Third World debt, for instance), or because of a victory of economic nationalism over the constraints of interdependence, or because of states' lack of control over the economic activities of private parties whose moves could provoke financial panics. Therefore, our third goal ought to be to bring about more order and more justice—to coin a phrase, a kinder and gentler world.

The domestic precondition for these new foreign-policy goals must be, of course, putting our economic house in order. What needs to be done in this sphere is too familiar from books and articles for me to repeat it here. I would only point to the price that our continuing budget crisis exacts from the pursuit of U.S. interests abroad. In Poland, for example, the pace and reach of reform will be less than if we had been able to make more money available to promote political pluralism and a market economy.

Goals are easy to describe. What matters more is a strategy for reaching them.

THE GORBACHEV OPENING

Even though the Bush administration appears to have emerged from its inauspiciously long initial phase of skepticism toward Gorbachev and grudging annoyance at the pace of his moves, much of what calls itself the enlightened public remains extraordinarily hesitant about what to do with the Soviet Union. The doubt takes two forms: fear that Soviet efforts at reform are still very much reversible, and questioning whether the United States really has an interest in "helping" Gorbachev. My answer is that of course much is reversible—in human affairs many things always are, and in politics nothing, not even totalitarianism, is ever definitive—but a great deal of the new thinking about foreign affairs which is going on in the Soviet Union is not tied exclusively to Gorbachev. It appears to be shared by much of a political generation, because it corresponds to almost desperate domestic necessities that are being proclaimed by a large number of Soviet people who have, by traveling around the world and by reading foreign works, been able to compare the Soviet performance with what goes on abroad. This is one of the interesting, welcome, and unexpected by-products of the détente of the 1970s. Also, the new thinking corresponds to a realistic reading by many Soviet leaders and experts of an international system in which the traditional Soviet mode of behavior—the attempt to impose political control and ideological conformity on others by force—yields limited results, often at exorbitant cost; in which the arms race and the logic of "absolute security" lead only to a higher, more expensive plateau of stalemate and to new forms of insecurity; and in which, in particular, the contest with the United States for influence in the Third World has turned out to be extraordinarily unrewarding. Thus, while Gorbachev may ultimately fail and be replaced, while some of his daring foreign-policy moves may be reversible, and while we may have only limited leverage over what happens in the Soviet Union, the important question is whether it is at all in our interest to undermine Gorbachev's innovations. The answer is obviously no, because the alternatives that one can think of are worse: a return to the militarized foreign policy that prevailed in the years of Leonid Brezhnev or a domestic triumph of the sort of Russian fundamentalism—anti-Western, chauvinistic, anti-Semitic, nationalist—that would make any kind of cooperation with the USSR much more difficult.

Thus it would be foolish for the United States to contribute to Gorbachev's fall, even if the contribution took the form of merely responding too grudgingly to some of his initiatives, and especially if it took the form of setting intemperate or untimely preconditions about internal changes or external retrenchment which could only embarrass and help derail him. Moreover, if Gorbachev should succeed, the result would not be a Soviet Union so much more efficient that it was more dangerous than the one we have known; in fact it would be less dangerous. *Glasnost* and *perestroika* are likely to produce a more open society, with a better informed and less manipulable public, with a greater role in the arena of interdependence and a smaller role in the military arena—precisely what we have always said we really wanted. Moreover, should Gorbachev fall after the United States had tried to cooperate with him, we would still have the means to return to our second nature—the Cold War—especially if we preserve our alliances while pursuing a new policy.

Therefore, it is in our interest to respond to Gorbachev's overtures, for all kinds of reasons. First of all, it is probably the best way of preserving the Western alliance; as the instructive few weeks before the NATO summit last spring showed, the more we drag our feet, the more divided we will be from at least some of our major allies—West Germany in particular.

And, then, we should respond in order to prevent the Soviets from getting too far ahead of us in a competition that Gorbachev seems to understand is more important than the classic military contest or the struggle for physical control of governments, peoples, and resources: the competition for influence. We should, when we celebrate the end of the Cold War as a victory for our past strategy and for our values, be careful not to nurture the illusion that Gorbachev wants to preside over the shrinking of Soviet foreign influence and the liquidation of the Soviet empire. In Europe, in the Middle East, in his relations with China, he acts like a man who understands that his country's best chances for affecting the course of world affairs lie in shedding counterproductive or fruitless burdens and attracting broad support, so that even suspicious powers (say, Israel and South Africa) will be willing to acknowledge a Soviet role. U.S. passivity would only play into his hands. Also, we have a chance, while Gorbachev is in power, of achieving with the Soviet Union not only a nonhostile relationship, which already would not be so bad, but also a number of cooperative arrangements in several areas.

Finally, we and the Soviets have a remarkably convergent interest in reducing the burden of arms that are very difficult to use and whose main purpose is to deter the other side from doing something that it has no particular desire to do. First, in arms control, the time has come to close the famous grand deal on strategic nuclear reductions that we might have obtained toward the end of the Reagan Administration, and that a large number of players in that administration wanted. It was blocked by the President, because he could not give up his Star Wars dream, even in exchange for drastic cuts in Soviet offensive weapons. The Strategic Defense Initiative may have been a clever bargaining chip, which contributed to Gorbachev's reversal of previous Soviet positions on verification and on cuts in heavy missiles, but the time has come to agree to limits on SDI in exchange for these reductions. Such limits would amount simply to recognizing the fact that the "Astrodome" concept is unrealizable, that no reliable deployment is conceivable for many years anyhow, and that there are ways of preserving land-based missiles that are cheaper and better than antiballistic defenses. A START agreement has also become snagged on the issue of sea-launched cruise missiles. The United States should agree to the Soviet proposal to limit these weapons, which might otherwise multiply threateningly and without any foreseeable possibility of verification. And the two sides should agree to ban antisatellite weapons.

The reduction of NATO and Warsaw Pact conventional forces, which experts have tended to present as a formidably difficult undertaking, appears far less so since the Soviets' agreement to the framework proposed by NATO and President Bush's decision to accept the inclusion of aircraft, on which the Soviets had insisted. The coming negotiations are still likely to be complicated, if only because of the number of parties engaged in them and the disagreements on the types of aircraft to be included and on the number of states that will have to reduce their armed forces. But the two sides have agreed to concentrate on those forces that are capable of surprise attack and on those weapons—such as tanks and armored personnel carriers—that are primarily offensive, and they have agreed to try to stabilize the restructured alliance forces at levels much lower than the present ones.

As for regional conflicts, whether in Afghanistan, the Middle East, or Central America, the imperative is clear: we must continue to cooperate with the Soviet Union in resolving them without being handicapped by the needless fear that by engaging the Soviets in such negotiations we legitimize their presence in those regions. They are there anyhow, whether we legitimize them or not. The "Finlandization" of Eastern Europe—the granting of internal autonomy in exchange for continuing membership in the Warsaw Pact—is not a fit subject for Soviet-American negotiations: the Soviets appear already to have granted Poland and Hungary the right to proceed in this direction, and evolution in East Germany and Czechoslovakia depends on the domestic situations there more than on Soviet, or Soviet-American, decisions. As for another suggestion that is sometimes made, that we negotiate the neutralization of Eastern Europe with the Soviets, it is most unlikely that they would accept this, and its necessary consequence, a total withdrawal of Soviet forces, without asking for at least a partial neutralization of Western Europe—including West Germany—and the departure of American troops and weapons. It would be unwise for us to accept this, because American forces would be even more difficult to send back to Europe in case of a crisis than Soviet forces would, and because neither great power has much interest in severing the ties that bind "its" Germany to it and to the other countries of its alliance. (Also, could two neutralized

Germanys remain separate for long? And would not a reunified Germany, even if formally neutralized, be a far more powerful and unpredictable independent actor than, say, a neutral Austria or Switzerland is?)

In the economic realm, the real question is not whether we should provide our chief military rival with high-tech goods and military technology; obviously the answer is no. But what the Soviet Union mainly needs is consumer goods, and the kinds of industries that can produce consumer goods. These are not strategically dangerous goods and industries, and are something we ought to be able to provide, in exchange for evidence of progress toward a more decentralized economy. If we don't act in this realm, our allies will anyhow. Finally, we should take advantage of the Soviets' cooperative strategy in order to involve them more, as they say they are willing to be involved, in international and regional organizations—including those that promote human rights.

AGAINST VIOLENCE

In the long run, strategy on the global front outside the Cold War is likely to be most important, and needs to become our main foreign-affairs priority. Much of what we will need to do between now and the end of the century can be grouped under three headings. The first of these is "Against Violence" in international affairs. Here the most urgent task ought to be the liquidation of the acute, dangerous, and lasting regional conflicts that are still with us.

In Central America we are a major part of the problem; we should leave the initiative as much as possible to the regional powers themselves. With respect to Nicaragua they seem to be doing a little bit better than we have done: our goal has been to overthrow the Sandinista regime, and it appears that we have finally given up on it, whereas President Oscar Arias Sanchez, of Costa Rica, and his colleagues can be counted on to keep applying pressure for democratization. In El Salvador it is up to us to make further military aid to the government contingent on the elimination of human-rights violations and the opening of serious negotiations with the opposition; the alternative is endless war and horror.

In the Middle East we are perhaps not a major part of the problem, but we are certainly a major part of the potential solution. There will be no solution if we continue to exert only mild pressure on Israel. The Israeli government's proposal for elections in the occupied territories is one more detour to avoid negotiating with the Palestine Liberation Organization and reaching a comprehensive settlement by means of an international conference. But if we want such elections, they will have, in order to be acceptable to the PLO, to include East Jerusalem and to occur in the absence of Israeli military control and without crippling restrictions being placed on the role of the elected representatives. If we succeed in obtaining free and open-ended elections, we will still ultimately need an international conference, because it is only with such a conference that some of the decisive parties—the PLO and Syria—could be involved and that each superpower would have an opportunity to exert some moderating influence on its allies or clients. If there should finally be a settlement of the Palestinian issue, which inevitably will be a Palestinian state (for the choice is either continuing occupation, repression and violence and the internal corruption of Israel, or a Palestinian state), the other American role will be to provide security guarantees for Israel after the state is established.

Another important priority in the area of violence will be to try to limit the risk of contagion from the fragmentary violence described earlier. This means taking more seriously, and backing with collective sanctions, the reinforcement of the nuclear nonproliferation regime, signing and enforcing a treaty against chemical warfare, and gradually negotiating both with the Soviet Union and with our allies (the latter being likely to prove resistant) limitations on the indiscriminate export of high-tech conventional weapons and missiles. These exports are already making even more dangerous a world in which many states have reached the stage of producing their own weapons—something about which we can do little. Both dynamics of the arena of economic interdependence—the traditional drive of states for comparative economic advantage and the logic of an open market that treats the trade in lethal goods like any other trade—threaten to make the strategic and diplomatic arena more deadly. Contrary to Kant's prediction, commerce detracts in this respect from the pacification of world affairs, which Kant thought would result from economic interdependence and the increasing horror of modern war.

AGAINST INJUSTICE

Under this second heading, "Against Injustice," we have a double mission. Some of what we should do derives from self-interest. In matters of distributive justice among states, economic interdependence means that we have an interest in the progress toward prosperity of many of the poorer societies, for they can provide us either with markets or with refugees. Moreover, if their states should collapse under the weight of debts, our international financial system might collapse also. But some of our duties go beyond self-interest. We have values, and it is perfectly normal to seek to promote them. In an increasingly open world of instant communications the claim of states to exert unlimited jurisdiction over the lives of their subjects is anachronistic and repugnant, because there is a connection between such a claim and the external behavior of a government, and because there is a constant demand by the American public in the realm of human rights abroad—an unease with any amoral foreign policy. This demand sometimes (as currently, with China) conflicts with the cold calculations of realpolitik, or else absolves the United States of its own exactions abroad, yet it cannot be ignored by American statesmen who seek legitimacy at home for their diplomatic course. We do not have to be apologetic about a human-rights policy as long as it is pursued without either hubris or illusions.

The main areas of policy against injustice would be the following: First, we continue to face the problem of the debt of numerous developing countries; here what is needed is, in the short term, extensive relief measures that will allow developing countries to concentrate on exports and to afford imports, rather than having to spend their resources on servicing their debt. We also need a reform of the conditions ritually imposed by the International Monetary Fund, because those conditions have so often turned out to be politically disastrous and recessionary. Any American policy on human rights must seek to be an international strategy; the United States cannot by itself redress injustices against human beings all over the world. If we look at South Africa, we realize quickly how limited American leverage is: American sanctions are not insignificant, but by themselves, they are not very effective. The United States *can* stop providing military and economic support to, or encouraging its companies to invest in, countries where serious human-rights violations take place. Moreover, there are many parts of the world where the United States by itself can have a considerable influence on the fate of human rights: those areas where it continues to be dominant and where it could use the tools of policy at its disposal to prod clients toward democracy and freedom.

FOR A MORE BALANCED ORDER

Under this last heading, "For a More Balanced Order," come the steps we must take in the 1990s to resolve numerous problems resulting from changes in the global distribution of power over the past fifteen or twenty years. We ought to adjust our burdens and privileges to our (relatively shrinking) power, and encourage others to play the roles and carry the responsibilities their power now requires. We should encourage the Western Europeans to develop and strengthen their identity. Whether or not they succeed in establishing a unified market by 1992 is a detail; it is not the timetable that matters but the process itself. It may take a little longer, because the issues of pooling sovereignty over money, taxation, and fiscal policy, for instance, are very complicated, and because Margaret Thatcher exists, but even without Thatcher the issues would be difficult, and what counts is that things are again in motion. Fears that a "Fortress Europe" will exclude American goods are not justified; many powerful forces in Europe, including Great Britain and West Germany, and many multinational businesses operating in Europe, will not allow this to happen. It is in the American interest, in the long run, to encourage the European Community to play a larger role in diplomatic and security affairs, an arena where progress among the twelve members has so far been very limited. If we succeed in lowering the level of armaments in Europe, in agreement with the Soviets, the moment will come when we will indeed be able to withdraw a part of our forces. The NATO alliance will then become more of an even partnership between the United States and its European associates. They are more likely to cooperate with one another on defense if the level of defense is lower overall than the present one. The situation that President Dwight D. Eisenhower, many years ago, thought would come very quickly will finally arrive: we will be able to disengage somewhat, and our allies will engage more. Western Europe has an extremely important diplomatic role to play in the eastern half of the continent. There the American and European objective ought to be to encourage as much Finlandization as possible. Each country in Eastern Europe is different, and it is much easier for the Western Europeans to pursue a discriminating policy—helping with economic ties and cultural agreements those countries that liberalize most convincingly—than it has ever been for the United States.

We should encourage Japan to be more active in international organizations, particularly in world institutions of assistance, development, and finance. Greater Japanese efforts at helping the developing countries would allow a partial reorientation of Japanese trade away from the developed world, where resistance to the volume of Japanese exports has been growing. Japanese consumers are likely to demand that their nation's economy also shift from the conquest of new external markets to the satisfaction of long-repressed domestic needs.

The last part of a policy toward a more balanced order should consist of deliberately strengthening international and regional organizations. Their decision-making machinery—especially that of world economic and financial organizations—needs to be reformed, so that the distribution of power, which now reflects the realities of the 1950s, will express the realities of the 1980s and 1990s. This means more power for Japan and Western Europe in the World Bank, the International Monetary Fund, and the General Agreement on Tariffs and Trade. We will need international and regional organizations as peacekeepers in areas of conflict. We will need them for information and for inspection. And we will need them on all the economic fronts, where self-help no longer gets one anywhere. There, such collective frameworks for bargaining are likely over time to affect the way in which states define their interests—

by injecting a concern for the long term and for the survival of international institutions. A collective defense of the environment is inconceivable without them. But we will also need to strengthen and spread such institutions in the field of security, in particular, for the prevention and limitation of regional conflicts and the monitoring of agreements against the proliferation of conventional and nuclear arms.

A PUBLIC AHEAD OF THE ESTABLISHMENT

There are formidable domestic obstacles to the policy I have sketchily described here. One—with us for so long that it is pointless to pin the blame on any administration—is the disjointed way in which American foreign policy is made. We can deplore this, but we could also try to do something about it, so that the amount of disorganization and fragmentation that inevitably results from our constitutional system is minimized. This requires a strongly engaged President (not one like Reagan, who concentrated on only a few, largely ideological concerns), a State Department that tries to balance the need to pursue a strategy abroad and the need to cooperate with Congress (instead of sacrificing one to the other), and a National Security Council staff that can effectively coordinate, but avoids making, policy. It also requires a sharp reduction in the covert role of the Central Intelligence Agency, a role that not only creates more bad will than successes abroad but also often threatens to divert American policy into uncontrolled, harebrained schemes.

Another obstacle is the disorientation of the foreign-policy establishment. It has become accustomed to American predominance and to the comforting ideas that only the United States has a sense of "world responsibility" and that it has a single permanent enemy and a number of reliable but dependent allies. A world that is more fluid, in which we remain "No. 1" but without the ability to control, is unsettling. A world in which the main perils are abstract—damage to the environment, the risk of a global recession, the possibility of regional arms races—is less easy to understand than a world dominated by a contest between two countries representing rival value systems. The Bush Administration is largely made up of conservative men, whose formative experiences occurred from the 1950s to the 1970s, and while their pragmatism has been evident, they seem, as in the case of the NATO summit, to have been pushed and pulled into the new world, rather than to have devised a coherent and long-term strategy for dealing with it.

However, there is at least one element favorable to the redirection of American foreign policy, and it has to do with the public. If one looks at opinion polls, one sees that the public, while quite wisely cautious toward the Soviet Union, is less mired in old modes of thinking than it has been in a long time. It is sufficiently worried about domestic economic trends to believe that the first priority is indeed putting our house in order. The shackles that opinion sometimes puts on the perceptions of leaders are not apparent for the time being.

In conclusion, in the world we have entered there will be many things that the United States can do nothing about. We should accept this state of affairs and, incidentally, perhaps even be grateful for it. It is a world in which war is no longer the principal and often inevitable mode of change; change comes more often now from domestic revolutions, about which we can and should do very little, because usually we do not understand the political cultures and trends of other countries and often we make mistakes. Change also, now that the pressures exerted by the Cold War are easing, comes from the rebirth of nationalisms. Many of the new forces of nationalism may lead to explosions and revolutions, about which, again, there will be very little that we or anybody else in the West can do. The task therefore is not to eliminate trouble everywhere in the world. Instead, we must devise what could be described as a new containment: not of the Soviet Union (although this will be part of it, insofar as conflicts of interest with the Soviets will continue) but of the various forms of violence and chaos that a world no longer dominated by the Cold War will entail. It is a complicated agenda, but it is at least different from the agenda we have had for so long.

If, as I have indicated, statesmen and citizens now operate not in a single international system but in two different fields, with different logics, actors, and hierarchies and tools of power, the question remains whether this duality can persist. An imperative for the United States is to prevent it from ending in the wrong way, as in the 1930s, when economic power was widely used for either self-protection or aggression. This is why we need to strive for the devaluation of hostile forms and uses of power in the strategic and diplomatic arena, and against a major recession in the field of economic interdependence. Our new strategy must aim at spreading the sense of common interests in the former and at strengthening it in the latter. It will require more "internationalism" than before, and the novel experience of cooperating widely with associates who are no longer satellites or dependents—as well as with the enemy of the past forty years.

15

Coping with the '90s

CHARLES WILLIAM MAYNES

In his White House memoirs, former Secretary of State Henry Kissinger concludes that since 1945 Japan has been better led than any other major country. Over this period, he writes, Japanese leaders simply proved to be more "farsighted" and "intelligent" than their counterparts. Leadership, in other words, can make a difference. Less than 50 years after the nadir of 1945, wise leadership has brought Japan to its current pinnacle.

Today, the extraordinary developments in U.S.-Soviet relations, the Soviet withdrawal from Afghanistan, the apparent willingness of Vietnam to pull its troops out of Cambodia, and the announced willingness of the Cuban forces to leave Angola all give many Americans a sense that their country is on a roll. But it would be unfortunate if understandable pleasure over these developments continued to ripen into a form of national self-satisfaction, blinding Americans to longer-term and more important trends of economic, military, and political significance. For the contrast between America's position in the world today and its position only a few decades ago is sobering.

In 1960 the United States was responsible for nearly one-half of the gross national product (GNP) of the world's market economies. Today it is responsible for only about one-third. For a period after World War II the United States enjoyed a nuclear monopoly. Today the USSR enjoys a position of nuclear parity with the United States; U.S. influence in the Western Hemisphere—so enormous in the 1950s that Washington could overthrow a left-leaning Guatemalan government with a minimal covert effort—had so diminished by the late 1980s that the Reagan administration was unable to force out of office a minor-league dictator in Panama, a country actually created by Washington and controlled by American officials for decades. Perhaps the extent of the change in America's international position can be summed up in a fact and a question. Between 1948 and 1952, the United States provided in today's dollars roughly $100 billion in grant assistance to Western Europe under the Marshall Plan. Does anyone believe that a U.S. administration today could persuade Congress or the country to make an investment of that size to further the country's international agenda?

Reprinted with permission from *Foreign Policy* 74 (Spring 1989). Copyright by the Carnegie Endowment for International Peace.

Note: It is a violation of the law to reproduce this selection by any means whatsoever without the written permission of the copyright holder.

Why did this shift in America's international standing occur? Poor leadership obviously played a role. Few would contend that the United States was well led after about 1965. It was also inevitable that major states like France, Japan, and West Germany would regain a major place in the international system. Crushed in World War II, they nonetheless retained the basic source of their earlier strength—talented, hard-working, well-educated populations.

What is puzzling about the decline in America's global fortunes is a sense not of steady decline but of sudden discontinuity. Something happened in the early 1970s that appeared to alter permanently America's place in the international system, however much American political figures have tried to pretend otherwise, particularly in a presidential campaign. What were the factors at work? . . . It will be impossible to understand, much less master, the new diplomatic agenda unless an attempt is made to answer this question.

In retrospect it seems clear that the decisive changes—those that transformed America from the world's pre-eminent power into only the world's most important power—took place, or came to light, during the presidency of Richard Nixon. The three pillars on which the United States had built its postwar hegemony suddenly buckled in the early 1970s, and none of the compensatory steps taken by administrations since then have succeeded in repairing the damage.

The three pillars were America's basic nuclear superiority, its control of the world's energy industry, and the pre-eminent role the dollar enjoyed in international trade and finance. In the early 1970s the Soviet Union, though still some distance from numerical equality in strategic warheads, attained rough nuclear parity. Meanwhile, the Organization of Petroleum Exporting Countries (OPEC) took control of the world's oil industry away from America, and Western allies began to compete effectively with the United States in the field of nuclear power. Finally, the United States abandoned the Bretton Woods system of fixed exchange rates based on a dollar standard for a regime of floating exchange rates. The marketplace rather than senior American officials began to dominate the world's monetary system.

Such relatively abrupt changes in such critical areas would have adversely affected the international position of any country, however well or poorly led at the time. America was no exception. Yet physical factors alone cannot explain the transformation that was taking place with respect to America's role in the world. Psychological forces were also at work; they are often overlooked but deserve more careful examination.

One explanation for the early postwar successes of U.S. policymakers is a hidden diplomatic advantage that America alone enjoyed in the same full measure: the positive image of America and its system of government in world eyes and the resulting deference toward its policies that many felt in other parts of the globe. This deference helps to explain the special international role the United States was able to play.

Any order, domestic or foreign, requires a certain measure of deference to remain stable. Otherwise police or troops would be stationed at every corner to compel obedience. The issue is why deference develops. In past centuries deference arose from the authorities' willingness to use almost unlimited force to compel it. The British could rule half the globe with only 100,000 soldiers. Whenever colonial figures failed to show sufficient deference, British authorities moved quickly to punish them. The machine gun was always there, if necessary, to snuff out more widespread rebellion. The white supremacy that reigned in the southern United States for many decades after the Civil War also rested on deference. Whenever blacks failed to show the proper measure of subservience toward whites, the hooded riders of the Ku Klux Klan soon mounted up.

In the Middle East, until recently, the Israelis could control the occupied West Bank and Gaza Strip with only weekend soldiers. No longer is this possible. The Israeli army is now trying to re-establish deference—in the words of Prime Minister Yitzhak Shamir, to put the "fear of death" back into the minds of the Palestinians—through the brutal tactics that have convulsed public opinion not only in the outside world but in Israel itself.

Some governments are obviously willing to go much further than others to force deference from citizens or subjects who may feel that the authorities no longer merit it. In Central America and Eastern Europe, governments have at times in effect suspended the rule of law in an effort to make average citizens once again deferential in their approach toward those in power. That has been the purpose of officially inspired death squads in Central America and officially supported show trials in Eastern Europe. And the Syrian government re-established deference by using artillery to level an entire city, Hama.

THE REWARDS OF DEFERENCE

Like other empires, the postwar American "empire" also benefited from deference. Yet it rested on an entirely different basis. Unlike more traditional imperial orders, until its disastrous involvement in Vietnam the American empire enjoyed the advantages of deference not so much because others feared the United States as because they respected it. The deference that existed in the British Empire, the American South, and the other examples cited rested primarily on brute force. The authorities had all the guns, or most of them, and were determined to use them if necessary. Except perhaps in areas like Central America, the postwar deference accorded the United States was quite different. Foreign observers saw America as the model of what a modern society should be. Their respect often bordered on awe because the attractiveness of the American model was coupled with phenomenal resources. Thanks to its overwhelming capabilities, America seemed in a position to accomplish whatever it set out to do. It could save Europe economically, block the Soviets militarily, and lead the world technologically. Most Americans do not reflect on the consequences of this deferential view of their country. Because it existed, for much of the postwar period challenges to American leadership and authority were fewer in number, less in intensity, and shorter in duration.

If the developments mentioned help to explain the relative decline in American power in recent years, are new developments likely to take place in the 1990s that will restore America to its earlier postwar role? In the military field some believe that the development of so-called smart weapons can restore the edge America once enjoyed. The U.S. Commission on Integrated Long-Term Strategy, whose members included such foreign-policy luminaries as former national security advisers Zbigniew Brzezinski and Kissinger, envisaged in its January 1988 report "dramatic developments in military technology" over the next 20 years. According to the commission, the exploitation of microelectronics and the development of directed energy will enable combatants through "greater precision, range, and destructiveness" to "extend war across a much wider geographic area, make war much more rapid and intense, and require entirely new modes of operation." The goal will be "to use smart missiles that can apply force in a discriminate fashion and avoid collateral damage to civilians."

If such weapons were created with the requisite degree of precision, their political impact almost certainly would be greater in the Third World than in the First World. For even if it is assumed that the Soviets would be unable to make comparable advances—a hazardous assumption in light of the history of the arms race—it is difficult to see how "smarter" U.S. weapons could have any impact on the existing military stand-off in Europe except to reinforce it further. Even if it gained a military advantage, the West would be unwilling to exploit it except for defensive purposes. With regard to the Third World, however, smarter U.S. weapons might persuade some that the U.S. military would from then on be in a much better position to use force against Third World states whose policies angered American officials. With such weapons, for example, the Reagan administration might have been in a better position to strike Libya or Syria with impunity because of the support each apparently had given to terrorist groups around the world. Particularly in areas where there was slight possibility of escalation to a superpower confrontation, the United States, armed with smart weapons, could punish malefactors with few civilian casualties and no U.S. losses.

There are important reasons, however, for believing that, even if successfully developed, smarter weapons will not give the United States the edge envisioned. First, in this area the technologists often promise more than they can deliver. In other words, the weapons are unlikely to be as smart as their creators say they will be. It is not reassuring to recall that the United States used "smart bombs" to attack Libya and was embarrassed when they turned up in the French ambassador's garden and other civilian sites, killing large numbers of innocents in Tripoli. Second, it seems unlikely that intelligence will be as smart as the weapons developed. Probably no site was more carefully scrutinized than North Vietnam's Son Tay prisoner-of-war camp, which American commandos assaulted at great risk in November 1970, only to find that the North Vietnamese had moved their American captives before the commandos struck.

Third, it is vital to recognize that, precisely because America's earlier hegemony rested on a deference of respect, not of fear, efforts to use military force to restore the earlier level of deference are by definition bound to fall short of official expectations. Military force may cow a few radical states, but it is unlikely to have the anticipated effect on others. If an operation is carried out recklessly, the use of force can even reduce respect for the United States in the world at large. In this regard, many American commentators overstate the meaning of the so-called Vietnam syndrome. They seem to argue that the key task of American foreign policy is to make others fear the United States again. On the contrary, the task is to make them respect America again. Placing as much emphasis on the use of force as some U.S. public figures do will serve not to increase the respect foreigners accord the United States but to lessen it. The image of the reckless, if well-meaning, cowboy will replace that of the benevolent, if firm, uncle. It is instructive to recall that respect for the Reagan administration was highest when it was negotiating with the Kremlin, not bombing Libya.

Are other, nonmilitary, sources of postwar U.S. power likely to be restored to their previous position of strength? In the eyes of a growing number of specialists, the financial capital of the world has shifted from New York to Tokyo as the Japanese propensity to save has outstripped that of any other major country. Any effort by the United States to regain its earlier financial position is hindered by its new position as the world's largest debtor. The United States must now tailor its economic policies to accommodate foreign creditors whose capital it cannot do without. It will take years to reduce America's trade deficit significantly. Even then, restoring the dollar to its earlier status in international financial transactions may be beyond America's reach, for Western Europe has regained its pre-World War II place in the international economy, and Japan has even gone beyond its earlier position.

America's loss of control over the world's energy supply also seems permanent. Indeed, if the United States does not manage its affairs wisely, OPEC may again achieve oligopolistic control over the world's energy markets. The National Petroleum Council has warned that net U.S. imports of crude oil and refined products are likely to rise from 27 per cent of consumption in 1985 to 30–40 per cent in 1990 and to 47 per cent in 1995. This oil will have to come from existing producers. For even if new oil fields are found, they take an average of 7 years to develop.

What about the factor of deference? Here there is room for constructive change because even though others have shown declining respect toward U.S. policies in recent years, many major opportunities remain to alter foreign perceptions. Events in even the last several months again demonstrate that the United States remains the critical link in the solution of almost all significant international problems. For that reason other states must be concerned with the American position. Wise leadership can enhance America's international image and the degree of its international influence. It will not be possible to return the United States to the extraordinary pre-eminence of the immediate postwar period. But the country should be able to improve on the record of the last few decades.

Past successes and failures provide the setting. Are there new realities that will alter this backdrop as the United States attempts to address its diplomatic agenda in the 1990s? There are, in fact, two: the resource gridlock and the information revolution.

Books by David Calleo, Robert Gilpin, and Paul Kennedy, among others, have opened up an important debate in the United States: Can America afford the international costs of its traditional postwar foreign policy?[1] On one side of the debate it is asserted that the United States is contributing to its own decline by channeling too high a percentage of its resources into the defense sector while its commercial rivals, primarily the West Europeans and the Japanese, are taking advantage of their lower defense burden to forge ahead economically. According to this argument, the United States must move more of its defense burden onto the shoulders of its allies so that the American economy can regain a sustainable level of international competitiveness.

On the other side of the debate are the alliance traditionalists who, while not disagreeing that the West Europeans and the Japanese should assume a larger share of the costs of maintaining the current international system, stress that, viewed historically, the American defense burden of the late 1980s is not excessive. In the words of the most prominent among the alliance traditionalists, former Secretary of State George Shultz, Americans enjoyed their highest economic growth in the 1950s and 1960s, precisely "when our military expenditures averaged 9.2 per cent of GNP, a much higher proportion than the 6.7 per cent we spend today."

Perhaps one reason neither side in this debate persuades the other is that the arguments of both sides are correct. It seems incontestable that, other things being equal, a country carrying a much smaller defense burden will have a commercial advantage over a country carrying a much larger burden. At least some talented people will be drained off into fields of endeavor valuable for national defense but not so valuable for international trade. And at least some of the money that the American government has spent on defense could have been channeled into areas like education and infrastructure that over time could have substantially improved America's ability to compete overseas.

At the same time, the traditionalists are right: America's defense burden, while significant, has not been so great that the United States could not have done what it needed to do in other areas by making an additional effort at home—for example, through economic policies that encouraged saving and productive investment. There is no fixed formula that determines when the size of the defense budget becomes counterproductive.

The key issue, in fact, is political. Both major party candidates for president in 1988 and leading pollsters agree that Americans are unlikely to make the same relative sacrifices for international affairs in the 1990s that they were willing to make in the mid-1950s. But this widely accepted point does not mean that the population has gone soft. Rather, various political sectors have become more conscious of their rights. In the mid-1950s the underprivileged members of American society were less likely to demand a fair share of the national income than they are today. Most blacks in the South in the 1950s did not even have the vote. Neither did many poor whites.

For many decades after Reconstruction southern political leaders skewed the electoral rules to disenfranchise blacks. But to avoid northern charges of discrimination they also disenfranchised whites in comparable economic and social conditions. The result was that while black political participation virtually ceased, white participation also fell precipitously. By the 1920s black voting in the South had effectively ended, and white voting had fallen by more than 50 per cent from the 1876–1892 period. In some years, only a little more than 30 per cent of the white population turned out to vote in presidential elections. The South thus became a reactionary anchor for the rest of the country.

But those days are gone. The Reverend Martin Luther King, Jr.'s civil rights revolution enfranchised not only blacks but also poor whites. Those concerned with the defense debate would be foolish not to recognize the altered nature of the country in which they live. Not only do the poor have a greatly increased ability to press their claims on the federal government, but entitlements and other programs benefiting the middle class have also increased dramatically as legislators have shaped social programs to maximize political support. In an indirect way, therefore, the earlier disenfranchisement of blacks and the earlier high political support for larger defense budgets may have been related.

It will now take a major international crisis to galvanize the American people into making the same kind of defense effort in the 1990s that they made in the 1950s. And the threat will have to be real. Mere rhetoric will not be enough. For another recent trend in American politics has been the steady de-demonization of America's principal international foe. Even before Mikhail Gorbachev became general secretary of the Soviet Communist party, it was becoming ever more difficult for American policymakers, though some tried, to contend that the Soviet Union of the 1980s was the evil empire of Joseph Stalin's era. The sharp public criticism of the Reagan administration's initial harsh rhetoric expressed eloquently the change that has taken place in popular American attitudes.

In the 1990s American diplomacy will also find itself steadily constrained in its freedom of movement by the information revolution, which includes not only the development of new communications technology but also the growing ability of large numbers of people to receive and understand the information sent to them, thanks to education and urbanization. Literacy is key. Many Americans fail to see the enormous political impact that literacy has already had on the postwar world. In the United States, for example, it helps to put the civil rights revolution into perspective. In 1940 only 11.6 per cent of black adults between the ages of 25 and 29 had 4 years of high school or any university-level education. By 1970 that figure was 55.4 per cent. During those years blacks also poured out of the rural South into America's great cities where ideas flow back and forth more easily than in the southern countryside. From this politically fertile urban soil came the chief commanders of King's civil rights army.

Take another country and a completely different system of government. Gorbachev's revolution can be understood not simply by studying his powerful personality and political acumen but also by examining the levels of education and urbanization reached in his country. In 1987, 89 per cent of the Soviet adult population had at least a 10th-grade education. The comparable figure in 1939 was 10 per cent, and even in 1959 it was only 32 per cent. A rural society when Stalin died, the Soviet Union is now nearly as urbanized as the United States.[2]

Then there is the crisis in Central America. It has many sources, but certainly one is the rising level of literacy. In Central America between 1960 and 1976 the literacy rate rose from 44 per cent to 72 per cent.

In the remaining years of this century there is every reason to believe that the cumulative impact of education, communications technology, and urbanization will continue to revolutionize politics and diplomacy in virtually every country. Illiteracy will continue to fall. The communications revolution will continue on its accelerating trajectory and people will continue to flock to the cities. This does not mean that all countries will evolve in a similar fashion; nor does it mean that the results will always be peaceful or desirable. But everywhere, governments will find it harder to control the direction of change within their own societies. They will find it harder to prevent new voices from speaking out and playing a role in policymaking—whether these voices are found in the business community, the academic community, or the churches and mosques. The direct-dial telephone, the videocassette, the short-wave radio, and the personal computer all will facilitate a rising degree of cross-penetration of every political system. The development of the video telephone may even facilitate cross-border alliances without the necessity of travel.

A hint of the future can be found in such different developments as the role of foreign clerics in the politics of Central America, Eastern Europe, and the Middle East; the direct party-to-party negotiations between the West German Social Democratic party and East German Communist party officials; and the new ventures into foreign policy by more than 1,000 U.S. state and local governments.

Governments that try to stop or control these activities will fail. Those that understand their direction and make an appropriate adjustment in their diplomatic efforts may succeed. In the 1950s U.S. diplomats saw themselves as creators or builders. In the 1990s they will be navigators, trying to captain a ship of state whose new crew members are difficult to lead and may mutiny if they lose respect for the captain.

CHALLENGES OF THE FUTURE

Against that backdrop, four fundamental problems face the United States in the 1990s: the economic challenge, the security challenge, the Latin American challenge, and the global challenge.

· In the 1990s, for the first time since the interwar period, economic issues will rival political issues as America's number one diplomatic priority. This shift will radically alter American diplomacy as most observers have understood it in the postwar period. After 1945 America, unlike most countries, was in a position to elevate security issues to the realm of high politics and to relegate economic issues to the realm of low politics. This ordering of U.S. objectives permitted U.S. officials, almost alone among the officials of the major Western powers, to sacrifice economic objectives in pursuit of security objectives. The United States could tolerate trade restrictions against itself if such concessions helped to rebuild Western Europe and consolidate NATO. It could purchase disengagement agreements in the Middle East through massive increases in American aid to Egypt and Israel. It could also use aid and trade throughout the Third World to shore up American friends and weaken American adversaries.

Now U.S. diplomats will join diplomats of other major countries in according priority to economic issues. Can U.S. diplomats be as successful in the future as in the past when they will be losing a tool critical to their earlier success?

A key issue is whether the United States can persuade others to join in common sacrifices sufficient to preserve the postwar economic system. Among the tasks facing U.S. policymakers in the 1990s will be maintaining and improving an open trading system, solving the Third World debt question, establishing a more stable currency regime, and finding new means of ensuring a reliable flow of capital to the developing world now that the United States is unable to fulfill this function.

Resource requirements are going to force the United States to link economics and security in a fashion that administrations have avoided for 40 years. Because the United States can no longer provide the capital and additional market access necessary to revive Third World, and thus global, growth, it must make clear to Western Europe and Japan that if they are unwilling or unable to assume a greater share of the military burden, the new security bargain requires them to take on a new role in the development field. Their willingness to assume new responsibilities is all the more important because the world economy needs a new source of growth, and revived development efforts in the Third World seem the principal hope in this regard.

Finally, in the 1990s the United States and its partners must find a way to integrate the communist world into the international economy. Whatever the future of the current reforms in the People's Republic of China, the Soviet Union, and other communist countries, there seems to be a systemwide determination among communist countries—except for Cuba and North Korea—to participate actively in the international economy so that they can become competitive economically and technologically. Over the long run, the West will be unable to deny them the right to participate, but it is not yet clear what conditions can be reasonably imposed for them to become full members of the international economic system.

· In dealing with security, the second challenge for the 1990s, American policymakers probably will have to work with their allies to develop a new defense structure in both Western Europe and Northeast Asia. Nuclear proliferation, both vertical and horizontal, among states other than the superpowers is changing the balance of power in the world in ways still not fully comprehensible. For example, as a result of the nuclear arms modernization programs being undertaken by Great Britain and France, by the end of this century these two powers will have increased the number of land- and sea-based missile warheads they deploy from the current level of roughly 300 to approximately 1,200. Unless there is some serious breakthrough in national defense against missile attack, this increase will revolutionize the defense of the West. By 1995 France alone will be able to kill 80 million Soviet citizens and destroy two-thirds of Soviet industrial capacity. Britain may be able to inflict as many as 68 million Soviet fatalities and incapacitate one-half of the Soviet production base.[3] The commander of a single British or

French nuclear submarine will have enough power under his command to wipe out every major and medium-sized city in the Soviet Union.

The momentous change the British and French modernization effort will bring can best be understood by recalling that in 1967 Robert McNamara, then U.S. secretary of defense, suggested that the destruction of perhaps one-fourth of the Soviet population and between one-half and two-thirds of Soviet industrial capacity would mean the "elimination" of the Soviet Union as "a major power for many years." Yet the 100 largest cities in the Soviet Union house one-fourth of the Soviet population and hold one-half of its industry. Thus, after their nuclear modernization programs are complete, Britain and France will have the capacity to destroy the Soviet Union many times over.

Meanwhile, according to the International Institute of Strategic Studies, China has on order eight ballistic missile nuclear submarines, with more planned. The Commission on Integrated Long-Term Strategy has predicted by the year 2010 China may become the world's second largest economic power. In addition, India and Pakistan seem to be acquiring nuclear weapons status as well as growing capabilities to deliver a nuclear device. These apparently include ballistic missiles. And Israel is believed to have more than 25 aircraft-deliverable nuclear weapons and has tested a missile with a range sufficient to hit southern parts of the Soviet Union. Other countries are undoubtedly engaged in similar activities. It is estimated that at least 20 countries currently possess or are striving to acquire ballistic missiles capable of carrying a chemical or nuclear charge.

Barring a degree of security cooperation between the United States and the Soviet Union that seems beyond reach, the United States has no interest in blocking the growing ability of Western Europe to defend itself. Indeed, in the 1990s the United States should do more to strengthen that ability. Although it should take no precipitous action, the United States should declare its intention over time—assuming appropriate developments in the Warsaw Pact—to limit its military commitment to NATO primarily to the air and sea, leaving only token ground troops in Western Europe. It should cut the special tie to Britain to end that country's illusion that it has an alternative to closer cooperation with its European partners; and, in continuing further nuclear cooperation with Britain, it should encourage Britain to work with France in nuclear targeting and acquisition.

The United States has an interest in seeing that the transition to a new security order is peaceful. It has a strong interest in preventing or slowing the proliferation of nuclear weapons to states such as Israel or Pakistan that face the kind of security threat that may someday tempt them to use their nuclear arsenals. For that reason, in the Bush administration and into the 1990s the United States should begin discussions, initially with allies and perhaps later with other major powers within the framework of the U.N. Security Council, on the contours of a new security order. Some observers may bridle at the mention of the United Nations in this highly sensitive field, but in September 1987 Gorbachev issued an important statement on common security in which he reversed traditional Soviet positions on such issues as U.N. peace keeping and the role of international law in settling disputes. He developed these ideas further in a remarkable speech before the U.N. General Assembly in December 1988. Key details are still lacking, but the United States has an important interest in exploring with the Soviet Union and other permanent members of the Security Council the seriousness behind his ideas.

Some might dismiss such discussions as utopian in light of the history of the earlier attempt at U.S.-Soviet détente undertaken in the Nixon administration. But it is time that Americans and others understand why détente in the early 1970s failed and why a new effort may have a greater chance for success. There is a tendency on the part of many who have assessed the wreckage of what might be called Détente I to search for scapegoats. The critics of the Nixon administration charge that officials of that administration oversold détente and practiced a deceitful foreign policy that finally destroyed public confidence. Former Nixon administration officials countercharge that détente failed because the opposition exploited the Watergate crisis for partisan purposes and destroyed the ability of the executive branch to act decisively in foreign affairs.

In fact, the objective conditions for a lasting relationship of détente did not exist. This can be seen by looking at the nuclear arsenals of the two sides. At the beginning of the Nixon administration the United States was at the end of a major defense acquisition cycle. Under McNamara's direction the United States in the 1960s had increased its submarine-launched and intercontinental ballistic missiles eighteenfold. For many Americans who did not understand these realities, Détente I meant Soviet acceptance of the status quo, which in turn meant Soviet acceptance of the American build-up and the existing gap. For the Soviets, détente undoubtedly meant permission to catch up. But no American administration could publicly defend arrangements allowing the Soviet Union to catch up with the United States militarily.

By the early years of the Reagan administration, the Soviets had actually succeeded in their effort. The number of warheads deployed on systems with ranges greater than 1,000 miles was roughly equal—about 11,000 on each side. Therefore, objective conditions for a more lasting relationship of détente had arrived, provided the strategic arms limitation talks weapons ceilings remained in place. In general, they have.

· William Colby, the former director of the CIA, has contended that the major security threat facing the United States in the remaining portion of this century is more likely to be uncontrolled immigration from Latin America than a missile attack from the USSR. Clearly he is correct that the former will continue, whereas it seems almost inconceivable that the latter will happen. Yet uncontrolled immigration from Latin America can radically change the character of the American body politic, perhaps at a speed that will create political instability if effective measures to manage it are not taken in time.

Because of sharp reductions in the death rate, Mexico alone must create 1 million new jobs a year for the next 15 years if it is to avoid a political explosion. This is a daunting task, since there are only 20 million permanently employed Mexicans currently on the official job rolls. Moreover, such an achievement has no historical precedent. Mexico did create 700,000 jobs a year during the 1970s, but annual growth rates then were as high as 6 per cent. Now growth has virtually ceased because of the debt crisis. What will keep these young Mexicans from moving north when they reach the age of maturity?

If political unrest in Central America continues, another stream of immigrants will flow northward. Finally, the meager economic prospects for the people living in the Caribbean ensures that a third immigration stream will swell in the coming years. Stringent enforcement of America's new immigration laws will not keep out these millions with no other place to go except the bread line.

A major challenge for the 1990s, therefore, will be to create a political and economic order in America's southern neighbors of sufficient decency to persuade people to remain in their own countries. The Bush administration should develop with its Latin neighbors, particularly Mexico, a massive jobs program to provide employment opportunities to the new generations in their own countries.

Regrettably, barring a major change in Americans' attitude toward the national tax burden, it will not be possible for the United States to undertake this task unless it cuts back its profile and commitments elsewhere. At this point a reallocation of America's international burden can only mean cuts in funds dedicated to NATO and the Middle East, the major beneficiaries of America's current international priorities. The allies are able to shoulder a larger share of the burden even though this task is politically difficult. Israel is in a more precarious position, but in the past internal U.S. government reviews have concluded that U.S. military aid to Israel could dip below $1 billion without threatening Israel's margin of superiority. Such programs as U.S. support for the Lavi fighter, now canceled, suggest that the U.S. aid program for Israel could be more efficiently managed. Most observers harbor similar views with respect to the U.S. aid program to Egypt.

Also affecting U.S. views will be the evolution of the Arab-Israeli conflict. Originally internationalized, it is steadily being internalized. This process can only lead to civil strife inside Israel. The U.S. government has repeatedly proved its willingness to finance Israel's security against outside aggression. Is it as likely to be willing for a sustained period to finance Israeli efforts to repress a large Palestinian minority insisting on its political rights? It seems unlikely that Americans will be comfortable supporting the permanent suppression of another people.

The Bush administration may have a last chance to develop a meaningful peace process in the Middle East before the process of internalizing the Israeli-Palestinian conflict has gone beyond the point of no return. If this negotiation effort fails, the United States should cut back its commitment to the Middle East in order to devote a greater share of its funds and energy to problems more pressing for American security. In this regard it should attempt to deal with international concerns about the security of Persian Gulf oil by probing more seriously Soviet proposals or those of former Secretary of Defense Elliot Richardson and former Secretary of State Cyrus Vance for a multilateral naval role. The Soviet withdrawal from Afghanistan should enable the United States to look at the entire region through a new optic. After all, America's major concern over the Soviet move into Afghanistan was the location of Soviet military bases closer to the Persian Gulf. Now these bases will close.

· In addition to nonproliferation, the United States and the world face a growing list of global challenges: apartheid, acquired immune deficiency syndrome (AIDS), the greenhouse effect, the international drug trade, acid rain, and the steady destruction of tropical forests, which serve as the globe's vital agricultural gene pool. Some of these issues pose a new challenge for international institutions: Formerly their main task was to facilitate the exchange of information and to encourage the establishment of global standards that member states would accept. Tomorrow their main task may be international regulation of economic behavior at the national level. This transformation will open a new chapter in the history of international organizations and will severely test their ability to assume new and daunting responsibilities. A symbol of the future was the treaty signed in 1987 to reduce the consumption of materials destructive of the atmosphere's ozone layer. In that treaty signatory powers accepted the obligation to reduce the use of materials that at the national level are profitable but that at the global level are dangerous.

In addition, in the 1990s the world community will face a major human and developmental tragedy in Africa. It is clear that many of the countries on that continent will never be economically viable. If millions are not to suffer or even die unnecessarily, the international community in the 1990s will have to turn its attention to the task of redrawing the economic map of Africa. Programs must be designed to induce or compel African states to cooperate more closely with one another. Special multinational programs must be launched to secure the funding that will be necessary to save much of Africa from a human catastrophe.

Few countries easily accept the need for a change in direction. Most require a crisis of sufficient magnitude to force new thinking. The 1990s may bring precisely such a crisis. In December 1987, 33 of the world's leading economists met in Washington and warned of a grave international economic crisis in the coming administration—saying that "the next few years could be the most troubled since the 1930s"—unless key countries took actions that now seem unlikely.[4] In the military field the 1990s could bring a dramatic increase in the number of nuclear powers or in the number of powers armed with chemical weapons on ballistic missiles. The 1990s seem virtually certain to impose a serious social and economic crisis on Mexico and Central America, which will adjust by encouraging more of their people to move to California and Texas. Finally, as the AIDS crisis demonstrates, new global problems can surface at unexpected moments.

In short, the challenges that seem likely to confront U.S. policymakers in the 1990s appear so urgent that it does not seem wise to allow events themselves to set the country's agenda. Japan prospered in the last four decades because its leaders faced up to new realities, shaped a coherent national response to deal with them, and then pursued with determination the long-range objectives they had set. With wise leadership, America also should be able to protect its security and enhance its welfare in the very different world that will arise in the 1990s.

NOTES

1. David P. Calleo, *Beyond American Hegemony: The Future of the Western Alliance* (New York: Basic Books, 1987); Robert Gilpin, *The Political Economy of International Relations* (Princeton: Princeton University Press, 1987); and Paul M. Kennedy, *The Rise and Fall of the Great Powers* (New York: Random House, 1987).

2. See S. Frederick Starr, "Soviet Union: A Civil Society," FOREIGN POLICY 70 (Spring 1988): 28–29.

3. John Prados, Joel S. Wit, and Michael J. Zagurek, Jr., "The Strategic Nuclear Forces of Britain and France," *Scientific American* 225 (August 1986): 36.

4. *Resolving the Global Economic Crisis: After Wall Street*, Institute for International Economics, Special Report no. 6 (Washington, D.C., 1987), vii.

RELIGIOUS AND ETHNIC NATIONALISM

16

Post-Communist Nationalism

ZBIGNIEW BRZEZINSKI

I

The time has come for the West to confront as a policy issue a problem that for years most Western scholars have tended to ignore and that all Western policymakers still consider to be taboo: the rising tide of nationalism in Eastern Europe and especially in the Soviet Union itself. This long-dormant issue is now becoming, in a dynamic and conflictual fashion, the central reality of the once seemingly homogeneous Soviet world. Indeed, whereas Marx once described the tsarist Russian empire as the prison of nations, and Stalin turned it into the graveyard of nations, under Gorbachev the Soviet empire is rapidly becoming the volcano of nations.

Until recently, the West preferred to downplay the reality of East European national aspirations and to downgrade the implications of non-Russian national awareness within the Soviet Union. Moreover, most Westerners perceived the Soviet Union as identical with Russia and assumed almost automatically that any Soviet citizen was a Russian. This has now changed. National conflicts have ruptured the illusion of communist brotherhood and the mirage of some sort of supra-ethnic Soviet nationhood. Henceforth, the ongoing crisis of communism within the once homogeneous Soviet bloc is likely to define itself through increased national assertiveness and even rising national turmoil. In fact, there is a high probability that the progressing self-emancipation of the East European nations and the growing sense of

Reprinted by permission of *Foreign Affairs*, Winter 1989–1990. Copyright 1989 by the Council on Foreign Relations, Inc.

Note: It is a violation of the law to reproduce this selection by any means whatsoever without the written permission of the copyright holder.

national distinctiveness among the non-Russian nations of the Soviet "Union" will soon make the existing Soviet bloc the arena for the globe's most acute national conflicts.

None of this should be construed as a lament for communism. Its fading is a liberation for those who have had to live under its stultifying and dehumanizing regime. Moreover, though it proclaimed itself to be a doctrine of internationalism, communism in fact intensified popular nationalist passions. It produced a political culture imbued with intolerance, self-righteousness, rejection of social compromise and a massive inclination toward self-glorifying oversimplification. On the level of belief, dogmatic communism thus fused with and even reinforced intolerant nationalism; on the level of practice, the destruction of such relatively internationalist social classes as the aristocracy or the business elite further reinforced the populist inclination toward nationalistic chauvinism. Nationalism was thereby nurtured, rather than diluted, in the communist experience.

As the communist veneer now fades and nationalism surfaces more assertively, the time is thus becoming ripe for the West to define more deliberately its interests. What sort of Eastern Europe do we wish to see emerge from Soviet domination? Is the secession of some or all non-Russian nations from the Soviet Union something that the West ought to encourage? Should we discriminate in that regard between the various Soviet nations? How should we react if the Kremlin again adopts a more repressive attitude toward non-Russians? What should be our attitude toward Great Russian nationalism, especially as it too becomes more openly assertive? What are the international strategic and economic implications of these issues? How does all this relate to our commitment to the cause of human rights?

II

This large agenda of related issues must be examined in the context of a historically grounded understanding of the phenomenon of nationalism in the Soviet world. While that phenomenon has rather different meanings in the East European and Soviet contexts, the two are also politically related. As a result, they cannot be treated as entirely separate and distinct issues. What happens—indeed, what is already happening—in Eastern Europe is bound to affect the internal affairs of the Soviet Union. Evidence abounds to demonstrate that the events in Poland have directly affected the Baltic states, and mounting evidence is coming to light that the Ukraine and Byelorussia are becoming susceptible to the ripple effects of events immediately to their west. It may thus be only a slight exaggeration to aver that the potential "Balkanization" of Eastern

Europe could be paralleled by the eventual "Lebanization" of the Soviet Union.

Conversely, massive national repression in the Soviet Union would affect adversely the process of democratization in Eastern Europe, but also arouse stronger nationalist passions within the region. Any such repression would have to be based on Great Russian nationalism—and its assertion would be likely not only to have a chilling effect on democratic hopes but also an intensifying impact on East European nationalisms, only thinly veiled by communist internationalist phraseology.

Eastern Europe has only two ethnically homogeneous states—and none without potentially severe territorial-national conflicts with their immediate neighbors. Poland is nationally and religiously the most cohesive, with 95 percent of its almost 40 million people both ethnically Polish and Roman Catholic. Hungary, 90 percent of whose 11 million people are Magyar, is the second most ethnically cohesive country, though more fragmented in its religious affinities. Every other East European state either has significant national minorities or is even ethnically diverse.

The two most diverse societies are those of Yugoslavia and Czechoslovakia. Yugoslavia is an amalgam of six nationally distinct peoples, further divided by differences in religion. The politically dominant Serbs, with nine million of the country's 24 million people, represent the most significant plurality, though their dominance has made them the object of considerable animus on the part of the economically more advanced but outnumbered Croats and Slovenes and the intensely nationalistic Albanians. Czechoslovakia is a federation between the more numerous and developed Czechs, who represent ten million of the country's 16 million people, and the somewhat resentful Slovaks, who for a brief time during World War II had their own state. Both Romania and Bulgaria also have substantial national minorities.

Moreover, all these states have borders that are potentially subject to revisionist aspirations on the part of their neighbors. Poland has a lingering, though not acute, territorial grievance against Czechoslovakia, and Poland itself could be the object of German territorial revanchism. Already in the 1980s, a sharp dispute developed over the maritime border between the communist governments of Poland and the German Democratic Republic, including access to the Polish port of Szczecin. In addition, possible countervailing territorial claims exist between Poland and its currently Soviet neighbors to the east: Lithuania, Byelorussia and the Ukraine. Czechoslovakia and Hungary also harbor some resentments over the treatment of their respective national minorities living within the other's frontiers, and these could mushroom into border disputes.

Much more serious and potentially even explosive is the openly antagonistic Hungarian-Romanian dispute over Transylvania, currently a part of Romania but once part of the Austro-Hungarian Empire and inhabited by several million Hungarians who have been oppressed by the dominant Romanians. Romania, in turn, has historical claims against the Soviet Ukraine over Bessarabia and against Soviet Moldavia, and a potential one against Bulgaria over the Black Sea region of Dobruja. To complete the circle, Bulgaria nurtures national ambitions regarding Yugoslavia's Macedonia. Yugoslavia in the meantime has a rapidly growing and increasingly restless Albanian majority in the region of Kosovo, which itself could soon become the object of Albanian irredentism.

This mosaic of unsatisfied territorial desires and of national antagonism—in itself not necessarily more complex than that of many other parts of the world, including Western Europe—is aggravated by the historical immaturity of Eastern Europe's nationalisms. While most of the region's nations are historical entities, with some legitimately boasting national histories comparable to those of any of the West European nations, Eastern Europe's nationalisms still tend to be more volatile, more emotional and more intense than those in the West. Moreover, the separate East European national states lack the tempering experience of genuine regional cooperation that in recent decades has emerged in Western Europe, starting with the Marshall Plan, continuing with the European Coal and Steel Community and eventually maturing into the supranational European Community, with its region-wide elections to the European Parliament.

Instead, while under Soviet domination and even while their regimes proclaimed fidelity to an allegedly internationalist doctrine, the East European states developed their economies and consolidated their political systems as hermetically sealed national entities. Moscow permitted no real economic cooperation among them. Polish-Czechoslovak plans, developed during World War II, for a genuine federation between the two states were scuttled by the Kremlin, as was the postwar initiative by the communist leaders Tito and Georgi Dimitrov for a confederation between Yugoslavia and Bulgaria. Instead, all lines of cooperation ran vertically to Moscow, not horizontally among the regional states. The Warsaw Pact and the Council for Mutual Economic Assistance served essentially as instruments of Soviet control.

Otherwise, each state was strictly isolated from its neighbors: Barbedwire fences separated communist states as much from one another as they did from the ideologically alien West. Travel was strictly controlled, and so was the flow of press and of educational exchanges. Bilateral economic cooperation was also discouraged in favor of national economic autarky, the latter only restrained by the policy of promoting some degree of economic dependence on the Soviet Union. With Moscow encouraging each state to cultivate both its official ideology and its distinctive nationalism, under Soviet domination East European nationalisms were further intensified and in some cases even warped into chauvinism.

The threat of Balkanization of the region as it emancipates itself from Soviet control is thus real. Economically retarded by the communist experiment, with narrow chauvinism intensified, Eastern Europe is faced with the prospect of internal and external strife as it gropes its way back to a closer relationship with the Western Europe it has always admired. That danger need not express itself in a replay of the old Balkan wars, but can do so through acute ethnic violence, local national clashes and even territorial collisions. The Albanian-Serb confrontations in Kosovo and the Hungarian-Romanian tensions over Transylvania could be portents of wider things to come. In brief, the de-Sovietization of Eastern Europe is not likely to be automatically tantamount to the peaceful expansion of all-European cooperation, with the European Community serving as a model.

III

These dangers pale in significance compared to the growing prospect of truly intense and potentially quite bloody international strife within the Soviet Union. Its various non-Russian nationalisms are less fulfilled and thus even more emotionally charged than those of Eastern Europe, in some cases with less historically defined borders and yet with even more commingling of potentially hostile peoples. Moreover, any attempts by Moscow to satisfy the desires of the historically more recognized nations—notably the Baltic ones, which have been contagiously influenced by developments in Poland—is likely to precipitate claims from newer national aspirants for equal treatment.

The scale and complexity of the Soviet national problem is striking. Of the Soviet Union's 290 million people, roughly 145 million are Great Russians. The other 145 million—who soon will outnumber the Russians because of more rapid demographic growth—are dispersed among 14 main nations with their own so-called Soviet republics, accounting for approximately 120 million of the 145 million non-Russians. Another hundred minor ethnic groupings have been organized or reorganized in a variety of autonomous republics or national regions. Complicating the picture further—and representing a potential time bomb for truly violent national feuding—is the fact that about 25 million Great Russians live scattered among the non-Russians, and more than 40 million non-Russians live outside their ethnic territories. These "outsiders," who number more than 65 million combined, represent the potential precipitating cause, as well as the likely victims, of any large-scale national strife.

Indeed, not a single non-Russian nation in the Soviet Union exists without significant intermingling of Russian or some other ethnic minority (see Table 1). In some, the major potential line of conflict runs vertically—against the Great Russian Kremlin and its local Russian settlers. That is the case, for example, with Estonia (with its population 25 percent Russian), Latvia (30 percent Russian), Kirghizia (also 30 percent Russian) and Kazakhstan (60 percent Russian or Ukrainian), and potentially the Ukraine (about 20 percent Russian). In others, the lines of conflict tend to be more horizontal—either against some other non-Russian minority (as with the Georgian animus toward the Abkhazians) or against a neighboring Soviet nation (as with the strife between Armenia and Azerbaijan, each of which has significant minorities from the other). In others still, the lines of conflict are likely to be both vertical and horizontal, as is the case in central Asia, where considerable commingling exists among local ethnic groups and Slavic settlers.

Moreover, quite unintentionally, the Soviet regime has created institutional vessels that now can be easily filled with nationalist content. The Soviet political structure has consisted for decades of allegedly sovereign republics, each even enjoying the right to secede from the Soviet Union (although, under Stalin, communist non-Russian leaders were quite often shot for allegedly planning to avail themselves of this "constitutional" option). In fact, offsetting that formal structure was the real system of centralized power, located in Moscow and wielded largely by Great Russians, reinforced by a doctrine of Soviet "nationhood" based on the Russian language and history. Nonetheless, the fictional political structure of separate national republics continued throughout the Stalinist era; a political framework for the eventual expression and then asser-

TABLE 1   NATIONAL COMPOSITION OF SOVIET UNION REPUBLICS

Republic	Population (millions)	Native (percent)	Russian (percent)	Others (percent)
Russian	137.6	83	83	17
Ukrainian	49.8	75	19	6
Uzbek	15.4	66	13	22
Kazakh	14.7	33	42	25
Byelorussian	9.6	81	10	9
Azerbaijan	6.0	74	10	16
Georgian	5.0	67	9	25
Moldavian	3.9	65	12	24
Tajik	3.8	56	12	32
Kirghiz	3.5	44	29	27
Lithuanian	3.4	80	9	11
Armenian	3.0	89	3	9
Turkmen	2.8	57	15	29
Latvian	2.5	57	30	13
Estonian	1.5	68	25	7

Note: Based on 1979 census data.

tion of ethnic aspirations was, therefore, ready and waiting for the day of national awakening.

That time arrived with Mikhail Gorbachev's *demokratizatsia* and perestroika. Gorbachev's realization that the Soviet system could not be revitalized without a significant decentralization of economic decision-making and without a broader democratization of the political system inherently meant that the national units would have to be endowed with greater authority. That automatically created an opportunity for long-suppressed national grievances to surface and for national aspirations to focus on the quest for effective control over the potentially significant local instruments of power. Hence, again quite unintentionally, Gorbachev's emphasis on greater legality—so necessary to the revival of the Soviet economy—gave the non-Russians a powerful weapon for contesting Moscow's control over their destiny.

In doing so, they seized on the provisions of the hitherto largely formalistic Soviet constitution. As Article 76 of that constitution states, "A union republic is a *sovereign* Soviet socialist state that has united with other Soviet Republics in the Union of Soviet Socialist Republics" [emphasis added]. The document even affirms in Article 80 a union republic's "right to enter into relations with foreign states, conclude treaties with them" and refers again in Article 81 to "the sovereign rights of the union republics." Indeed, Article 72 even states, without any qualification whatsoever, that "each Union Republic shall retain the right freely to secede from the U.S.S.R." Accordingly, a constitutional framework for the full assertion of national sovereignty has formally existed, almost inviting the increasingly assertive leaders of the non-Russian nations to take deliberate advantage of it.

Paradoxically, the expansion of the Soviet empire into Eastern Europe also helped to legitimate ideologically the national aspirations of the non-Russian Soviet peoples. As long as the Soviet Union was an isolated "socialist" state, Moscow could claim that the union was necessary to preserve "the sacred gains of socialism." But once other communist states had come into existence, even communist non-Russians could claim that there was no longer any doctrinal reason why, for example, a separate but still communist Estonia could not now exist outside the Soviet Union—as was the case with the communist-ruled states of Eastern Europe. The spread of the Kremlin's power beyond Soviet frontiers thus provided additional ideological ammunition, sustaining the national ambitions of the Soviet non-Russian communists.

Finally, the manifest failure of the Soviet system more generally discredited not only the official ideology but especially the practical consequences of the so-called union. Most non-Russians increasingly came to view the very existence of the centralized Soviet state as the cause of their relative impoverishment. In that context, the progressive self-emancipation of Eastern Europe from Moscow's control exercised a special attraction, particularly for those contiguous non-Russian nations located at the western end of the Soviet Union. For them, the gradualist strategy of the Polish independent trade union Solidarity in contesting communist rule served as an organizational model for their own grass-roots mass movements—the Popular Fronts—that have sprung up in several of the non-Russian republics.

Five broad stages can be discerned in the expanding process of non-Russian national awakening and growing self-assertion. In the first stage, nationalism typically has tended to focus on demands for the preservation in some significant fashion of the national language, which represent an almost instinctive desire for national self-preservation from progressive Russification. In the second stage, initial success in linguistic self-preservation then normally generates a wider insistence on the promotion of distinctive national cultural autonomy. In the third, this prompts demands for national economic self-determination. In the fourth, the foregoing combination then quite naturally fosters a struggle for national political autonomy. In the fifth, non-Russian nationalism is but a step away from openly proclaimed dreams of national sovereignty.

Generalizing boldly, the politically aroused peoples of the Baltic republics, independent between the end of World War I and 1940, and in Georgia, a historical kingdom prior to the nineteenth century and briefly independent from 1918 until 1923, are now moving from the fourth to the fifth stage. The extremely important Ukraine, which numbers more than 50 million people, has at least reached the second stage, though political winds in Kiev and especially in Lvov point clearly toward the fourth and beyond. Byelorussia and Moldavia are still in the first or second stage. Most of the Soviet central Asia republics—with their Islamic self-confidence heightened by the Soviet debacle in neighboring Afghanistan—are moving from the third stage into the fourth.

In all of the non-Russian republics, however, national passions are being unleashed. Russification is being openly denounced—occasionally in turbulent demonstrations—in literally every non-Russian republic. National-minded elites who do not hide their desire for eventual sovereignty already dominate the Baltic republics politically. Most of the other republics are experiencing similar pressures from below, generated largely by their national intelligentsias. Moreover, intense interethnic violence has also broken out in hundreds of localities, with some thousands killed in communal clashes. It has been officially admitted that hundreds of thousands of refugees have fled national persecution, with, for instance, 350,000 Armenians and Azerbaijanis made homeless by national strife. In all likelihood, the problem will get worse, rather than better.

The national issue has become the central dilemma of Soviet political life, overshadowing even the economic crisis. It affects and vastly complicates almost every dimension of the political and economic perestroika. It expresses itself in a variety of ways. It manifests itself—as in the Baltic republics—in the peaceful constitutional struggle for the devolution of power from Moscow and even in unilateral legislation mandating the termination of central control over national resources. It explodes periodically—as in Kazakhstan's Alma Ata in 1986 or Georgia's Tbilisi in 1989—into violence directed at Great Russian domination, with strong overtones of a national liberation struggle against the foreign "occupiers." It takes the form—as in Armenia, Azerbaijan, Georgia, Uzbekistan and elsewhere—of bloody interethnic pogroms, unleashing the most primitive passions. And it infects those scores of smaller peoples who do not even have their own nominal Soviet republics, prompting further demands for the national diversification of what is rapidly becoming the Soviet "Disunion."

Last but by no means least, all of the foregoing is made even more combustible by the extensive commingling of the Russians and non-Russians. With some 65 million people living outside their ethnic homelands and thus in potentially hostile environments, the grim possibility has been placed on history's agenda that Russia's empire, Marx's "prison of nations," could now spin out of control, becoming a battlefield of nations.

Such an outcome would be particularly ominous for the Great Russians. Their empire has expanded over the last several hundred years at a rate equivalent to approximately one Vermont (or Holland) per year. In the process, Russia has become the world's largest and—until now—most enduring multinational empire, controlling by far the largest piece of global real estate. Yet for the foreseeable future, the Great Russians now face the unpleasant dilemma that either a policy of repression of non-Russians or a policy of acquiescent passivity poses an acute threat to their own well-being.

To complicate matters even further, a painful nexus exists between the challenge of East European nationalism and the escalating aspirations of the Soviet non-Russians. The Kremlin would not find it easy to separate a policy of domestic repression of non-Russians from a policy of toleration for the East European nationalisms. It would be even more difficult to continue the domestic perestroika while engaging in repression of the non-Russian half of the Soviet population. Indeed, much of the recent national self-assertion within the Soviet Union was stimulated by the successful precedents set by Solidarity and the Catholic Church in Poland. Repression of non-Russian nationalism within the Soviet Union, combined with toleration of it within the Soviet sphere in Eastern Europe, would mean that the external contagion would persist, with the emboldened Poles and Hungarians publicly voicing their support for the suppressed non-Russians, and perhaps with such Soviet "allies" providing political beachheads for continued national agitation within the Soviet Union.

Thus a domestic crackdown would require some turning of the screws in Eastern Europe, even if short of direct intervention. Any such effort would entail real costs, political and economic. Moscow would have to channel its energies and resources into intimidating and bribing the East Europeans, and would have to do so without precipitating highly disruptive outbreaks in the region itself. And the last thing the Kremlin could now wish would be a conjunction of East European and internal Soviet national disorders.

The domestic consequences of the physical suppression of the non-Russians would also entail high costs. A policy of repression would have to be based on intensified Great Russian chauvinism. That, in turn, would breed even more widespread anti-Russian sentiments. Moreover, any attempt at reimposition of centralized Muscovite control would be met with political and perhaps even physical resistance. The non-Russians are no longer the pliant and illiterate peoples colonized by the tsars or the decapitated victims of Stalinism. They now have their own national intelligentsias and their own aroused students and, above all, their own awakened sense of national identity.

Repressive measures would require severe enforcement. That would be likely to jeopardize any serious pursuit of economic decentralization. As a practical matter, effective repression would require enhanced concentration of political power in Moscow, and that would not be compatible with continued economic decentralization. Since even the most modest scenarios of a successful perestroika hinge on enhanced economic activity, especially among the non-Russians, some of whom are the most productive contributors to the Soviet economy, it follows that domestic repression would simply kill perestroika. In effect, repression to preserve the empire would require self-abnegation by the Great Russians. They would have to forsake any dreams of greater democratization and of enhanced prosperity for themselves. The brutal fact is that their empire can be maintained only as an impoverished Great Russian national garrison state.

The prospects for the Great Russians, however, are even grimmer if the process of national self-assertiveness continues dynamically to percolate in the fashion of the last two or three years. If the Kremlin acquiesces while the economic perestroika falters, the non-Russians will become even more insistent on retaining the tangible fruits of their labors, to the disadvantage of the Great Russians. Ironically, to the extent that perestroika prospers, it is likely that the non-Russians—and not the Great Russians—will be its principal beneficiaries. It is among the Balts, the Jews, the Georgians, the Armenians, the Uzbeks and others that the traditions of commerce, entrepreneurship and private initiative have been least suffocated by the Soviet experience. The non-Russian peoples have also partaken much less in the Great Russian tradition of subordinating economic activity to state control. These subjective factors, combined with the objective reality of the greater access of the non-Russian regions to world trade and also the relatively greater concentration of natural resources in their lands, make it quite probable that a successful perestroika would leave the non-Russians considerably better off than the Great Russians.

In fact, stripped of any real degree of effective control over the non-Russian lands, the Great Russian plurality could find itself, quite literally, in a genuinely serious crisis of biological survival. The non-Russians have become not only more assertive but also more prolific. Demographic trend lines indicate quite clearly that the Russians are becoming outnumbered. The approximately 50 million Soviet Muslims currently produce as many babies per year as do the 145 million Russians.

To make matters worse, the Great Russian homeland lacks commercial outlets to the world's oceans, adequate arable land and natural resources. It is also cursed by an inhospitable climate and lacks clearly defined natural or ethnic boundaries. Thus any widespread implementation of national separatism would inevitably produce bloody collisions, not to speak of the mind-boggling prospect of an impoverished Russia having to accommodate millions of Great Russian expellees from the non-Russian lands.

IV

The Great Russians therefore have no choice but to conclude that they are doomed to some form of relatively intimate coexistence with their neighbors. However, the two likely policy responses to the rising difficulties of that coexistence—repression of the challenge, or reactive evasion of the problem in the hope of preserving the essence of the status quo—offer true Hobson's choices. The first policy would retain for the Russians effective political power, but engage them in prolonged and costly efforts to crush national liberation movements, both within the currently Soviet nations and perhaps even within some of the East European ones. The Soviet Union would thereby become a Northern Ireland writ large. A policy of brutal repression would probably also help to rekindle the cold war, guaranteeing for the Russians continued poverty.

The second option—that of largely reactive maneuvering to preserve political power and economic privilege—is unlikely to prevent the empire's fragmentation. In the absence of positive change, the Baltic republics would doubtless attempt to secede and to become somehow associated with the Scandinavian states. That might well lead to a subsequent effort at secession by Georgia, and also to rising demands in some of the central Asian republics for completely independent statehood. It would be only a matter of time before the Ukraine, and eventually even Byelorussia, followed the same route. Russia would suddenly be thrust back to its frontiers of the mid-seventeenth century. The process would most certainly be a bloody one, potentially reminiscent of the Indian-Pakistani population transfers of the late 1940s, perhaps with some painful similarities to the Lebanese tragedy of the 1980s.

What real policy choices do the Great Russians then have, given current dynamics? Quite naturally, they would prefer to maintain the status quo, at a minimum of cost. If forced to choose, they are more likely to opt for all-out repression, though preferably as a last resort. With Great Russian nationalism on the rise, that option is bound to gain more adherents in the near future, especially as acquiescence begins to look more and more dangerous. There is already again much talk among the Russians of the unique mission of their nation, with its historically fated leadership role. At the same time, their concern and sense of frustration are likely to grow as national turbulence intensifies and as the communist ideology—which has masked Moscow's rule with a convenient veneer of transnational rhetoric—continues to fade.

A mood of desperation among some Russians has already surfaced in the course of the sessions of the new Congress of People's Deputies. Speaking in early June 1989, one deputy, V. G. Rasputin, a writer, evoked the memory of the great prerevolutionary tsarist prime minister, Stolypin, in castigating non-Russian speakers with a paraphrase of his famous words: "You, sirs, need great upheavals—we need a great country." To the applause of the deputies, Rasputin charged that the alleged "chauvinism and blind pride of Russians are but fabrications of those who are playing upon your national sentiments, respected brothers." Lamenting the lack of gratitude among the non-Russians for the sacrifices made on their behalf by the Russian people, he asked:

> Would it perhaps be better for Russia to leave the union. . . ? We still have a few natural and human resources left, our power has not yet withered away. We could then utter the word 'Russian' and talk about national self-conciousness without the fear of being labeled nationalistic. . . . We would be able to gather the people together into a unified spiritual body.

Again, the Russian deputies responded with applause, and many would doubtless also applaud a repressive effort to sustain the Great Russian empire.

For the time being, however, the Great Russians in the Kremlin are most likely to strive to preserve the status quo by some combination of manipulative repression, selective accommodation and limited constitutional reform. The first involves the continued application of the tried and true policy of *divide et impera,* playing off one non-Russian nation against another, with Moscow acting as arbiter and protector and even using some nationals as enforcers of its will against others. The second entails some specific concessions to the more established and cohesive national republics, in the hope that their aspirations will thereby be satisfied, but without setting off a system-wide chain reaction. That has already happened with respect to the Baltic republics, which are gaining real autonomy. Such preferential treatment for some could be coupled with intensified suppression of the geopolitically crucial Ukrainian and Byelorussian nations, including even the arrest and exile of the nationalist leaders. Finally, Moscow is planning some changes in the existing constitution, to enhance the real powers of the non-Russian entities, especially in the socioeconomic realm.

Nonetheless, it is more than doubtful that any of these measures will suffice either in resolving or in containing the dynamics of national awakening within the Soviet Union. The old empire is just no longer tenable. The fact is that the status quo, even in some modified fashion, will no longer satisfy the national aspirations of the nationally awakened non-Russians. They may not all be in the same stage of national development, they may not be able to coalesce against Moscow, and they may have different demands and even conflicting goals (notably territorial ones). But their nationalism cannot any more be squared with continued Great Russian political and economic domination, even if masked and made somewhat gentler.

Moreover, as already noted, the internal problem is being compounded by the national self-assertion of the East Europeans. Their success has had, and will continue to have, a direct impact on popular attitudes in the Baltic republics, the Ukraine, Byelorussia and Georgia. Central Asia has also been fired up by the almost parallel cases of successful Iranian and Afghan national and religious defiance of the superpowers. All of that creates a conundrum of problems, linking closely the threat of East European Balkanization with the potential for Soviet Lebanization, thereby vastly complicating Russia's imperial crisis.

V

The specter that haunts the Russians in the Kremlin is that of nationalism—both within the Soviet Union and in Eastern Europe. The only constructive response to that condition is for the Russian people to be given the opportunity to shed their messianic complexes—either that of a Third Rome or of some "internationalist" Leninist mission—and to accommodate themselves to the necessity of coequal cohabitation with other nations. After three hundred years of almost continuous expansion, but now increasingly showing symptoms of imperial fatigue, the Russian people would be the principal beneficiaries of such a change in their national ethos.

The West can especially help the Russians at this crucial historical juncture by not only articulating positive visions of a confederated but nonthreatening Germany, of a regionally more cooperative Eastern Europe engaged in all-Europe institutions, and of a post-imperial Russia within a Soviet confederation, but also by indicating its readiness to assist very tangibly the translation of such visions into a mutually beneficial reality. Over the years, the West has propagated pluralism, democracy and the market system as the superior social combination—while the Soviet propagandists derided these notions. Yet today these ideas dominate even Soviet discussions of perestroika. Similarly, the West should now take the lead in advocating open and voluntary confederation arrangements as the only solution to the potentially lethal challenges of nationalism in the emerging post-communist era.

17

The Coming of Africa's Second Independence

COLIN LEGUM

Signs of mounting discontent across the entire African continent are reminiscent of the anticolonial storm that gathered after World War II and bear some resemblance to the current movement of dissent in Eastern Europe. Whereas the anticolonial movement spearheaded a revolt against alien rule, the present targets are the postindependence African ruling classes and, especially, the political systems they built and now defend. Although challenges to rulers and regimes have been endemic ever since the first army coup d'état in Togo against President Sylvanus Olympio in January 1963, the significant difference now is the thrust of opposition against the existing *political systems* and not just against a particular ruler or regime.

During the first 30 years of postcolonial independence, the overthrow of rulers and regimes seldom produced fundamental change, despite outward changes in the style of government and an often temporary rearrangement of priorities. In 28 of the continent's 51 states civilian

Reprinted from *Washington Quarterly*, Winter 1990, by permission of the MIT Press.

Note: It is a violation of the law to reproduce this selection by any means whatsoever without the written permission of the copyright holder.

governments were overthrown by military coups d'état that were primarily bloodless; but military regimes were composed more of co-opted civil servants than soldiers. The military used its power to exercise authority but, with few exceptions such as Niger under Lieutenant Colonel Seyni Kountche, military governments had little influence, mostly because they lacked the consent of an electorate. Even the initial popularity that often greeted the overthrow of an unpopular regime quickly evaporated because of the harshness and general ineffectiveness of military rule.

With only three notable exceptions—Burkina Faso under Thomas Sankara, Ghana under Jerry Rawlings, and Ethiopia under Mengistu Haile Mariam—no serious attempt was made to create new institutions with political and economic programs that differed radically from those of their predecessors. Sankara survived for less than four years, and his assassination ended his radical reform policies. Rawlings has lasted for 10 years, but he has shifted away from his Nkrumaist socialist ideas, becoming one of the favorites of the International Monetary Fund (IMF).[1] In Ethiopia—the only African country where a serious attempt has been made to build a structured Marxist state—the revolution has been obstructed, probably permanently, by the obdurate resistance of nationalist forces in Eritrea, Tigre, and Oromo-inhabited regions. Of all the states beyond the borders of sub-Saharan Africa, only Libya so far has succeeded in creating a wholly different system—the *Jamahiriya*—that has existed since 1977; but this theoretically decentralized system of power exercised by people's committees actually is dependent on the leadership of the idiosyncratic Colonel Mu'ammar Qadhafi, and it is unlikely to survive his personal rule.

Military coups also produced relatively brief tyrannical dictatorships in Uganda under Idi Amin, the Central African Empire (now the Central African Republic) under Emperor Jean-Bedel Bokassa, and Equatorial Guinea under Francisco Macias Nguema. These three nasty regimes, relatively short-lived, were aberrations both in their brutality and in the fact of their being the only properly classified dictatorships to have emerged in sub-Saharan Africa. These three exceptions gave rise to the popular Western misconception of Africa as a whole being under despotic rule.

The first 30 years of African independence witnessed two major political phenomena: the rise of the single-party state and army coups d'état. The latter have occurred with the breakdown in postcolonial institutions, when internal conflicts, economic failure, corruption, nepotism, and repressive laws paralyzed governments and provoked varying degrees of popular discontent. The rise of the single-party state, on the other hand, was a response to the political, economic, and security problems that faced postindependence leaders.

THE POLITICAL PHENOMENON OF THE SINGLE-PARTY STATE

Upon independence, the former colonies that had achieved independence without a violent struggle against the metropolitan power adopted a multiparty parliamentary system fashioned along Western democratic lines. One notable exception was Tanganyika (now Tanzania), whose ruling party won over 95 percent of the vote in preindependence elections supervised by the colonial power; this gave some legitimacy to its decision to turn the country into a single-party state. Only six countries have maintained multiparty parliamentary systems with regular and, more or less, free elections: Botswana, The Gambia, Djibouti, Mauritius, Tunisia, and (arguably) Morocco. These exceptions suggest that multiparty political systems can be maintained, even in societies as culturally cleaved as Mauritius and Djibouti, and perform at least as well as, if not better than, most single-party states.

Although it is convenient to speak of the "single-party state," there are substantial differences among the states. Some countries with one-party rule, like Tanzania, provide for a reasonable level of genuine democratic participation in the election and deselection of members of parliament, while others such as Uganda, Burundi, Zaïre, and Somalia lack any democratic pretensions.

Protagonists of the single-party state advance several reasons for its advantage over multiparty democracies in developing societies. Former president Julius Nyerere of Tanzania and others have argued that consensus politics is the traditional form of government in precolonial African societies. This is a myth.[2] Some claim that democracy is a luxury that developing societies cannot afford because of the curbs on policy-making imposed by often ethnically centered oppositional politics. Others claim that the task of nation-building in new states—themselves not yet nation-states—is retarded by allowing free play to political parties that, in the nature of most Third World countries, are ethnically or regionally based. A combination of these three reasons provides the rationale for the claim that new states in their formative stage of becoming nation-states, during a period of rapid modernization and in urgent need of economic growth, demand single-party rule. Accordingly, the one-party governments will allow for as large an element of democracy as is thought will not obstruct the objectives of national unity and economic growth.

Without, for the moment, examining the merits of single-party rule over a multiparty democracy, it must be conceded that some of the more fragile, young sovereign states would have fallen prey to civil war or violent conflicts, might have risked splitting up into one or more separate states, or might have been consumed by ethnically charged politics. One example of an arguably justified decision to move toward single-party rule was the agreement by Zimbabwe's two major leaders, Robert

Mugabe of the ruling Zimbabwe African National Union (ZANU) and Joshua Nkomo of the Zimbabwe African People's Union (ZAPU), to merge their parties as a means of healing the breach between the Shona and Ndebele people. Their decision certainly has helped to ease one major problem, but it has exacerbated others. For example, the merger led to the breakaway of one of ZANU's founding leaders, Edgar Tekere, who formed his own left-wing opposition party.

With only few exceptions, crises occured in the new African states within months of their independence and at a time when the new governments still were struggling to establish themselves. The origin of these postindependence crises was the political composition of the anticolonial liberation movement. In the majority of cases, there were coalitions between left-wing and right-wing parties and of different ethnic and regional groups. Once the colonial rule was driven out, the interests of the different groups that formed the new government diverged. This resulted in the breakup of most independence movements, made for serious and often ethnically based conflict, and destabilized the new state. Therefore, the rapid shift of many African governments from the parliamentary system inherited from the colonial period to a single-party system is understandable. In many cases, however, this move was made not because of any serious danger to the state, but simply in order to entrench the power of a particular ruling group.

Single-party states diverge from each other not only in different levels of their democratic content, but also in their choice of economic systems. For example, Côte d'Ivoire, Gabon, Cameroon, and Kenya opted for private enterprise, and free market, and foreign capital and entrepreneurial assistance; other states, including Algeria and Tanzania, opted for non-Marxist socialism; a few countries nailed their flag to the Marxist mast. This last group, confined to small francophone countries like Benin and the Congo, used Marxist rhetoric but made no serious attempt to create the structures of a Marxist state. Ethiopia, as already mentioned, was the exception. Although the liberation movements of Angola and Mozambique were committed to Marxism, the civil wars and economic collapse the two countries have faced since independence have impeded the implementation of such ideology.

Irrespective of whether the ruling parties were pro-capitalist or pro-socialist, they created parastatal corporations to take control of their principal resources and financial institutions. A basic reason for this continental pattern was the perceived need to replace the former colonial control over major economic sectors with an economic instrument of the state in order to achieve effective control over the policies and revenues of the major wealth-earning crops, minerals, and enterprises, thereby establishing national priorities for both economic and social development. Unfortunately, these parastatals mushroomed into large, centralized bureaucracies that were quite often corrupt and in many, if not most, cases inefficient. In some countries, these parastatals became so powerful that they were virtual states within the state. Because of their inflexible bureaucracies and particular priorities for investment and developments, instead of being the motor to drive the economy forward, the parastatals had become a major obstacle to developments.

Those governments that had opted for the socialist path of development saw the parastatals as the means of gaining control over the major components of the economy—a lesson learned from the Labour Party in Great Britain and the Socialist Party in France. In spite of whatever benefits there may be to nationalized industries in the West European countries, the developing countries mostly lacked the expertise to manage large corporations and the governmental institutions to monitor and control them. Thus, instead of building socialist institutions, most African countries succeeded only in establishing state capitalism, in an inefficient version more appropriately named unfree capitalism. The expensive failure of the parastatal policy was one major cause of economic decline and helped to discredit governments. In a speech delivered to the University of Zimbabwe in Harare, Julius Nyerere admitted that if there were a parliamentary opposition in Tanzania, many of the malpractices and inefficiencies of parastatals might have been avoided, but he added that the disadvantages of oppositional politics outweighed the advantage of having a watchdog to prevent the slackness, nepotism, and corruption of single-party rule.[3]

All African governments currently are engaged in either privatizing their parastatals, substantially reducing their number, or turning them into joint state–private sector enterprises as part of the IMF structural adjustment programs. Africa's experience with parastatals is one expensive lesson about the advantages of an open society, where a parliament, political parties, professional and other associations, and the media are free to criticize government policies. Now that most African governments increasingly are adopting free enterprise or market economy systems, the logical question is whether it is feasible to open up the economy without also opening up the political system. Mikhail Gorbachev's twin policies of glasnost and perestroika demonstrate an understanding of the reality that one cannot be accomplished without the other, whereas the Chinese leaders' attempt to open up the economy while maintaining a party dictatorship led to the disaster of Tiananmen Square.

Two major claims were made for the advantages of a single-party state in a developing society. First, the one-party state system was claimed to be the most effective way of integrating a large variety of ethnic communities and of harmonizing the interests of the modern urban sector with the traditional rural sector. Second, the system was deemed to offer the quickest way of promoting balanced economic development. After the experience of 30 years, both of these claims appear to be seriously flawed. There is no evidence that the half-dozen African states that have retained multiparty parliamentary systems have fared worse in the promotion of national unity or economic development than those governed by a single ruling party. Botswana with its nine ethnic groups and Mauritius with its dynamic heterogeneous society are, in many respects, prospering more than most other countries. The experience of other countries has been like that of Kenya, which today is more ethnically divided than before the government of President Daniel T. arap Moi turned the country into a single-party state.

It might be argued that it is easier to maintain a democratic system in small countries such as Botswana and Mauritius rather than in larger ones. If this were the case, if tiny Djibouti can be democratic, then why not the minuscule Comoros; and if in The Gambia why not in Gabon? If a country the size of Senegal with its acute cultural and sectarian diversities is now democratic then why not the other smaller countries in the region, Sierra Leone and Liberia, for example? Size and the degree of cultural cleavage in societies are undoubtedly important factors that determine the governability of states. Yet, India, one of the world's largest and most culturally divided countries, has managed to retain a multiparty parliamentary system for almost 40 years. Explanations other than just size and cultural diversities must be sought to justify the single-party state. Its protagonists have been put on the defensive over their failure to justify the claim that the suppression of opposition parties is necessary in order to achieve rapid economic growth.

Nevertheless, the fact that most sub-Saharan African countries are worse off today than they were a decade ago cannot be ascribed simply to their political systems. Adverse international factors affecting commodity prices, an inequitable world trading system, the quadrupling of oil and fertilizer prices, drought, locust plagues, and other deleterious climatic conditions have all contributed to the grave decline in most African countries.[4] Still, these negative factors, although beyond the control of local governments, need not have been so severe were it not for the failure of governmental policies and the unresponsiveness of state bureaucracies to popular opinion, especially from the peasantry that constitutes over 70 percent of the population of most sub-Saharan countries. Ethiopia, to cite but one example, is in desperate economic straits not just because of drought and eroded land, but because a tiny elite of soldiers and intellectuals have remained determined to nail down an unpopular Marxist system on an unwilling population, instead of tackling the fundamental problem of establishing a viable constitution acceptable to a majority of Ethiopians and Eritreans. Sudan is wallowing in war, misery, and economic hardship because a section of the community is intent on imposing the *Shari'a* (Islamic law) on both the sizable non-Muslim minority in the south and on the influential secularists in the Muslim north.

Wars are now being fought in several parts of the continent—not for revolutionary ideologies, but in the name of democracy. Today, the advent of the end of the first period of African liberation—from colonial or other forms of alien rule or domination—is heralding the beginning of a second period of liberation from unpopular, unsuccessful, and undemocratic governments. It is a time of turbulence and uncertainty. What will result from this transitional period is still unclear. It is clear, however, that the tide is turning against the political systems devised to cope with the difficult problems of the immediate postcolonial era.

THE DEMOCRATIC TIDE

The evidence that Africa has reached a watershed between the first and second periods of its liberation is to be found in five developments: the breakdown of political and economic institutions; the growing number of countries abandoning the experiment in single-party states; the establishment of centers for the promotion of pluralist political systems in the continent; the growing chorus of outspoken dissent from single-party rule; and the spread of a human rights movement initiated by Africans themselves. Each of these developments merits separate consideration, although they are directly interconnected.

Over the last three years, the number of countries with a multiparty political system has increased from six to eight, with a ninth, Nigeria, now poised to return to parliamentary democracy. In two of the six countries that previously had maintained a framework of parliamentary democracy, Morocco and Tunisia, the scope for broader political security has been enlarged. The two countries that have abandoned single-party rule are Senegal and Algeria. The Algerian change is particularly significant because following the country's emergence from a long and bitter independence struggle as a single-party state in 1962, it rigorously had repressed any sign of serious political dissent. The extent of the existence of clandestine opposition was revealed when no fewer than 20 political parties surfaced after the ban against them was lifted. With the transformation of Algeria's political system, the entire North African littoral (except for Libya), now possesses the rudiments of parliamentary democracy.

Senegal, which had a brief flirtation with single-party rule, now displays a vibrant, open political system with no fewer than 17 competing parties (seven of them Marxist factions). This new system already has stood the test of two elections. Nigeria—the continent's most populous state with almost 100 million people, 4 distinct national groups, and over 20 sizable minority groups—is set to return to parliamentary government in 1992. Four military governments failed to quell the popular demand for democracy. Instead, they fueled the unpopularity of nonelective governments. Especially encouraging about developments in Nigeria is that it is the only African country that has taken steps to devolve central power by expanding its federal system.

Sudan's experience closely resembles that of Nigeria. Successive attempts to institutionalize military-political regimes have ended in failure; each failure has resulted in a return to civilian government. The country is once again under military rule, but after only a relatively short period signs have emerged that it will fare no better than its predecessors. The bitter armed struggle waged by the Sudan People's Liberation Movement (and the Sudan People's Liberation Army [SPLA]) led by Ohio University trained Dr. John Garang, has as its goal the creation of a democratic, secular Sudan. The earlier civil war between the predominantly Muslim north and the non-Muslim south has given way to a national struggle to establish a single united nation under a democratic parliamentary government.

This trend away from the single-party state is infectious, inspiring the growth of democratic opposition in other African countries. The earlier taboos that inhibited challenges to the notion that Africans are better governed under single-party rule are being eroded. It is no longer fashionable to accuse those favoring democratic parliamentary systems of wishing to imitate Western political systems. In the current political debate, emphasis is placed on the universality of principles that govern democratic parliamentary institutions.

The impression that parliamentary democracy was a foreign-inspired import to the continent undoubtedly was strengthened in the past by Western-based organizations that pressed for African democracy, including Harvard University's Center for African Democracy and the National Endowment for Democracy (NED) funded by the U.S. Congress since 1983. Under their auspices, African politicians and intellectuals were invited to seminars held in the United States. Now, centers for studying and promoting democratic ideas are establishing their own bases on African soil. The Center for the Study of Research of Pluralistic Democracy in the Third World has been established in Dakar, Senegal under the presidency of Jacques Mariel Nzouankeu, a professor of law and economics at Cheikh Anta Diop University. In a recent speech, Nzouankeu spoke of an "atlas of democracies" beginning to spread across the continent and citing recent elections in a half-a-dozen countries, he commented: "In every case, democratic principles were put to the test . . . and in every case those countries showed that they are moving away from authoritarianism and towards greater democracy."[5] The former Nigerian Head of State General Olusegun Obasanjo has established the Africa Leadership Forum at his successful poultry farm in Ota, Nigeria. At the inauguration of the Forum, the General described its aim as preparing African leaders for the task of undertaking the "profound changes" necessary to halt the backward movement of the continent and to correct "our false political start." The problems now facing Africa, he added, "stem from a human failure to establish institutions that make for a human society . . . . In the last resort, only we ourselves know what is really amiss with us and, what is more, only we Africans can tell it as it is to ourselves."[6] A number of other centers for the study and promotion of democracy are emerging in other parts of the continent.

This movement for democracy is fueled by the increasingly outspoken dissent expressed by academics, journalists, and politicians in books, articles, and seminars. Writers like the Nobel prize winner Wole Soyinka of Nigeria are in the forefront of the campaign against misgovernment and abuses of human rights. It is not enough, they say, to inveigh against the misdeeds of the apartheid regime in South Africa while ignoring the offenses of African governments. Among those in the vanguard of the demand for the creation of open societies are politicians who earlier were prominent in boosting the advantages of single-party states but who have themselves become victims of their system. Edem Kodjo, the former secretary general of the Organization of African Unity (OAU), who is now in exile in France, has severely attacked African leadership in a recent book.[7] Another former African minister, Abdulrahman Mohamed Babu, who first came to prominence as a leader of the Zanzibar revolution, was later detained for seven years in Tanzania. His political writings in the London-based *African Events* and in other publications argue passionately for the need for political democracy. A dozen African academics, who organized a workshop in Kenya to review the past and future of democracy, recently produced the book *Democratic Theory and Practice in Africa*.[8] Peter Wanyande, a lecturer in government at the University of Nairobi, summed up their conclusions:

> Partly as a result of their failure to meet the popular and legitimate demands of the people, the one-party states have not only become sensitive and insecure, but also very oppressive and unresponsive to the demands of the mass of people whom they rule. They have tended to control and limit the rights and freedoms of the people who would want to participate voluntarily in the political life of the nation. Institutions such as parliaments have been rendered largely ineffective as sources of legitimacy for government decisions. The people, therefore, no longer control and limit governmental authority in the one-party states of Africa.[9]

The fact that these intellectuals, who were mainly from Kenya, had the courage to launch a methodical attack on the idea of a single ruling party in a country whose leadership is particularly "sensitive and insecure" is representative of the resolution and concern of the great majority of the continent's intellectuals who, today, fill the void created in most single-party states that deprive ordinary people of effective participation. The situation is better in a country like Tanzania where the *wananji* (the ordinary people) do enjoy the right to select and deselect their parliamentary representatives, but where other essential aspects of democratic government, including a free press and the right to organize opposition parties, are absent.

President Jimmy Carter was correct in making human rights an essential feature of U.S. foreign policy. Despite the inability of his and subsequent administrations to apply the principle consistently, the focus has given a fillip to the human rights movement in the Third World and has provided a cutting edge to the campaign for wider democratic rights. Speaking up for human rights has become respectable and hard to oppose, except by such uncaring despots as Zaïre's President Mobutu Sese Seko who, especially in the post-Carter administration, has been allowed to get away with murder, figuratively speaking. It is no longer possible to campaign for human rights without linking them to the abuse of undemocratic governments. The growth of the human rights movement in Africa is an intrinsic element in the growth of the democratic movement.

That human rights is an idea whose time has come is evidenced by the OAU's adoption of the *Charter of Human and People's Rights* that has been ratified by over two-thirds of its 51 member states. Notable among those who have so far refused to ratify the Charter are the governments of Colonel Mu'ammar Qadhafi of Libya and President Mengistu Haile Mariam of Ethiopia. The African Commission for Human and People's Rights (ACHPR) has been established with headquarters in Banjul, The Gambia, in recognition of President Dawda Jawara's initiation of the Charter. The purpose of the ACHPR as outlined at the 1989 OAU summit is to make Africans aware of and to promote their rights and obligations, and to ensure that these are properly protected. Just how these rights are to be protected properly in those countries that imprison and subsequently often torture dissenters remains to be tested. Two years after its establishment, the Commission so far has received 30 complaints that are still under investigation. The 11-member Commission has been selected by the OAU heads of state for "their integrity and morality." It appears that the first 11 measure up to those standards. Ten years ago, the idea of such a Charter and Commission was inconceivable; that these pan-African institutions exist today is a measure of the changing climate of political opinion in the continent.

The African Lawyers Association, whose membership includes lawyers and judges, has played a major role in the campaign for human rights. Its meetings are noteworthy for the freedom and outspokenness of lawyers to expose the injustice and political interference in the judicial processes of many countries.

If one takes account of the five trends described above, it is hard to escape the conclusion that the protest movement against undemocratic government is gathering in strength and importance. The possibility of new tyrants emerging in Africa—equal to the likes of Amin, Nguema, and Bokassa—cannot be ruled out. What seems more certain, however, is that the African silence that shrouded their misdeeds is much less likely to occur in the future. Still, one cannot be too confident so long as criticisms of Qadhafi, Mengistu, and Mobutu remain muted. What is important, nevertheless, is that their misdeeds should be trumpeted by Africans—rather than by Americans or Europeans.

IMPACTS ON AFRICAN DEMOCRACY

Many, if not all, of the nastier regimes were able to survive in Africa because of their client relationship with some of the major powers. The Americans have supported and continue to support Mobutu's regime in Zaïre and, formerly, President Jaafar al-Nimeiri's in Sudan. The Soviets supplied arms to Amin and give strong support to the Mengistu regime in Ethiopia. The British provide substantial aid to Moi in Kenya. The French encouraged and supported Bokassa until nearly the end. Without such foreign support, usually accompanied by an uncomfortable silence about the behavior of the client regime, such dictators would not have survived for as long as they did. Now that the major powers' struggle in Africa seemingly is coming to an end, it could be easier for the major powers either to withhold support from crass offenders or, at least, to speak out against them, which would be a major contribution to the evolving democratic challengers.

African democrats perceive the new thrust of Western policy as exporting the idea that capitalism is the answer to the continent's problems; that privatization, à la the government of Margaret Thatcher, should be the keynote of development, and that the writ of the International Monetary Fund shuld extend continent-wide. Governments that are willing to toe this line are more likely to figure prominently with regard to the allocation of Western resources. Whereas Moscow sought to export Marxism, the major Western countries now seek to export their versions of capitalism.

This development is likely to produce new tensions among Africans, including between those favoring democracy and the West. What African democrats are seeking is both freedom from their own unrepresentative governments and freedom from foreign economic dictates. Not all African democrats embrace capitalism as the answer to the continent's problems. Many, possibly the majority, favor a mixed economy along the lines of European social democracies. Out-and-out democratic socialism, as in Tanzania, has its adherents; while others favor a diluted form of socialism, as in Sweden, France, and Spain, or as advocated by the British Labour Party and the West German Social Democrats. The future of African democracy is likely to be as diverse as it is in Western

Europe. Undiluted capitalism has little support—not even among those who nail their flag to the mast of free enterprise, as in the Côte d'Ivoire.

On the other hand, communism is no longer a lodestar—even for African radicals. Some still aspire to their invention of African Marxism, but the recent developments in Eastern Europe already have had a visible impact on African political thinking and practice. The formerly small, but tenacious, Marxist people's democracies in Benin and the Congo already have abandoned even their slender pretensions of being Marxist states. The Frente de Libertação de Maçambique (FRELIMO) government of Mozambique recently erased Marxism from its program. Angola can be expected soon to follow suit. Only the Mengistu government in Ethiopia still clings to the bloody, tattered flag of its Communist revolution, but its survival is doubtful, to say the least. The African National Congress (ANC) of South Africa never has been a Marxist movement, despite its convenient alliance with the South African Communist Party and Moscow; but the bitterness of the anti-apartheid struggle in South Africa—where apartheid understandably is linked to capitalism—has bred a new generation of younger black leaders who see a Marxist state as the only way of transforming the country's inequitable political and economic system. Nevertheless, the *rigor mortis* of West European communism and Gorbachev's *perestroika* cannot fail to affect the continent's future political climate, even in South Africa.

China, once seen as the alternative lodestar to the Soviet Union, lost its attraction with the demise of Mao Zedong and the rise of the revisionist government in Beijing. The last lingering doubts about the "Chinese model" seem to have been dissipated finally by the revolt in Tiananmen Square. In a summing up of the uprising of Chinese students and workers, Ghanaian journalist Baffour Ankomah has written:

> The ignorance of the Chinese people about politics made it possible for the dictators to hold power so tightly for so long. It used to be so in Africa, today it is all changing. Like Chinese students, Africans are now a widely travelled people and can compare the differences between countries. They know we have chains to break at home, and are angry . . . The fact that so few African leaders have condemned the killings in China shows how guilty they feel about repression at home . . . But, thank God, Africa has precedents and time on its side. We can begin, today, to reform our political systems, to do away with the "culture of silence," to restore basic personal freedoms to our people—before the bubble finally bursts.[10]

What of Cuba—that island of communism? Fidel Castro undoubtedly still has his admirers in Africa. Many Africans feel a sense of gratitude for the Cuban support of the Angolan government's resistance to South Africa's military pressure. Nevertheless, this kind of appreciation does not translate easily into influence. Africans seem to understand that Castro's Cuba was made possible only by the solid support of pre-

Gorbachev Moscow. Because Gorbachev is perceived widely in Africa as having abandoned the earlier policy of solidarity with the international working class, Africans no longer put their faith in the possibility of "new Cubas" in their continent. Anthony Lewis recently wrote that "Marxism is *passé*" in Africa.[11] He would have been more accurate if he had said that the Soviet Union is *passé*. Although Marxism still has its supporters, there seems little chance that it will offer the new wave for a continent in transition from one generation of politicians to the next.

Finally, one possible development that could affect progress toward the achievement of democracy in Africa is the Islamic factor, in countries with large Muslim populations. Sub-Saharan countries have been relatively untouched by the rise of Islamic fundamentalism in Africa's northern littoral. This type of Islam undoubtedly constitutes a challenge in the countries of the Maghrib—notably Tunisia, Algeria, Libya, and (arguably) Morocco—as well as in Egypt, Sudan, and, more marginally, Somalia. Whereas frustration and disillusionment in sub-Saharan Africa have led to an awakening of interest in the alternative of multiparty parliamentary government, in countries with strong Islamic ties, such frustrations and disillusionment have produced a reaction favoring religious fundamentalism.

The Muslim Brothers have strong pockets of support in North Africa. One case is Sudan, where the promise of a return to parliamentary democracy has been checked, at least temporarily, by a military coup with links to the local Islamic fundamentalist organization. Unless democracy can be implemented in Algeria, Tunisia, and Egypt, those countries risk a strong challenge from religious fundamentalism.

CONCLUSION

Africa stands poised for its second period of liberation. The current dominant trend strongly favors the seeding of democratic ideas. Historic change, however, is seldom swift, never easy or harmonious, and always unpredictable.

NOTES

1. Kwame Nkrumah, prime minister of Ghana from 1952 to 1960, led that country to independence in 1957. Serving as Ghana's first president from 1960 to 1966, Nkrumah pursued policies of African socialism and pan-Africanism and helped establish the Organization of African Unity. While there is no agreed definition of African socialism, African leaders widely subscribed to the philosophy, especially during the 1960s and 1970s. Generally, African socialism emphasizes equitable development and a major role for the state in its pursuit.

2. For a convincing exposure of this myth, refer to Vincent Simiyu's writing in *Democratic Theory and Practice in Africa* (London: James Curry, 1986).

3. *Guardian* (London), June 11, 1986.

4. Refer to Carol Lancaster, "Economic Reform in Africa: Is It Working?" in *Wash. Quarterly*, Winter 1990, Vol. 13, No. 1, pp. 115–128.

5. Cited in the United States Information Agency, *Africa Wireless File* (Paris), May 3, 1989.

6. Quoted by Flora Lewis, *International Herald Tribune* (Paris), October 31, 1988.

7. Edem Kodjo, *Et Demain l'Afrique* (Paris: Stock, 1985).

8. *Democratic Theory and Practice in Africa*.

9. *Ibid.*

10. *New African* (London), August 1989.

11. *International Herald Tribune* (Paris), January 31, 1989.

HAVES AND HAVE-NOTS: UPHEAVAL BETWEEN NORTH AND SOUTH

18

South–North Dangers

IVAN L. HEAD

I

The North has discovered the South any number of times; we have given it—or parts of it—a variety of names (sometimes in error), and have defined its interests almost always from our own exclusive perspective. Curiosity, greed, fear, evangelic fervor and the zeal to civilize; the motivation for contact or disengagement has ranged from the loftiest to the basest. Northern observers have generally chosen the more generous interpretation; Southerners have less often shared that point of view.

North–South economic linkages have proved the most enduring and have taken several forms. Trade has been foremost. Trade generally consisted of commodities from the South—spices, fibers, precious metals and gems, beverages, slaves, sugar and tobacco; and manufactured goods from the North—trinkets, cloth, weaponry, implements and machinery. During the Industrial Revolution a global pattern of trade evolved; not vis-à-vis the Southern trading partners, which was assumed, but against Northern competitors. This was followed by the North's need to protect and secure its interests, initially against other Northern rivals and adversaries, local ruling classes and occasional brigands, and later against religious sects and sometimes entire local

Reprinted by permission of *Foreign Affairs*, Summer 1989. Copyright 1989 by the Council on Foreign Relations, Inc.

Note: It is a violation of the law to reproduce this selection by any means whatsoever without the written permission of the copyright holder.

populations. From time to time the North settled segments of its surplus population in the South: sometimes forcibly, as to America and Australia, and other times peacefully, as to Canada and parts of Africa.

The direction and the result of these settlements were always the same: from North to South, infrastructure was installed, principles of governance were introduced and technologies were transferred. It was assumed that the North's techniques and technologies were superior, relevant and sustainable. Much more frequently than admitted, these assumptions have proved false.

In North–South terms, the year 1945 was a turning point both in activities and in expectations. Throughout the South, long-festering independence movements burgeoned into prominence. In the North, where interests are increasingly defined in terms of security and stability, a sterile bifurcation began to divide East and West. Not surprisingly, the definitions of security and the criteria for stability differed when viewed from the North or from the South. Of the human attributes, arrogance has not been absent in either hemisphere. Humility, however, has seldom been present in the North when it looks South. The absence of this trait, unless overcome, will continue to weaken the North both in image and in substance and will be critical to Northern welfare as the century turns.

The North–South relationship is a diverse and confusing web. To understand, to respond effectively and to ensure a constructive outcome is as demanding a task as any that faces humankind. It is demanding not only in terms of substance, but also because of attitudes well entrenched in both North and South. It is moreover the most important task, since it subsumes—or inevitably will subsume—all the others. We in the North may be most in peril (as those in much of the South have long been) because the momentum of events impacting upon us is in excess of our willingness to respond. If we are not willing to become aware, to change our unsustainable attitude of superiority, and to take action to reduce dramatically in the South the broad incidence there of absolute poverty, then our own economic welfare, our own social tranquility and our own political stability will not simply be at risk—increasingly they will be in jeopardy.

The phrase "North–South relations" was reportedly first used in the late 1950s by Sir Oliver Franks, then British ambassador to the United States. In the three decades since, the definition of the term has become as elastic as the relationship it describes has been turbulent.

This has happened, perhaps, because of the multitude of variables encompassed in the phrase: the formation of 100 or so newly independent states; the desire on the part of governments rich and poor that broad disparities in wealth be reduced; the hard evidence in a variety of places that violence is still all too often regarded as an acceptable option; the stark reminders of the strengths of tribalism, feudalism and fun-

damentalism; and the ubiquitous obstacles to change—lack of awareness, absence of preparedness, inadequacy of commitment, retention of
privilege.

Though imprecise, even inaccurate, the term "North–South" is reso-
nant of human expectations and by far richer in its range of connotations
than its contemporary, "East–West."

The notion of "development" has been consistently present in those
connotations. The word itself is now permanently associated with the
nonindustrialized, often recently independent countries. Gradually, the
concepts of "economic advancement and social security" included in the
1941 Atlantic Charter by Churchill and Roosevelt, and reformulated in
the U.N. Charter in 1945, have come to occupy a central position in
international relations, but without a uniform interpretation. Politicians,
popes, academics and journalists have all put forward definitions and
proposals, some quite contradictory.

II

Policymakers in the immediate postwar period grappled with development issues framed by the experience of the colonial era and the anxieties of an increasingly polarized world. Initial development efforts
emphasized, on the one hand, flows of technical assistance and improved market access for primary commodities and, on the other, efforts
to bolster friends and strategically located countries against the perceived threat of communist aggression or subversion. Environmental
awareness was generally absent. In all too many instances there was a
failure to respond effectively to the underlying social and economic
problems facing the developing countries. In the absence of accurate
diagnosis, the tendentious policies of the industrialized countries were
not surprising. In particular the rapid and vigorous employment by
Europe of generous U.S. assistance in the late 1940s led to assumptions
that similar programs in developing regions would be equally successful. The Marshall Plan was not applicable, however, to the dissimilar
circumstances of the developing countries.

The turmoil of governments in Western Europe in the seventeenth
and eighteenth centuries, as they grappled with governance issues, appears minimal compared with the plight of the new postwar states. In
the twentieth century, modern communications technologies have acquainted even the most remote communities with a knowledge of the
much higher standards of living enjoyed elsewhere. Alternative social
and economic images are projected and debated with the ferocity of the
antagonists within Europe during the Reformation, but today's images
are joined by an excess of weaponry and an intrusion of ideology that
turns local dissidents into pawns on a global chessboard.

As they attained independence, developing countries found themselves wooed by East and West, not always in benign fashion. Many were alternately confused and exhilarated by the apparent choices open to them. To governments ill-equipped to shape their own societies, and impotent to respond to such indignities as the Hickenlooper Amendment, which required suspension of U.S. assistance to countries that nationalized U.S. property without speedy compensation, the planetary struggle for hearts and souls appeared in many instances as a bargaining card.

The development debate soon transformed itself from local social and economic imperatives into broad political divisions argued out in regional and interregional assemblies. Western politicians saw that more was involved here than the provision of rural health clinics or the importation of unprocessed primary commodities. The North–South relationship was no longer an engagement of cooperative activity; it had become a battlefield in which human ideals, vested interests and concepts of strategic security tussled and jousted. Throughout the 1950s the legal basis for U.S. development assistance was security—The Mutual Security Act. South Korea and Taiwan became major aid recipients, and Western financing for the Aswan High Dam was withdrawn when Egypt presumed to accept Soviet military assistance.

Then the United Nations declared the 1960s a "Development Decade," and the Organization for European Economic Cooperation became the Organization for Economic Cooperation and Development (OECD). The creation of the United Nations Conference on Trade and Development (UNCTAD) in 1964 eloquently signaled that the South regarded its plight as one anchored in the current international economic structure. "Trade, not aid" became a rallying cry, one which led to the formation of the Group of 77 and a determination by the nations of the South that they would form and maintain a unified bargaining position. If the North controlled the economic agenda, the South moved to assert the political agenda.

Throughout the 1970s, with mixed results, that agenda remained. The General Agreement on Tariffs and Trade (GATT) added Part IV to accommodate the particular problems of developing countries, and UNCTAD produced a resolution on a generalized system of preferences that was later adopted by OECD members. The strident call for a New International Economic Order issued from a nonaligned summit in Algiers in 1973 on the eve of the success of the Organization of Petroleum Exporting Countries in quadrupling oil prices within a year.

The intensity of the North–South debate escalated during the two special sessions of the General Assembly, and led to efforts to mute the language and restore some orderliness to the dialogue. The World Bank and the International Monetary Fund introduced new facilities to meet the needs of those countries grievously wounded by the rise in oil prices. The Common Fund emerged in mid-decade as the dominant demand of the South, but diminished in importance as its complexity proved to be unmanageable and as the attention of the world turned increasingly to the fate of the low-income, oil-importing countries. The South, wearied by the reluctant responses of the North, turned to South–South cooperative initiatives but found its unity shattered with the second oil shock of 1979.

At the end of the 1970s the Brandt Commission signaled alarm that Northern interests were imperiled by the inability of the South to better meet its needs, but it was unable to attract the attention of the new U.S. administration. The 1980s ushered in the great debt crisis of the developing countries, with coincidental circumstances of extreme drought and famine in much of Africa, and unprecedented economic vitality and export performance in the newly industrialized countries of Asia. The Brundtland Commission warned that, in the absence of sustainable development practices, the planet would lose its life-support abilities.

In 1989 it seems clear that the governments of the North have not yet been able to muster resolve and effective response to these bewildering circumstances.

There are a number of reasons. First, much as we in the North lose patience with our efforts to eradicate pockets of poverty in our midst and turn our attention elsewhere, the North seems unable to muster the stamina needed for the lengthy period of transformation in the South. The nations of the North evolved over many centuries as they tackled problems associated with the absence of infrastructure, inadequate education and social diversity. The struggles in the South are no less challenging and require a continuing commitment.

Second, arrogance and ignorance combine to prescribe inept remedies. Technologies that are inappropriate and ineffective continued to be transferred from North to South. When they fail, the South is blamed. Third, outrageous abuses of human rights, corruption and privilege in some developing countries are ready excuses for reluctance to respond adequately anywhere. And fourth, a latent fear of competition from low-wage producers deters full cooperation. In the end, evolving economies are often denied access to Northern markets, or are forced to absorb subsidized agricultural produce from the North at the expense of their own farm sector.

III

As in the arcane and isolated world inhabited by arms controllers, so in the supercharged atmosphere of development, sheer quantity of activity can leave the false impression of accomplishment.[1] In most developing countries individual standards of living have dropped, political instability has increased, and the likelihood of sustained economic growth has now diminished. From the perspective of hundreds of millions of inhabitants of developing countries, life remains a wretched, uncertain prospect. One out of five persons lives in "absolute poverty"—the World Bank's definition of the state of those persons suffering from malnutrition "to the point of being unable to work." For all too many, the likelihood of a dignified, fulfilling livelihood is as distant as it was a generation earlier.

North–South relations are now in a state of disequilibrium, which makes the status quo unsustainable. The most obvious of the disequilibriums are environmental degradation, economic uncertainty, social unrest and political instability.

Population

On July 11, 1987, the world's population passed the five-billion mark. In the first full year following, a net growth of another 83 million took place, an increase greater than the entire population of Mexico. The size of the planet did not increase, nor will it. In some respects, the planet has become smaller. The amount of arable land is actually decreasing. In those same 366 days, arable land diminished by 8,700 square miles— more than twice the size of the island of Jamaica.

From prehistory until about the year 1000, the world's population did not increase by much. In earliest times, life was so precarious and food supplies so unreliable that a rough balance was maintained between births and deaths, notwithstanding an undoubtedly high fertility rate. The introduction of agricultural practices around 8000 B.C. lent a greater certainty to food supply, but for a long time it was largely offset by recurring crises of other sorts—plague, war, etc. Population growth was modest for many centuries—from about 300 million at the time of Christ to some 800 million in the mid-1700s. The doubling took about 1,500 years. Equally important is the fact that the rate of growth was approximately the same in all populated regions of the world.

From about the year 1850 onwards, the rate of population growth immensely accelerated. Mortality decreased with progress in science and technology. The next doubling period was reduced by 90 percent; the world required only 150 years to grow from 800 million to 1.7 billion in 1900. That acceleration has continued. By 1950 the figure had reached 2.5 billion; by 1987, five billion: doubling the world's population, which had once taken 1,500 years, had been accomplished in 37 years. The World Bank states that the best estimate for the year 2000—just 11 years from now—is an increase of 1.2 billion, for a total world population of 6.2 billion at the close of the century.

Those figures are difficult to digest. They work out to an annual increase of close to 100 million persons. One hundred million is about the population of Bangladesh. From now to the turn of the century, then, the world's population will grow by the equivalent of one new Bangladesh every year. Accepted projections distribute the population for the year 2000 as 4.9 billion for the developing countries and 1.3 billion for the industrialized countries. This is disequilibrium.

In increasing numbers, from countries far and wide, the wretched and the persecuted seek entry into the industrialized countries in search of refuge and opportunity. Neither physical barriers nor bureaucratic labyrinths can stem this human tide. The only effective constraint is hope and security within the developing countries. The problem is rapidly worsening, however, by reason of the changing demographic composition.

By the year 2000, 51.2 percent of the world's population will be urban. Forty-five of the 60 largest cities will be in the South, 18 of them larger than ten million. While populations are aging in the North, the reverse is the case in the South. The residents of Southern cities will be overwhelmingly young. In the developing countries, 35 percent of the total population will be under the age of 14. In ever-increasing numbers these youths find themselves on the streets: abandoned, uneducated, unemployed, alienated from any societal norms, without any loyalties except to their own gang or their own ideology or their own religious zealotry.

The rural populations find themselves forced to degrade the environment in an incessant quest for food, firewood and forage. Planetary forest cover was reduced from 25 percent of the earth's surface to 20 percent in two decades, according to the Brandt Commission. Today, the Brundtland Commission estimates, for every tree planted in the tropical regions, ten are destroyed; in sub-Saharan Africa, the ratio is one to 29.

Economic Wealth

The broad interstate disparities in wealth and income have long been recognized. A new factor has recently reemerged: financial transfers from South to North. Reemerged, for it was also a common occurrence in earlier colonial periods.

Capital flows to developing countries fall into two broad categories, private and official. The latter may be on concessional or commercial terms and found in both bilateral (national) and multilateral (international) institutions. Funding of these kinds is as targeted as in the case within industrialized countries, and takes several different instrumental forms: export credits, direct investment, grants and loans.

Until recently, the volume of capital flows to and from developing countries represented only a small proportion of the international total. The composition of those flows has varied considerably. Prior to World War I, the only countries then independent but regarded as developing were in Latin America. Virtually the only capital flows to the South were from private sources; overwhelmingly they were employed to finance the construction of railroads and utilities. In the interwar period, government borrowings became common, and sometimes loans were obtained to finance commodity stocks in the face of falling prices. With the Great Depression came defaults often spurred by protectionist trading policies that effectively prevented debtor countries from earning export-generated surpluses with which to service foreign debt.

The Bretton Woods Conference in 1944 sought to address the frailties of the international system through the creation of the World Bank and the IMF. A third, critically important institution, the proposed International Trade Organization, failed to emerge.

In the post–World War II period, financial flows to the poorest of the developing countries began to emerge from the new multilateral sources, initially from the International Development Association, then from the new regional development banks. With trade liberalization, both trade finance and private direct investment increased. The IMF began to finance restructuring efforts.

The oil-shock-induced current account deficits were in most instances financed from the unprecedented liquidity in the oil-producing countries, increasingly through the intercession of private banks. Since 1970 developing countries' external liabilities of all kinds, including obligations to the IMF, increased significantly. The current total is in excess of $1.3 trillion, the greater part of it denominated in U.S. dollars. Debt service payments have risen more than tenfold in the same period. Rising interest rates have resulted in interest payments accounting for more than 50 percent of debt servicing. What was once a condition of illiquidity in much of the South has now become a condition of insolvency.

The unprecedented exposure of the private banks has considerably reduced fresh credits. This—combined with the successful, though painful, servicing efforts of the majority of debtor countries—has led to a sharp reversal of the earlier transfers, with negative net transfers recorded successively since 1983. In 1988 the net negative flow (i.e., from South to North) from the 17 most highly indebted countries was $31 billion. The figure for all developing countries last year was in excess of $43 billion.

These negative flows are particularly evident in the World Bank and the IMF. The World Bank shifted from being a net provider to the tune of $2.6 billion in 1985 to a net taker of $350 million in 1987. Net flows of resources from the developing countries to the IMF increased from $2.7 billion in 1985 to $8.6 billion in 1987. However, the recently agreed upon credits from the IMF are desperately needed. Continuing net financial transfers of this magnitude from the developing countries to the industrialized countries and the international financial institutions are not sustainable. The increasing structural dependence of Northern countries upon this type of transfer is dangerous. This is disequilibrium.

A factor contributing to the growing magnitude of this imbalance is found in the terms of trade between developing and industrialized countries. It is more acute in some regions than others. The Economic Commission for Latin America and the Caribbean found that terms of trade for Latin American countries deteriorated 16.5 percent between 1980 and 1985.

Relative to gross domestic product, the external debt of the developing countries in the Western Hemisphere was 44.5 percent in 1988 (up from 34.5 percent in 1980); in Africa, 54.4 percent (up from 28.3 percent); and in Asia, 26.4 percent (up from 17.2 percent).

In the same period the ratio of external debt to exports was 322.4 percent for developing countries in the Western Hemisphere (up from 183.6 percent), 237.7 percent for Africa (up from 92.5 percent) and 81.8 percent for Asia (up from 72.1 percent). The economic downturn in the South in the past seven years has led to the loss of 130,000 Canadian jobs and some $24 billion (in Canadian dollars) in export revenues. In the United States, diminishing exports to Latin America alone has meant the loss of 340,000 jobs.

Scientific Activity

In the late 1960s the inquiries launched by the Pearson Commission revealed that expenditures committed to research and development in Latin America, Asia and Africa lagged far behind the outlays in the industrialized countries. An earlier U.N. study estimated, on the basis of admittedly uncertain data, that of all the funds committed to R&D worldwide, less than three percent were expended in the developing countries. Expenditure at these levels means that the indigenous scientific communities are inadequate in size even to identify problems, let alone deal with them effectively across the entire spectrum of natural and social sciences. In an age where technological advances are occurring with breathtaking speed, the gap in capacity between North and South is rapidly widening.

This lack of capacity is particularly distressing in light of the incontestable fact that technology, throughout history, has been the most effective of all agents for change. Contrary to popular opinion, the knowledge now available with respect to agricultural production, primary health care, pedagogy and economic analysis is not simply transferable; rather, it needs to be understood, then revised and absorbed by developing countries in order to be utilized in a geographically and culturally sensitive fashion. Developing countries must acquire the means to pursue the newer biological and physical science technologies and adapt them to their own needs. In their absence, the employment and benefit opportunities that these technologies promise will not be obtained.

UNCTAD figures show that the distribution of scientists and engineers worldwide is overwhelmingly concentrated in the North. The rate per 10,000 inhabitants is 95 in the developing countries compared with 285.2 in the industrialized market economy countries and 308.2 in the East European countries. That average figure of 95 for the South, not surprisingly, is not evenly distributed. The range is from 157.6 in Asia to 9.6 in Africa. The figure for technicians is even more dramatic, revealing a difference between North and South of an order of magnitude of ten.

The number of scientists, engineers and technicians engaged in R&D in the developing countries is less than 1.5 per 10,000 inhabitants, compared with 16.6 in the market economies of the North. It follows that R&D expenditures as a percentage of GNP heavily favor the North. In Africa and Latin America the figure is only 0.2 percent, and in Asia 0.5 percent. These figures have shown no significant increase in the past two decades.

No form of public-sector investment has paid greater dividends over time than investment in people through education and training. Yet no investment is slower in its returns (an entire generation is needed at minimum) and few are more controversial; witness the funding crisis now faced by school boards and universities throughout the United States and Canada. Even the most enlightened of developing countries' governments are unable to muster and retain the political courage required to invest in the future while denying immediate needs of a basic kind to populations that are not, historically, acquainted with the advantages of education. In the result, these countries are condemned for the foreseeable future to pursue outmoded, low-valued economic activity of a kind that is increasingly irrelevant to world market demand. In human terms it means that the grip of absolute poverty will not be eased and that the scourges of malnutrition and ill health will persist.

The impact of this disequilibrium takes many forms, many of them with negative effect upon the North: in the current Uruguay Round of GATT negotiations as developing countries resist the inclusion of services and proprietary knowledge in trade preferences; in the world's stock markets as they reflect the decreasing absorptive capacity of developing countries for imports of high-price, high-tech manufactures; in the health care systems of Europe and North America where tens of billions of dollars must be dedicated each year to life-support systems for incurably ill patients; in community concern over the spread of narcotics imported from regions unable to earn foreign exchange from any other economic activity; and in climate changes which are attributed in many instances to unsustainable agricultural practices and tropical rain forest destruction.

Military Power

In contrast to the three previous sectors of activity, this one suffers not from neglect but from too active a stimulus. The issue is not so much that the North is enormously more richly endowed in military prowess than the South; it is that the countries of the South in many instances choose to mimic the industrialized states in placing high priority on defense-related expenditures at the expense of social needs. The result is a perverse imbalance. In the North are quantities of nuclear weapons, many mounted on long-range delivery systems of great accuracy, supported by highly trained personnel and sophisticated techniques for command, control and communications. These are weapons that are intended not to be used. In the South are increasingly available arsenals of conventional weapons ranging from rockets through aircraft and tanks to machine pistols, the specter of chemical weapons in some instances, much of this too often within the reach of inadequately trained or commanded troops. These are weapons that are intended to be used.

The sheer volume and transportability of modern weapons guarantees the porosity of once impervious membranes. No longer are deadly devices tightly held by national armed forces. The arsenals of heavy weaponry now in the hands of informal, sometimes unidentifiable, groupings is the equivalent of those in many legitimate armies. The firepower available to street gangs in some American cities exceeds that of World War II infantry platoons. And from both sides of the North–South divide, weapons and munitions make their way into the hands of terrorists.

The industrialized states are not entirely to blame for these circumstances, but neither are they entirely without responsibility. The conscious extension of East–West rivalries into the developing countries has certainly encouraged the latter to dedicate scarce resources to military activities. The perception that interregional rivalries are not only worthy of armed conflict but are also subject to military resolution (both assumptions highly questionable in most instances) is still another reason for high defense spending. The assumption that strong military forces are the best guarantee of a nation's ability to govern itself further supports these expenditures. Until relatively recently, the military academies of Europe and the United States were preferred training institutions for future leaders in the South, often with the active encouragement of Northern governments.

Not only have the military capacities of a number of Southern countries become considerable, including arsenals of increasingly potent weapons and delivery systems, but there has also been a tendency to rely on military force to the detriment of democratic processes. The combination of eager buyers in the South and willing sellers in the North has created a North-to-South weapons market of tens of billions of dollars annually, and the proliferation of an unhealthy community of arms brokers and military advisers.

Still another anomaly has emerged. The high cost of arms imports and the images of successful defense industries, projected unconsciously by such countries as the United States and France, have encouraged increasing numbers of developing countries to become weapons manufacturers. The result is an increasing South–South arms trade, and an economic dedication in the South to defense industries, to the disadvantage of the civilian sector. Some countries are more successful than others in their search for markets. The Jaffee Centre for Strategic Studies at Tel Aviv University has calculated that arms exports represent nearly 20 percent of all Israeli manufactured exports and some 10 percent of all exports.

Even as Northern policy analysts express alarm at the current chemical and the emerging nuclear capabilities of increasing numbers of developing countries, there is precious little evidence that Northern governments are willing to address seriously the underlying social and economic conditions that have spawned subversive movements and prompted armed retaliation.

This form of disequilibrium—military disequilibrium—is not one that should be balanced by major increases in expenditures and activity in the developing countries. The entry into a developing region of new types or levels of weaponry can be as destabilizing as would be the case in central Europe, and undoubtedly more destructive. Yet the tendency is in that direction.

As East–West tensions relax in the NATO region, the possibility of a power vacuum in the developing countries into which the East–West conflict could move is distressingly high, despite the welcome assurances of the Soviet Union to the contrary. To military planners in the North and South, security is often defined in military terms with consequences all too evident in any number of developing countries where defense expenditures rival or exceed expenditures on basic social requirements, to the detriment—not the enhancement—of political stability and, often, of military security as well: Lebanon, Afghanistan, El Salvador, Ethiopia—the tragic list goes on and on.

IV

The consequences of these and other disequilibriums are not always predictable, and sometimes not even discernible during real-time human observation. The political unit of time measurement in the industrialized democracies is four or, at most, five years. Events that mature on a longer cycle are seldom visible, and are certainly not influential, in the time frame occupied by decision-makers. Absent a political equivalent of time-lapse photography, governments of the North are unlikely to commit resources now to influence or control events in the distant future. If development is investment, as we encourage the developing countries to believe, we in the North offer little evidence of our own commitment to invest in the South's development.

Population, properly supported, is an immense natural resource and an incomparable source of accomplishment. Wretchedly poor people, however, without basic necessities or the hope of attaining them, turn upon themselves and upon their landscape with distressing results. Governments in North and South alike must acknowledge that population pressures are inconsistent with a wholesome environment and demeaning to human dignity, make a social contract impossible, and contribute to political and economic insecurity. Humane, effective programs of fertility control must attract sustained support, as must programs for the development and enhancement of individual human beings.

Sustainable economic growth is no longer severable as between North and South. Development assistance programs that are designed primarily for the benefit of the Northern donors—to reduce agricultural surpluses, to create employment in sluggish sectors of the economy, or to spur the export of military hardware—must be recognized for their inherent cynicism and their eventual ineffectiveness. In the interests of the North, the economic well-being of all countries must be accepted as a policy goal to be factored into all resource allocations.

Scientific activity must be encouraged within the developing countries to permit them to identify their own problems and gain the competence to resolve many of them. This approach demands programs designed to permit Third World scientists to engage in research of their own choosing in their own institutions on problems seen by them to be of priority. It demands as well a dedication to the sharing of knowledge and a utilization of the new computer and satellite technologies to permit a worldwide dissemination of information now in the public domain. The new biotechnologies promise to meet the food production requirements of many developing countries as well as utilize, for the benefit of North and South, the rich genetic biomass resources that can be cultivated only in the tropical regions and that have immense potential in so many sectors of application.

Military prowess in the North intended primarily for deterrence of worst-case fears has now surpassed the economic ability of either superpower. Technological spin-offs into the civilian sector have long since ceased to be cost-effective. Each new threshold in technology results in the release to Third World markets of massive quantities of powerful obsolescent weaponry. Governments North and South must accept that military prowess is not the normative indicator of accomplishment, that military prescriptions for the symptoms of socioeconomic distress reveal ignorance, not resolve.

What is needed is an attitudinal change of profound quality, of the kind that visits humankind only infrequently. To encourage a fresh perspective, we might borrow from Cornwallis' decision at Yorktown to order his bands to play "The World Turned Upside Down." We could begin by abandoning the misleading term "North–South" and substitute for it the now more accurate "South–North."

The South–North matrix is extensive and complex; it does not translate readily into simple patriotic imagery. It does not respond to simplistic "if only they were like us" solutions. It cannot even be defined in purely statistical terms. It is an embarrassment to Northern governments for it is at once a reminder of barren colonial legacies, compelling evidence of the failure of humankind to accomplish even a passing degree of social equity and proof that international arrogance is, in the end, hollow. And all the while, time is not on the side of the North any more than it favors the South.

Measured against the relentless momentum of current phenomena, indifference is not benign. Humility is needed, as is sustained dedication, if there is to be any reduction in magnitude of the disequilibriums now evident. The crafting of mutually beneficial dynamic relationships cannot wait for the emergence of a brilliant universal accord; it must emerge from a series of what Saburo Okita called "creative patchworks." In their absence, the present and growing imbalances threaten an uncontrollable Newtonian reaction of the kind prophesied a few years ago by François Mitterrand: "I am convinced that the balance between the two parts of the world, the industrialized nations and the others, will be one of the causes of the most serious tragedies at the end of the century, to be explicit, of world war."[2]

NOTES

1. In a number of sectors, accomplishment has resulted. In the 24-year period 1960–84, the average annual per capita growth of GDP for all developing countries, excluding China and the oil-exporting countries, was 2.8 percent. If those countries were included, the average would be 3.4 percent. In that same period, remarkable gains were recorded in literacy, in reducing infant mortality and in increasing life expectancy. Cereal grain production increased; smallpox was eradicated.

2. Interview with James Reston, *The New York Times*, June 4, 1981.

19

Slaying the Drug Hydra

SCOTT B. MACDONALD

THE SCOPE OF THE PROBLEM

In almost any basic international relations course, a fundamental point about the change in mankind's relationship with iteslf is the globalization of communications. To state it simply, the world has become a smaller place, and access to almost any point on the globe is much easier and faster. Advancements in the telecommunications, computer, aerospace, and shipping industries have revolutionized daily life, especially in the post–World War II era. In terms of free capital movement from country to country, transactions can be completed within a minute using telecommunications technology. Transportation of goods, such as cocaine and heroin, takes hours instead of months. Consequently, the globalization of communications has contributed greatly to the internationalization of the drug trade, shortening the flow time between producers and markets and accelerating the pace at which supply can meet demand.

However, the globalization of communications would have had little effect on the drug trade had a drug industry not already been in existence. The global drug trade largely involves Asian and Latin American producers, although production of illicit drugs and their use are also evident in parts of Africa, Europe, and North America (marijuana is the second-largest cash crop in the United States). Asian production centers around areas known as the Golden Crescent and the Golden Triangle, although opium production continues in parts of the Middle East, namely Turkey and Lebanon. The Golden Crescent production area, including parts of Pakistan and Afghanistan, and the Golden Triangle, in the remote mountainous area where Burma, Thailand, and Laos converge, is largely oriented toward the conversion of opium to heroin. In 1987 alone, Burma exported an estimated 65 metric tons of heroin destined for North America, Europe, and Australia. Hong Kong, with its extensive offshore banking facilities and secrecy laws, has emerged as a

Excerpts reprinted by permission of the *SAIS Review*, Vol. 9, No. 1, 1989. Copyright 1989 by Johns Hopkins Foreign Policy Institute, SAIS.

Note: It is a violation of the law to reproduce this selection by any means whatsoever without the written permission of the copyright holder.

major money-laundering center for converting narco-dollars into legal tender and investing the money into legitimate businesses.

Both of Asia's illicit production centers are strengthened by extensive international networks. Almost 90 percent of the Golden Triangle's opium is produced in Burma, where two major groups hold sway over the trade—the Maoist Burmese Communist Party (BCP) and the Shan United Army (SUA), led by a Chinese warlord, Khun Sa. An estimated eight other groups of such insurgents also sustain the drug trade. These groups fall into four broad categories—ethnic insurgents, revolutionary movements, warlord organizations, and syndicates and consortia.[1] During several decades these groups transformed what had been an indigenous cottage industry into a global heroin enterprise, complete with brand names, such as 999, Red Lion, and Double Globe. What was their incentive to go into the drug business? As one source noted, "Under any name, the economics are alluring: a batch of opium that costs $170 in northern Burma yields $2 million or more in American and European cities after relatively cheap processing and dilution."

Drug organizations such as the SUA and the BCP maintain sizable armed forces to protect production centers, which are usually located in difficult to reach, mountainous areas. As in many regions of the Andes in South America, the remote border regions of Burma, Laos, Thailand, Afghanistan, and Pakistan are usually well beyond the reach of government authority. Regional development in these rural areas has often lagged behind that of national urban centers and coastal zones, and political, administrative, and economic integration there is much weaker and less firmly implanted. In many respects these conditions make for ideal "hot houses" for the drug trade, whether dominated by criminal syndicate or by Maoist guerrillas.

The involvement of insurgents in the trafficking of narcotics has often been referred to as the "drug insurgency nexus."[3] This is defined as the involvement of insurgent groups in any or all of the following capacities: (1) producing, refining, and selling cocaine, heroin, opium, or any other illicit drug; (2) functioning as "protection" for drug dealers; (3) functioning as intermediary agents for small-scale peasant cultivators. In the Asian production areas the highly complex drug insurgency nexus has put right-wing Islamic Afghan rebels fighting Soviet troops in the same loose category of insurgent involvement as the Burmese Communist Party.

In Latin America the drug insurgency nexus plays an important role, especially in the Andean states of Colombia and Peru. This arrangement is usually a marriage of convenience between drug traffickers (narcotraficants) and leftist revolutionary groups, such as Colombia's M–19 or Peru's Sendero Luminoso (Shining Path). The drug smugglers are usually conservative and status quo-oriented (especially in Colombia), while the leftist groups are usually seeking to transform radically their respective societies by overthrowing the government and implementing a revolutionary new order, usually based on an offshoot of Marxist-Leninist or Maoist ideology.

The incentive for ideologically guided insurgent groups and drug traffickers to join forces is simple. In most cases they share a preference for remote border regions beyond the government's reach, and clashes between the two groups have been costly. Cooperation usually means shared profits for cash-starved revolutionary groups, such as the *Sendero Luminoso*, as narco-money is an easy and ready way to fill the war coffers. Moreover, Latin leftist groups (including the Cuban and Nicaraguan governments) regard drug abuse as a weapon to be used against the United States. For their part, the drug traffickers get additional military clout. This was reflected by the November 1985 assault on Colombia's Palace of Justice in Bogotá by M–19 guerrillas. Although a majority of the sixty guerrillas perished in the army's successful assault on the palace, nine Supreme Court judges involved in narcotics cases were killed. Valuable files were destroyed that could have resulted in the extradition of defendants to the United States for trial.

The Latin American drug trade encompasses the Andean countries of Colombia, Bolivia, and Peru, which are the leading cocaine producers; the lesser cocaine producers of Ecuador, Brazil, and Venezuela; and the transit states of the Caribbean and Central America. Brazil, Venezuela, and Chile in particular have emerged as key transit points to North America, Australia, and Europe. The Caribbean, Belize, and Paraguay have become significant exporters of marijuana, joining the ranks of transit states. Other key transit states are the Bahamas and Panama (two countries particularly well known for both corruption of government officials and as major laundering points). Some Caribbean officials, for instance, in the Turks and Caicos Islands, Suriname, and Haiti, have been charged and put on trial in the United States for offering services of their states as transit points. Mexico has become a key transit point for South American cocaine but is also a major exporter of marijuana and supplies one-third of the U.S. heroin market.

Latin America's major traffickers are dominated by the Colombian Medellín Cartel and the smaller Cali Cartel (which control between 60 and 80 percent of cocaine entering the United States) and smaller, less organized groups of families in Peru and Bolivia. Many drug kingpins are wealthy, such as Bolivian Roberto Suárez Gómez and Colombian Pablo Escobar. These men have considerable political and economic influence and represent a powerful challenge to Latin governments as well as the populations of transit states in the Caribbean Basin and North America.

The power of the *narcotraficantes* has been magnified considerably by the debt crisis, which has weakened legal economies and cut enforcement budgets throughout the region. The contrast between austerity from adjustment programs and the easy wealth of the drug business has made it exceedingly difficult to contain the trade and to check the spread of domestic abuse. Furthermore, many opposed to the drug trade, such as Lara Bonilla, Colombia's justice minister, who launched a major assault against the Medellín Cartel, have been slain by hired assassins. *Narcotraficantes* in Bolivia, Colombia, and Peru have even offered to help pay off their nations' external debt—a tempting offer not yet accepted.

Thus, the major components of the drug trader's external side— production countries, the drug insurgency nexus, the corruption and involvement of governments (for example, Panama, Cuba, and Laos), and money laundering—interrelate and often overlap, greatly complicating progress toward international cooperation and interdiction.[4]

Their importance would be meaningless, however, without the demand side of the equation. It is here perhaps that the United States can make the greatest contribution. The U.S. market is the most lucrative in the world, with an estimated retail value of $100 billion and 27–30 million consumers.[5] The market divides roughly between 20 million who smoke marijuana, about 6 million who regularly use cocaine, and the half million that take heroin. This sector of the population represents growing health care costs, lost work hours, and related violent crimes. In New York, Washington, D.C., Miami, Los Angeles, and other cities, entire neighborhoods have been taken over by dealers and gangs, while drug corruption has permeated even law enforcement agencies. Consequently, the drug problem has become one of the major issues confronting the American city in the late 1980s.

NOTES

1. Kraar, "The Drug Trade," 37.

2. Jon A. Wiant, "Narcotics in the Golden Triangle," *The Washington Quarterly* (Fall 1988).

3. Renssalaer W. Lee, Jr., "The Latin American Drug Connection," *Foreign Policy*, vol. 61, no. 4 (Winter 1985–86): 153–57.

4. For further information see Scott B. MacDonald, *Dancing on a Volcano: The Latin American Drug Trade* (New York: Praeger, 1988).

5. Kraar, "The Drug Trade," 37.

20

The Political Economy of the Andean Cocaine Industry

RENSSELAER W. LEE III

The control of narcotics, once an issue far outside the diplomatic main-stream, has become a vital component of U.S. relations with Latin America. Indeed, eradicating drug production and export is officially the highest U.S. diplomatic priority in Colombia and one of the top priorities in Bolivia and Peru. U.S. economic aid is allocated accordingly: narcotics-related assistance rose from 30 percent of total aid to Colombia in fiscal year 1984 to 90 percent in FY 1988. Moreover, Congress now ties foreign aid to recipient countries' drug-control efforts. Thus, in the last two years, the United States has withheld $17.4 million in aid from Bolivia, primarily because coca crop eradication targets were not met.

It is noteworthy that Washington does not practice drug diplomacy worldwide, but restricts it largely to Latin America and the Caribbean. There has been no serious threat to cut off economic and military aid to Pakistan (the world's largest heroin producer) or to stop supplying Stinger missiles to the *mujahidin* of Afghanistan (who cultivate opium). In these places, obviously, there are higher priorities than narcotics control.

Within Latin America, too, there are priorities. Although Latin America supplies most of the marijuana, about 40 percent of the heroin, and all of the cocaine entering U.S. markets, cocaine is easily the biggest concern at the moment. The fight against America's cocaine epidemic—an estimated six million people regularly use this highly addictive drug—consumes the bulk of the federal government's drug-fighting resources. But the cocaine industry is a powerful antagonist. Having cultivated extensive ties with the economic and political power struc-tures of the Andean countries, it poses a difficult challenge to U.S. policy.

First published as "Why the U.S. Can Not Stop South American Cocaine." Revised and reprinted from *Orbis,* A Journal of World Affairs, with permission from the Foreign Policy Research Institute, Philadelphia.

Note: It is a violation of the law to reproduce this selection by any means whatsoever without the written permission of the copyright holder.

WHO PRODUCES COCAINE?

The business of cocaine differs from one country to the next. In Colombia, two coalitions of criminal families headquartered in the cities of Medellín and Cali control—directly or through affiliate organizations—an estimated 70 to 80 percent of that country's cocaine exports. Bolivia's cocaine trade is dominated by some twelve to twenty-five families, most of whom also run cattle ranches or commercial farms in the Beni, Cochabamba, and Santa Cruz regions. In Peru, on the other hand, the industry is highly fragmented and, to a large extent, dominated by Colombian traffickers.

Colombia is clearly the linchpin of the South American cocaine industry. The Medellín-Cali syndicates, which control most Andean cocaine exports, procure raw materials in Peru and Bolivia, manufacture refined cocaine in Colombia, ship it in large loads of 300 kilos or more to the United States, and market the cocaine wholesale within the United States. They may also be expanding into the even more profitable phases of distribution, where a kilo of cocaine is subdivided into small lots, adulterated with an inert substance, and sold in small packages for about double the wholesale price. By the end of the 1980s these organizations probably grossed at least $7 billion annually from international cocaine sales, primarily to the U.S. market. About 50 to 60 percent of this amount was profit.

The Medellín and Cali syndicates do not function as cartels in the true sense of the term. As a recent congressional study notes, "There is no evidence that the Colombian groups set prices on cocaine by the kilo or that they make arrangements on how much cocaine will be introduced in a given period of time."[1] In fact, average per-kilo wholesale prices for cocaine plummeted from $45,000 to $55,000 in 1983 to $10,000 to $15,000 in 1989. Furthermore, bad blood flows between the Medellín and Cali groups, stemming from the Medellín's attempts to encroach on Cali's sales territory in New York City. (In addition, the Medellín mafia's addiction to using violence as a political tool is perceived by Cali as dangerous and counterproductive.) Yet, considerable business collaboration occurs within each group—traffickers coinsure cocaine shipments, engage in joint smuggling or production ventures, exchange loads, and jointly plan assassinations. Moreover, cocaine barons share a common agenda that includes blocking the extradition of drug traffickers and immobilizing the criminal justice system.

Production within the cartels is relatively dispersed—that is, many organizations operate cocaine laboratories; however, distribution is relatively concentrated. Colombia's major drug kingpins—the men at the apex of the trafficking pyramid—are responsible for smuggling cocaine to the United States and other overseas markets. For many years, the kingpin list included Cali traffickers Gilberto Rodríguez Orejuela, his brother Miguel Angel Rodríguez, and Jose Santa Cruz Londoño; and Medellín traffickers Pablo Escobar Gaviria, Jose Gonzalo Rodríguez Gacha (now deceased), and the three Ochoa brothers (Jorge, Fabio, and Juan David). The organizations headed by Orejuela, Santa Cruz, Escobar, Rodríguez Gacha, and Ochoa are vertically integrated enterprises—they maintain their own refineries and transport capacity as well as their own networks of wholesalers in the United States. They also handle the cocaine produced by other suppliers in the Medellín and Cali coalitions. The leading traffickers control their export and distribution networks in part by offering suitable suppliers an insurance package for their shipments. That is, the traffickers guarantee 100-percent replacement of any cocaine shipments that are lost or seized.

The 20 to 30 percent of Colombia's cocaine industry not under the syndicate is shared by scattered small processors and refiners, some of whom have links to guerrillas of the Revolutionary Armed Forces of Colombia (FARC). FARC also has its own cocaine-processing capabilities in some regions. The small producers do not appear to have access to the cocaine elite's distribution capabilities; they rely heavily on mules (hired couriers) to smuggle cocaine into the United States.

THE BENEFITS OF COCAINE

All together, South American drug traffickers earn an estimated $9 to $10 billion each year. The bulk of these funds remains abroad, stashed in offshore tax havens such as Panama and the Cayman Islands, or invested in U.S. real estate, securities, and business. In 1983, Colombian drug traffickers reportedly held $10 to $11 billion worth of assets in the United States.[2]

Between $1.5 billion and $2.5 billion annually may return to the principal cocaine-producing countries—Colombia ($800 million to $1 billion), Bolivia ($400 to $600 million), Peru ($500 to $700 million). In terms of these repatriated dollars, cocaine exports could equal 10 to 15 percent of Colombia's 1988 legal exports, 20 to 25 percent of Peru's, and 60 to 90 percent of Bolivia's. The economic impact of these funds is not clear, however, for the relationship between the drug industry and prosperity is far from direct.[3] When spending their repatriated dollars, traffickers tend to short-change core economic activities. As *The Economist* recently noted, "the economic impact of $1 billion spent bribing politicians and buying status symbols will usually be less than that of $1 billion spent building roads and electricity generators."[4]

And much is spent on bribes. Because cocaine is a criminal industry, the producers spend 10 to 20 percent of all operating expenses to create a secure climate for business operations. The money goes for weapons and private security forces, information networks, bribes to law enforcement officials, contributions to political campaigns, and "war taxes" paid to guerrilla groups.

Conspicuous consumption is another hallmark of the cocaine industry, giving rise to absurdly unbalanced development in the remote South American jungle regions that cultivate coca. The town of Tocache in Peru's Upper Huallaga Valley has six banks, six Telex machines, several stereo dealerships, a discotheque, and one of the largest Nissan outlets in Peru. Tocache also has no paved streets, no drinking water, and no sewage system.[5] In Medellín and Santa Cruz, cocaine capos flaunt ostentatious lifestyles—buying luxury high-rise apartment buildings, Mercedes-Benzes and BMW's, helicopters, and antiques. Last January, after a bomb exploded in front of Monaco, one of Pablo Escobar's Medellín houses, police reportedly discovered in the wreckage a veritable fortune in Ming dynasty vases, Greek sculptures, paintings (including works by Botero, Morales, and Obregón), and a collection of thirty antique cars.[6]

In the attempt to buy status, drug traffickers in South America, Jamaica, and Honduras also devote funds to social welfare programs, earning the traffickers a significant popular following. Pablo Escobar, for example, built 450 to 500 two-bedroom cement-block houses in a Medellín slum that has now been renamed the "Barrio Pablo Escobar." Reportedly he has built more public housing in Medellín than the government. Escobar also financed many other Medellín projects—sewer repair, educational facilities, clinics, and sports plazas. Carlos Lehder organized and funded a major earthquake relief effort in the city of Popayan and also built a housing project for the poor in his native Armenia, the capital of Quindío department. Gonzalo Rodríguez Gacha donated an outdoor basketball court to his native town of Pacho, Cundinamarca, and repaired the façade of Pacho's town hall. Roberto Suarez, the "king of cocaine" in Bolivia, paves streets, restores churches, and donates sewing machines to poor women in his Beni home town of Santa Ana de Yacuma. Suarez reportedly provides college scholarships for needy students in the Beni region.[7]

The cocaine industry also generates genuine economic activity. It directly employs more than a million people in the Andean region. Two-thirds to three-quarters of these are farmers (mostly in Peru and Bolivia) who cultivate and harvest coca leaves. Several hundred thousand are engaged in downstream functions: macerating coca leaves, building maceration pits, buying and selling leaves or paste, refining and smuggling cocaine, building clandestine airstrips, and smuggling precursor chemicals (used to convert coca into cocaine). An estimated 350,000 to 400,000 Bolivians (5 to 6 percent of that country's population) work directly in one phase or another of the trafficking cycle.[8] For many, however, these activities do not provide full-time work; in Bolivia, some farmers cultivate coca in the Chapare during the summer months and farm their traditional crops in the Upper Cochabamba Valley during the winter. Coca cultivation often makes the difference between subsistence and a decent standard of living.

Thus, drug-related business serves as an important economic safety valve, especially in Peru and Bolivia, providing income, jobs, and foreign exchange when the formal economy falters. According to a Bolivian government document, "Triennial Program of the Battle Against Drug Trafficking," while Bolivia's gross national product declined 2.3 percent per year from 1980 to 1986, production of coca grew an estimated 35 percent per year over the same period. The official unemployment rate more than tripled from 1980 to 1986 (from 5.7 percent to 20 percent), but so did the number of families reportedly growing coca.[9] During 1986, over 20,000 Bolivian miners lost their jobs; as many as 5,000 may have sought work in the coca fields. From 1984 to 1986, when world prices for oil, tin, and natural gas declined, Bolivia's exports shrank by 25 percent and Peru's by 20 percent; cocaine exports compensated for the loss.[10]

Cocaine production has an economic ripple effect. A proportion of drug traffickers' earnings goes for the purchase of the means of production (farm equipment, chemicals, and other tools of the trade) and export (clandestine airstrips, transportation, etc.). Local industrialists create new manufacturing capacity to provide goods, while new services (banks, law firms, and accounting firms) spring up to cater to the cocaine syndicate. Even the expenditures on conspicuous consumption have an effect. The demand for luxury housing has been a boon for building contractors and for producers of such construction materials as cement, bricks, and glass.

Some drug money is invested in quite ordinary economic outlets, though these tend to be in agriculture and services rather than in the more traditional areas, such as extraction, manufacturing industries, and infrastructure projects. The Rodríguez Orejuela family put together an extensive business empire in Cali which at one time included banks, construction companies, pharmaceutical companies, sports clubs, private security companies, automobile dealerships, twenty-eight radio stations, and two higher educational institutions, the Fundacion Educativa de Estudios Superiores and the Faculdad de Formación de Empresarios. Several of the Medellín-based traffickers (José Gonzalo Rodríguez Gacha, Pablo Escobar, and the Ochoa clan) own dairy farms, cattle ranches, and horse ranches. In Bolivia, where the cocaine dealers are largely coterminous with the rural elite, traffickers invest drug profits into expanding herds, cross-breeding cattle, or improving cotton and sugar cane yields. Characteristically, the major drug lords also invest in executive air-transport services (which may be used for drug trafficking), restaurants, and resort hotels (especially on Colombia's Caribbean coast and on San Andrés Island).[11] Even while they remain theoretically dedicated to combatting drug traffic, Andean governments encourage the inflow of narcotics profits. As a Colombian banking official remarked in a 1986 interview, "Why should we drive all this money into the black market and into foreign banks?"[12] Toward this end, tax amnesties were declared in Colombia at the beginning of the last four presidential administrations. In Peru and Bolivia, traffickers who repatriate hard currency are protected by government decree from tax penalties and to some extent from criminal investigation. Such money now replaces the international loans which are no longer forthcoming from commercial bankers. Peru's nationalistic economic policies exclude it from receiving loans from any international sources, and Peruvian banking officials make no secret of their view that cocaine dollars partially substitute for foreign investment and bank loans.[13] In an apparent effort to draw in more cocaine dollars and to keep them in Peru, the government has overvalued the local currency (the INTI) and provided high INTI interest rates for depositors. In sum, drug dollars create pockets of prosperity, stimulate certain industries, stabilize the currency, and help finance exports. Were the industry suddenly shut down, economic chaos would reign in Bolivia and Peru, and possibly in Colombia too.

THE DRUG PRODUCERS' CLOUT

The cocaine industry's enormous wealth, its large popular base upstream, and its formidable organization downstream combine to give it great political influence in the Andean countries. It has two especially powerful constituencies: the farmers who defend their right to cultivate coca, and cocaine dealers who exert a range of influences over the criminal justice system and the state generally.

Coca Farmers

Farmers who cultivate illicit coca make up the most visible cocaine constituency, for they are highly organized and sometimes well armed. They can exert tremendous pressure on governments.

In Peru's Upper Huallaga Valley, where more than 90 percent of farm income derives from coca cultivation, coca farmers are represented by provincial and district self-defense fronts (FEDIPs). FEDIPs are heavily influenced by the parties of the United Left (Izquierda Unida), and may also have been infiltrated by the Sendero Luminoso and Tupac Amaru guerrilla movements.[14] FEDIPs lobby for the legalization of coca cultivation and challenge government eradication teams with sit-ins, demonstrations, roadblocks, and other mass mobilization tactics. The coca growers' opposition and the security threat from Sendero forced the virtual halt of a U.S.-Peruvian eradication project in the Valley in late

1989. The presence of Sendero clearly limits the political space for eradication. As the military commander of the Upper Huallaga security zone, General Arcenio Arciniega noted in a 1989 interview: "There are 150,000 campesinos cocaleros in the zone. Each of them is a potential *subversivo*. Eradicate his field and the next day he'll be one."[15] In Bolivia, the political dynamics are even worse, for 70,000 coca-growing families are organized into ten regional federations comprising several hundred syndicates. These receive direct political support from national mass membership organizations, including the 1.3-million-member Bolivian Workers Congress and its main affiliate, the Confederation of Bolivian Peasant Workers. In a country of only 6.4 million people, such support significantly deters narcotics control programs. U.S.-Bolivian efforts to pressure coca farmers by destroying crops or regulating the sale of coca leaves trigger organized resistance on a national scale. The Bolivian coca lobby has the power to shut down parts of Bolivia's fragile transportation system. For example, coca farmers and their worker-peasant allies have sealed off Cochabamba, Bolivia's third largest city, four times since 1983 to protest various anti-coca policies of the Bolivian government. The Bolivian authorities did eradicate 2,500 hectares of coca between 1987 and 1988, but only by undertaking a complex process of bargaining with federations and individual syndicates and by paying peasants $2,000 for each hectare eradicated. Involuntary eradication on any significant scale is probably politically impossible in Bolivia.

Traffickers

U.S. officials sometimes characterize the narcotics industries as a direct threat to democracy in the Western Hemisphere and as a danger to U.S. security interests in the region.[16] Such characterizations are not entirely accurate. To be sure, traffickers do not hesitate to use violence against government officials and public figures to promote their political objectives, such as deactivating the U.S.-Colombian extradition treaty. But unlike leftist guerrillas, whose objective is to seize power, traffickers are not ideologically committed to destroying the political system in which they survive.

Nevertheless, when an industry as large as the cocaine one searches for protection, it spawns corruption on a massive scale. Cocaine traffickers can manipulate the key institutions of public life, including the political parties, the press, the police, the military, and the judiciary. Traffickers exercise enormous influence in such major cities as Medellín and Cali; they even dominate entire regions, including parts of Córdoba, Meta, and Antioquia in Colombia and much of the Beni region in Bolivia.

The strategy of self-protection operates on seven different levels. First, drug lords make large outlays for weapons and guard forces to protect laboratories, clandestine airfields, drug shipments, and key personnel. Traffickers are in general better armed than national police forces, use better communications equipment, and deploy faster aircraft.

Second, traffickers attempt to neutralize the effectiveness of law-enforcement institutions by paying police or military officers to overlook cocaine refineries or drug-smuggling operations. Chapare traffickers in Bolivia pay police $20,000 to $25,000 for a seventy-two-hour window of impunity for loading major shipments by air, land, or river.[17]

Third, the drug lords maintain elaborate networks of informants that provide advance information of the exact plans for raids or checkpoints, thus enabling the traffickers to escape police dragnets and to live fairly comfortably in such major cities as Medellín and Cali. The Ochoa family of Colombia reportedly has informants in the Ministry of Justice and the Ministry of Foreign Affairs.[18] A few U.S. narcotics specialists in Bogotá believe that the Medellín syndicates have infiltrated the U.S. Embassy, and that traffickers' informants read some of the Embassy's cable traffic.[19] The cocaine chiefs could conceivably be privy to secret U.S.-Colombian deliberations on drugs and plans for major anti-drug initiatives. No wonder that a Colombian opinion survey taken in March 1987 reports that nearly half the population believes drug traffickers are too powerful to combat.[20]

Fourth, traffickers undermine the judicial system. When caught in the net, they pay the police to release them. Pablo Escobar, Colombia's biggest cocaine dealer, was arrested by accident in November 1986 at a police checkpoint in Southern Antioquia; he was quickly released after paying a bribe of some $250,000 to $375,000.[21]

If traffickers cannot escape the police, judges presiding over drug trafficking cases in Colombia are offered the choice of *plomo o plata* (lead or silver)—death if they convict, a bribe if they set aside the charges. Nor surprisingly, few judges opt to convict. In the past two years, criminal court judges either released from jail or dropped the charges against four major cocaine dealers: Gilbert Rodríguez Orejuela, José Santa Cruz Londoño, Evaristo Porras (a mid-level capo from the city of Leticia), and Jorge Luis Ochoa. In fact, Ochoa was released twice within sixteen months, and corrupt judges appear to have played a role on both occasions. Recently in Medellín, police arrested a middle-ranking trafficking chief implicated in the murder of Guillermo Cano (the editor of the Bogotá daily *El Espectador*). After several days in jail, he was released because no judge in Medellín was willing to try the case.[22]

If traffickers do end up in jail, they usually can bribe their way out. The second time Jorge Ochoa escaped, according to a Western diplomatic source, his clan paid $3 million to get him out of jail and an additional $20 million to arrange every step of his escape route so that he would not be murdered or recaptured. At the moment of writing, no major traffickers are in jail anywhere in Colombia, although one Medellín kingpin, Gonzalo Rodríguez Gacha, was killed in a shootout with police in December 1989.

With respect to drug-trafficking cases, then, the Colombian criminal justice system has almost ceased to function.

The fifth level of self-protection exercised by the drug lords in Colombia includes influencing public opinion and the political process. Publications such as Carlos Lehder's *Quindío Libre* and the Escobar family's *Medellín Cívico* carry out an unremitting campaign against the U.S.-Colombian extradition treaty, portraying it as "a monstrous legal absurdity" and "the ultimate surrender of sovereignty."[23] These publications depict drug dealers as progressive and public-spirited citizens. *Medellín Cívico* praises Escobar's "great human and social sensitivity" and his dedication to "redeeming the forgotten people of Antioquia."[24] Mafia-controlled columnists in more respectable publications convey the same message. In addition, as noted above, sponsoring public works and social services in communities that governments have failed to reach wins good will for the drug lords. Although the cost of such projects represents a tiny fraction of overall cocaine resources, the political impact is incalculable.

Sixth, cocaine traffickers become power brokers. In Colombia, where political campaigns are not funded from the state treasury, drug money is an important underpinning for the entire democratic process. Traffickers contribute indiscriminately to campaigns—often through front organizations—to hedge their bets. Pablo Escobar is affiliated with the Liberal party, but he gave money to both candidates in the 1982 Colombian presidential campaign.[25] Sometimes traffickers prepare their own slate of candidates for local political office, as does the "political group" of Evaristo Porras in Colombia's Amazonas Department.[26]

Seventh, and finally, the cocaine mafia protects itself by using violence to shape the laws and policies governing narcotics control. In Colombia, the main perpetrators of anti-state violence have been the Medellín syndicates; the syndicates' aims are to halt the extradition of drug traffickers to the United States, to discourage high-level investigation of criminal activities, to mobilize a public consensus against the drug war, and to force official recognition of traffickers as "political" criminals who, like guerrillas, would be eligible for amnesty. From 1986 to 1989, Medellín henchmen murdered several prominent Colombians who supported extradition or who otherwise crusaded against the cocaine industry: the editor of *El Espectador*, a Colombian Supreme Court Justice, the former head of Colombia's anti-narcotics police (who was preparing a "black book" on the mafia's activities, a governor of Antioquia and the leading Liberal party candidate for president. Violence and threats virtually paralyzed Colombia's criminal justice system and influenced the Supreme Court in June 1987 to strike down legislation enabling the government to implement the extradition treaty with the United States.

After the death of presidential candidate Luis Carlos Galan in August 1989, the government issued emergency decrees reviving extradition administratively (i.e., without benefit of a prior court decision or a functioning instrumental treaty) and confiscating traffickers' real estate and bank accounts. The Medellín mafia responded by launching a campaign of bombings and kidnappings—actions that had hitherto been more characteristic of terrorists than of drug dealers. The Colombian government and populace may not be able to sustain this level of hostilities much longer; as of this writing there is tremendous public pressure on the Colombian government to reach some kind of peace settlement with the drug lords.

RELATIONS WITH GUERRILLAS

Perhaps because of the cocaine industry's multi-front attack on the government's control, Washington expressed concern about a connection between the cocaine industry and Marxist guerrilla groups. Indeed, in its early days, the Reagan administration analyzed the drug problem within the framework of the East–West conflict. Administration officials spoke publicly and privately about a "deadly connection" and an "unholy alliance" between cocaine kings and guerrillas.[27] A U.S. government report in 1985 on Soviet influence in Latin America warned of an "alliance between drug smugglers and arms dealers in support of terrorists and guerrillas."[28] This report, however, may have exaggerated the depth of the narco-guerrilla connection.

To be sure, drug dealers, especially the larger operators, do share some of the guerrillas' anti-establishment views: for example, they are both strongly anti-American. In Colombia, major guerrilla groups and cocaine syndicates oppose as "Yankee imperialism" the extradition treaty that allows traffickers to be tried in the United States under American judges and U.S. law. In both Colombia and Peru, therefore, guerrilla organizations have cultivated ties with coca growers.

In addition, the drug lords generally advocate a more egalitarian social structure. Pablo Escobar, for example, espouses the cause of slum dwellers and of "marginal people" in general. The Escobar family newspaper, *Medellín Cívico*, professes strong support for the Liberal party but has a decidedly populist orientation. Recent articles in the newspaper, though not praising the cocaine traffic as such, have criticized "the fabulous profits" of industrialists, claimed that "we are good friends of the working class," and advocated "employment for all, education for all, health for all, and bread for all."[29]

The nationalist-populist fervor of Colombian narcotics traffickers reached its most extreme form in the bizarre political philosophy of Carlos Lehder, who founded a political movement in his native department of Quindío—the Movimiento Latino Nacional (MLN). The MLN's *raison d'être* was campaigning against the extradition treaty, but the party also had a full-blown international political program that included the struggle against "communism, imperialism, neocolonialism, and Zionism" and favored the replacement of Colombia's traditional political parties with mass popular organizations. In the 1986 presidential elections, his party supported the extreme leftist UP candidate, while Lehder himself maintained ties with several Colombian revolutionary organizations, including the Quintin Lamé and the April 19th Movement (M–19). He may even have helped to finance the M–19's raid on Colombia's Palace of Justice in November 1985—a raid culminating in a holocaust in which eleven Supreme Court justices and scores of other people were killed.

Lehder's extreme radicalism, however, was not shared by his colleagues, who generally prefer to work within the system. Many Colombian observers believe that the Medellín syndicates viewed Lehder as an embarrassment, were eager to cultivate a pro-establishment image, and consequently betrayed the trafficker to authorities.[30] Lehder now is in jail in the United States, probably permanently.

At any rate, whatever ideology the drug lords may espouse, on the level of "turf," clashes with guerrilla groups have been common. Guerrillas increase the cocaine industry's overhead costs—traffickers must either pay protection money (war taxes) to guerrillas or make large outlays to guard their drug shipments, laboratories, supply routes, clandestine airfields, and exports. The Colombian cocaine leadership—which invests much of its new-found wealth in farms, ranches, and landed estates in Colombia's relatively unprotected hinterland—is vulnerable to extortion by FARC guerrillas.

Because their interests in these legitimate properties are similar to the interests of Colombia's traditional elite, drug traffickers have spearheaded efforts to organize ranchers and farmers to resist attacks by local guerrilla forces. Colombian cocaine barons have invested some of their profits in acquiring vast tracts of land in the countryside—reportedly at least one million hectares of land in the past 5 years—in Cordoba, Antioquia, Meta, and other Colombian departments. Many of the recently purchased tracts of land lie in "zonas rojas"—areas where predatory guerrillas maintain a strong presence; hence, the new landed narco-gentry has found itself on the cutting edge of Colombia's guerrilla conflict.

This historically significant process has revived and overhauled the local self-defense forces or has created such forces where none previously existed. In certain cases, cocaine barons or their representatives assumed the leadership of, and most of the financial responsibility for, such groups. Consequently, self-defense networks have become a significant political and military force in some regions. For example, as of mid-1989, a paramilitary network centered in Puerto Boyacá (in the Middle Magdalena Valley) reportedly operated its own fleet of planes, helicopters, and launches, jeeps and bulldozers, a printing press, a clinic, and a training school, not to mention maintaining vast stores of ammunition and automatic and semiautomatic weapons.[31] Five Israeli mercenaries and perhaps 10 former members of the British Strategic Air Services came to Puerto Boyacá to train mafia soldiers in counterinsurgency techniques. The network, with the tacit or active support of local landowners, businessmen and military commanders, apparently succeeded in sanitizing the Puerto Boyacá, Puerto Triunfo, and Puerto Berrío region of the Valley—an area that had apparently been a FARC sphere of influence in the early 1980s.

Furthermore, the paramilitary movement is acquiring a political face. Puerto Boyacá, which calls itself the "anti-subversion capital of Colombia," is the center of a new political phenomenon, the so-called Movement for National Restoration (MORENA). As the ideological expression of the self-defense groups that operate in the Middle Magdalena Valley, MORENA aspires to "free our beloved country of the infamous communist guerrillas." MORENA seeks status as a nationwide political party and plans to field its own presidential candidate in 1990. Such a strategy would accord MORENA roughly the same relationship to the paramilitary movement in Colombia that the Unión Patriótica has to the FARC. MORENA is not simply a front for cocaine traffickers, because it is also backed by legitimate landowners and businessmen. (MORENA's leaders deny any connection with the cocaine trade.) Yet, the influence of cocaine traffickers, who have been prime movers in establishing the Middle Magdalena's self-defense network, almost certainly pervades MORENA. Needless to say, traffickers could acquire substantial political legitimacy in Colombia if MORENA successfully achieves the status of a nationwide political party.[32]

An integral part of the traffickers' anti-communist political strategy has been the systematic extermination of visible members of the extreme left. Such "soft targets" have included labor organizers, civil rights workers, peasants, activists, intellectuals, and politicians. About one-third of the Union Patriotica (UP) mayoralty candidates (the UP is an umbrella organization for Colombia's Marxist group) were massacred, many by drug traffickers in the six months preceding the March 1988 elections. According to Colombia's justice minister, Rodriquez Gacha paid 30 million pesos (about $120,000) to one of his henchmen to arrange the October 11, 1987 assassination of Colombia's foremost leftist leader, Jaime Pardo Leal, the head of the UP.[33] According to an article in *Samana*, drug traffickers were responsible for murdering nearly 1,000 UP members between 1985 and 1989.

In Peru, the Upper Huallaga Valley hosts many bloody confrontations between cocaine-trafficking gangs and Sendero Luminoso guerrillas. In mid- and late 1987, clashes were recorded in or near the Valley towns of Sion, Uchiza, and Paraíso. According to an article in Bogotá's *El Tiempo*, Colombian crime syndicates recently dispatched 300 heavily armed traffickers to the Upper Huallaga Valley to help Peruvian traffickers protect cocaine shipments and supply routes against Sendero Luminoso attacks.[34] The efforts by "Machis," one of the Valley's leading cocaine dealers, to organize residents of the Uchiza district against the guerillas led to an ambush against him at Paraíso by Sendero Luminoso on October 10, 1987. Machis got the worst of it, and was encircled by the guerrillas. At this point, he let himself be rescued from certain death by the Peruvian anti-narcotics police flying in U.S.-piloted helicopters; he is now in a Peruvian jail.[35] However, Peruvian traffickers, unlike their Colombian counterparts, lack a common anti-leftist agenda. Sendero has made inroads into the cocaine trade by exploiting rivalries among Peruvian traffickers as well as their sense of nationalism (i.e., their hostility toward Colombian buyers). By the late 1980s, Sendero had become a powerful force in the Valley and was earning up to $30 million a year by taxing coca plantations and shipments of cocaine paste or base. In some areas (such as Uchizo district in Tocache province), traffickers paid off military and police commanders, municipal councilmen, and Sendero guerrillas for the same planeloads of cocaine leaving the Valley.

Although guerrillas can successfully tax cocaine traffickers in areas where they maintain a preponderance of power, traffickers often respond to a guerrilla threat by developing "certain forms of cooperation and tacit alliance with the state."[36] Thus, during a 1984–85 state of emergency in the Upper Huallaga Valley, Peruvian military commanders relied heavily on local cocaine dealers for information on the whereabouts, strengths, and weaponry of Sendero Luminoso forces. There were reports in 1989 that cocaine traffickers, under prodding from the Peruvian military, were financing electrification and road-building projects to woo local peasants away from Sendero.[37]

Conversely, Colombian military units occasionally protect cocaine laboratories against FARC extortion attempts; in a November 1983 incident, a Colombian Special Forces team from Villavicencio helped a cocaine trafficker move an entire laboratory complex from an area controlled by the First FARC Front to a safer location near the Brazilian border. The operation, which involved five officers and forty-three NCOs, required twenty-six days.[38] From the state's perspective, guerrillas present a larger threat, or at least a more obvious threat.

Narcos allied with guerrillas appear more dangerous than plain narcos, but the cocaine industry is essentially a para-establishment political force. Episodic and opportunistic links to Marxist guerrilla organizations are far less important than penetrations of legitimate economic and political institutions. The cocaine traffickers' vast financial resources, military and logistical capabilities, and power to corrupt represent a challenge to government authority—but not an ideological challenge to democracy. In the end, the narco-guerrilla theory advanced by Reagan administration officials such as former ambassador to Colombia Lewis Tambs and Assistant Secretary of State for Inter-American Affairs Elliott Abrams was designed primarily to get the attention of Latin American governments.

WHY THE SUPPLY CANNOT BE STOPPED

U.S. and Latin American efforts to curb the supply of cocaine have failed abjectly. Some 300 to 400 tons of cocaine may flow into U.S. markets yearly; as University of Michigan researcher Lloyd Johnston notes, "the supply of cocaine has never been greater in the streets, the price has never been lower, and [the] drug has never been purer."[39] South American coca cultivation increased 44 percent from 1985 to 1989 according to the State Department's Bureau of International Narcotics Matters.[40] The U.S. government plans to spend $2.2 billion on narcotics-related programs in the Andean countries over the next five years, but even this sum is a pittance when compared to the South American cocaine industry's earnings of $9 to $10 billion a year. Anyhow, more resources may not be the answer. Structural barriers block effective drug enforcement in poor countries, and such barriers could well be insurmountable.

First, Andean governments worry about the impact of successful drug-control programs. The consequences would be exacerbated rural poverty and new legions of the unemployed, both of which would strengthen anti-democratic or communist movements. Imagine 200,000 coca-growing peasants marching on Bolivia's capital, La Paz. In Peru and Colombia, the war against drugs has proved difficult to reconcile with the struggle against communist insurgency. The threat of eradication alienates coca growers from the government and enhances the appeal of insurgent groups. In the Upper Huallaga Valley, for example, the U.S.-backed eradication effort has doubtless driven many peasants into the ranks of Sendero Luminoso. In Colombia, the government's persecution of the Medellín drug lords has tied down roughly one-third of Colombia's 110,000-man army, mostly in occupying estates belonging to traffickers. Such a huge diversion of manpower has enabled guerrilla organizations to regroup, expand their strength, and launch new offensives against military and civilian targets.

Second, many Latin Americans see the economic benefits of drug trafficking. Colombia's controller general, Rodolfo Gonzales, has publicly hailed the contribution of drug dollars to national economic growth. Leading bankers in Peru talk about the importance of cocaine earnings in stabilizing the country's currency. Bolivia's president Victor Paz Estenssoro remarked in 1986 that "cocaine has gained in importance in our economy in direct response to the shrinking of the formal economy."[41]

Third, Latin Americans tend to see U.S.-imposed drug enforcement measures as infringements on their national sovereignty. According to recent polls, two-thirds of Colombians oppose the extradition of drug traffickers to the United States.[42] This feeling may be heightened because some of the leading candidates for extradition, such as Colombia's Pablo Escobar and Bolivia's Roberto Suarez, provide support for charitable activities and so are popular in their countries. Arresting and extraditing such traffickers would be difficult politically. Officials undoubtedly recall the violent anti-American outbursts in Honduras following the April 1988 extradition of Juan Matta Ballestreros, a narcophilanthropist who cultivated a Robin Hood image.

Fourth, governments often exercise little or no control over territories where drug production flourishes, for these are remote from metropolitan centers, relatively inaccessible mountainous or jungle terrains which are patrolled by guerrillas or other hostile groups. In this way, drug traffic encourages territorial disintegration. The Peruvian government, for example, is losing control over the Upper Huallaga Valley, the region which ships its most important export, coca paste, to Colombia and in return receives money, weapons, and some economic leadership. Colombian aircraft maintain this connection by flying in and out of Peruvian airspace with virtual impunity. Colombian middlemen increasingly buy paste directly from peasants in the Valley rather than through Peruvian dealers. The Upper Huallaga is becoming less a part of Peru and more a part of Colombia.

Finally, corruption severely undermines criminal justice systems in cocaine-producing countries. Law enforcement in Latin American countries often represents simply a way to share in the proceeds of the drug trade: the police take bribes not to make arrests and seizures. When the police do make successful busts, the drugs are often resold on the illicit market.

These barriers mean that anti-drug activities in Latin American countries are largely cosmetic. Governments draw up elaborate plans to eradicate coca—the police make a few highly publicized arrests and cocaine seizures, fly around the countryside in helicopters, terrorize villages, and knock out an occasional cocaine laboratory—but with little effect. The core structure of the cocaine industry remains, and the industry's agricultural base continues to expand. Farmers in the Upper Huallaga Valley plant four to five acres for every hectare of coca eradicated, according to a professor at the Agrarian University of Tingo María, the capital of an important cocaine-growing province in the Valley.[43]

At the same time, governments resist the only effective method for controlling coca cultivation, herbicides. Herbicides toxic enough to kill the hardy cocaine bush may also be dangerous to agricultural crops, wildlife, fish, and even humans. The herbicide tebuthiuron ("Spike"), manufactured by Eli Lilly, is "one of a class of toxins that has caused liver damage and testicle tumors in rats." Lilly has refused to sell the herbicide to the State Department, apparently fearing a rash of liability lawsuits stemming from improper use.[44]

Governments fear ecological damage from the use of toxic chemicals, but they are even more concerned about the social effects: the prospects of massive rural unemployment and (in Colombia and Peru) the aggravation of a festering insurgency problem.

As a result, Bolivia has ruled out chemical eradication entirely. In Colombia, an experimental spraying program has been halted because the government is reportedly afraid of "criticism by environmentalists, the political opposition and peasants involved in drug cultivation." In Peru test spraying has been underway since October 1987; however, the Peruvian government's willingness to move toward full-scale chemical eradication seems contingent on assurances "that the herbicide is not harmful to other plants, animals and human beings." Given the recent publicity surrounding "Spike" and other toxic chemicals, the Peruvian government may opt to remain at the testing stage indefinitely.[45]

THE U.S. POLICY DILEMMA

A 1988 Department of State report noted that Latin American governments do not yet recognize that coca growing and cocaine trafficking "pose serious threats to their own survival."[46] Be that as it may, many Andean leaders are concerned that the suggested cures would be worse than the disease.

To a degree, that concern must also be the concern of Washington, which wants to encourage stable, economically viable governments in the region; to promote democracy; and to suppress leftist insurgent movements. America's war against its drug addiction is not necessarily compatible with these other priorities, at least in the short run. In fact, the argument can be made that the United States and its Latin American allies have a common interest in minimizing the intensity of the drug war. Yet this may be hard for Washington to do—there are real public pressures to do just the opposite. A *New York Times*/CBS News poll shows that Americans perceive drug trafficking as a more important international problem than arms control, terrorism, Palestinian unrest in Israel, or the situation in Central America. Another poll reports that Americans perceive stopping the drug dealings of anti-communist leaders in Central America as more important (by a vote of three to one) than fighting communism in the region. A third poll notes a public preference for U.S. government policies that reduce the supply of illicit drugs entering the United States over policies that focus on persuading Americans to stop using drugs.[47] A *Wall Street Journal*/NBC *News* poll in September 1989 showed that Americans by a 58 percent to 34 percent margin favored sending troops to fight drug trafficking in Colombia if the government there requested them.[48]

Nevertheless, the State Department report is certainly correct if it means that the status quo is not in the long-term interests of the Latin American countries. At issue is not so much democracy as the deterioration and de-modernization of political and economic institutions. As U.S. Ambassador to Colombia Charles Gillespie recently remarked, "The traffickers have already penetrated the fabric of Colombian life . . . [T]his penetration will lead not to the downfall of Colombia and its institutions but rather to a serious and lasting corruption."[49] Other political problems include the governments' weakening hold on their territories, their deteriorating reputation, and discrimination against their citizens and products.

Unfortunately, there may be no useful way to upgrade the war against cocaine that is not counterproductive. Virtually every prescription under discussion carries major disadvantages.

Enhancement of Drug-Fighting Capabilities in Producer Countries

Under this proposal, Andean governments would be provided with firepower, transport, communications, and intelligence support to establish their authority in drug-trafficking zones and destroy the cocaine industry's infrastructure. But the prevailing pattern of corruption in Andean countries makes many U.S. observers skeptical of the utility of such buildups. RAND economist Peter Reuter has suggested that better-equipped governments might mean no more than greater payoffs from the drug traffickers.[50]

Direct U.S. Military Intervention

The classic example of the approach was Operation Blast Furnace, the U.S. army-supported operation against cocaine laboratories in Bolivia in the summer of 1986. Blast Furnace was apparently a technical success since it virtually shut down the Bolivian cocaine trade for three months, but such operations can undermine the political legitimacy of host governments. All segments of Bolivia's political establishment condemned the government for inviting in American forces, and a leader with less stature than Victor Pas Estenssoro probably could not have survived the political fallout. South American countries today do not want foreign military forces stationed in their territories. Sending in military units or even large numbers of armed Drug Enforcement Agency agents risk landing the United States in a Vietnam-type morass: an unpopular confrontation with a powerful and elusive enemy on the enemy's own turf.

Income Replacement

"If we are to make a difference in cocaine control," declares a Department of State report, "a massive infusion of economic assistance will be required."[51] Such assistance compensates countries for the economic and social costs of shutting down cocaine production. Possible measures include hard currency loans to compensate for the reduced flow of dollars and lowering import barriers for legitimate products, such as textiles and sugar.

But what about the hundreds of thousands of small farmers who cultivate coca? A coca farmer in the Bolivian Chapare can net up to $2,600 per hectare per year, over four times what he can earn from cultivating oranges and avocados, the next most profitable traditional crops.[52] Thus crop substitution offers few attractions. The U.S. government is now indirectly paying $2,000 for each hectare of coca eradicated in Bolivia, but the Bolivian government estimates that the social costs of eradication—the cost of redirecting farmers into the licit agricultural economy—would be at least $7,000 per hectare.[53] For Bolivia, where coca grows on 50,000 to 70,000 hectares, the cost of total eradication would be a mind-boggling $350 to $490 million. Even if the money were available, it might be misspent; there are persistent rumors that some coca farmers in the Upper Huallaga Valley and the Chapare have used the cash payments for eradication to underwrite the costs of planting new coca fields in other locations.[54]

Sanctions

Perennially popular with Congress, this course of action includes withholding aid, prohibiting trade, cutting off international lending, and restricting the flow of travelers. Yet the record shows few cases where sanctions have achieved the desired objective. To cut off aid to the Andean countries would probably provoke intense anti-Yankee feelings, poison the diplomatic atmosphere, and reduce the resources available for anti-drug campaigns.

In addition, sanctions are a blunt instrument for specific problems. Thus, when Jorge Ochoa was released from a Colombian jail on December 30, 1987 (the second such release in sixteen months), the U.S. government singled out Colombian passengers and products for special customs checks at U.S. ports of entry. Yet the Colombian government had no jurisdiction over the criminal court judge who ordered Ochoa's release, and it had taken extraordinary measures to ensure that Ochoa could not escape from jail. Hence, the U.S. sanctions were misplaced—they will not bring Ochoa back to jail, nor will they make Colombia's criminal justice system less porous. Worse, they doubtless added to the unpopularity of the war against drugs. As Carlos Mauro Hoyas, Colombia's recently murdered attorney general, remarked, "Reprisals against innocent tourists create anger and resentment as well as a sort of solidarity with the drug bosses, not as traffickers but as fellow Colombians."[55]

Negotiating Cutbacks in Drug Production

This approach requires a dialogue with the Escobars, the Ochoas, the Rodríguez Gachas, and the other chief executives of the cocaine industry. The idea of a dialogue has enormous public support in Colombia. Supporters include a number of distinguished figures: a former head of Colombia's State Council (the country's top administrative court), a former acting attorney general, two Catholic bishops (of Popayan and Pereira), the mayor of Medellín, the president of the Chamber of Representatives, and several congressmen and academics. An ABC/*Washington Post* poll released in February 1990 indicated that nearly six out of ten Colombians favor giving amnesty to drug traffickers if they abandon the drug traffic, free their hostages, and end the violence.[56] The traffickers themselves made a formal offer to the government in 1984—to withdraw from the cocaine industry, to dismantle their laboratories and airstrips, and to repatriate their capital. In return, they wanted guarantees against extradition, which would have amounted to a safe haven in Colombia. The Medellín mafia advanced similar peace initiatives in September 1988 and January 1990. The Colombian government has said officially that it will not negotiate with traffickers.

Certainly, selective amnesty arrangements for criminals can and have been tried as tools of law enforcement. (The United States has its own witness protection program, for example.) Cocaine chiefs could reveal much about the structure and operations of the international cocaine industry—its supply channels, distribution networks, personnel policies, financing, and the names of corrupt U.S. officials who abet the trade. They could also provide information about guerrilla operations, for the two often use the same territory, the same clandestine methods, the same smuggling channels, even the same overseas banks.

Yet it is hard to see how the proposal would work in practice. For example, monitoring an amnesty arrangement—the repatriation of capital and the shutting down of a multi-billion-dollar industry—would present fundamental problems. How many Colombian and American law enforcement officials would it take to oversee such a program, and who would monitor the monitors? Too, the traffickers might be unable to deliver on their promises. Is the cocaine industry so tightly structured that a few kingpins can command a larger number of lieutenants to order an even larger number of managers, suppliers, and transporters to withdraw from a business that earns so much? Possibly, but an amnesty might constitute little more than a retirement program for the chief executives of the cocaine industry. They would have to make a practical demonstration of their market power—say, by shutting down 80 percent of Colombian cocaine production for a six-month period. A negotiated settlement is at best a futuristic option. The idea has some theoretical merit, but it would be extremely difficult to implement.

These difficulties suggest that curbing the supply of cocaine from producer countries may not be effective, no matter how much money the United States government devotes to overseas programs.

Are there better ways to spend the U.S. drug-enforcement dollar? The options seem to be increased interdiction, stepped-up enforcement against drug dealers and pushers, and such demand-reduction steps as stiffer penalties for users, "Just Say No" programs, and drug testing. Many U.S. experts expect these measures also may not work very well.[57] Moreover, as the national controversy over drug testing indicates, there are political and legal limits to controlling drug consumption, just as there are limits to controlling production in the Andean countries. Short of legalizing cocaine use (which carries the danger of stimulating even more addiction) or changing the habits and preferences of U.S. consumers, there seems to be no way out of the cocaine morass.

The solution, if there is one, lies not in the Andean jungles but in the United States. The six million people who now consume cocaine must be persuaded to change their habits and preferences. Perhaps they will grow tired of cocaine and switch to designer drugs; or perhaps they will find more productive and healthy forms of recreation.

NOTES

1. U.S Senate Committee on Governmental Affairs, "Hearing on Structure of International Drug Cartels," Washington, D.C., September 12, 1989, p. 14.

2. Committee on Foreign Relations, U.S. Senate Subcommittee on Terrorism, Narcotics and International Ammunition Hearings, "Drugs, Law Enforcement and Foreign Policy: Panama," Washington, D.C., Part 2, February 8, 9, 10, and 11, 1988, p. 245.

3. Kevin Healy, "The Boom Within the Crisis: Some Recent Effects of Foreign Cocaine Markets on Bolivian Rural Society and Economy," in Coca and Cocaine, ed. Deborah Pacini and Christine Franquemont (Peterborough, N.H.: Transcript Printing Company, 1986), pp. 101–43.

4. "Colombia: The Drug Economy," The Economist, April 2, 1988, p. 63. For a general discussion of the cocaine economy in South America, see Rensselaer Lee, The White Labyrinth: Cocaine and Political Power (New Brunswick, N.J.: Transaction, 1989), chapter 1.

5. Scott L. Malcomson, "Cocaine Republic," The Village Voice, August 26, 1986, p. 18; "Tocache: Some Things Go Better With . . .," The Andean Report, December 1985, pp. 242–43.

6. "¿Quién Fue?" Semana, January 25, 1988, p. 24.

7. Author's March 1998 trip to the Barrio Pablo Escobar and to Pacho. Hernán Gavíria Berrio, "Letter to Fabio Castillo," Medellín Cívico, April 1987, p. 13; "Civismo En Marcha," Medellín Cívico, March 1984, p. 2; Jorge Eliecer Orozco, Lehder: El Hombre (Bogotá: Plaza y

Janes, 1987), pp. 60, 120; "A Self-Styled Robin Hood," *Time*, February 25, 1985, p. 33; *The New York Times*, August 15, 1982.

8. Rensselaer Lee, "Drugs," in *The U.S. Economy and Developing Countries: Campaign 88 Briefing Papers for Candidates*, ed. Richard Feinberg and Gregg Goldstein (Washington, D.C.: Overseas Development Council, 1988), p. 2. See also Congressional Research Service, *Combatting International Drug Cartels: Issues for U.S. Policy* (Washington, D.C.: Government Printing Office, 1987), p. 32; and Institutio Nacional de Planificación, "Plan Nacional de Eliminación del Narcotrafico" (Lima, 1984), p. 4.

9. Government of Bolivia, *Triennial Program of the Battle Against Drug Trafficking*, November 1986, pp. 5–6.

10. *Latin American Regional Reports: Andean Group*, March 3, 1988, p. 8. Export data from author's conversations with U.S. Treasury officials, March, 1988.

11. Fabio Castillo, *Los Jinetes de la Cocaina* (Bogotá: Editorial Documentos Periodistos, 1987), pp. 124–48.

12. Interview with the author, April 1986.

13. "Governments' Sweetheart Deals and Subsidies Attempt to Stop Widening the Gaps in the Financial Circuit," *The Andean Report*, October 1986, pp. 141–42.

14. Raúl Gonzáles, "Coca and Subversion in the Huallaga," *Quehacer* (Lima), September-October 1987, pp. 55–72.

15. Michael Massing, "In the Cocaine War the Jungle Is Winning," *The New York Times Magazine*, March 4, 1990, p. 90.

16. *The Washington Post*, February 24, 1988; "Aboga Abrams por Más Ayuda a Gestiones de América Latina Contra Narcóticos," USIS news release in Spanish, Bogotá, February 1986, p. 4.

17. *INCSR*, 1987, p. 70.

18. *El Tiempo*, January 10, 1988.

19. Author's interviews with U.S. narcotics experts in Bogotá, March-April 1986.

20. Author's interview with the staff of Invamer, a Colombian polling organization, Medellín, March 9, 1988.

21. "El Dossier de Medellín," *Semana*, January 27, 1987, p. 25.

22. *El Tiempo*, February 9, 1988.

23. See, for example, "La Patria Acorralada," *Quindío Libre*, October 1, 1983; "No a la Extradición,"*Medellín Cívico*, March 1984, p. 7; and Gilberto Zapata, "El Triunfo Es de Colombia," *Medellín Cívico*, July 1987, p. 3.

24. Berrio, "Letter to Fabio Castillo."

25. "El Dinero Caliente Pretende Entrar en Politica," *Guión*, July 15–21, 1983, p. 21; Jorge Child and Mario Arango, *Los Condenados de la Coca* (Medellín: Editorial J.M. Arango, 1985), p. 107.

26. Castillo, *Jinetes*, p. 105.

27. USIS, "Aboga Abrams," p. 4; *The Washington Post*, November 14, 1987.

28. Ibid. For a detailed analysis of the narco-guerrilla connection, see Lee, *The White Labyrinth*, chapter 4.

29. "Los Barrios Pobres y la Eradicacion de la Pobreza," *Medellín Cívico*, October 1986, p. 3; "La Paz Es la Justicia Social,"*Medellín Cívico*, November 1986, p. 3; "Mientras el Pueblo Padece Hambre, Varias Industrias Se Enriquecen," *Medellín Cívico*, April 1987, p. 4; Berrio, "Letter to Fabio Castillo"; and "Existen Mas de Dos Millones de Desempleados," *Medellín Cívico*, May 1987, p. 6.

30. Orozco, *Lehder: El Hombre*, p. 235.

31. "El Dossier Paramilitar," *Semana*, April 11, 1989, p. 28.

32. "MORENA se destapa," *Semana*, August 15, 1989, pp. 21–26.

33. *El Tiempo*, November 13, 1987. See also: *The Washington Post*, November 14, 1987, and Ayatollah, *El Tiempo*, November 15, 1987.

34. *El Tiempo*, February 22, 1988.

35. Interview with staff of CORAH (Coca Reduction in the Alto Huallaga), Tingo María, October 12, 1987; interviews with U.S. pilots, Upper Huallaga Valley, October 13, 1987; interview with U.S. narcotics official, Lima, October 15–16, 1987; interview with General Juan Zarate of Peru's narcotics police, Lima, October 16, 1987; and *The Miami Herald*, October 14, 1987.

36. Alfredo Molano, *Selva Adentro* (Bogotá: El Ancora, 1987), p. 134.

37. Cristian Bofill, "Arciniega: The Coca Paste General," *Estado de Sao Paolo*, Sao Paolo, October 29, 1989, p. 16.

38. For accounts of this operation, see Castillo, *Jinetes*, p. 235; and Fabio Castillo, "Operación Encubierta para Proteger Laboratorio de Coca," *El Espectador*, August 1, 1985.

39. Quoted in *The New York Times*, April 12, 1988.

40. State Department, *International Narcotics Contol Strategy Report*, Washington, D.C., Bureau of International Narcotics Matters, 1987, p. 24, hereafter INCSR; *The New York Times*, March 2, 1990.

41. "Reactivación Economica por Dinero Caliente," *El Espectador*, October 3, 1987; "Directive del BCR del Peru Habla Sobre Narcodolares," *El Comercio*, October 8, 1987; *The Washington Post*, July 17, 1986.

42. *The Washington Post*, February 2, 1988, and ABC/*Washington Post*, Colombia Poll, February 8, 1990.

43. *The Washington Post*, April 16, 1987.

44. *The Washington Times*, June 8, 1988.

45. INCRS, March 1, 1988, pp. 8, 75, and 91, *The New York Times*, June 28, 1988.

46. INCRS, 1988, p. 8.

47. *The New York Times*, April 10, 1988.

48. Michael McQueen and David Shribman, "Battle Against Drugs Is Chief Issue Facing Nations," *The Wall Street Journal*, September 22, 1989, pp. A1, A14.

49. Quoted in *The Los Angeles Times*, February 21, 1988.

50. Congressional Research Service, *Combatting International Drug Cartels: Issues for U.S. Policy*, Report for the Caucus on International Narcotics Control, U.S. Senate (Washington, D.C.: Government Printing Office, 1987), p. 13.

51. INCSR, 1988, p. 8.

52. Gerald Owens, "Costs of Production: Coca," Unsolicited report to AID, December 31, 1986, p. 6.

53. Peter McFadden, "New Eradication Program Winning Over Coca Farmers," Associated Press, December 31, 1987.

54. Interviews with Peruvian officials, Upper Huallaga Valley, October 10–14, 1987. (In Peru, farmers get up to $300 for each hectare of cocaine destroyed.) Also, telephone interview with a U.S. expert on Bolivian rural development, June 26, 1988.

55. *The New York Times*, January 13, 1988.

56. ABC/*Washington Post*, Colombia Poll, February 8, 1990.

57. *The New York Times*, April 12, 1988.

21

Robbin' Hoods: How the Big Banks Spell Debt "Relief"

JEFFREY SACHS

Last September [1988] American banks were singing the praises of their latest "debt relief" agreement with a Latin American nation. Citicorp, which had led the banks in negotiations with Brazil, said the resulting deal contained the "most extensive and innovative menu of options of

Reprinted by permission of *The New Republic*, © 1989, The New Republic, Inc.

Note: It is a violation of the law to reproduce this selection by any means whatsoever without the written permission of the copyright holder.

any package to date." Five months later the deal is virtually dead. Brazil has descended more deeply into economic crisis, with an inflation rate that exceeds 2,000 percent. The Brazilians have suspended the agreement, and President Jose Sarney warned recently that the March interest bill could go unpaid. With the ink on the September agreement barely dry, the Brazilian government is once again searching for new financing.

Were the banks foolish? Did they overestimate the power of their agreement with Brazil? No, the banks knew exactly what they were doing: lulling the public, claiming to have found a solution to Brazil's debt problem, when in fact their overriding motivation was short-term profit. The September agreement, notwithstanding Citicorp's sunny rhetoric, was plainly unrealistic. It forced Brazil to use billions of dollars in scarce foreign exchange reserves to pay all of its overdue interest. These payments were completed last fall, leading to record profits for big American banks in the fourth quarter of 1988.

It was clear from the beginning that the payments might well trigger runaway inflation. But this prospect didn't deter the banks, for two reasons. First, they are notoriously shortsighted. (Remember, they helped create the debt crisis.) Second, they knew that even if putting the squeeze on Brazil left it incapable of continuing its payments, someone else could probably be convinced to pick up the tab: the International Monetary Fund, the World Bank, or the U.S. government (in all three cases, read "American taxpayers"). Indeed, over the past few years, the largest banks have succeeded remarkably in using other people's money to shield themselves from the fallout of the bad loans they made in the 1970s.

The gap between rhetoric and reality has never been as wide as it is now. The banks continue to tout their constructive role highly. (They have been "innovative in responding to the financing needs of the debtors," says a recent study by the bankers' lobby, the Institute of International Finance.) And they continue to refuse to offer real debt relief. Meanwhile Latin American nations, many of them frail democracies, continue to sink into unprecedented chaos. There is hyperinflation in Argentina, Brazil, and Peru. There is a high risk of political instability in these countries as well as in Mexico. And a growing number of nations are far behind on their debt payments, including Argentina, Bolivia, Costa Rica, the Dominican Republic, Ecuador, Honduras, and Peru.

In persisting with their upbeat rhetoric, the large U.S. banks are trying to hide a simple truth—that a real solution to the crisis would require them to accept a significant loss on their loans, by reducing the interest or reducing the principal. The longer the banks can manage to conceal that fact, the better their chances of shifting the losses to others, notably you.

You can say lots of nasty things about this strategy, but you can't say it hasn't worked. There are about 40 countries, with 800 million people, in financial distress over the debt crisis. Since 1982 these countries have signed over 90 "debt restructuring" agreements with the banks. Many of these countries don't have a prayer of servicing more than a tiny fraction of their debts in the long term. Yet there hasn't been a single restructuring in which the commercial banks have agreed to submarket interest rates, or to an across-the-board cut in the amount of debt.

Instead, there have been various more convoluted forms of "relief," virtually none of which fulfill the meaning of that word. The big banks have lately become quite adept at flashing around refinancing tools that have impressive-sounding names—debt-equity swaps, "voluntary" debt reduction—but that either have no real effect or actually compound the debt crisis.

In rejecting the call for straightforward debt reduction, the banks say that Latin America's problems are self-inflicted. That is partly true, and there is no doubt that Latin America needs economic reform—more responsible fiscal policy, and the loosening up of markets and of trade policy. Further, this reform should precede, not follow, debt reduction. But bold reforms have already been forthcoming in many countries, including Bolivia, Costa Rica, Ecuador (most recently) Venezuela, and, most important, Mexico, which has slashed its budget deficit and its tariffs and joined the General Agreement on Tariffs and Trade. Reforms could be extracted from Brazil and other countries, too. The problem is that reforms can't be sustained without a significant reduction of the debt burden. The debtor governments need economic breathing space to impose reforms. And besides, no leader can gain support for reforms that have little payoff at home and instead serve mainly to facilitate interest payments to foreign banks.

At its core, the sound solution to the debt crisis is comparable to a simple bankruptcy case, in which the debtor's burden is comprehensively reduced, and all creditors share the losses. This is almost invariably to the collective benefit of the creditors; after reducing the debt to a reasonable amount, they can expect to receive that amount in full, whereas leaving the debt at its original level could worsen the debtor's crisis and lead to a complete halt of payments. Still, individual creditors may try to resist comprehensive debt reduction, and get other creditors to absorb the losses. Bankruptcy law arose for this very reason; bankruptcy judges impose settlements in which all creditors share the burden and all ultimately benefit.

In the debt crisis that now faces developing countries, there is no bankruptcy judge. Instead, agreements are fashioned by a few big banks sitting on committees that negotiate with the debtor nations. The biggest U.S. banks—led by Citicorp and including the Bank of America, Manufacturers Hanover, Chase Manhattan, and Chemical Bank—have systematically resisted an orderly solution to the crisis (a simple cut in interest rates, say), because they have had the incentive and the opportunity to pawn off some of their losses on other players in the game, including the smaller banks as well as the taxpayer.

Their surprising ally in this game of delay and buckpassing has been the U.S. Treasury. It has exercised its influence within the International Monetary Fund to keep the IMF from stepping in and playing the role of bankruptcy judge. The Treasury has also, under the Baker plan, sent a clear message to debtor countries: if you push for real debt reduction, and especially if you try to force concessions from the largest banks, we will not take it kindly. The Treasury has been vague about what the retaliation might be, but less favorable trade status and less generosity from world lending institutions are among the likely candidates.

Thus did Secretary of State James Baker personally derail the Brazilian negotiations in the fall of 1987, back when he was treasury secretary, by warning Brazil's finance minister that his proposal for submarket interest rates was a "non-starter." Of course, no one knew until recently one possible reason for Baker's intense support of the banks: his holdings in Chemical Bank, which had more than half of its shareholder equity lent to Brazil alone.

The Treasury has also helped the big banks pass much of the bill to the taxpayer, by supporting their lobbying for increased lending from the IMF and the World Bank. Loans to developing nations from those institutions have traditionally supported economic stabilization and economic development. Under the influence of Baker and the big banks, though, they are devoted increasingly to helping the debtor countries pay the interest on their bank debts. This amounts to a money laundering operation in which taxpayer dollars are diverted to the commercial banks via world lending institutions and Latin America. Maybe all this helps explain why Baker, not generally a big fan of multilateral aid, was an avid supporter of the $14 billion of new lending authority given by the United States to the World Bank last year.

The big banks support this lobbying with a steady stream of publicity to convince the public of their good intentions. They tirelessly tell us about the "new money" they're making available to debtors, even though out of the 40 or so debtor countries, exactly one signed a "new money" agreement that was actually put in operation last year. That was Brazil, and we've seen what became of its new money.

Notwithstanding the p.r. virtuosity of the big banks, the past year has seen growing political support for debt relief that would actually do what the term implies. Faced with this threat, the banks have upgraded their rhetoric, while holding firm to their basic strategy. They have lately become champions of "voluntary debt reduction," in which an individual bank can choose to give up part of its claim on the debtor country in return for a safer asset. For example, last year the banks were given the option of trading their claims on Mexico for a new Mexican "exit bond" that had a smaller principal than the original loan, but came with (among other things) collateral that the bank could seize in the event of default. There were a few takers, and Mexico reduced its debt, but only marginally.

One reason the relief was only slight is that voluntary debt reduction suffers from a basic problem—the general problem of trying to negotiate debt relief without the equivalent of a bankruptcy judge. If individual banks actually granted enough voluntary debt reduction to restore Mexico's creditworthiness, the remaining Mexican debt would rise sharply in value (it now sells for 37 percent of face value), as repayment prospects improved. But knowing this, each individual bank is inclined to hold on to its Mexican debt, waiting for the other banks to provide relief. In the end, little real debt reduction will occur unless all banks are somehow compelled—either through mutual agreement or by an external authority such as the IMF—to share the cost.

From the big banker's point of view, of course, voluntary debt relief is a smashing success. It helps them look earnest and conscientious, a perception that comes in handy when they're trying to lobby for taxpayer contributions to the World Bank and IMF. Also, the big banks can reap monetary benefits if smaller banks can be tempted into giving up their claims on a developing nation and thereby raising the value of remaining claims. And the smaller banks, which tend to have less equity tied up in these loans, are often willing to cave in and take a loss, just to clear their books of the mess once and for all. Citicorp chairman John Reed was recently quite candid on this point: ". . . Some smaller banks that have very different interests [from ours] are selling out at prices that, frankly, are quite convenient to those of us who are going to stay in for the long haul."

This enthusiastic championing of debt reduction—so long as it's done by others—has become the standard pose of big banks. Last year Bolivia arranged a "buyback" in which it repurchased its debts at a discount from any bank willing to sell. Bank of America played a large role in negotiating the arrangement, and praised it in testimony before Congress. But when the time came for the actual buyback, Bank of America refused to sell Bolivia more than 16 percent of the debt it held, keeping Bolivia in hock on the rest. Citicorp also praised the deal in Congress while refusing to sell most of its claims on Bolivia.

Another part of the game plan for the largest banks, particularly those with a network of branch banks in Latin America, is to press hard for more "debt-equity swaps," which are fast becoming the banks' favorite kind of voluntary debt reduction. These have been widely touted as a partial solution to the debt crisis, even though they have proved disastrous in most countries that try them. In a debt-equity swap, the bank typically sells its debt to another firm, which in turn sells it to the central bank of the debtor country. The central bank may buy the debt at a modest discount, or even at face value, despite the fact that the debt trades at a deep discount in New York and was bought cheaply by the intermediary firm. That firm then uses the proceeds to invest in the local economy.

The debtor country typically loses big. The central bank does not usually have enough cash on hand for the deal. (After all, it didn't have the money to pay the interest, so how can it suddenly retire the principal?) Therefore, the central bank must print money, or float new internal debt. The upshot is that debt-equity swaps typically fuel inflation, or sharply raise domestic interest rates, or both.

So why do the debtor nations sign on to these deals? Sadly, some local officials consent to the swaps in exchange for a kickback or in response to more subtle pressures from local firms that benefit from them. Also, debt-equity swaps are often foisted on debtor nations by big banks as a precondition for restructuring agreements. This was painfully true in the case of Brazil, where Citicorp relentlessly insisted on a swap program—the last thing a country on the verge of hyperinflation needed. Brazil was committed to repurchase $1.8 billion of its debt at face value, despite the fact that the debt was selling in the New York market at less than 40 cents on the dollar. Of course, in agreeing to the swap, Brazil raised the debt's value in New York markets, which was exactly what Citicorp had in mind.

From the point of view of U.S. foreign policy, the most pressing need for debt reduction is in Mexico, which is currently negotiating a new restructuring agreement. There is no doubt that debt reduction would help keep the Mexican government viable. Nor is there doubt that the government has undertaken heroic economic reforms. The country deserves and needs to have the interest rate on its debt cut to four or five percent, from the current 11 percent.

Could Mexico's creditor banks be convinced to agree to such a cut? Almost certainly, if there was adequate support from the U.S. Treasury, finance ministries in other creditor countries, and the IMF. The first step would be a clear signal that the U.S. government wants real relief, and that the Treasury will not pressure Mexico to keep paying 11 percent interest. The United States could also make clear that it will continue to support lending by the IMF and the World Bank, but will not press Mexico into using those funds to pay market interest rates to banks. The Treasury has many other carrots and sticks at its disposal. And the IMF and World Bank could encourage debt reduction by guaranteeing the reduced interest payments.

Japan has already signaled its willingness to help finance those guarantees, not only for Mexico, but for other debtors as well. But so far the Treasury has pushed away Japan's offer, partly out of fear of surrendering IMF voting power to Japan, and partly, it seems, to keep American banks from getting cornered into actual debt relief. Once again the

Treasury has proved more attentive to the interests of large banks than to those of taxpayers or U.S. foreign policy.

Granted, in theory, the taxpayers *could* foot the entire bill for genuine and lasting debt relief. And they assuredly will keep footing some of the bill, whatever happens. But banks deserve to shoulder a large share of the burden in both a moral and practical sense. It was they, and not the taxpayers, who made the bad loans. (Their claims that they did so under government pressure just don't wash.) And accepting the consequences for bad loans of the past is supposedly what discourages bad loans in the future. Of course, the same can be said for debtors; and you can rest assured that, even in the best of cases, the developing nations will live with collapsed living standards for years to come as a result of their overly aggressive borrowing.

Under the current Treasury, which so far looks disturbingly like the Baker Treasury, the banks are not likely to pay their fair share anytime soon. Instead, we will be told that no bank should be "pressured" into anything. And we will be told once again that the problem is very complicated, requiring new IMF and World Bank inflows into Mexico, co-financing arrangements with third countries, a "new money" package from the banks, contingency clauses, and a menu of options for debt-equity swaps and exit bonds for the smaller banks. And so on.

Mexico, like Brazil before it, may knuckle under to the Treasury; its internal economic and political crisis—the very reason it urgently needs relief—robs the government of the vigor to challenge the Treasury's position. But as in Brazil, we should expect the current policy to produce rising instability rather than renewed creditworthiness and growth. And you know who, in addition to Mexico's impoverished people, will pay in the end.

REVOLUTION: THE WEAK RESPOND

22

Eastern Europe: The Year of Truth

TIMOTHY GARTON ASH

1.

Last year communism in Eastern Europe died. 1949–1989 RIP. And the epitaph might be:

Nothing in his life
Became him like the leaving it.

The thing that was comprehensively installed in the newly defined territories of Poland, Czechoslovakia, Hungary, Romania, and Bulgaria, and in the newly created German Democratic Republic after 1949, the thing called, according to one's point of view, "socialism," "totalitarianism," "Stalinism," "politbureaucratic dictatorship," "real existing socialism," "state capitalism," "dictatorship over needs," or, most neutrally, "the Soviet-type system"—that thing will never walk again. And arguably, if we can no longer talk of communism we should no longer talk of Eastern Europe, at least with a capital "E" for Eastern. Instead, we shall have central Europe again, east central Europe, southeastern Europe, eastern Europe with a small "e," and, above all, individual peoples, nations, and states.

To be sure, even without a political-military reversal inside the Soviet

Reprinted with permission from *The New York Review of Books*. Copyright © 1990 Nyrev, Inc.

Note: It is a violation of the law to reproduce this selection by any means whatsoever without the written permission of the copyright holder.

Union there will be many further conflicts, injustices, and miseries in these lands. But they will be different conflicts, injustices, and miseries—new and old, post-communist but also pre-communist. In the worst case, there might yet be new dictators; but they would be different dictators. We shall not see again that particular system, characterized by the concentration of political and economic power and the instruments of coercion in the hands of one Leninist party, manifested sociologically as a privileged new class, and initially aspiring to total control, in states with arbitrarily limited sovereignty.

Of course, if we walk the streets of any Eastern European city we can still find the gray, familiar traces: the flattened neoclassical Stalinist facades on all the Victory Squares, the Lenin Boulevards, Steelworks, Shipyards, the balding middle-aged officials with their prefabricated lies, the cheap paper forms for completion in quadruplicate, the queues, the attitude of "we pretend to work and you pretend to pay us." Yet even the physical evidences are being removed at a speed that must cause some anxiety to conservationists. (In Poland there is a scheme for preserving all the old props in an entertainment park. The proposed name is Stalinland.)

If 1989 was the end, what was the beginning of the end? To read the press, or hear Mrs. Thatcher talk, you would think history began with Gorbachev. At the other extreme, some would say communism in Eastern Europe was doomed at birth. This thesis may, in turn, be advanced in several forms. One can say that communism was incompatible with the political culture of East Central Europe, although why that political culture should suddenly stop at the quite arbitrary Western frontier of the Soviet Union is not clear. Alternatively, one can say that communism was a wonderful idea that was doomed only because the people of Eastern Europe did not find their way to it themselves, but had it imposed on them by a foreign power, which itself did not understand it. Or one can say that communism is incompatible with human nature, period. Whether by congenital deformity or merely as the result of a ghastly forceps delivery, the death was preordained at birth. In between these two extreme positions, some people in the countries concerned would point to various supposed "missed opportunities" or turning points at which Eastern European history failed to turn. In this class, 1956 and 1968 are the leading candidates.

As usual, there is an element of truth in all these claims, though in some more than others. Churchill declared, "I have not become the King's First Minister in order to preside over the liquidation of the British empire," and proceeded to do almost exactly that. Gorbachev came to power proposing to save the Soviet empire and presides over its disintegration. That Moscow has permitted the former "satellite" countries to determine how they want to govern themselves was clearly a sine qua non for what followed.[1] But the nature and direction of the processes of domestic political self-determination cannot be understood by studying Soviet policy. The causes lie elsewhere, in the history of individual countries, in their interactions with their Eastern European neighbors, and with the more free and prosperous Europe that lies to the West, North, and South of them.

If I were to be forced to name a single date for the "beginning of the end" in this *inner* history of Eastern Europe, it would be June 1979. The judgment may be thought excessively Polonocentric, but I do believe that the Pope's first great pilgrimage to Poland was that turning point. Here, for the first time, we saw that large-scale, sustained, yet supremely peaceful and self-disciplined manifestation of social unity, the gentle crowd against the Party–state, which was both the hallmark and the essential domestic catalyst of change in 1989, in every country except Romania (and even in Romania, the crowds did not start the violence). The Pope's visit was followed, just over a year later, by the birth of Solidarity, and without the Pope's visit it is doubtful that there would have been a Solidarity.

The example of Solidarity was seminal. It pioneered a new kind of politics in Eastern Europe (and new not only there): a politics of social self-organization aimed at negotiating the transition from communism. The actors, forms, and issues of 1980–1981 in Poland were fundamentally different from anything seen in Eastern Europe between 1949 and 1979: in many respects, they presaged those seen throughout Eastern Europe in 1989. If there is any truth in this judgment, then there was something especially fitting in the fact that it was in 1989 that the Russian leader and the Polish Pope finally met. In their very different ways, they both started it.

To find a year in European history comparable to 1989, however, we obviously have to reach back much farther than 1979, or 1949: 1789 in France? 1917 in Russia? Or, closer to home, 1918–1919 in Central Europe? But 1918–1919 was the aftermath of world war. The closer parallel is surely 1848, the Springtime of Nations. In the space of a few paragraphs such comparisons are little better than parlor games. Yet, like parlor games, they can be amusing, and sometimes help to concentrate the mind.

According to A.J.P. Taylor, 1848 erupted "after forty years of peace and stability," while Lewis Namier describes it, with somewhat less cavalier arithmetic, as "the outcome of thirty-three creative years of European peace carefully preserved on a consciously counter-revolutionary basis." The revolution, Namier writes, "was born at least as much of hopes as of discontents." There was undoubtedly an economic and social background: lean harvests and the potato disease. But "the common denominator was ideological." Namier quotes the exiled Louis-Philippe declaring that he had given way to *une insurrection morale*, and King Wilhelm of Württemberg excusing himself to the Russian minister at Stuttgart, one Gorchakov, with the words: *"Je ne puis pas monter à cheval contre les idées."* Namier calls his magnificent essay "The Revolution of the Intellectuals."[2]

The Revolution of 1989 also erupted out of celebrations of "forty years of peace and stability in Europe." Remember NATO's fortieth anniversary in May? With the "Yalta Europe," as with the "Vienna Europe" in the previous century, the question was always: Peace and stability *for whom*? Ordinary men and women in Central and Eastern Europe felt the rough edge of both. Here too, a stricter arithmetic might reduce the forty years to thirty-three, for perhaps it was only after crushing the Hungarian revolution of 1956 that Soviet leaders could be quite sure that the West would not intervene militarily to disturb this "peace"—carefully preserved on a counterrevolutionary basis.

A revolution born as much of hopes as of discontents? Yes, again. To be sure, the economic "discontents" were there, acutely in Poland and Romania, increasingly, though less dramatically, elsewhere. In this connection, Fritz Stern has aptly recalled Mirabeau's declaration on the eve of the French Revolution: "the nation's deficit is the nation's treasure." Substitute "hard currency debt" for "deficit" and you have one of the main reasons why it was Poland and Hungary that led the field in the first half of 1989. But, unlike in Poland in August 1980, it was not a turn of the economic screw that precipitated mass popular protest in any Eastern European country in 1989. It was political hopes—and outrage at the repression with which the local regimes attempted to curb those hopes.

As with 1848 this, too, might be called a "revolution of the intellectuals." To be sure, the renewed flexing of workers' muscle in two strike waves in 1988 was what finally brought Poland's Communists to the first Round Table of 1989. To be sure, it was the masses on the streets in demonstrations in all the other Eastern European countries that brought the old rulers down. But the politics of the revolution were not made by workers or peasants. They were made by intellectuals: the playwright Václav Havel, the medievalist Bronislaw Geremek, the Catholic editor Tadeusz Mazowiecki, the painter Bärbel Bohley in Berlin, the philosophers János Kis and Gáspár Miklós Tamás in Budapest, the engineering professor Petre Roman and the poet Mircea Dinescu in Bucharest. History has outdone Shelley, for poets were the acknowledged legislators of this world. The crowds on Wenceslas Square chanted "Long live the students! Long live the actors!" And the sociology of the opposition forums (New, Democratic, Civic), parties, and parliamentary candidates was distinctly comparable to that of the Frankfurt Parliament or the Slav Congress at Prague in 1848. *Hundert zwanzig Professoren. . . .*

As in 1848, the common denominator was ideological. The inner history of these revolutions is that of a set of ideas whose time had come, and a set of ideas whose time had gone. At first glance this may seem a surprising statement. For had not the ideology ceased to be an active force many years before? Surely the rulers no longer believed a word of the guff they spouted, or expected their subjects to believe it, or even expected their subjects to believe that they, the rulers, believed it? This is probably true in most cases, although who knows what an old man like Erich Honecker, a Communist from his earliest youth, still genuinely believed? (One must never underestimate the human capacity for self-deception.)

Yet one of the things these revolutions showed, ex post facto, is just how important the residual veil of ideology still was. Few rulers are content to say simply, "We have the Gatling gun/ and you do not!" "We hold power because we hold power." Ideology provided a residual legitimation, perhaps also enabling the rulers, and their politbureaucratic servants, at least partly to deceive themselves about the nature of their own rule. At the same time, it was vital for the semantic occupation of the public sphere. The combination of censorship and a nearly complete Party–state monopoly of the mass media provided the army of semantic occupation; ideology, in the debased, routinized form of newspeak, was its ammunition. However despised and un-credible these structures of organized lying were, they still performed a vital blocking function. They no longer mobilized, but they did continue to prevent the public articulation of shared aspirations and common truths.

What is more, by demanding from the ordinary citizen seemingly innocuous semantic signs of outward conformity, the system managed somehow to implicate them in it. It is easy now to forget that until almost the day before yesterday, almost everyone in East Germany and Czechoslovakia was living a double life: systematically saying one thing in public and another in private. This was a central theme of the writings of Václav Havel over the last decade and one he movingly returned to in his 1990 New Year's address as president.[3] The worst thing was, he said, the "contaminated moral environment":

> All of us have become accustomed to the totalitarian system, accepted it as an unalterable fact and therefore kept it running. . . . None of us is merely a victim of it, because all of us helped to create it together.

The crucial "line of conflict," he wrote earlier, did not run between the people and the State, but rather through the middle of each person, "for everyone in his or her own way is both a victim and a supporter of the system." A banner I saw above the altar in an East Berlin church vividly expressed the same basic thought. It said: "I am Cain *and* Abel."

In order to understand what it meant for ordinary people to stand in those vast crowds in the city squares of Central Europe, chanting their own, spontaneous slogans, you have first to make the imaginative effort to understand what it feels like to live a double life, to pay this daily toll of public hypocrisy. As they stood and shouted together, these ordinary men and women were not merely healing divisions in their society; they were healing divisions in themselves. Everything that had to do with the word, with the press, with television, was of the first importance to these crowds. The semantic occupation was as offensive to them as military occupation; cleaning up the linguistic environment was as vital as cleaning up the physical environment. The long queue every morning in Wenceslas Square, lining up patiently in the freezing fog for a newspaper called *The Free Word*, was, for me, one of the great symbolic pictures of 1989.

The motto of the year—and not just in Czechoslovakia—was *Pravda Vítězí*, the old Hussite slogan, adopted by Masaryk, "Truth shall prevail," or, in the still more ancient Latin, *Magna est veritas et praevalebit*. As one speaks in English of a "moment of truth" for some undertaking, so this was a year of truth for communism. There is a real sense in which these regimes lived by the word and perished by the word.

2.

For what, after all, happened? A few thousands, then tens, then hundreds of thousands went onto the streets. They spoke a few words. "Resign!" they said. "Free elections!" "Freedom!" And the Berlin Wall opened. And the walls of Jericho fell. And with the walls, the Communist parties simply crumbled. At astonishing speed. By the beginning of 1990 the Hungarian Socialist Workers' party had split in two, with the majority of its members leaving for good. In Poland, the Polish United Workers' party held its last Central Committee meeting in the first week of January, resolving thereafter to change its name, statutes, and character. Within two months, East Germany's Socialist Unity party lost its leading role and almost half its members. The inner decay of these parties recalled the remark of a German poet in 1848: "Monarchy is dead, though monarchs still live."

With the single, signal exception of Romania, these revolutions were also remarkable for their almost complete lack of violence. Like Solidarity in 1980–1981 they were that historical contradiction in terms, "peaceful revolution." No bastilles were stormed, no guillotines erected. Lamp posts were used only for street lighting. Romania alone saw tanks and firing squads. Elsewhere the only violence was that used at the outset by police. The young demonstrators in East Berlin and Prague laid candles in front of the police, who responded with truncheons. The Marseillaise of 1989 said not *"aux armes, citoyens"* but *"aux bougies, citoyens."* The rationale and tradition of nonviolence can be found in the history of all the democratic oppositions of East Central Europe throughout the 1980s. Partly it was pragmatic: the other side had all the weapons. But it was also ethical. It was a statement about how things should be. They wanted to start as they intended to go on. History, said Adam Michnik, had taught them that those who start by storming bastilles will end up building their own.

Yet almost as remarkable, historically speaking, was the lack (so far, and Romania plainly excepted) of major *counter*revolutionary violence. The police behaved brutally in East Germany up to and notably on the state's fortieth anniversary, October 7, and in Czechoslovakia up to, and notably on, November 17. In Poland the systematic deployment of counterrevolutionary force lasted over seven years, from the declaration of a "state of war" on December 13, 1981, to the spring of 1989. But once the revolutions (or, in Poland and Hungary, "refolutions"[4]) were under way, there was an amazing lack of coercive countermeasures. The Communist rulers said, like King Wilhelm of Württemberg, "I cannot mount on horseback against ideas." But one is bound to ask: Why not? Much of the modern history of Central Europe consists precisely in rulers mounting on horseback against ideas. Much of the contemporary history of Central Europe, since World War II, consists in rulers mounting tanks against ideas. Until 1989 the most fitting motto for any history of this region was not *"Pravda Vítězí"* but some lines from the nineteenth-century Polish poet Cyprian Norwid:

> *Colossal armies, valiant generals,*
> *Police—secret, open, and of sexes two—*
> *Against whom have they joined together?*
> *Against a few ideas . . . nothing new!*

So why was it different in 1989? Three reasons may be suggested. They might be labeled "Gorbachev," "Helsinki," and "Tocqueville." The new line in Soviet policy, christened by Gennady Gerasimov the Sinatra doctrine—"You do it your way"—rather than the Brezhnev doctrine, was self-evidently essential in making the revolutions possible. In East Germany, Moscow not only made it plain to the leadership that Soviet troops were not available for the purposes of domestic repression, but also, it seems, went out of its way to let it be known—to the West, but also to the population concerned—that this was its position. In Czechoslovakia, the Soviet Union helped the revolution along by a nicely timed retrospective condemnation of the 1968 Warsaw Pact invasion.

Throughout East Central Europe, the people at last derived some benefit from their ruling elites' chronic dependency on the Soviet Union, for, deprived of the Soviet Kalashnikov crutch, those elites did not have another leg to stand on. Romania was the exception that proves the rule. For it is no accident that it was precisely in the state for so long the most independent of Moscow that the resistance of the security arm of the powers-that-were was most fierce, bloody, and prolonged.

Nonetheless, the factor "Gorbachev" alone does not suffice to explain why these ruling elites did not more vigorously deploy their own, still-formidable police and security forces in a last-ditch defense of their own power and privilege. Is it too fanciful to suggest that the constant, persistent harping of the West on certain international norms of domestic conduct, the Eastern European leaders' yearning for international respectability, and the sensed linkage between this and the hard-currency credits they so badly needed—in short, the factor "Helsinki"—played at least some part in staying the hands of those who might otherwise have given the order to shoot?

Yet none of this would have stopped them if they had still been convinced of their right to rule. The third, and perhaps the ultimately decisive factor, is that characteristic of revolutionary situations described by Tocqueville more than a century ago: the ruling elite's loss of belief in its own right to rule. A few kids went into the streets and threw a few words. The police beat them. The kids said: You have no right to beat us! And the rulers, the high and mighty, replied, in effect: Yes, we have no right to beat you. We have no right to preserve our rule by force. The end no longer justifies the means!

In fact the ruling elites, and their armed servants, distinguished themselves by their comprehensive unreadiness to stand up in any way for the things in which they had so long claimed to believe, and their almost indecent haste to embrace democratic capitalism. All over Eastern Europe there was the quiet flap of turning coats: one day they denounced Walesa, the next they applauded him; one day they embraced Honecker, the next they imprisoned him; one day they vituperated Havel, the next they elected him President.

Eighteen-forty-eight was called the Springtime of Nations or the Springtime of Peoples: the *Völkerfrühling, wiosna ludów.* The revolutionaries, in all the lands, spoke in the name of "the people." But the international solidarity of "the people" was broken by conflict between nations, old and new, while the domestic solidarity of "the people" was broken by conflict between social groups—what came to be known as "classes." "Socialism and nationalism, as mass forces, were both the product of 1848," writes A.J.P. Taylor. And for a century after 1848, until the communist deepfreeze, Central Europe was a battlefield of nations and classes.

Of what, or of whom, was 1989 the springtime? Of "the people?" But in what sense? *"Wir sind das Volk"* said the first great crowds in East Germany: the people against the self-styled people's state. But within a few weeks many of them had changed the definite article. *"Wir sind EIN Volk,"* they now chanted: that is, we are one nation. In Poland, Hungary, Czechoslovakia, Romania, the crowds were a sea of national flags, while the people raised their voice to sing old national hymns. In Hungary and Romania they cut the communist symbols out of the centers of their flags. In East Germany there were, at first, no flags, no hymns. But gradually the flags came out, plain stripes of red, black and gold without the GDR hammer and dividers in the middle: the flag of Western and before that of united Germany. And the chant taken up by a very large part of the crowds was *"Deutschland, Einig Vaterland!"*—the line on whose account the so-called "national" anthem of the GDR had not been sung officially since the early 1970s.[5]

In every Western newspaper commentary on Eastern Europe one now invariably reads that there is a grave danger of something called "nationalism" reviving in this region. But what on earth does this mean? Does it mean that people are again proud to be Czech, Polish, Hungarian, or, for that matter, German? That hearts lift at sight of the flag and throats tighten when they sing the national anthem? In that case I must warn the world against one of the most rabidly "nationalist" countries I know. It is called the United States of America.

Patriotism is not nationalism. Rediscovered pride in your own nation does not necessarily imply hostility to other nations. These movements were all, without exception, patriotic. They were not all nationalist. Indeed, in their first steps most of the successor regimes were markedly less nationalist than their Communist predecessors. The Mazowiecki government in Poland took a decisively more liberal and enlightened approach to both the Jewish and the German questions than any previous government, indeed drawing criticism, on the German issue, from the communist–nationalists. In his first public statement as president, Václav Havel emphasized that he would be the president of "all Czechs, Slovaks, and members of other nationalities." His earlier remark on television that Czechoslovakia owes the Sudeten Germans an apology for the way they were expelled after World War II was fiercely criticized by—the Communists.[6] In Romania, the revolution began with the ethnic Romanian inhabitants of Timisoara making common cause with their ethnic Hungarian fellow citizens. It would require very notable exertions for the treatment of the German and Hungarian minorities in postrevolutionary Romania to be worse than it was under Nicolae Ceauşescu.

Of course there are counter-examples. One of the nastier aspects of the German revolution was the excesses of genuine popular support for a Party-government campaign against Polish "smugglers and profiteers," and abuse of visiting black students and Vietnamese *Gastarbeiter*. In Hungarian opposition politics, the fierce infighting between the Hungarian Democratic Forum and the Alliance of Free Democrats was not without an ethnic undertone, with some members of the former questioning the "Hungarianness" of some members of the latter. Thousands of Bulgarian oppositionists protested against the new government giving the Turkish Muslim minority its basic minority rights.

If one looks slightly further ahead, there are obviously potential conflicts over other remaining minorities: notably the Hungarian minority in Romania, the Romanian minority in the Soviet Union (Moldavia), the German minorities in Poland, Romania, and the Soviet Union, and Gipsy minorities in several countries. There are the potential political uses of anti-Semitism. There is the difficulty of finding a combination of Czecho- and -Slovakia fully satisfactory to both Slovaks and Czechs.[7] And there are the outstanding frontier questions, above all that of the post-1945 German–Polish frontier on the Oder-Neisse line.

Yet compared with Central Europe in 1848 or 1918–1919 this is a relatively short list. Most nations have states, and have got used to their new frontiers. Ethnically the map is far more homogeneous than it was in 1848 or 1918; as Ernest Gellner memorably observed, it is now a picture by Modigliani rather than Kokoschka. (The main artists were, of course, Hitler and Stalin: their brushes being war, deportation, and mass murder.) National and ethnic conflicts may grow again between and within these states, as they did in Eastern Europe before the last war, especially if their economic situation deteriorates. Or those national and ethnic conflicts may progressively be alleviated, as were those of Western Europe after the last war, especially if these countries' economic situation improves in a process of integration into a larger European common market and community. We shall see. But the historical record must show that 1989 was not a year of acute national and ethnic conflict in Eastern Europe west of the Soviet frontier. Quite the reverse: it was a year of solidarity both within and between nations. At the end of the year, symbolic and humanitarian support for the people(s) of Romania came from all the self-liberated states of East Central Europe. A springtime of nations is not *necessarily* a springtime of "nationalism."

In any case, what was most striking was not the language of nationhood. That was wholly predictable. What was striking was the other ideas and words that, so to speak, shared the top billing. One of these was "society." In a country often stigmatized as "nationalist," Poland, the word most often used to describe the people as opposed to the authorities was not "nation"; it was *społeczeństwo*, society. In Czechoslovakia the word "society" was used in a similar way, though less frequently, and here it could not simply be a synonym or euphemism for "nation" because it covered two nations. In both cases, it was as meaningful to talk of social self-determination as it was to talk of national self-determination. Everywhere stress was laid on the self-conscious unity of intelligentsia, workers, and peasants.

Of course in part this unity was created by the common enemy. When communist power had been broken, and real parliamentary politics began, then conflicting social interests were robustly articulated. Thus probably the most distinctive and determined group in the new Polish parliament was not the Communists or Solidarity, left or right, but peasant-farmers from all parties, combining and conspiring to advance their sectional interests.

Nonetheless, the social divisions were nothing like as deep as in the nineteenth or early twentieth century, and they did not undercut the revolutions. There is an historical irony here. For in large measure communism created the social unity that contributed decisively to the end of communism. The combination of deliberate leveling and unintended absurdities resulted in a distribution of wealth throughout most of society that was not so much egalitarian as higgledy-piggledy. A professor would earn less than a miner, an engineer less than a peasant-farmer. A plumber with a few dollars or Deutschemarks would be better off than a prince without hard currency. A worker lived in the same house as a doctor, an engineer, or a writer, and the ground plans of their apartments were almost certainly identical, even if the décor differed.

At the same time, they were all united by consciousness of the one great divide between the communist upper/ruling class, the *nomenklatura*, and all the rest. In all these countries the former were "them": *oni* (a word made famous by Teresa Torańska's book of interviews with Polish Stalinists), the *Bonzen*. "They" were identified by their clothes, their black-curtained cars, their special hospitals and shops, their language, and their behavior. When the dense crowds in Prague were asked to clear a path for an ambulance, they did so chanting, "We are not like them! We are not like them!"

At the same time, there was a remarkably high level of popular political awareness. Again, this was partly a result of the system. Everyone had at least a basic education, and from the earliest years that education was highly politicized. Many people reacted against this politicization with a determined retreat into private life, and an almost programmatic apoliticism. But because of the politicization of education, and the ubiquity of ideology, no one could be in any doubt that words and ideas mattered, having real consequences for everyday life.

A concept that was central in opposition thinking during the 1980s was that of "civil society." The year 1989 was the springtime of societies aspiring to be civil. Ordinary men and women's rudimentary notion of what it meant to build a civil society might not satisfy the political theorist. But some such notion was there, and it contained at least three basic demands. First, there should be forms of association, national, regional, local, professional, that would be voluntary, authentic, democratic, and, first and last, not controlled or manipulated by the Party or Party–state. Second, people should be "civil": that is, polite, tolerant, and, above all, nonviolent. Civil and civilian. Third, the idea of citizenship had to be taken seriously.

Communism managed to poison many words from the mainstream of European history—not least, the word "socialism." But somehow it did not manage to poison the words "citizen" and "civic," even though it used them, too, in perverted ways: for example, appeals to "civic responsibility," meaning "keep quiet and let us deal with these troublesome students." Why it did not manage to poison those words is an interesting question—to which I have no ready answer—but the fact is that when Solidarity's parliamentarians came to give their group a name, they called it the *Citizens'* Parliamentary Club; the Czech movement called itself the *Civic* Forum; and the opposition groups in the GDR started by describing themselves as *Bürgerinitiativen*, that is, citizens' or civic initiatives.[8] And the language of citizenship was important in all these revolutions. People had had enough of being mere components in a deliberately atomized society: they wanted to be citizens, individual men and women with dignity and responsibility, with rights but also with duties, freely associating in civil society.

There is one last point about the self-description of the revolution which is perhaps worth a brief mention. As Ralf Dahrendorf has observed. Karl Marx played on the ambiguity of the German term *bürgerliche Gesellschaft*, which could be translated either as civil society or as bourgeois society. Marx, says Dahrendorf, deliberately conflated the two "cities" of modernity, the fruits of the Industrial and the French Revolutions, the *bourgeois* and the *citoyen*.[9] I thought of this observation when a speaker in one of the mass rallies in Leipzig called for solidarity with the *bürgerliche Bewegung* in Czechoslovakia. The bourgeois movement! But on reflection there seems to me a deeper truth in that apparent malapropism. For what most of the opposition movements throughout East Central Europe, and a large part of "the people" supporting them were in effect saying was: Yes, Marx is right, the two things are intimately connected—and we want both! Civil rights and property rights, economic freedom and political freedom, financial independence and intellectual independence—each supports the other. So, yes, we want to be citizens, but we also want to be middle class, in the senses that most citizens in the more fortunate half of Europe are middle class. We want to be *Bürger* AND *bürgerlich!* Tom Paine, but also Thomas Mann.

So it was a springtime of nations, but not necessarily of nationalism; of societies, aspiring to be civil; and above all, of citizens.

3.

The springtime of citizens has already changed the face of Europe. What seemed only possible at the beginning of 1989 seemed certain at the beginning of 1990. There would be a new Europe, for which the term "Yalta" would no longer be an appropriate shorthand. This Europe would have a different place for the countries formerly described as East European, and, at the very least, a less divided Germany.

The Revolution of 1848 ended badly because of the combination of internal and external forces of reaction: but in East Central Europe the external ones were decisive. No comparable external forces of reaction were visible at the beginning of 1990. The Prussians were making their own revolution, not crushing those of their neighbors. The Austrians were not repressing the Hungarian reform-revolution, but helping it along. And the Russians? Here the transformation was miraculous, to the point where senior American and British officials indicated that they might actually welcome a Soviet military intervention to smash the Securitate death squads in Romania. But no, for Romania, as for Czechoslovakia, Hungary, Poland, and Bulgaria, Soviet leaders and commentators from Gorbachev down assumed a saintly expression and said they would never dream of interfering in the internal affairs of another country.

Yet the popular movement for national and social self-determination did not stop neatly at the western frontier of the Soviet Union. What happened in Eastern Europe directly encouraged the Baltic States, not to mention the Romanians of Soviet Moldavia. And what if the political earth began to move in the Ukraine? At the beginning of 1990 it was therefore all too possible to imagine some backlash or reversal inside the Soviet Union. But it seemed reasonable to doubt whether even a conservative–military leadership in Moscow would attempt to use armed force to restore Russian domination west of the Soviet frontiers of 1945. Would they not have more than enough on their hands trying to preserve the empire inside the postwar Soviet frontiers? Logically, if they invaded one Eastern European country they should now invade them all. And then, what would they "restore"? The shattered Humpty-Dumpties that were yesterday's Eastern European Communist parties? Obviously a reversal inside the Soviet Union would make life much less comfortable in the new Europe, and directly affect developments in a Germany still partly occupied by Soviet troops. But it would not in itself suffice to turn the map back to what it was before 1989.

About this new Europe there are countless questions to be asked, of which the most obviously pressing is: How can the West help the transformation of formerly communist states into liberal democracies? I ask myself a less obvious question: not "How can we help them?" but "How might they help us?" What, if anything, can these nearly one hundred million Europeans, with their forty years of hard experience, bring to the new Europe, and to us in the West? The Czechs were delighted to point out that 89 is 68 turned upside down. But one of the notable differences between 1968 and 1989 was a comparative lack of Western intellectuals discovering, in these exotic regions, new utopias, such as "socialism with a human face" and the fabled Third Way.[10]

Of course there is a kaleidoscope of new parties, programs, and trends, and it is little short of impudence to subsume them in one "message." Yet if you look at what these diverse parties are really saying about the basic questions of politics, economics, law, and international relations, there is a remarkable underlying consensus. In politics they are all saying: There is no "socialist democracy," there is only democracy. And by democracy they mean multiparty, parliamentary democracy as practiced in contemporary Western, Northern, and Southern Europe. They are all saying: There is no "socialist legality," there is only legality. And by that they mean the rule of law, guaranteed by the constitutionally anchored independence of the judiciary.[11]

They are also saying—and for the left this is perhaps the most important statement—there is no "socialist economics," there is only economics. And economics means not a socialist market economy but a social market economy. Not Ota Sik but Ludwig Erhard. Of course there are grave differences between, for example, Friedmanites and Hayekites. A good word might even be heard for Keynes. But the basic direction is absolutely plain: toward an economy whose basic engine of growth is the market, with extensive private ownership of the means of production, distribution, and exchange. The transition to such a system poses unique problems, for which original solutions will have to be found. In most of these countries there is still widespread support for relatively egalitarian distribution of the wealth thus created, and for a strong welfare state. But the basic model, in the three essentials of politics, economics, and law, is something between the real existing Switzerland and the real existing Sweden.

Sweden—or, as one leading Soviet economist carefully stressed *southern* Sweden—now seems to be the accepted ideal for virtually everyone who styles themself a socialist between Berlin and Vladivostok. But if Marx came back to earth, would he not describe the predominant mode of production in Sweden as capitalist? In other words, the fundamental argument from the left is no longer about the best way to produce wealth, only about the best way to distribute it. (The more fundamental critique of the successful forms of production comes from Greens rather than socialists.)

For purely practical and historical reasons, the State will clearly play a larger part in most Eastern European countries than in most Western European countries, for some years to come. But this does not necessarily mean that people will *want* it to. On the contrary, having had so much state interference for so long, they might decide they want as little of it as possible. Public opinion polls and sociological surveys are not much use here, since most people have only just begun to think about these issues, let alone to confront them in the hard reality of economic transition. The proof of the pudding will be in the eating. Among the intellectuals who have begun to confront these issues there is, it seems to me, an opposite danger: that of regarding the free market as a universal cure. Hence the popularity of Hayek. The free market, one might say, is the latest Central European utopia.

It is easy now to forget that communism claimed to have found not only new and better forms of politics, law, and economics, but also a new and better way of organizing relations between states. This new way was called "socialist internationalism," and counterposed to "bourgeois nationalism." What we have seen in practice is the rise of socialist nationalism and bourgeois internationalism. There are many examples of bourgeois internationalism—IMF, NATO, GATT, OECD—but in the perspective of European history the most dramatic is the European Community. Now there are proposals, too numerous even to list, for new forms of interstate relations in the former Eastern Europe. To give but one example, leading Polish politicians have revived the idea of a confederation of Poland and Czechoslovakia. But if you ask what is the basic, underlying model for the new relations between these states, and for the resolution of their outstanding national, ethnic, and economic conflicts, then the answer is clear. The basic model is the European Community—the one and only, real existing common European home.

This means not only that they would like to join the present EC, as fully as possible and as soon as possible. It also means that they hope their outstanding historic conflicts and enmities can be overcome in the same kinds of ways that, say, those between France and Germany have been overcome. This is true, it seems to me, even of those groups that would not explicitly acknowledge the EC as a model. Certainly, you have to go far in Western Europe to find such enthusiastic "Europeans"— that is, supporters of a supranational community called Europe—as you will find at every turn in Eastern Europe. Traveling to and fro between the two halves of the divided continent, I have sometimes thought that the real divide is between those (in the West) who have Europe and those (in the East) who believe in it. And everywhere, in all the lands, the phrase people use to sum up what is happening is "the return to Europe."

Yet what, to repeat the original question, can these enthusiasts bring to the new Europe? If I am right in my basic analysis, they can offer no fundamentally new ideas on the big questions of politics, economics, law, or international relations. The new ideas are the ideas whose time has passed. The ideas whose time has come are old, familiar, well-tested ones. So is all they have to offer us their unique, theoretically intriguing but practically burdensome problems? Do they come, as it were, like mendicants to the door, bearing only chronicles of wasted time?[12] Or might they have, under their threadbare cloaks, some hidden treasure?

Traveling through this region over the last decade, I have found treasures: examples of great moral courage and intellectual integrity; comradeship, deep friendship, family life; time and space for serious conversation, music, literature, not disturbed by the perpetual noise of our obsessively telecommunicative world; Christian witness in its original and purest form; more broadly, qualities of relations between men and women of very different backgrounds, and once bitterly opposed faiths: an ethos of solidarity. Here the danger of sentimental idealization is acute, for the privileged visitor enjoys these benefits without paying the costs. There is no doubt that, on any quantitative or utilitarian reckoning, the costs have been far higher than the benefits. Yet it would be even more wrong to pretend that these treasures were not real. They were. And for me the question of questions after 1989 is: What if any of these good things will survive liberation? Was the community only a community of fate, a *Schicksalsgemeinschaft?* Were these *just* the uses of adversity?

Even if there is no reversal in the Soviet Union, no violent backlash or undemocratic and illiberal turns in this or that Eastern European country, won't these treasures simply be swept away in the rush—the all too understandable rush—for affluence? As a Hungarian friend wryly remarked: "I have survived forty years of communism, but I'm not sure that I'll survive one year of capitalism." And this will not just be the atomizing impact of developed consumerism, one of the most potent weapons known to man. It will be the still rougher and more traumatic impact of the attempted transition from a planned to a market economy, with all the associated blows of unemployment, dislocation, and injustice.

Wishful thinking helps no one. One can, alas, paint with a rather high degree of analytical plausibility a quite dark picture of the prospect for the former Eastern Europe in the 1990s: a prospect in which the post-communist future looks remarkably like the pre-communist past, less Central Europe than *Zwischeneuropa*—as I wrote in these pages just over a year ago—a dependent intermediate zone "of weak states, national prejudice, inequality, poverty, and *Schlamassel.*"[13] The year 1989 might then appear, to participants and historians, as just one brief shining moment between the sufferings of yesterday and those of tomorrow.

This fate is not inevitable. Whether it can be avoided depends to a very significant degree on the commitment and ingenuity of the West in general, Western Europe in particular, and above all on West Germany—or rather, to put it in terms more appropriate to the new Europe, on a Germany remaining Western.

Yet even if the darker prospect were to be realized, something would remain, at least in memory, in culture, in spirit. At the very least the Europeans from over there would have offered us, with a clarity and firmness born of bitter experience, a restatement of the value of what we already have, of old truths and tested models, of the three essentials of liberal democracy and of the European Community as the one and only, real existing common European home. Intellectually, dare I say spiritually, "1989" in Eastern Europe is a vital complement to "1992" in Western Europe.

"Litwo! Ojczyno moja! ty jesteś jak zdrowie," begins the most famous of all Polish poems, Adam Mickiewicz's *"Pan Tadeusz"*:

Lithuania, my fatherland, thou art
  like health;
How much we should value thee
  he alone learns,
Who has lost thee.

If we put in place of "Lithuania" the word "Europe," we may have the deepest lesson of that year of wonders, 1989.

NOTES

1. At the time of writing, the one crucial reservation expressed by the Gorbachev leadership concerns the independent statehood of the German Democratic Republic.

2. Intellectuals . . . a term Namier uses with all the scorn of his acquired Englishness for that suspect Continental breed.

3. See Václav Havel, *Living in Truth* (London: Faber, 1988), and the account in my *The Uses of Adversity* (Random House, 1989). Havel illustrates his argument about people "living a lie" with the example of a greengrocer who puts in his shop window, among the onions and carrots, the slogan "Workers of the World, Unite!" "Why does he do it?" Havel asks. "What is he trying to communicate to the world? Is he genuinely enthusiastic about the idea of unity among the workers of the world? Is his enthusiasm so great that he feels an irresistible impulse to acquaint the public with his ideals?" Of course not. He is signaling his readiness to conform. But "if the greengrocer had been instructed to display the slogan 'I am afraid and therefore unquestioningly obedient,' he would not be nearly as indifferent to its semantics, even though the statement would reflect the truth." Today that greengrocer's shop window probably displays a photograph of Václav Havel.

4. Reform-revolution, see the last chapter in my *The Uses of Adversity*.

5. The transitional government led by Hans Modrow gave instructions that it could be sung officially again.

6. Cardinal Tomásek was also initially reported to have disagreed with Havel on this point. But he subsequently issued a statement in which he described Havel's apology as "an important step for the development of relations between the Czech and German nations." The statement also said that "these illegal, inhuman acts have left a stain on our national honor."

7. The hyphenated form, Czecho-Slovakia, was favored by Slovak autonomists between the wars.

8. The actual word is probably imported from West German usage, but the fact remains that they chose this rather than some other term.

9. See Ralf Dahrendorf, *The Modern Social Conflict* (London: Weidenfeld and Nicolson, 1988).

10. But writing in the London *Sunday Times* (January 7, 1990), the thoughtful editor of *Marxism Today*, Martin Jacques, suggests that "the innovations of Prague and Leipzig are there to influence and inspire would-be imitators in western Europe. It is difficult to believe that forum politics as practiced by Civic Forum in Czechoslovakia and Neues Forum in East Germany will have no impact on the west European left." Whether that would increase the left's chances of being elected is another question!

11. At one moment in the Magic Lantern, the Civic Forum headquarters in Prague, I overheard the historian and lawyer Petr Pithart trying to reason with some striking students: "But you can't say 'we'll continue on strike until we've built a state of law!' because that will last years." The students seemed rather taken with the idea.

12. Of course one must beware of being ahistorical. It is legitimate to ask what other paths to modernization were open in 1945. Even with forty years of democratic capitalism, Albania would not be Switzerland. But the Czech lands? Central Germany? There is no deeper historical reason at all why they should not have a level of development comparable to that of Austria.

13. See "Reform or Revolution?" in *The New York Review*, October 27, 1988; also reprinted in *The Uses of Adversity*.

23

Can South Africa Change?

GEORGE M. FREDRICKSON

1.

In the spring of 1989 I visited South Africa for the first time in fifteen years. When I had been there in 1974, apartheid was flourishing. Signs designating facilities for "whites only" or "non-whites only" were omnipresent, and I had the unforgettable experience of riding in unproud isolation on the lower deck of a double-decker bus in Cape Town, the top of which was filled to capacity with the black people who had been fortunate enough to get aboard at all. The sight of blacks left on the curb rather than taking seats in the virtually empty "white" part of the bus brought home the meaning of segregation as social humiliation and personal hardship.

The university where I was doing research had a handful of black students admitted under some loopholes in the educational apartheid laws (usually because they were studying, or supposedly studying, subjects not offered at all at the segregated black institutions popularly known as "bush colleges"), but they kept to themselves. The black protest of that period was in itself segregated, as militant young blacks, influenced to some extent by black power rhetoric imported from the United States, refused to make alliances with liberal whites, and rallied around the separatist "black consciousness" movement. The African National Congress, which had been banned in 1960, seemed to be no more than a memory within South Africa, and its longstanding goal of "nonracial" or "multiracial" democracy was likely to strike a dispassionate observer as utterly unrealistic.

When I came back this year for a month of historical research, I was impressed by the changes that had taken place. I had kept up to some extent with developments in South Africa and was of course aware that some aspects of apartheid had been relaxed or even abolished. But I was not quite prepared for the degree to which some of the most conspicuous trappings of segregation had disappeared. In the large cities that I visited—Johannesburg, Bloemfontein, and Cape Town—I found no

Reprinted with permission from *The New York Review of Books.* Copyright © 1989 Nyrev, Inc.

Note: It is a violation of the law to reproduce this selection by any means whatsoever without the written permission of the copyright holder.

signs of racially restricted facilities. As far as I could see, hotels, restaurants, movie theaters, buses, and trains were open equally to all races. If Johannesburg of the 1970s was like Birmingham in the 1950s, then Johannesburg of the late 1980s was, on the surface at least, strikingly like the Birmingham of the early 1970s.

In some respects, Johannesburg seems more integrated than many large American cities. The lower-middle-class neighborhood of Hillbrow, which was all white when I was there in 1974, is now racially mixed to a degree that would be hard to duplicate in a similar neighborhood in the United States. The notorious Group Areas Act, which restricts residence in designated urban areas to members of a single racial group, is still on the books, but it is not consistently enforced, and the government has recently proposed to modify it by formally assigning "mixed" status to some neighborhoods. Public swimming pools are still segregated in Johannesburg, but pressure is building to remove this vestige of purely social apartheid. Desegregation of beaches has begun in many coastal cities. (Some beaches previously reserved for whites have been opened to all races, and the last two "whites-only" beaches in Cape Town have been the target of recent black protests.)

It would appear that the kind of everyday segregation that went under the name of Jim Crow in the United States is becoming a thing of the past in the major cities. (Since my visit, "white" hospitals, under pressure from nonviolent protesters, have begun to admit blacks.) Small towns undoubtedly lag behind, and municipalities under the control of the far right Conservative party have attempted to reintroduce mandatory segregation of public facilities. But successful black boycotts of white merchants are putting heavy pressure on Conservative local authorities to rescind these actions.

At the "English-speaking" "white" universities, the situation is again reminiscent of post–Jim Crow America. On their own initiative, these universities have recently carried out something very like the vigorous affirmative action programs of the late Sixties and early Seventies in the United States. There have been dramatic increases in the numbers of black students, who now make up close to one quarter of the total enrollment at the universities of the Witwatersrand (in Johannesburg) and Cape Town.

As in most American universities, black and white students have little to do with one another socially; indeed voluntary segregation in South Africa's "integrated" universities also includes a black boycott of extracurricular activities, including sports. But black and white students come together to protest against the regime. While at the University of the Witwaters, I observed a demonstration of roughly a hundred students, about a quarter of whom were white, to commemorate the anniversary of the Sharpeville massacre of 1960. When all the participants raised their fists in the ANC salute and sang the ANC anthem,

I sensed the immediate and practical meaning of the ANC's nonracial nationalism.

The ANC position is that members of the white minority are not to be allowed to determine the content of South African nationality; but if they are willing to accept the ideas and symbols associated with a nation under black majority rule, most African resisters seem willing to regard them as compatriots despite the color of their skin and their European ancestry. Most black activists now reject the position of the black consciousness movement that whites should be excluded from the struggle against apartheid. I saw another example of racial inclusiveness when the leader of a black jazz band in Cape Town said he would lead a predominantly white audience in "the national anthem" at the end of a concert in a public auditorium. Clasping one another's raised hands and swaying to the music, whites joined with the small number of blacks in the audience singing the ANC hymn. Many blacks and at least some whites are openly behaving as if a transfer of power from the white minority to the black majority has already taken place. Such scenes would have been unimaginable fifteen years ago.

But of course power has not really been transferred or even "shared." "Petty apartheid" may be on the way out, but "grand apartheid"—the denial to Africans of the right to own land outside the 13 percent of the country "reserved" for them and the restriction of African political rights to the election of local authorities in "homelands" and segregated townships—remains in force. Furthermore, under the state of emergency first declared in 1985, and redeclared for a third time in 1988, all black protest activities and organizations are illegal. The difference one senses from the early 1970s is a new self-confidence and assertiveness among blacks that cannot be repressed by the kind of martial-law measures currently in effect. Blacks may not be on the verge of seizing power, but one gets the impression that they will never again be reduced to a state of acquiescence to white rule. On my earlier visit, I was often addressed as *baas* (master), but on this occasion even blacks with service jobs scrupulously avoided such terms and looked me straight in the eye in a way that would once have been regarded as "cheeky."

Such impressions of a visitor raise more questions than they answer. To explain and assess the significance of the kinds of changes that I observed during my month in South Africa requires some immersion in the enormous literature on the recent history and current state of the South African republic. A good place to begin for anyone not already familiar with the history is Martin Meredith's *In the Name of Apartheid*, a perceptive and readable popular history of South Africa since 1948. Although clearly opposed to apartheid and sympathetic to the blacks' struggle for liberation, Meredith has no special ax to grind or panacea to propose. A journalist who also did historical research at Oxford, he is content to call our attention to the major elements in an unfolding story that has not yet reached its climax.

Meredith recalls the coming to power in 1948 of the Afrikaner Nationalist party, with its plan for total racial segregation, or apartheid, and he describes how the party imposed on South Africa an elaborate body of legislation designed to entrench white power and privilege for all time. He also describes the black political reaction to this systematic assault on such limited rights as blacks had managed to salvage from previous white supremacist governments. After a passive resistance campaign in the early 1950s had failed to stop the flood of apartheid legislation, African nationalist leaders, Nelson Mandela among them, tried to organize more militant protests, including mass demonstrations and civil disobedience. This led to the Sharpeville massacre of 1960, when dozens of blacks engaged in a peaceful march were killed, and the banning of the principal black protest movements. During the 1960s and early 1970s, the Nationalist government increased its hold over the white electorate and maintained repressive policies that drove internal opposition to the regime far underground.

During this period the Bantustan, or homeland, policy was in its heyday; hundreds of thousands of blacks who were living in largely white districts were forced to move to already overcrowded black enclaves that supposedly would become "independent homelands." A nightmarish form of racist central planning and social engineering resulted in blacks being shunted back and forth from the "white" urban and industrial regions to the homelands; the aim of the planners was to exploit black labor power while denying them any basis for political participation and democratic rights. Full-blown apartheid was very expensive, but, fortunately for the regime, South Africa was in a boom period and was receiving heavy foreign investment. Its growth rate was among the highest in the world.

By the early 1970s, however, the white leaders began to run into problems. As manufacturing expanded, a serious shortage of skilled labor developed that could not be met by the white population. In 1973, Prime Minister John Vorster began in a small and inadequate way to soften the policy of "job reservation" that had officially given white workers a monopoly of skilled occupations. (When I visited South Africa in 1974, I frequently saw blacks doing skilled construction work, although always under the close supervision of white foremen.) According to Meredith, relaxing the job reservation system was "the first significant retreat in the apartheid system since 1948."

A wave of strikes by black workers in search of higher wages also began in 1973, and the government began to recognize that some of the fruits of prosperity would have to be allowed to trickle down to black labor if industrial peace were to be maintained. During the 1970s, black wages increased dramatically, and the black share of personal income in

South Africa increased from 19 percent of the total to 29 percent. The Nationalist politicians saw that black labor had to be accommodated within an industrializing South Africa that lacked enough whites to man the factories. In 1980 they recognized and allowed negotiations with black trade unions, in an effort to bring them under control through the pressures of the industrial bargaining process.

Meredith also provides a useful summary of events since the mid-1970s—the Soweto uprising of 1976, the growth of an enormous state security apparatus, Botha's political reforms, the arrests in townships between 1983 and 1986, and the crackdown on black political groups and the press in 1985 and 1986, when martial law was imposed. But the reader seeking a concise historical introduction to South Africa since 1976 might be better served by the first chapter of *South Africa: No Turning Back*, edited by Shaun Johnson. The work of a British study group assembled in 1987, this book is among the best I know of recent collections on South Africa.

The opening historical essay on the period from the Soweto uprising to the end of the township revolts of the 1980s, written by the two most prominent British historians of South Africa, Shula Marks and Stanley Trapido, takes note of the economic gains made by blacks in the 1970s but argues that "these increases should be set against rapidly increasing unemployment and the further deterioration of rural resources." In other words, the blacks lucky enough to have jobs were better off than employed blacks in the past, but the proportion of blacks who had no jobs at all and were living wretchedly in shantytowns outside the cities or within the "homelands" was growing. The economic situation of the "superfluous" or "redundant" blacks became even more desperate when recession hit the South African economy in the early Eighties. During my own recent visit to Soweto, I was struck by the contrast between the improved housing available to employed Africans and the squalid shantytowns with long lines outside their few latrines that are increasingly the refuge of the unemployed.

The Soweto uprising of 1976 was in large part the result of government efforts to expand secondary education for blacks in order to provide a more skilled work force for South African industry but without providing money for enough teachers or adequate classroom facilities. The efforts to enforce laws making Afrikaans obligatory in half of the courses taught in African schools set off the student rebellion in the townships near Johannesburg. Black high school students, conscious of the inferiority of their education, unsure of their job prospects, but convinced that English was the language of economic advancement, began a protest that became more and more vehement as young students threw stones at the police, provoking a bloody response when trigger-happy officers fired on the students, killing some 575 people. The black consciousness movement, with its emphasis on black pride and assertiveness, acted as a catalyst for this children's revolt.

Although the wave of disorders that spread outward from Soweto lasted only a few months, and the heavy hand of government repression fell on the black consciousness organizations, a new spirit of resistance to apartheid was born in 1976 and 1977; it was to reemerge in the broader based and longer lasting revolts in the townships during the 1980s. The government's response to Soweto was not simply to ban the militants but also to undertake reforms designed to defuse black discontent. "As it became apparent that the existing system was producing instability incompatible with the needs of industry," Marks and Trapido write, "there was an intensified demand for reform from both local and foreign capital."

Between 1978 and 1981, the government pursued economic measures, including subsidies for black education and urban housing, that it hoped would bring the business community, which favored such reforms, into more effective cooperation with the state. It was during this period that black unions were recognized and began to grow rapidly. In retrospect, Marks and Trapido point out, it is clear that the government's willingness to spend larger and larger sums of public money to improve black economic conditions depended on the temporary revival of prosperity at the end of the Seventies and the beginning of the Eighties and that it could not survive the deep recession that began in 1982. Botha then introduced his proposal for a new constitution providing for a separate parliament representing "coloureds" (people of mixed racial origin) and Indians but conspicuously excluding Africans.

The response of black leaders was to organize the United Democratic Front, a broadly based federation of black community organizations and a few white liberal groups, which took the ANC's Freedom Charter as its manifesto and won the endorsement of the ANC leaders in Zambia. The revival of the nonracial philosophy of the ANC and the eclipse of the black consciousness doctrine that blacks could go it alone were the most important changes in black political thinking during the 1980s. As blacks who were drawn to the ANC and the UDF demonstrated in the townships, and sought, sometimes violently, to purge their ranks of informers and collaborators with apartheid institutions, troops moved in; the violence that we saw on television in 1983 and 1984 threatened to plunge South Africa into civil war. Less widely observed than Botha's feeble and self-defeating efforts at "power sharing" was his simultaneous remodeling of the constitution in order to create an all-powerful office of the president, who could act independently of parliament through the elaborate state security system.

In summing up the changes between 1976 and 1986, Marks and Trapido stress the transformation of black consciousness, the rise of a skilled and unionized black industrial working class, the challenge to the established order posed by the "combination of worker and community organization" in the UDF, and the control that a transformed Afrikaner Nationalist party has nevertheless continued to maintain over South African society, even though its limited and narrowly self-interested reformism provoked several hundred thousand right-wing Afrikaner voters to secede from the party and join the intransigently racist Conservative party. The result, they conclude, is "an oppressive stalemate."

This pessimistic perspective is evidently influenced by the Marxist view that apartheid and capitalism are so closely bound together that it would take a social revolution to bring equality to blacks. According to the interpretation of Marks and Trapido, the relation of apartheid that I observed this spring might be seen as the residue of a program that failed to achieve its objective of defusing black protest and creating a climate of opinion conducive to capitalist development. In 1987, when Marks and Trapido wrote their essay, the Nationalist government remained strongly opposed to negotiations that would give blacks any form of political power; but it was unable to resume its policy of the mid-1970s of trying to take the edge off African discontent by providing better living conditions and opening purely economic opportunities for blacks in the cities. In the recent depressed state of the South African economy, according to Marks and Trapido, the material circumstances of blacks would seriously improve only if the whites were willing to reduce their own standard of living, something no white electorate is likely to support.

The remaining essays in *No Turning Back* provide further insights into the current situation in South Africa. Howard Barrell, a longstanding observer of the ANC, reports on the outlawed black resistance movements and describes, although he does not fully explain, the congress's remarkable revival in the 1980s at the expense of orthodox African nationalism or separatist black consciousness. The ANC recognized that the South African situation was unique. In contrast to other African countries where white Europeans held control, the powerful white minority in South Africa is determined to stay, and there is no colonial power to preside over negotiations leading to African independence. The ANC's policy of organizing a multiracial popular front is therefore more effective than any effort to imitate the liberation movements that succeeded in throwing off European rule in the rest of Africa. Yet for all its strength and flexibility, as Barrell argues, the ANC still lacks the capacity to mount a successful revolution.

Shaun Johnson's essay is an incisive analysis of how young people brought up on the black consciousness rhetoric of the Seventies rediscovered their past—the record of black resistance in South Africa on "nonracial" principles during the 1950s and 1960s. The conversion of youth politics from orthodox black consciousness to "charterism"—adherence to the ANC's broadly inclusive Freedom Charter of 1955—was partly the result, according to Johnson, of the government's decision to send the young activists of the late 1970s to Robben Island prison, where they learned of the ANC and its traditions directly from Nelson Mandela and the other ANC leaders who had been held there since the early 1960s. In his discussion of the new youth revolt or "children's crusade" of the 1980s, Johnson shows how a tendency toward violence and anarchy on the part of young people became a matter of concern to older members of the UDF, who have tried to curb it, with some success. He concludes that young people who refuse to accept the apartheid system and are relatively fearless in their opposition to it remain a central force in the South African struggle.

Other essays in *No Turning Back* provide accounts of the black trade union movement, the United Democratic Front, and other internal resistance movements, the Afrikaner establishment, the military and police forces, the impact of the divestment movement, and Inkatha—the Zulu ethnic movement led by Chief Gatsha Buthelezi that seems destined to be the wild card in any efforts to reach a political settlement. The general impression that these essays convey is that no single ethnic group or political strategy can control what happens in South Africa. So many different forces are now taking part in the contest to shape the destiny of South Africa that confident prediction is impossible and neat solutions are unrealistic.

It is noticeable, however, that no political force readily identifiable as liberalism or a liberal establishment has had any large part in the contest for power described by the contributors to *No Turning Back*. Some might argue that the ANC and the UDF have liberal programs or connections, despite the alliance of the ANC with the South African Communist party. But it makes more sense to describe the members of the popular opposition in South Africa as "radical democratic" rather than liberal; they put emphasis not on individual or minority rights or on preserving a capitalist or mixed economy but rather on turning over power to an underprivileged and dispossessed majority that will likely prefer socialism and the redistribution of wealth. (The ANC has agreed in principle to a bill of rights protecting personal liberties, but not, as yet, to an independent judiciary.) The clear implication of *No Turning Back* is that democratic capitalism along British or American lines is an unlikely prospect for South Africa. If the implication is valid, then many of the current opponents of apartheid in the United States are bound to be disappointed.

2.

Three recent books deal directly with the possibilities of democratic liberalism in South Africa. Janet Levine's autobiography *Inside Apartheid* is the memoir of the agony of conscience of a white liberal. A longtime supporter and associate of the Progressive Federal party leader Helen Suzman, Levine tells how, as a young woman from a well-to-do Jewish family, she early became aware of the injustices of apartheid. She not only joined with other white liberals to protest against the regime, but also, as a member of the Johannesburg city council, tried to act as the spokeswoman for black municipal workers in their struggle to get decent treatment from the city authorities. She was deeply involved in efforts to establish a black taxi cooperative in Soweto.

By the early 1980s, however, she became convinced that her kind of liberalism no longer had a part to play in the anti-apartheid movement. She saw herself and other white liberals as

> caught in the Kerensky trap, wedged tightly between the conflicting forces of reactionary white desperation and militant waves of black nationalism surging toward political domination.

When other white liberals found it possible to back the United Democratic Front—which invited white support but not white leadership—she decided she could not do more "because what you believed in was of little value to those around you—black and white—whose narrow nationalism superseded your liberal value system."

After emigrating to the United States in 1984, she gave talks to American liberal audiences which shocked them by expressing her fear that a "militaristic black oligarchy" would replace a white one; she also threw cold water on their favorite anti-apartheid initiative by arguing that campaigns for disinvestment and sanctions are the very opposite of what is needed in South Africa. In favoring increased foreign investment and contacts with Western businessmen as liberalizing influences, she is, of course, echoing the longstanding views of Helen Suzman; but it is also worth noting that in May a Gallup poll in South Africa found that approximately six out of ten blacks would oppose sanctions, even if sanctions would cause the government to resign in five years. This survey, sponsored by the South African Chamber of Mines, contradicts earlier polls, and one has to wonder whether blacks would be trustful enough to respond honestly. But it does raise some difficult questions for proponents of sanctions.

Levine is an intelligent, experienced, and sensitive observer, and her views deserve to be taken seriously. Still, her opinions are somewhat at odds with those of the other white liberals with whom I spoke on my recent trip. Despite all that has happened recently in South Africa, they had not given up hope or concluded that the black opposition had embraced a "narrow nationalism" no better than that of the Afrikaners. Like Levine, they understand that whites cannot expect to lead a black liberation struggle or control its ideologies and programs, but many of them have nevertheless found good reasons to choose one side over the other. In his contribution to a recent symposium, *Democratic Liberalism in*

South Africa, F. Van Zyl Slabbert, an Afrikaner who was formerly a member of parliament and leader of the Progressive Federal party, argues that "in a broad sense there is a choice between the 'struggle for freedom' and opposition to the struggle, between 'liberation' and 'oppression,' or between 'stability' and 'freedom.' He defined that choice as follows:

> The government has appropriated "stability" together with its own interpretations of concepts such as "negotiation," "reform," "constitutional change," and "consensus," and has effectively debased them as instruments of incremental change by linking them to repression. The "struggle" has appropriated "freedom," together with "people's power," "liberation," "justice," "equality," "boycotts," and "sanctions," and has very effectively inflated them as instruments of revolutionary change.
>
> The traditional liberal political response would be to say: "I like this on that side and this on the other and dislike the following in both" and then proceed to present a coherent and rational alternative position to a potential constituency. Unfortunately, there is no such coherent and rational constituency of any significance available in our present polarized situation. The primary question now that liberals are forced to face is: "Where do you stand in the struggle? For freedom or stability?" They may refuse to choose by calling a plague on the irrationality of both houses and hover around in a fit of sullen irrelevancy. If they do, the struggle for freedom will become the exclusive preserve of the revolutionary, and the maintenance of stability the preserve of increasing repression.

Some of the contributors to *Democratic Liberalism in South Africa* seem to believe that they can avoid making this kind of choice. The result of a 1985 symposium underwritten by the Chairman's Fund of the Anglo-American Corporation, the volume attempts to show that liberalism is still a strong force in South Africa and offers a workable middle ground between African and Afrikaner nationalism. But the absence of black contributors to this collection of papers by white, mostly South African, academics may be a clue to the weakness of this proposition. The essays are of high quality and provide some of the most perceptive analyses of South African history, politics, and economics to be found anywhere. Such articles as David Welsh's commentary on the theoretical arguments about what determines inequality in South Africa and David Yudelman's analysis of the relation between the state and capitalist development in South Africa are examples of liberal social science at its best.

One can agree with much in this book, as I do, and one can respect its view of the superiority of liberal conceptions of individual and minority rights over a neo-Marxian or black populist tendency to remove, in the name of democracy, all restraints on the actions of a proletarian African majority. At the same time one must ask just how this kind of liberalism can be applied to contemporary South Africa.

First of all, the contributors suggest no plausible way to give democratic liberals the power to take a decisive or even a very influential part in South Africa's future. At the moment they are a tiny, mostly white, minority with little power outside the English-speaking universities (even there they seem to be in retreat before exponents of more radical viewpoints influenced by Marxist ideology). Second, there is no single liberal point of view, and South African liberals have no single position on what kind of economic system would be right for a postapartheid South Africa. The money to support such liberal initiatives as the symposium comes from the business community, whose members are ideologically committed to free-market capitalism and are anxious about the effects of majoritarian democracy on their lives and businesses. Some of the academic liberals, however, believe that the values of a political democracy are more important than laissez-faire capitalism and seem willing to accept some form of democratic socialism, or egalitarian social democracy, as the inevitable and justifiable outcome of reforms that would extend political power to a black majority.

Whatever one may think about capitalism and socialism in the abstract, it seems clear that the vast inequities resulting from South Africa's long history of racial privilege and discrimination require action by the state to redistribute wealth and resources. Liberalism cannot make common cause with the black liberation struggle unless it puts itself at some distance from orthodox free-market formulas that in the US would be considered "conservative" rather than liberal.

A contrary point of view is advanced in Francis Kendall and Leon Louw's *After Apartheid*. Here we find free-market "liberalism" carried to its libertarian extreme and offered as "the solution for South Africa." Louw is a South African émigré who is executive director of the American Free Market Foundation, and Kendall is editor of an American Libertarian paper, *The Individualist*. The book was published with much fanfare in the United States after being a best seller in South Africa, and carries the endorsements of Winnie Mandela, Bayard Rustin, and Alan Paton.

In view of their prestige and the seemingly impeccable anti-apartheid credentials of its sponsors, I was led to expect a convincing contribution to the debate on South Africa. I was disappointed. The main proposal is that South Africa be reorganized politically on the Swiss canton model, turning the existing 305 magistrate districts into essentially self-governing units. As a result of such radical decentralization, the central South African government would have severely limited powers. It would be elected by black majority vote, but this would not mean that other racial groups "would be ruled by blacks, because the central government would not have the power to impose its policies or values on anyone."

Essentially this is a strategy for preventing Africans from controlling

South Africa by making it impossible for anyone to control it. Economic, welfare, and educational matters would be under the exclusive control of the cantons, which would choose capitalism, socialism, or some kind of mixed economy, as local voters determined. A bill of rights would protect individuals and minorities from government repression or discrimination.

Kendall and Louw make it clear, however, that they would prefer not to protect individuals or groups against private discrimination or segregation by voluntary associations. Anything resembling affirmative action would be beyond the pale in the "colorblind . . . entirely nonracial" society that they favor. Mixed in with their constitutional proposals are a number of the familiar, and still largely untried, economic proposals of the libertarian right, such as replacing public schools by a voucher system, and abolishing most health and safety regulations for industry, or at least reducing them to something Kendall and Louw call "third-world" standards. In short, privatize everything in sight and get the government off the backs of both white and black South Africans, who will then proceed to build a prosperous and happy society.

The first problem with the proposal for constitutional decentralization is that there is not a chance in the world that the black majority will accept anything of the sort. The African National Congress and the United Democratic Front have often made it clear that they will settle for nothing less than majority rule in the South African state as it is now defined, a position that is based on the fateful white decision to create a centralized state in South Africa in 1910 and on the precedent of every successful nationalist or independence movement in the third world. If a white-dominated government were to attempt to impose decentralization of the kind Kendall and Louw are recommending, Africans would likely regard it as merely the latest ruse of the whites in their desperate struggle to keep power. And I am not sure that they would be wrong. If no effective central political authority existed in South Africa, who then would have de facto power over the whole? Presumably those who possess economic power through the ownership of productive resources, primarily white-owned corporations and large white landowners. Afrikaner nationalist domination would not survive the reforms of Kendall and Louw, but de facto white supremacy would remain intact and would in fact become virtually unchallengeable under the constitutional structure they propose.

Kendall and Louw show they are to a degree aware of how the long history of racial oppression has stacked the deck against blacks in a free-market economy. They propose that blacks be paid compensation for past discrimination by distributing to them the proceeds of government assets sold to private interests. Beyond that, however, they would rely on the entrepreneurial efforts of Africans in a competitive, laissez-faire economy to bring about the redistribution of wealth.

Doctrinaire free-market ideology of the kind advanced by Kendall and Louw is deeply ahistorical. The notion that every country, whatever its history and circumstances, should have the same extremely limited government and the same kind of freedom of enterprise is every bit as unrealistic, and potentially as disastrous, as the contrary notion that centralized state socialism is the only path to prosperity. At a time when the failures of state socialism have become apparent in Eastern Europe, the Soviet Union, and China, and the virtues of pluralism and market activity are being recognized in much of the Communist world, it is easy to forget that capitalism was unable to cope with the Great Depression of the 1930s and had to be modified in significant respects. In such different capitalist economies as those of West Germany and Sweden, government intervention, directly or indirectly, redistributes income, maintains elaborate welfare and education systems, and attempts to protect the safety of workers in factories and the health of the population generally—all functions that are suspect to Kendall and Louw.

Moreover, even the most doctrinaire free-enterprisers would agree that government has to take a hand in times of great natural disasters, such as famines and earthquakes. The current economic plight of South African blacks, as presented with great force and authority in the Carnegie Corporation study *Uprooting Poverty*, by Francis Wilson and Mamphela Ramphele, in fact borders on a disaster, and it is hard to imagine any solution that would not involve the use of substantial power by a central government. The misery, desperation, and death discussed in *Uprooting Poverty* may make the reader impatient with utopian fantasies of pure market theory and uncertain whether the sources of power and wealth that already exist can be mobilized to avert a human catastrophe.

Uprooting Poverty is the report of the Second Carnegie Inquiry into Poverty and Development in Southern Africa. The first inquiry, which resulted in a five volume report published in 1932, concentrated on "poor whites," implicitly assuming white poverty in a multiracial society was unnatural, whereas black poverty was the inevitable consequence of a lack of "civilized" development. The report helped to rationalize government efforts to improve the conditions of the white population at the expense of the blacks and thus contributed to the growth of racial discrimination and segregation. It is a measure of the shift of international opinion away from a white supremacist bias that the Carnegie Corporation should now sponsor a study of black poverty based on the assumption that white rule in South Africa has been unjust and exploitative. One of the authors, Francis Wilson, is a white South African economist known for his studies of the migratory labor system that has made South African industrial capitalism unique in the world; the other, Mamphela Ramphele, is a black physician and founder of community health centers who was a close associate of Steve Biko in the black consciousness movement of the 1970s.

Their study does not offer political solutions or endorse in so many words any of the competing ideologies of reform or revolution in South Africa. It mainly describes the acute economic needs and social degradation that any new system would have to confront. It nevertheless argues explicitly that the current policies of the Nationalist government have contributed to impoverishing the black population, and that radical changes in the power relations between the privileged white minority and the deprived black majority are preconditions for a successful campaign against poverty.

Most reports of this sort are full of statistics, and this one is no exception. The figures are truly alarming. According to the best available information, 50 percent of the total South African population and almost two thirds of the African population earn less than is required for subsistence. One third of all black children (this figure includes "coloureds" and Indians as well as Africans) are victims of malnutrition. The infant mortality rate, estimated at between 94 and 124 per thousand births during the early 1980s, is considerably higher than that of the more prosperous African countries (such as Kenya and Zimbabwe) and roughly equal to some of the poorest. Although reliable unemployment statistics are hard to come by, the best available estimates put the jobless rate at around 20 percent for the labor force as a whole, and up to 50 percent or even higher in districts where blacks are concentrated.

Shocking as such statistics are, they fail to convey the full human meaning of these conditions. Aware of this, the authors depart from the normal pattern of social-scientific surveys by providing case studies of poor families and interviews with them. They also give accounts of a farming community where the soil is nearly all gone and only bedrock remains; of a child who subsists almost entirely on coffee, sugar, and Cremora; and of a woman who set herself on fire with paraffin because she could not feed her children. In describing the fear and insecurity of the poor, the authors quote a "coloured' woman in Cape Town:

> You suffer—you are not certain of your life or anything else. I lost my job because of my nerves. Because there is no crèche to look after my children while I am working, I used to fear for their safety.

They add that she was shortly evicted for not paying her rent and had a premature baby as a result.

To some extent, poverty in southern Africa is caused by geography: the region is naturally arid, drought is frequent, and a rapidly growing population puts pressure on available land and resources. Yet South Africa is able both to export food and to support a very high standard of living for the white minority. It has in fact the most unequal distribution of wealth and income of any country in the world. Wilson and Ramphele make it clear that much of the misery of South African blacks is not only man-made but the result of deliberate government policies. The destitution of women and children is closely related to the migratory labor system, which takes men away from home for extended periods and fails to pay them enough to sustain both themselves and their families or even to insure that they contribute something to their kin left behind in "homelands." (Recent reforms abolishing the pass laws have not eliminated this problem, because those reforms do not apply to most of the roughly nine million Africans who are citizens of "independent" homelands; furthermore, the government can still limit the urban migration of families by failing to provide housing for new arrivals.)

The government has also impoverished blacks through its "removals" policy. Between 1960 and 1983, nearly 3.5 million blacks were forced to move from one place to another against their will in order to bring about the territorial separation required by apartheid laws. People were often transferred to regions where chances of employment or agricultural subsistence were fewer than in the places they had left. In some cases, they were dumped in villages where the only possible way to survive was through migratory labor or by commuting enormous distances each day. (Some African workers spend up to six hours a day on buses getting to and from their jobs.) As South African agriculture has been mechanized since World War II, the proportion of the African work force employed on white farms has dropped from one third to one fifth; but displaced agricultural workers have not, for the most part, been permitted to move to the cities—the usual pattern of "modernization" in other countries. They have instead been forced into already overcrowded "homelands" where they have little chance of earning a living.

In short, the South African government has deliberately created conditions that are conducive to extreme poverty and everything that goes with it—demoralization, crime, disease, high mortality rates. The black population clearly exceeds the numbers that can be employed in the current white-dominated economy, and policies that send the people to "surplus" remote areas under life-threatening circumstances have a certain brutal logic to them.

Unless major changes come quickly, the conditions that Wilson and Ramphele describe are likely to get worse. While standards of living improve for blacks fortunate enough to live in cities and have steady jobs, they are deteriorating for those lacking regular work. Average wages for black workers are going up but so is the rate of unemployment. The stagnation of the South African economy and the growth of mechanization in agriculture and automation in manufacturing make it more difficult than ever to create enough jobs for a rapidly growing black population. It is hard to see how establishing a free market and turning all government functions over to private hands—the solution of

Kendall and Louw—can deal with these deep-rooted conditions. Wilson and Ramphele acknowledge that private economic initiatives and voluntary action are important to the struggle against poverty but they insist that state action to relieve misery and redistribute wealth is also clearly required. Kendall and Louw are noticeably silent about the crisis in African health and how it would be dealt with under their decentralized laissez-faire regime. Presumably they favor a private health care system. Wilson and Ramphele, on the other hand, have no doubt that South Africa urgently needs a national health service. One does not have to be a socialist, only a practical humanitarian, to recognize that a public health disaster requires state action.

Uprooting Poverty is not simply another plea for helping the poor through public programs conducted by a state more benevolent than the current one. The authors also recognize that there are some things the poor themselves can do in the meantime to improve their immediate circumstances—form cooperatives and community organizations, for example. But there can be no decisive, long-term improvement in the condition of South Africa's poor until political democracy is introduced. In the authors' words, "an essential prerequisite for uprooting poverty in South Africa is a redistribution of political power," but even a representative government will face enormous difficulties in undoing the legacy of more than three centuries of white domination.

How close is South Africa to political changes that affirm basic human rights and begin to address the huge economic and social problems left by apartheid? Wilson and Ramphele are not very optimistic, writing in their introduction that

> there is virtually no likelihood of the present government (or some revised version of it) either voluntarily handing over power to democratic rulers or finding itself coerced by guerrilla activity, economic sanctions and other pressures into negotiating away its entrenched position, in the immediate future.

The liberation struggle, they conclude, has "long years to run."

A recent symposium addressed precisely the question of how long the white minority can retain power and thwart democratic aspirations and makes a similar assessment. *Can South Africa Survive?*, edited by John Brewer, brings together an international panel of experts to consider the immediate and long-range prospects for South Africa. The book is more unified and coherent than most symposiums because the contributors all take as their point of departure R. W. Johnson's influential book of 1977, *How Long Will South Africa Survive?*[1] Countering the expectation, common in writings about South Africa in the 1960s and the early 1970s, that the apartheid regime would soon be overthrown, Johnson argued that white domination was likely to survive for a considerable period. Although many of the preconditions for a black revolution existed, he argued that they were not sufficient to threaten the regime in the short-to-medium run. The clock, Johnson said, is stuck at five minutes to midnight.

The contributors to *Can South Africa Survive?* review the events that have taken place since Johnson wrote his book, and try to decide what difference they have made. They generally find that pressure on the regime has increased but not to the point where radical change is likely to occur. As John Brewer sums up the consensus, using Johnson's metaphor,

> The balance of forces in South Africa still excludes a revolutionary overthrow of the government, but the government's capacity to maintain the present pattern of political power has weakened. If the militarised and centralised state is as yet unassailable, the system is becoming more ungovernable. So while the clock is still at five minutes to midnight, it is no longer riveted in this position.

In coming to such conclusions, the authors give Johnson credit for anticipating the regime's overall capacity to adjust to new challenges and endure. What he did not expect, as the essays by Brewer and Tom Lodge show, was that internal black resistance would become as intense and irrepressible as it did in the past decade. He also overestimated the solidarity of the white minority, and failed to foresee how Afrikanerdom would fracture along class lines between middle-class pragmatists, who also are at last willing to talk of changing the system, and members of the white working class, such as miners or factory workers who fear that liberated blacks would take over their jobs and incomes, and who have become members of the intransigent Conservative party. (Herman Giliomee describes this schism in his fine essay on Afrikaner politics.)

Johnson's skepticism toward Western economic sanctions was borne out by the failure of the measures taken by the US and European community to have dramatic effects; but he may have underestimated the cumulative impact on an already weak South African economy of the limited international actions against apartheid, which, at the very least, have raised the cost of doing business. Nevertheless, if we are to believe the economist T. C. Moll, the survival of white South Africa in the short run is quite possible, even in a siege economy that has been cut off from virtually all Western trade. Furthermore, he warns that if blacks come to power only after a long period of economic decline, they may find the country so deeply impoverished that it would be very difficult to revive it economically. "In short," he concludes,

> precisely because of its current resilience, policies to undermine the South African economy could have multiplied negative effects on the political system that replaces apartheid, which poses a difficult tactical dilemma for those who seek an end to white political supremacy.

In other words, sanctions should only be used with careful calculation of their practical effects, not simply as a way of pacifying the consciences of some people in Western countries.

The authors of the essays in *Can South Africa Survive?*, like those in *South Africa: No Turning Back* and *Uprooting Poverty*, give little or no support to those who believe that a negotiated settlement of the South African conflict is possible in the near future.[2] But all these assessments were written before the Namibian agreement, the replacement this year of P. W. Botha by F. W. de Klerk as president and as head of the ruling Nationalist party, the emergence of an impressive new campaign of nonviolent mass protest by blacks, and, most recently, the Nationalists' loss of a substantial number of seats to both the Conservative party and the liberal Democratic party in the elections of September 6, 1989. Do these developments provide grounds for new hope that an end to apartheid can be achieved with the long-lasting, intermittently bloody, and economically devastating struggle that practically all the writers under review seem to regard as the most likely prospect for South Africa?

Perhaps they do, although predicting the immediate future remains treacherous. De Klerk is committed to a change in the constitutional system and to some form of negotiations leading to the extension of limited political rights to Africans, but he has yet to agree to talk with the genuine leaders of the black resistance in the ANC and the UDF; and he remains adamantly opposed to the kind of constitutional change that would meet the demands of these leaders for a majoritarian democracy. Despite the proclamation of the unusually repressive state of emergency in February 1988, nonviolent black protest, under the leadership of Archbishop Desmond Tutu and the Reverend Allen Boesak, reemerged in the summer of 1989. The protest movement now has more popular support than ever before and appears to be both more disciplined and more effective.

The Nationalists emerged from the election on September 6 with a greatly reduced majority, losing seats in approximately equal numbers to the staunchly pro-apartheid right and the moderately liberal left. Having come dangerously close to losing its overall parliamentary majority for the first time since 1948, the Nationalists will have to bend one way or the other to halt the erosion of their strength. With the Afrikaner white working class turning to the Conservative party, the Nationalists are no longer supported by a majority of the Afrikaners, and are now dependent on English-speaking voters, some of whom defected to the Democrats in the election.

The central question now is whether the ruling party will seek the support of white liberal opinion at the expense of the conservative Afrikaner hard core and even seek to reach an accommodation with the Democrats, whose leaders include recent defectors from the Nationalists. Referring to the points of agreement between the Nationalists and the Democrats, de Klerk said on the day after the election that nearly three quarters of the nation's voters had now endorsed a change of direction in South African politics; but building a white majority consensus behind pragmatic reform and limited concessions to black protesters will not be easy. If it is to be convincing it would require further steps by de Klerk and his allies to eliminate formal apartheid and to lift the provisions of the state of emergency. It would also probably require a willingness on de Klerk's part to consider constitutional changes providing for the inclusion of Africans in the political system, and to undertake negotiations with black leaders such as Nelson Mandela and Archbishop Tutu on the extent and character of African enfranchisement. So far, it must be said, de Klerk has taken none of these steps.

Still, it seems to me somewhat more likely that the de Klerk government would move in this direction than that it would try to protect its right flank by stealing the thunder of the Conservative party. More perhaps than Botha, de Klerk is responsive to the parts of the business community and a white middle class (including many Afrikaners) that are currently more concerned with saving the South African economy than with guaranteeing white supremacy in every aspect of South African life. His government may be disposed to see if a deal can be cut with the African resistance movement, including the African National Congress. If that is so, then the big question is whether or not the spokesmen of the black majority are likely to have a similar disposition to compromise and conciliation.

If we take literally the rhetoric and official positions of the ANC, the UDF, and the new Mass Democratic Movement (essentially the UDF under another name), it would seem unlikely that anything even a relatively more liberal and accommodating white government would propose as a basis for negotiations would be acceptable. The formal aim of the resistance is immediate black majority rule under a one-person-one-vote electoral system, something no white government could agree to without committing suicide.

But it is not inconceivable that black leaders would settle for something like the proposal made by a Soviet expert on South Africa in an essay written in 1986—a two-house assembly, with each chamber elected by universal suffrage but with one chamber based strictly on population—one man, one vote—and the other on the equal representation of the four racial groups. Giving the second chamber a veto on legislation would mean that no single ethnic community could impose its will on the rest.[3]

It is still not clear whether this is indeed the Soviet Union's official position or that the USSR would be ready to use its considerable leverage as the main arms supplier to the ANC to induce the ANC leaders to consider some such form of minority veto under a cloak of universal suffrage. If Gorbachev is moving in this direction then there could well be something to talk about with a white government, especially if it were under pressure from Britain and the United States to agree to such a scheme. A shared desire by the superpowers to bring peace and stability to southern Africa under an arrangement for power sharing that the international community would find tolerable could bring results within the next few years.

In any case, things are changing rapidly in South Africa. The black opposition is gaining strength and unity; the whites are more divided than they have ever been on how to respond to the black liberation movement, although for the first time there seems a white majority in favor of some kind of African enfranchisement, and the government is apparently edging toward negotiations with Nelson Mandela and the ANC. In mid-September, confronted by marches in several cities of thousands of blacks and whites protesting the killing of twenty-nine people on election day, the de Klerk government took no repressive action despite the illegality of such demonstrations and ordered the police to accept the marchers' petitions to end police brutality. But the banning of a women's march on September 23, and the beating of those who attempted to march despite the ban, show that the government still has a long way to go before it allows full rights to peaceful protest. Those who hope for a relatively peaceful transition from a minority racial tyranny to an arguably democratic multiracial polity may still be looking at the world naively, but, unless the repression in Pretoria indicates a reversal of de Klerk's proclaimed new openness to dialogue with anti-apartheid forces, they have more good reasons for cautious optimism now than at any other time since 1948.

NOTES

This chapter is a review of the following works: Martin Meredith, *In the Name of Apartheid: South Africa in the Postwar Period* (New York: Harper and Row, 1988); Shaun Johnson, ed., *South Africa: No Turning Back*, foreword by Lord Bullock (Bloomington, Ind.: Indiana University Press, 1989); Janet Levine, *Inside Apartheid: One Woman's Struggle in South Africa* (Chicago: Contemporary Books, 1988); Jeffrey Butler, Richard Elphick, and David Welsh, eds., *Democratic Liberalism in South Africa: Its History and Prospect* (Middletown, Conn.: Wesleyan University Press, 1987); Frances Kendall and Leon Louw, *After Apartheid: The Solution for South Africa*, foreword by Samuel Motsuenyane (San Francisco: Institute for Contemporary Studies, 1987); Francis Wilson and Mamphela Ramphele, *Uprooting Poverty: The South African Challenge* (New York: W. W. Norton, 1989); and John D. Brewer, ed., *Can South Africa Survive? Five Minutes to Midnight* (New York: St. Martin's Press, 1989).

1. New York: Macmillan, 1977.

2. See Mark R. Hoffenberg, "Falling Apartheid," *The New Republic* (July 31, 1989), pp. 16–17.

3. This proposal by Gleb Starushenko, published by the Africa Institute in Moscow, is described by G. R. Berridge in *Can South Africa Survive?*, p. 18.

24

The Impact of the Intifada

BISHARA A. BAHBAH

Last year, the Arabic word *intifada* was incorporated into the English language. The word *intifada*, which means "uprising," has come to symbolize the Palestinian people's revulsion with and resistance to 22 years of Israeli occupation of the West Bank and the Gaza Strip.

Although the nature and timing of the intifada, which erupted on December 9, 1987, took both Palestinians and Israelis by surprise, it was bound to happen. Since 1948, which marked the creation of the state of Israel on almost two-thirds of the land of Palestine, Palestinians have been reduced to a stateless nation. Half of them reside as refugees in neighboring Arab countries and the other half still lives in Palestine but under Israeli control. Over the years, Palestinians tried different approaches to regain all or part of Palestine. All have failed and none has provided as much hope as the intifada.

In 1948, Palestinians and neighboring Arab countries failed to stop the Zionists from establishing a Jewish state in Palestine. Having just emerged from colonialism themselves, most independent Arab countries at the time were militarily weak and unskilled in the art of diplomacy. Despite the Arabs' defeat, the Palestinians, who strongly believed in Arab nationalism, adopted a strategy that relied heavily on the Arab world's participation and assistance in helping to liberate Palestine. Palestinians and other Arabs wanted nothing less than the entire land of Palestine and the elimination of the state of Israel, which they viewed as a foreign entity in the midst of the Arab world.

For the next 20 years, the Arab world talked about liberating Palestine and annihilating the Jewish state. But Arab leaders failed to back up their threats with a corresponding military buildup. Moreover, the Arab countries underestimated the strength, discipline, and skills of the Israeli army. Less than a week after the June 1967 war broke out, the armies of Egypt, Syria, and Jordan were summarily defeated by the Israeli army. As a result, Israel occupied the remaining parts of Pales-

This article appeared in the September 1989 issue and is reprinted with permission from *The World & I*, a publication of the Washington Times Corporation, copyright © 1989.

Note: It is a violation of the law to reproduce this selection by any means whatsoever without the written permission of the copyright holder.

tine—the West Bank and the Gaza Strip. It also seized the Sinai from Egypt and the Golan Heights from Syria.

The Palestinians were shocked and dismayed but, more importantly, they were awakened. Many felt that it was a mistake to have relied so much on other Arabs. They strongly believed that from that time on, the initiative in liberating any part of Palestine should be Palestinian, albeit unavoidably with Arab assistance.

Prior to 1967, the Palestinians had conducted limited armed raids against Israel, beginning in the early 1950s. In 1957, the Palestinian Liberation Movement (Fatah), headed by Yasser Arafat, started to organize and prepare for the fight against Israel. As the idea of armed struggle by Palestinians gained popularity, the League of Arab States, during its first summit meeting in 1964, decided to establish the Palestine Liberation Organization (PLO) and a traditional army.

The Palestine Liberation Army, which was made up primarily of infantry units, fought and was defeated in the 1967 war. Like other defeated Arab armies, it lost its credibility. A major turning point in Palestinian history occurred on March 21, 1968, when Palestinian guerrillas fighting alongside the Jordanian army were able to halt and force the Israeli army to withdraw during an attack on the village of Karameh in the Jordan River Valley. This victory reinforced the belief that only armed struggle could defeat the Israelis. Within a few months, the ranks of the Palestinian guerrillas grew in numbers, with the new members challenging the traditional leadership of the PLO and taking control of the organization. Arafat was elected chairman of the Executive Committee of the PLO at that time.

"Armed struggle is the only way to liberate Palestine," stated Article 9 of the Palestine National Charter, which was amended in July 1968 by the Palestine National Council, the supreme body within the PLO. Politically, Palestinians espoused the establishment of a secular state in Palestine, where Arabs and Jews could live side by side in peace. Israel completely rejected this notion and continued to hold on to the Palestinian territories it had occupied.

A new phase in Palestinian history began to unfold. Palestinian guerrillas escalated their attacks against Israeli targets inside and outside occupied Palestine. Palestinian guerrillas were accused of engaging in acts of terror. Although the PLO was successful in drawing the attention of the world to the plight of the Palestinian people, it was often negative attention.

In the meantime, Israel was consolidating its hold on the newly occupied lands. Thousands of Palestinians were imprisoned, often without due legal process; homes were demolished to punish alleged security violators; curfews were imposed; and large portions of the West Bank and Gaza were confiscated either for military use or for the building of Jewish settlements.

REASSESSING STRATEGY

The inability of Syria and Egypt to defeat Israel during the October 1973 war helped convince Palestinians that a military victory over Israel was far-fetched. This, in addition to the international backlash engendered by the PLO's use of what was described as terrorism, forced the PLO to reassess its strategy toward Israel. A resolution adopted by the Palestine National Council at its 1974 meeting called for the establishment of a Palestinian state on "any part of liberated Palestine." This was seen as a very significant departure from previous positions that called for the end of the Jewish state.

Palestinians were slowly coming to the realization that armed struggle, although an important element in the fight against Israel, was not leading to the liberation of Palestine. Hence, they adopted a new, two-pronged strategy. One aspect of this strategy called for the continuation of armed struggle against Israel, while the other called for a diplomatic offensive aimed at gaining recognition for the PLO and acceptance of a two-state solution.

The PLO's diplomatic offensive quickly paid off. In 1974, the League of Arab States recognized the PLO as the sole legitimate representative of the Palestinian people. In November of that year, Arafat was invited to address the UN General Assembly, and the PLO was granted observer status by the General Assembly. By 1980, 115 countries had recognized the PLO. Nevertheless, these diplomatic victories had little effect on the Israelis, who continued to suppress Palestinians living under occupation.

The Palestinians now believed that the best vehicle to settle the Arab-Israeli conflict was the convening of an international peace conference with the participation of all the parties concerned, including Israel and the PLO. This approach was derailed in 1977 by the decision of Egyptian President Anwar Sadat to enter into direct negotiations with Israel. These negotiations resulted in the return of the Sinai Peninsula to Egypt in exchange for a peace treaty between Israel and Egypt. This Egyptian-Israeli agreement left Israel with little incentive to come to terms with the Palestinians. With Egypt's military threat against Israel neutralized, Israel annexed the Golan Heights, attacked a nuclear reactor in Iraq, and invaded Lebanon in 1978, 1981, and 1982 in order to crush the PLO. Israel was hoping that defeating the PLO would help convince Palestinians in the West Bank and Gaza Strip that their only recourse was to accept an offer of local autonomy under continued Israeli control.

Israel's wish to see the PLO destroyed did not materialize. Although the PLO's forces had to be relocated into a number of Arab countries following Israel's 1982 invasion of Lebanon, and a revolt within Fatah—the largest guerrilla group—was instigated by Syria, Arafat survived as the leader of both Fatah and the PLO. From 1982 to 1987, the PLO expended its energies in rebuilding its forces and bases. In the meantime, Israel continued to be adamant about not dealing with the PLO and not recognizing Palestinian aspirations for a state of their own.

A UNIQUE PHENOMENON

Then the intifada erupted. Although neither planned nor anticipated, it has done more to advance the cause of the people of Palestine than major wars and years of diplomacy. The intifada is a unique phenomenon in the history of the Arab-Israeli conflict for a number of reasons.

First, it is a mass movement among Palestinians from all walks of life, including women and children. Although throughout the years of Israel's occupation of the West Bank and the Gaza Strip many acts of resistance against Israel's occupation took place, they were rarely on such a large scale and were always short-lived. In contrast, every Palestinian plays a role in the intifada. Merchants open their shops only when told to by the leadership of the intifada. Youths battle Israeli soldiers and settlers with stones. Women and even children have joined ranks with the men in confronting the Israelis. The intelligentsia has mobilized to tell the world about Israeli's oppressive occupation.

Second, the objective of the intifada is to end Israel's occupation through nonmilitary means. Stones and Molotov cocktails are the primary weapons of the intifada. Both from a pragmatic and a public relations point of view, the use of firearms has been forbidden by the Palestinian leadership. Realistically, the Palestinians have few weapons and cannot match Israel's firepower. More importantly, Palestinians realize that world sympathy usually sides with the underdog.

Third, the intifada is changing Israel's image throughout the world. No longer is Israel viewed as David fighting the Arab Goliath. It is now the other way around. The intifada, in that regard, has helped expose Israel's brutality. According to the 1988 human rights report issued by the U.S. State Department, 366 Palestinians were killed in 1988 by Israeli soldiers and settlers, over 20,000 were wounded or injured by the Israeli army, at least 13 Palestinians were beaten to death, more than 154 houses were demolished, and 36 people were deported. The list of Israeli abuses goes on.

Fourth, the intifada helped shatter Israel's invincibility in Palestinian eyes. Israel's control of the West Bank and the Gaza Strip is at best shaky. There are Palestinian liberated villages that the Israeli army has not set foot in for months. The intifada has convinced many Palestinians that the end of Israel's occupation is inevitable, if not near.

Fifth, the intifada has proven to be a tremendous economic burden on Israel. Aside from the cost of maintaining a large military presence in the occupied territories, Palestinians have refused to pay the taxes that Israel had formerly collected. Moreover, the occupied territories are no longer Israel's second largest export market after the United States. The $900 million worth of products that the West Bank and Gaza imported from Israel has dwindled. Tourism to Israel, which is a major foreign currency earner, has suffered significantly since the beginning of the intifada. At the same time, the Palestinians themselves have been adversely affected. Their standard of living has declined, and the flow of outside aid has been severely restricted. Nevertheless, Palestinians have been willing to sacrifice in order to see an end to Israel's occupation.

Sixth, the intifada has refocused the attention of the Arab world and the international community on the plight of the Palestinian people. Only months before the beginning of the intifada, the Arab League Summit that was held in Amman, Jordan, dedicated most of its energies to the Iran–Iraq War and paid little attention to the Palestinian issue. The most important effect that the intifada has had on the Arab arena was the decision of Jordan's King Hussein to sever all legal and administrative ties to the West Bank. That clearly meant that the king no longer viewed as feasible the possibility of ever governing the West Bank. Internationally, the intifada has generated tremendous sympathy and support for the people of Palestine. During the first few months of the intifada, the Western media diligently covered Israel's attempts to suppress the uprising.

Finally, the intifada's success provided the Palestinian leadership with new-found confidence to take risks on the political front and to adopt a new course of action. In November 1988, a special session of the Palestine National Council proclaimed the establishment of the state of Palestine and made key decisions, including a call for the convening of an international peace conference on the basis of UN Security Council resolutions 242 and 338. These resolutions called for Israel's withdrawal from territories it occupied in 1967 but referred to Palestinians as refugees only, which was the main reason they were rejected by the Palestinians. This was the first time that Palestinians officially accepted these UN resolutions.

The newly declared Palestinian state quickly gained recognition from more than 100 countries. However, the United States, which is viewed by many Palestinians as the only country with some influence over Israel and capable of affecting the course of events, remained adamantly supportive of Israel.

On December 14, 1988, Arafat declared at a news conference in Geneva, Switzerland, that the PLO recognized UN resolutions 242 and 338. He also stated "in no uncertain terms" that "we totally and absolutely renounce all forms of terrorism, including individual, group, and state terrorism." Arafat added that he recognized Israel and its right to live in peace and security. Hours later, the United States announced that the PLO met the conditions it had imposed to enter into a dialogue with the PLO. This was yet another crucial development that could be attributed to the intifada.

The euphoria following the United States' decision to enter into a substantive dialogue with the PLO was short-lived. Few meetings have taken place through the U.S. ambassador in Tunisia, the only authorized channel to talk to the PLO. The United States has been unwilling to act as either a partner or a mediator between the PLO and the Israelis. The United States has viewed its role as merely that of a facilitator.

In April of this year, Israeli Prime Minister Yitzhak Shamir proposed holding elections in the West Bank and Gaza for local representatives to negotiate with Israel on limited self-government for the Palestinians. The United States supported the elections plan, which was vehemently opposed by Palestinians. In July, Shamir agreed to add limits to his elections proposal so that it excluded both the creation of a Palestinian state and the relinquishing of any Palestinian lands. For the Palestinians, that ensured outright and absolute rejection of the Shamir plan.

There are few encouraging signs as far as the future is concerned. The Palestinians have made the intifada their new way of life. They are willing to continue battling Israel until the latter recognizes the right of Palestinians to self-determination and withdraws from the West Bank and the Gaza Strip. The Palestinians have paid a dear price to make the intifada a success and are determined to maintain pressure on Israel.

Israel's policies, on the other hand, are hardening. Israel's Likud government is not willing to negotiate with the Palestinians on the basis of a land-for-peace settlement. The United States, although it now talks to the PLO, continues to pursue a staunchly pro-Israeli policy and shows little willingness to put pressure on Israel to withdraw from the occupied territories.

What we will certainly continue to witness is an escalation of violence between Palestinians and Israelis. The Palestinians are hoping that eventually Israel might want to cut its losses and agree to a land-for-peace arrangement. After all, they believe, unless Israel is made to pay a heavy price for its occupation, it will have little incentive to withdraw.

25

The Perils of a Palestinian State

STEVEN L. SPIEGEL

In the mid-1970s we heard much about the human rights violations of the Shah. America and Iran, it was said, would be well rid of him. As the Iranian protest movement grew, many American observers came to believe that our interests and values would be best served by a nationalist, neutralist government in Tehran. Of course, taking this scenario seriously required us to believe that the Ayatollah Khomeini, the leader in exile of this Persian *intifada*, was a well-meaning and ultimately harmless man. So we did: he might emerge as a figurehead, we said, but he would not rule. Perhaps he would retreat to study theology at Qum. And even if he retained political influence, he would not impose his fundamentalism on the government. The Ayatollah was a "saint," according to our U.N. ambassador, and anyway, Iran was too modern to become an Islamic state. The Shah's collapse was greeted with a combination of relief and heady expectation.

Today we see Israeli soldiers shooting at Palestinian children in the West Bank and the Gaza Strip, and we are understandably troubled by the image. Many in the West are convinced that sweeping changes are necessary in the Holy Land, just as they were said to be in Iran a decade ago. Indeed, there is now a cottage industry devoted to the proposition that PLO-Israeli dialogue leading to a Palestinian state will rid us of our Mideast dilemmas once and for all. There is even the Palestinian equivalent of the Ayatollah: Yasir Arafat, whose character is being willfully distorted in order that we may believe in his good intentions.

Before the optimism grows any further, a cold look at the likely implications of a sovereign Palestinian state is in order. Although the idea of a new political arrangement that would end the trouble once and for all is seductive, the stakes are too high for decisions to be made on the basis of faith and hope. And close analysis suggests that a new Palestinian state could well become, in broad terms, a replay of the new Iranian state: a victim of continued domestic turmoil and a source of new international turbulence; a solution that brings short-term relief for Western guilt, but only at great long-term cost.

To begin with, there are the many old, familiar arguments against a

Reprinted by permission of *The New Republic,* © 1989, The New Republic, Inc.

Note: It is a violation of the law to reproduce this selection by any means whatsoever without the written permission of the copyright holder.

Palestinian state, which are no less valid for being old and familiar. After the creation of such a state, two sovereign peoples whose histories show almost unrelenting mutual antagonism would be locked together in a tiny territory the size of New Jersey. A terrorist incident, a volatile speech by one leader or another, or the machinations of an outside power could result at any time in war. Of course, in its first few years the Palestinian state would be demilitarized and patrolled by some kind of international force, but a few years is not a long time.

It is far from clear that a Palestinian state would be economically viable. In the tiny Gaza Strip there are about 600,000 Arabs living under ghastly conditions. In the West Bank, there are more than 900,000 Arabs. And the numbers are increasing. In these two areas, over 400,000 live in refugee camps, and they would undoubtedly expect to be re-settled if a Palestinian government were established. Without consider-able aid from the Japanese, Americans, Europeans, and other Arabs, the Palestinian state would be a hotbed of unemployment, poverty, and frustration. Matters would be even worse if Palestinians were not al-lowed to work in Israel; yet if they were, the possibility of terrorism would be that much larger. And what of all the Palestinians—twice as many as in the occupied territories—who now reside in surrounding Arab countries or elsewhere around the world? Many of them are from within the frontiers of pre-1967 Israel (Haifa, Jaffa, Lod, Safad, etc.), and neither Israel nor Palestine would be equipped to take them in. If a Palestinian state did try to accommodate them, the result would be havoc. If it didn't, they would suddenly be its enemies. Certainly this Palestinian ministate would not sate their grievance. It might even in-tensify it.

Most advocates of a Palestinian state seem to envision a Palestinian Israel or perhaps an Egypt or a Jordan—in other words, a state that is either democratic or moderately authoritarian, and is in either event at least minimally stable. But is a democracy really plausible? As of now, there is no such thing as an Arab democracy. Could a mildly authori-tarian regime prove stable? Probably not. Even a well-intentioned Pales-tinian leadership would confront citizens of wildly varying interests, ideologies, and backgrounds—a bewildering mélange of nationalists, traditionalists, fundamentalists, irredentists, and radicals. It would be a gargantuan task to mold these factions into a viable polity without civil strife and even civil war. The need to control internal tensions would probably require military force, which is likely to be limited in any settle-ment acceptable to Israel. In the end, there would be no easy way for Israel to be confident that an assassination, a coup, or even a more peaceful change wouldn't produce a radical or fundamentalist regime.

Remember, the Middle East is not a nice place. Has anyone been in Beirut lately? Do we forget the carnage of the Iran–Iraq war so quickly? It is ironic indeed that a Palestinian state of potentially fundamentalist character is gaining in popularity at the very moment when the world is awash in headlines about Khomeini's death sentence against Salman Rushdie. Westerners are finally coming to realize that Western rules of law, order, and equity often do not apply in the Middle East. Yet they continue to expect Israel to welcome an unpredictable Palestinian state on its frontier.

In some respects it is not surprising that the idea of a Palestinian state has gained currency. As a recently published report from the Jaffee Center of Tel Aviv University makes clear, all other currently discussed Israeli options have serious deficiencies: the status quo, with the *intifada* and the demographic time bomb; annexation and mass transfers, which would alienate the rest of the world, including the United States, and divide Israel; Palestinian autonomy, which the Palestinians will not accept without guarantees of eventual statehood; a deal with King Hussein, which, for the moment at least, does not seem feasible; a unilateral withdrawal from the occupied territories, the consequences of which are entirely unpredictable.

It's no wonder, then, that everyone is eager to see a new moderation in Arafat and his entourage. But the defenders of Arafat have no idea what he will do if he comes to rule a Palestinian state. They are heartened by his talk of a two-state solution, and they want to believe he has really forsaken the goal of destroying Israel. But the record is not encouraging. Here is a leader with a long history of cowardice and deceit. He has alternately been aligned with Syria, Iraq, the Ayatollah, Qaddafi, Jordan, and Egypt, in a revolving door of intrigue and mutual duplicity. Until 1988 Arafat has always genuflected to the radical wing of the PLO. Since the *intifada*, he has moved toward compromise but only under the kind of duress that will not be permanent; he has renounced terrorism, but when terrorism occurs he claims he does not control the particular PLO faction responsible. He may be right, and if so that is just another shadow over the whole Palestinian enterprise.

It has become fashionable to describe the Arab-Israel conflict as a dispute that has returned to its roots: the Arab and Jewish communities of the former British mandate of Palestine. But this wrongly suggests a comfortable insulation from the rest of the Middle East. As the Arab states interfered many times before in Palestine, they can do so again. So any solution must take into account the relationship of the Palestinians to their neighbors. If Syria attacks Israel, for example, what does a Palestinian state do? If there is Palestinian unrest in either Jordan or Israel, does a Palestinian state ignore it? As the Israelis often point out, even if a Palestinian state were demilitarized, a lightning attack against Israel could be launched by Jordan with Palestinian consent. Alternatively, Palestine could be the base from which terrorists either conducted raids or lobbed rockets into Jerusalem or Tel Aviv. A Palestinian leadership might be unable or unwilling to control this activity; in fact, such activity is likely to please at least some of this leadership, which even under the best of circumstances won't behave like a single rational actor.

These scenarios are not new, of course. But the problem goes much deeper than they suggest. In myriad ways, a Palestinian state would complicate geopolitics throughout the Middle East and, indeed, on the larger international stage, substantially increasing the range of combustive possibilities. That is why the technical solutions to Israeli security concerns—an international peacekeeping force, etc.—are not adequate. The political genie unleashed by a new Palestine is the real problem to be addressed.

Fundamentally, the question is the international constellation into which a Palestinian state would fit. First, what would its relations be with the great powers, especially the United States and the U.S.S.R.? Second, what of its relations with the other Arab countries and Iran? Would it be closer to radical countries such as Libya, Iraq, Syria, and Iran, or to conservative states such as Saudi Arabia, Morocco, and Egypt? Finally, what would its relations be to its two critical neighbors, Israel and Jordan? And would the answers to these questions, once they materialized, remain stable? Who could prevent a Palestinian leader from switching allies as Arab nations often have in recent years? Remember, in the 1960s Libya was a conservative monarchy and Egypt a radical client of the U.S.S.R.

As the new Palestinian state emerged in the region, it would assume a role in what the late Malcolm Kerr called "the Arab cold war." If its role were passive, and if focused on the Herculean task of constructing a new polity, it would invite pressures from outside states. Defenders of the "true Palestinian faith" like a Qaddafi or an Assad or a Khomeini would not forgive the settlement with Israel. They would argue that the Jewish interloper must be destroyed. Inevitably there would be resonances in the new Palestine (and beyond). Today, as Palestinian mobs demonstrate in the territories and in Jerusalem, they not only shout, "Allah is great." They add, "Death to the Jews." If the Palestinian leadership refused to participate in this holy war, which might be only a war of attrition, such states would seek to destabilize the regime. They might well succeed.

The leadership of the Palestinian state—presumably the Fatah wing of the PLO—would be sensitive to these perils and the consequent need to be active in the region. The Palestinian leadership would no longer need its Arab brethren to attain a state, but it would need them for protection from whichever Arabs opposed the regime in power. After all, Arafat's wing of the PLO was unable to maintain its alliance with all Arab states when Arafat represented the most unifying theme in Arab politics—the idea of a Palestinian state. He certainly would be unable to retain consensual support once he actually ruled as a sovereign (especially since for many Arab regimes, the public advocacy of such a state has been more than matched by a secret fear of its emergence). Assad, for example, could not condone a Palestinian state that contradicts his own view of Syria's destiny. He has not yet been heard from on the idea that evokes so much exuberance from others. And there is no reason to think that he'd be bought off by the restoration of the Golan Heights to his control. There is also no reason for the Israelis to contemplate such a restoration: there isn't even the problem of a restive local population, which makes Palestinianism so salient.

Once the Palestinian state was engaged in the intrigues of intra-Arab politics, its choice of allies would depend partly on domestic politics and rivalries within the regime. If the Palestinians moved in a radical nationalist direction, opportunities for coalitions with states as varied as Libya, Syria, Iraq, and Iran would emerge. As we have seen over the last decade, these countries are often hostile to each other and often at war. Engagement with them could focus Palestine on foreign adventures— efforts to thwart regimes in Damascus or Baghdad, or to establish a client regime in Lebanon; attempts to use the "overseas Palestinians" to overthrow the Saudis; efforts to promote Islamic fundamentalism or to sponsor terrorist campaigns in Europe. Radical nationalists have proved repeatedly that they have a rich ingenuity when it comes to fomenting trouble. Some of these projects might have the effect of directing the Palestinians' mischief away from Israel. But does anyone doubt that in an atmosphere of radical anti-Westernism, Israeli security and American interests would suffer?

Critics will claim that the Palestinians are too educated and advanced to engage in such foolishness. We should recall similar arguments about the Iranians. But let us cede the point that a Palestinian state is more likely to align with more moderate regimes, such as Egypt, Saudi Arabia, or Jordan. Even this arrangement could dangerously strain relations with Israel. In the Middle East, conservative regimes are ever fearful of radicals and fundamentalists, and commensurately reluctant to do business with Israel. Even the most courageous and powerful government of all the Arab regimes—the Egyptian, which actually made peace with Israel—has been terrified of the "Arab consensus" since the death of Sadat. The cold peace between Israel and Egypt is exactly ten years, and both countries deserve credit for its maintenance. But the gradually deteriorating quality of the relationship is hardly cause for optimism. And remember: unlike Egypt, the new state of Palestine would have the fundamental problem of a dissatisfied diaspora constituency spread across the Arab world, with significant numbers residing in extremist countries.

So if the Palestinian regime were to pursue a conservative policy, most likely the Israelis would be reduced to delicate isolation, waiting to see if it could withstand the angry tide of regional Arab politics. After 50-

odd years of Jewish statehood, Israel would still be a pariah, vilified by part of the Middle East and kept at arm's length by the rest. This would be an even more precarious existence than Israel endured in the 1960s, when the West Bank was controlled by a Jordanian regime that was solidly in control of its power base.

And this is actually a relatively sunny scenario; a Palestinian state nominally aligned with the conservative Arab states might well pursue an actively hostile foreign policy. A relatively responsible regime could soon conclude that unless it adopted a dynamic approach it would fall prey to its adversaries. It might foment terrorism against Israel and attempt to dilute the peace agreement. It might move against Jordan and/or Lebanon, attempting by subversion to emerge with a sympathetic or subservient regime in these countries. Such a Palestinian thrust toward *lebensraum*, motivated also by the desire to integrate the surrounding Palestinian diaspora into the new society, would pose an immediate concern to any Israeli government, and tensions would heighten. There is also the likely risk that a semi-independent Palestinian entity in confederation with Jordan—which has a Palestinian majority—could nurse ambitions of taking over the entire kingdom.

In theory, of course, there could emerge a Palestinian state that would espouse a doctrine of partnership with Israel. Cooperation between the two former adversaries, as well as the Palestinians' sponsorship of close Israeli relations with other Arab countries, might create an environment conducive to peace. Indeed, perhaps a grand alliance among the two and Egypt, Jordan, and Saudi Arabia would develop. But if this is what Arafat has in mind, it is a well-kept secret. Nothing in his record or background suggests he would be prepared to challenge his Arab and Palestinian enemies by entering into an alignment with Israel (if it were willing) that would invariably leave him the junior partner. And even if he did, no one could rely on his maintaining power, or even staying alive. After all, this has been tried before by Arabs: King Abdullah, Anwar Sadat, Bashir Gemayel—all of whom died at the hands of assassins. Arafat knows firsthand how far death squads can reach, and of the power of the nationalist, radical, and fundamentalist forces that would be aligned against him.

Alluding to the vivid dangers that Israel now confronts in the frenzy for a Palestinian state seems churlish and ungenerous. The apprehensive are seen as the world's biggest party poopers. This is particularly the case when their anxiety is compared with the beguiling optimism of Palestinian spokesmen and their surrogates. But a relentless skepticism is in order; it is the utopians who should be under suspicion. Whenever someone imagines a new Marshall Plan as a deus ex machina for the region or conjures up the Benelux countries as a model for Middle East regional cooperation, that someone is blowing smoke in your eyes. He is trying to evade the concrete and intrinsic impediments to peace by mustering a fantasy.

Is the seemingly inexorable movement toward a Palestinian state truly inexorable? No. The *intifada*, literally the "dusting off," may threaten Israel's economy, its social and political unity, and its moral standing, but it does not threaten its survival. (Of course, the uprising is also a low-cost operation for the Palestinians, particularly when measured against the norms of how insurgencies are dealt with in the Arab world.) And certainly, the United States is not as pressured as the advocates of a Palestinian state suggest. What, after all, are the real American interests in Nablus and Ramallah? Moreover, Soviet foreign policy is in transformation. Improved relations with the United States are a major priority, and Moscow's dialogue with Israel has advanced much further than Washington's with the PLO. As the Arab states have done for decades, the Russians may well find themselves swearing eternal fidelity to the Palestinians while compromising that fidelity as soon as convenience dictates. Just ask Syrian president Assad about the Kremlin's capacity to redefine past commitments.

All of this puts Washington in a peculiarly favorable position to make the Soviets our partners in the search for durable peace. As for Israel's course of action: its security could never be significantly enhanced without bilateral discussions with at least several key Arab states. The question is what to do if Israel is offered a series of such discussions that entails discussions with Arafat. The Israeli government would then have to decide whether it could more effectively expose the weakness of a Palestinian state through this option or through continued isolation.

No matter what course is taken, we must recognize that we will not reach the end for many years, and perhaps decades. Reaching a point where Arafat's PLO is even indirectly involved in some kind of Palestinian self-rule will require a virtual revolution, and moving beyond that point will be even harder. Whether the eventual result is confederation with Jordan or Israel or an independent state, it will require a gradual process in which perceptions slowly change and building blocks are arduously moved into place. Those who believe in the instantaneous satisfaction of a TV extravaganza are destined for disappointment. Those who are patient enough to live with uncertainty for many years may be rewarded. Engineering a livable future in Palestine is a delicate, painstaking operation. For now, the Israelis are doomed to live dangerously.

26

Terrorism: A Balance Sheet

SHIREEN T. HUNTER

During the past decade, what has been variously called state-sponsored terrorism, secret warfare, or low-intensity conflict—a phenomenon mostly originating from or related to the Middle East—has been a principal foreign and domestic policy problem for the West, especially for the United States.

No doubt, terrorism—both indigenous and Middle East-originated— was already a problem in the 1960s and 1970s. Then it was mostly limited to Europe and was of much lesser magnitude and frequency. For instance, few terrorist acts during that period could compare with the Iranian hostage crisis of 1979–1981, to the bombings of the U.S. Embassy and marine barracks in Beirut in 1983–1984, or to the wave of kidnappings and hijackings that swept the Middle East in the mid-1980s.

Thus, preoccupation has grown with problems of defining the nature of terrorism and finding ways to combat it. This preoccupation has been accompanied by a sense on the part of vastly superior powers that they are impotent and beleaguered in the face of terrorist actions.

It is indisputable that the concept of terrorism still presents significant definitional problems. It is equally clear that no one has found a single effective way to combat terrorism or to resolve its causes. However, although people in the West understandably feel impotent and beleaguered, their response is exaggerated. Indeed, the record of the last 10 years shows that, despite creating wrenching human dramas and causing temporary policy setbacks, terrorism has not in any significant or lasting way affected the regional or international balances of power. Nor has it in any significant way undermined the economic well-being, military power, political influence, or prestige and standing of Western countries. Moreover, experience during the last decade shows that states engaged in sponsoring terrorism and the perpetrators of terrorist acts have suffered more than have the victims in terms of national and human losses, as well as in terms of power and prestige.

This is not to deny that terrorism is a serious problem requiring serious and concerted efforts on the part of all states to prevent it or respond to it. Rather, dealing successfully with the problem and developing an

Reprinted from *Washington Quarterly*, Vol. 12, No. 3 (Summer, 1989) by permission of the MIT Press.

Note: It is a violation of the law to reproduce this selection by any means whatsoever without the written permission of the copyright holder.

appropriate framework within which states can coordinate their antiterrorist activities requires understanding its nature correctly.

TERRORISM: SOME DEFINITIONAL PROBLEMS

The international community has grappled for nearly a quarter of a
century with the problem of defining terrorism. Yet, consensus is not
greater today than it was in the 1960s. Indeed, the well-worn but still
current cliché that "one man's terrorist is another man's freedom
fighter" illustrates the deep divisions that remain. Nor is there a consensus on the underlying causes of terrorism.

Yet, some agreement on these issues is essential to develop antiterrorist policies that can be acceptable to a sufficiently wide group of
countries and, certainly, to elaborate international legal instruments that
could be ratified and implemented by a large number of states. The
sharpest division of opinion is still between the advanced industrial
nations and the so-called Third World countries. The latter believe
that—given the nature of the current international system that is still
dominated by a few countries—a narrow definition of terrorism, limiting it to acts committed by Third World nationals and governments,
would delegitimize any action by them for the purpose of what they call
national liberation, whether liberation from a foreign power or from an
oppressive internal regime.

These countries worry that such a definition of terrorism would exclude indirect meddling, especially by great powers, in the internal affairs of other states. This meddling can include the provision of military
and financial support for opposition forces and ethnic minorities
fighting against a Third World government, as well as other political,
economic, and military pressures brought to bear on a state to change its
political system or behavior. For example, should a great power's sponsorship of a coup d'état against a legal—and even a popular—government in the Third World or the military and economic sponsorship of
groups fighting a legal government be considered acts of terrorism?
Only by addressing these issues from the perspective both of great
powers and of Third World countries is it possible to understand the role
played by acts of intervention and violence, whoever perpetrates them.

This situation also raises a moral dilemma. Should any act of violence,
even against totally innocent people, be justified if its goal is supposedly
national liberation, ending corruption and oppression on earth, fighting
communism, or achieving a socialist, Islamic, or some other kind of
utopia? This, of course, is not a novel inquiry; rather another manifestation of the perennial problem of when, under what circumstances,
and for what purpose is the use of violence morally justified. Indeed,
many Middle Eastern terrorists have proclaimed themselves to be
mujahid (holy warriors) engaged in *jihad* (holy war), which in legal

and moral terms is the equivalent of the Western Christian concept
of just war.

Nevertheless, there is considerable agreement that such acts as
hijacking airplanes and abducting protected persons (for example,
diplomats and officials of international organizations) cannot be justified on the grounds of struggle for national liberation or similar
pretexts.[1]

A similar difficulty exists in identifying the causes of terrorism, where
there are two broadly defined categories of opinion. The first emphasizes the social, economic, and political causes of terrorism. The second
ascribes terrorism to the peculiarities of certain cultures, religions, or
political ideologies, as well as to the general laxity of the civilized
world—meaning the Western world—in dealing with acts of terrorism.

Thus, in explaining the phenomenon of Shi'a terrorism in Lebanon,
the adherents of the first theory point to the long history of the Shi'as'
suffering and their efforts to obtain social, economic, and political justice. The supporters of the second theory point to the Messianic dimensions of Shi'ism and to its cult of martyrdom to explain Shi'a terrorism,
as well as the inability or unwillingness of its victims to retaliate swiftly
and strongly.

In reality, however, both types of causes affect the emergence and the
development of modern-day terrorism. Thus, responses designed to
deal with terrorism must also address both of them. For example, retaliatory actions that deprive a group or a state of its economic and military
means to perform terrorist acts or that raise the costs of such acts do
have an impact in reducing terrorist incidents over time. However, if
other causes of terrorism are not dealt with in the meantime, the respite
gained will likely be short-lived.

Two points need emphasis. First, states are more likely to attribute
terrorism to social, economic, and political factors—thus to recommend
long-term solutions rather than short-term retaliation—if they have not
themselves been frequent targets of terrorism. Second, the sociopolitical
explanation of terrorism, although important, is insufficient because it
ignores the fact that specific conflicts that cause terrorism often go beyond material factors to involve opposing visions of what is good and
just. In these cases, the only solution would be either to develop some
from of convergence or compromise between the conflicting visions or
to see one defeat the other. This means that purely moralistic, legalistic,
or even sociological approaches to defining terrorism or to designing
measures to deal with it are inadequate.

TERRORISM AS A POLITICAL PHENOMENON

With few exceptions (such as acts commited for nihilistic purposes),
terrorism is a political phenomenon aimed at achieving politically deter-

mined goals. This does not mean that, in the eyes of those who are pursuing these goals, they lack moral or religious dimensions, rather that, in their essence, the goals are political. They are aimed, first and foremost, at changing power relationships between groups and countries at the national, regional, and international levels, and, second, at affecting the distribution of goods, whether of a material or spiritual nature—such as wealth, political independence, prestige, or the supremacy of a particular ideology. By contrast, most of those who complain about terrorist acts want to maintain the existing power equation that favors them and to limit the spread of ideas that could undermine the existing balance of power. In other words, terrorism, especially Third World terrorism, is another aspect of the struggle between the forces of change and the forces of the status quo and between competing visions of what constitutes a just and good order.

As a political phenomenon, terrorism or secret war is also a manifestation of changes in the international political system and in the nature of warfare. For example, the development of weapons of mass destruction, the strategic stalemate between the two superpowers, the ideological and power competition between East and West, the emergence of international institutions, and the development of norms and regulations have together made the open and frequent use of force to achieve national goals or to settle disputes more difficult, although by no means impossible. These circumstances encourage more indirect uses of force. Thus, if the United States and the Soviet Union could not risk a war with one another, each would use proxies or try to undermine the other's position by destabilizing the regional and international environments within which the rival has to operate. Alternatively, if big powers are inhibited in using direct military force against weaker states, they try to preserve and advance their interests by the use of coups d'état or other pressure tactics known as covert operations. The fragile and unsettled character of most societies: their social and economic problems, their political, ethnic, and religious divisions; and their lack of solid institutions for making decisions and resolving political disputes make such operations tempting.

Another feature of the international system during the last several decades has been the effort by the great powers to enhance their influence among Third World nations by spreading their value systems and their concepts of a desirable world order. This practice has been called "competition for the hearts and minds" of Third World peoples. Together, all these techniques are what George Liska called the "new statecraft."

What has been new in the last 20 years is that, increasingly, Third World nations have also become players in the game of indirect warfare and practitioners of the new statecraft. Often they have justified their actions in terms of broad ideologies, such as Arab nationalism, anticolonialism and national liberation, revolutionary Islam, or socialism. Ultimately, they view the current international political system as heavily weighted against them; thus, at heart their purpose has been political: to try changing the power equation at the national, regional, and international levels.

TERRORISM AS AN INSTRUMENT OF POLICY

The use of terrorism by three Middle Eastern states—Iran, Syria, and Libya—illustrates its political nature. There are many similarities in the Iranian, Syrian, and Libyan uses of terrorism as an instrument of policy. Their practice, however, differs in significant ways.

First, transcendental ideals have played a greater role, at least in the initial stages of involvement, in Iranian and Libyan activities as opposed to Syrian. In Iran's case, this has meant the spread of revolutionary Islam, efforts to unify the Muslims and other so-called oppressed of the world, and efforts to eliminate the influence of the great powers from the Muslim world. In the Iranian view, achievement of these goals would lead to the creation of a more just world order. Such goals as eliminating corrupt regimes in the Muslim world, restoring Muslim rights in Palestine, and creating an Islamic government in Lebanon are preliminary steps to achieving the ultimate goals of Muslim unity and a just world order.

In Libya's case, ultimate goals have been the achievement of Arab unity—which is a prerequisite for the liberation of Palestine—the unification of Muslims (especially in Africa), the spread of Arab-Muslim influence, and promotion of the principles of Colonel Mu'ammar Qadhafi's Green Book. Qadhafi, too, believes that the spread of his revolutionary ideals would benefit all the Third World, if not all mankind. As with Iran, dispensing with those individuals and governments considered hindrances to reaching these objectives has been a secondary, albeit essential, step. In the broad ideological schemes of Iranian and Libyan thinking, the West—especially the United States—is viewed as the principal hindrance to the achievement of lofty goals because of its role in supporting those regimes and individuals who are viewed as enemies of Arabs and Muslims.

Yet, deep ideological divisions and rivalries exist between the Iranian and Libyan worldviews and objectives. Indeed, Ayatollah Ruhollah Khomeini's brand of revolutionary Islam is quite different from Mu'ammar Qadhafi's Islamic socialism, and many of their regional political goals also differ. These factors limit the potential for their cooperation and, in some cases, they compete. For example, Iran and Libya have supported different factions in Lebanon.

Furthermore, power within the Iranian leadership is more diffuse than is true in Libya, despite Khomeini's special role. Unlike Libya, the

Iranian leadership holds deep differences of opinion regarding a wide range of issues. These include Iran's goals and the means to achieve them, especially the role of terrorism and subversion as an instrument of state policy. During the last several years, this diffusion of power has resulted in parallel and often contradictory actions undertaken by different factions within the leadership or elements outside the governmental organizations.

This issue also points to an important difference between Iran and Syria. Power in the Syrian government is both highly centralized and personalized. President Hafiz al-Asad and a handful of his close associates make and implement policy, including whether to engage in terrorism. Unlike Iran and Libya, in Syria transcendental ideals have played little role in deciding its involvement in terrorist and subversive activities. Instead, its activities have largely been determined on the basis of their contribution to achieving Syria's power ambitions. Thus, its activities have been focused on the Arab-Israeli conflict, on efforts by others to resolve it, and on the impact of a resolution on Syria's regional position.

IRAN

Since the 1979 Islamic revolution the more exaggerated view of Iran's role in the international terrorist network has portrayed it as a center for training, financing, and indoctrinating potential terrorists. Iran is also viewed as a center for sending terrorists to various Muslim countries to spread the message of the Iranian revolution, to foment similar upheavals, and to eliminate the Western presence in the Middle East, as well as using existing terrorist and dissident networks, particularly Muslim fundamentalists.

No doubt, Iran has been involved in terrorist and subversive acts, although the extent of this involvement and the support that it has enjoyed within the leadership are less clear. Indeed, both Iran and its foes have tended to exaggerate its role: Iran to demonstrate to its own public and to the region the attraction and sweep of its revolution[2] and others to justify a variety of policies from support for Iraq and arms sales to the Persian Gulf Arab states to the readmission of Egypt into the Arab world. This attitude confirms the political nature of terrorism.

Meanwhile, the definitional problem remains about what constitutes subversion. The West extends the term to cover 1) the exaltation of the virtues of Islamic revolution, 2) calls to Muslims to unify and fight against Islam's enemies, and 3) efforts to attract Muslim youths to Iranian centers of religious learning and to acquaint them with the principles of Islamic revolution. Applied in this sense, subversion would encompass most nations, as either practitioners or victims. Iran would itself be considered a prime target of subversion by regional countries, the Soviet Union, and others, which have criticized its regime and called on Iranians to free themselves from its yoke.[3]

Moreover, the extent and intensity of Iranian involvement in terrorism have been largely determined by its domestic development and foreign-policy goals. For example, the most blatant act of Iranian terrorism—the U.S. hostage crisis—was the direct result of an internal struggle for power. The official government, headed by Mehdi Bazargan, not only was uninvolved but also was itself a prime target of the so-called students who seized the U.S. embassy. They opposed Bazargan and his liberal nationalist colleagues, suspecting them of having pro-U.S. sympathies.[4]

The hostage crisis was the first manifestation of two sets of conflicts within Iran's revolutionary groups—namely, between religious factions and a variety of secular forces, from liberal nationalists to different types of leftist groups, and between two diverging tendencies within the religious group.

Within the religious leadership, the moderate tendency holds a traditional interpretation of Islam and favors a free market economy. In foreign policy, it supports nonalignment but is more suspicious than the radicals of the Soviet Union and the Eastern bloc, thus favors Iran's opening up to the West—including, ultimately, the United States. It supports the spread of Iran's revolution but only through peaceful means and by setting a successful example of Islamic government.[5]

In contrast, a radical tendency has a more revolutionary interpretation of Islam, favors a state-controlled economy, massive land reforms, and an egalitarian socioeconomic system. In foreign policy, they are virulently anti-American, take a much more benign view of the Soviets, favor closer Soviet-Iranian ties, and support a much more active policy of exporting revolution, including the use of subversive and terrorist acts.[6]

Since the consolidation in 1981 of the power of the religious factions, neither of these two tendencies has gained the upper hand, although, periodically, power has shifted relatively in favor of one or the other.[7] However, even at times when the moderates have ascended somewhat, the radicals have continued to sabotage their efforts to moderate Iran's external behavior and to improve its international ties, especially with the West. This strategy has included the kidnapping of Western nationals and other terrorist acts.

For the victims of Iranian terrorism, the fact that these divergences exist within its leadership is meager satisfaction. Nevertheless, they must be kept in mind in devising responses, so they will not have the effect of weakening the more moderate tendency, thus undermining long-term Western interests.

Iran's involvement in terrorism has also been related to its assessment of whether these actions have helped or hindered the pursuit of specific policy goals. Furthermore, its resort to terrorism can be explained in large part in terms of its inability to retaliate against hostile actions taken against it through conventional means.

Thus, Iran's involvement in the truck bombings of the U.S. embassy compound in Beirut on April 18, 1983, the truck bombing of the U.S. Marine and French contingent headquarters in Beirut on October 23, 1983, the truck bombing of the U.S. and French embassies in Kuwait City on December 12, 1983, and the hijacking of TWA flight 847 on June 14, 1985, were—in one form or another—related to Iran's foreign-policy goals. These goals were focused on the war with Iraq. In part, Iran undertook these actions in retaliation for support rendered to Iraq by such countries as France and Kuwait. Rather than illustrating Iran's power and influence, however, the terrorist actions reflected its military weakness and its inability to stop external assistance to Iraq through other means.

On the Lebanese front Iran intended its role in the attacks to achieve several goals: 1) to increase its credibility with the Lebanese Shi'as and segments of Palestinian and Arab populations, by demonstrating its seriousness in confronting Israel and its prime supporter, the United States; 2) to increase its influence in Lebanon by forcing the departure of Western forces; 3) to encourage the Lebanese to resist Israeli and U.S. pressures by demonstrating their vulnerability; and 4) to help create conditions in Lebanon that could lead to the establishment of an Islamic republic on the Iranian model.

In this context, too, Iran's role in the Lebanon bombings was related to its broader foreign-policy goals, although for some Iranians, certainly Khomeini, these goals went beyond mere political aspirations and were viewed as a religious duty deriving from the Koranic injunction to "enjoin to good and warn from evil." The Iranian goals also were derived from the impulse common to all states—namely, to try to affect positively their strategic and political environment by surrounding themselves with like-minded countries.[8] In this sense—judged within a purely political context and without making any judgment about the inherent merits of U.S., Iranian, or socialist values—Iran's behavior has not been much different from, say, that of the United States, which has wanted to "make the world safe for democracy," or from the Soviet Union in attempting to spread communism.

SYRIA

Syria's experience also confirms the political nature of terrorism. Three themes have been constant in its terrorist acts, namely, opposition to any solution to the Arab-Israeli conflict without Syria's involvement and without taking into account its interests, prevention of the formation of regional groupings or understandings detrimental to Syria's position, and ensuring that countries both within and without the region consider Syria seriously in any arrangements regarding major issues. Over the years, the pattern of Syrian involvement has varied from the direct use of its own intelligence services to reliance on non-Syrian terrorist groups with bases and training facilities in Syria and Syrian-occupied areas of Lebanon—such as the notorious Abu-Nidal group, an extremist Palestinian splinter faction.[9]

Targets of Syrian-sponsored terrorism have been mostly moderate Arabs and anti-Syrian or independent Palestinian figures, especially if they have been suspected of willingness to engage in any kind of dialogue with Israel. As a rule, therefore, in the past the surge in Syrian terrorism has been related to regional and international efforts to advance the Arab-Israeli peace process. Thus, when King Hussein—with Egypt's backing—launched his initiative in February 1985 to develop a joint Jordanian-Palestinian negotiating position with Israel, Jordan became a target of Syrian-supported terrorism. One should also regard in this context the sea-jacking of the Italian cruise ship, *Achille Lauro*, from Port Said in Egypt on October 7, 1985, by a breakaway Palestinian group.[10]

Syria was directly implicated in the abortive attempt by Nizar Hindawi, a Jordanian national, to blow up an El Al flight from London to Tel Aviv on April 17, 1986, and in the earlier March 29 bombing in West Berlin of the German-Arab Friendship Union.[11] One Syrian purpose for undertaking these terrorist attacks was to make it difficult for Western governments to deal with the Palestine Liberation Organization (PLO) by exacerbating their public's anti-PLO feelings. Another objective was to intimidate Yasir Arafat and his supporters into backing away from cooperation with Arab moderates. Syria achieved both objectives.[12] Earlier, in 1983, Syrian-supported terrorism in Lebanon—including the assassination of the Lebanese Falangist leader, Bashir Gemayel—helped scuttle Western-Israeli plans to establish a new political order in Lebanon.

LIBYA

Of the three countries under discussion, Libya's involvement in terrorism and subversion is the most diversified and widespread geographically. Libya has the most extensive links with subversive and terrorist organizations in Europe and Latin America, including links to the Provisional Irish Republican Army (IRA).[13] Libya has justified its support for the IRA on the basis of its commitment to national liberation movements. In reality, however, Qadhafi's support for the IRA has generally depended on the state of Libya's relationship with Britain. Support for Italian-based and other European terrorists has derived from a general anti-Western sentiment and opposition to Western Europe's alliance with the United States.[14]

In Latin America, Libya's longest association has been with Cuba. It has also provided arms to the Sandinista regime in Nicaragua and the Salvadoran guerrillas. Again, anti-Americanism has been the principal reason for Libyan assistance for Latin American extremists.[15] Qadhafi feels justified in doing so because he perceives a U.S. fight against the Arab nation and the Palestinians through its support for Israel and its intervention in such places as Lebanon. In Qadhafi's words:

> When we ally ourselves with the revolution in Latin America and particularly Central America, we are defending ourselves. This Satan (the United States) must be clipped and we must take war to the American borders just as America is taking threats to the Gulf of Sidra and to the Tibesti Mountains.[16]

Qadhafi also sees these revolutionary organizations as national liberation movements—in the mold of the Palestinians'. Similar motives also lie behind Qadhafi's support for such disparate groups as the Muslim separatists in the Philippines and the autonomists in French New Caledonia.

Libya's involvement in terrorism and subversion derives from a mixture of universalist idealism and cynical power ambitions. As in the case of other countries with such aspirations, idealism often tends to rationalize rather than to motivate Libyan actions, including subversion and terrorism. Whenever necessary, Libya has shown an ability for tactical flexibility. Nothing illustrates this better than its alternation of subversion against its neighbors, including Morocco and Tunisia, with its effort to merge with one or both of them as a first step toward Arab unity. Nevertheless, Qadhafi's ideological beliefs have been important in that they have formed the prism through which he sees the world and Libya's role in it.

TERRORISM: A BALANCE SHEET

The answer to one question, more than anything else, may determine the fate of international terrorism and certain types of subversion: Has terrorism benefited states that have, in one form or another, engaged in it to advance their foreign-policy goals and international standing? The answer to this question is "No." With a few limited exceptions, the three states considered here have suffered more than they have gained as a result of their terrorist activities.

In Iran's case, the U.S. hostage crisis did serve the interests of radical factions within the Iranian leadership, and it achieved its twin goals of preventing any improvement in U.S.-Iranian relations and of eliminating U.S. influence from Iran. Nevertheless, the hostage crisis could not guarantee for them the decisive control of the government. U.S. prestige did suffer during the crisis, and U.S. pride was hurt. All the U.S. hostages came home safely, however, and, overall, U.S. power and influence remained intact, both within the region and elsewhere.

Meanwhile, during the course of the war with Iraq, Iran reaped the bitter harvest of its terrorist acts. Indeed, it is doubtful that, without the U.S. hostage crisis and Iran's international isolation, Iraq would have dared to invade Iran—thereby receiving assistance from both regional and great powers. This war has cost Iran more than $400 billion in economic damage and even more in terms of human loss and psychological scars. Iran also suffered what was, in effect, retribution for its earlier actions when, during the skirmishes of 1988 in the Persian Gulf, the United States destroyed valuable Iranian oil fields and a third of the Iranian navy and accidentally shot down an Iran Air passenger plane, with the loss of 300 civilians. Western economic and trade embargoes also contributed to Iran's economic difficulties.

Iran's subversion in the Persian Gulf has also failed to dislodge the existing Arab regimes or intimidate them into following its dictates. On the contrary, Iran's challenge brought the Persian Gulf Arabs closer together, stiffened their resistance, and made them more determined to help Iraq. Countries, such as Saudi Arabia, retaliated against Iran by using their oil power and by waging virtual economic warfare. The Iranian threat also strengthened military cooperation between the Persian Gulf Arabs and the United States and, ironically, led to a greater U.S. presence in the Persian Gulf.

Iran's resort to terrorism also deeply disillusioned most Muslim populations, undermined its prestige, and eroded early enthusiasm for its revolution. As a result, Iranian terrorism and subversion hurt rather than helped the exportability of the Islamic revolution.

In Lebanon, terrorism—in which Iran partook—may have helped cause the departure of U.S. Marines and the rest of the Multinational Force (MNF), while also scuttling U.S.-Israeli plans for Lebanon's future. In fact the impact of these incidents was secondary. Without them, the MNF might have stayed in Lebanon somewhat longer, but it is unlikely that it would have been able to pacify Lebanon, dispose of the Syrians, and create a stable Christian-dominated government willing to make peace with Israel.[17] To assume otherwise would be to show a serious lack of understanding of the basic psychological and demographic changes—including growing Shi'a self-awareness—which Lebanon has undergone during the last two decades.

Libya has had a similar experience. Qadhafi has little standing in the Arab world and in Africa, his mixed ideology of Islam and socialism has little appeal, and Libya is internationally isolated. Meanwhile, Africa has not succumbed either to Libya's ideological appeal or to its more direct subversion. Economically, during the last few years terrorism—combined with falling oil prices—has been costly to Libya. It has also suffered military humiliation in Chad, during the 1981 Gulf of Sidra crisis, from the April 1986 U.S. bombing, and from the November 1988 downing of two jets.

Syria has fared somewhat better, avoiding the disastrous consequences endured by Iran and Libya. Syria's successes, however, have been more negative than positive. It has managed to foreclose some options and prevent some outcomes, but it has not been able to bring about desired changes. Thus, on the Palestinian front, Syria contributed to Jordan and the PLO's inability to accomplish key goals, but it failed to subdue either of them. Nor was Syria able to prevent either a change in the PLO's attitude on recognizing Israel's right to exist or the establishment of a U.S.-PLO dialogue. Yet, all these developments have radically reduced the importance of Syria in any future Arab-Israeli peace process.

In Lebanon, meanwhile, Syria was able to prevent the consolidation of a Christian-dominated regime, but it failed to impose its solution on the country. In general, it has become more isolated politically. The establishment of the Arab Cooperation Council—among Egypt, Iraq, Jordan, and North Yemen—is further proof of the erosion of Syrian influence in Arab politics. Furthermore, Syria's international prestige has suffered severely.

In short, after nearly 10 years of resorting to terrorism, the power and influence of Iran, Libya, and Syria has dramatically declined, and the position of the regional and extraregional countries which have been victims of their terrorism has improved. Meanwhile, all three countries have become targets of what can be called retaliatory subversion. Jordan, for instance, has helped Syria's dissident Muslim fundamentalists, Egypt has tried to overthrow Qadhafi, and a host of countries has helped the opponents of the Islamic Republic of Iran.

RESPONSES TO TERRORISM

During the last several decades, states that have suffered from terrorist and subversive attacks have been preoccupied with finding means of halting them. Until recently, however, only underdeveloped nations of the Third World were the battleground of competing political forces—including those aligned with either the Eastern or the Western bloc—through proxies, coups, countercoups, guerrilla warfare, assassination, and manipulation of ethnic and other divisions.

As far as the great powers have been concerned, this type of subversive activity, with few exceptions (such as Vietnam and Afghanistan) has not involved massive commitment of financial and human resources over a long period of time. However, during the last 15 years, some terrorist acts, such as airplane hijackings, kidnappings, hostage takings, bombings, and assassinations, carried out against nationals of Western countries and in their national territory have made terrorism and the response to it a domestic political issue.

This domestication of terrorism has given a sense of urgency to finding responses. In democratic societies, the terrorism issue has become important in elections. For example, the issue of U.S. hostages in Iran and the Carter administration's handling of it became campaign issues and were manipulated by the Republican party. Statements made at the time by the Republican candidate, governor Ronald Reagan, about "swift retribution" against terrorists and not "negotiating" with them would later haunt him as president. They would lead to such totally different types of responses as the U.S. bombing of Libya in April 1986 and the U.S. arms-for-hostages deal with Iran. Likewise, the French socialists lost the parliamentary elections in 1985, partly because they could not gain the release of French nationals held hostage in Lebanon.

The most vexing aspect of dealing with terrorist acts has been their impact in temporarily rendering even overwhelming power inadequate for achieving desired goals. Thus, the issue has not been merely whether military power should be used against the terrorists in order to demonstrate opposition but also whether it would yield the desired results. Even after the U.S. raid on Libya in 1986 and the U.S. bombing of Iran's oil and naval installations in 1988, U.S. nationals are still being held hostage in Lebanon, and several Western hostages were executed in retaliation for the U.S. raid on Libya.[18] This explains terrorism's attraction because, if only momentarily, it can sometimes overcome sizable disparities in power among states.

Other difficulties involved in responding to terrorism relate to identifying the perpetrators and determining responsibility. For example, should retaliation be against the individuals or groups that commit the actual act, or should it be against their sponsors? It is also difficult to define sponsorship. Does the provision of money, weapons, or safe haven constitute sponsorship? Or does sponsorship require more direct involvement in planning and executing a terrorist act? Under the first definition, such countries as Saudi Arabia or Kuwait that finance the PLO would have to be considered sponsors of international terrorism. A further difficulty is the issue of the proportionality of response to threat so that other, more important, interests are not endangered in the process of trying to deal with terrorism.

These difficulties mean that there cannot be any standard formula for responding to terrorism. Instead, states must determine the response by a careful calculation of costs and benefits, based on domestic political considerations, the impact on other objectives, and the regional and international configuration of power.

During the U.S. hostage crisis, for example, the United States refrained from using force against Iran partly because of concern over possible Soviet military intervention. Yet, because of changes since 1985 in U.S.-Soviet relations and in Soviet attitudes regarding regional conflicts, the United States was able to use force against Iran in 1988 without fear of Soviet retaliation. That fear has also been largely responsible for U.S. unwillingness to use military force against Syria. The same factor was also partly responsible for U.S. hesitancy in striking Libyan territory until 1986, when circumstances indicated that the USSR was unlikely to endanger its broader agenda with the United States in order to protect Libya. Indeed, many have argued that the United States chose Libya as a target for a showdown on terrorism, not some other country, because of Libya's relative insignificance in the region, thus the low costs to U.S. interests.

The same arguments apply to the use of economic and other sanctions. Nations have long used these means, based on the same calculations of costs and benefits. In recent years the United States has often accused European countries of sacrificing the fight against terrorism for commercial gain. However, some Europeans have felt that the damage done to their national well-being as a result of economic sanctions would be greater than that done by sporadic terrorism. Thus, the response to terrorism is a political decision taken on the basis of what the impact will be on the protection of a state's short- and long-term interests.

Legal instruments—national, bilateral, or multilateral—also have a role to play in the response to terrorism and could form an important part of the panoply of means required. Yet, because terrorism is a political phenomenon, legal remedies at the international level are likely to be ineffective in the absence of a broad political consensus. Indeed, there exist international conventions banning some types of terrorism, such as the hijacking of airplanes, and attacking so-called protected persons, such as diplomats. Nevertheless, with the current state of the international system and the existence of sharply clashing views regarding how representative and just this system is, there are no means of enforcing these conventions. Regarding subversion, the United Nations Charter already banned the "interference in the internal affairs" of other countries, but this legal ban inhibits few countries.

In a more general sense, the often selective approach to the application of international norms and regulations has weakened the role of law in settling international disputes and strengthening the world legal order. Until that situation changes, international action on terrorism must also be political. Those countries that feel their well-being and interests to be endangered by terrorism must cooperate on security, intelligence, and other preventive measures. In general, the cost of engaging in terrorism should be made as high as possible for its perpetrators. In the long term, if the scourge of terrorism is to be reduced—if not eliminated—the social, economic, and political roots beneath politically motivated terrorism should also be addressed. The international system must also become more responsive to the needs and grievances of the less powerful. International norms and regulations must apply irrespective of whom they favor.

NOTES

Acknowledgment: The opinions expressed in this essay are the author's own and do not represent those of her institution. This article is based on a larger study written by the author for the United States Peace Institute.

1. See The Report of the United Nations Ad Hoc Committee on International Terrorism, supplement no. 28 (A/9028). Also, The International Convention Against the Taking of Hostages, December 17, 1979.

2. Of course, Iranian leaders have denied involvement in terrorist actions, such as the hijacking of airplanes or assassination attempts. They have not denied, however, what they consider to be Iran's support for Islamic revolutionary forces and for other liberation movements of the so-called oppressed peoples.

3. By the same token, Iranian embassies are often accused of subversion because they distribute pamphlets and are involved with Islamic communities. If so, then similar activities by other governments should also be considered subversive. In fact, much of Iran's propaganda activities are representative of efforts by Third World nations in the global competition for people's hearts and minds.

4. Even after the fall of Bazargan, not all individuals and groups that in one form or another held power in Iran or that were involved in competition for power condoned this act, although all of them manipulated the crisis for their own purposes. Indeed, some of them, such as Abol-Hassan Bani-Sadr and Sadiq Qobtzadeh, lost power—and Qobtzadeh his life—as the result of power struggles intimately linked to the hostage crisis. See Richard W. Cottam, *Iran and the United States: A Cold War Case Study* (Pittsburgh, Penn. University of Pittsburgh Press, 1988).

5. Because of these characteristics, the proponents of this trend have been accused of adhering to what the radicals call "American Islam." See the interview of Hodjat al-Islam Koeiniha in Foreign Broadcast Information Service (FBIS), Middle East and South Asia Report, January 28, 1988, p. 54.

6. Members of this group have been accused by the moderates of being, in the words of Iran's foreign minister Ali-Akbar Velayati, "leftists with an Islamic veneer." See Velayati's speech, *The Washington Post*, November 27, 1986, p. A25.

7. For a more detailed study of these divisions, see Shireen T. Hunter, "After the Ayatollah," *Foreign Policy*, no. 66, Spring 1987, pp. 77–97.

8. For an elaboration of these themes, see Hunter, "Iran and the Spread of Revolutionary Islam," *Third World Quarterly* 10:2, (April 1988), pp. 730–749.

9. See "Syrian Support for International Terrorism: 1983–86," *Department of State Bulletin*, vol. 87, February 1987, pp. 73–76.

10. There was no evidence that Syria was involved in the incident. Nevertheless, the fact that the group had its headquarters in Damascus does make Syria an accomplice. Indeed, one of the problems of assessing a given state's degree of support for terrorism is whether to take into account only its involvement.

11. "Syrian Support for International Terrorism"; and Nicholas Wood, "Syrians Given 14 Days to Go," *Times* (London), October 25, 1986, p. 1.

12. Of course, divisions also prevailed within Arafat's own Fatah movement and the PLO's desire to maintain a semblance of unity even if this meant paralysis on the political front.

13. Indeed, in 1985 Qadhafi stated the reason for his support for the IRA in the following terms: "We were obliged to support the cause because we think it is a just cause." See Richard Ford, "Libya Backs IRA with Weapons and Cash Aid," *Times* (London), October 27, 1986.

14. See Vitto Franco S. Pisano, "Libya's Foothold in Italy," *The Washington Quarterly* 5:2 (Spring 1982), pp. 179–182.

15. Indeed, Qadhafi said, "We must force America to fight on 100 fronts all over the earth . . . in Lebanon, in Chad, in Sudan, in El Salvador, in Africa." Quoted in the report of the Senate Subcommittee on Security and Terrorism, p. 22.

16. Ibid.

17. Anti-French terrorism also failed in its objectives, namely to prevent France from supplying sophisticated weapons, including Exocet missiles and Super-Etendard aircraft, to Iraq.

18. Three Britons were executed by pro-Libyan Lebanese factions.

PART THREE
The Crisis of Institutions

In Part Three we deal with a variety of institutions: international and domestic, political and economic. We also examine the roles of individuals in these organizations, as bureaucrats and as leaders.

Many analysts concerned about bringing order to world politics have been intrigued by the possibility of world government—a global union in which a United States of the World would provide supervision over and restraint to the management of relations among nations. Through an international parliament with binding powers on its members, conflict would presumably be restricted. Others have viewed this solution as either unachievable, undesirable, or downright utopian; instead, they advocate the concept of collective security as embodied in the charters of both the League of Nations and the United Nations. Although the organizational differences between these two institutions are great, both were founded on the belief that international politics could be partially ordered by an agreement among states to defer and control their conflicts. The League of Nations ended in dismal failure, and today many are disillusioned with the United Nations, which they see as a tool of national interests (its organs constituting a weapon in the hands of those who can obtain a majority in a given dispute) and a dangerous impediment to conflict reduction.

Not everyone agrees with this assessment. In "Exploiting the Recent Revival of the United Nations," Frederick Lister explains that with the abatement of the cold war, the great powers are finding the United Nations to be a useful instrument in their pursuit of conflict-limitation policies. Lister also examines the role played by the Third World bloc, which constitutes a majority in the General Assembly and has had enormous influence in recent years. He scrutinizes the United Nations' record in promoting peace and security, as well as in less controversial welfare activities. Finally, he considers how the United Nations might become a more effective institution over the next several years.

One instrument that promotes the worldwide role of international institutions is international law. Louis Henkin, in "Influence, Marginality, and Centrality in the International Legal System," examines the position of international law in world politics. This article reviews the history and evolution of international law and its impact on both the superpowers and Third World nations. Henkin argues that, although nations initially challenged the established order, they have come to accept the efficacy of the existing but limited international legal system. Nevertheless, states are still sovereign and individually determine which laws they will recognize. Henkin applies this rubric to several cases, including the law of the sea, the new international economic order, the use of force, and human rights. Drawing a conclusion similar to the one Lister came to in the case of the United Nations, Henkin believes there is great room for improvement in the sphere of international law. Under current conditions, law remains an "instrument of politics," its acceptance dependent on the political will of individual states.

From the international arena, we move next to national institutions. In this edition I have chosen to focus on the United States and the Soviet Union because they are currently reexamining their institutions in the wake of the end of the cold war. The selections reflect this transition. First, Richard J. Barnet's "Reflections: After the Cold War" is a comprehensive summation of the details of Soviet-American relations in the post–cold war world. He discusses a variety of issues affecting America's changing position as a superpower, including a united Europe, a unified Germany, Latin America, Asia, technology, the arms race, Soviet history, and the potential of a U.S. trade war with Japan. Barnet is convinced that the Soviet Union has altered its direction, and he questions whether the United States will also do so. I have placed this article in this section because Barnet bases his argument on the idea that the roots of change lie in the organizations of both societies. Although he criticizes American institutions and the mind-set of decision makers of both superpowers, he particularly targets those of the United States, who appear unable to adjust to a changing world. Barnet argues that the "national-security thinkers" and their institutions are at the substantive heart of the problem of producing a new American policy.

Institutions, of course, exist within the society that creates them. As Michael Vlahos points out in "The End of America's Postwar Ethos," "the culture of a society—its ethos—defines distinctive patterns of individual and group behavior." Thus, it seems particularly appropriate that our institutions section should include an article showing how institutions function within a series of constraints that originate in both society and the broader international system. Vlahos identifies two American groups: "progressives," who see America as a model that demands involvement, and "purifiers," who maintain that the United States exists as a model for a corrupted world. The purifiers believe that Americans must remain detached if they are to avoid being ruined by engagement with the outside world. Both purifiers and progressives believe that the United States should fight only if a war is just and the cause is righteous. Vlahos demonstrates how the national consensus deteriorated over Vietnam, a war that deeply divided Americans. Finally, in the Reagan era, tension grew between the president and those who began to see that Americans needed to adjust to an era of limits. The basic attitudes toward military institutions and activities have continued, but they have become more subtle. According to Vlahos, although Americans are concerned about defending themselves, they also believe the American model can be applied elsewhere, as long as U.S. military activity in the world remains limited.

Vlahos also demonstrates the impact of the successes and failures of individuals and foreign policy elites in terms of their abilities to remain compatible with prevailing American myths. In order to understand foreign policy decisions, the role of individuals in American institutions and in society as a whole is essential. A determined individual or group at the pinnacle of a governmental hierarchy can greatly affect that government's policies as well as the international order. Mikhail Gorbachev's impact on world politics and on changes that are occurring in Eastern Europe and the Soviet Union marks him as this type of influential leader. However, it remains unclear whether Gorbachev's impact is due to personal initiative or to his acceptance of the inevitability of altered conditions. Moreover, continuing fears exist that he will not survive politically but will be buried in the turmoil he is confronting.

The last two articles in this section, though sharing an understanding of the tension between domestic and foreign policies, present different views of Gorbachev. George W. Breslauer analyzes Gorbachev's overall agenda in "Linking Gorbachev's Domestic and Foreign Policy Agendas." He emphasizes developments within the Soviet Union and the influence these events will have on the Soviet economy and polity. Although the United States may be unable to aid Gorbachev materially with his internal challenges, America should respond to his conciliatory gestures, Breslauer argues.

The anonymous "Z" provides a very different perspective in "To the Stalin Mausoleum." "Z" believes that "the Soviet socialist 'experiment' has been the great utopian adventure of our century." However, Gorbachev's monumental attempts to restructure the economy and refashion socialism are being frustrated by the Soviet nationalities problem. "Z" describes Gorbachev's efforts at perestroika, glasnost, and democratization and, like Breslauer, asks whether Gorbachev will succeed and whether the United States should support him. His answers differ markedly from Breslauer's, however. While "Z" sees the possibility of Western aid in reducing the Soviet arms burden and in developing a private sector, he generally derides the idea of successful reform in the Soviet Union and doubts that Gorbachev will be able to fulfill his promises to the Soviet people. "Z" views the crisis in the USSR in starker terms than most analysts. He argues that a breakthrough to democracy and to a stabilized international situation, especially in Europe, will be a longer, more painful process than most analysts have suggested. Readers must judge for themselves the accuracy of these predictions in the light of ongoing developments.

THE CRISIS OF
INTERNATIONAL INSTITUTIONS

27

Exploiting the Recent Revival of the United Nations

FREDERICK LISTER

Over the past year, the United Nations, long written off by many as useless or worse, has re-emerged in the international limelight. Its patient mediation has culminated in the Iran–Iraq ceasefire and at least a temporary ending of the bloodiest confrontation since World War II. Even if the ceasefire is not followed by a full-scale peace settlement, it seems unlikely that the exhausted contenders will return to the battlefield in the near future. The United Nations has also demonstrated its value in other trouble spots, for example in Afghanistan, in the long-smouldering Western Sahara, in Namibia, and the list may soon be lengthened to include Cambodia. Why has this long-moribund body suddenly shown such vitality? Might not a clearer understanding of its potential (and of the limitations of that potential) enable national leaders to use it increasingly to defang other serious international problems?

The world should have learned since 1945 that certain approaches often work well for the United Nations, while others are almost always counterproductive. Obviously, it would make sense for the Organization to focus on the former and to steer clear of the latter.

On the positive side, the United Nations has long played a useful part in the realm where its potential has been disparaged for so long—that of international peace and security. Its services in three confrontations be-

From *International Relations*, vol. IX, no. 5, May 1989, David Davies Memorial Institute of International Studies.

Note: It is a violation of the law to reproduce this selection by any means whatsoever without the written permission of the copyright holder.

tween the superpowers may be cited in this connexion. For example, as soon as the 1962 Cuban missile crisis erupted, Secretary-General U Thant addressed identical letters to President Kennedy and Chairman Khrushchev asking the former to suspend the quarantine measures against Cuba and the latter to suspend all arms shipments to Cuba. It so happened that the request provided a convenient pretext for Khrushchev to stop his arms-laden ships headed for Cuba, and this step proved a key factor in providing the time needed for the crisis to be peacefully resolved. In the crucial negotiations that followed in which the United Nations was not involved, it was agreed, *inter alia*, that the world organization would monitor the withdrawal of the Soviet missiles already in Cuba. Although Prime Minister Castro later vetoed this arrangement, it had already contributed to defusing the crisis. Thus, in these two ways, the United Nations had a tangential yet significant role in staving off armed conflict between the superpowers.[1]

Eleven years later, at the end of the Yom Kippur war between Egypt and Israel, the superpowers again found themselves in the midst of an unwanted confrontation. The Israelis had overwhelmed the Egyptian forces that had attacked them and were threatening to annihilate those forces. The Soviets declared that they had to come to the aid of their Egyptian client, if necessary by flying in their own forces. The Americans took the position that they could not allow this, even though they were invited by the Soviets to join them. That this second, less celebrated crisis was nearly as serious as the first is shown by the massive Soviet troop movements actually underway and the declaration by the United States of the highest state of emergency in peacetime. The United Nations was able to resolve this stand-off by the simple expedient of quickly interposing units from its international peace-keeping force already in Cyprus, thus saving face all around.[2]

More recently, the United Nations has played a central part in resolving the less tense but prolonged superpower confrontation over Afghanistan. After years of efforts by a UN negotiator, the moment came when the parties were ready for serious negotiations, and the talks soon produced signed agreements.[3]

The United Nations used a variety of approaches in these three cases: written pleas to the principals and simple availability (Cuban missile crisis); patient mediation (Afghanistan); and the interposition of a peace-keeping force (Egypt/Israel). It should be noted that in none of these situations did the Security Council act alone. The Secretariat's quiet negotiations proceeding along lines tacitly or openly set by the Council were equally essential to the favourable impact.

The United Nations and its specialized agencies have also shown that they can be useful in many less dramatic situations. They have become centres for consensus-building and for concerting the actions of their members on the basis of broad agreements. For example, many multilateral treaties have been concluded under their auspices in such domains as outer space, the law of the sea, narcotic drug control and terrorism. All of these treaties are based on a large measure of world-wide consensus and require those party to them, usually most of their member states, to act in certain pre-agreed ways. The most recent example of this process at work is the Protocol—ratified unanimously by the US Senate—providing for world-wide co-operation to counter the alarming depletion of the ozone layer that protects us against the sun's ultraviolet rays.[4] This success may pave the way for further pacts dealing with other environmental problems such as the "greenhouse effect" and acid rain. Indeed, the stakes for humanity in finding ways to deal effectively with key environmental problems may be about as high as they are in the realm of world peace.

Finally, the United Nations and its specialized agencies have also demonstrated that they can often provide useful services that go beyond workaday reporting and data-gathering. These include neutral peace-keeping and truce supervision forces and practical assistance to vulnerable groups such as children and refugees and to poverty-ridden countries. By far the largest part of the money spent on UN services goes for activities of this kind that command almost universal support.

Thus, the United Nations is at its best when it serves as the agent of a united world community in pursuing agreed and clearly-defined objectives and functions, for example when it is involved in preventing the outbreak of wars, when it is promoting consensus-building among its member states, and when it is performing services that are needed and non-partisan in character.

The other side of the picture is obviously a darker one. The United Nations tends to fare less well when it takes on controversial functions and proceeds on the basis of majority rule rather than consensus. There are a number of fairly obvious reasons why this should be so: (1) The Organization is an association of *sovereign* states and yielding meekly to the majority viewpoint is not commonly associated with sovereign status; (2) Most UN decisions are recommendations which are not legally binding on governments which are thus free to ignore them or set them aside;[5] (3) Even when decisions are binding, the Organization has generally found it impossible to impose them upon the states towards which they are directed.

Inevitably, the United Nations has found itself in the middle of tense confrontations between its member states that could not be resolved by negotiation. When the majority, in frustration, sought to break through the impasse by voting in UN organs, a parliamentary-type victory all too often had little impact outside the meeting-room. In most cases, voting settled nothing and sometimes even made matters worse. For, in the context of the United Nations, the majority can seldom successfully impose itself on a determined minority, and its inability to do so involves the United Nations as an institution in the stigma of a highly-visible failure. Because of the publicity attending such failures and their frequency, governments and the public generally have tended, unfairly but understandably, to downgrade the potential value of the United Nations to the world community. Yet these failures have come about not from any defect in the machinery but from a persistent refusal to acknowledge the limitations on what can be expected of any world organization in a society of sovereign states.

Let me analyze briefly how this refusal has affected the United Nations' political evolution. In its earlier years, the United States and its supporters could muster a comfortable two-thirds majority—the Soviet Union called it a "mechanical majority" and U Thant referred to it in his *View from the UN* as a "one-party system."[6] This also coincided with the tensest period of the Cold War. Predictably, the Western allies sought to use their voting advantage in the Organization as a weapon in that confrontation. While the USSR could thwart action by the Security Council by using its veto power, the mechanical majority could use its voting-power in the General Assembly and other bodies to make the world organization take sides—its side!—in the Cold War. It could and did secure the adoption of resolutions calling for almost any action it wished. The limitations of this approach, however, soon became apparent. The Soviet Union could not be coerced or intimidated by such resolutions. The Western allies discovered that the United Nations could bring them little in the way of practical advantage in their confrontation with the USSR that they did not already have through the NATO alliance.

The very limited practical utility of majority rule in the context of the United Nations became apparent when the North Koreans suddenly invaded South Korea at a time when the Soviet Union had temporarily withdrawn from its seat in the Security Council. For the first and only time, the road was open for the United Nations to test its ability to bring into play the collective security provisions of the Charter. Instead, however, the Council took the short-cut of recommending that members make available military forces and other assistance to a "unified command" under the United States. While they derived a certain moral and propaganda advantage from having UN support, the United States and its NATO allies still had to bear virtually the entire military burden of the war that followed, which was deeply resented by American public opinion. The Organization's value to the majority thus proved, even in circumstances unlikely ever to be repeated, much less than had been supposed. And the United Nations itself was somehow diminished by having its forces placed under the control of one of its leading members.[7]

From beginning to end, the attempt of the United States and its supporters to use the United Nations as an instrument against the Soviet

Union proved ill conceived. It gained them little aside from a rather dubious moral legitimacy. It alienated the Soviets from the Organization; they are only now beginning to regain (as the Americans have been losing!) confidence in an organization that so consistently aligned itself against them. It tended, if anything, to widen rather than to narrow the gap between the superpowers. And, finally, by demonstrating over and over that the United Nations could not get members to heed its edicts, it concealed the potential that the Organization might have if and when it was properly used.

In more recent times, the ability to command mechanical majorities has been transferred to the Third World countries, which now comprise 120 of the 159 member states. The period of their voting strength has also coincided with a less dramatic but still very real confrontation between these countries and much of the Western world. And, like the Western group before them, they have often been unable to resist the temptation of turning from seemingly hopeless and endless negotiations to the short-cut of voting. And they have discovered, in their turn, that the UN's writ often begins and ends at Turtle Bay. They have had little luck in compelling the economic great powers to address the imbalances and inequities that characterize so many aspects of their position in the world economy.[8] Impolite resolutions have merely led those powers to switch the main action to organizations such as the IMF, GATT and the World Bank where they continue to be very influential.

In short, the efforts of Third World members to use the United Nations as an instrument against the West are proving as futile as the latter's effort to use it against the Soviet Union. It has gained them little in concrete terms; it discourages the use of the United Nations as a forum for mediating international economic issues; and it has produced frustration on all sides.

Even when the United Nations majority is overwhelmingly large, and the minority consists of only one target country with perhaps a few reluctant supporters, the effort to apply effective sanctions through the General Assembly has proved uphill work. The impact achieved thus far by the hundreds of resolutions directed against Israel and South Africa confirms the limitations of what may be described without too much hyperbole as the "bulldozer approach." In a few cases—one is obviously South Africa—the United Nations may be obliged for moral reasons to call for sanctions against states engaged in unacceptable behaviour even when it knows that such measures have little chance of success. But it should only do so when absolutely necessary since, by displaying its own impotence, it may harm itself more than the offending country.

Worst of all, it may undermine its own acceptability as a vehicle for carrying out the functions for which it is better qualified. To the extent that the Organization is perceived as a neutral bastion that can be trusted to approach disputes among its member states in a non-partisan spirit, its role as mediator and arbitrator will be strengthened. But when the same majorities regularly outvote the same minorities, the latter may come to suspect that the Organization is more in the service of those majorities than of all member states equally. As a result of this perception, these members may not be ready even to lend their support to the UN's consensus-type activities.

There is, of course, nothing inherently wrong with partisanship and majority rule. They are regarded as natural and normal by most people in the Western world and, increasingly, in other parts of the world as well. They form two of the essential props of parliamentary-type government, and have proved their value in helping to bring about a reasonable degree of democracy at the national level over the past two centuries. Any American who suggests that they should not govern the procedures of international organizations is likely to be accused of sour grapes or worse.

Yet in analysing the working of government, pragmatism and experience must be allowed to have the final say. There is no blinking the fact that, in the United Nations, giving a free rein to partisanship and majority rule has not worked very well. This is because in the global context unbridled partisanship has proved overly divisive, and the majority has found that it can not rule effectively. The evidence all points to the conclusion that in world-wide bodies, partisanship needs to be kept within bounds and majorities restrained.[9] These needs should be met in any effort to re-orient international bodies towards approaches and procedures that they can pursue successfully.

Of course, no political body—least of all a global one in which almost all the peoples of the world with their infinite variety of cultural, social and ideological beliefs are represented—can escape controversy and confrontation. Its debates are sure to become, from time to time, heated and even bitter. This need not be harmful and is often a healthy thing. But a world body's rules and procedures must also protect it lest such conflicts—natural though they may be—jeopardize its basic mission. Its rules and procedures should try to ensure that member states do not come away from such exchanges (except when they have been involved in truly unconscionable acts) with the impression that the United Nations as an organization is aligned against them.

Fortunately, there is already an abundance of evidence that the United Nations is now moving away from the excesses of majority rule and towards the consensus-based approach that seems so much more promising for international associations composed of sovereign member states. The rest of this article will focus on how this change in the UN's *modus operandi* could contribute to its performance in the areas where it has already established its credentials: global peace-keeping and general welfare activities. It also suggests certain ways in which the Organization's services in these areas might be modestly broadened and strengthened.

INTERNATIONAL PEACE AND SECURITY

The need to keep the peace among its member states in an age of nuclear weapons remains in 1989, as it was in 1945, the principal raison d'être of the United Nations. Accordingly, it is inevitable that governments and people generally will judge the Organization's performance in terms of its capacity for dealing with international crises and armed conflicts. Since the United Nations has clearly not come close to solving all crises or preventing all conflicts, it must expect and has in fact received a good deal of criticism. If the Organization is to come into its own, it needs to make a greater, and above all a more visible, impact in its key role as peace-maker.

Let us briefly examine in turn the Organization's Charter mandate, its performance over the years and finally how that performance might be made to come closer to meeting world needs.

The Charter has given the United Nations two distinct, quite different roles in maintaining the peace. The one is based on traditional diplomatic procedures while the other is innovative in the extreme.

The first role is delineated in Chapter VI of the Charter which prescribes that the parties to disputes likely to endanger international peace and security *must* seek a solution "by negotiation, enquiry, mediation, conciliation, arbitration, judicial settlement, resort to regional agencies and arrangements or other peaceful means of their own choice." It provides that the Security Council should be involved in this process in the ways set forth in Articles 34 and 36–38 of the Charter. Under these procedures, the Council might go so far as to try to influence the situation by making recommendations to the parties, i.e. exercise its powers of persuasion.

The second role is elaborated in Chapter VII "Action with Respect to Threats to the Peace, Breaches of the Peace and Acts of Aggression." When the Council acts under this chapter, it is mostly in the guise of judge and imposer of sanctions. As judge, it is called upon to decide when there is a threat to the peace or an act of aggression (Article 39). As imposer of sanctions, including the use of armed force, it decides what measures are to be applied against states that persist in threatening the peace or in committing aggression (Articles 41–48). To ensure that the Council's decisions are carried out, Articles 25 and 49 read as follows:

> The Members of the United Nations agree to accept and carry out the decisions of the Security Council in accordance with the present Charter.

> The Members of the United Nations shall join in affording mutual assistance
> in carrying out the measures decided upon by the Security Council.

The United Nations's current credibility problem arises from the fact that neither approach has come close to meeting the high expectations held for international co-operation in 1945. At that time, internationalists had pinned their hopes to the far-reaching powers confided to the United Nations in Chapter VII. This constituted a second effort (the League of Nations having made the first) to translate the concept of collective security into a working reality.[10]

Unhappily, the Organization's procedures for applying sanctions have not succeeded any better than did those of the League. Modalities for the national stand-by forces that were to have been placed at its disposal—these forces were supposed to become the centrepiece of its authority as peacekeeper—could never be agreed upon. This was only partly because of the damper imposed by the Cold War. More basically, it is attributable to the great political obstacles and risks involved in using such forces in a society of still sovereign states.[11]

In all the years since 1945, the Security Council has invoked the sanctions available to it in Chapter VII only twice (against Southern Rhodesia and South Africa) and then not the military ones. On one other occasion, when South Korea was attacked, the United Nations assumed a collective security stance without, however, turning to the mandatory provisions of Article 42.[12] The results in these three cases have pleased only the sceptics. South Africa remains, as we know, defiant. Southern Rhodesia became Zimbabwe not so much as a result of the UN-led blockade but because the country's Caucasian minority came to recognize that it could not indefinitely dominate twenty times its number of indigenous Blacks.[13] Finally, as was noted earlier, the decision to come to South Korea's defence led to a bloody war run not by the United Nations but by one superpower against the client of the other superpower.

There are many reasons why the provisions of Chapter VII have turned out to be ill-adapted to the maintenance of the peace in the post–World War II era. For one thing, there have been few cases of unequivocal aggression of one member state against another. Instead, the world community has been faced with an intense political and ideological rivalry between the superpowers which has spilled over into and complicated most of the serious regional and world crises since 1945. Moreover, most armed conflicts have not been between member states. Instead, they have involved divided countries such as Korea and Vietnam and civil wars within member states (e.g. China, Cambodia, Pakistan, Nigeria, Angola, El Salvador and Nicaragua). Almost invariably, these have been situations best handled on the negotiation track.

This may have been lucky, for it is quite clear that the concept of collective security rests on rather flimsy foundations, particularly in a world flooded with nuclear arms. For example, if a nuclear power were to turn rogue (à la Hitler), the Security Council would face the dilemma of either doing nothing or of risking unacceptable world-wide destruction. Even in less dramatic circumstances, few governments would probably be ready to risk the lives of their citizens on a massive scale to counter distant aggressions posing no immediate threats to their interests.

In these circumstances, the United Nations has had little choice but to fall back on the traditional approach of diplomacy, mediation and arbitration. As noted earlier, this approach has sometimes produced valuable results. But often it has produced mixed results or no results at all. Unless adversaries are ready to negotiate in a serious way, a condition that is very often lacking, third parties can seldom come up with full-scale solutions. Yet we have been discovering that, even when final settlements are out of reach, much may still be done via the traditional approach. And even when only a little can be done, that little may still be very much worth doing as it was in the case of the Cuban missile crisis. Thus, the Security Council and successive Secretaries-General have been quietly carving out a significant niche for themselves in this grey area of conflict control.

But governments and people generally still need to acquire a clearer understanding of the kind of role that the United Nations can realistically be expected to play at times of international crisis. It is simplistic to suggest that the Organization must somehow find final "solutions" to such crises or be labelled a failure. It must usually deal with each threatening situation as best it can. This commonly involves searching for ways to improve matters, even marginally, for modus vivendi, and very often for devices to forestall any further deterioration in the relations between disputants. Sometimes, the UN's negotiators must deal with governments that refuse to have direct contacts with one another, as Iran and Iraq did, much less to negotiate in any serious fashion. Particularly in such cases, as we are now seeing, an uncommitted third party may serve as a useful intermediary. The success of such efforts generally depends heavily on timing, that is to say on capitalizing on the fleeting moments when the disputants have become eager to reach some resolution of their differences. Quiet diplomacy of this kind is usually best conducted without much public fanfare or media attention. Yet, perversely, this may deprive it of public recognition of its existence, much less its importance.

In recent years, the UN's contribution towards the maintenance of the peace has involved members of the Security Council and successive Secretaries-General in carefully orchestrated activities, particularly in situations where the permanent members are not at loggerheads. Usually, the Council undertakes preliminary consultations on the procedures to be followed in dealing with a situation being brought to its attention. If hostilities have actually broken out, it may call for a ceasefire. It may open up the process of substantive negotiation. But the main burden of negotiation and mediation is more readily borne by individuals than by corporate bodies, and thus it has come to fall more and more often on the Secretary-General or his representatives. The two roles are interlocking and require the latter to operate within a negotiating framework, very often implicit rather than explicit, that is acceptable to the Council's members.

To permit him to act in this capacity, a doctrine has evolved whereby the Secretary-General may exercise "inherent powers" that do not stem from specific provisions of the Charter or from resolutions of the UN's principal organs. These are diplomatic in nature and form the basis for initiatives that successive Secretaries-General have taken to avert or alleviate conflicts and confrontations of international importance. Such initiatives are called "quiet diplomacy" or "preventive diplomacy." Though this doctrine has nowhere been formally approved, its tacit acceptance by most member states has endowed it with strong customary authority since the times of Lie and Hammarskjöld.[14]

The UN's role as monitor and mediator is tested and assumes a special importance for those crises and confrontations that drag on interminably. The Arab-Israeli situation and the three-cornered dispute involving Cyprus, Greece and Turkey come to mind in this connection. When bitterly opposing claims could not be reconciled over long periods of time, the United Nations has devised modus vivendi which include observer groups to reassure suspicious adversaries and peace-keeping forces to help minimize direct contacts likely to lead to further friction and enmity.

Even though their curative effects may be limited, such devices should be seen as the beginning of the development of a capacity to deal with the most recalcitrant international quarrels in a constructive way. In this sense, the United Nations has been developing techniques and instruments for countering the scourge of war in much the same way as the medical profession has been mounting its equally difficult campaign against cancer. Attention should be focused principally on the marginal successes and even more on the methods by which those marginal successes have been achieved.

The moment may have come to take further steps. This section will conclude with a general indication of three main directions in which further progress seems feasible.

1. *Information and Intelligence.* Knowing when and how to intercede effectively in unstable situations depends upon having steady and reliable channels of information. Without good intelligence, mediation efforts may be futile and sometimes even counter-productive. The UN's capacity independently to monitor peace-threatening situations clearly

needs to be strengthened. An important first step in this direction has been the creation at UN Headquarters of a new Office for Research and the Collection of Information. The information circle now needs to be completed to provide the Security Council and the Secretary-General with their own sources of information in member states on behind-the-scene political developments in trouble spots or potential trouble spots.

As it happens, the United Nations already has representatives stationed in most national capitals, carrying out public information and technical assistance functions. The persons serving in these capacities, if properly chosen, could also be called upon to undertake monitoring functions and to develop the necessary contacts to serve this additional need. With such a network, the Secretary-General would be in a better position to work with the Council in conducting "preventive diplomacy" and to reach conclusions on when it would be useful to take the formal step of bringing a threatening situation to its attention as he is authorized to do under Article 99 of the Charter.

2. *Good Offices and Mediation.* In recent years, there has been a growing tendency for disputants to turn to the Secretary-General or one or two other top UN officials for help in dealing with their disputes. This is a positive development that seems to signify that disputants have come to value not only the mediating skills of the incumbents of that office but also to recognize the impartiality of its occupants and of the Secretariat generally. This trend towards developing a "good offices service" within the Secretariat seems a positive one deserving of further thought and development.

At present, the group providing such services consists of the Secretary-General himself and two of his senior assistants. Occasionally other senior assistants with different regular duties may be pressed into such service. Since, in some situations, one or other of these persons may have a nationality that is not acceptable to one or other of the disputants, the UN's pool of skilled mediators should perhaps be modestly increased. It may be added that becoming part of such a pool need not disqualify anyone from being responsible for other functions within the Secretariat. Perhaps the panel available to the Secretary-General might also include some experienced national-level negotiators who would be available to the Organization on request for mediation-type services.

3. *Operational Capacity.* The United Nations's most promising innovation has been its development of non-fighting operational units to help with on-the-spot peace-keeping. Such units can reassure former combatants that the terms of their truce are being observed (the Iraq–Iran observer group provides a current example); they can impose a *cordon sanitaire* between hostile forces (the force imposed between the Egyptian and Israeli armies has already been mentioned); and they can sometimes provide a stabilizing presence (the forces in Cyprus and Southern Leba-

non have this goal). Indeed, trained soldiers serving in military detachments have proved quite successful as observers and peace-keeping policemen.

The moment has come when operational devices such as these could be used more widely. Cease-fire negotiations might be more regularly tied in with the interposition of observers, and sometimes observers might even be put into place as a step to avoid the outbreak of fighting. Taking advantage of the turnabout in the Soviet Union's position on UN peace-keeping, it may now be timely to establish a UN roster of available national contingents and to systematize their advance training—already conducted in some countries—as truce supervisors and peace-keepers. The technique might also be adapted to other contexts. For example, there might be inspectorates for monitoring arms limitation agreements, perhaps drawing on the experience of the International Atomic Energy Agency with respect to atomic power plants.

Any such expansion of the UN's activities with regard to international crises and confrontations depends on two things. The Organization has continually to demonstrate that it can carry out such activities in an apolitical, impartial way. Secondly, it will need more assured financial resources if it is to continue its involvement in large-scale field operations.

The first aspect could become a major roadblock, as we know from the many complaints over the UN's so-called "politicization." The Security Council is, of course, a political forum in which its members have always manoeuvered for political advantage. It could hardly be otherwise. At the same time, the Secretary-General and his staff occupy a quite different position. Under Article 100 of the Charter, they must not seek or receive instructions from any government or indeed from any authority external to the Organization. This pledge of political non-involvement sets them apart from the struggle for political advantage and seems to have made their good offices widely acceptable to member states in need of them.

The recent readiness of even unpopular member states to call upon the Secretary-General's good offices probably depends, at least in some measure, on their awareness that the Security Council allows him considerable latitude in exercising these good offices. This is true not only for his mediation efforts where it could hardly be otherwise but also for his management of the truce supervision and peace-keeping units (awarded the Nobel Peace Prize in 1988) which have established a notable record for impartiality. Members of the Council have seemed to recognize that this is the only way that a highly political organization such as the United Nations can also become the force for peace that is needed. The Secretary-General's latitude in carrying out these delicate functions needs to be maintained and perhaps even reinforced.

The problem of financing peace-keeping operations also looms large.

Now that it is established that these forces can function effectively, it would seem that the funds to finance them, which are quite modest in terms of the military alternatives, could surely be found. Unfortunately, that has not been the experience to date. A renewed effort is needed by the world community to set aside the jumble of *ad hoc* financing arrangements by which these forces have been financed in the past and to establish an agreed system under which all of the UN's member states will regularly contribute in proportion to their ability to do so. Unless this can be done, even some existing forces may have to be phased out with unpredictable consequences.

GENERAL WELFARE ACTIVITIES

While world peace is a goal that is widely understood and supported, the UN's general welfare activities serve a diversity of goals that are unobjectionable but too broad, too ambitious and too difficult of attainment to win the same kind of understanding and support. For example, the Charter calls upon the Organization to promote social progress and higher living standards; to secure justice and respect for obligations under treaties and other sources of international law; to bring about full employment and to solve other economic, social, health and related problems, and, last but not least, to promote universal respect for, and observance of, human rights and fundamental freedoms for all without distinction as to race, sex, language or religion (Articles 1, 55).

This call for the United Nations to bring about a better world suggests that the founding fathers foresaw an organization that would play a major part in all of these sectors, though some of them doubtless regarded the highly ambitious goals as window-dressing for over-optimistic idealists and internationalists.[15] They must have known that to make appreciable progress toward any of these objectives—let alone all of them at once—would tax the resources, management capacity and resolve of even the richest and most efficiently-run government. To do so on a world-wide basis would obviously be many times harder.

The United Nations's member states have never been ready to provide it with financial or other resources in any way commensurate with such an ambitious mandate. This has confronted the Organization's policy-makers and programme managers with a challenge that they have thus far been unable to meet: to establish an appropriate division of labour between governments working at the national level on behalf of these same goals and international organizations working at the global level.

This is not to imply by any means that the Organization is not already providing many important general welfare services. But because it has never been able to establish rational priorities, its limited resources have tended to be thinly spread over hundreds of lightly-funded activities that are conducted year after year with little or no visible impact in many programme sectors where the same job can be done equally well or better at the national level. As in so many bureaucracies, activities of relatively little value and without wide political support tend to continue even in periods of financial crisis.

Governments, collectively, must come to the realization that they could, if they would only bestir themselves, have a much more useful world organisation. Only they can bring about a suitable allocation between what is better done in their own countries and the relatively limited number of specialized functions that can be carried out with greater impact at the global level. Conceptually at least, the road to follow may be mapped out fairly easily. This involves identifying high-priority activities that the United Nations should be able to carry out, because of its central position and the need for a co-operative approach organized by a non-partisan manager, with a comparative advantage over national governments working independently of one another. For example, in multilateral treaty-making, the comparative advantage of international organizations is obvious and generally recognized. Examples of programme sectors that would seem to qualify under this criterion are:

· global environmental activities;
· regulation of international "commons," such as outer space, deep seabeds and other places not coming under the sovereignty of any national state;
· world-wide problems that require international co-operation for their solution, e.g. terrorism, international drug trafficking; illegal migrations across national borders; the wholesale destruction of tropical forests; and epidemics such as AIDS;
· standard-setting for human rights; and the application of pressures on countries that flagrantly violate the human rights of large groups of their own citizens;
· direct assistance to governments, with no political or ideological strings attached, to help them deal with delicate internal problems, such as improving their public administrations and formulating family planning policies.

Even within such qualifying sectors, it is important to establish realistic, achievable objectives and to formulate programmes and projects that would draw upon the United Nations's strengths and take into account the constraints inherent in all internationally-managed activities. Also, in order to let the Organization make the greatest impact it can in its areas of comparative advantage, member states and the secretariat staff should work together to winnow down the great proliferation that has occurred in the UN's activities, retaining only those that truly serve the world's urgent needs.[16]

In general, each activity the United Nations carries out should satisfy four conditions:

1. Just as in determining the priority sectors, preference should be given to activities within each sector that can not be carried out equally well (or better) at the national level by governments or private entities, i.e. activities where the UN's comparative advantage is readily demonstrable.
2. Each activity's objectives should be framed in such a way that visible progress may be made towards their attainment within a reasonable time-frame.
3. United Nations members, collectively, should not only support the activity concerned, but must also be ready to furnish whatever resources, financial or otherwise, may be needed to attain such visible progress.
4. Finally, there should be broad (though not necessarily unanimous) agreement within each of the UN's main groups of states that the activity is one that it is suitable and necessary for the Organization to carry out on behalf of the world community.

Prescriptions such as these are more easily made than followed. Governmental and secretariat programme planners will need to approach their task much more conscientiously and pragmatically than they have in the past. Hitherto, despite complex programming procedures, the substantive programme managers have often used the resources available to them pretty much as they pleased. The following suggestions are offered in the hope of turning the Organization into a more effective—and more widely-respected—purveyor of general welfare services to the world community.

1. Setting the United Nations's priorities and formulating the activities that it will carry out in accordance with them requires a "think tank" type of analysis of the various alternatives and possibilities. This task needs to be carried out on a non-partisan, non-ideological basis. The Secretary-General and his international staff are uniquely placed to make such an analysis on behalf of the world community as a whole.

The Secretary-General and his staff should also be required to take on a leadership role in programme planning, that is to say they should be expected not only to analyze the various programme alternatives and possibilities but to come forward with their suggestions of programme sectors meriting priority treatment and of activities within each such sector that would yield the highest return in terms of money spent.

2. At the same time, it must be recognized that the foregoing function is not one that the Secretary-General and his staff can carry out

entirely on their own. The beneficiaries, the governments and peoples of the UN's member states, also need to be deeply involved in that process. The desirability of this parallel involvement has long been recognized, but the means to achieve it have eluded policy-makers. Concerns of this kind underlay the creation of the UN's Committee for Programme and Co-ordination (known as the CPC). However, over the quarter century of its existence, CPC has had only a marginal impact on the UN's programming process, and recent attempts to strengthen it have not worked very well. The main obstacle seems to be that the UN's activities are too complex and variegated to be mastered and governed by government representatives who can focus on them for only a few weeks each year.

Perhaps the CPC might be better able to fulfill its assignment as the United Nations's board of programme directors if it had a small steering group of governmental representatives seconded to the Organization who would spend their entire time working with their counterparts in the Secretariat. They might be involved in both aspects, setting priority areas and formulating appropriate activities to be carried out in each such area. This would ensure that the Secretary-General and his staff would have a readily-available governmental sounding-board for their ideas. At the same time, it would provide an informal channel through which national concerns, wishes and expectations could be phased into the planning of general welfare activities.

3. Making a global-scale impact is such a challenging and uncertain business that no group of mere mortals, no matter how great their combined competence, can hope to anticipate all the pitfalls of what they propose. Activities that may seem highly promising sometimes turn out badly. This has long been understood by those close to the UN's programme planning process. Yet attempts to establish effective evaluation of the impact and utility of what the Organization does have never been very successful.

To make programme evaluation more effective, it needs to be conducted outside the process of programme formulation and execution, with inputs from national as well as from Secretariat officials. Thus, the machinery for this type of evaluation must be placed in a separate compartment from the rest of the Secretariat, and its head should report directly to the Secretary-General. National officials should also be seconded to this unit, but should mainly work in their own countries to ascertain the effectiveness of what the United Nations does at the national level. The findings reached could then be fed back into the process of programme planning to permit the UN's on-going work to be adjusted periodically in order to have an increasing impact and utility.

4. General welfare activities to be effective at the global level require highly-qualified managers and staff. The United Nations now finds itself in a vicious circle in this respect. If what the Organization does is mar-

ginal with little impact (rightly or wrongly, the prevailing view in many quarters), governments can justify placing second-rate persons in its ranks on the ground that little harm will be done. However, with such persons, its activities, no matter how well conceived they may be, will probably not be conducted in a way likely to enhance the Organization's reputation. Thus, the Secretary-General, working with governments that grasp the potential of global co-operation, will need to seek ways of making the United Nations once again a place where highly-qualified people can expect to find stimulating and rewarding careers. Some ideas on how to do this are discussed later.

DECISION-MAKING PROCEDURES

To be viable, any decision-making system has to produce decisions whose legitimacy and binding force will be generally recognized and which can be carried out and have the impact intended for them. This kind of decision-making is carried out by most national governments on the basis of majority rule. In democracies at any rate, minorities are trained to accept as legitimate and binding the decisions that they have opposed. And there is an executive to ensure that such decisions are carried out and enforced.

At San Francisco, decision-making by majority rule was adopted for the United Nations.[17] However, the Organization's founders did not fully grasp how different the circumstances of associations of sovereign states are from those of national governments. They did not see the extent to which those differing circumstances affect the way in which it would be best for international bodies to take their decisions. For example, the subjects of these decisions are not individuals but sovereign governments, and the Organization's "government"—in reality not a government at all, but only an international Secretariat—has no means of imposing implementation on states that disagree with the decision concerned or merely, as very often happens, just can not be bothered to carry it out. As was pointed out earlier, in the United Nations, majorities, far from automatically ruling, are more often frustrated by their inability to prevail. In any case, most decisions of the General Assembly and of other UN organs are not legally-binding; so far as governments are concerned, such decisions are merely recommendations that they are free to accept, reject or ignore.

All of this signifies that the Organization's decision-making needs to be carried out in very different ways to that of national legislatures. Recent years have witnessed the slow and grudging acknowledgment of these realities and of the consequent need to adjust the Organization's decision-making system to accommodate them. While the process is far from complete, there is widespread awareness, first, that to be viable, its decisions must enjoy a much higher preponderance of support than would be required in national legislatures, and secondly that the role of negotiation and of somehow accommodating all points of view is accordingly much more crucial than voting.

Moreover, since compliance is largely voluntary, those whose cooperation in implementation is indispensable must not merely be in half-hearted agreement; they must be ready to lend their active support in carrying out the decision concerned. This has led to a trend in the United Nations to take more and more decisions on the basis of consensus (without voting) or at least broad agreement. And majorities now know that decisions taken in the face of significant opposition assume the character of referenda of the state of world-wide opinion rather than any serious effort to generate global action.

In an effort to make its decision-making procedures more productive and less time-consuming, the United Nations has come to conduct its parliamentary business through groups of its member states that share common interests and caucus regularly to formulate common positions on issues coming before the Organization. These groups are unlike the political parties of national governments in that they cluster states rather than cut across them. They thus tend to reflect regional rather than horizontal common interests. For most issues, there are three main groupings: the Western developed countries (including Japan) with free enterprise economies; the Soviet Union and the socialist countries affiliated with it; and the more than 120 "developing countries" which form the largest and most heterogeneous of the three groups, running the gamut from wealthy Kuwait to impoverished Haiti. Almost every member state belongs to one or another of the three groups, and increasingly this machinery is used by negotiators to shape the kind of broad agreement that the Organization has found to be a prerequisite for viable decision-making. This means that, before a draft resolution is adopted, efforts are made to ensure that it has wide support not just within the membership as a whole but within each of the three groups.[18]

For example, at the General Assembly's 1987 session, only twenty-seven resolutions and decisions of the 317 adopted were opposed by four or more members. Many of these twenty-seven were referenda-type resolutions taking controversial stances on what was happening in Kampuchea, Afghanistan, Falkland Islands, Iran, Chile and New Caledonia. None of the twenty-seven was action-oriented in the sense of calling for significant expenditure. At the same time, the UN's programme budget for 1988–1989 was adopted with the nearly unanimous support of all three groups (only Israel voted against it, while Australia, Japan and the United States abstained).[19] In 1988, the revised 1988/9 programme budget was adopted by acclamation.

While the need for acting on the basis of broad agreement is now widely recognized, there is equally wide resistance to the notion that any member or any handful of members should be able to block the Organization's action. Even a superpower, except in the Security Council, should not have this power. To insist on a unanimity rule, it is felt, would give too much leeway to obstructionists and would too often keep the Organization from acting at all. Moreover, if the majority accepts, reluctantly, the principle of decision-making by broad agreement, minorities must respond by exercising their greater influence in a responsible way, that is by abstaining from the vote when their fundamental interests are not affected by the decision being taken. It has been the reluctance of the United States to go along with this *quid pro quo* that lies at the heart of the Organization's recent political and financial crisis.

The following suggestions are offered in part as a kind of codification of the UN's evolving decision-making process and in part as ideas on how the spirit behind that practice might be translated into further concrete steps:

1. All members, large and small, would retain their right under the Charter to insist that votes be taken in accordance with its provisions, i.e. by simple and two-thirds majorities of those present and voting. However, they would agree that, under ordinary circumstances, they would not exercise this right with regard to decisions calling for UN action or expenditure.
2. Action-oriented decisions would normally be adopted on the basis of "broad agreement," and such "broad agreement" would require a large preponderance of support within each of the three main groups. What would constitute such a large preponderance of support would have to be worked out and agreed upon by the membership of each group for that group.
3. Every member state should be entitled to join one and only one group, and this should ordinarily be the group of its choice. If a state concludes that its interests have become more closely akin to those of another group, it should be possible for it to switch to that other group.
4. The present threefold grouping of the UN's member states is, for the time being, suitable for governing much but not all of the UN's decision-making. Where it is not (for example, with regard to law of the sea matters), other groupings could be established around common interests. The time may come when the main threefold grouping will need to be reorganized, and the possibility of this should be provided for.

The foregoing procedures place the main burden of decision-making where it belongs in any association of sovereign states, on the skills of negotiators. It is to be hoped that their skills will be addressed less to finding ambiguous, mutually acceptable wordings than to working out agreements on what the Organization will do. Of course, the processes of negotiation are time-consuming and likely to slow down the taking of decisions (maybe not such a bad thing, after all!). Moreover, this approach would tend to reduce the number of unimplementable decisions; it would re-assure individual members that the Organization could not be used in ways that they deemed threatening to their fundamental interests; and it would at the same time protect the United Nations from being used by any group, as has very often been the case in the past, as an instrument of its partisan policies.

ENHANCING THE UNITED NATIONS'S CAPACITY TO ACT EFFECTIVELY

It is not enough to produce implementable decisions; there must also be well-oiled machinery capable of carrying them out. Smoothly-functioning peace-keeping and general welfare services require a Secretary-General and a central staff capable of organizing and maintaining them on a sufficiently high level of efficiency and effectiveness. But national leaders and their diplomatic representatives seem to have lost sight of the high stake they have in ensuring that the most highly qualified individual available is chosen for the office of Secretary-General and in providing whomever it may be with an efficient, highly-motivated staff. They seem equally reluctant to recognize that long-time international civil servants are usually capable of attending to their UN duties with a global rather than a narrowly nationalistic outlook. Those that can not do so usually prefer to pursue their careers elsewhere.

The staffing of international organizations is particularly vulnerable to patronage pressures. Member states find it all too easy to apply relentless pressures on the Secretary-General, who is dependent upon them in so many ways and has no independent constituency of his own, to hire and promote their nationals.

At the outset, the United Nations was somewhat shielded from such pressures. The framers of the Charter and the organizers of the Secretariat were, many of them, steeped in civil service traditions. In 1945, they had just experienced the terrible consequences of a breakdown in international co-operation. In drafting the Charter and at the UN's Preparatory Commission in London, they understood the need for having an elite international civil service. In those optimistic times, it was relatively easy to staff the Secretariat on a merit basis from among the many qualified applicants who offered their services to a new and prestigious world body. At the outset, the UN Secretariat was probably the equal of the better civil services in its member states.

Since then, the pressures for patronage have steadily increased on all sides. Sadly, the nationalities of candidates for Secretary-General now assume greater importance than their qualifications. And the Secretariat is being filled with the friends and relatives of the patronage-dispensers in member governments. More attention is paid to keeping national quotas of Secretariat posts filled than to ensuring that each post is occupied by someone who is competent to carry out its responsibilities.[20] Worse yet, as the UN's attractiveness as a place to work has faded, the quality and dedication of the candidates for posts in the Secretariat has tended to decline.

This lowering of the capabilities and of the morale in the UN's executive branch must be countered if the Organization is to continue to be of use to its member states.

The ultimate responsibility for dealing with this situation obviously rests with these same member states, using perhaps the same group machinery they now employ to co-ordinate their positions on other global issues. But they must first become convinced of the need for having highly competent and motivated staff at all levels from Secretary-General down to the bottom rungs of the Secretariat. Once convinced of that need, they may wish to consider steps such as the following:

1. The International Civil Service Commission might be transformed from the quasi-political body it has become into a smaller expert group, with each member chosen for his or her long experience in civil service management. This group might have as its main task the revival of civil service standards within the Secretariat as a whole.
2. The Secretary-General and Director of Personnel might be provided with the necessary powers to hire new staff solely on the basis of competitive examinations and personal suitability.
3. Every effort should continue to be made to find and hire staff on the widest geographical basis but without lowering standards of competence and suitability.

Measures such as these are sure to be strongly resisted and unpopular in many quarters. But they are the alternative to a gradual undermining of the usefulness of the Organization.

Member states, of course, play a direct part in carrying out the recommendations made to them. They need to take such recommendations more seriously than they have in the past. When they vote in favor of a draft resolution, they must usually carry out or abide by its provisions. When they fail in this respect, they must be reminded of their delinquency. If there are many delinquents, there should be further discussions to see why and perhaps to modify the proposed course of action to gain wider support for it. In associations of sovereign states, this process should be treated less as one of "enforcement" than one of maintaining the standing and purposefulness of the decision-making process itself. It is one of preserving the Organization's reputation as a place where serious business can be carried on.

CONCLUSION

To the extent that they are controlled by anyone, governmental institutions evolve in line with the decisions taken by politicians. Reforms that seem sensible and necessary to knowledgeable observers often do not attract much political support. This general rule holds for associations of sovereign states where the "politicians" are the national leaders and diplomatic representatives of those states. Thus, the United Nations can be developed only in ways that those leaders decide that it should.

Accordingly, any deliberate reorientation of the world body depends on two factors: the expectations and judgements of those leaders and diplomats with regard to its potential for effective action; and the external pressures on them to turn to global institutions. Let us take up each of these factors in turn.

In 1945, the winners of World War II, appalled at the price that their countries had paid to escape Hitlerian tyranny, conceived over-blown expectations of what could be brought about through organized international cooperation. They quickly found that the new world organization could not become the kind of "cure-all" for humanity's "war problem" that they had had in mind. Since the 1940s, there has been a steady downscaling of the UN's potential until now the present pessimism has become as unrealistic as was the earlier over-optimism. What is needed is a more balanced assessment of what it would be sensible to expect from international entities in the way of peace-keeping and general welfare services. The reorientation suggested in this paper would aim to strengthen the United Nations so that it might more nearly realize this potential. Once the Organization is in a position to confirm its usefulness, national leaders are likely to turn to it more often.

The United Nations's potential for dealing with international peace and security problems remains limited but nonetheless important. With its mediation services and observer and peace-keeping forces, the Organization has shown that it can often help angry and suspicious member states resolve or live with their differences. It can step in whether military operations are underway or not provided that the parties each want its assistance. Once this condition is met, the UN's services may prove very valuable indeed, as we are now finding in Afghanistan, Iran–Iraq and elsewhere. At such times, the extent to which the Organization is trusted by the parties determines whether it will be permitted to undertake politically delicate functions. The Security Council may help in this process by applying pressures equally on all of the parties, and by making the war option less attractive to leaders flirting with it. Such pressures are most effective when the great powers are not directly involved and can apply them in unison. In all of these functions, there is room for improvement, and some suggestions towards that end have been made earlier.

The external pressures nudging national leaders towards greater use of world-wide organizations are strongest in the realm of general welfare services. More and more problems call for a global co-operative effort because of their interlocking impact on people everywhere. A few of these problems are beginning to loom very large. These include the tearing of the ozone protective layer, the "Greenhouse effect," the massive destruction of the tropical forests, and the spread of AIDS. In countering threats such as these, national leaders may become readier to accept a more highly organized and categoric form of international co-operation than they have in the past. Moreover, the older problems— refugees, international terrorism, the international drug traffic, excessive trade and foreign exchange imbalances, endemic poverty in Africa and other parts of the Third World, illegal migrations across national boundaries, growing congestion and confusion in international "commons"—remain unsolved, and progress towards solving them is very difficult in the absence of world-wide co-operation. Problems such as these combine to make a cogent case for taking such co-operation more seriously. In fact, national leaders already turn to entities that they see working tolerably well. These include the World Health Organization, the International Atomic Energy Agency, the International Civil Aviation Organization, the IMF, the World Bank and the GATT. A main purpose of any re-orientation of the United Nations must be to restore it to its rightful leadership position in the network of international organizations.

It is difficult to see how such a turn-about in the UN's world-wide standing can come about unless its member states moderate the confrontational approach that pits groups of states against one another. Forty-four years of experience have shown the futility of such confrontations. These same forty-four years have demonstrated the many ways in which organized international co-operation is in the interest of all groups. This record of UN service would surely be much improved in the future if each group of states, freed of fears of being outvoted, outmanoeuvered and out-propagandized on the parliamentary front, could more confidently support its activities and its involvement in tense situations. The changes in voting procedures suggested in this paper would help the United Nations to concentrate on the approaches that have worked well and to steer clear of those that have proved counterproductive.

This might clear the way for the gradual evolution of a world organization that would be equipped to deal effectively with the massive needs likely to emerge in the context of an increasingly complex global economy and society in the twenty first century.

NOTES

1. U Thant, *View from the United Nations,* (Garden City, N.Y.: Doubleday, 1978), pp. 154–94; Seymour Maxwell Finger, *American Ambassadors at the United Nations,* (New York: Holmes and Meier, 1988), pp. 121–2; Sir Brian Urquhart, *A Life in Peace and War* (New York: Harper & Row, 1987), pp. 192–3.

2. Finger, op. cit., pp. 228–9; Urquhart, op. cit., pp. 236–43.

3. Contrasting accounts of these negotiations will be found in Rosanne Klass, "Afghanistan: The Accords," *Foreign Affairs,* 66 (Summer 1988), pp. 922–45, and Selig S. Harrison, "Inside the Afghan Talks," *Foreign Policy,* 72 (Fall 1988), pp. 31–60.

4. Montreal Protocol on Substances that Deplete the Ozone Layer and Final Act, 1987, published by the UN Environment Programme in document Na. 87–6106.

5. Articles 13, 38 and 62 so limit the powers of the General Assembly, the Security Council (when it acts under Article 38 of the Charter) and the Economic and Social Council, respectively. Under Chapter VII, the Security Council *is* entitled to take decisions that are legally binding on member states.

6. U Thant, op. cit., pp. 34–5.

7. Seymour Maxwell Finger, op. cit., pp. 58, 60. Finger acknowledges that "in retrospect, it appears that the military aspect of the Korean War would not have been much different if the UN had not existed." Alfred O. Hero, Jr, in "The United States Public and the UN", states that disillusionment with and disapproval of the UN reached a high point during the Korean War. (See David A. Kay (ed.), *The Changing United Nations,* New York: Academy of Political Sciences, 32, 4 (1977), pp. 12–29.

8. For example, the call for a new International Economic Order and a programme of action to bring it into being (General Assembly resolutions 3201 (S–VI) and 3202 (S–VI) of May 1974) has been quietly ignored by most of the developed countries to which it was addressed.

9. Charles Kindleberger sums up the situation very well: "The essence of democracy is not that the majority rules, but rather that the majority and the minority both understand—because their positions might one day be reversed—that the majority acts with restraint towards the minority. . . .
The restraint of the majority towards the minority is an implicit contract necessary to democracy." *International Organization,* 40 (1986), p. 846. Restrained majority rule is much more difficult to bring about in international bodies because, *inter alia,* member state majorities tend to be stable over long periods, leaving member state minorities more or less permanently out in the cold.

10. The extent to which planning for the new world organization was focused on the enforcement provisions is well documented by Ruth Russell and Jeannette Muther, *A History of the United Nations Charter* (Washington, D.C.: Brookings Institute, 1956), Chapters X, XIX and XXVI. The authors comment (p. 227): "In fact, the *enforcement* aspect of security so dominated most governmental thinking on the subject that the *peaceful settlement* aspect was not given the attention it deserved until relatively late."

11. Evan Luard, *The United Nations,* (New York: St. Martin's Press, 1979), pp. 20–1. While the Cold War was the proximate cause of the failure to establish such forces, Russell and Muther describe the many political and technical obstacles that would have had to be overcome first (op. cit., pp. 234–8), which raise many doubts whether the provisions for enforcement spelt out in Articles 43–50 could have ever been carried out in any circumstances.

12. See page 422 and footnote 7 above.

13. France, Japan, Netherlands, the Soviet Union, Switzerland, the United States (openly) and West Germany were among the many countries that did not fully maintain the blockade. The value of Rhodesian imports was substantially higher in 1972 than it had been in 1965, the year the country declared its independence. (Frederick Kirgis, *Interna-*

tional Organizations in Their Legal Setting [St. Paul, Minn.: West Publishing Co., 1977], p. 596.) At the same time, the Zimbabwean guerillas persisted in a series of morale-breaking attacks on the White settlers for which David Caute, in *Under the Skin, the Death of White Rhodesia* (Evanston, Ill.: Northwestern University Press, 1983), provides a detailed account.

14. Leland M. Goodrich, Edvard Hambro, and Anne Patricia Simons, *Charter of the United Nations: Commentary and Documents*, 3rd and revised ed (New York: Columbia University Press, 1969,) pp. 588–93.

15. Senator Arthur Vandenberg, for example, argued with wide support against any attempt "to spell out a do-gooder program for the whole world" but was prepared to compromise with other delegates who wanted to expand the UN's mandate in this sphere.

16. The United Nations's biennial programme budget, essentially a voluminous listing of projects, contains more than 1,000 single-spaced pages and is very difficult to absorb. (See, for example, the *proposed Program Budget for 1986–1987*, General Assembly, Official Records, 40th Session, Supplement no. 6 [A/40/6], 2 vols.)

17. See Articles 18, 67 and 89 of the Charter.

18. Although the group system remains largely informal, i.e. it is unmentioned in the official rules of procedure of UN bodies, its impact on the decision-making process is very great indeed. The groups regularly caucus to co-ordinate their positions on pending resolutions, and group spokesmen often present these positions in the General Assembly and other UN bodies. Caucus groups are often furnished with conference rooms and interpretation services, and official meetings are sometimes postponed to accommodate them. Final negotiations on important and controversial resolutions often take place in "contact groups," that is, in small committees composed of representatives from each of the three main groups. In recent years, the system has become essential to consensus decision-making, though of course sometimes agreement can not be reached. In that case, the majority may either insist on voting formally or postpone the taking of any decision.

19. A surprising number of the General Assembly's resolutions are now adopted unanimously or even without any voting. (See the details for 1987, the forty-second session, in the Department of Public Information's 646-page presentation of the Assembly's resolutions and decisions, Press Release GA/7612, 13 Jan. 1988.)

20. Every year, the Secretary-General must submit to the Assembly an exhaustive statistical analysis of the number of staff members from each member state, broken down by grade level and sex. These are then weighed against the "desirable range" of staff for each state, with the result that some members are over-represented and others under-represented. The Secretary-General is under pressure in his recruitment to bring each member state's staff contingent within the range designated for it. The system is further complicated by the fact that the formula for establishing "desirable ranges," based on such factors as minimal number for each member, population, and contribution rate to the UN budget, is frequently changed. A recent report by the Secretary-General on the composition of the secretariat will be found in UN document A/42/636 of 16 Oct. 1987.

28

Influence, Marginality, and Centrality in the International Legal System

LOUIS HENKIN

International law is the law of the international state system, serving purposes and ends like those that law serves in national societies—order, predictability, efficiency, convenience, the promotion of common or dominant values (individual and common good and the general welfare? autonomy? equality? justice?). As in national societies, international law is made by political actors through political processes for political ends. Perspectives on the political influence of states and of regions, on equality or hierarchy, on marginality or centrality, apply to the legal dimension of the system as well. But international law also has its own laws, modifying those that govern international politics generally.

INTERNATIONAL LAW AND ORDER

International law aims at international order. International order—more precisely, interstate order—suggests order in a system of states, not the order that might be achieved by hegemony of a single power (such as a *Pax Romana*) or by world law under world government. Order in a system of states, moreover, is not a single, defined concept. From Westphalia (1648) to San Francisco (1945, the UN Conference), the order for which international law strove was that of a "liberal" system of states,[1] one that aimed at a maximum of liberty—sovereignty, being let alone—for each state, consistent with similar liberty for other states.[2] The international liberal order was enhanced in our day by the law of the UN Charter, which prohibited the use of force by any state against the political independence or territorial integrity of any other state. Equal liberty for equal states was enhanced also by adopting into law the principle of self-determination, which in effect outlawed involuntary colonialism.

Reprinted from *Jerusalem Journal of International Relations*, Vol. 11, No. 3, 1989, by permission of the Johns Hopkins University Press. Copyright 1989 by The Hebrew University of Jerusalem.

Note: It is a violation of the law to reproduce this selection by any means whatsoever without the written permission of the copyright holder.

The liberal state system and its law are committed to peace and order, to respect for state autonomy and to *"pacta sunt servanda"* (agreements are to be kept); the state system is not a "welfare system" dedicated to ensuring that every state can meet its basic needs and those of its inhabitants, or to reducing inequalities among states. Since 1945 the system has taken small steps away from strict liberalism: the UN Charter dedicated the UN Organization, among other purposes, to promoting the welfare of states and the human rights of individuals, and during forty years the United Nations has established international human rights and promoted economic development. But the international system has remained essentially liberal and international law continues to reflect that liberalism. The system exerts influence for internal change and for interstate cooperation, but in principle states remain autonomous. Internal changes must come from internal forces; cooperation is voluntary. International law has little to say about constitutional government or democracy within a state. No state is required to adhere to any human rights covenant or convention.[3] No state is required to help another state meet the needs of its inhabitants. Foreign aid, development assistance, have remained voluntary.

International law promotes a liberal state system because international political forces are committed to that system. In the political system law is neither central nor marginal. International law has no ends of its own; it is a means and a dimension of politics. Law confirms, it does not lead; it cannot get ahead of politics; law is a result, not a cause of politics.[4]

The Law and Politics of International Law

International law is a particular political instrument for ordering interstate relations. Making and maintaining international law are political processes, and the axioms, norms, procedures, and institutions of the law reflect political forces effectively brought to bear within the system. But the politics of lawmaking has its own process and its own laws of continuity and change.

International law consists principally of customary law and treaties. Treaties are made by agreement and a treaty is binding only on states that are parties to it. Customary law is the result of state "practice," and is generally binding on all states.

It is useful to distinguish between two kinds of customary law. Traditional customary law was largely "constitutional," fundamental, consisting of the basic principles of the state system and the basic norms of any legal system. These included: the concept and definition of the state, the implications of state sovereignty (including territorial integrity and inviolability), the norms of diplomatic intercourse, principles of property, contract, tort (delict) in relations between states. It included also the law of "commonage," governing common domain and common resources, notably the law of the sea. But custom continues to be available also as a means of legislating new, contemporary norms—for example, some new customary law of human rights. The traditional customary law is binding on all states, including states that have become states (and entered the state system) recently, and such customary law has remained largely immune to contemporary political forces. New customary law, on the other hand, results only when contemporary political forces will it.

Treaties too may be subdivided along lines of political significance. Bilateral treaties serve the needs of the two state parties and respond to their bargaining interests and powers. Multilateral agreements—which are also binding only on states that adhere to them—are used for general (or regional, or other group) legislative purposes, and are the product of a complex of political forces brought to bear at a particular time, on a particular issue, often in a particular forum.

In the latter half of the twentieth century, the state system has resorted to treaties for codifying and developing customary law. Like other treaties, "codificatory" treaties, such as the Vienna Convention on the Law of Treaties or the Vienna Convention on Diplomatic Relations, are binding only on states that adhere to them, but since they largely correspond to customary law they serve also as an authoritative restatement of the obligations of all states under customary law.

Whether as customs or by treaty, international law is made by the states themselves; there has been no representative body to legislate for the system. By the "constitutional" theory of the system, all states are autonomous and equal in status and authority. In principle—sometimes called the principle of unanimity—no state can be compelled to accept law to which it objects before it becomes law; no state can impose law on any other, unwilling, state.[5] That principle does not prevent those who wish to make law for themselves from doing so; it does not give others a veto. But opposition by one or more important states can preclude general law, and abstention by one or more states may sometimes undermine law made by other states for themselves, as when a few states refrain from adhering to an anti-hijacking agreement and serve as a haven for hijackers. International law, therefore, is difficult to make and difficult to change, and the laws of lawmaking favor nonregulation, state autonomy, laissez-faire, reliance on market forces, the status quo.

Law is made by governments, by politicians (not by lawyers). Since law results from agreement of many states or from their practice in relation to each other, lawmaking is a complex of actions by political actors and of layers of negotiation. Subject to the principle of unanimity, the forces that exert influence in the political system generally do so as well in the complex process of lawmaking. In bilateral negotiations, in conferences convened for the purpose of developing and concluding international agreements, in international organizations, in special bodies established to promote lawmaking (such as the International Law Commission), states are subject to persuasion, and political forces reflect political centrality, marginality, and other influences as in the system at large.[6] Group commitments may also have particular significance in lawmaking. Military allies, members of regional or economic groups, tend to seek law reflecting their common interests, and they will frequently support each other in promoting or resisting or shaping law on other issues as well. In recent decades, I shall suggest, the Third World has exhibited "solidarity" in the lawmaking process even on issues that do not involve their obvious common interests. Particular states have important, often dominant influence in resisting or shaping international norms that would regulate activities or interests in their possession or under their control.

Since the Second World War, international organizations have contributed to the development of international law. International (intergovernmental) organizations are generally established by treaty, and such treaties become part of international law. Some constitutive treaties also include normative principles of major significance, such as the UN Charter provisions prohibiting the use of force. In general, international organizations have no legislative authority, but resolutions of major organizations, such as the UN General Assembly, contribute to the development of international law: they may declare or clarify the state of the law on a particular matter; they may constitute state practice contributing to the development of customary law; they may encourage and promote the negotiation of treaties and help shape the content of such treaties.[7] The contribution of international organizations to lawmaking is shaped in part by political forces brought to bear in those organizations.

FROM EUROCENTRICITY TO UNIVERSALITY

For hundreds of years, the state system was centered in Europe and its politics were the politics of European powers. International law too, therefore, was inevitably Eurocentric. The core of customary international law was created and developed by the practice of European powers, and then also of their offspring in the Western Hemisphere. As a result of colonialism, that law applied also to much of Asia and Africa.

After the Russian Revolution, the USSR challenged the traditional law and insisted that it would be bound only by treaties (not by the traditional customary law), and only by treaties of its own making (not those of the czars). But the USSR soon found that it valued, as much as did its capitalist neighbors, the fundamentals of the customary law—state sovereignty, the principle of unanimity, territorial inviolability, sovereign and diplomatic immunities, *pacta sunt servanda*, and so on. Basic elements of traditional international law, moreover—its conceptions of status, contract, tort (delict), property—correspond to those of any organized legal system and there has proved to be little in customary law to offend the socialist states.[8]

Half a century later the advent of many new states led to the emergence of the "Third World," consisting of a large majority of the states of the world, tied by bonds of common colonial experience and consequent grievance, of non-European history and culture, and underdevelopment. Common interests and a sense of ideological-political solidarity have fused them into a large bloc that has proceeded to dominate international organizations (notably the United Nations) and lawmaking conferences (e.g., the UN Conference on the Law of the Sea). Western powers and major socialist states competed for their favor, enhancing their political influence. To date, however, because of the laws of lawmaking, the impact of the Third World on the legal system has proved to be marginal.

The new postcolonial states also began with a disposition to challenge existing international law as European, Christian, colonial, capitalist. But every newly independent country accepted the state system, eagerly sought statehood, and fought for entry into the state "club," the United Nations and its specialized agencies. Like the USSR earlier, the new states too soon realized that the values and principles of the traditional customary law were dear to them and favored their interests too. Like the USSR, the new states accepted the customary principle of *pacta sunt servanda* and did not press for radical change in the law of treaties.[9]

As regards the law generally, the Third World states pressed not for radical change but only for reexamination and codification, asserting their right to participate in the process of lawmaking and to free themselves from the history of the law (and the need to develop expensive expertise and archives). They influenced the codification and development of customary law, but in only a few respects (noted below) did they seek to change it radically, or to promote interests not shared by the older "worlds."

In a few respects, Third World influence was determinative. Rapid and near-total decolonization confirmed that self-determination—meaning, at least, freedom from Asian-African territories from traditional forms of Western colonialism—had become an established principle of politics; the new states helped confirm that principle in law, and they wrote it firmly into various international instruments.[10] They challenged various forms of "extraterritoriality" for foreign nationals that they saw as remnants of colonialism. Comprehensive racial discrimination, i.e., apartheid, became general anathema.

But in view of the unanimity principle, the established character of existing law, and the forces of continuity and inertia, the Third World could not make new law, or change old law, over determined resistance.

For notable examples, efforts to achieve big-power disarmament and to outlaw nuclear weapons have had little success. Attempts to change the international law governing foreign investments failed, and a major effort to achieve a New International Economic Order has not flourished. Foreign aid for development has continued to depend on grace, not on law. A new regime for the deep seabed, which some had hoped would lead to some redistribution of wealth and of influence at sea, floundered and its future remains uncertain. On the other hand, if the Third World has not been able to make new law or modify established law in its own image and interest, it has been able to prevent the emergence of law that it did not favor. What some Third World states opposed, others also disfavored in expression of Third World solidarity—for example, laws against terrorism, or stronger international institutions for enforcing human rights (other than against apartheid).

Influence, of course, is not either/or, all or nothing. Third World solidarity, and the competition of others for their favor, exert strong political pressure focused in international bodies. Once skeptical about customary law, often champion of the principle of unanimity, the Third World has sought to move—subtly, cautiously—toward majority control. It has launched resolutions by consensus, creating pressures on resisting states to acquiesce, and has influenced the content of resolutions creating practice (the stuff of customary law) and affecting the interpretation of treaties.

The influence of particular groups, and influence within groups, are often determined by leadership and initiative of particular states or of individual representatives of stature. Influence within groups such as the Organization of American States, the Organization of African Unity, the Arab League, the Council of Europe, NATO, or COMECON carries over into larger bodies. Mao's China once aspired to join and lead the Third World; for a while, India exercised moral leadership in the United Nations. For some years the oil states had the prestige of their power as a counterforce to the big powers and the middle European powers, and their influence was enhanced by promises of oil and aid. At the Law of the Sea conference, radical and moderate groupings emerged, competed, compromised. On some issues one strongly concerned group—such as an African leadership in the struggle against apartheid—can command solidarity of the Third World and shame the rest into unanimity. Blocs join on some issues in exchange of favors or the hope of favors, as when Arab and socialist states joined to oppose the establishment of more effective human rights institutions such as a UN high commissioner for human rights.

I have stressed the Third World because its members are many, and despite the unanimity principle—numbers weigh heavily for change, in and out of international organizations and conferences.[11] But politics are a web with few seams, and the forces that influence law are part of those that shape the international system generally. The political influence of powers and superpowers, of the mighty and the rich, or of voices for freedom and justice, human rights and human welfare, make themselves felt in the legal system too. In the legal system too, moreover, interests do not correspond to ideological or economic categories exclusively; surely, the vast Third World is hardly monolithic. States share other characteristics or qualities, for example, as "coastal states" or as "maritime states," or "oil states," or "oil-hungry states," that often override ideology and solidarity. States have particular interests and can exert influence for or against change in the law by unilateral action that others are unable to resist: many states have pursued huge arms arsenals and some have sought nuclear weapons; coastal states have extended their interests into the sea; resource states control their produce, investing states their capital, the economically developed retain the advantages of "the market"; "haven" states refuse to agree to extradite hijackers and other terrorists.

THE POLITICS OF LAW OBSERVANCE

International law serves its purposes in very large (though widely underappreciated) measure. Almost all principles of international law and almost all international agreements are observed almost all the time. There are important exceptions—where a norm has been formally accepted without authentic commitment to it (as, by some countries, to respect human rights, or, some would say, the prohibition on the use of armed force); where a state values the short-term advantage of a violation over its less palpable, long-term costs; when an agreement has ceased to be satisfactory and the costs that will be incurred by its breach do not appear to be compelling.

Influence for compliance with international law is diffuse. The principal inducements for a state to comply with general international norms or with its own international agreements are its commitment to the system and to the particular norm or agreement, and reluctance to incur the reaction of the victim of the violation. For some norms and agreements violation is also deterred by the threat of reaction by the victim's allies, by bodies particularly charged with responsibility for assuring compliance, or by the community at large.[12]

In general, violations are "torts" (delicts), offending only the particular victim, not "crimes" against the larger community. Every violation can become a source of friction and thereby a threat to "international peace and security," but that has not in fact made the ordinary violation a matter of general concern. Political influence within the community of states in support of law is ordinarily a consideration only for particular norms of general interest: those governing the common interest (the seas, the environment); the world economy; the use of force; selected human rights norms (anti-apartheid).

INFLUENCE IN CONTEXT

Influence in making and maintaining law can be illuminated by reference to several major issues. The development of the law of the sea in the past two decades affords perhaps the best and most various lessons. A few other cases deserve brief mention.

The Law of the Sea

In 1967 Dr. Pardo, the representative of Malta, placed the future of the resources of the deep seabed on the agenda of the UN General Assembly. Governments generally were surprised, wholly unprepared, and ignorant even of their own interests in the subject. But Third World states quickly embraced the item and fired it with rhetoric, determined perhaps to strike a blow against "economic imperialism" by the developed states, which might be disposed to exploit deep-sea minerals. Some states perhaps dreamed dreams of great wealth from the sea that would transform the world economic system and eliminate the chasm between rich and poor. Third World states led the Assembly to declare the seabed beyond national jurisdiction to be the "common heritage of mankind."[13] The Pardo initiative addressed only mining in the deep seabed; Third World states succeeded in expanding the agenda to cover all sea issues, and launched the largest and longest multilateral negotiations and international conference in the history of international relations. Fifteen years after Pardo's initiative, there emerged a new and comprehensive Convention on the Law of the Sea.

The 1982 Convention was shaped by a complex process, involving novel procedures and imaginative adaptations of old ones, intricate negotiations within and between blocs and sub-blocs, and the interplay of personalities. But, at bottom, the law that emerged was the result of "political vectors," the interaction of political forces reflecting the influence of governments (and of domestic influences on governments) trying to realize national interests as they saw them. Of course, these included interests, sometimes common, sometimes competing, in and about the sea; but they also included the relevance of sea issues to other economic-political issues, and their place in the totality of national interests in an interdependent, highly complex international system. The forces were modified by the process, by the stronger desire of some states to obtain agreement, and by different advantage or disadvantage for different states if the conference failed. The vectors were drawn at conference tables, but the forces had their interplay elsewhere, everywhere, before as well as during the actual conference proceedings. Some of the resulting law was effectively realized even before the conference formally began; most of it, surely, before the conference ended.

The UN conference dealt with the law of the sea as a whole and negotiations on each issue could not be isolated from bargaining on other issues; there were repeated references to the resulting draft as a "package deal." But inevitably negotiations on every major issue brought particular forces to bear on its resolution. The Maltese initiative was directed to the resources of the seabed "beyond national jurisdiction" but, ironically perhaps, its principal impact was on the extent and character of "national jurisdiction," of the rights of coastal states in the seas. Although at first attention and discussion focused on the mining of the deep seabed in the future, developing coastal states concentrated on modifying immediately the reach of national jurisdiction. They sought to persuade their fellow members of the Third World that coastal claims were an aspect of "economic self-determination" and that fishing and mining by distant states was "economic imperialism." The "geographically disadvantaged" states—those that were landlocked, had short coastlines or narrow submerged land masses, or whose coastal areas were not rich in minerals or fish—stood to gain nothing from coastal-state expansion; indeed, they might have benefited from resisting that expansion so as to leave more of the seas as "the common heritage of mankind" in which they might claim a share. But apparently they deemed the demands of Third World solidarity more compelling, perhaps seeing all Third World interests in the seas as an aspect of a drive for a new economic order. Perhaps they expected some compensation from their coastal-state neighbors who would gain from this expansion. Perhaps they did not perceive their particular interests clearly, or organize themselves effectively and in time.

In the early stages of the negotiating process, developed maritime states maintained their earlier resistance to coastal-state expansion. As distant fishing states, they rejected the notion that a coastal state might exclude them from wide coastal zones in which they had long fished. Developed maritime states feared, too, that if the coastal state acquired exclusive fishing rights, its jurisdiction would expand to govern other uses and would interfere also with navigation, military use, and scientific research in wide coastal zones. But developed maritime states are also coastal states, and some of them had important national interests that stood to gain from coastal-state expansion. Some also had some sympathy for the economic needs of poor coastal states. Maritime states were reluctant to enter into political confrontation with developing coastal states (supported by the rest of the Third World), especially since the coastal states had effective "possession" of the coastal areas and could seize them (or threaten to seize them) unilaterally. Pressed from without, and by some national interests within, the maritime states acquiesced in the concept of an exclusive economic zone.

It was a foregone conclusion that an exclusive economic zone for coastal states would be written into law if the conference succeeded; it would probably emerge as the law in fact, even if the conference failed. That doubtless strengthened the hand of developing coastal states to resist limitations on their authority in such a zone. The geographically disadvantaged states sought to impose some limits on coastal states' claims, insisting that coastal states should share some revenues with the rest of mankind and afford special rights to neighboring disadvantaged states. But although the geographically disadvantaged were sufficiently numerous, if united, to prevent the conference from taking decisions, they had made their commitment to Third World solidarity and had few bargaining chips left.

The direction and magnitude of the forces brought to bear on the regime to govern mining the deep seabed were different and produced a different result. Whereas no government had cared to dissent when the UN General Assembly declared that the seabed beyond national jurisdiction was "the common heritage of mankind," governments disagreed widely as to what that concept implied and differed as to what they hoped to make of it. Perhaps because it soon appeared that the wealth of the deep seabed would not in fact produce tremendous wealth, surely not right away, the general agreement on "common heritage" was soon submerged beneath other, largely ideological differences. "Radical" Third World states sought arrangements that would not only give the Third World virtually all the economic benefits of deep-sea mining, but would also give the right to mine exclusively to institutions that the Third World would control, and that would enable Third World governments and citizens to have access to and be educated in the technology and to manage as well as operate the enterprises.[14] From a different perspective, some developing states sought such control in order to prevent exploitation of deep seabed minerals that would compete with their land-based minerals in world markets. The United States and other developed states, on the other hand, insisted on a regime that would permit free enterprise and profit for states or for their companies. The communist states, although generally fearful of multilateral institutions and desiring to retain a role for their state enterprise, did not favor a large role for Western companies and banks. On these issues, the pressures of majority votes and rhetoric were not determinative, since the developed states had "possession"—the technology and the capital as well as the ability in fact to "go it alone," as domestic forces were pressing the United States to do.

Whether the 1982 Convention comes into effect by general agreement or as a result of customary law deriving from the LOS Conference, from unilateral state actions and reciprocal national legislation, and from smaller international agreements, the law of the sea will not be the same in 2000 as it was in 1960.[15] The principal outcome will be something that Ambassador Pardo of Malta surely did not intend or anticipate, but probably helped to achieve. By throwing open the law of the sea to change at a time of political militancy and daring by small nations, he unleashed, in particular, egoistic nationalist forces of coastal states blessed by geography, which, by expanding their coastal jurisdiction, were reaching for immediate gains at the expense of both traditional freedom of the sea (i.e., laissez-faire) and the common heritage. Beyond national jurisdiction, the Third World saw an opportunity to develop new institutions that they might control, to extend their authority and preclude that of developed states in the large oceans, and to add a dimension to their drive for a New International Economic Order. There, however, they met strong opposition from established law and expectations, and from the powerful, wealthy, and technologically developed states whom established law (or freedom from law) favored. And when all the compromises were done, the Reagan administration frustrated them, insisted on "going it alone," and pursued private arrangements with a few like-minded states.

As of now, the tug of political forces continues and its outcome still remains to be seen.

The New International Economic Order

Beginning in the 1970s, the states of the Third World undertook a massive effort to achieve a new international economic order. They declared the right of all peoples to economic self-determination and to sovereignty over their national resources. They challenged the traditional norms of customary law that recognize special obligations toward foreign nationals, including a requirement of full compensation if foreign properties or investments were nationalized. They sought to improve their situation in the financial markets and in international financial institutions. They pressed for "more equitable" terms in trade that would assure poor states higher prices for their exports and afford them technology and other manufactured goods at lower than "market" prices.

Since they had "possession" of their natural resources, since "gunboat diplomacy" and other military intervention were no longer acceptable in the international system, Third World states succeeded in ending many concessions to foreign investors and in renegotiating foreign investment on a new basis in various forms of "joint ventures," with greater governmental control and a larger share for the host state. Third World states also joined in the United Nations to adopt resolutions denying any international obligation to compensate for expropriation of foreign properties or investments.[16] But Third World states needed foreign investment and, as a condition of investment, Western states effectively compelled importing states to acquiesce in an obligation under international law to compensate for expropriation, or to conclude specific agreements assuring such compensation.[17] In time, states that had previously expropriated agreed to "lump-sum" settlements, sometimes in order to open the way to future investments and to improve relations generally.

Perhaps the greatest Third World failure and disappointment was in its effort to achieve a new order in trade. All the poor states together could not change the law of the free market, although the General Agreement on Tariffs and Trade (GATT) permits some special concessions to developing states.[18] Arguments based on "community" and interdependence, and claims for "reparation" against former colonial powers, invoked international morality, not law. Appeals to self-interest urging that development and new arrangements would benefit all did not persuade those who had to be persuaded. Foreign aid to developing countries has remained essentially voluntary; the UN Development Program has provided assistance to the extent that the rich states could be pressed or shamed into contributing; banks and governments and international institutions provided some debt relief, but those concessions granted from sympathy or prudence have not acquired normative character.

The Use of Force

Until 1945 war was not unlawful, but lesser uses of force required justification and were subject to principles of necessity and proportionality. In the UN Charter, the nations agreed to outlaw war and other uses of armed force, except in self-defense against armed attack. They also established institutions, notably the Security Council, to enforce the prohibitions of the Charter and maintain international peace and security. The major powers insisted on and obtained a veto in the Security Council.

The Security Council, all know, has been rendered largely ineffective to date by big-power conflict and the big-power veto, and the United Nations has exerted only marginal influence on enforcing the law of the Charter, principally through its peacekeeping activities. The law against war and other uses of force has suffered. To be sure, the big powers have been deterred from overt resort to war by mutual fear of terrible weapons, but recurrently they have been involved in surrogate wars or in interventions and counterinterventions—Korea, Czechoslovakia, Vietnam, Afghanistan, Nicaragua. Big-power hostility, and their competition for the favor of small powers, has limited big-power influence against war by smaller powers. The mass of nations in the United Nations, and smaller groups in regional organizations, have not been sufficiently committed to the law of the Charter, have not cared enough to attempt to prevent, deter, or terminate war, and some states have even resisted such efforts by others. As a result, some states (other than the big powers or their allies) have felt free to engage in war, regardless of law. The Middle East has seen several wars between the Arab states and Israel, the lengthy war between Iran and Iraq, and interventions and counterinterventions in Cyprus and Lebanon. There have been small wars and other illegal uses of force in Africa, in Asia, in Central America, and between Argentina and the United Kingdom. Law has not been irrelevant, but it has had insufficient effect.

For decades, the big powers have not seen it as in their common interest to support that law and to impose or strongly press for peace; they have not themselves been scrupulous to respect the law. The USSR has generally seen its interest in maintaining or spreading communism, or expanding Soviet influence, as greater than any interest in peace. The United States was firmly committed to the law of the Charter, but also to the containment of communism. In the Reagan years, the United States was seen as moving beyond its earlier insistence on the right to engage in collective self-defense against armed attack and against indirect aggression, and proclaiming the right to use force to prevent or undo communist regimes (even if not externally imposed), to spread democracy, and to respond to terrorism (Libya). That policy has been attacked by other states and by many in the legal community; some of these actions have been declared illegal by the International Court of Justice.[19]

In 1988, the USSR began the process of fully withdrawing its forces from Afghanistan. The United States suspended arms assistance to the Contras fighting in Nicaragua. The big powers agreed on, and the United Nations helped achieve, a cease-fire between Iraq and Iran. It remains to be seen whether in the post-Reagan years the United States will revert to greater attention to the law of the Charter and to a renewed commitment to enforcing it against other states. It remains to be seen, too, whether the United States and the USSR might begin to cooperate to that end.

Most of the uses of force in the past decades have been internal— rebellions and civil wars—with interventions and counterinterventions by other states, notably by the big powers or their surrogates. International law has not attempted to and could not regulate internal uses of force, but it has attempted to regulate external interventions by force in such internal struggles. Some of these interventions of recent decades were illegal by international norms; the legality of other forms of support or intervention is uncertain.

Law is made by states through incumbent governments, all of which wish to be free to receive aid, including armed support against rebellion, even in civil war; all incumbent governments desire law forbidding intervention in support of rebellion or civil war. On the other hand, opposition forces seek support from other states, and some states have given such aid, including armed support.

There is a need to define and refine the law governing intervention in rebellion and civil wars. But the principal "would-be" intervenors and countervenors are the superpowers and their allies or surrogates, and no new law, or clarification of the existing law, is likely unless the superpowers agree to have it.

In the enforcement of the law against war, I regret to conclude, all states (and the United Nations) have been more or less marginal. One may hope that in the future, big-power cooperation will justify a different conclusion.

Human Rights

Human rights is a Western idea, but it has been universally accepted, at least nominally. The Universal Declaration is repeatedly invoked; the various covenants and conventions are adhered to by states from every region and of every ideological hue. More than half of the states have adhered to the International Covenant on Civil and Political Rights; the Genocide Convention and the Convention on the Elimination of All Forms of Radical Discrimination, in particular, have received overwhelming support.

The enforcement of universal standards has been less successful. The commitment to human rights has been insufficiently strong to mobilize effective (and sometimes costly) collective actions, though the determination of Black Africa to eradicate apartheid has moved other states, too, to take some measures against it. In international bodies, particular countries—for example, the Scandinavian states—have sometimes taken the lead to nudge the majority toward constructive action. But the United Nations has been "politicized," and, except when directed against South Africa, Israel, or Chile, there have been only spasmodic efforts to address human rights violations. Politicization is particularly strong and rampant in larger political organs such as the UN General Assembly; increasingly, it has been possible to address egregious human rights violations in smaller, less prominent bodies, notably the Human Rights Commission. Regional organizations and other groupings sometimes provide inducements to comply with human rights law. European institutions, and increasingly those of the American states, have helped maintain universally accepted norms. It remains to be seen whether the African states will develop effective means to implement the African Charter of Human and People's Rights. The Commonwealth and the French Community have exerted some informal influence against egregious violations. Arab states have not yet moved effectively to adopt common standards and effective machinery to enforce them.

Individual states—notably the United States—have sought to address "consistent patterns of gross violations" by refusing economic and arms assistance, but it is difficult to assess the deterrent effect of such sanctions, or of public condemnation or of "quiet diplomacy" by the United States, other countries, nongovernmental organizations, and international communications media.

POLITICAL-ECONOMIC MARGINALIZATION AND INTERNATIONAL LAW

In the international system, lawmaking and law enforcement are collective political acts. In the complex processes involved, no state or group of states and no particular region consistently wields extraordinary influence, and none has been wholly marginal. Political and economic power is persuasive in these political acts as in others, but general law requires general agreement. By its numbers and solidarity, the Third World has generally been an impressive force, but it is a negotiating bloc, not a legislative body.

The international system is not in perfect health, and its law reflects its weaknesses. The hopes of 1945 for a peaceful world are frayed, and the law on the use of force is in some disarray. The interdependence of states demands ecological and economic regulation, but there has been insufficient success in achieving it. Technology continues to aggravate inequalities, but there are no law and legal institutions to make the economic system more just and efficient, to reduce gross inequalities, or even to create a minimal "welfare system" that would assure that the basic human needs of all are met. One can expect some firm agreement on the law of the sea. One can hope for an emergence of political forces that would lead to law against terrorism. There is little basis for expecting radical change in the law generally: one cannot predict the unpredictable.

A basic order is in place, reflecting established customary law, confirmed and extended by contemporary multilateral treaties and by a network of bilateral arrangements. For the rest, the system—and the rules and the politics of lawmaking—favor state autonomy, laissez-faire. That leaves many needs of the system and of individual countries unmet. There is urgent need for new law, but law is an instrument of politics; there can be no effective law if politics does not will it. Political will to make law requires general agreement, which requires a will by some—the rich, the mighty, the wise, the brave—to lead, and by all— including the many poor—to join and help. Will it require world economic crisis, world environmental crisis, world nuclear catastrophe, to forge that will?

NOTES

1. As the word *liberal* is used in the term *liberal state*, i.e., a state that does not have its own conception of the good but whose purpose is to maximize the realization of every individual's conception

2. Hedley Bull described the state system as an "anarchical society."

3. The modest customary law of human rights has also come about by state consent, though the system has effectively outlawed apartheid over the resistance of the Republic of South Africa.

4. See generally L. Henkin, *How Nations Behave: Law and Foreign Policy*, 2nd ed. (New York: Columbia University Press, 1979).

5. But by the rules of the system, preexisting customary law is binding on new states entering the political system.

Traditional international law did not refuse effect to unequal, even unconscionable bargains, even to treaties imposed by force; since World War II, treaties imposed by use or threat of armed force are illegal and not enforceable, but agreement is not vitiated because it results from economic coercion or unequal bargaining power.

6. Nongovernmental entities can influence the process of influencing states.

7. General Assembly resolutions have made notable contributions to the law of human rights and the law of the sea.

8. Issues of the law governing foreign nationals and foreign investment will be addressed below.

9. For a time there was uncertainty about succession to treaties, but decolonization provided its own rules: in large measure the older states allowed the new states to choose among the treaties of their colonial predecessors, succeeding to the treaties they desired and rejecting the others. With decolonization virtually ended, the law of state succession has receded in significance.

10. See, e.g., Article 1 of the International Covenant on Economic, Social and Cultural Rights, and Article 1 of the International Covenant on Civil and Political Rights.

11. By the principle of unanimity no state is compelled to adhere to any international agreement, but generally the content of an international agreement is determined in organizations or conferences governed by majority or two-thirds vote.

12. In a real sense, peace within Eastern Europe is maintained by the USSR, peace within Western Europe by regional forces.

13. See UNGA Res. 2749 (1970).

14. Some observers think that "radical states" saw effective control of mining as a step toward Third World control of other uses of the oceans, and in turn a step toward establishing other powerful institutions with authority in other aspects of international life.

15. See Restatement, Third, Foreign Relations Law of the United States, Introduction to Part V (1987).

16. See the Charter of Economic Rights and Duties of States, GA Res. 3281 (1974).

17. Latin American states have resisted such agreements.

18. See Restatement, §810.

19. It is not clear that the United States itself is prepared to support generally the view that it is legal for any country to intervene or to counterintervene in other countries, or to attack states believed to be responsible for terrorism.

THE CRISIS OF
NATIONAL INSTITUTIONS

29

After the Cold War

RICHARD J. BARNET

As the decade draws to a close, the globe seems to be spinning faster than at any time in forty years, blurring long-familiar landscapes. The surprises of the past two years have been breathtaking: The Soviet Union, dropping its elaborate mask, displays the weakness and discontent of seventy years of rule under the Communist Party, withdraws its troops from Afghanistan, and opens up an exciting but perilous process of debate and reform. Poland has a free election, and a leader of Solidarity becomes Prime Minister. Hungary announces that it is a People's Republic no more, stops calling its ruling party Communist, and proclaims Imre Nagy, the symbol of the struggle against Soviet tanks in Budapest in 1956, a national hero. Todor Zhivkov, the Stalinist leader of Bulgaria for thirty-five years, is ousted. In one long weekend in November, East German soldiers bulldoze parts of the Berlin Wall and announce that everybody is free to go to the West. The hard-liners in Czechoslovakia capitulate to a week of massive demonstrations, and the Czech Communist Party gives up its claim to play "the leading role." Alexander Dubček, who twenty-one years ago tried to create "socialism with a human face" and was crushed by Soviet tanks, returns in triumph. Even within the Soviet Union itself Mikhail Gorbachev's uncertain strategy for maintaining control of the non-Russian republics encounters defiance in Lithuania and results in bloody clashes in Georgia, Azerbaijan, and Uzbekistan. In the heady atmosphere of *glasnost*, the failures and disappointments of *perestroika* are undisguised. Officials

Reprinted by special permission; © 1990 Richard J. Barnet. Originally in *The New Yorker*. All rights reserved.

Note: It is a violation of the law to reproduce this selection by any means whatsoever without the written permission of the copyright holder.

and pundits in the West, unable to comprehend, much less to predict, the speed and magnitude of these changes, routinely assert that Gorbachev will fall. Some assume that the breakup of the Soviet Union is inevitable.

The nations of Western Europe agree to open a highly integrated regional super-market and trading bloc in 1992—an event no less stunning than the dissolution of Communism in Eastern Europe. The leaders of the Soviet Union and China meet and announce a rapprochement, but the massacre in Tiananmen Square is a sober reminder that dramatic changes can be dramatically reversed. Japan becomes the world's most successful trading nation, the world's greatest exporter of capital, the leading supplier of foreign aid, and the financier of the United States budget deficit. As pressures build on both sides of the Atlantic for withdrawals of American troops from Europe, the United States and West Germany artfully downplay their deepening split over the future of nuclear weapons on the Continent. But within half a year the dispute over whether to have a new generation of short-range nuclear missiles in West Germany aimed at East Germany is overwhelmed by the dramatic events in the German Democratic Republic. Suddenly, an issue that most non-Germans and many Germans would like to avoid—the reunification of the two Germanys—is on the table.

Thus, many of the long-declared aims of Cold War policies over more than forty years—a "mellowing" of the Soviet system, a tempering of revolutionary zeal, support of United Nations peacekeeping efforts, improvements in human rights, greater respect for religion in the Soviet Union, a willingness to negotiate a less threatening military posture, reductions in Soviet military spending, encouragement of greater democracy and diversity in Eastern Europe—are, to a remarkable extent, moving toward realization. The conversion of the Soviet Union from a revolutionary power seeking to replace the world capitalist system into a traditional nation-state seeking membership in that system is proceeding with great rapidity.

For almost forty-five years, the Cold War has served as the organizing principle of United States strategy. Virtually every foreign relationship has been viewed as an aspect of the global struggle with Communism. The Cold War has defined American priorities and American purposes, and its approaching end offers a historic opportunity for the United States to take stock of what has happened, to reexamine its foreign-policy goals and strategies, and to redefine its role in world affairs. For the first time since 1946, this country is being forced by events to rethink the meaning of national security in a basic way. It is a time, like the end of the Second World War, for Americans to revive old dreams of a world at peace, stabilized not by military force and hostile alliances but by political, economic, and legal institutions that respond to the cry for democracy now heard around the world. Prudence, pragmatism, and caution are admirable watchwords for confronting a time of upheaval, but if there is no larger American vision of a new world order Americans will have little choice but to accommodate or to resist the visions of others. It may now be possible to transcend the politics of the past, and to marshal resources in new ways to face the very different sorts of security problems of the future. The United States has a major role to play in the great transformations that lie ahead, but a different role, surely, from the one it played two generations ago.

So far, however, this country, the prime architect of the postwar world, is moving slowly in response to the end of the Cold War, content to let the nations of Europe take the initiative. After the months of tumultuous change that have taken place in his first year in office, President Bush has adopted a rhetoric that has begun to acknowledge the waning of the Cold War, but the impact on United States policy is as yet far from clear. The President presents the astonishing events of recent weeks as a well-earned reward for maintaining "steady" Cold War policies all these years. He sounds as though the ideas, institutional arrangements, and spending priorities that won the long war needed only to be modified to serve equally well in a post-Cold War world. Such a response to the rush of unanticipated events could have been predicted. The United States, like all the other players, was unprepared for this moment. There are file drawers of contingency plans in the Pentagon for fighting all kinds of wars that can never be fought, but the White House clearly had no contingency plans for what to do in the face of Cold War victory. President Bush was curiously low-key in his first reactions to the dramatic developments in Germany last November, giving the impression that he didn't know quite what to do but was determined to do it prudently. The contours of the new world in the making are murky, and there are no maps. As the new decade begins, the Administration seems elated by its sense of Cold War victory, careful not to press its advantage in Eastern Europe too far, and anxious about venturing into the uncharted waters of the post–Cold War world.

The United States of the early postwar years, rich beyond measure and invulnerable to attack, entered the era of its supreme power with both euphoria and apprehension. The men around President Truman, though aware of the power of the United States and the weakness of the Soviet Union, wondered whether public opinion in the United States would support a permanent global mission or whether the economy could sustain it. Fears of a revived Depression were widespread. The choices then seemed clear, and stark. Stalin's despotism, secrecy, and cruelty gave credibility to "worst case" thinking. The fateful underestimation of Hitler in the nineteen-thirties made the most pessimistic assumptions about Stalin's expansionist plans seem nothing more than elementary good sense.

The atmosphere of fear generated by the atomic bomb and by the spread of Soviet influence in Europe served American leaders as a license—even an obligation—to organize the non-Communist world under American leadership and to prepare for nuclear war. The obvious course was to adapt the strategies that had been used against Hitler to defeat the next totalitarian threat. The United States stepped easily into Britain's role of leadership as the exhausted British Empire dropped its mantle, and within months the traditionally isolationist continental nation had become the world's first truly global power. In the world of 1945, ideology offered a clear benchmark for distinguishing friend from foe: on the creed of anti-Communism and the "lessons" of Munich, Pearl Harbor, and Hiroshima, a global strategy was built.

Of all the perquisites of office, the one that bureaucracies are most reluctant to give up is the world view on which their existence depends. Political rhetoric is more easily changed than the unstated assumptions on which national-security establishments operate. If, as John Maynard Keynes lamented, modern society is in the grip of defunct economists, it is equally in the thrall of early-twentieth-century geopoliticians. In the prism of geopolitics, the Soviet Union, however profound its reforms, remains a permanent enemy of the United States by virtue of its size, its history, its huge military potential, and, above all, its geographical position. All these factors give it the opportunity—which has never been realized—to dominate the heartland of Europe. The United States fought two world wars to prevent another aspiring power from achieving such a goal. Those who look at the world through the traditional geopolitical prism view with considerable apprehension the conversion of the Soviet Union from an enemy of West Germany into an economic collaborator.

It was thus hardly surprising that the initial policy review of the Bush Administration came up with a clarion call for "the status quo plus." But the pressure of events—Gorbachev's steady stream of intriguing offers and beguiling statements, the collapse of Communism in Eastern Europe, and the domestic pressures to cut the United States military budget—has impelled the Administration toward a complex and comprehensive negotiation with the Soviet Union over the direction of the arms race, the future of Europe, and the redefinition of United States–Soviet relations. Such negotiations, as Ronald Reagan discovered, have a momentum of their own, and without a clearly articulated set of goals the United States will find it hard to keep control of the process. The Soviet Union today is a far more tractable negotiating partner than it was in the late nineteen-forties, when the pillars of United States postwar foreign policy were implanted, but the United States no longer enjoys the overwhelming power it had then to convert other nations to the American view of reality. Some of President Bush's caution reflects an awareness that whatever new American vision is proclaimed will not be easily sold.

Bureaucracies with a heavy investment in the world view of the Cold War have an inexhaustible supply of arguments for clinging to something called the status quo even as it disappears. Not so long ago, the argument for avoiding a political settlement of the Cold War rested on the absence of leadership in the U.S.S.R. Soviet leaders were dying every fifteen months or so. Before that chain of events started, Soviet leaders were seen as too fanatical (Stalin), too mercurial (Khrushchev), or too euphoric about their own historical prospects (Brezhnev in the post–Vietnam years) to make acceptable negotiating partners. (Only in the years when the United States was embroiled in the Vietnam War did it feel sufficient pressure to make negotiations with the Soviet Union an essential part of its security strategy. The result was the Nixon–Kissinger détente, a managed arms race, and a formal recognition of the division of Europe.) For most of Bush's first year in office, Soviet weakness provided as good a reason to keep to the old course as Soviet strength once did.

At the beginning of the process of *perestroika*, the reflex response in Washington was to dismiss it as a media campaign. When it became clear that it was much more than that, a second response was to cast doubt on Gorbachev's survival, as if it were axiomatic that the democratization process inside the Soviet Union and the "new thinking" on foreign policy could not survive this remarkable personality. But as Gorbachev appeared to consolidate his power over an increasingly exposed and troubled empire the case for United States passivity shifted again. Why take the political and military risks of negotiating fundamental changes in the relationship with an adversary in crisis?

During the 1988 Presidential campaign, George Bush vigorously resisted the notion that the Cold War was over. His closest advisers at the time believed that Ronald Reagan's embrace of Mikhail Gorbachev was the naïve response of an old man in a hurry to make history. For most of its first year in office, the Bush Administration was divided on how to confront the radical new world in the making. The majority position was that nothing was to be lost by proceeding with great caution, for events were moving America's way. The Administration greeted the accelerating changes with a series of politically adept gestures, mostly rhetoric, that seemed calculated to slow the call for a significant response from the United States. But in the last weeks of 1989 the Administration began to take friendlier note of Gorbachev's lavish menu of reforms. In its annual report, "Soviet Military Power," the Pentagon downgraded the Soviet military threat, and the Central Intelligence Agency has estimated that last year the Soviet Union cut its military expenditures by perhaps as much as two per cent of its gross national product. In the last four years, the United States military budget, under the pressures of the national budget deficit, has been about seven per cent lower than what the Pentagon requested. After the December summit, in Malta, President Bush discouraged the notion that a sizable "peace dividend" was in the offing. Under-Secretary of Defense for Policy Paul Wolfowitz testified last month that, despite the reduction in the United States' assessment of the Soviet threat, "the fundamental unpredictability" of the political situation in Eastern Europe precludes anything more than modest cuts in defense spending.

Gorbachev's eagerness to make a deal, Administration officials believe, is the best reason not to be rushed into making one. The more severely Gorbachev is pressed by a growing awareness of the gravity of the Soviet situation, the more favorable the negotiating climate becomes. After all, it is the Soviet Union that wants basic changes. Gorbachev and his advisers believe that only increased productivity can meet the demands of the Soviet people for more goods and better services. The legitimacy and the survival of Communist Party rule are at stake, yet the achievement of those economic goals requires changing the incentive system and integrating a private-enterprise sector into an essentially state-managed economy. It is not clear that such radical shifts can be achieved without unleashing considerable conflict within the Soviet Union—or, indeed, that they can be achieved at all. Why should the United States exchange the global security system—the set of political and military relationships around the world—that has brought it victory in the Cold War for the risks and uncertainties of Gorbachev's "new thinking"? Even as the Secretary of State and the President issue upbeat statements about improved United States–Soviet relations, Vice-President Quayle expresses doubt that much has changed in Soviet foreign policy. Cold War diehards dream of unconditional surrender. The Soviet leader, they point out, is asking for quarter in an arms race he cannot afford. The forty-year effort of his predecessors to achieve true superpower status has failed. He wants time to reform his distressed economy, to increase Soviet influence by deemphasizing military power and acting in non-threatening ways, and to integrate the Soviet Union into the world economy. But why should the United States settle for this? Why not push Gorbachev or his successors to the wall and enjoy a lasting victory: not only the collapse of the Communist system but the disintegration of the Soviet Union itself?

By contrast, Gorbachev's grand strategy has become clearer. He is undertaking the risks of a thoroughgoing reconstruction of the Soviet system and a reshaping of the Soviet role in the world because nothing less will rescue the Soviet Union from decline and decay. Domestic reform requires a major shift in energy and resources. The recapitalization of the Soviet economy can be accomplished, he believes, only by a significantly greater integration of it into the world economy, and that cannot be achieved without radical changes in foreign policy. Contrary to the prevailing assumptions from Lenin to Chernenko, neither the ideological mission of spreading socialism nor the game of great-power politics is useful either for rebuilding Soviet society or for achieving national security. Neither is affordable. Almost seventy-five years after the Bolshevik Revolution, the Soviet people are impatient with making endless sacrifices for the class struggle, "internationalist duty," and the building of socialism in faraway places. "Now we have parity with the United States," goes a bitter remark currently making the rounds in Moscow, "and you can see the results in the shops." Gorbachev has spelled out a long-term vision of "common security" which is mostly borrowed from intellectuals and critics in the West. He articulates it with a knowledge and a passion unmatched by any other world leader. At the heart of Gorbachev's world view is the conviction that war in Europe is implausible, and permanent mobilization for such a war weakens the Soviet Union. Stalin seized Eastern Europe as a buffer zone, to keep any future European war from Soviet territory, but Gorbachev understands that trying to hold on to it by force would doom *perestroika* and preclude advantageous political and economic relations with the West.

His ultimate goal, it must be assumed, is to make socialism work under a regenerated Soviet Communist Party: to the extent that that happens, the power and influence of the Soviet Union in the world will increase. His tactics are not mysterious. He is bent on removing the threatening image of the Soviet Union and on breaking out of the isolation of the late Brezhnev years. "We are going to deprive you of the enemy," Georgi Arbatov, the leading Soviet Americanologist, tells American audiences. Polls show that the strategy is working. At the same time, Gorbachev is busy repairing relations not only with the United States but with Japan, China, Iran, and Western Europe—most significantly, West Germany.

When I visited Moscow last February, a senior foreign-policy analyst told me that Germany—by which he meant the Federal Republic—was "the natural partner of the Soviet Union in Europe." My mind flashed back to my last visit, four years earlier, in the final days of the Chernenko regime, when more than one Soviet researcher spoke hysterically about a "revanchist" Germany locked in a secret nuclear embrace with Mitterrand's France. Now some Moscow academics mention West Germany (right after Sweden) as a possible model for a reconstructed socialism in the Soviet Union. But as these ideas make their way into the press, increasing numbers of Soviet workers worry that the "cooperative sector"—restaurants, small businesses, and private farms—is creating a new class of entrepreneurs and hucksters, thereby threatening the achievements of the revolution while providing no assurance that *perestroika* will improve the standard of living of the majority.

The contrast between the intellectual ferment of the new thinking in Moscow and the sober, cautious reshuffling of old thoughts in Washington over the past year is striking. The differences in approach reflect differences in outlook. The crisis of the Soviet system is too profound to ignore, and Gorbachev's *glasnost* has stimulated an astonishing process of self-examination and self-criticism. The United States, on the other hand, is in a relatively buoyant mood. Inflation is down. Employment is up. The stock market has been booming. It is widely believed in official circles that the spurt of military spending in the nineteen-eighties increased the respect of other nations for the United States, and despite the evidence that public opinion imposes sharp limits on the actual use of military power, the national-security establishment of the United States feels vindicated by events and shows no enthusiasm for making major reductions in force levels and expenditures.

The second major difference between the superpowers flows from the first. There is a great disparity in the importance each attaches to its relationship with the other. Both the United States and the Soviet Union, judged by their recent histories, their problems, and their rhetoric, are in decline, but, just as they were never equal in power or reach during the brief "American Century," their declines differ from each other sharply. The word "superpower" has always had a hyperbolic ring to it, as if large stockpiles of nuclear weapons could be translated into world hegemony. The history of the last forty-five years suggests that this was never the case—not even when the United States had a monopoly on nuclear weapons, for those were the years of Soviet expansion in Eastern Europe and maximum Soviet influence in Western Europe. As the weapons stockpiles of the superpowers mounted, both the United States and the Soviet Union lost much of the extraordinary power they had briefly wielded over their allies and clients. The phenomenal influence that the United States exerted all over the world in the early postwar years was due primarily to its undamaged economy, its reputation as a successful democracy, its brilliantly conceived foreign-assistance programs in Europe, its economic dynamism and political stability, and, most important, the unique circumstances of that historic moment. The United States was the *only* nation with a global vision and the economic and military means to bring it into being. The Soviet Union under Stalin had to content itself with the consolidation of its dominion over Eastern Europe.

Under Khrushchev, the Soviet Union sought recognition as a superpower through boasts, threats, and promises. It also discovered the Third World, which Stalin had largely dismissed, and the worldwide battles for decolonization and independence became the arena for United States–Soviet confrontations. Under Brezhnev, the Soviet Union asserted a "parity" built upon a large increase of nuclear missiles and an unprecedented investment in an oceangoing Navy. The Politburo tried to dramatize its new status by actively aiding struggling revolutionary movements around the world, fourteen of which came to power in the latter half of the nineteen-seventies.

A central feature of Gorbachev's "new thinking" is that the Soviet

Union is not a "superpower," either in the sense that it can afford to install, buy, or prop up governments around the world or in the sense that it has the resources to maintain military and naval forces with a global reach. Numerous articles in Soviet journals and statements of Soviet diplomats and academics make the point that supporting regimes and revolutionary movements is expensive, that client governments not only drain resources needed in the domestic economy but contribute little to Soviet power or prestige. Gorbachev knows that he must alter the relationship with the United States if he is to break free of failed Cold War policies. Unless the United States cooperates, he cannot cut the military budget below a certain figure or stabilize a more heterogeneous and independent Eastern Europe—a state of affairs he has done much to encourage. Nor can he court the Federal Republic of Germany without creating dangerous tensions. Above all, the United States, as President Bush noted last May, holds the Soviet Union's ticket of admission to the "community of nations," symbolized by membership in the General Agreement on Tariffs and Trade (GATT), the World Bank, and the International Monetary Fund.

The leaders of the United States, on the other hand, see the Cold War with the Soviet Union, despite its risks and costs, as a success on many levels. For the West, the Cold War years have been a period of phenomenal growth, prosperity, and commanding power. The Cold War prism has served to simplify and explain world events, to set limits on undesired domestic social spending—especially in the nineteen-eighties— and to shift the domestic political consensus to the right. The preoccupation with the United States–Soviet relationship has provided the justification for investing in the arms race rather than in the solution of urgent global economic and ecological problems—the latter a course that involves hard decisions and prickly dealings with banks, industry, and foreign governments. Serious attention to the world-debt crisis has been little and late. During the nineteen-eighties, more dollars have been sucked from poor countries through interest payments and flights of capital than have flowed into them. Despite all the infusions by private investors, the International Monetary Fund, and the World Bank, and from various national aid programs, the world has been witnessing a Marshall Plan in reverse.

Other critical "north–south problems," relating to trade and development, were swept from the agenda in the Reagan years. The accumulating hazards to the earth's atmosphere which threaten the continuation of human life itself were given the barest fraction of White House attention, which was reserved for Soviet missile production and tank maneuvers. Even as aging military alliances have crumbled and economic competition has intensified, little has actually been done to restructure relationships within the industrial world or to address in a fundamental way either the transformation of United States–European relations or the worsening of United States–Japanese relations or the crisis of under-development. Instead, progress is asserted in upbeat communiqués after largely inconclusive high-level meetings. The Soviet Union is showing a new interest in using the United Nations as an instrument of diplomacy, rather than just a propaganda forum, but the United States, after a decade and a half of U.N.-bashing, has yet to design a strategy for developing international organizations as practical vehicles of cooperation in a radically new world, where global institutions are indispensable.

In the 1980 election campaign, Ronald Reagan attacked Jimmy Carter for being obsessed with vague notions of world order and environmental concerns to the neglect of the real security threat from the Soviet Union. For eight years, he made the United States–Soviet relationship once again the centerpiece of United States foreign policy. But in truth the mounting economic and social problems faced by the United States in the nineteen-eighties have had almost nothing to do with the Soviet Union, except for the crushing costs of the arms race.

The Soviet Union continues to serve the United States as the organizing principle of world politics, while Gorbachev is trying with almost frantic haste to fashion a strategy that does not depend so heavily on the bilateral relationship with the United States. But he realizes that he must alter the relationship with the United States in order to escape the grip of military spending and to be able to divert capital to invigorate the Soviet economy. The United States feels no similar need for escape. The idea of a "peace dividend" is popular. But the proposition that the national security requires a vast shift in spending priorities is still a minority position in both political parties, even though polls show that the American people rank the Soviet Union far down in the list of national-security threats. (Drugs, the economic future, Japan, and environmental disaster are viewed with greater concern.) Despite the American military-budget cuts in the offing, the Soviet adversary continues to serve as the prime rationale for keeping the present national-security arrangements intact.

A post-Cold War military budget based on a fundamental reassessment of the threats facing the United States and on what the military forces can and cannot do to reduce those threats is needed. If war in Europe is no longer plausible, if Europe can once again take primary responsibility for its own defense, and if the Cold War rationale for unilateral United States military intervention in the Third World is gone, it should be possible to make major shifts in strategic thinking. And those shifts should yield substantial amounts of money and energy for reinvestment in American society. A shift in resources to invigorate education and to encourage the restructuring of American industry would make a crucial difference to the United States in facing increasingly tough commercial competition from Europe and Japan. But a significant transfer of resources from military production to nonmilitary purposes requires a national policy on industrial conversion. Without such a policy, communities, corporations, workers, scientists, engineers, and millions of other Americans who are dependent, directly or indirectly, on Cold War spending will oppose a massive change in spending priorities and end up as a powerful constituency in favor of continuing Cold War priorities—even if at somewhat reduced levels. Conversion of industrial, technological, and educational institutions from military to civilian pursuits is not an insurmountable task, as the experience immediately after the Second World War reminds us. But the problem is harder than it was then, because now the American people are not starved for more consumer goods. The major shift of resources to post–Cold War purposes requires more interventionist federal policies than the Bush Administration would welcome.

As old enemies are transformed, new enemies float into view. National-security bureaucrats, no less than generals, tend to prepare for the last war, and so it is not surprising that they view the post–Cold War world through the Cold War prism. Old assumptions, old war plans, and old force structures remain essentially undisturbed as politicians and strategists around the globe turn their attention to new threats. Welcome though the peaceful rhetoric emanating from so many world leaders may be, peace is not yet breaking out.

There have been, to be sure, a series of ceasefire agreements on a number of battlefields across the world. Major military engagements in Asia, Africa, and the Middle East have ended or are winding down. Yet for millions of people around the world there is no peace. More than twenty wars still rage across the planet. The economic and paramilitary war against the Sandinistas in Nicaragua continues even as the Contras have been pensioned. The carefully cultivated myths of moderation and democracy have lapsed in El Salvador, and violence and repression are escalating in that brutalized country. Peru is dissolving, partly under the attacks of the Shining Path guerrilla movement. The Philippines are the locale of another protracted war, with increasing involvement by the United States.

Leading military officers argue that the major challenges to the armed forces of the United States in the coming century are revolutionary strife, random violence, nuclear terrorism, and drug-running—all of them primarily in the Third World, which has been the only actual theatre of combat over the last forty years. As the Cold War mold breaks, nations, tribes, and religious sects take up centuries-old battles once more, free at last to be full participants in their own histories. And as these newly emerging or reemerging forces in world politics jockey for position, jump at new opportunities, and rethink their security needs, the world as it is seen from Washington and Moscow in some ways looks more dangerous: high-technology weaponry is being distributed at an ever faster pace as more and more nations seek to profit from the arms trade, and nuclear proliferation, an issue that has been largely ignored over the last twenty years, is now a reality. With the shadow of nuclear weapons hovering over the conflicts of the Middle East, the Indian subcontinent, and Southern Africa, the case for increasing deterrent forces, covert operations, and actual military intervention can be made to sound plausible in the absence of more sensible approaches. Military forces are being drawn into "the war on drugs," and "narcoterrorists" are replacing the Marxist variety. Both the United States and the Soviet Union are well aware that political struggles in faraway places can be contagious. The rise of Islamic consciousness in the Middle East has contributed to the unrest in the Muslim republics of the U.S.S.R. War and brutality in Indo-China, the regional war in Central America, and the deepening crisis in Mexico have triggered a huge migration, which has already transformed the demography of the United States and will have a steadily increasing impact on its politics and its culture.

In the nineteen-eighties, the United States stepped up its military intervention in the Third World. It introduced the concept of "low-intensity conflict"—a global approach to what war planners call "ambiguous" military activities in the Third World, which range from drug-running to revolutionary guerrilla wars. "Low-intensity conflict" is a curiously callous description of what is a most intense experience for those caught in the cross fire—fifty thousand of whom have been killed in Nicaragua over the last dozen years, and more than seventy thousand in El Salvador. "Ambiguous warfare has exposed a chink in our armor," Secretary of State George Shultz declared at the National Defense University in 1986. Low-intensity conflict borrows heavily from the counterinsurgency doctrines of the early Vietnam War era. Conflict is protracted. The hope is not quick victory but the avoidance of defeat through wars of attrition. Defeat means either that undesirable—usually leftist—guerrillas come to power or, if they are already in power, that they succeed in establishing a viable government. Low-intensity conflict is fought with political, economic, and cultural weapons as well as specially designed military technology.

In the plans developed by the Reagan Administration for fighting low-intensity conflicts, there were two critical new elements, and they have achieved certain successes. The first has been the "covert" but highly publicized support of insurgents against target governments designated "Marxist-Leninist." Thus, the supplying of Stinger missiles to the Mujahideen in Afghanistan raised the cost of Soviet intervention and helped persuade the Soviet Union to withdraw its troops. As the late C.I.A. director William Casey put it, "whereas in the nineteen-sixties and nineteen-seventies anti-western causes attracted recruits throughout the third world, this decade has emerged as the decade of freedom fighters resisting communist regimes."

The second innovation of the Reagan years was "public diplomacy"—greatly increased attention to the mobilization of domestic support for foreign intervention. The mobilization was carried out by using on the American people sophisticated propaganda techniques that had hitherto been reserved for foreign countries. United States public opinion continues to oppose a military operation of the size and duration needed to overthrow the government of Nicaragua, and no evidence has come to light that the Reagan Administration ever intended to undertake such an operation, for the opposition of the Joint Chiefs of Staff was implacable. But the American people acquiesced in a large-scale war of harassment, which continues to this day.

The end of the Cold War offers a unique moment for rethinking the meaning of national security in the light of two closely related historic developments. One is the growing global consciousness that nonmilitary concerns now affect the freedom, well-being, and physical safety of people more profoundly and more dramatically than any military development in any nation. The threat to human life posed by man's destruction of the environment far surpasses any threat posed by increases in the weapons stockpiles. For inner-city Americans and suburban families, the narcotics economy poses an immediate threat to physical security for which no adequate system of deterrence, let alone defense, exists. It is increasingly evident that this nation's future is more imperilled by its own improvident economic decisions, by its permissiveness with respect to environmental destruction, and by its neglect of health and education than by the warmaking power of any other nations.

The second development is the transformation of consciousness about war. Since the early years of the century, a long process of rethinking has been under way about the uses of military power to advance national political and economic interests. Gorbachev's "new thinking" is grounded in some of the obvious lessons of the twentieth century. The First World War nearly obliterated the distinction between victor and vanquished; Britain and France suffered such grievous casualties and economic costs that they could sustain neither their empires nor stable economies and robust democracies at home. The Second World War made it clear that high-technology "conventional warfare," however noble the cause, could not be repeated without reducing whole continents to rubble. It was immediately apparent that the atomic bomb was not a weapon in the strict sense, because it could be effectively used only by *not* using it. Today, there is a growing consensus that a large-scale nuclear war would destroy all that was to be defended. Even smaller wars produce few triumphs. The long, bitter war between Iran and Iraq exacted a heavy price from both societies and resulted in victory for neither. The United States, despite its huge investment in the military, has not had a clear-cut tactical victory since General Douglas

MacArthur's triumphant landing at Inchon in the summer of 1950, during the Korean War, and, that victory notwithstanding, the war ended in stalemate. The pressures of public opinion now exact political costs on adventurous, desperate leaders, even in the Soviet Union. The anger and disillusionment of Soviet citizens over the Afghanistan invasion was a significant factor in Gorbachev's decision to end it. In the Reagan Administration, the Secretary of Defense, speaking for the uniformed military, proclaimed the "Weinberger Doctrine": the armed forces will not willingly fight wars that the political leaders cannot induce the American people to support. Since Americans quickly sour on wars, even when they are successful, the doctrine is a recognition that public opinion now sets real limits on United States military operations.

But, as the United States' Panama operation last month shows, war has not become obsolete. All that can be said is that the nature, the function, and the scope of war have radically changed. The only politically successful wars are limited operations, short in duration, against small and weak nations. Britain's war for the Falkland Islands and the United States invasion of Grenada are prime examples. Politicians are still tempted to use a splendid little war as a piece of political theatre, provided the risks appear minor. Whenever public frustration runs high about a challenge to public order and individual security, as in the case of terrorism or drug-running, there is a strong temptation to find a military solution. The involvement of the United States military in the "war on drugs" is increasing, even though there is no prospect of victory.

Even as the utility of fighting wars has sharply declined, the political and economic advantages of preparing for them are widely perceived to have risen. Military budgets have themselves become weapons. Members of the Bush Administration believe that Ronald Reagan's decision to challenge the Soviets to a spending race helped stimulate Gorbachev's new thinking. It may have been a factor, but the crises of political legitimacy at home and diplomatic isolation abroad were the prime considerations. Under those pressures, the Soviet élite were forced to reassess what their expensive military buildup was buying them.

Today, the most compelling arguments for military spending are psychological. The advantageous impact that such spending will have on adversaries, allies, and clients is simply asserted, since it can be neither reliably predicted nor proved. As the future wars in the voluminous Pentagon contingency plans come to look increasingly unlikely and unwinnable, and the political dividends of protracted low-intensity conflicts appear more and more problematical, the maintenance of large, mobile military establishments and the production, stockpiling, and deployment of advanced weapons will be justified on the ground that they deter (or encourage) a wide variety of political behavior.

The degree and kind of military power required to protect United States security in this world of new and decentralized threats is not easily measured. Such old benchmarks as the missile tally and the conventional-arms "balance" seem beside the point. Unlike old-fashioned strategies for fighting wars, the new strategies for deterring conflicts and challenges are seldom put to the test. Victory is easily proclaimed whenever the fearful contingencies in the war plans do not materialize. The irrelevance of the forces to most of the wars, violence, dissolutions of nations, and acts of terrorism that do occur is not a matter for discussion.

There are, to be sure, certain short-term economic and political interests to be served by the production of weapons and the maintenance of large military forces. As every nation becomes more and more integrated into the world economy and hence more dependent on exports, many feel increasing pressure to participate in the global arms trade to earn hard currency. The Soviet Union, for example, which was the world's largest supplier of arms in 1987, the most recent year for which figures are available, is reexamining the *political* benefits of spreading high-technology arms around the planet, but the *economic* pressures to export weapons to finance needed imports of civilian technology are stronger than ever.

While some national-security thinkers triumphantly proclaim the impending death of Communism as America's supreme Cold War victory, a better case can be made that the real winners in this long struggle are the defeated enemies of the Second World War, Germany and Japan. Both contestants in the superpower arms race have been losers. After spending more than four trillion dollars on its global security system, the United States is much less secure and much less in command than it was in 1945. The most serious national-security problems facing the country are economic, and the source of the problems is capitalist nations, not the Communist world. Like the Soviet Union but unlike Japan and Germany, the United States has systematically sacrificed economic strength to the accumulation and projection of military power. In the process, the sinews of nationhood have become frayed. Neither the neglected education system of the United States nor the country's weakened industrial base can support the global role to which our national-security élites have aspired. However, Germany and Japan, thanks in large part to their catastrophic experience in the Second World War, and the disarmament imposed upon them at its end, have built their recovery on economic power and subtle diplomacy rather than on military aspirations. Both now have impressive military establishments, more than capable of deterring any plausible military threat, but their growing influence in the world rests on an understanding of technological development, a skill in managing the character and pace of the integration of their economies into the world economy, and a discipline in husbanding resources for long-term investment which surpasses anything demonstrated in recent years by the United States.

Ironically, Japan and, to a lesser extent, the Federal Republic of Germany have become formidable economic competitors by willingly taking the path to which the early postwar leaders of the United States beckoned them. Both have denounced their militarist pasts and have become successful trading nations. The irony is a source of bitterness. The Japanese feel victimized when they catch glimpses of Japan-bashing in the United States. They are delivering a blunt message, in words that have lost some of the tact for which their nation is famous: "You made the rules. We did as you wished. What right do you have to be angry that we are beating you at your own game?" But people in the United States feel victimized as well. "We rebuilt your country," they say. "We fed you at the end of the war more generously than we did the surrounding peoples of Asia, whom you ravaged. For forty years we have defended you, and in the process of fighting in Korea and Indo-China in behalf of the free world to which we have admitted you, we made you rich." Japan was the staging area in both wars, and the huge inflow of dollars was an important contributor to the Japanese economic miracle. "We sacrificed our own economy to carry your defense burden, and you repaid us by closing your markets to us and by creating Japan, Inc., an ingenious capitalist mutation that turns the huge Japanese trading corporations into weapons of economic warfare."

The end of the Cold War greatly increases the risks of serious confrontation between the United States and its Pacific ally. The two nations are locked in a potentially dangerous embrace: each is now extremely dependent on the other. The United States market is crucial for Japan, and the United States finances its government deficit in significant part with Japanese capital. This sort of interdependence does not augur good relations. To resolve the growing economic confrontation requires major changes in cultural habits in both countries. The United States needs to husband resources for tomorrow, and Japan is under growing pressure to raise consumption levels today.

Both societies are beset by problems of national identity as each finds itself increasingly integrated into a world system that is new and in many ways mysterious. The very concept of nationhood is changing radically, and the confused response is nationalist nostalgia. The manifest revival of nationalism in both societies is evidenced in a variety of ways, but none is more disconcerting than the reappearance in Japan of militaristic textbooks that gloss over Japanese responsibility for the war in Asia. The United States has recently been caught up in flag hysteria, the trampling of cloth calling forth more passions than can be aroused by the trampling of lives.

United States–Japanese relations are at a turning point. The United States has overemphasized the military relationship with Japan and underestimated the seriousness of the economic and technological competition. Japan plays a critical role in United States plans for fighting a future war in the Pacific against the Soviet Union. For years, the United States has been urging Japan to shoulder more of the "burden" of defense, on the ground that it was unfair for Japan to use its "free ride" under the nuclear umbrella to surge ahead of the United States in the competition over exports and finance. The world awoke not so long ago to the realization that Japan, long famous in the West for producing junk, had become the master of advanced technology, and now the Japanese are handing the world another surprise: not only is Japan the third largest military power in the world, as measured by military budget, but it has become evident in recent years that Japan's edge in such civilian technologies as semiconductors, data processing, and tele-communications has important military implications. Even as United States–Japanese economic friction has intensified over the past decade, the United States has grown more dependent on access to Japanese technology for military purposes. Former Secretary of Defense Harold Brown has predicted that Japanese achievements in high-temperature ceramics could be "the stepping stone to a Japanese lead in military aircraft engine design and development." In 1987, the Reagan Administration blocked the Japanese computer firm Fujitsu from acquiring Fairchild Semiconductor, a firm that produces both nuclear-missile components and superconductors, on the ground of national security.

The Japanese are in a position to be major players in the high-technology-arms trade. The only restraints are the vestiges of the political culture imposed upon the Japanese under General MacArthur's "peace constitution." For more than thirty years, American leaders have been pushing the Japanese to play a larger military role, and, with United States encouragement, the Japanese government has been chipping away at the spirit of the postwar constitution. Japan's impatience at not having a political role commensurate with its economic might appears to be increasing along with its historic feelings of vulnerability and isolation.

In the United States, verbal attacks on Japan make good politics. In Japan, America-bashing is at least as popular, especially after clips of United States congressmen taking sledgehammers to a Toshiba cassette player were relentlessly rerun on Japanese television. "While one can always find an American voice of reason to counter every act of Japan-bashing in Washington," the Washington correspondent for the Japan *Times* Ayako Doi writes, "it is hard to find a Japanese who would publicly counter America-bashing in Japan." The new focus on the United States–Japanese relationship is feeding hostility in both countries, because the problems underlying the relationship are not being adequately addressed. A prominent United States business leader, a Democrat of liberal persuasion, recently observed that the United States could not afford to take Gorbachev up on his offer to demilitarize the Pacific, because it would mean abandoning the region to the Japanese. Some public-opinion polls already show that popular sentiment in the United States is more concerned with the economic threat posed by Japan than with the military threat posed by the Soviet Union.

There is a danger that the United States and Japan will slip into a new sort of Cold War. The original Cold War was a global ideological and geopolitical contest with a powerful emotional appeal, but, for all the thundering rhetoric that has continued ever since, the great issues that gave rise to the Cold War were settled by the late nineteen-forties, and the de-facto division of Europe was accepted by both the United States and the Soviet Union. All during that period, despite two Asian wars and frightening moments like the Cuban missile crisis and the crises over Berlin, the Cold War was remote from the day-to-day experience of most Americans. The wars in Korea and Indo-China and the back-alley duels of the rival intelligence agencies were fought in the name of that great crusade, but the wars were unpopular in the United States and the duels were largely unknown. (Curiously, the high point of United States–Soviet relations before Gorbachev was 1974, when Soviet arms were pouring into Vietnam to assure the final defeat of the United States in Indo-China.) The bilateral disputes between the United States and the Soviet Union were trivial. The Cold War rested on the implicit premise that there were no life-or-death issues dividing the superpowers, and thus each could take its victories and defeats in stride. For the overwhelming majority of the American people, the Cold War was a spectator's contest that generated jobs and money but required little sacrifice. On the other hand, the economic, technological, and psychological issues dividing the United States and Japan and—depending on what happens in the next few years—dividing the United States and Europe, too, affect the fundamental development strategies of the advanced industrial nations. These disputes could well touch the populations of the contending nations more deeply than the Cold War did because settling them, or even managing them, might require painful domestic changes. The current drift in United States–Japanese relations is dangerous.

Despite these shadows, the possibilities for making hopeful changes in the international system are greater than they have been at any time since 1945. The Soviet Union under Gorbachev appears eager to call off the ideological Holy War. The common security concerns of all humanity, and not class struggle, are the moving force of history, the Soviet President says. The Soviet Union has announced a freeze on aid to Cuba and a cutoff in military aid to Nicaragua, and Gorbachev is signalling in many other ways that he intends to fulfill his "internationalist duty" by promoting cooperation rather than conflict. As yet, the United States has shown no interest in shifting to a less ideological policy in Latin

America. There has been no suggestion that either a non-Communist Eastern Europe or an end to Soviet support for guerrilla movements would be met by a non-interventionist policy in Washington. The United States continues a contradictory policy in El Salvador, supporting political compromise in theory while supplying hundreds of millions of dollars in arms to a right-wing government that came to power threatening "total war" and is now seeking a military victory over the guerrillas using American high-technology weapons to bomb and strafe civilian neighborhoods. The United States is openly intervening in the forthcoming Nicaraguan elections: the President received the opposition candidate at the White House, and everyone assumes that American money is flowing freely in Nicaragua to defeat the Sandinistas at the polls.

The muting of the Holy War offers a historic opportunity for curbing the numbers and mitigating the destructiveness of wars in the Third World, which have so often been encouraged and supplied by both the United States and the Soviet Union. The primary rationale for the United States policy of engaging in counter-guerrilla warfare has been that the fall of governments to "Marxism-Leninism" strengthens the hand of the Soviet Union as a global power. It would be difficult to see how Nicaragua, a desperately poor country of under four million people, could otherwise pose a threat to the United States, however it organized its economy and whatever rhetoric it chose to adopt. The arguments for military interventions will now be harder to make, but this in itself does not mean that they will cease. There can be no real development in poor countries, however, until the superpowers stop using them as Cold War battlefields. Beleaguered landowners in Central America who face armed political movements for redistribution and social justice have a strong interest in keeping the Cold War going, for United States aid offers them their only chance of survival, but the real interest of the United States is to negotiate an end to the warfare that is reducing a neighboring region to a shambles.

The idea that human progress can be achieved by ideological warfare is a dangerous reactionary notion. Perhaps more than any other factor, the dogmatic faith that military power can be used to fight, defend, or establish ideas created the conditions under which nuclear war could actually happen. (It is difficult to explain the 1962 Cuban missile crisis in any other terms.) All over Latin America, political élites, having experimented with socialism, military dictatorship, and faltering efforts to reestablish viable democracies, are deeply pessimistic about their societies' ever evolving into stable political communities under any of the old formulas. The realization that the nostrums of both the right and the left work badly leads, on the one hand, to extremist movements such as the Shining Path, in Peru, and, on the other, to a strong desire for compromise, pragmatism, and moderation. Of all the nations of the hemisphere, Cuba and the United States seem the most inextricably caught in the time warp of the Cold War.

It is ironic and disturbing that as the Soviet Union mutes the cries of ideological warfare and tries to come to terms with the failures of socialism, the United States finds itself in a complacent—even congratulatory—mood. (That the United States ever felt deeply threatened by revolutionary ideology and experiments in the Soviet Union and other underdeveloped countries reflected a failure of confidence rather than a realistic assessment of the competition.) There is in fact no ideological victory to celebrate. The revival of unfettered free enterprise in Great Britain and the United States seems to have run its course, and the pressures to deal with the wreckage of the new capitalist prosperity— the ravaging of the environment; the abuse, waste, and neglect of what we now call human resources, principally our children; the potentially explosive increase in inequality—will eventually force another swing of the pendulum in market economies. The influence and leadership of the United States are measured not by Soviet failure but by American success.

The Cold War was about many things, but, despite the extravagant claims on both sides, it was never "a clash of two systems." Both United States-style "capitalism" and Soviet-style "socialism" are the legacies of nineteenth-century dogmas, and both are in continuous, profound transformation. The differences between "capitalism" in Japan and "capitalism" in the United States are as significant as the similarities. For the past forty years, there has been only one "system" that has expanded throughout the world, not two. (The Soviet Union was unable to permanently impose its "system" even on Eastern Europe, despite military occupation.) That system is the product of a process of global integration which exerts unrelenting pressure on every country. The product of a series of mutations in early-twentieth-century capitalism, it is fuelled by profits and the accumulation of private property. But it borrows heavily from socialism—indeed, from one of its most discredited features, which is to say, highly centralized planning by anonymous bureaucrats. The bureaucrats are servants of global corporations and banks, which by convention we call "private," and of international financial institutions such as the World Bank and the International Monetary Fund, which we call "public." These planners operate largely beyond the reach of the electorate in any nation, and mostly out of the public view.

This system is not controlled by the United States, and indeed the United States finds its own options narrowed by an increasingly integrated world economy, over which it exercises less and less control. Everywhere on the planet, the same twin processes appear to be at work—rapid economic integration accompanied by accelerating social and political disintegration. For some farmers, workers, regions, and city blocks all around the world, there is unparalleled prosperity, and for many others there is crushing poverty. This growing disparity at every level—neighborhoods, cities, continents—is promoting the dissolution of political communities, and especially of nation-states.

These same processes of change—what the economist Joseph Schumpeter called "a gale of creative destruction"—are also at work in developed countries, including the United States, where the gap between rich and poor, between cities or regions with a future and those with memories of a once prosperous past, has widened dramatically in the nineteen-eighties. It was such wrenching effects of technological and economic change that gave rise to the political, economic, and spiritual impulses out of which socialism was born. Running nations by dictatorship, whether of the left or the right, offers no way out of poverty, but the yearning for a decent society in which people can build communities without gross exploitation, without worshipping money and defiling nature, and without creating walls between a few rich and many poor is as powerful a human impulse as it ever was. Nineteenth- and early-twentieth-century road maps to the good society, however, are not much help.

The highly publicized failures of socialism in underdeveloped countries and the extraordinary prosperity within the United States in recent years make the idea of an American *perestroika* seem preposterous. Yet the United States is squandering capital to maintain an ephemeral prosperity that is politically unstable, because it is based on increasing inequality. Consider the cumulative consequences of these conditions, which the United States finds itself facing: a unique dependence on foreign financing of its debt; the paucity of long-term investment in industrial production, the modernization of services, or public infrastructure; the lack of a coherent policy on technological development, which puts the country at a serious competitive disadvantage; a frenzied, "get rich quick" economy, in the grip of takeovers, leveraged buyouts, and other manifestations of what Keynes called the "casino" economy; the descent into poverty of almost a fifth of the nation's children; the growing disparity between cities and regions with rising prospects and the large areas of the nation that are being abandoned by both government and industry; and a seeming inability to reduce significantly a military establishment much of which is increasingly irrelevant to real security needs. Still used to thinking of ourselves as "the No. 1 nation," as President Lyndon Johnson did twenty-two years ago, the people of the United States have actually fallen behind the people in other leading industrial countries with respect to maternal health, literacy, infant mortality, drug dependence, and education. We are five per cent of the world's population, and it appears that we consume more than half the hard drugs on the global market. By these crucial measures, the security of the United States is eroding.

A truce in the ideological war between mythic systems may now make it possible to redirect energy from crusades and propaganda wars to the resolution of urgent problems. Instead of mindless attacks on "government"—the rhetoric of Thatcherism and Reaganism—it may now be possible to ask, What are the proper functions of the nation-state in the world waiting to be born, and how can they be performed most efficiently and humanely? Instead of celebrating "the market," it may now be possible to ask how it could be made to work better in the service of social goals, and what should be done when it does not work. Instead of talking about "incentives" as if they were a sort of miracle drug, we may be able to look at how incentives actually operate under our system, and to strengthen those that produce desirable results, and seek to change those that produce perverse results.

A global understanding of national security is now essential, for the United States is organically connected to societies across the planet which are in a position to export considerable misery to our shores. In the nineteen-nineties, the revenge of the poor, unintended though it may be, is likely to be far more devastating than either the fiery rhetoric of the guerrilla movements of the nineteen-sixties or the challenge of the abortive oil cartel of the nineteen-seventies. Communist regimes export refugees, but military dictatorship, poverty, and war in Central America have been responsible for many more immigrants into the United States, most of them unwelcome. The effects of the worldwide boom in the narcotics industry, the spread of ozone-depleting agriculture, and the public-health crises in distant, poor countries cannot be kept from American shores by military means or, it seems, by any other—except the building of stable economies and a more equitable social order within those societies.

During the decades of the Cold War, domestic political, economic, and technological decisions made by the United States have had such an impact on other countries that foreign leaders sometimes facetiously suggest that they should have a vote in United States elections. Now it is becoming clear that the choices of underdeveloped countries can have a profound impact on life in the United States. Brazil's decisions on the rain forest affect the air quality in Chicago. Public-health policies in Zaire may have been responsible for the most serious epidemic in the history of the United States. The real security problems are global in character, and the solutions are global.

The long joust we call the Cold War no longer serves the interest of either the United States or the Soviet Union. But both societies have organized themselves on the basis of the Cold War and remain heavily dependent on the mind-set and the structures of the Cold War—large military forces, espionage, secrecy, and military production. The institutions of the Cold War will survive the normalization of relations between the United States and the Soviet Union and will set limits on the process

unless the transformation of domestic institutions in both countries becomes the central focus of the process. The great challenge of the next
decades is to make the domestic institutions of nations reflect the political, economic, and ecological realities of the post–Cold War world.

30

The End of America's Postwar Ethos

MICHAEL VLAHOS

I

National security policies reflect the culture of the society creating them.
Each society's forms of war and politics express its unique culture. The
United States has taken this truth as its own. From the beginning this
nation imposed upon itself a self-conscious identity distinct from the
European world. It was a New World torn from the Old. Americans
continue to seek to strengthen our self-described uniqueness, and our
national security policy has always been asked to reinforce our identity.

More than other modern societies, America relies, even depends, on
myth to cement its confidence in current policies. Americans are profoundly ahistorical; we do not share a coherent sense of our own history
in formal, academic terms. Popular culture, not an educational system,
shapes our common sense of identity.

Our national myths are not tall tales, nor are they untruths, but they
are both representations of identity and the actual instrument of acculturation. Myths give each of us our sense of belonging, our actual membership as Americans. This process of acculturation through myth,
moreover, is achieved through what many believe is simply entertainment: television and movies. Even the way in which we choose to represent ourselves is uniquely American, however chaotic and random in
appearance.

It is nonetheless extremely effective. The American ethos is no less
entrenched for its lack of a formalized historical-literary tradition sternly
taught in state schools. The imagery of American myth, one might ar-

Reprinted by permission of *Foreign Affairs*, Summer 1988. Copyright 1988 by the Council
on Foreign Relations, Inc.

Note: It is a violation of the law to reproduce this selection by any means whatsoever
without the written permission of the copyright holder.

gue, is actually more passionate and more powerful given its screen presentation. The problem for Americans is the translation of inchoate images of self into a coherent mental concert for the development of foreign and national security policies. The culture of a society—its ethos—defines distinctive patterns of individual and group behavior. Culture shapes the way we look at the world. Whatever our immediate group membership, our final sense of identity is shaped by larger cultural patterns.

If we define ourselves according to myth, what kind of worldview has it given us?

First, at the core, Americans share an essentially religious value system. The primal myth of our origin is that of the "Pilgrim's Progress," with the Plymouth Colony completely overshadowing Virginia and its lineal transplanting of British class and caste. We believe that the source and inspiration of America is bound up in religion: religious freedom, but also the moral vantage of Calvin. The impact of Protestant thought is felt in the ways we talk about mission, service, sacrifice, restraint. It underlies the sense that Americans share of serving a higher calling. This underpinning remains dominant today even though it is highly secularized, and transmuted into legal, constitutional language.

Second, Americans still hew, if unconsciously, to the symbolism of a New World. This symbolism has given rise to a set of specific myths about the United States. One of these is that America is the source of human progress and can achieve perfection as a society. The sense that we strive to create "a more perfect union" is embedded in our policy-making.

Americans believe that there has never been a society quite like our own. This American "exceptionalism" suggests that we are a people graced with unusual natural endowments. We think of ourselves literally as a "people of plenty." But our mythology also reminds us that this land was a great "untamed wilderness," a "land of savagery." It was the exceptional will, unity and vision of the American people and their beliefs that transformed the landscape. The twin icons of national bounty and national achievement have inspired two senses of an American national purpose: a conviction that the United States should serve as an example to the world, that America and its people are the model for all human development; and an impulse to change the world for good, to become the active agency of human progress. Tyranny and resistance to change are so entrenched in the world that only direct American intercession can shift the direction of history. America's gifts demand that it assume a missionary role.

But there are two tendencies. Does this nation exist as a model to a corrupted world, where existence is contingent on separation? Or does our existence demand engagement, so that a corrupted world ultimately may be reformed? Engagement risks mirroring that from which we fled.

The hazard is that in reforming evil we will inevitably, naturally incline toward its forms of subjugation—war and tyranny—even if pursued for good. But aloofness implies its own corruption, encouraging evil by celebrating detachment from the very fledgling movements America's existence hopes to inspire.

Our national irony is that both strands must coexist and even be woven together politically for this nation to remain uncorrupted. There is an American mission, and it is composed of two apparently contradictory parts. It must preserve itself from the world at the same time it proselytizes to that world. Even the earliest American immigrants knew that there was no escape, that by leaving Europe they must eventually return, that there could be no reconciliation between good and evil belief systems. After two world wars, Americans remain united around this recognition.

In functional terms there are only two identifiable American political groups. One seeks to preserve the purity of the American ethos, to keep our society unsullied, a more perfect model. At the other extreme is a broad group committed to the progress of world reform. Between the two is the political center, always shifting in emphasis, attempting to balance both interpretations of national purpose as they are translated into policy.

The most important thing to understand is that this basic split in American politics is not linked to party affiliation. Both major parties historically have had to balance "purifiers" and "progressives."

II

Purifiers and progressives, however, share a set of assumptions about the outside world that binds them together as Americans. These assumptions—a set of cultural theses—emerged from core national myths and were shaped at the beginning, as America struggled to free itself from Europe. Even today, many of the images we paste onto the wider world were cut in the eighteenth century.

A basic thesis was the rejection of the European concept of "grand strategy." Grand strategy was the agenda of monarchs, serving their needs at the expense of their people.

The very execution of a grand strategy implied an exaltation of the power of the state: it required centralized if not absolute state control over society in order to mobilize national energy. The monarch was thus the arbiter of an entire people's energy; he personally calibrated the limits of their capacity for sacrifice. Grand strategy required domestic political servitude.

If the monarch's personal goal was simply the pursuit of power, then it was the merest cynicism to say, for example, that "France aspired to greatness," if such greatness was simply the whim of a single man, and purchased with the blood, treasure and freedom of twenty million Frenchmen. It is understandable that Americans today mistrust the word "realism" in the conduct of foreign policy, where realism is seen as no more than the cynicism of equating state interests to national interests.

The objective of grand strategy itself was also intrinsically corrupting: at home through the enslavement of popular will to the state, and abroad through the enslavement of others in imperial wars. Even if called forth by the collective will of an entire people, the quest for great power status as a norm, an acceptable end in itself, was wrong. It must be remembered that throughout the eighteenth century North America was the imperial battleground par excellence for endless wars in which Indian nations served as the "Third World surrogates" of European kings.

If imperial wars were the rituals of grand strategy, then the professional military castes of Europe were its instruments. This led to an American rejection of the European norm of "professional" or state-controlled military institutions. Professional armies were at best an unaccountable mechanism of royal power over society, encouraging legal absolutism. At worst, they could create the eighteenth-century equivalent of the totalitarian state. The European officer corps was seen as a pylon of an unjust class system. War was also a king's domestic political safety valve, used to channel the energies of the aristocracy while encouraging patriotic allegiance to the commander-in-chief: the state.

Completing the American antipathy to standing armies was the nineteenth-century emergence of the iconography of the Prussian General Staff. A general staff existed to prepare for war, to present the state with the most encouraging and attractive motivation for initiating war.

Taken together, these cultural theses mean that any American engagement must be a "just war" with moral aims. In our history, the Civil War serves as the grand prototype of the "good war." Our twentieth-century world wars were deliberately given the mythic trappings of 1861–65. Each became a just war the moment each became explicitly a war for human freedom. The power of this moral aim was redoubled in the Civil War by the need for full national mobilization in the North to defeat the Confederacy. The aim was elevated and enshrined by the sense that all citizens were fully committed to its attainment.

The totality of war also made the enormous sacrifices required easier to bear. In fact, sacrifice became a positive force after war, the "honored dead" giving inspiration and moral force to those who would shape America's future course. Finally, war was made to remake a world. "Reconstruction" was a necessary part of the process.

War demands cathartic action to justify it. War must celebrate American values and materially advance the American mission. Limited wars do not easily satisfy these needs, especially limited wars on foreign soil. Where America has intervened abroad, such actions have been politically satisfying only to the extent that they perpetuated national myth. In the postwar era, Korea just barely passed popular muster, and Vietnam failed altogether. Our failure in the latter conflict was in many ways a judgment on a leadership that ignored the centrality of the Civil War in national myth.

Both progressives and purifiers accept the legitimacy of the just war, and both interpretive strands have been intertwined through American enlistment in the war-as-moral-crusade, in 1861, 1917 and 1941. Since 1945, however, nuclear arms have negated the only kind of war that could be considered positive in our national ethos: one that is capable of unifying our national identity. Limited war is almost always unacceptable to purifiers, and an uncomfortable choice for progressives.

If military force is to be used it demands a unanimous definition of the national interest. But what are our vital interests? An attack on American citizens abroad has always been one of the few provocations for which military intervention was considered necessary. But purifiers at times have taken exception even to this: the Barbary outrages and today's terrorist assaults are two examples. But when American interests are linked to economic investments or geopolitical "stakes," support for the use of force in their defense is readily likened by critics to the European imperial prototype: American boys are dying to protect a depraved potentate or a banker's profits.

Finally, the whole issue of force and interest returns to the primal question of national purpose. If we must be committed to the world for our own values to survive, then its defense is a necessary risk. If commitment to an imperfect world, however, ends only in the defense of the morally indefensible, then the use of force must sap those values. We do not reform the world; the world succeeds in corrupting us.

Today, the stress between the two visions of American national purpose is greater than at any time since 1939. From the unity forged by world war, we have come to doubt ourselves. A national mission accepted as orthodoxy for a generation—from the late 1940s to the late 1960s—is now in shards. The world has changed, but so have we. It is important to show, in contrast to national myth and historical tradition, how Americans came to construct an essentially progressive mission, how purifiers came to be excluded from that mission, and how, ultimately, the mission foundered. Only then can we discern the state of the American ethos today.

III

The breathtaking experience of global war, where war with unconditional aims seemed to succeed completely, gave us enormous national self-confidence. Not only had the war justified our sacrifice, the completeness of the success made an ambitious national vision seem within reach: true world reform. It was the ultimate progressive mandate, and yet purifiers could embrace it. The Old World was so prostrate that, without the scheming Clemenceaus and Lloyd Georges of 1919, it could pose no threat of corruption. The world was ours, to remake in our image.

Several historical recognitions only reinforced this new tableau of American mission. One was a revision of historical myth. Pearl Harbor seemed a judgment on the isolationist legislation of Congress during the 1930s. After 1945, this assessment was extended. America was not attacked simply because it failed to respond to a threatening world; the very progress of evil, going from strength to strength, was a function of American withdrawal from the world. The United States actually encouraged the path of the dictators by its willful abstention.

America as a model to the world during the 1930s, moreover, now appeared vain, self-serving and farcical. Shackled by Congress, Franklin D. Roosevelt, with his gestures and pleas for peace, looked absurd in retrospect. From the vantage of 1945 our behavior appeared doubly pernicious: it did nothing to preserve world peace, and it made American foreign policy seem a posturing, useful only to stroke our national sense of self-righteousness.

In contrast to the lamentable moral aversion of the 1930s, World War II created a satisfying symbiosis: American moral imperative was indissolubly linked to absolute evil (i.e., Nazi tyranny). In this sense, American involvement was necessary to evil's abolition.

The depth of national emotional commitment was presented as equivalent in moral content to the fight against slavery. And just as the Emancipation Proclamation transformed a war of rebellion into a revolutionary struggle, so the Atlantic Charter, the "Four Freedoms" and the United Nations created for global war the same constitutional imperative. They elevated our passion to one of national crusade.

Our national sacrifice made sense only within the moral embrace of a natural extension of war into peace. World War II existed not merely to end a threat, but to remove the very source of threat. Before America's entry into the war, the pieces had already been put into place: a transformation of the world system was made the ultimate goal. Going into battle, Americans understood that the peace settlement would not hew to Old World tradition. This time, unlike the squabbling at Versailles in 1919, there was to be no balance-of-power solution. The world was not to be remade in favor of great power aggrandizement among the victors. The model of 1815 was to be forever left behind.

This charge ensured that the primary task of the postwar era would be to create a true liberal world order, to do what had been left undone in 1919. In American expectations, this new order was to be evenhanded: the Soviet Union must accept international standards and restraints on its behavior, while the colonial powers, especially Britain and France, must accept decolonization as their post-imperial fate.

IV

Between 1945 and 1950 Americans yielded to the charge of global mission. It began with a gathering sense of failure in transforming victory into peace. The Yalta agreement began to seem a little like appeasement, certainly an arrangement more at ease in the world of 1815 than the new world of 1945. How could the Soviet Union be coopted into a universe of liberal values if we began by bartering for its good behavior with the freedom of whole peoples? The vision of future world stability anchored in U.S.-Soviet cooperation vanished in the confrontation over Germany. The American effort to resolve the new German question was blocked by a Soviet cement-brick wall. Beyond this "diplo-deadlock," the rapacity with which Stalin seized his war spoils shocked even the practitioners of accommodation. His ruthless subversion of Eastern Europe at once evoked the imagery of the late 1930s. Appeasement again had led to aggression and enslavement, but this time the United States was acquiescing to evil directly. How easy it was for us to recreate the masque of the prewar world. Stalin became Hitler: threatening, fomenting, saber-rattling.

It is only understandable that the Munich metaphor returned to those who had held junior positions in 1938. It is also understandable that their response should be "never again." All of the new myths of recent war informed Americans: the fruits of appeasement were war; it was better to stand up for our values earlier than later; evil understood only force; with a broken Europe before us nothing could stop the march of evil but the United States.

The myths were already there, and Stalin was foolish to give them renewed life. He unwittingly forced a fusion of "truths" from the recent past to expectations of the future. History would repeat itself—unless America intervened.

The shock of the Soviet atomic bomb, however, twisted the context of national mission. America's commitment to a liberal world order was unchanged, but the form of mission-as-crusade changed subtly. Nuclear weapons forced an abandonment of the just war as an instrument of reform. If the Soviet Union became the focus of contemporary evil, then it could not be tackled directly. Communist Eurasia could at best be "contained" while the rest of the world, the "free world," together held the line until a true and complete liberal world order could be reestablished. The free world rubric reflected a return to the language of 1942, when F.D.R. used the term "United Nations" to identify not merely the allied coalition, but the legitimacy of a universal world order to come.

Nuclear weapons also changed the style of American strategy and diplomacy, as well as its objectives. Partly in response to nuclear ambiguity, Americans tentatively accepted a partly European approach to great power diplomacy. The early 1950s marked the emergence of a guiding guild of pragmatists who tried to manage America's global commitment in a classical manner, while publicly genuflecting to the rhetoric of a progressive mission. They tended to see the United States as a mature great power, inheriting the mantle of Britain. America indeed took responsibility for the stability of the world system, but it could do so only by tempering its impulse toward moral absolutism.

At first the pragmatists believed that Americans might also be forced to live under a permanent war-mobilization. The West would have to mirror evil's power to contain it successfully. The world of containment and NSC-68 was a dark one, almost Orwellian, where we would live on the edge of apocalypse for a generation, waiting out the Soviets. In this sense the neo-British metaphor hearkened to the 1930s, not the sunny climes of Victoria's stewardship.

Eisenhower tried to leash the trend toward an American mission that would abridge ultimately the very values it sought to defend. Ike sought a "middle way": moderating defense expenditure while promoting a strategic doctrine that would skirt the tar pits of limited war. He recognized the danger that active containment would come to be seen as corrupting our national ethos. But his instrument of cultural moderation appeared immoderate. The "New Look" (NSC-162/2) quickly became "massive retaliation," an apparent prescription for atomic war. It was in any event evanescent, for it could survive politically only as long as it was not tested. As Americans became aware of their vulnerability to atomic attack, their acceptance of the threat of nuclear first use in support of crisis diplomacy became a political taboo.

V

The great postwar consensus was always more fragile than it appeared. It was finally riven over Vietnam. And Vietnam was the centerpiece of the Kennedy Administration, a buoyant reenactment of NSC-68 after eight years of Republican timidity. What Eisenhower had feared, Kennedy embraced. Everything seemed in place in 1961 for a testing of American mission: a resurgent economy, dominance in the nuclear balance and a fine-tuned, conscripted army. In contrast to 1950, the vantage of the new decade was infused with traditional American optimism. A permanent war-economy was unnecessary to contain communism. Americans could have both "guns and butter," and social reform at home would mirror our missionary energies abroad. An unsullied, supremely confident American ethos could go on a progressive offensive.

Vietnam can be seen as a flamboyant failure by the postwar pragmatists to apply their own historical vision. As an elite, they envisaged themselves as latter-day Foreign Office archons, guiding America's way in the world. They were like Palmerston or Grey, modulating world affairs for good, but with realism and restraint. When they came into office they found an emotional allegiance among Americans to a progressive interpretation of national mission. It was this popular support that could be exploited in the pursuit of their strategic theories. The majority of Americans appeared to believe in a rigorous, "symmetrical" application of containment. So be it.

But their war went awry.

Intended as a kind of Yankee affirmation of the British imperial model, Vietnam soon was leashed by deeper native values. At first, the foreign and defense elite prosecuted a "brushfire war" as would Garnet Wolseley or Kitchener, but they did so with a draft army of civilians. The war could not, as in British experience, continue as long as was necessary. There was no tough, professional, all-but-impressed clutch of battle-hardened veteran regiments to battle the Ashanti or Zulu. Americans do not go to war unless it is a revolutionary, liberating, all-embracing struggle for reform. A coldly calculated exercise in great power diplomacy, playing with the lives of American boys, had always been taboo.

Worse, the war trampled upon the old myths of America itself. In Vietnam we were fighting like a corrupted European monarchy, insensitive to the squandered blood of our young men, pursuing objectives defined by a pseudoaristocratic elite. That this war was prosecuted by the party of reform and revolution (in recent mythic terms) and that its members developed the callous theories of "graduated response" and "signaling" only heightened the perception of corruption. The military was fighting the war, but a sinister band of academic and political sorcerers was pulling the strings.

It was the beginning of the end of the postwar world. In the process of defending the free world, the very values cherished by Americans (in contrast to their subjugation elsewhere) were diminished. It was inevitable tragedy to watch Lyndon Johnson (painted as an archetypal American) destroyed by the vanity that he could remain untarnished while aping empire; it was inevitable that we should also await the transmission of that corruption to us. Having essayed an imperial mission, what we did abroad had to come home.

Watergate only seemed to complete the prefigured denouement. It became an equally emotive symbol of America's fall from grace, straight from the vision of our own ancestors. The patterns of an evil foreign policy had in fact clearly permeated the very fabric of American life, and the soul of our political institutions.

Although it was the Democratic pragmatists among the Washington elite who created Vietnam (and their indistinguishable Republican counterparts who extended the metaphor to domestic corruption), it was the progressive mission that suffered. Its calling was crippled. It had failed because Vietnam was presented as an authentic American vision—hardly as an imperial venture—and that vision had gone terribly wrong.

The mission-standard Americans had followed after 1950 was discredited. There was a resurgence of a traditional, even nativist American worldview, for the most part strongly puritanical. Its shamans sought to purge us of our sins, to bring those who had led America astray back to grace. The tide crested in 1972, when the "corrupt" within the Democratic Party were purged. Purifier values had suddenly, strongly reasserted themselves in the definition of American foreign policy.

Ultimately, nativisms of the left and right margins captured the center, and the center ceased to dominate. In foreign policy, Jimmy Carter and Ronald Reagan—both outsiders "running against Washington"—defined an authentic, even parochial sense of American mission, much to the horror of the foreign policy "community."

The pragmatic practitioners of the cold war foundered because they did not recognize the pervasive power of American myths, because they did not understand their own national ethos. They sought to emulate models that American people have characteristically found uncomfortable; worse, they practiced their arts without reference to the will of the people. Current pragmatic practitioners would do well to remember this.

VI

Ironically, Vietnam brought us back more intently to the myth of World War II, to the restatement of the just war, or as Studs Terkel cunningly sensed, *The Good War*, that it represents. By the end of the 1970s Americans could imagine such a war fought only in the strict image of France under Nazi jackboot or Britain under Nazi blitz. But a rerun was conceptually impossible: a Soviet assault implied almost certain nuclear escalation. We would destroy ourselves to save ourselves. Deterrence might work, but there could be no just nuclear war.

The severe restriction of our conception of the just war and of the national interest during the 1970s was reinforced from without by a popular sense of major change in world conditions. This American perception of a changing world was used, however unconsciously, to underscore the traditional revision of national mythos.

First, the image of the enemy was gradually reduced to adversary, then to mere competitor. This process was in part a natural product of the selling of détente. It promised "a generation of peace," in itself a pernicious pledge. Far worse was its implicit revision of the Soviet-American confrontation. If, after an epoch standoff at the brink, old cold warriors could suddenly link arms over champagne, then why the years of nuclear strain?

Through the Strategic Arms Limitation Talks, détente also revived the American purifier tradition of "peace reform." The old equation of peace through arms control and disarmament could be reestablished. The postwar truth of peace through strength then could be dismantled.

Second, world conditions as a whole seemed to have changed. The world system had been transformed again. What in 1945 had been beleaguered democracies were now healthy, powerful economies. Former enemies were now buttresses of the Western alliance. The vast colonial world was now the "developing world," calling itself the "Third World" between East and West.

America was reexamining its commitments to Western Europe and Japan. The dependence of their fat economies upon our defense began to look like usury to many Americans. Why, asked the most inflammatory, should we be saddled by perpetual strategic dependents who seemed intent on making us their economic dependents? Moreover, a young "Euro-generation" vocally equated the U.S. and Soviet states as morally equivalent. Why did the United States "pick up the bill" for defending Europe, and even go so far as to accept nuclear destruction in its defense, when its thronging demonstrators screamed that this was the last thing on their minds?

The Third World had once been the focus of our postwar proselytizing: we saw in the newly independent states of Africa and Asia the hope of the future. Americans were confident that they would trust us, for had we ever intentionally sought overseas colonies? Had we not been the instrument of postwar decolonization? We lavished foreign aid upon them and waited for them to become, in Jefferson's phrase, little "eaglets" of the United States.

Instead, in the 1970s they turned on the United States. In the United Nations, in the form of the Group of 77, they took over the General Assembly and many U.N. agencies, and used the liberal forum of F.D.R. to attack America. The unfinished architecture of that dream of world order became the leasehold of squatters. The stature of the United Nations gave them an opportunity to promote their own local agendas and enhance their international standing—at America's expense.

Many Americans accepted the public lashing. It was even embraced as a kind of deserved public punishment for recent crimes, a cleansing at the hands of world opinion. It did not matter that many of the regimes excoriating the United States were themselves tyrannies of the most loathsome sort. In Vietnam, America had lost the right to judge others. Indeed, taken to its extreme, liberal values ended by declaring that all value systems were equal, and that for the United States to force its beliefs on other cultures was the worst form of imperialism.

The American breast-beating of the late 1970s was less a rejection of fundamental national myths than a celebration of them in their original form. American exceptionalism, American perfection, America as a model for others—these were myths stained by a long episode of national intervention. Only by returning to traditional values could America be cleansed, and rediscover itself. Both national parties made this quest their theme in 1976 and 1980; although the Democrats couched this process in terms of universal human rights and the Republicans in terms of particular domestic values, the goal of national purification was, and is, shared.

VII

Where does the American approach to the world stand in the 1980s? The dominant sense of American foreign policy behavior in this decade has been one of limitation. These limits can be described as a set of precepts, a rough chart of the ways domestic values are shaping foreign policy and national security:

· Traditional (pre-1939) attitudes about the nature of America's relationship to the world coexist uneasily with postwar norms. Officially the United States is still committed to the defense of Western Europe, Japan and South Korea. The ANZUS and Rio treaties are still on the books, barely. The United States still swears to defend its commitments with nuclear force if necessary. Both Democrats and Republicans still pay lip service to a grand strategic concept of containing Soviet power. But the visible superstructure of the postwar world is gone. No one today could certify the strength of American commitment to others, as they could not measure others' ultimate fidelity to us.

· Major nativist lobbies in both the right and left wings of the major parties reinforce the sense that domestic political support of the postwar global mission continues to erode. There is a generalized belief that alliances remain stable only in the absence of crisis; but there is an equal apprehension that the continued absence of crisis also accelerates the process of dissolution.

· A pattern of American use of force has emerged during the last decade that implies very clear domestic limits on military action. The duration and scale of the response, and the political capital expended in doing anything military at all are advertisements to our adversaries. By choosing the time and place well, and by exploiting American public opinion, a skillful adversary can almost ensure American military abstention from regional crises.

· This emerging conviction on the part of friend and foe alike that American words are seldom backed by deeds creates a special pressure on U.S. diplomacy. Forceful diplomacy must be confined to the initial period after an election (which historically is the time when an American president is least capable of foreign policy assertion), when domestic political support should be greatest. Foreign perception of an American president's strength is seen today as a function only of his electoral charisma.

· The collective "truths" that emerged from American wars are unchanged. In this sense the received truths of Vietnam do not in themselves constitute a rejection of World War II, and ultimately of the Civil War model. To the contrary, Vietnam has been incorporated into the larger body of American myth. Both purifiers and progressives join ranks in longing for the just war. But as World War II becomes even more mythic as its veterans pass on, its iconography seems ever more rigid and unbending. It is harder than ever for younger American generations to relate contemporary conditions to the world of the 1930s, and yet that world, threatened by Hitler and fascism, is the only setting in the picture of national myth legitimizing the just war.

Any effective use of American military force must forge a bond with World War II and its transcendental heroic imagery; but perceived world conditions today evoke no resonance. The gap between myth and its reassertion was vividly evoked in the 1984 film *Red Dawn*. The only way in which director John Milius could bridge the distance between mythic American wars and his vision of a contemporary just war was to force a situation so absurd as to negate the idea itself: a Soviet invasion of the United States from Mexico and Alaska! His artistic desperation mirrors a profound American dilemma.

VIII

These precepts describe only limits. How did these limits operate during the Reagan era?

To some, Ronald Reagan appeared an atavism, an unregenerate cold warrior (or musing hoplite) seeking to recapture a halcyon age of American dominance. Given that he was born at around the same time, one might suggest that he be painted as an aged Jack Kennedy. Certainly his campaign rhetoric in 1980 echoed J.F.K. on the stump in 1960.

But for all his talk, Reagan's policies and programs reflect an emerging American nativism. At the end of his watch, Reagan has come to the arms control altar as eager as a Nixon or a Carter. Military force has been used, as it has been without exception since Vietnam, only when there has been no danger of escalation, only when such action could be limited in advance, and only where a sure escape route existed if things went sour. Reagan's trumpeted nuclear buildup has yielded a minor cache compared to Kennedy's majestic atomic arsenal. And his Strategic Defense Initiative frames an almost frantic appeal to a changing American worldview. The vision of strategic defense hearkens to an older, cherished picture of national security.

Weapons trumpeted for a cold war arsenal in 1981 have since been pitched in tones richly appealing to the old image of the "Shield of the Republic." Reagan has abetted an erosion of the postwar paradigm of containment at its foundation: extended deterrence. Serious strategic defenses deny the legitimacy of nuclear use, and readiness for nuclear use *is* extended deterrence. Although Reagan was yielding to a yearning among Americans to "escape the nuclear trap," the snare was laid less by the weapons themselves than by the ironclad resolve that they be used.

Ultimately, Reagan's desire to make nuclear weapons "impotent and obsolete" is less important than his intent to do so. SDI reflects more than a generalized antinuclear yearning. It signals a renewed American urge, however latent, to revise the cold war commitments symbolized by nuclear use. Revision came with the treaty on intermediate-range nuclear forces, but the terms had been couched years earlier. Remember, the "zero option" was Reagan's; the call for weapons, Europe's. Reagan's initial zest as a progressive shows in the early bidding on strategic nuclear forces. The zest was gone by 1984.

It is quite clear that Reagan did not succeed in reasserting the postwar progressive mission. The United States undertook no offensives against tyranny; in contrast, the progressive image of America as champion of freedom was reduced to furtive arms smuggling to the mental rimlands of civilization, in Angola, Nicaragua, Afghanistan. In the places where we actually used military force, our late twentieth-century behavior began to mirror nineteenth-century antecedents: our Libyan raid evoking the Barbary Coast in 1804 and our Iranian combats the quasi war with France in 1799. In practical and popular terms, America's armed forces had come again to protect Americans abroad. Their use might even be justified as necessary to uphold ancient liberal notions like the right of free passage at sea. But there has been no hint since 1980—not even in Reagan's most expansive speeches—of another crusade.

If anything, Reagan's exertions served to exhume the mythology of the American postwar progressive mission for examination, only to have the people reject it. If a single postulate could be found, a kind of core reality underpinning American attitudes about how we should approach the world, it is that the postwar world is over. This means three things.

First, Americans see a world different from the one to which we pledged our lives and fortunes in 1950. We fought and remained ready to fight through three generations to build a world out of our beliefs: a democratic free world. It paid off. The states of the West are rich and free, and appear to be in no danger. The so-called Third World has gone its own way. It is not necessarily a bad world, but it is not necessarily worth dying for.

Second, although many Americans would be willing to fight for values at the core of our national myth—the "American way of life"—we question whether these values are really threatened the way they were in 1941. The Soviet Union seems in serious decline. The threat has receded each year since 1981. In contrast, our allies promise to challenge the American way more than any rogue Leninist. So the need for sacrifice, too, is gone.

Third, if national values are no longer threatened at the center, as they were during the postwar era, then the danger is at the margins, in the Third World. Here in the galaxy of the American belief system are both good and bad states, people some want to help and societies some long to reform. Reagan sought to help rebels in Angola and Afghanistan and Nicaragua. His loyal opposition would do the same for dissident groups in South Africa. The impulse to intervene is the same. So are its limits. In contrast to the postwar era, the reasons for intervention now emerge from a domestic debate over the American identity and our national purpose. No longer do our allies rally to consensus calls for the defense of the free world.

What was left of the good-war-as-crusade died in Vietnam. Today, as in earlier times, the United States has its interests and the lives of its citizens to defend. We continue as well to call (according to domestic political stripe) for the nurturing of new "eaglets" in the Third World, as long as their suckling or succoring does not risk our own corruption.

The American approach to the world shifted after 1980. We simply have not yet surveyed the watershed.

31

Linking Gorbachev's Domestic and Foreign Policy Agendas

GEORGE W. BRESLAUER

There has always been a close relationship between internal and external affairs in Soviet history.[1] What is distinctive about the current situation is the leadership's sense of urgency about the need to actively create an international environment conducive to the realization of leading domestic policy priorities, without sacrificing Soviet hard-won positions as a military and diplomatic superpower. In many cases this poses contradictions and forces the regime to make hard choices, as, for example, in the decision to withdraw from Afghanistan. Moreover, the search for new strategies at home and abroad is taking place in a domestic political context that is highly diverse and conflictual. Advocates of less innovative foreign and domestic policy agendas remain entrenched in positions of power and influence. They are ready to bemoan the costs and risks of current changes, and they are searching for a persuasive alternative conception that may replace the Gorbachev agendas if conditions permit.

This chapter specifies the main components of Mikhail Gorbachev's domestic and foreign policy agendas, and then analyzes the ways in which Gorbachev has defined the relationship between the two agendas, both in his long-term vision and in his short-term political strategy. I will also examine the factors likely to facilitate and frustrate Gorbachev's efforts, and inquire into whether it is in the U.S. interest that Gorbachev succeed.

GORBACHEV'S VISION

Gorbachev has attempted to legitimize the need for radical changes in domestic and foreign policy by portraying the turn of the twenty-first century as the time by which the country must have reversed its decline and begun gaining momentum in the direction of a more prosperous and proud international actor. He has starkly posed the question of whether the Soviet Union will enter the new century "in a manner

Published by permission of the *Journal of International Affairs* and the Trustees of Columbia University in the City of New York.

Note: It is a violation of the law to reproduce this selection by any means whatsoever without the written permission of the copyright holder.

worthy of a great power," both militarily and economically. He and his advisers have expressed additional fears that a U.S. crash program based on the Strategic Defense Initiative (SDI) could lead to military breakthroughs during the 1990s that would pose fundamental national security threats to the USSR. His time-perspective is also evident in the argument that reform of the Soviet political and economic systems will require a generation to put in place, and even longer thereafter to bear continuing fruit. Finally, Gorbachev realizes that, during the next ten years or so, he will have to make his mark on Soviet history. He will turn seventy years of age in March 2001.

By that time, Gorbachev hopes to have firmly turned things around. This will be a truly imposing and daunting task, given the numerous obstacles at home and abroad. And Gorbachev knows as much. He has spoken publicly of the difficulties and of the uncertainty of success. But he has also insisted that there is simply no alternative to reforming the current system, that the Party has nothing to turn back to. Thus, Gorbachev looks to the future with both an optimistic vision and a deep apprehension; apprehensive, if not fearful, of what might result for Soviet domestic stability and national security if the nation fails to realize much of his vision.

Gorbachev is a visionary and a political risk-taker. He is bold. He has consolidated power faster, though not more fully, than any leader in Soviet history. He has proposed reforms that would significantly alter, if not replace, the current system. He has openly challenged cherished values. He has unleashed social forces that he has not always been able to control. He has taken these risks because he has become convinced that only a frontal assault will overcome the entrenched political interests, behavior patterns, and attitudes that accompanied Soviet stagnation of the late 1970s and 1980s.

Gorbachev does not have in mind a detailed blueprint for how much to reform the system. He may be a visionary, but he is not omniscient. We know, for example, that Gorbachev wants to partially decentralize the Soviet economic system. But we also sense that he has been feeling his way, unsure of *how much* marketization will be required to effect a sustained improvement in the performance of the economy. Similarly, we know that Gorbachev has greatly liberalized the opportunities for people to speak out on issues. But we also sense that he has not quite known whether or where he may eventually have to draw the line (for example, with respect to the nature and scope of public demonstrations and disruption, when used as a political resource by the disaffected). And we know that Gorbachev wants to democratize political relationships within the factories, the governmental structures (the soviets), and the Communist Party itself. But we also sense that he has not known how far this democratization process will ultimately go, once it has gathered steam and goes on to precipitate new autonomous interest group formations, alternative programs within the Communist Party based on "factionalism," regular public challenges to the rights of those who manipulate the nomination process, or a multiparty political system. The recent constitutional and public order crisis over Armenian versus Azerbaidjani rule in Nagorno–Karabakh provides a vivid example of some of these dilemmas and of Gorbachev's uncertainty over how to handle them.

All this uncertainty is compounded by the scope of the risk involved. Gorbachev is by far the most powerful member of the Politburo, but power in Soviet politics (as in U.S. politics) is not a currency that can be purchased and hoarded. It must be invested in policy initiatives and programs that promise to improve the country's condition at an acceptable cost. If these initiatives ultimately fail to meet their objectives, the investment may fail. The politician's authority will decline—perhaps to the point that he or she is ousted from office. Gorbachev surely hopes to remain in power for many more years, and he hopes to be presiding at that time over an incipient Soviet renaissance. But he cannot know very far in advance just how far the Politburo and the Central Committee will allow him to go in the direction of decentralization, liberalization, and democratization in pursuit of his vision of a prosperous, powerful, and proud Soviet Union. And, of course, if he fails, he cannot know whether he will be allowed to remain in office.

Given all these uncertainties—about how much the system needs to be reformed and how much it will be allowed to be reformed—Gorbachev conceives of changes as a *process* that will continue to unfold throughout the 1990s. This view of change applies to both his domestic and foreign policy agendas.

REFORM AND RECONSTRUCTION AT HOME

Essentially, there have been four elements to Gorbachev's ambitious program for reform and reconstruction at home, each of which was originally conceived of as part of a long-term process. The first element involved efforts to crush or restrict the most deviant and dysfunctional features of social and political behavior, and it was coercive in nature. Campaigns against alcoholism, labor indiscipline, and official corruption initially imposed very severe restrictions and penalties, with varying degrees of success, in the finest Russian and Soviet disciplinarian traditions. At first, such efforts were viewed as a prerequisite for, and an accompaniment of, a long process of changing behavioral patterns, individual attitudes, and, ultimately, social and political consciousness. Eventually, they were largely abandoned or scaled back. The anti-alcohol campaign proved ineffective; campaigns for labor discipline proved inconsistent with a greater emphasis on democracy and material incentives as spurs to initiative; and anti-corruption campaigns, while continuing, have been more frequently initiated "from below," by angry citizens demanding removal of corrupt local mafias. Nonetheless, the social forces Gorbachev encourages, rewards, and protects are those that seek to overcome the attitudes and behaviors that were characteristic of the Brezhnevite period of "stagnation."

The second element of Gorbachev's program involved liberalization of public expression. There has been an opening up of the media, along with a tolerance for, and even encouragement of, iconoclasm in all areas of cultural, social, economic, and political life. Yesterday's dissent has become today's reformist mainstream. Although Gorbachev probably never envisaged how much *glasnost* would snowball once the restrictions were removed or relaxed, he has been able to use it as an instrument for both building a political constituency and overcoming the demoralization of many strata within Soviet society. He has come to view *glasnost* as a prerequisite for raising public consciousness, for training people to become involved in a tolerant, democratic political process of give-and-take, and, more importantly, for instilling confidence in people that whistle-blowing will be neither futile nor dangerous. Finally, Gorbachev views *glasnost* as a means of activating and generating a broad societal constituency that will conceive of the reformist alternative as desirable, necessary, *and* feasible. However, achieving such a change in public consciousness and behavior patterns will take time.

The third element in Gorbachev's program involved partial marketization of the socialist economy. New laws have been enacted permitting limited private and cooperative enterprise, especially in the agricultural and service sectors, and have resulted in an explosion of localized and very small-scale private enterprise. A schedule of reforms has been announced for expanding the autonomy of state enterprises in the industrial sectors. In practice, however, the process of marketization of the state sector has barely gotten off the ground. Partial measures have been enacted that are frequently being sabotaged in the course of implementation or that cannot be effective until other features of the command economy are changed. For example, questions of price reform, inflation, bankruptcy, private property, and job security have yet to be tackled or resolved. New laws on some of these matters have been enacted by the Supreme Soviet (apparently at Gorbachev's instigation or with his consent), but they have been marked by ambiguity and compromise. For the most part, the crucial issues, such as price reform, have been postponed for several years. Thus, Gorbachev has treated reform of the economy as a lengthy process that will unfold in stages. He has begun the process, but the most difficult choices have been temporarily deferred.

The fourth element has been Gorbachev's program for political democratization. This program, first outlined in January 1987 (when Gorbachev began to radicalize his entire approach to reform), has been geared toward redefining the hierarchical character of political relationships throughout the system. The components are familiar to anyone who has been following Soviet developments even casually: multiple candidacies and secret ballots in factory, governmental, and party elections; limits on the length and number of terms held by elected officials; extensive revisions of the legal code to provide greater guarantees to citizens against bureaucratic and political arbitrariness; greatly increased powers for the nominally legislative councils (soviets) at all levels of the hierarchy; freedom for citizens to organize themselves into informal groups to articulate and press their demands; and the creation of a Congress of People's Deputies and a new Supreme Soviet to serve as a genuine Parliament, at the expense of many of the powers of the CPSU's Central Committee. Informal groups, which now number well over 50,000,[2] have mobilized millions of Soviet citizens, especially young people. The Supreme Soviet and the Congress have met several times and have proved to be, on balance, a radicalizing force as well as a mobilizer of public activism among their constituents. The creation of a "law-governed state" has not yet been accomplished, and local political machines in many areas still exercise considerable control over electoral nominations. Nonetheless, in just three years great strides have been taken in the direction of genuinely competitive elections and political accountability to constituents. In addition to all these changes, strikes have been legalized, and legitimate, independent trade unions would appear to be on the horizon. Gorbachev has also pressed the Central Committee to abrogate its constitutionally guaranteed right to monopolize party politics (thus setting the stage for legitimate opposition parties and multiparty contestation). And he has initiated legislation to specify conditions under which minority republics might secede from the Soviet Union.

These processes, unless aborted by backlash, will continue to expand. Thus, like economic reform, political democratization is a process unfolding over time; it is not an event. It will require substantial elaboraton and an ongoing struggle to be effective. Thus far, Gorbachev has pushed it more rapidly than he has pushed economic reforms, both because he has often been reacting to, and trying to keep up with, released social forces, and because he has defined political democratization as a prerequisite for effectively implementing a program of partial marketization of the economy.

OBSTACLES AND REQUIREMENTS

The obstacles to realizing these programs are formidable. One set of such obstacles stems from the political and social malaise bequeathed by Brezhnev; a deeply entrenched bureaucracy that has spent decades smothering independent initiatives and justifying that repression in ideological terms; widespread corruption of the administrative and political elites, which extends to their families, friends, and all those dependent on them for supplies, perquisites, and largesse; and large social strata that, for whatever reasons, have become demoralized, nonentrepreneurial, or risk-averse in their orientations to economic and political life.

A second obstacle to reform is budgetary stringency. The combination of a bloated military-heavy industrial sector and huge state subsidies of basic consumer necessities has created a severely stretched budget.[3] In the absence of a large redistribution of resources across budgetary categories, the leadership is impeded in its ability to attend to new needs, to pump those sectors of the economy that are being reformed, or to buffer those social strata most dependent on the social safety net, which is itself weakening during the process of reform.

Certain features of the traditional political culture can also impede reform prospects. Widespread envy of those who get ahead is a significant constraint on marketization. Traditional Russian and Soviet xenophobia, though significantly diluted by time and generational change, still provides a social base in a Time of Troubles for chauvinist appeals and a "pogrom" mentality against minorities, intellectuals, and the Westernizing thrust of reforms.[4] These behavioral predispositions, combined with the objective economic and social conditions of the 1980s, mean that, in the Soviet Union today, a social basis for fascism exists, though its size is difficult to estimate. A counter-reform coalition of disenfranchised bureaucrats, unskilled masses threatened by inflation, unemployment, and social differentiation, and authoritarian chauvinists can come together if conditions get sufficiently bad.

A fourth obstacle might be called global overextension. Worldwide Soviet foreign policy commitments are a continuing drain, not only on Soviet resources, but also on the attention span of Soviet leaders, who can attend meaningfully to only so many problems and crises at once.

What Gorbachev needs in order to revitalize the Soviet system, then, is a foreign policy that allows him (1) to concentrate attention on the home front; (2) to counter xenophobic tendencies within the Soviet establishment and society; (3) to save money and divert it to new priorities; (4) to inspire people with a new sense of drama and mission; (5) to mobilize pressures for entrepreneurialism within Soviet society; and (6) to achieve "wins" internationally that will bolster his authority in the absence of demonstrable, short-term domestic progress. Much of Gorbachev's foreign policy can be seen as an effort to forge an international environment that will facilitate his achieving these immediate objectives.

GORBACHEV'S FOREIGN POLICY AGENDA

It cannot be denied that Soviet leaders *still* maintain autonomous foreign policy goals and that some foreign policy changes have roots in the

Brezhnev era. These changes have been facilitated by elite learning regarding the ineffectiveness of previous policies and assumptions about international politics. But a decisive change in the domestic policy agenda has made it possible for Gorbachev to formulate and legitimize an equally decisive change in a large number of interrelated foreign policies. Put differently, it is difficult to imagine that Gorbachev's immediate predecessors would have adopted such a far-reaching change in foreign policies and perspectives. Both a generational change in the context of a political succession, and a domestic crisis of huge proportions, were required to justify what Gorbachev has done.

In the area of *arms control,* Gorbachev has made a series of surprising concessions in order to achieve an INF treaty, advance the cause of major reductions in strategic missiles, and hopefully effect an end to the U.S. Strategic Defense Initiative. He has accepted the U.S. double-zero option on medium- and short-range missiles in Europe and Asia, has expressed willingness to cut back sharply the Soviet heavy missile arsenal, and has accepted intrusive on-site verification as a requisite of treaty enforcement. He has also initiated potentially major changes in Soviet military doctrine and has made large unilateral concessions geared toward substantial conventional force reductions in Europe.

Clearly, Gorbachev viewed it as worthwhile to make these concessions in order to achieve several of his goals. These include stabilizing the U.S.–Soviet relationship in order to allow him to concentrate on repairing the home front; breaking through the siege mentality that prevailed under Brezhnev and prevented highly flexible negotiating terms; avoiding the economic cost of a strategic defense race with the United States; and, not least, bolstering his political authority at home by delivering progress in the pursuit of peace.

Another area in which Soviet foreign policy became concessionary is *Afghanistan.* The withdrawal from Afghanistan, completed in February 1989, was intended to service higher priority goals. It removed an albatross (what Gorbachev called "a running sore") from around the necks of a leadership that, for the most part, was not involved in the original decision to intervene. It allows them to concentrate on the home front and to reduce the ruble cost of their foreign policy. It heads off the disaffection that was spreading in Soviet society as a result of the war, and thus it assists the effort to overcome societal demoralization. And it contributes to the larger goal of stabilizing East–West, as well as Sino-Soviet, relations during the concentration on domestic tasks. Although it may have the unintended effect of unleashing debates over "who lost Afghanistan," or over the morality of the enterprise to begin with, the current leadership's lack of responsibility for the original decision may allow it to deflect such criticism. Moreover, the absence of an ongoing war effort should facilitate the discrediting of xenophobes who point to embattlement as a justification for maintaining strict "order" at home.[5]

The Soviets have also made efforts to be conciliatory in order to advance the cause of *Sino-Soviet* reconciliation. Gorbachev conceded to the Chinese position on border modification. Even though the strategic significance of the concession was negligible, its significance as a precedent was potentially great, which explains why this was the first Soviet border concession on any front since 1956. The Soviets have somewhat reduced their troop strength on the Sino-Soviet border and in Mongolia. They have met the Chinese condition of withdrawal from Afghanistan. And they have used their leverage with Vietnam to secure a Vietnamese withdrawal from Kampuchea and to secure Vietnamese cooperation with a Southeast Asian negotiating process on a Kampuchean political settlement. China had defined the issue of Vietnamese withdrawal from Kampuchea as the most important and necessary precondition for Sino-Soviet reconciliation. Soviet willingness to attempt to influence Hanoi on this matter can only be understood as a product of their policy toward China. That policy was again derivative of Gorbachev's effort to defuse antagonisms with foreign neighbors and adversaries in order to focus on domestic problems, to reduce the economic costs of his foreign policy (troop concentrations on the Chinese border are far more expensive to maintain than are strategic nuclear arsenals), to reduce the credibility of xenophobes and others who possess a siege mentality, and to bolster his personal image within Soviet politics as an effective problem-solver in international affairs, by breaking gordian knots and advancing the cause of peace and international security. From this perspective, Gorbachev's summit meeting in Beijing with Chinese leader Deng Xiaoping was viewed in Moscow as a potentially major political asset for Gorbachev, just as Ronald Reagan's visit to Moscow boosted Gorbachev's political standing. Unfortunately for Gorbachev, the summit in Beijing (May 1989) coincided with the student occupation of Tiananmen Square. In light of the subsequent Chinese crackdown, some of the luster of that summit was lost, and Gorbachev's political dividends from the meeting were cut.

Elsewhere in the *Third World*, we see further evidence of Gorbachev's efforts to defuse potentially confrontational situations in order to stabilize East–West relations. In the Middle East, where progress is largely dependent on the dispositions of local elites, Gorbachev has reached out to Israel on matters of diplomatic recognition and Jewish emigration, has reconciled with several moderate Arab states, and has marginally softened Soviet negotiating terms for a settlement of the Arab-Israeli conflict. In Southern Africa, Moscow was a "silent partner" in the complex negotiations that resulted in a political settlement of the interconnected issues of Angola, Namibia, Cuba, and South Africa, assisting the negotiating process among these four parties and the United States, while also pushing for a softening of Cuban/Angolan negotiating terms. In Ethiopia, Gorbachev has put the Mengistu regime on notice that Soviet military assistance will be declining and that Mengistu will be well advised to seek a political settlement of the civil war in his country. In Nicaragua, Gorbachev pressed the Sandinista government in 1987 to negotiate with the Contras, cut back Soviet oil deliveries to the hard-pressed Nicaraguan economy, and, in 1989, cut back (some say, cut off) military assistance as well. Most recently, in February 1990, Moscow has accepted the results of the electoral defeat of the Sandinistas. In general, although the Soviets have tried not to abandon their allies (indeed, military support of Angola, Ethiopia, Cuba, and Syria continued and, in some cases, increased), they have decidedly subordinated the radical activist strand of their Third World policy to the crisis-prevention strand of that policy.[6] Again this is consistent with Gorbachev's larger strategy of stabilizing East–West relations, reducing the cost of foreign policy, and concentrating on domestic, or high priority foreign policy, concerns. To the extent that success is achieved in settling any of these regional conflicts, it also has the added benefit of bolstering Gorbachev's standing as a peacemaker.

Soviet policy toward *international organizations* has also changed in ways consistent with these goals. Since the fall of 1987, Moscow has been touting the United Nations as an organization that should become more fully involved in regional conflict resolution. The Soviets have offered to pay up their long-delinquent financial obligations to the UN. They have called for the creation of multilateral negotiating formats and policing operations. They have agreed to allow their personnel in international organizations to become genuine international civil servants. How far this will go remains to be seen. But again, it is consistent with the goals of demilitarizing and pacifying the international environment by depolarizing regional conflicts. This would contribute to the stabilization of East–West relations and would reduce the force of xenophobic sentiments by embracing a more ecumenical, and less sectarian, approach to integration into the international political order.[7]

A similar trend is evident in Soviet *foreign economic relations*, where Gorbachev has moved toward fuller Soviet integration into the capitalist international economic order. Joint venture legislation, however imperfect in the absence of price reform, now allows foreign capitalists to own majority equity in projects within the USSR. Moscow has applied for observer status in GATT (the General Agreement on Trade and Tariffs) and has indicated an interest in eventually joining the International Monetary Fund and the World Bank as well. The goals of these changes have largely been economic, for they are most directly related to Soviet budgetary stringency and to the evolving process of economic reform. But they also have social and political functions to perform. They help to mobilize international pressures for entrepreneurialism within the USSR, and they blunt the edge of xenophobic insularity by exposing the country to foreign economic benefits as well as methods. This could backfire, of course, by fueling the arguments of those who claim that the country is being sold to foreign capitalists. But Gorbachev is betting that integration into the capitalist international economic order will increase Soviet capacity to compete in its foreign economic relations.

Another feature of Gorbachev's policy might be called *partial Westernization*. This spans the divide between domestic and foreign policy and is closely related to the policy of *glasnost*. It entails reducing anti-Western propaganda and opening the electronic and print media to a wide range of Western culture, news, and scholarship (Western movies, interviews with Western antagonists, televising of European rock groups, tours of U.S. rock groups, and so on). Gorbachev seeks to integrate the USSR into European culture, not just the European economy. He openly refers to the USSR as an abnormal society and now praises the "normal," "civilized" societies of the West. This represents a natural elaboration of the effort to appeal to the new middle class and the "yuppies" who have become so numerous in Soviet urban society. But it also has the intended effect of overcoming demoralization among the cosmopolitan strata of society, of activating new social forces, of creating external sources of irreversibility for the reform process, and of countering xenophobic insularity.

In his policy toward *Eastern Europe*, Gorbachev's foreign policy suddenly changed dramatically in 1989. Initially, he flirted with the idea of pushing *perestroika* onto reluctant East European elites, but he appears to have tempered the urge. His strategy became one of temporizing: buying time and hoping that instability would not break out in that region, with all this might imply for the legitimacy of reform in the USSR, or for the stability of East–West relations should another Soviet invasion be deemed necessary. But in 1989, when matters came to a head in Poland and when the examples of Poland and Hungary, along with revulsion against the "Chinese solution," emboldened social forces in Czechoslovakia and East Germany as well, Gorbachev decided to rely on his earlier instincts. He informed recalcitrant East European conservative elites that the Soviet Union would not protect them against their enraged populations if they refused to sanction reform. This opened the dike, and a flood of popular protest brought down regimes throughout the region. Gorbachev's decision to remove the security guarantee, to sanction Jaruzelski's capitulation to a Solidarity-led government, and to allow the Berlin Wall to be breached allowed 1989 to be a year of areawide revolution. To this point, Gorbachev has even accommodated himself to the prospect of German reunification. His unwillingness to try to prevent radical change in Eastern Europe, and in Europe at large, reflects the magnitude of the economic, political, and ethnic crisis within the USSR, and his felt need to accommodate adversaries abroad in order to build an international environment supportive of his domestic policy agenda.

These foreign policy objectives add up to a vision of a world ten to twenty years hence in which the arms race has been harnessed, and the maintenance of a credible and adequate defense has been made more affordable—a world in which détente with major neighbors and with the United States allows for a cultural and political renaissance inside the USSR, along with cultural integration into Western civilization, and in which Soviet integration into the global economy yields substantial benefits to the Soviet developmental program. Gorbachev recognizes that the achievement of this vision will require a sustained process of negotiation and adjustment. That is why he considers it so important to create momentum in these directions, and to harness both domestic and international resources toward the maintenance of that momentum. In most cases, Gorbachev has been reacting to forces not under his control. But his reactions are unique in Soviet history. He has made virtues out of necessities, proving himself willing to live with turmoil (indeed, in some cases encouraging or eliciting it). There will be continuous elaboration of Soviet legislation and negotiating positions. Indeed, in some areas of domestic policy, and in foreign economic relations, this will be necessary to keep the process from bogging down. Continuous leadership skills and energy will therefore be required.

It is worth reemphasizing the *limits* of the changes Gorbachev seeks to introduce. Although he does not have a clear conception of how far he will have to go in the direction of democratization and marketization at home, or conciliation abroad, he probably has a relatively clear conception of what he hopes to *avoid*. Gorbachev's agenda is to alter, not abandon, the Soviet system. He hopes to create a political order in which a revitalized, more social-democratic Communist Party maintains a leading political role by virtue of its moral appeal. He does not appear eager to do away with central planning in the heavy industrial sectors. Similarly, his agenda abroad is to alter, not abandon, Soviet foreign policy commitments and identity. This entails maintaining Soviet status as a competitive global power, as a co-equal superpower, and as a great power that preserves a distinctive socialist identity even as it Westernizes and integrates itself into the international political and economic orders. Whether Gorbachev can avoid testing these limits remains to be seen. Only one year ago (early 1989), he surely did not anticipate having to broker the reunification of Germany. Other surprises may be in store for him.

How far things go will depend not only on Gorbachev's leadership capacities, but also on the answers to certain empirical and theoretical questions. Can the Soviets, for example, achieve a balance between market and plan that will substantially, and on a sustained basis, improve the performance of their economy? Many people say no, either because the political obstacles appear to be too formidable or because these people believe that only a fully marketized economy can break through Soviet stagnation.

Can the Soviets achieve a more democratic polity that inspires its citizens to contribute more willingly? Many people say no, viewing the party apparatus and the ministries as a relatively monolithic aristocracy that will defend its privileges to the end. Others argue that only full democratization and open politics can overcome the cynicism and corruption rampant in the Soviet Union today.

Can the Soviets create an international environment supportive of these efforts? Some say no, because the competitive ideological impulse in Soviet politics remains strong and will frustrate efforts at reconciliation. Others doubt that the United States, NATO, or China will cooperate to the extent required or that the international economic order will permit integration of the Soviet economy at a price the Soviets will be willing to pay.

Counsels of despair frequently predominate in Western journalistic and scholarly analyses of the chances that Gorbachev will succeed in reversing (not just stemming) the decline in Soviet fortunes at home and abroad. That is understandable, given the numerous obstacles. For that very reason, however, it is worth reviewing the factors that both impel and facilitate reform of the Soviet system, those factors that would support a probabilistic (and optimistic) conclusion that, with luck, Gorbachev *can* succeed.

WHY GORBACHEV CAN SUCCEED

A number of factors facilitate continued expansion of the restructuring process—both in the economy and the polity.[8] Without assigning relative weights to these factors, let me check them off.

1. *A New Social Structure*. This includes the new middle class, the skilled blue-collar stratum, and, from a generational standpoint, the "yuppies." Collectively, these strata number in the tens of millions, and many are eager to employ their skills and initiative in a context that will promise a payoff (either public or private). Many of them may not be willing to stick their necks out to advance the cause of *perestroika*, but they may be willing to fight to prevent the process from being halted or rolled back. Indeed, with the *glasnost* genie now out of the bottle, so many social and political forces have been unleashed that an effort to roll back *perestroika* or *glasnost* could elicit rage from many thousands (perhaps millions) of articulate, influential people.

2. *Elite and Specialist Learning*. Brezhnev's longevity contributed to the eventual reform process by thoroughly discrediting conservatism, which is now treated as synonymous with stagnation (*zastoi*). As a result, within the upper reaches of the political establishment, there is a widespread sense that no alternative to reform exists, although battles rage over how far the process should be allowed to go. Moreover, thirty years of experimentation with more modest reform efforts, both in the

USSR and in Eastern Europe, have given Soviet social scientists and their political sponsors a deeper understanding of a number of processes including the nature of systemic interdependencies, the limits of the capacity of the unreformed system to perform, the inevitability of corruption and stagnation in the absence of reform, and the potential negative consequences for Soviet competitiveness internationally should the reforms fail.

3. *Psychological and Ideological Factors.* Both psychologically and ideologically, Soviet elite political culture displays an aversion to stagnation and a need for a sense of progress, drama, and mission. This helps to foster, and then legitimize, transformative leadership. Khrushchev tried to stimulate such missionary drama, following the stagnation of late Stalinism, with his anti-Stalin campaign and his campaign to construct full communism. The former proved to be too negative, and the latter too incredible. The New Right in the Soviet Union today proposes Russian chauvinism or "National Bolshevism" which, to this point, the politicians have treated as too dangerous and counterproductive. That leaves *perestroika* or "socialist democracy" to provide the sense of progress and drama. At the moment, the other competitors lack legitimacy, lending strength to the Gorbachev claim that "there is no alternative."

What's more, the ideological heritage, as Stephen Cohen has argued with great eloquence, is substantively dualistic. Lenin's last writings and the New Economic Policy (NEP) of the 1920s can be cited as precedents to justify both political and economic *perestroika*.[9]

4. *A Non-monolithic Party Apparatus.* Were the party apparatus united in its definition of where its interests lie, the task of *perestroika* might be an impossible one. Fortunately for Gorbachev, who himself is a product of that apparatus, there are heterogeneous dispositions and interests within the Party apparatus. The Party includes reformists as well as conservatives, cosmopolitans as well as parochials, ascetics as well as "aristocratizers," regionalists as well as centralists, anti-corruption fighters as well as the corrupted. This provides Gorbachev with the opportunity to alter recruitment patterns and to build coalitions within the apparatus as he tackles the difficult intellectual and political task of maintaining the momentum of change.

5. *A Manipulable Political Order.* Two, apparently contradictory, features of the Soviet political order also facilitate the task of reform. First, the advantages of centralization make it easier for Gorbachev to transform the bureaucracy from above, by mobilizing supporters through the patron–client machinery on which much of his raw power is based. Second, the nominally legislative arenas of the system (the Soviets and the party committees [as opposed to bureaus]), though subordinated to the executive structures for seventy years, are available for resuscitation. Gorbachev is currently seeking to do so, and thereby provide an alternative arena of power in which he can mobilize political leverage against

the bureaucrats. Such resuscitation can also be justified with reference to the "pure ideology" of the regime.[10]

6. *International Impulses.* Throughout both Imperial Russian and Soviet history, there has existed a strong relationship between modernization strategies and perceived international security imperatives.[11] To cite but one example of recent memory, Stalin justified the tempo of industrialization in 1931 by arguing that the alternative would be to be crushed by foreign predators. Similarly, Gorbachev justifies *perestroika* in part in precisely such terms. He cites the economic and military security implications of technological backwardness, and he holds out the prospect of the USSR slipping to second-class power status in the absence of reform. This may explain, incidentally, why Gorbachev chose to reform the urban-industrial sector before reforming the agricultural sector. His greater concern, or that of his political constituents, may well have been international competitiveness rather than consumer satisfaction.

There are other international impulses that stem less from perceived security requirements than from ideological and patriotic forces. Soviet elite political culture has viewed the USSR as the natural ideological hegemon within the world communist movement. It has fused communism with nationalism in expressing pride in the USSR's (not just Russia's) status as a great power. In proving to all audiences the higher worth of the socialist social system, it has also viewed the USSR as the leading ideological competitor of the West. To the extent that successful reform in Eastern Europe allows these countries to make major progress in the direction of consumer societies, and to the extent that the capacity to export manufactured goods, the technological levels, and the consumer affluence of capitalist, newly industrialized countries (NICs) come to exceed those of the USSR, severe ideological and national embarrassment is eventually likely to be the Soviet response. Fear of these potentialities facilitates the efforts of Soviet reformists to legitimize their case.

To this combination of compelling and facilitating factors in the USSR today we may add a number of theoretical insights. First, with respect to the presumed need for full marketization to reverse the fortunes of the economy, it is necessary to bear in mind that hybrid mixtures of market and plan, and even of market and command, are not only viable but also typical in the world today. The question is: which combinations optimally advance the causes of growth, consumption, and equity? Economic science does not have a ready answer to that question. Second, with respect to the lengths to which democratization will have to go, we should remember that intermediate forms of partially democratic, partially authoritarian politics not only exist in the world today, but are also frequently capable of managing conflict. The question is: which combinations "work" in given political cultures? Political science does not have a ready answer to that question. As to whether the Soviets can fashion an international environment that will facilitate their domestic efforts, international relations theory is currently cast at too high a level of abstraction to allow us to deduce the viability of different mixtures of collaboration and competition between great powers in the nuclear age. All we can say is that no existing theory persuasively rules it out.

Finally, we can draw some encouraging lessons from the literature on democratization in Western Europe.[12] One lesson is that there are many roads to, and forms of, democracy. A second is that democratization generally emerges through phases and that the first phase requires at least a generation to take hold. A third is that democracy may emerge from a preparatory stage of protracted, deep conflict and struggle between radical and conservative forces. Fourth, in the course of that struggle, circumstances may often force or lure nondemocrats into democratic forms of behavior, which they later rationalize by adopting democratic beliefs or values. Fifth, rarely was democracy historically the primary goal; it was sought as a means to some other end (usually, as the British statesman James Bryce pointed out, to "the wish to be rid of tangible evils"). The parallels with the USSR are obvious, including the wish to be rid of technological backwardness for the sake of international security and regime security.

These, of course, are not iron-clad laws, and they do not imply that the Soviet Union will necessarily follow the path, or reach the end-point, achieved by Western Europe. Moreover, although the Soviet Union may end up with a mix of market and plan, democracy and authoritarianism, the greatest challenge it now faces is to break out of Leninism by *creating* a market to subsequently regulate and by *creating* a multiparty system to be tempered by authoritarian elements. That is no mean feat. Nonetheless, these comparative observations at least lend perspective to the tortured process which the USSR is currently undergoing, and alert us to the probability of some unexpected, and apparently paradoxical, outcomes.

IS IT IN THE U.S. INTEREST THAT GORBACHEV SUCCEED?

Should we be "rooting" for Gorbachev? Some people answer no, arguing that Soviet conciliation abroad is tactical, geared toward winning a "breathing spell," during which they will recover economically and emerge as a more capable and self-confident competitor of the United States throughout the world. Although anything is possible, I find the arguments positing that Gorbachev's success is in the American interest to be more compelling. Much depends here on the definition of "success" and the time-frame of prediction. I do not see any chance that Gorbachev or his successors will succeed to the point of attaining standards of living, national economic efficiency, or broad-based technological innovation akin to those currently, much less prospectively, existent in the United States, Japan, West Germany, or Sweden. Hence, I do not expect the USSR to be able to afford an abundance of consumption, growth, equity, and military capacity as well.

Moreover, to institutionalize a process of reform that moves the country decisively in those directions will require at least fifteen to twenty-five years, while to deepen the reforms and see them achieve "self-sustaining" growth, both economic and political, will probably require another generation thereafter. All this also assumes unilinear development, which itself is a dubious premise, since the long-term process of reform is likely to proceed in fits and starts. It seems to me, therefore, that it is in the American interest that the Soviet Union remain engrossed in this lengthy process of reform, at home and abroad. A Soviet Union that is absorbed in improving the quality of life of its citizens, the accountability of its officials, and the efficiency of its economy is a Soviet Union that will be more predictable and less adventuristic in its international behavior. On the other hand, a Soviet Union that has given up on the process of reform and is unstable, desperate, or seized by stagnation or, worse, a right-wing reaction, is likely to be a more unpredictable and aggressive adversary.

If we look beyond the perspective of one or two generations into the future and inquire not into the process of transition but into the outcome of that process, we find still another argument for perceiving the Gorbachev revolution to be in our interest. The radical reformists in the USSR today are, in many cases, people who have not been advocates of radical activism or expansionism abroad. They may be great power nationalists, but they are neither xenophobes nor ideologues of proletarian internationalism. Nor do they view the current changes in Soviet thinking about foreign policy as a merely tactical respite. Rather, they seek to integrate the USSR into the international cultural, political, and economic order *as an end in itself*. Thus, if Gorbachev and his successors actually transform the country into a more efficient and affluent hybrid of market and plan, and into a social democracy, the system is likely to be run by people whose outlooks on the international system are quite different from those that have prevailed in the past. They will be operating in a situation in which the costs of attacking the international order will have been raised substantially. What is more, the domestic legitimation needs of a more relaxed Soviet political order will no longer require either an attack compulsion or a siege mentality toward the outside world.[13]

Whether the United States ought to fashion its policies in ways likely to assist the process of *perestroika* is a much more complex matter. We have very little reliable information about political interactions within the ruling circles of the USSR. Hence, the fine-tuning of U.S. policies to affect the constellation of forces within the Kremlin could be misguided.

On a more general level, however, I have argued that Gorbachev needs a relatively benign international environment to further the cause at home and to bolster his personal authority. Since he is willing to be conciliatory to achieve those ends, it is in the United States' and Gorbachev's common interest that Washington be receptive to Soviet conciliatory gestures and be adroit at fashioning arrangements that would reciprocate genuine Soviet conciliation (for example, in the area of conventional force reductions in Europe). Gratuitous U.S. efforts to block instances of mutually economically advantageous Soviet integration into the international economic order would also be unwise. Overreaction to the periodic incidents and accidents that inevitably take place would likely be counterproductive. And an atmosphere of international crisis, born of a military effort to roll back Soviet positions in the Third World would also be likely to delegitimize both Gorbachev and his program. In sum, the United States has primarily *negative power* in the current situation: the power to undermine Gorbachev and *perestroika*. It does not have enough information to know how to advance the cause of *perestroika*. Yet this country does have a positive stake in the success of Gorbachev's efforts, regardless of whether success in decisively reforming the Soviet system may currently appear to be uncertain.

NOTES

1. I would like to thank the Carnegie Corporation of New York for support while this article was written and, later, updated. The earlier version of this article appeared in *Journal of International Affairs*, Vol. 42, No. 2 (Spring 1989). The update was written in February 1990.

2. Victoria Bonnell, "Voluntary Associations in Gorbachev's Reform Program," in George W. Breslauer, ed., *Can Gorbachev's Reforms Succeed?* (Berkeley, Calif.: UC Berkeley, Center for Slavic and East European Studies, 1990), p. 64.

3. Of the 450 billion ruble budget, 90 billion, or 20 percent, goes to subsidizing basic goods such as bread, meat, milk, eggs, butter, housing, transport, and children's clothing. In addition, budgetary stringency is compounded by the huge budget deficits only recently admitted to by Soviet leaders.

4. For the most elaborate exposition of this viewpoint, see Alexander Yanov, *The Russian Challenge and the Year 2000* (London and New York: Basil Blackwell, 1987). For the argument that xenophobia marked the Lenin and Stalin periods, but that it has gradually dissipated since Stalin and is being decisively subordinated by generational change today, see Jerry Hough, *Russia and the West: Gorbachev and the Politics of Reform* (New York: Simon and Schuster, 1988).

5. On the other hand, disaffected Afghan veterans could provide a constituency for right-wing demagoguery.

6. For further discussion on the four strands of Soviet Third World policy under Brezhnev and Gorbachev, see George W. Breslauer, "All Gorbachev's Men," *The National Interest* 12 (Summer 1988), pp. 91–100.

7. I owe this distinction between sectarian and ecumenical approaches to my colleague, Ken Jowitt.

8. For a much fuller discussion of these and other factors assisting the reform process, see my "Thinking About the Soviet Future," in Breslauer, ed., *Can Gorbachev's Reforms Succeed?*, pp. 1–34.

9. Stephen Cohen, *Rethinking the Soviet Experience* (New York: Oxford University Press, 1985).

10. On the distinction between "pure ideology" and "practical ideology," see Franz Schurmann, *Ideology and Organization in Communist China*, 2nd edition (Berkeley, Calif.: University of California Press, 1968), ch. 1. For an example of reference to the pure ideology to justify democratization, see Roy A. Medvedev, *On Socialist Democracy* (New York: Alfred A. Knopf, 1976).

11. Theodore H. Von Laue, *Why Lenin? Why Stalin?* (Philadelphia and New York: J. B. Lippincott Company, 1964).

12. This paragraph summarizes the themes of Dankwart Rustow's seminal article, "Transitions to Democracy: Toward a Dynamic Model," *Comparative Politics*, 2, no. 3 (April 1970), pp. 337–363.

13. On these points compare Jack Snyder, "The Gorbachev Revolution: A Waning of Soviet Expansionism?" *International Security* 12, no. 3 (Winter 1987–1988), and R. Judson Mitchell, *Ideology of a Superpower: Contemporary Soviet Doctrine on International Relations* (Stanford, Calif.: Hoover Institution Press, 1982). See also Snyder's brilliant "International Leverage on Soviet Domestic Change," *World Politics* XLII, no. 1 (October 1989).

32
To the Stalin Mausoleum

Z

The most dangerous time for a bad government is when it starts to reform itself.
—Alexis de Tocqueville, anent
Turgot and Louis XVI

I

The Soviet socialist "experiment" has been the great utopian adventure of our century. For more than seventy years, to millions it has meant hope, and to other millions, horror; but for all it has spelled fascination. Nor does age seem to wither its infinite allure.

Never has this fascination been greater than since Mikhail Gorbachev launched *perestroika* in the spring of 1985: a derivative painting in the Paris manner of 1905, a Beatles' vintage rock concert, or a *Moscow News* article revealing some dark episode from the Soviet past known to the rest of the planet for decades could send tremors of expectation throughout the West if it were datelined Moscow. So conservative-to-centrist

Reprinted by permission of *Daedalus,* Journal of the American Academy of Arts and Sciences, "Eastern Europe . . . Central Europe . . . Europe," Winter 1990, Vol. 119, No. 1, Cambridge, Massachusetts.

Note: It is a violation of the law to reproduce this selection by any means whatsoever without the written permission of the copyright holder.

Margaret Thatcher and Hans-Dietrich Genscher have vied with the liberal-to-radical mainstream of Anglo-American Sovietology in eulogizing Gorbachev's "modernity." Even though after seventy years, the road to the putative "radiant future" of mankind no longer leads through Moscow, the road to world peace still does. And who is against world peace?

But this is not the whole explanation: Moscow is still the focus of a now septuagenarian ideological fixation. On the Right there is the hope that communism may yet repent of its evil totalitarian ways and evolve into a market democracy of sorts (into the bargain putting down the Western Left). On the Left there is the wish that the "experiment" not turn out to be a total loss (if only so as not to comfort the Western Right) and yet acquire something approximating a human face. So on all sides alleged connoisseurs of the *res sovietica* are anxiously asked: Are you optimistic or pessimistic about the chances for perestroika? Can Gorbachev succeed? Will he survive? Should we help him?

These questions, however, presuppose answers with diverse ideological intonations. To what is no doubt a majority in Western opinion, Gorbachev's reforms mean that Stalinism and the Cold War are over and that democracy is at hand in the East, bringing with it the end of global conflict for all. For a smaller but vocal group, the Cold War is indeed over and the West has won, a victory that presages the global triumph of capitalism, the end of communism, indeed even the "end of history."[1] A third group, once large but now a dwindling phalanx, holds that communism remains communism for all Gorbachev's glitter, and that *glasnost* is simply a ploy to dupe the West into financing perestroika until Moscow recovers the strength to resume its inveterate expansionism.[2]

Yet the two dominant Western perspectives on Gorbachev have one element in common: the implication that our troubles with the East are over, that we are home free, at the "end of the division of Europe" and on the eve of the Soviet Union's "reintegration into the international order," a prospect first advanced by Gorbachev but eventually taken up by a hesitant President Bush. So in an odd way the perestroika pietism of the Gorbophiles and the free-market triumphalism of the Gorbophobes converge in anticipation of a happy dénouement of a half-century of postwar polarization of the world.

And, indeed, in this avalanche year of 1989 we are surely coming to the end of a historical epoch. It is hardly so clear, however, that we are entering a simpler, serener age: decaying superpowers do not go quietly into the night. It is not even clear that we are asking the right questions at all about Gorbachev. Certainly Western Sovietology, so assiduously fostered over the past four decades, has done nothing to prepare us for the surprises of the past four years.

Nor is the predominant Western question about Gorbachev's chances for success the most pertinent one, or at least the first we should ask. The real question is: Why is it that seventy years after 1917—which was to have been the ultimate revolution, the revolution to end all further need of revolutions—Gorbachev proclaims *urbi et orbi* that Soviet socialism urgently requires a "new revolution," a "rebuilding" of its fundamental fabric? What is so drastically wrong as to require such drastic action? And what, after four and a half years of increasingly frenetic activity, has in fact been accomplished?

The most natural way to approach this question is to focus on personalities and policies: on Gorbachev and his "conservative" opponents; on "perestroika," "glasnost," and "democratization." And it is this preoccupation which explains the cult of his personality in the West. But if fundamental revolution is now really on the Soviet agenda, then our focus of inquiry ought to be the *longue durée* of deep structures and abiding institutions. And these, as Gorbachev constantly reminds us, were created "sixty years ago," a euphemism for Stalin's "Year of the Great Break," 1929. For this was the beginning of the forced collectivization of agriculture through "dekulakization," together with "full steam ahead" in industry for a "First Five-Year Plan in four years," policies that created the Soviet system as it exists in its main outlines to the present day. In short, Gorbachev is calling into question the very basis of the Soviet order and the historical matrix of what until now was called "developed" or "real" socialism. Perestroika is thus not just a reform of a basically sound structure, but the manifestation of a systemic crisis of Sovietism per se. . . .

II

. . . Awareness that something was seriously amiss with Sovietism first came to the surface in 1983 under Andropov. As head of the KGB, he knew far better than his colleagues the true state of affairs; and he took the novel step of calling on intelligentsia specialists, especially economists and sociologists from the Academy of Sciences, to consult on possible remedies, an enterprise in which his protégé Gorbachev was involved. This endeavor produced the *Novosibirsk Report* by the sociologist Tatania Zaslavskaia, who argued that the Soviet system of centralized planning had become obsolete, a fetter on production, and that Soviet society, far from being a harmonious unity, was riven by the conflicting interests of both the ruling and the ruled—an analysis that implied the necessity of radical restructuring for sheer survival. This document, leaked to the Western press in the once putatively fatal year of 1984, first alerted the world to the impending end of Soviet stability.[3]

At the beginning of his general secretaryship, Gorbachev may be considered as Andropov redux, though the younger leader was driven by a much more acute sense of crisis and a correspondingly bolder willingness to experiment. His initial program of perestroika as controlled economic reform from above therefore quickly branched out in new directions under the pressure of events. *Perestroika* soon came to stand for "radical reform," then "revolutionary change"; and further policies were added to it: "new thinking," or retrenchment, in foreign relations, and "acceleration," "glasnost," and "democratization" domestically. It is in this historical sequence that its course will be examined here.

When Gorbachev first launched perestroika in April 1985, it had the relatively limited purpose of producing a rapid acceleration, or *uskorenie,* of national economic performance; and his method was similar to Andropov's: reliance on administrative action from above in consultation with intelligentsia experts and operation within the existing structures of the Plan and its attendant ministries. For *perestroika* means, literally and simply, refashioning an existing edifice, or *stroika,* the root also of the Russian term for the "building" of socialism. Thus, while he summoned Zaslavskaia and the Novosibirsk economist Abel Aganbegyan to Moscow and positions in Academy of Science think tanks, his basic approach was to jump-start the stalled Soviet productive mechanism by the classic administrative methods of exhortation and bureaucratic reorganization.

An example of the first tack was his 1986 anti-alcohol campaign. This measure backfired, however, by increasing the budget deficit through loss of sizable vodka sales, which now went to the "black" economy. An example of the second tack was the "quality control" of industrial products by state inspectors, whose power to refuse substandard goods, and hence also to lower enterprise revenues, generated insecurity among both managers and workers. In addition, Gorbachev regrouped ministries and replaced cadres on a scale not seen since Stalin. As a result of this, by the fall of 1986 strong resistance emerged among the apparat to further changes, whether of policy or of personnel.[4]

Gorbachev therefore embarked on a second policy, glasnost. In this he was advised by his chief theoretician, Alexander Yakovlev, who had become a connoisseur of modern, Western ways during a decade as ambassador to Canada, an experience that both sharpened his appreciation of Russia's backwardness and acquainted him with the contemporary television techniques required to stimulate innovation. In choosing this new course, Gorbachev was guided by two considerations. As a question of conviction, he recognized that a dynamic economy could not be built with a passive population, isolated from knowledge of the modern world, ignorant even of real conditions within the Soviet Union—a state of affairs that produced Chernobyl, for example. Glasnost was thus intended to energize the nation. Also, as a matter of political tactics, he now made an all-out wager on the "creative intelligentsia" to bring pressure for reform on the recalcitrant apparat.

To signal this change, and to give the intelligentsia assurance that they could speak up without fear, he made a dramatic telephone call to Sakharov in Gorki in December 1986 to summon him back from exile. During the next eighteen months the liberal intelligentsia, in the press and on television, began to criticize society's ills, and to fill in the "blank spots," in Gorbachev's expression, of the Soviet past, with a fervor born of the twenty years of frustration that had built up since the previous thaw under Khrushchev. They did this with all the more passion since it was only by owning up to the errors of the past that they could attack the problems it had created for the present.[5]

In the course of this glasnost explosion, both Gorbachev and his supporters radicalized as they encountered resistance from "conservative" (or more accurately, old socialist) forces under Ligachev. A note of desperation crept into the debate, and on both sides. Ligachev and his allies asserted that the liberal intelligentsia's criticism was leading the country to ruin by undermining the institutions and values that had built socialism and won the Fatherland War. Gorbachev and his supporters answered that the situation was so far gone that there was "no alternative to perestroika": to continue the policies of stagnation would lead to the rapid obsolescence of the economy, loss of superpower status, and ultimately the death of the system. As Yakovlev, in early 1989, put it more bluntly than Gorbachev himself would have dared, "We probably have no more than two to three years to prove that Leninist socialism can work."[6] Thus in 1987 and 1988, the initially self-confident campaign for perestroika of 1985 took on the air of an increasingly desperate gamble, an ever more urgent race against time; and by 1989 matters had acquired the aura of a crisis of survival, which recalled, though in different form, the disaster years of 1921, 1932, and 1941.

The flood of candor under glasnost did indeed produce the consequences of which the conservatives complained, and in a form more radical than during Khrushchev's thaw. For each new revelation about past crimes and disasters did less to stimulate the people to new effort than to desacralize the system in their eyes; it did so all the more thoroughly since the Myth was long since dead, especially among the young. Repressed awareness of the Lie poured forth in a flood progressing from the publication of Anatoli Rybakov's mild novel *Children of the Arbat* in 1986 to that of Solzhenitsyn's outright anti-Soviet *Gulag Archipelago* in 1989. In the process, not only were the long decades of Stalin and Brezhnev swept away, but the very foundations of Sovietism, the economic theories of Marx and the political practices of Lenin, were touched. By 1988 Marxism-Leninism was a shambles; and by 1989 it could be openly denounced by leading intellectuals, such as the historian Iuri Afanasiev, as a dead weight on the mind of the nation.[7]

In the midst of the turmoil unleashed by glasnost, the system was threatened by still another danger: the nationalities crisis and the beginning of the breakup of the empire. The leadership had known from the start of perestroika that it faced an economic problem, but in its Russocentric naiveté was quite unaware it had an equally grave nationalities problem. So the mass strikes of February 1988 in Armenia over the issue of Nagorny-Karabakh came as a total surprise, a "moral Chernobyl," as one Soviet leader put it. But soon autonomist, even separatist, agitation spread to the Baltic states, then to Georgia and Azerbaijan, and by 1989 to the vital Ukraine.

These movements, moreover, everywhere assumed the form of "popular fronts," grouping all classes of the population against the Party apparat (or in the Baltic virtually taking the Party over), a pattern reminiscent of the "dual power" that existed between the original "soviets," or workers' councils, and the Provisional Government in 1917. The cause of this sudden explosion lay in the same process of desacralization that was undermining all Soviet institutions. The fiction that the Party-state was a federal "union" was perhaps the most egregious form of the Lie, for all the border "republics" had in fact been conquered by the Great Russian central region beginning in 1920, with the Baltic states and the Western Ukraine added only as recently as 1939–1944, and then only after a deal with Hitler. When the freedom to criticize released these border populations from fear, the result was a national as well as an anti-Party upsurge; for them *perestroika* came to signify "sovereignty," by which they really meant independence.

With this danger added to the other strains produced by glasnost, the old-line socialists, or conservatives, redoubled their efforts to retain control of the apparat, where the general secretary still lacked an unquestioned majority, from the Politburo down to the base. Given the constraints of Party discipline, this resistance could express itself in public only obliquely, but behind the scenes, what liberals called a bloodless civil war in fact was raging. Its most open expressions were the firing of Boris Yeltsin as Moscow Party chief in the fall of 1987 and the national-Communist, anti-Gorbachev manifesto, known as the "Nina Andreeva Letter," published in much of the press in the spring of 1988.

In response to these pressures, the general secretary moved to a third and still more revolutionary policy: democratization. First bruited in early 1987, this meant double or multiple candidacies in elections and fixed terms of office for all Party and state, or Soviet, posts. This policy was first applied to the Party by convening a Special Party Conference (in effect, a mini-Congress) in June 1988 in an effort to gain at last the majority necessary for a renewed attempt at economic reform. Yet this device, like glasnost, overshot the mark assigned to it, while at the same time it fell short of achieving its intended positive function. The conference turned out to lack the necessary majority of proreform delegates for a purge of apparat deadwood. Yet it began the politicization of the hitherto quiescent Russian lower classes, since the partially televised proceedings revealed the once monolithic and mysterious Party to be a fallible and quarrelsome body of self-seeking interests.

Failing to revitalize the Party, Gorbachev then upped the ante of democratization by using it the following year to reanimate the hierarchy of state administrative bodies, the soviets. Taking up the 1917 slogan "all power to the soviets," he sought to give real political life to both halves of the system of dual administration, in which all power, since Lenin, had belonged to the Party. Again his motives were mixed. There was first his Leninism—by no means a mere ritual invocation—which he vaunted as the "pragmatic" capacity to adapt policy rapidly to changing circumstance and the constant willingness to risk a gamble. Then, too, democracy, like glasnost, was necessary to galvanize the population for perestroika. But above all, Gorbachev sought to give himself a structure of power parallel to the regular apparat. He sought this in part so that he could not be deposed by a Central Committee coup as Khrushchev had been in 1964—a precedent on everyone's mind in the perestroika era—and in part to give himself an independent instrument for putting through his stalled economic programs.[8] And, as some Soviets noted, this effort to outflank the old guard by a parallel power was reminiscent, *mutatis mutandis*, of the way Stalin had used the NKVD against the mainline Party.

This second round of democratization overshot its intended mark far more widely than the first. This became apparent during the elections in March 1989 to a Congress of People's Deputies, whose function was to create a strong executive presidency for Gorbachev and to elect a Supreme Soviet, or national parliament, with some measure of legislative power, unlike its rubber-stamp predecessor. An unintended result of these elections, however, was to produce a resounding defeat not just for the apparat, as Gorbachev wished, but for the Party as an institution. For the first time in seventy years, the population had the possibility of saying no to official candidates, and did so, at least in the large cities, on a major scale. As a result, the "correlation of forces" within the country changed radically: the Party which had hitherto inspired fear in the people suddenly came to fear the population, and demoralization spread throughout its ranks.

This effect was compounded at the Congress meetings, televised live for two weeks during May and June. To be sure, Gorbachev got himself elected president and thus secured a buffer against a coup by the Party. He also obtained the selection of a new Supreme Soviet—in effect, a consultative assembly, rather than a genuine legislature—which he felt confident would do his bidding. But the authoritarian way he pushed these elections through the Congress caused his popularity, already low because of the economic and ethnic problems engendered by perestroika, to reach its nadir; he, too, was desacralized and made to appear as just a bigger apparatchik. Moreover, the liberal delegates, though a minority, dominated the proceedings with a barrage of exposés of all the ills with which the country is afflicted: the poverty, the abominable health service, the rising crime rate, the ecological disasters, the economic disintegration, the KGB's "secret empire," as one deputy dared call it, and the Party corruption. The net result of the Congress was, in the words of another deputy, "the demystification of power."

As a result, Gorbachev's initially demagogic slogan "all power to the people" began to acquire some real content. The Congress first of all produced an organized Left opposition to Gorbachev in the form of the Interregional Group, led by such figures as Sakharov, Yeltsin, Afanasiev, and the economist Popov, a loyal opposition to be sure, yet one that nonetheless insisted that real perestroika was still in the future. Even more boldly, this group broke the supreme taboo of communism and demanded an end to the leading role of the Party.[9] Simultaneously, the Congress debates produced a politicalization of the Great Russian and Ukrainian populations almost as intense as that of the border nationalities. And since the Congress had come up with no concrete remedies for the ills its debates had exposed, by July the population began to take matters into its own hands. The country was swept with a wave of self-organization from below; popular fronts and embryonic trade union associations appeared in the cities of Russia and the Ukraine. Thus "civil society," as the opposition called these new formations, began to emerge for the first time since it had been suppressed in 1918; and in some areas this movement edged off into a form of "dual power," as some radicals asserted, a phenomenon of which the Kuzbas and Donbas miners' strikes in July 1989 were only the most visible and spectacular manifestations.

III

While all this was going on, what had been accomplished in the economic sphere to produce the hoped-for "acceleration" that had been perestroika's starting point? The short answer is: nothing much. Or more accurately still, those measures that were taken led to an outright deterioration of the situation.

Gorbachev's economic program has thus far consisted of two main components, both formulated in 1987.[10] The first of these is the creation of small "cooperatives," in reality private ventures, in the service sector. But the impact of this cooperative sector has been derisory, since its services are priced far above the purchasing power of the 200-rouble-per-month average wage of the majority of the population. These enterprises have therefore become the focus of popular hostility to economic reform in general, since any form of marketization is perceived by "the people"—as the miners made clear during their strike—to benefit only "speculators" and the privileged—a reaction quite in conformity with the socialist egalitarianism the regime inculcated in the population for decades. Moreover, the cooperatives are harassed by the state bureaucracy, whose monopoly they threaten, and are often either taken over by, or made to pay protection money to, various Mafias from the "black" economy.

The second component of Gorbachev's economic reform is the Law on State Enterprises, providing for "self-management" and "self-financing." If actually applied, these provisions would significantly reduce the role of Gosplan and the central ministries by using self-interest to correct the predominance of administrative directives. This reform is thus an effort to return to the spirit, if not the precise institutions, of the NEP, and to its policy of *khozraschyot*, or businesslike management and accountability under a regime of state enterprise. In other words, it is a variant of the half-measures of soft communism, put forth periodically in Soviet history from Bukharin to Eugene Varga just after World War II to Kosygin, but never really implemented because they threaten the Party apparat's "leading role." And, indeed, this time too, the Law on State Enterprises has remained a dead letter ever since it took effect in January 1988, because the silent resistance of legions of apparatchiki has kept industry operating at 90 percent on "state orders"—that is, on the old Plan.[11]

In still other domains, Gorbachev's economic perestroika has met with failure, but this time without his having really tried to produce a program. In agriculture Gorbachev has spoken repeatedly of long-term leases of land, indeed up to fifty years, for the peasantry. But this proposal has gone nowhere, in part because of the resistance of the huge kolkhoz bureaucracy, in part because the peasantry has seen so many different agrarian reforms imposed from above that it will not trust the regime to respect leases of any duration and hence will not take up the government's half-offer.

Thus, Gorbachev is in a far more difficult position than his predecessors in communist economic reform. He no longer has the option of Lenin in 1921 at the beginning of the NEP, or of Deng Xiaoping in 1979 of reviving agricultural and artisan production rapidly by granting the 80 percent of the population that is peasant a free market. The Russian peasantry, now disproportionately aged and only 35 percent of the population, is too decimated and demoralized by over sixty years of collectivization to respond to any NEP-type initiatives. In consequence, Gorbachev has been obliged to begin his perestroika with industry, where the transition to marketization is far more difficult than in agriculture. Here the very success of Stalin in urbanizing Russia has created a cast-iron block to progress.

Another such block is financial and monetary policy. Heavy state subsidies to hold retail prices low, to keep unprofitable factories running, to maintain full employment, and to secure the safety net in place—what some Western specialists call the social contract between regime and people—cannot be abolished without unleashing inflation and thus igniting a social explosion. But unless these subsidies are abolished, or at least reduced, the economy cannot move to real prices; and without real prices there can be no dilution of the Plan by marketization or privatization; nor can there be convertibility of the rouble to reintegrate Russia into the international order. And without movement in these directions, there can be no revival of the economy. So the alternative before Gorbachev is either economic stagnation through subsidies or social upheaval through real prices.

And perestroika faces other problems as well: the infrastructure and the capital stock created by decades of extensive development are now approaching exhaustion. In a nationally televised address in October 1989, Prime Minister Ryzhkov warned that the overburdened railway system (Russia still lives basically in the railroad age) was on the verge of collapse. The country's enormous metallurgical plant is outmoded and unprofitable. Housing and administrative buildings are in a state of disrepair often bordering on disintegration. The extraordinary number of industrial "accidents," from Chernobyl to the gas-line and train explosions of June 1989 are usually due to functional breakdown or criminal neglect. All this exhausted equipment must be restored or replaced, and much of the work force retrained and remotivated.

Then, too, the stores must be filled again. Under the present conditions of collapse and penury, available goods are either siphoned off legally by state enterprises to supply their workers, or they disappear illegally into the black economy. But short of massive imports of foreign goods, stocking the shelves is an impossible task, since decades of wasteful investments and subsidies, and of printing money to finance both, have now created an enormous budget deficit and rapid inflation—both "discovered," or admitted, by the government only in late 1988. As a result of this, a movement away from the rouble to the dollar or to barter is well under way, a phenomenon that presages the collapse of the consumer market.

Under such conditions of near breakdown, any transition to real prices, self-management, and self-financing are quite out of the question for the foreseeable future; and the old reflexes of the command-administrative system are sure to persist, if only to ensure a modicum of order. Thus, active consideration of real market reform has been postponed time and again and is now slated, more or less, for the mid-1990s. Indeed, economic perestroika of any type has been stalled since early 1988.

Overall, then, the balance sheet of more than four years of perestroika has been that the half-reforms introduced so far have unsettled the old economic structures without putting new ones in their place.

And in this, perestroika resembles earlier failed halfway-house reforms in Central Europe: General Jaruzelski's reforms of self-management in 1982 and of self-financing in 1987 in Poland, and earlier still the failed, halfway New Economic Mechanism in Hungary. Yet, despite this accumulated evidence of failure, Gorbachev intends to stick to the unnatural hybrid of "market socialism," as his chief economic advisor, Leonid Abalkin, made clear in November 1989 in launching an updated plan of alleged "transition" away from statism.[12]

The current impasse of perestroika, furthermore, resembles the Soviet NEP, but in reverse. The NEP saw the progressive stifling of the surviving prerevolutionary market economy by the nascent ambitions of Party–state power. Gorbachev's perestroika has witnessed the tenacious resistance of an ailing but still massive Party–state structure to a fledgling yet corrosive market. Whereas it proved easy to move brutally from a market to a command economy, it is turning out to be inordinately difficult to make the more delicate reverse transition. Between Gorbachev and a neo-NEP stands the mountainous mass of decaying Stalinist success, whereas between Lenin and the first NEP there stood only the failed wreckage of War Communism. So Gorbachev is left with the worst of two possible worlds: an old one that refuses to die and a new one without the strength to be born.

At the same time, this failure of economic perestroika coincides with the runaway success of glasnost and the progress of democratization and popular politicalization. The result is a new kind of "scissors crisis," to appropriate a metaphor used by Trotsky during the unstable NEP to describe the upward curve of industrial prices when charted against the downward curve of agricultural prices. Similarly, under the unstable neo-NEP of perestroika, the curve of glasnost and politicalization is running alarmingly high, and that of economic restructuring is sinking catastrophically low.[13] So perestroika, like its predecessor, risks being destroyed by the widening gap of the scissors unless energetic emergency measures are taken soon.

By late fall 1989, Moscow began to hear rumors of a coup. Other rumors, more plausibly, offered speculation about an imminent state of emergency or of a mitigated form of martial law (*osoboe polozhenie*). To everyone, society seemed to be adrift in disorder. Fear of state authority had almost vanished during the summer after the Congress, and with it, so it seemed, the regime's ability to govern. When the emigré Andrei Amalrik twenty years ago published his *Will the Soviet Union Survive until 1984?* his question was met with incredulity, even derision.[14] Now it may well turn out that he was only a few years off.

In the midst of all this, what of Gorbachev, on whose person the West concentrates its attention and hopes? To the outside world, he passes for a bold and decisive leader, a mover and a shaker of major stature, especially in international affairs. When seen from Moscow, however, after his first initiative in unleashing the perestroika deluge, he has come to look more like a reactive than an active figure, a man increasingly incapable of staking out strong policy positions on the two make-or-break domestic issues of his reign, the economy and the nationalities. Instead, he appears essentially as a political tactician, fully at home only in Party maneuvering, now pruning the Politburo of conservative foes such as the former KGB chief, Chebrikov, or the Ukrainian Party boss, Shcherbitsky, as in the fall of 1989, now tacking from left to right and back again in the debates of the new Supreme Soviet. Indeed, by giving way totally and immediately to the miners' demands in July 1989, he appeared downright weak. And in all things he acts as if his economic problems could be solved by political means. Yet, since the direct road to economic perestroika is closed to him by structural blockage, this easier political route of glasnost and democratization is the only one left open to him.

Nor does he seem to be able to make up his mind whether he is head of state or head of the opposition. As one Soviet commentator put it, he is trying to be both Luther and the pope at the same time.[15] But in such a contradictory situation, for all his political prowess, he may yet turn out to be no more than the ultimate sorcerer's apprentice of Sovietism.

IV

As 1989 draws to a close, it is clear that it will enter history as the beginning of communism's terminal crisis, the year of the Second Great Break, but in the descending, not the ascending, phase of utopia in power; and this not just in Russia, but from the Baltic to the China Sea, and from Berlin to Beijing. It is also clear that perestroika and glasnost, welcome as they are in their intention, have in their application only aggravated the systemic crisis they were intended to alleviate. And they have done so because like all forms of soft communism, they go against the logic of the system they are trying to save. The internal contradiction of perestroika is that Gorbachev has been trying to promote soft communism through structures and a population programmed for hard communism. But the latter is the only variety of Sovietism that is the genuine article, for the essence of all varieties of Sovietism is Party supremacy. Thus, the instrument of Gorbachev's reform—the Party—is at the same time the basic cause of Sovietism's troubles. To adapt a diagnosis of Alexander Herzen regarding earlier revolutionaries, the Party is not the doctor; it is the disease.

And the way out of this contradiction then? As one Soviet reformer put it after the June Congress, "The country now stands at a crossroads. From here we either go the Chinese way or the Polish-Hungarian way." Although the speaker obviously wished for the latter course, the alternative he posed may well be a Hobson's choice. The Chinese way since June 1989 means relative, though now declining, market prosperity under a regime of political and military repression. Repression is certainly a possibility in Russia, but market prosperity is quite out of the question for the indefinite future. Conversely, the Polish-Hungarian way means genuine democracy, but this is being attempted in the midst of economic ruin so severe as to threaten the survival of the new constitutional order. In Russia the economic ruin is even worse than in Poland and Hungary, but real democracy, as opposed to mere democratization, is not even on the agenda. Thus, the Russian way could well combine the worst of the Chinese and the Central European scenarios: economic failure in conjunction with an inexpungeable leading role for the Party.

Indeed, all three paths of communist reform (we may leave out of consideration the frozen Albanias such as Romania, Cuba, and North Korea) seem to end in one or another type of impasse. In this way Leninist totalitarianism shows another facet of its difference from ordinary authoritarianism. As Polish radicals discovered in the early 1980s in looking for possible models of liberation, post-Franco Spain and post-Pinochet Chile could not serve as examples. For those countries were able to make the transition to democracy because they had only been political authoritarianisms, not economic, social, and ideological monoliths. And, of course, they possessed market economies, so when political tyranny was ended, civil society, which had never been destroyed, could emerge fully into the light of day. But Leninist regimes, when they enter their final decline, seem able only either to implode, as in Poland, Hungary, and East Germany, or to dig in their heels militarily to stave off implosion, as under Deng Xiaoping in 1989, or his favorite model, the General Jaruzelski of 1981.

Yet whether they implode or hang on for a last desperate stand, all that they leave behind is economic and social rubble—hardly the foundation for building a "normal" society, as the Poles call their hoped-for post-Leninist order. And the leaders of Solidarity are acutely aware of the enormous risk they are taking in assuming power under such parlous conditions. Yet they have no choice but to try, since after eight years of Jaruzelski's failed attempt at being a Polish Kádár—that is, repression followed by liberalizing economic reform—the Party was as bankrupt as the country.

V

This grim impasse at the end of utopia in power is the logical outcome of the structures which that power had built. The whole impossible enterprise of Lenin and Stalin was sustainable only as long as the human and material resources on which the system fed retained the vitality to endure the burden of the regime, and as long as some modicum of material success undergirded the Party's monopolistic position. But when these conditions ceased to hold, beginning with Deng Xiaoping's marketization of 1979 and Solidarity's revolt of 1980, the Communist parties' will to power began to flag and their people's habit of fear began to fade. This soon made necessary, for the Soviet Party–state's survival, the recourse to the expedients of perestroika and glasnost. But these are only pale substitutes for the market and democracy, halfway measures designed to square the circle of making the vivifying forces of a resurrected civil society compatible with the Party's leading role.

But this circle cannot be squared. If marketization and privatization are the economic goals of reform in communist countries, then Party planning becomes superfluous, indeed downright parasitical. If multiple parties, elections, and the rule of law are the political goals of reform in communist countries, then the dual administration of the Party–state becomes supernumerary, indeed positively noxious.

The Party is not a party, in the normal sense of an association for contesting elections and alternating in government under the rule of law. The Party is, rather, a self-appointed society for the monopoly of power. It can tolerate normal parties only as temporary expedients, satellites, or fronts when the political weather is stormy. Likewise, the dual administrative body of the Party–state is not a normal state, but a special instrument created by the Party to act as a transmission belt of its policies to the population through the nomenklatura. Such a state cannot therefore be turned into a normal polity simply by legalizing other parties, since they will not have equal access with the Party to the monopolistic facilities of the state apparatus, from its police to its press. Nor is socialist planning an alternative way to organize the economy; it is the negation of the economy, its death as a separate sphere of human activity through its subordination to politics and ideological imperatives. It is this total amalgam, this whole surreal world, that is summed up by the sacrosanct tenet of the leading role.

This role is in its essence inimical to all the professed goals of reform now echoing throughout the Soviet Union and Central Europe, whether glasnost, democratization, or multiparty elections. All these reforms imply that there is a third way, a halfway house between what the ideological call socialism and capitalism, or what the inhabitants of the East think of as Sovietism and a "normal society." But there is no third way between Leninism and the market, between bolshevism and constitutional government. Marketization and democratization lead to the revival of civil society, and such a society requires the rule of law. But civil society under the rule of law is incompatible with the preservation of the lawless leading role.

At some point, therefore, the redline will be reached where reform crosses over into the liquidation of the leading role and all the structures it has created. And both Russia and Central Europe are now reaching that critical line. The false problem of how to restructure Leninism is now giving way to the real problem of how to dismantle the system, how to effect at last an exit from communism. Perestroika is not a solution, but a transition to this exit. As Milovan Djilas foresaw early in perestroika: communism is not reforming itself, it is disintegrating.[16]

VI

As yet, the only country that has posed the problem of the exit from communism openly and as a matter of practical policy is Poland. Hungary so far has given up on communism and the leading role only verbally; and its free elections are still in the future. To be sure, changing the Party's name to "Socialist" caused membership to drop from 700,000 to 30,000; but even this rump party still controls all the institutional assets of the old Party-state and preserves the aim of maintaining some form of socialism. But Poland has already crossed the redline with a Solidarity-led government proclaiming a goal of full marketization, the phasing out of the nomenklatura, and the decommunization of the army, the police, and the public administration—in short, the end in fact, not just in law, of the leading role, indeed of the whole communist system.

But even in Poland all the structures and coercive power still remain in the Party's hands, and the Solidarity ministry is proceeding very cautiously with de-Sovietization for fear of provoking a "Kabul reaction," a bunker defense, among the 2-million-member Party. Simultaneously, the official trade union, larger than worker Solidarity, is now demagogically exploiting the socialist reflexes inbred by forty years of Sovietism to "defend the rights of workers" against the free-market policies of the Solidarity ministry. Such an attempt at destabilization should not be too difficult to promote amid the economic wreckage left behind after the Party's unexpected implosion during what were to have been the fail-safe elections of last June. (These elections were set up during the previous winter's round table negotiations with Solidarity, designed to give the Party a few more years of respite.) Under such unstable conditions, the oldest and most lucid critic of Polish communism, Stefan Kisielewski, concludes that it will take twenty years to de-Sovietize the Polish mentality and Polish institutions.[17]

So as we rub our eyes in astonishment at the most stunning communist implosions of all, the November collapse of the Berlin Wall and the ensuing Prague revolt, we should not conclude that the structures it shielded for so long can be transformed by a few reform decrees. The revolutionary rapidity of events in 1989 should not breed the illusion that the exit from communism these events presage will itself be a rapid process.

And the most difficult case of all will be the Soviet Union. There, unlike Central Europe, the real problem of dismantling, not reforming, communism is not yet posed, not even by the Interregional Group of People's Deputies: Russia, after all, has had seventy, not forty-five, years of Sovietism. Also, the Soviet Party is a national institution, not an alien imposition, with deep roots in the patriotic success of World War II. Finally, this national-imperial Party has the military apparatus of a superpower. To be sure, Gorbachev is clearly retrenching from the global overextension of the Brezhnev era. True also, in the course of the Polish elections of June, the Hungarian Party reforms and the East German and Czech *Zusammenbruch* of 1989, Moscow has clearly accepted the inevitability of the Finlandization of Central Europe, or national autonomy within the Warsaw Pact, and possibly even some type of Rapallo cooperation with West Germany to revive the ruined economies of the area. Nonetheless, the Soviet military budget has not significantly decreased, nor has modernization of its arsenal ceased. And these circumstances give to the Soviet Party's leading role vertebrae that its little brothers lack.

VII

Let us return now to the questions with which this inquiry began: Can Gorbachev succeed? Should we help him? It is now the official United States position, to quote President Bush, that Gorbachev is a "genuine reformer" and that we all "wish perestroika to succeed," a stance that implies at least moral help. But to answer these questions meaningfully, we must, as with the questions of Stalin's necessity, rephrase them first. Succeed at what? Help him to do what?

If by perestroika's succees we mean producing a communist system that is economically effective and politically democratic, then the answer must be no: the empirical record of seventy years shows that the fundamental structures of the Leninist system reached an inextricable impasse at the end of the 1970s; and the mounting contradictions of perestroika indicate that the system cannot be restructured or reformed, but can only either stagnate or be dismantled and replaced by market institutions over a long period of time. In this case, any aid the West might render to the Soviet state to save or improve the existing system would be futile: on this score, Gorbachev is beyond our help. Such aid would also work against the real interests of the restive Soviet peoples and thus of international stability. Like Western credits to Eduard Gierek and the Polish Party–state in the 1970s, aid to the Soviet government would simply prolong the agony of everyone concerned.

Yet if by perestroika's success we mean effecting a transition from a Party–state and a command economy to democracy and the market, then the answer, unfortunately, must still be no. First of all, such a transition is not the aim of Gorbachev's perestroika; its aim, rather, is to salvage what can be saved of the existing system by halfway-house concessions to economic and human reality, concessions moreover that are constantly being revised as new sections of the system give way and as the regime improvises frantically in the hope that something might turn the situation around. Second, and even more important, such a transition would bring the end of the cardinal leading role and hence would amount to the self-liquidation of communism, something Gorbachev clearly does not intend to do.

Still, events are pressing toward the eventual dwindling away of the system, whatever the Soviet leadership's intentions and whoever that leader might be in the future. And here Western help could play a constructive role. First, reducing the mutual burden of armaments, if carried out with due attention to legitimate security concerns, would ease the severity of the Soviet crisis (though it would not alter its structural causes). And Gorbachev has clearly indicated his willingness to engage in arms reductions, while at the same time taking care that the Soviets' international retreat does not turn into a rout.

Second, although Western aid should not go to shoring up Soviet economic institutions in the state sector, it could be usefully applied to the piecemeal development of parallel structures in a private sector operating on market principles so as to promote economic and eventually, political pluralism. This could take the form, say, of free economic zones operating under IMF conditions in such places as the Baltic states, Armenia, or the Soviet Far East. In this case, the expectation would be that such a parallel sector, perhaps with its own convertible currency, would eventually spread across the Soviet Union.

Such a policy is, indeed, the approach that the Mazowiecki government and its finance minister, Leszek Balcerowicz, are now attempting to inaugurate in Poland. But what Gorbachev is prepared to accept for his outer empire in Central Europe (where he effectively lost control over events sometime in 1988) would be much more difficult for him to accept for the inner empire of the Soviet Union itself, since foreign investment would imperil national sovereignty. So Western investment, in joint or other enterprises in Russia, would have to be handled without triumphalism about capitalism's superiority, and with due sensitivity to Soviet national pride. The West's aim should be to encourage the change of Soviet realities, while leaving the old labels intact—in a kind of socialist-emperor-of-Japan arrangement.

Yet, however the Soviet Union edges toward its particular exit from communism, this unchartered process can only be a long and painful one. Nor will it be a unilinear or an incremental progress toward integration in some "common European house." Instead, further crises will most likely be necessary to produce further, and more real, reforms. And a last-ditch attempt to stave off ruin by curtailing destabilizing reform altogether could lead to that military reaction so feared by Moscow liberals. And who knows, in this scenario Gorbachev might be agile enough to become his own successor, or if perestroika ends in another eighteenth of Brumaire, to be his own Bonaparte. Gorbachev would be hard to replace because his international reputation is now the Soviet Union's chief capital asset; yet he could not afford to be a very tough Bonaparte, since he has become the prisoner of his foreign policy successes.

Obviously, none of these prospects is a cheering one, and none would be easy for the West to live alongside. But it is better to look realistically at the genuine options in the East as they have been molded by seventy years of failed utopia than to engage in fantasies about Gorbachev as a demiurge of instant democracy or about the end of conflict in history. Nor should we forget that communism, though a disaster in almost every creative domain, has always been supremely successful at one thing: resourcefulness and tenacity in holding on to its monopoly of power. So the Soviet world's transition to normality will be a long time coming, for the Party, though now dyed with the hues of glasnost and democratization, will cling to the bitter end, like some poisoned tunic of Nessus, around the bodies of nations it has enfolded in its embrace for so many decades.

NOTES

1. Francis Fukuyama, "The End of History?" *The National Interest* (Summer 1988).
2. See, for example, Judy Stone, *The Coming Soviet Crash: Gorbachev's Desperate Pursuit of Credit in Western Financial Markets* (New York: The Free Press, 1989)—a bad title for an otherwise good book. The threat of financial crash is quite real, but until now Gorbachev has steadfastly refused to use foreign credit extensively for fear of compromising national independence.
3. Tatiana Zaslavskaia, "The Novosibirsk Report," *Survey* 28 (1) (1984): 88–108. An early and perceptive Western statement of the growing contradictions of Sovietism is Seweryn Bialer's *The Soviet Paradox: External Expansion, Internal Decline* (New York: Knopf, 1986).
4. The best treatment of the beginnings of perestroika is Michel Tatu's *Gorbachev: L'U.R.S.S., va-t-elle changer?* (Paris: Le Centurion-Le Monde, 1987).
5. The most comprehensive collection of reformist intelligentsia writings was issued for the June 1988 Special Party Conference. See *Inogo ne dano,* ed. Iuri Afanasiev (Moscow: Izdatel'stvo Progress, 1988). A partial translation exists in French under the title *La Seule Issue* (Paris: Alban Michel, 1989). For the genealogy of the submerged tradition of soft communism from the 1920s on, see Moshe Lewin, *Political Undercurrents in Soviet Economic Debates: From Bukharin to the Modern Reformers* (Princeton, N.J.: Princeton University Press, 1974).
6. Quoted in *Le Monde,* 20 December 1988.
7. Quoted in *Russkaia Mysl' (La pensée russe)* (Paris), 4 August 1989.
8. Igor Kliamkin, *Moscow News,* 15 April 1989.
9. Sakharov's speech at the Congress launching his idea was reproduced in *The New York Review of Books,* 17 August 1989, 25–26.

10. The best discussion of the background to Gorbachev's economic reforms and the development of his early programs is Ed. H. Hewett, *Reforming the Soviet Economy* (Washington, D.C.: The Brookings Institution, 1987). On the Soviet side see Tatiana Zaslavskaia, in *A Voice of Reform: Essays by Tatiana Zaslavskaia*, ed. Murray Yanovitch (Armonk, N.Y.: M.E. Sharpe, 1989) and especially Nikolai Shmelyov and Vladimir Popov's *Na perelome (At the Breaking Point)* (Moscow: Ekonomika, 1989).

11. The most informed, penetrating, and realistic study of economic perestroika's record to date is Anders Aslund, *Gorbachev's Struggle for Economic Reform* (Ithaca, N.Y.: Cornell University Press, 1989).

12. The best general treatments to date of the Gorbachev era overall are: Alec Nove, *Glasnost in Action: Cultural Renaissance in Russia* (Boston: Unwin Hyman, 1989), which is moderately pessimistic; and Walter Laqueur, *The Long Road to Freedom: Russia and Glasnost* (New York: Scribners, 1989), which is distinctly pessimistic. A strong statement of the internal contradictions of Gorbachevism is Vladimir Bukovsky's "Who Resists Gorbachev?" *Washington Quarterly* (Winter 1989).

13. The scissors metaphor was applied to Gorbachev by the historian Sergio Romano, Italian ambassador to Moscow during the last four years. It will be the theme of his forthcoming book, in Italian, on perestroika.

14. Andrei Amalrik, *Will the Soviet Union Survive Until 1984?* (New York: Harper and Row, 1970).

15. Andranik Migranyan, *Literaturnaia Gazeta*, 16 August 1989.

16. Milovan Djilas and George Urban, "Djilas on Gorbachev," *Encounter* 71 (September-October 1987): 3–19.

17. For an example of his thought, see Stefan Kisielewski, *Polen-Oder die Herrschaft der Dilletanten: Sozialismus und Wirtschaftspraxis* (Zurich: Edition Interform, 1978).

PART FOUR

The Problems of a Changing World: Will the World as We Know It Survive?

It has become commonplace to evaluate the problems of the future. Discussions of the year 2000, "future shock," the energy crisis, the food crisis, the environmental crisis, the economic crisis, and the population explosion have become widespread in the press and the media. Many people view postindustrial society as a scientific utopia that will solve many of our pressing material problems. Others think the new society is plagued by the poisonous fruits of science and technology. Intellectuals and professional elites view the effects of scientific progress and economic growth with increasing pessimism. Indeed, many observers consider issues like the balance of power trivial at a time when our future existence seems imperiled by environmental conditions and careless application of new technologies rather than exclusively by an atomic Armageddon. In one year, 1986, these fears seemed to be confirmed by the explosion of the *Challenger* space shuttle in January and by the accident at the Soviet nuclear power plant at Chernobyl in April.

The first article in this section responds to these problems directly. In "Redefining Security," Jessica Tuchman Mathews addresses the environmental problems that could eventually threaten life as we know it on planet Earth. As she points out, polluted coastlines, climatic extremes, and accelerating deforestation may be just the harbinger of new and threatening problems we are only beginning to address. Natural resource and population trends as well as the dangers of greenhouse warming produce dark projections of possible worldwide deterioration. Tuchman Mathews makes practical recommendations regarding the reversal of these ominous trends.

From this profound and bleak analysis, we move to a more optimistic article, "The Coming Global Boom" by Charles R. Morris. Unlike many of the articles in this volume which present deeply pessimistic views about future developments, especially concerning the American role in the world economy, "The Coming Global Boom" offers a very different picture. Morris's optimism is based on three broad factors: the globalization of the world economy; a growing number of politically active people in their forties; and the consequences of steadily falling interest rates. While Morris believes the United States is "too big, too rich, too resourceful" to be excluded form this global boom, he also believes the nation should avoid a protectionist trade policy. Overall, he is confident that the 1990s will be a period of growth, plenty, and progress.

The changing conditions which these two authors identify must be included in any consideration of the course of future society. As these articles illustrate, a consensus does not exist concerning the impact of scientific and industrial advances or the possibility of social and economic decline. Whether the issues are balance of power and nuclear proliferation or energy and food crisis, the problems of tomorrow are inextricably tied to justice and equality, scientific achievement and political wisdom. The future, whether it brings a new age of rare achievement or a turbulent era of escalating crises, may make our thermonuclear era appear tranquil by comparison.

Edmund Burke once wrote, "Society is indeed a contract. . . . It is a partnership in all art; a partnership in every virtue, and in all perfection. As the ends of such a partnership cannot be obtained in many generations, it becomes a partnership not only between those who are living, but between those who are dead, and those who are to be born."

In a new society of pain or plenty, the links between generations may be broken as technology or turmoil makes it increasingly difficult for us to identify with the wars of previous generations. Perhaps the greatest challenge of all in this future environment will be to maintain our links with tradition and to preserve the best human values as society continues to change. In the world arena, a search for links to the past may become central to the quest for a form of order that will maintain what Burke called "the great primeval contract of eternal society."

THE ENVIRONMENT

33

Redefining National Security

JESSICA TUCHMAN MATHEWS

I

The 1990s will demand a redefinition of what constitutes national security. In the 1970s the concept was expanded to include international economics as it became clear that the U.S. economy was no longer the independent force it had once been, but was powerfully affected by economic policies in dozens of other countries. Global developments now suggest the need for another analogous, broadening definition of national security to include resource, environmental and demographic issues.

The assumptions and institutions that have governed international relations in the postwar era are a poor fit with these new realities. Environmental strains that transcend national borders are already beginning to break down the sacred boundaries of national sovereignty, previously rendered porous by the information and communication revolutions and the instantaneous global movement of financial capital. The once sharp dividing line between foreign and domestic policy is blurred, forcing governments to grapple in international forums with issues that were contentious enough in the domestic arena.

II

Despite the headlines of 1988—the polluted coastlines, the climatic extremes, the accelerating deforestation and flooding that plagued the

Reprinted by permission of *Foreign Affairs*, Spring 1989. Copyright 1989 by the Council on Foreign Relations, Inc.

Note: It is a violation of the law to reproduce this selection by any means whatsoever without the written permission of the copyright holder.

planet—human society has not arrived at the brink of some absolute limit to its growth. The planet may ultimately be able to accommodate the additional five to six billion people projected to be living here by the year 2100. But it seems unlikely that the world will be able to do so unless the means of production change dramatically. Global economic output has quadrupled since 1950 and it must continue to grow rapidly simply to meet basic human needs, to say nothing of the challenge of lifting billions from poverty. But economic growth as we currently know it requires more energy use, more emissions and wastes, more land converted from its natural state, and more need for the products of natural systems. Whether the planet can accommodate all of these demands remains an open question.

Individuals and governments alike are beginning to feel the cost of substituting for (or doing without) the goods and services once freely provided by healthy ecosystems. Nature's bill is presented in many different forms: the cost of commercial fertilizer needed to replenish once naturally fertile soils; the expense of dredging rivers that flood their banks because of soil erosion hundreds of miles upstream; the loss in crop failures due to the indiscriminate use of pesticides that inadvertently kill insect pollinators; or the price of worsening pollution, once filtered from the air by vegetation. Whatever the immediate cause for concern, the value and absolute necessity for human life of functioning ecosystems is finally becoming apparent.

Moreover, for the first time in its history, mankind is rapidly—if inadvertently—altering the basic physiology of the planet. Global changes currently taking place in the chemical composition of the atmosphere, in the genetic diversity of species inhabiting the planet, and in the cycling of vital chemicals through the oceans, atmosphere, biosphere and geosphere, are unprecedented in both their pace and scale. If left unchecked, the consequences will be profound and, unlike familiar types of local damage, irreversible.

III

Population growth lies at the core of most environmental trends. It took 130 years for world population to grow from one billion to two billion: it will take just a decade to climb from today's five billion to six billion. More than 90 percent of the added billion will live in the developing world, with the result that by the end of the 1990s the developed countries will be home to only 20 percent of the world's people, compared to almost 40 percent at the end of World War II. Sheer numbers do not translate into political power, especially when most of the added billion will be living in poverty. But the demographic shift will thrust the welfare of developing nations further toward the center of international affairs.

The relationship linking population levels and the resource base is complex. Policies, technologies and institutions determine the impact of population growth. These factors can spell the difference between a highly stressed, degraded environment and one that can provide for many more people. At any given level of investment and knowledge, absolute population numbers can be crucial. For example, traditional systems of shifting agriculture—in which land is left fallow for a few years to recover from human use—can sustain people for centuries, only to crumble in a short time when population densities exceed a certain threshold. More important, though, is the *rate* of growth. A government that is fully capable of providing food, housing, jobs and health care for a population growing at one percent per year (therefore doubling its population in 72 years), might be completely overwhelmed by an annual growth rate of three percent, which would double the population in 24 years.

Today the United States and the Soviet Union are growing at just under one percent annually (Europe is gowing only half that fast). But Africa's population is expanding by almost three percent per year, Latin America's by nearly two percent and Asia's somewhat less. By 2025 the working-age population in developing countries alone will be larger than the world's current total population. This growth comes at a time when technological advance requires higher levels of education and displaces more labor than ever before. For many developing countries, continued growth at current rates means that available capital is swallowed up in meeting the daily needs of people, rather than invested in resource conservation and job creation. Such policies inescapably lay the foundations of a bleak future.

An important paradox to bear in mind when examining natural resource trends is that so-called nonrenewable resources—such as coal, oil and minerals—are in fact inexhaustible, while so-called renewable resources can be finite. As a nonrenewable resource becomes scarce and more expensive, demand falls, and substitutes and alternative technologies appear. For that reason we will never pump the last barrel of oil or anything close to it. On the other hand, a fishery fished beyond a certain point will not recover, a species driven to extinction will not reappear, and eroded topsoil cannot be replaced (except over geological time). There are, thus, threshold effects for renewable resources that belie the name given them, with unfortunate consequences for policy.

The most serious form of renewable resource decline is the deforestation taking place throughout the tropics. An area the size of Austria is deforested each year. Tropical forests are fragile ecosystems, extremely vulnerable to human disruption. Once disturbed, the entire ecosystem can unravel. The loss of the trees causes the interruption of nutrient cycling above and below the soil, the soil loses fertility, plant and animal species lose their habitats and become extinct, and acute fuelwood shortages appear (especially in the dry tropical forests). The soil erodes without the ground cover provided by trees and plants, and downstream rivers suffer siltation, causing floods and droughts, and damaging expensive irrigation and hydroelectric systems. Traced through its effects on agriculture, energy supply and water resources, tropical deforestation impoverishes about a billion people. This pattern is endemic throughout Central America, much of Asia, sub-Saharan Africa and South America.

The planet's evolutionary heritage—its genetic diversity—is heavily concentrated in these same forests. It is therefore disappearing today on a scale not seen since the age of the dinosaurs, and at an unprecedented pace. Biologists estimate that species are being lost in the tropical forests 1,000–10,000 times faster than the natural rate of extinction.[1] As many as 20 percent of all the species now living may be gone by the year 2000. The loss will be felt aesthetically, scientifically and, above all, economically. These genetic resources are an important source of food, materials for energy and construction, chemicals for pharmaceuticals and industry, vehicles for health and safety testing, natural pest controls and dozens of other uses.

The only reason that species loss is not a front-page issue is that the majority of species have not yet been discovered, much less studied, so that none but a few conservation biologists can even guess at the number and kinds of species that are vanishing. The bitter irony is that genetic diversity is disappearing on a grand scale at the very moment when biotechnology makes it possible to exploit fully this resource for the first time.

Soil degradation is another major concern. Both a cause and a consequence of poverty, desertification, as it is generally called, is causing declining agricultural productivity on nearly two billion hectares, 15 percent of the earth's land area. The causes are overcultivation, overgrazing, erosion, and salinization and waterlogging due to poorly managed irrigation. In countries as diverse at Haiti, Guatemala, Turkey and India, soil erosion has sharply curtailed agricultural production and potential, sometimes destroying it completely. Though the data are uncertain, it is estimated that the amount of land permanently removed from cultivation due to salinization and waterlogging is equal to the amount of land newly irrigated at great expense each year.

Finally, patterns of land tenure, though not strictly an environmental condition, have an immense environmental impact. In 1975, seven percent of landowners in Latin America possessed 93 percent of all the arable land in this vast region. In Guatemala, a typical case, two percent of the population in 1980 owned 80 percent of the land, while 83 percent of farmers lived on plots too small to support a household. At the same time, even in Costa Rica, with its national concern for social equity, three percent of landowners held 54 percent of the land. These large holdings generally include the most desirable land. The great mass of the rural population is pushed onto the most damage-prone land, usually dry or highly erodible slopes, and into the forests. Land reform is among the most difficult of all political undertakings, but without it many countries will be unable to create a healthy agricultural sector to fuel economic growth.

Environmental decline occasionally leads directly to conflict, especially when scarce water resources must be shared. Generally, however, its impact on nations' security is felt in the downward pull on economic performance and, therefore, on political stability. The underlying cause of turmoil is often ignored; instead governments address the poverty and instability that are its results.

In the Philippines, for example, the government regularly granted logging concessions of less than ten years. Since it takes 30–35 years for a second-growth forest to mature, loggers had no incentive to replant. Compounding the error, flat royalties encouraged the loggers to remove only the most valuable species. A horrendous 40 percent of the harvestable lumber never left the forests but, having been damaged in the logging, rotted or was burned in place. The unsurprising result of these and related policies is that out of 17 million hectares of closed forests that flourished early in the century only 1.2 million remain today. Moreover, the Philippine government received a fraction of the revenues it could have collected if it had followed sound resource management policies that would have also preserved the forest capital. This is biological deficit financing writ large.

Similarly, investments in high-technology fishing equipment led to larger harvests but simultaneously depleted the stock. Today, ten of 50 major Philippine fishing grounds are believed to be overfished; the net result of heavy investment is that the availability of fish per capita has actually dropped. These and other self-destructive environmental policies, combined with rapid population growth, played a significant role in the economic decline that led to the downfall of the Marcos regime. So far, the government of Corazon Aquino has made few changes in the forestry, fishery and other environmental policies it inherited.

Conditions in sub-Saharan Africa, to take another case, have reached catastrophic dimensions. In the first half of this decade export earnings fell by almost one-third, foreign debt soared to 58 percent of GNP, food imports grew rapidly while consumption dropped, and per capita GNP fell by more than three percent. A large share of those woes can be traced to Africa's dependence on a fragile, mismanaged and overstressed natural resource base.

Exports of mineral and agricultural commodities alone account for a quarter of the region's GNP, and nearly three-quarters of the population makes its living off the land, which also supplies, as fuelwood, 80 percent of the energy consumed. The land's capacity to produce is ebbing away under the pressure of rapidly growing numbers of people who do not have the wherewithal to put back into the land what they take from it. A vicious cycle of human and resource impoverishment sets in. As the vegetative cover—trees, shrubs and grass—shrinks from deforestation and overgrazing, soil loses its capacity to retain moisture and nourish crops. The decline accelerates as farmers burn dung and crop residues in place of fuelwood, rather than using them to sustain the soil. Agricultural yields then fall further, and the land becomes steadily more vulnerable to the naturally variable rainfall that is the hallmark of arid and semiarid regions, turning dry spells into droughts and periods of food shortage into famines. Ethiopia is only the most familiar case. The sequence is repeated throughout the region with similarly tragic results.

If such resource and population trends are not addressed, as they are not in so much of the world today, the resulting economic decline leads to frustration, resentment, domestic unrest or even civil war. Human suffering and turmoil make countries ripe for authoritarian government or external subversion. Environmental refugees spread the disruption across national borders. Haiti, a classic example, was once so forested and fertile that it was known as the "Pearl of the Antilles." Now deforested, soil erosion in Haiti is so rapid that some farmers believe stones grow in their fields, while bulldozers are needed to clear the streets of Port-au-Prince of topsoil that flows down from the mountains in the rainy season. While many of the boat people who fled to the United States left because of the brutality of the Duvalier regimes, there is no question that—and this is not widely recognized—many Haitians were forced into the boats by the impossible task of farming bare rock. Until Haiti is reforested, it will never be politically stable.

Haitians are by no means the world's only environmental refugees. In Indonesia, Central America and sub-Saharan Africa, millions have been forced to leave their homes in part because the loss of tree cover, the disappearance of soil, and other environmental ills have made it impossible to grow food. Sudan, despite its civil war, has taken in more than a million refugees from Ethiopia, Uganda and Chad. Immigrants from the spreading Sahel make up one-fifth of the total population in the Ivory Coast. Wherever refugees settle, they flood the labor market, add to the local demand for food and put new burdens on the land, thus spreading the environmental stress that originally forced them from their homes. Resource mismanagement is not the only cause of these mass movements, of course. Religious and ethnic conflicts, political repression and other forces are at work. But the environmental causes are an essential factor.

IV

A different kind of environmental concern has arisen from mankind's new ability to alter the environment on a planetary scale. The earth's physiology is shaped by the characteristics of four elements (carbon, nitrogen, phosphorous and sulfur); by its living inhabitants (the biosphere); and by the interactions of the atmosphere and the oceans, which produce our climate.

Mankind is altering both the carbon and nitrogen cycles, having increased the natural carbon dioxide concentration in the atmosphere by 25 percent. This has occurred largely in the last three decades through fossil-fuel use and deforestation. The production of commercial fertilizer has doubled the amount of nitrogen nature makes available to living things. The use of a single, minor class of chemicals, chlorofluorocarbons, has punched a continent-sized "hole" in the ozone layer at the top of the stratosphere over Antarctica, and caused a smaller, but growing loss of ozone all around the planet. Species loss is destroying the work of three billion years of evolution. Together these changes could drastically alter the conditions in which life on earth has evolved.

The greenhouse effect results from the fact that the planet's atmosphere is largely transparent to incoming radiation from the sun but absorbs much of the lower energy radiation re-emitted by the earth. This natural phenomenon makes the earth warm enough to support life. But as emissions of greenhouse gases increase, the planet is warmed *unnaturally*. Carbon dioxide produced from the combustion of fossil fuels and by deforestation is responsible for about half of the greenhouse effect. A number of other gases, notably methane (natural gas), nitrous oxide, ozone (in the lower atmosphere, as distinguished from the protective ozone layer in the stratosphere) and the man-made chlorofluorocarbons are responsible for the other half.

Despite important uncertainties about aspects of the greenhouse warming, a virtually unanimous scientific consensus exists on its central features. If present emission trends continue, and unless some as yet undocumented phenomenon (possibly increased cloudiness) causes an offsetting cooling, the planet will, on average, get hotter because of the accumulation of these gases. Exactly how large the warming will be, and how fast it will occur, are uncertain. Existing models place the date of commitment to an average global warming of 1.5–4.5°C (3–8°F) in the early 2030s. The earth has not been this hot for two million years, long before human society, and indeed, even Homo sapiens, existed.

Hotter temperatures will be only one result of the continuing greenhouse warming. At some point, perhaps quite soon, precipitation patterns are likely to shift, possibly causing dustbowl-like conditions in the U.S. grain belt. Ocean currents are expected to do the same, dramatically altering the climates of many regions. A diversion of the Gulf Stream, for example, would transform Western Europe's climate, making it far colder than it is today. Sea level will rise due to the expansion of water when it is warmed and to the melting of land-based ice. The oceans are presently rising by one-half inch per decade, enough to cause serious erosion along much of the U.S. coast. The projected rise is one to four feet by the year 2050. Such a large rise in the sea level would inundate vast coastal regions, erode shorelines, destroy coastal marshes and swamps (areas of very high biological productivity), pollute water supplies through the intrusion of salt water, and put at high risk the vastly disproportionate share of the world's economic wealth that is packed along coastlines. The great river deltas, from the Mississippi to the Ganges, would be flooded. Estimates are that a half-meter rise in Egypt would displace 16 percent of the population, while a two-meter rise in Bangladesh would claim 28 percent of the land where 30 million people live today and where more than 59 million are projected to live by 2030.

Positive consequences would be likely as well. Some plants would grow more quickly, fertilized by the additional carbon dioxide. (Many of them, however, will be weeds.) Rainfall might rise in what are now arid but potentially fertile regions, such as parts of sub-Saharan Africa. Conditions for agriculture would also improve in those northern areas that have both adequate soils and water supplies. Nonetheless, as the 1988 drought in the United States vividly demonstrated, human societies, industrial no less than rural, depend on the normal, predictable functioning of the climate system. Climate undergoing rapid change will not only be less predictable because it is different, but may be inherently more variable. Many climatologists believe that as accumulating greenhouse gases force the climate out of equilibrium, climate extremes—such as hurricanes, droughts, cold snaps and typhoons—will become more frequent and perhaps more intense.

Since climate change will be felt in every economic sector, adapting to its impact will be extremely expensive. Developing countries with their small reserves of capital, shortages of scientists and engineers, and weak central governments will be the least able to adapt, and the gap between the developed and developing worlds will almost certainly widen. Many of the adaptations needed will be prohibitively costly, and many impacts, notably the effects on wildlife and ecosystems, will be beyond the reach of human correction. A global strategy that relies on future adaption almost certainly means greater economic and human costs, and vastly larger biological losses, than would a strategy that attempts to control the extent and speed of the warming.

Greenhouse change is closely linked to stratospheric ozone depletion, which is also caused by chlorofluorocarbons. The increased ultraviolet radiation resulting from losses in that protective layer will cause an increase in skin cancers and eye damage. It will have many still uncertain impacts on plant and animal life, and may suppress the immune system of many species.

Serious enough in itself, ozone depletion illustrates a worrisome feature of man's newfound ability to cause global change. It is almost impossible to predict accurately the long-term impact of new chemicals or processes on the environment. Chlorofluorocarbons were thoroughly tested when first introduced, and found to be benign. Their effect on the remote stratosphere was never considered.

Not only is it difficult to anticipate all the possible consequences in a highly interdependent, complex system, the system itself is poorly understood. When British scientists announced the appearance of a continent-sized "hole" in the ozone layer over Antarctica in 1985, the discovery sent shock waves through the scientific community. Although stratospheric ozone depletion had been the subject of intense study and debate for more than a decade, no one had predicted the Antarctic hole and no theory could account for it.

The lesson is this: current knowledge of planetary mechanisms is so scanty that the possibility of surprise, perhaps quite nasty surprise, must be rated rather high. The greatest risk may well come from a completely unanticipated direction. We lack both crucial knowledge and early warning systems.

V

Absent profound change in man's relationship to his environment, the future does not look bright. Consider the planet without such change in the year 2050. Economic growth is projected to have quintupled by then. Energy use could also quintuple; or if post–1973 trends continue, it may grow more slowly, perhaps only doubling or tripling. The human species already consumes or destroys 40 percent of all the energy produced by terrestrial photosynthesis, that is, 40 percent of the food energy potentially available to living things on land. While that fraction may be sustainable, it is doubtful that it could keep pace with the expected doubling of the world's population. Human use of 80 percent of the planet's potential productivity does not seem compatible with the continued functioning of the biosphere as we know it. The expected rate of species loss would have risen from perhaps a few each day to several hundred a day. The pollution and toxic waste burden would likely prove unmanageable. Tropical forests would have largely disappeared, and arable land, a vital resource in a world of ten billion people, would be rapidly decreasing due to soil degradation. In short, sweeping change in economic production systems is not a choice but a necessity.

Happily, this grim sketch of conditions in 2050 is not a prediction, but a projection, based on current trends. Like all projections, it says more about the present and the recent past than it does about the future. The planet is not destined to a slow and painful decline into environmental chaos. There are technical, scientific and economical solutions that are feasible to many current trends, and enough is known about promising new approaches to be confident that the right kinds of research will produce huge payoffs. Embedded in current practices are vast costs in lost opportunities and waste, which, if corrected, would bring massive benefits. Some such steps will require only a reallocation of money, while others will require sizable capital investments. None of the needed steps, however, requires globally unaffordable sums of money. What they do demand is a sizable shift in priorities.

For example, family-planning services cost about $10 per user, a tiny fraction of the cost of the basic human needs that would otherwise have to be met. Already identified opportunities for raising the efficiency of energy use in the United States cost one-half to one-seventh the cost of new energy supply. Comparable savings are available in most other countries. Agroforestry techniques, in which carefully selected combinations of trees and shrubs are planted together with crops, can not only replace the need for purchased fertilizer but also improve soil quality, make more water available to crops, hold down weeds, and provide fuelwood and higher agricultural yields all at the same time.

But if the technological opportunities are boundless, the social, political and institutional barriers are huge. Subsidies, pricing policies and economic discount rates encourage resource depletion in the name of economic growth, while delivering only the illusion of sustainable growth. Population control remains a controversial subject in much of the world. The traditional prerogatives of nation states are poorly matched with the needs for regional cooperation and global decision-making. And ignorance of the biological underpinning of human society blocks a clear view of where the long-term threats to global security lie.

Overcoming these economic and political barriers will require social and institutional inventions comparable in scale and vision to the new arrangements conceived in the decade following World War II. Without the sharp political turning point of a major war, and with threats that are diffuse and long term, the task will be more difficult. But if we are to avoid irreversible damage to the planet and a heavy toll in human suffering, nothing less is likely to suffice. A partial list of the specific changes suggests how demanding a task it will be.

Achieving sustainable economic growth will require the remodeling of agriculture, energy use and industrial production after nature's example—their reinvention, in fact. These economic systems must become circular rather than linear. Industry and manufacturing will need processes that use materials and energy with high efficiency, recycle by-products and produce little waste. Energy demand will have to be met with the highest efficiency consistent with full economic growth. Agriculture will rely heavily upon free ecosystem services instead of nearly exclusive reliance on man-made substitutes. And all systems will have to price goods and services to reflect the environmental costs of their provision.

A vital first step, one that can and should be taken in the very near term, would be to reinvent the national income accounts by which gross national product is measured. GNP is the foundation on which national economic policies are built, yet its calculation does not take into account resource depletion. A country can consume its forests, wildlife and fisheries, its minerals, its clean water and its topsoil, without seeing a reflection of the loss in its GNP. Nor are ecosystem services—sustaining soil fertility, moderating and storing rainfall, filtering air and regulating the climate—valued, though their loss may entail great expense. The result is that economic policymakers are profoundly misled by their chief guide.

A second step would be to invent a set of indicators by which global environmental health could be measured. Economic planning would be adrift without GNP, unemployment rates, and the like, and social planning without demographic indicators—fertility rates, infant mortality, literacy, life expectancy—would be impossible. Yet this is precisely where environmental policymaking stands today.

Development assistance also requires new tools. Bilateral and multilateral donors have found that project success rates climb when nongovernmental organizations distribute funds and direct programs. This is especially true in agriculture, forestry and conservation projects. The reasons are not mysterious. Such projects are more decentralized, more attuned to local needs and desires, and have a much higher degree of local participation in project planning. They are usually quite small in scale, however, and not capable of handling very large amounts of development funding. Often, too, their independent status threatens the national government. Finding ways to make far greater use of the strengths of such groups without weakening national governments is another priority for institutional innovation.

Better ways must also be found to turn the scientific and engineering strengths of the industrialized world to the solution of the developing world's problems. The challenges include learning enough about local constraints and conditions to ask the right questions, making such research professionally rewarding to the individual scientist, and transferring technology more effectively. The international centers for agricultural research, a jointly managed network of thirteen institutions launched in the 1960s, might be improved upon and applied in other areas.

On the political front, the need for a new diplomacy and for new institutions and regulatory regimes to cope with the world's growing environmental interdependence is even more compelling. Put bluntly, our accepted definition of the limits of national sovereignty as coinciding with national borders is obsolete. The government of Bangladesh, no matter how hard it tries, cannot prevent tragic floods, such as it suffered last year. Preventing them requires active cooperation from Nepal and India. The government of Canada cannot protect its water resources from acid rain without collaboration with the United States. Eighteen diverse nations share the heavily polluted Mediterranean Sea. Even the Caribbean Islands, as physically isolated as they are, find themselves affected by others' resource management policies as locusts, inadvertently bred through generations of exposure to pesticides and now strong enough to fly all the way from Africa, infest their shores.

The majority of environmental problems demand regional solutions which encroach upon what we now think of as the prerogatives of national governments. This is because the phenomena themselves are defined by the limits of watershed, ecosystem, or atmospheric transport, not by national borders. Indeed, the costs and benefits of alternative policies cannot often be accurately judged without considering the region rather than the nation.

The developing countries especially will need to pool their efforts in the search for solutions. Three-quarters of the countries in sub-Saharan Africa, for example, have fewer people than live in New York City. National scientific and research capabilities cannot be built on such a small population base. Regional cooperation is required.

Dealing with global change will be more difficult. No one nation or even group of nations can meet these challenges, and no nation can protect itself from the actions—or inaction—of others. No existing institution matches these criteria. It will be necessary to reduce the dominance of the superpower relationship which so often encourages other countries to adopt a wait-and-see attitude (you solve your problems first, then talk to us about change).

The United States, in particular, will have to assign a far greater prominence than it has heretofore to the practice of multilateral diplomacy. This would mean changes that range from the organization of the State Department and the language proficiency of the Foreign Service, to the definition of an international role that allows leadership without primacy, both in the slogging work of negotiation and in adherence to final outcomes. Above all, ways must soon be found to step around the deeply entrenched North–South cleavage and to replace it with a planetary sense of shared destiny. Perhaps the successes of the U.N. specialized agencies can be built upon for this purpose. But certainly the task of forging a global energy policy in order to control the greenhouse effect, for example, is a very long way from eradicating smallpox or sharing weather information.

The recent Soviet proposal to turn the U.N. Trusteeship Council, which has outlived the colonies it oversaw, into a trusteeship for managing the global commons (the oceans, the atmosphere, biological diversity and planetary climate) deserves close scrutiny. If a newly defined council could sidestep the U.N.'s political fault lines, and incorporate, rather than supplant, the existing strengths of the United Nations Environment Programme, it might provide a useful forum for reaching global environmental decisions at a far higher political level than anything that exists now.

Today's negotiating models—the Law of the Sea Treaty, the Nuclear Nonproliferation Treaty, even the promising Convention to Protect the Ozone Layer—are inadequate. Typically, such agreements take about 15 years to negotiate and enter into force, and perhaps another ten years before substantial changes in behavior are actually achieved. (The NPT, which required only seven years to complete these steps, is a notable exception.) Far better approaches will be needed.

Among these new approaches, perhaps the most difficult to achieve will be ways to negotiate successfully in the presence of substantial scientific uncertainty. The present model is static: years of negotiation leading to a final product. The new model will have to be fluid, allowing a rolling process of intermediate or self-adjusting agreements that respond quickly to growing scientific understanding. The recent Montreal agreement on the ozone layer supplies a useful precedent by providing that one-third of the parties can reconvene a scientific experts group to consider new evidence as it becomes available. The new model will require new economic methods for assessing risk, especially where the possible outcomes are irreversible. It will depend on a more active political role for biologists and chemists than they have been accustomed to, and far greater technical competence in the natural and planetary sciences among policymakers. Finally, the new model may need to forge a more involved and constructive role for the private sector. Relegating the affected industries to a heel-dragging, adversarial, outsiders role almost guarantees a slow process. The ozone agreement, to cite again this recent example, would not have been reached as quickly, and perhaps not at all, had it not been for the cooperation of the chlorofluorocarbon producers.

International law, broadly speaking, has declined in influence in recent years. With leadership and commitment from the major powers it might regain its lost status. But that will not be sufficient. To be effective, future arrangements will require provisions for monitoring, enforcement and compensation, even when damage cannot be assigned a precise monetary value. These are all areas where international law has traditionally been weak.

This is only a partial agenda for the needed decade of invention. Meanwhile, much can and must be done with existing means. Four steps are most important: prompt revision of the Montreal Treaty, to eliminate completely the production of chlorofluorocarbons no later than the year 2000; full support for and implementation of the global Tropical Forestry Action Plan developed by the World Bank, the U.N.'s Development Programme, the Food and Agricultural Organization, and the World Resources Institute; sufficient support for family planning programs to ensure that all who want contraceptives have affordable access to them at least by the end of the decade; and, for the United States, a ten-year energy policy with the goal of increasing the energy productivity of our economy (i.e., reducing the amount of energy required to produce a dollar of GNP) by about three percent each year. While choosing four priorities from dozens of needed initiatives is highly arbitrary, these four stand out as ambitious yet achievable goals on which a broad consensus could be developed, and whose success would bring multiple, long-term global benefits touching every major international environmental concern.

VI

Reflecting on the discovery of atomic energy, Albert Einstein noted "everything changed." And indeed, nuclear fission became the dominant force—military, geopolitical, and even psychological and social— of the ensuring decades. In the same sense, the driving force of the coming decades may well be environmental change. Man is still utterly dependent on the natural world but now has for the first time the ability to alter it, rapidly and on a global scale. Because of that difference, Einstein's verdict that "we shall require a substantially new manner of thinking if mankind is to survive" still seems apt.

NOTE

1. E. O. Wilson, ed., *Biodiversity*, Washington, D.C.: National Academy Press, 1988, pp. 5–18.

THE ECONOMY

34

The Coming Global Boom

CHARLES R. MORRIS

The prevailing economic opinion in the United States, it sometimes seems, is one of unrelieved Spenglerian gloom. The world creaks beneath hopeless burdens of debt and deficit. Japan is destroying the international trading economy with its single-minded drive toward mercantilist conquest. America is besotted by the bright torrent of electronic gewgaws from Asia. Europe is retreating into its "Fortress 1992."

Latter-day Jeremiahs draw dire conclusions. Ravi Batra's warnings of a thunderous seven-year depression, starting next year, are runaway best sellers. Batra is a disciple of an obscure Indian historian, P. R. Sarkar, and he insists that Sarkar's theory of social cycles, which stresses the increased concentration of wealth and the buildup of debt of all kinds, points to a collapse in commerce and prices, a free fall into the abyss. The best place for your money, according to Batra, is a safe-deposit box or a mattress. Paul Erdman, the Swiss banker turned novelist and prognosticator, expected "the panic of '89" to be a deflationary downward spiral like Batra's, if not so prolonged a one. Erdman counsels investors not to buy stocks until the Dow Jones hits 1200.

Mainstream economists, like Stephen Marris and C. Fred Bergsten, of the Institute for International Economics, in Washington, D.C., worry about the tendency of Washington's persistent budget deficits to leach away savings, drive up consumption, and suck in imports. Unless America takes hold of its economic destiny, they warn, the future offers a choice of horrors. Feckless consumerism might ignite runaway inflation, or the Federal Reserve might jack up interest rates so high—both to head off inflation and to attract foreign savings to float the buying spree—that it will cause a worldwide recession.

Reprinted by permission of Russell & Volkening as agents for the author. Copyright © 1989 by Charles Morris. Originally published in *The Atlantic* Oct. 1989.

Note: It is a violation of the law to reproduce this selection by any means whatsoever without the written permission of the copyright holder.

A. Gary Shilling, the president of his own economic advisory firm, with a blue-ribbon list of Wall Street and corporate clients, expects a near-term global recession, followed by a long and painful cycle of deflation. "The world's debt load has far outrun its collateral," he says, "whether you're talking about the Third World, farm land, corporations, consumers, everything. It will take a major global recession to force a debt restructuring. But even coming out of the recession there will be a fierce battle for exports—there's a lot of extra capacity coming on line in the developing countries—and a protectionist scramble. Governments won't help. Military spending is dropping; Star Wars will turn into Trade Wars. It's hard to foresee a happy resolution even longer-term."

These are all serious and respected thinkers. Even Batra, whose reading of history is sometimes comically simplistic, has made substantial contributions to the theory of international trade. But there is another view. A small but growing group of economists makes a strong case that the world and the United States, instead of teetering on the edge of disaster, are really on the threshold of an almost unprecedented long-run economic boom.

THE CASE FOR OPTIMISM

The intellectual icon of the new optimists is Joseph Schumpeter, an Austrian economist who did much of his work in the United States. Schumpeter, who died in 1950, was one of the first to develop the theory of business cycles. He believed that economies progress in fitful starts and stops, interspersing long periods of economic dislocation with stretches of sustained growth and development. The driving forces behind Schumpeter's cycles of boom and bust are the pace of industrial innovation and the diffusion of new technology. In Schumpeter's terms, the optimists see the long run of economic turmoil that began in the early 1970s as a period of dislocation that is the prelude to a new industrial golden age.

Although there is some overlap between the new optimists and the supply-side publicists—the people, that is, who predicted we could have tax cuts without budget deficits—their case is not just blind Panglossism. It rests on sophisticated arguments, derived from economic and demographic developments around the world and in the United States. The gap between the optimists' view and that of most economists, according to Edward Yardeni the chief economist at Prudential-Bache Securities, who is one of the most vocal of the optimists, is that mainstream economics focuses too much on formal macroeconomic models. "Most economists don't look much at the real economy," Yardeni says. "It's messy and doesn't translate well to models. But when you stop and look, the case for a long-run boom is almost over-whelming."

The optimists' arguments reduce essentially to three. The first is the integration of the global goods markets. Everyone knows about global *financial* markets. Stocks, bonds, and bank deposits surge around the world in nanoseconds, riding the twinkling green blips on trading-room computer screens. Integration of the manufacturing economy is an even newer development. High-productivity manufacturing technology, much of it pioneered in Japan, is spreading rapidly throughout the world, at the same time that big companies, and even many medium-sized companies, are operating more and more on a global scale. The result is relentless global competition on price and quality, a steady, even startling, worldwide increase in manufacturing productivity, and solid increases in real world output.

The second argument is a demographic one. The population profile of the United States has been wildly misshapen over the past twenty years. Tens of millions of young adults born during the Baby Boom years of 1946–1964, unskilled, semischooled, and very unsettled, streamed into the job queues, playing havoc with the unemployment rate, personal savings, and the quality of American work output. The populations of Japan and Germany, in contrast, have been much more heavily weighted toward mature adults in their forties and early fifties. Starting just about now the center of gravity of the American population is shift-ing radically once again. For most of the next two decades the age mix in America will be very much like those in present-day Japan and Ger-many. The labor force will grow very slowly, if at all; the demographic pressures making for unemployment will decline; output, income, and savings per worker should go up steadily.

Finally, the optimists foresee a steady decline in interest rates. Big-country governments, as a group—including the United States—have halved their budget deficits, measured as a percent of national income, over the past few years; some are already buying back their bonds. Over time reduced borrowing should mean lower rates. Meanwhile, global competition is already keeping a tight lid on inflationary wage and price increases. About half the long-term interest rate is a hedge against higher future inflation. As investors slowly come to believe that inflation isn't about to run out of control, the size of that hedge will drop. What's more, for a variety of complicated reasons, the demand for housing is expected to drop sharply. Real estate has absorbed an absurdly high proportion of American wealth over the past twenty years. Over the next ten much of that capital will become available for productive busi-ness investment, helping to keep interest rates low.

It is important to be clear about what the optimists are *not* saying. No one is claiming that recessions are a thing of the past. Indeed, some of the optimists, like many other economists, believe that after seven years of uninterrupted growth there is considerable likelihood of an American recession late this year [1989] or sometime in 1990. But recessions in the 1990s should be short-lived and shallow—more like the twenty years after the Korean War, when the American and world economies grew smoothly and steadily, with occasional pauses, to be sure, but without the jagged bounces, the stomach-churning spurts and plunges, that we saw from 1973 to 1982.

Nor is the boom absolutely guaranteed. No one should underestimate the ability of governments to derail a drive for efficiency and productivity in the name of local special interests. And while the United States will prosper mightily during a long-run cycle of global growth, there is no assurance that it will remain the world's economic kingpin, the imperious proclaimer and disposer of the postwar years. Indeed, that is not at all likely to be the case.

Finally, the optimists tend to ignore the darker side of the boom. It will be some time, perhaps a decade or more, before the boom's blotched underbelly draws much public attention. Some of the issues of public policy will be momentous: What, for example, is the relation between a government, no matter how powerful, and a company that is truly global in its operations, it management, and its ownership? But there will be few hardy contrarians to point out the problems of the boom. For the foreseeable future, if the optimists are right—and their case is a strong one—powerful industrial, economic, and demographic forces will be converging in a way that will offer a welcome respite from the traumas of the past two decades.

BIG BUSINESS GOES GLOBAL

Lee Iacocca's television ads blared, "Here's to You, America," as jet planes streaked red, white, and blue exhausts across the sky. There is no subtlety in the appeal: buying from Chrysler is your patriotic duty. But the pitch is more than normally disingenuous. For behind the smoke and clamor of the trade wars, Chrysler and the rest of the world's automotive majors are frantically forming engineering, production, and marketing alliances, literally carving up the world, to buttress their positions in the struggle for global car-sales supremacy. Who the eventual winners will be is far from certain, but what is clear is that only a small number of global companies will survive, and it is increasingly meaningless to speak of them as "American" or "Japanese" or "European" companies. (Even in Iacocca's ad the planes are French.)

The global restructuring of the automobile companies is being driven by the hurricane-force wind from East Asia that hit the industry in the 1970s, capitalism's "perennial gale of creative destruction" extolled by

Schumpeter. In a world where no market is safe, only the biggest and strongest companies can thrive. The alliances of the automotive majors look like the intricate crisscrossing battle lines in the Oriental game of Go. Take Chrysler itself: For all of Iacocca's red, white, and blue bunkum, auto-industry analysts say that Chrysler has the lowest percentage of American-made parts in its cars of any of the Big Three. It also owns 24 percent of Mitsubishi Motors and, through Mitsubishi, a share of the South Korean upstart Hyundai. Mitsubishi has long made cars under Chrysler's label, and the two companies run a fifty-fifty joint venture in Normal, Illinois, which will be producing 240,000 vehicles under both nameplates by the end of next year [1990].

Ford, with one third of its sales outside the United States, owns 25 percent of Mazda. Mazda makes cars in America for Ford; Ford will reciprocate by making compact trucks for Mazda; and the two companies trade parts. Each owns a piece of Korea's Kia Motors, which produces the Ford Festiva for export to the United States. Ford and Nissan, Japan's No. 2, swap vehicles in Australia and are planning a joint mini-van program in America. Ford and Volkswagen have merged into a single company in Latin America, which exports trucks to the United States.

General Motors holds a 41.6 percent stake in Isuzu, which is starting a joint venture in America with Subaru, which is partly owned by Nissan. GM also owns half of Daewoo Motors, Hyundai's major competitor in Korea. Daewoo makes Nissan cars for Japan and Pontiacs for America; soon it will be selling cars that were primarily designed by GM-Europe to Isuzu in Japan. GM has also teamed with Japan's No. 1, Toyota, to produce cars under both companies' labels in America and Australia. Their joint American operation will be turning out 100,000 small cars and trucks by 1991.

Europe is laced with partnerships, joint ventures, and production agreements. Honda America sells more cars in America than its parent does in Japan—its Accords were the seventh best-selling American-made car in 1988—and some analysts see the power balance within the company shifting to the American subsidiary. Honda plans to be exporting 70,000 cars from the United States by 1991.

Whether the Chryslers, or even the Hondas, can survive is far from clear. The weaker Japanese companies, like Daihatsu, are already dropping by the wayside. But no one can deny that cars, particularly American cars, are much better than they used to be. The American industry still isn't up to the level of the best Japanese companies, but standards are tighter, the work force is leaner, and the cars are more competitive. They have to be, because the Big Three can no longer be rescued by import controls. In a year or so global Japanese companies will be turning out two million high-quality American cars a year, with American workers, in American plants.

THE THIRD INDUSTRIAL REVOLUTION

The automobile industry is not the only one to have felt the competitive lash. For sheer compressed, earth-scorching savagery, it is difficult to match the violent recession that struck American manufacturing industries in 1981–1982. Whole sectors of the economy were brought to the brink of destruction. Just a few statistics convey the speed and extent of the humiliation. In 1975 America's machine-tool manufacturers dominated the world markets; by 1985 machine-tool exports were virtually nonexistent and German and Japanese machine tools were standard throughout American industry. In just a few years America's share of world semiconductor fabrication dropped from 60 percent to 40 percent. For all practical purposes, American companies simply exited the consumer electronics industry. *No* home radios, phonographs, black-and-white televisions, or cassette players are made in the United States any longer; American companies' share of the color-television market is minuscule. No American company makes VCRs or CD players. Industry after industry told the same story. "We were oxyacetylened," one Rust Bowl executive says—it was like being taken out with a blowtorch.

In retrospect, the storm warnings had been flying for years. American companies, feeling secure in their big home market, were complacent and lazy, running smug big-union and big-management cartels, turning out shoddy products that cost too much. And in industry after industry there are the same frantic struggle for global position and scrambling for strategic alliances that are reshaping the automobile industry. Texas Instruments and the Japanese computer-maker Hitachi are partners in developing the next-generation computer memory chip, the 16-megabit DRAM. The Japanese earthmoving-equipment-maker Komatsu is partnering with Dresser Industries in manufacturing and marketing throughout North and South America.

Whirlpool has joined with the Dutch electronics giant Philips to operate six major appliance factories in the Common Market. Philips has also joined with a group of American executives and the Taiwanese government to create an advanced semiconductor-fabrication plant in Taiwan, where Texas Instruments is also building an advanced chip factory with a Taiwanese partner. Ball, of Muncie, Indiana, has entered into a series of joint ventures around the world to market and manufacture its lightweight containers for soft drinks. The list goes on and on—USX and Kobe Steel, Armco and Kawasaki Steel. The misnamed National Steel Company is a fifty-fifty joint venture between an American and a Japanese company. Most of the pharmaceutical majors have entered into extensive cross-licensing agreements covering one another's products. Japan's robotics leader, FANUC, has partnerships with General Motors in robots, with General Electric in computerized factory control devices, and with the German firm Siemens in electronics.

The drive for global market share is forcing what Stanley Feldman, of Data Resources, calls the Third Industrial Revolution. A wholesale reordering of production technology is under way—computerized factory schedules and inventory controls to cut costs, intelligent production machinery that can shift processes in the middle of an assembly line. The object is to produce local products adapted to local markets, but reap world economies of scale in research and development, raw-materials sourcing, and production balancing.

IBM makes almost all its products in its local markets, but no other company can match its worldwide research-and-development base; and it enjoys the luxury of global sourcing of selected products from highly specialized factories. Sony has been steadily moving the design and production of its televisions to Europe and America, but a common worldwide chassis gives a cost advantage no local competitor can match. Engineers at General Electric–FANUC design factory controllers around the clock—at the end of each day the Americans download their work to a satellite link to Japan and then pick up the next morning where the Japanese left off. A global competitive standard squeezes out the small inefficiencies that build up in protected national markets—traditional labor practices, fustian management. "If you let your costs or your quality get out of line almost anywhere, someone is moving in to take advantage," says Steven Nagourney, the chief international strategist for Shearson Lehman Hutton.

Support for the optimists' claims comes from the striking rise in global manufacturing productivity during the 1980s. Manufacturing productivity in the United States has grown at an annual rate of 4.3 percent since 1982, one of the fastest sustained run-ups on record. (American steel is now actually cheaper than Japanese steel.) After slipping badly three years ago, Japan has surged back to the head of the productivity-league tables, with a 5.9 percent growth rate over the same period. And right behind Japan is Great Britain, for twenty years the living symbol of "Eurosclerosis." Europe's second fastest rate of output growth was in Italy—yes, *Italy*—just a hair faster than the rate in the United States. France, Germany, and Sweden are clustered behind the United States, with quite respectable rates of improvement.

Edward Yardeni, of Prudential-Bache, suspects that globalization is already a factor in the eerie lack of an American recession, the missing guest at the economic table whose absence has been so glaring for the past several years. He thinks there may be a new pattern of "rolling recessions" that affect whole industries around the world a cluster at a time, rather than the individual national recessions that economists are accustomed to looking for. He points to the recession in the computer industry in 1983–1984: computer and computer-component manufacturers were severely depressed globally, but not enough to take the steam out of the rest of the economy.

Even accepting the optimists' claim that the world is on the brink of an industrial boom, the question remains whether the United States will get much benefit from it. National economic behavior for the past two decades has not been impressive. The problem seems almost to be a moral and intellectual flabbiness—an inability to make spending choices, a low savings rate, a culture of self-centered consumerism and restless mobility, a lack of commitment and loyalty on the part of careless workers and job-hopping executives. The optimists' answer is that the past twenty years have been a most unusual period in American economic history.

THE COMFORTS OF DEMOGRAPHY

The world sings the praises of the "Great American Job Machine." Over the past twenty years the United States has created jobs for 38 million new workers, 17 million of them in the past seven years alone, when employment was virtually flat in almost every other industrial country. But in the same breath economists lament the slowdown in American productivity; manufacturing excepted, the output of American workers has been stagnant since the early 1970s.

The strong performance in job creation and the weak performance in productivity are, of course, two sides of the same coin. New workers swelled the American labor force by about 50 percent in the past twenty years, shifting the average age and experience of workers sharply downward. Not surprisingly, with lots of cheap new workers mobbing the doorway, businessmen increased hiring instead of investing in labor-saving machinery—a fancy industrial robot costs about as much as a year's wages for a hundred entry-level workers. Real wages and productivity were stagnant, and the business success stories were companies, like McDonald's, that learned how to pan for gold in that low-wage pool.

The transformation of the work force in the 1990s will be just as dramatic. People born at the Baby Boom's peak are in their thirties. About five years from now two thirds of the Baby Boomers will be over thirty-four. Walking shoes are already pushing high-priced running shoes off the sports-store counters. Another sign of the times is that McDonald's is beginning to invest in labor-saving machinery—two-sided grills, for instance. As the size of the work force begins to stabilize, and the average age and experience of workers move rapidly upward, business will start substituting equipment for low-wage workers. Capital spending, in fact, has been strong throughout the 1980s expansion, and with time productivity should soar. "Couch potatoes" are not exciting people. The soul does not thrill at the sight of forty-year-old workaholics, raising kids and paying their mortgages, but as the economy's centerweight, they have it all over the long-haired pot-smokers of a couple of decades ago.

The critical variable will be the American savings rate, which, in fact, has shown signs of rising again after hitting an all-time low in 1987. Personal savings are the ultimate source of all productive investment. It is the high Japanese savings rate—as much as 18 percent of all personal income—that has financed Japan's global industrial conquest. It is the high savings rates in other countries, as well, that have allowed America to dance through the economic raindrops in recent years; foreign capital picks up the tab for the American budget and trade deficits. The optimists argue, plausibly enough, that an older, more productive work force, with higher real incomes, will save more. Yardeni expects a 10 percent savings rate in the mid-1990s, roughly double the current one.

Unfortunately, for all its importance, the personal savings rate is one of the least precise of statistics. The number is merely a residual of two huge data series, for personal income and personal spending, each of which involves thousands of samples, estimates, and interpolations. The difference between the two is "savings." Tiny estimating errors or changes in method in calculating the two big series can cause proportionally enormous swings in the residual. "There are no data relating savings to age group," John Gorman, a key analyst at the Department of Commerce, says flatly. "None."

Yardeni points to sample data indicating that people under thirty, particularly those with lower incomes, are "dissavers"—they spend more than they earn. People over forty, particularly those with higher incomes, do most of the saving. Other economists challenge those findings, citing studies that show only inconsistent relationships. All the studies have major methodological problems. For anyone who wants to believe that the optimists are right, though, this is the vital sign that bears the closest watching.

Interestingly, the demographic tides in Japan suggest that the long surge of Japanese industry is reaching a cyclical peak. An International Monetary Fund study says that the impact of demographic change in Japan will be the "most extreme" of any in the industrialized countries, as the number of aged dependents doubles starting about 1995.

Bill Emmott, the business-affairs editor of The Economist, foresees a steadily Westernizing Japanese economy in an important new book, The Sun Also Sets. The very high Japanese savings rate will drop as the workers now in their fifties reach retirement age and begin to draw on their savings, at roughly the same time that American savings, one hopes, will begin a long rise. Consumer spending is already rising strongly as young Japanese adults, with no memories of the postwar deprivations, begin to insist on the same amenities in housing and public services, and the same range of specialty consumer items, enjoyed by other rich nations. Emmott suggests that spending on overseas travel and other services could equal or exceed the return on overseas investment income. He assumes that Japan will continue to be a formidable competitor, of course, but eventually as the leader of a bloc of yen-oriented industrial powers—much as West Germany is the leader of a de facto European bloc—rather than as a world-conquering golden horde.

OF GOVERNMENTS, REAL ESTATE, AND INTEREST RATES

The last thread in the bright economic tapestry the optimists are weaving is the forecast of steadily falling interest rates. Falling rates would ease debt pressures and spur industrial investment. The array of forces lining up to push rates down is, in fact, an impressive one. In the first place, interest rates are partly an anticipation of inflation. There is a good argument that global competitive pressures clamp a firm ceiling on prices. Coopers & Lybrand, the international accounting and consulting firm, says flatly that only the "fierce worldwide competition in price and quality" can explain the tame behavior of prices during the prolonged American economic expansion. Alan Greenspan, the chairman of the Federal Reserve, says that "integration of the world's production facilities" heads off inflation by unstopping production bottlenecks.

At the same time, government borrowing is declining in virtually all the industrial countries, which should press rates down further. Roland Leuschel, the chief investment strategist at Banque Bruxelles Lambert, has even raised an unfashionable alarm over "a looming shortage of government bonds." On average, government borrowing as a percent of national income fell by about half from 1984 to 1988—in the United States from five percent of GNP in 1985 to about three percent now (or two percent if state and local surpluses are counted, as they should be). Britain is already in surplus, retiring perhaps $23 billion of debt this year. Australia and Denmark are running surpluses, as will Japan and Germany within a year or two. America's cash deficit will disappear sometime after 1995, as collections for the next century's Social Security overhang begin to accumulate. Scarcer bonds mean higher bond prices—another way of saying lower interest rates.

Even more important is the expected drop in housing demand in the United States. Housing was the characteristic American investment of the 1970s and 1980s. Not only did the sheer number of young adults increase sharply, but they moved out of their parents' households sooner, got married later, and formed more separate households. To further boost housing demand, the next-fastest-growing age group consisted of those over sixty-five, who for the first time ever decided to keep their own houses instead of living with married children.

Throw in a tax code that depressed the real cost of mortgages, an inflationary psychology that encouraged people to borrow against real property, and truly spectacular capital gains from leveraged real-estate investments—and housing starts exploded. All those factors will run in reverse in the 1990s. The number of young adults will drop, and the number of people over the age of sixty-five will stabilize. More-traditional family relationships among aging Baby Boomers will reduce the number of separate households. A Brookings Institution study forecasts about a 30 percent drop in demographically driven housing demand through the decade of the 1990s. Already the inventory of single-family homes for sale has risen about a third since 1982. A shift of savings away from real estate to bank deposits or stocks and bonds would mean some rough adjustments for homeowners who are still hoping to make a killing on their houses, but would be a major shot of adrenaline for American industry.

Yardeni has pulled together all the roses blooming in the economic garden into a bouquet he calls New Wave Economics. "After the stock market crashed in 1987," he says, "and everyone was filled with gloom, I decided to look at what might go right. Frankly, I was amazed at how positive all the fundamentals were. The work force is getting older, more skilled, and more productive. Savings should rise just as government borrowing and the demand for housing slow down. Global competition and a resurgence in manufacturing are a lid on inflation. We're looking at low interest rates, a long-term shift from housing to business investment, and a big increase in productivity and real incomes. It's a cycle that could go on for a long time."

BUT WILL IT HAPPEN HERE?

There is still the pervasive worry that American industry has been weakened to the point where we are slipping to second-class economic status. It is a serious issue, and there *is* genuine cause for concern in specific industries.

But the question of America's future success in a global economy is too often confused with the issue of our regaining our postwar position as economic dictator to the world. That role is gone forever, and no one should wish it otherwise. The income of urban adults in the major industrialized countries is now practically uniform. That was the explicit objective of American statesmanship at the end of the war, the crowning adornment of our postwar foreign policy, a grand aim expressly adopted, pointedly pursued, and unambiguously attained. To seize upon that success as an index of relative "decline" is to miss the point.

The shock of the economic turmoil of the 1970s, the recessionary gales of the early 1980s, and the sudden onslaught of the Japanese have tended to exaggerate the perception of decline. There are real problems in many American industries, but they need to be kept in perspective. Some statistics:

- According to a detailed study recently completed by the British Treasury, real output per American worker, abstracted from currency fluctuations, is still the highest in the world, and perhaps half again higher than output per worker in Japan.
- Over the past twenty years American companies have increased their share of world exports. But American companies have spread their operations around the globe, and their sales overseas do not show up in American trade data.
- The U.S. share of world output actually increased slightly during the 1980s. Asian and Japanese shares of world output also increased, but at the expense of Europe, not of America.
- The United States never "de-industrialized." Manufacturing's share of GNP, at about 23 percent, has been virtually unchanged since 1947.

The world-thumping success of Japanese companies in high-visibility consumer-product manufacture obscures how staggeringly unproductive the greater part of the Japanese work force is. The ratio of wholesale to retail sales, for instance, a measure of how long it takes goods to get to consumers, is more than double that in America. Food is extremely expensive, partly because of agricultural protectionism and partly because there are no world-class Japanese food-processing and distribution companies. According to Nomura Securities, Kraft could import cheese to Japan and sell it for half the price charged by local businesses, which, of course, are clamoring for import protection.

The Japanese pharmaceutical market is the second largest in the world, but there are no world-class Japanese pharmaceutical companies. The largest Japanese chemical company, Asahi Chemical, would barely make the list of the top ten in America. The Japanese construction industry is notoriously fragmented, inefficient, and mobster-ridden. It is also politically powerful, and has managed, by and large, to exclude much more capable American companies from bidding on major public projects.

The importance of agriculture, mining, and logging in America is sometimes viewed as a measure of backwardness. But as practiced in the United States, these are becoming high-tech industries. The price of coal has dropped by about a fifth in recent years, primarily because of improvements in mining machinery. The continuing flaps over bovine somatotropin, the hormone that boosts cows' milk production, and over the use of recombinant gene products as pesticides or crop enhancers demonstrate the impact of technology on the modern farm.

And the American high-technology position is still very strong. In the booming market for mini-supercomputers—miniaturized powerhouses that can chew through scientific problems that would tie up even the largest business computers for years—the only manufacturers are still American. In the computerized-work-station market—very high-powered personal computers—Sony is still chasing the medium-sized California firm Sun Microsystems in Japan. America has no peer in medical technology, fiber optics, genetic engineering, or computer-aided design.

Clearly, there are problems with American competitiveness, as was documented most recently by MIT's Commission on Industrial Productivity last spring. Michael P. Schulhof, the vice-chairman of Sony Corporation of America, points to an American penchant for quick fixes. "American businessmen seem to think they can catch up in high-definition television with a year or so of federal funding," he says. "That's not true. We've been building those technologies for twenty years. Besides that, I won't believe American companies are serious until they stop trying to sell left-hand-drive cars in Japan."

Schulhof's comment is on the mark. When American import restraints and the falling dollar raised the price of Japanese cars, American automobile executives, for all their Iacoccan swagger, took the easy way out: instead of winning back their markets, they raised prices, trumpeted a turnaround, and paid themselves multimillion-dollar bonuses with the windfall profits. Christopher Willard, at Dataquest, a high-technology market-research firm, says, "There's nothing wrong with American technology. But there is an attitude difference. American companies won't manufacture complicated low-volume chips if they can't make a profit on them. Japanese companies will take the job if they think they'll learn something that will help them later on, regardless of the short-term profits."

The American lead in high technology, indeed, is part of the problem. American R&D expenditures, as a percentage of GNP, are actually slightly higher than Japan's, but about a third of them are defense-related. America has more scientists and engineers than Japan, Great Britain, and West Germany combined, but much of their work is devoted to building weapons. As a consequence, America has unmatched high-end machining, for example—missile gyroscopes and submarine propeller blades must be finished to exquisitely precise standards—but has been thoroughly outclassed in mid-technology applications.

America is too big, too rich, and too resourceful to be shut out of the global boom. Even the pessimist Gary Shilling sees America as regaining much of its competitiveness longer-term: "Japan may actually have a tougher time than the United States," he says, "because of demographics and excess capacity."

As global companies continue the relentless push into local markets, America will become a haven for high-productivity manufacturing.

American companies will be clear winners in some global industries, and American companies that have taken to heart the lessons of the past ten years will be winners in every industry. To be sure, a large number won't make the grade and will be swallowed up by stronger Asian or European competitors, but it will be increasingly difficult for consumers or workers to tell the difference.

CAN THE BOOM BE STOPPED?

Even the most convinced optimists concede that there is a long parade of horribles capable of pushing the world off a fast-growth track. Some of them are unpredictable and probably uncontrollable. Can the world ecosystem sustain a prolonged cycle of global industrial growth? Images arise of a Bhopal or a Chernobyl on a tremendous scale, setting back economic development for a generation. Might there be a new Ice Age in the Cold War? A world nervously fingering triggers in the wake of, say, a revolution in Eastern Europe might snuff out the free flow of goods and wealth-creating technology essential to a sustained cycle of world economic development.

But the most dangerous obstacle to a new industrial golden age, and the only one really within our political control, is the economic national-ism brewing in the halls of Congress and the councils of Europe. Europe is the prime example: it has attempted to protect its markets and its national producers for forty years. Engorged with government sub-sidies, the British automobile industry simply rolled over and died. None of the global car companies that will survive a decade from now is likely to be European. Semiconductor and computer "initiatives" pro-liferated throughout Europe in the 1970s; the result was a virtually com-plete takeover by the Americans, as national resources were dissipated on losers.

There are some signs that American businessmen recognize that pro-tectionism is against their interests. Caterpillar, for example, has op-posed the recent steel and ball-bearing import restraints, because they raise the cost of its production. "Managed" semiconductor prices made American computer companies less competitive, and managed trade in cars drew the Japanese into the high-profit luxury segment of the Ameri-can market.

It may, in fact, be too late for the protectionists to do great damage; the interventions required would need to be truly malign and persistent. Political consensus tends to coalesce slowly, and the trade spats already have an anachronistic air. The rapid movement of global companies into local markets, the intricate networks of partnerships, joint ventures, and cross-ownership, make a mockery of the instinct to throw up ramparts. In 1986 American overseas sales were three times as large as American merchandise exports; half the trade deficit represents imports from American companies. The Japanese tire company Bridgestone is investing $1 billion to upgrade the North American operations of Firestone, its new American acquisition. Goodyear, the world's leading tire manufacturer, is increasing its investment to keep pace. The country and the economy are the winners.

The more challenging problems, in fact—ones that the optimists rarely allude to—will be the problems of success. In the late 1950s John Kenneth Galbraith complained about the slothful market-fixing practices of big American companies. He was right, and the complacent giants got their comeuppance in the surprise Japanese onslaught of the 1970s. But a decade or so from now, when a handful of global automobile companies, global computer companies, global chemical and food companies, global steel and consumer-electronics companies, emerge from the fierce competitive struggle in clear leadership positions, who will keep them in line? Where will Schumpeter's cleansing gale come from? From competitors on Mars? In an outcome that would be much to Schumpeter's chagrin, the global competitive struggle we are now witnessing may end in the Marxist nightmare of global monopolies.

Robert Reich, of Harvard University, worries that global competition, while opening unprecedented opportunities for educated manipulators of symbols, like lawyers, investment bankers, design engineers, and marketing experts, will impose iron limits on the wages of ordinary workers. At the very least, there is cause for grave concern about a laggard national educational system, turning out a class of permanent social dependents who are squeezed out of any meaningful economic role by the better schooling and work ethos prevailing abroad.

Success, in short, will bring momentous problems of its own. But if the optimists are right, and the world really is on the brink of a Schumpeterian golden age, there should be energy and resources enough to solve them.

Contributors

Timothy Garton Ash is a fellow at St. Antony's College, Oxford.

Bishara A. Bahbah is editor in chief of the *Return*, a Palestinian monthly magazine.

Richard J. Barnet is senior fellow of the Institute for Policy Studies in Washington, D.C., and the author of numerous books on international relations, most recently *The Rocket's Red Glare: When America Goes to War: The President and the People.*

George W. Breslauer is associate professor of political science at the University of California, Berkeley.

Zbigniew Brzezinski is professor at the Paul Nitze School of Advanced International Studies at Johns Hopkins University and counsellor at the Center for Strategic and International Studies. From 1977 to 1981 he served as President Carter's national security adviser.

Charles H. Ferguson is a postdoctoral research associate at the Center for Technology, Policy and Industrial Development at the Massachusetts Institute of Technology.

George M. Fredrickson is Robinson Professor of American History at Stanford University.

Raymond L. Garthoff is a senior fellow at the Brookings Institution. He served as executive officer of the U.S. delegation to the Strategic Arms Limitation Talks and has held various positions in the State Department.

Robert Gilpin is Dwight D. Eisenhower Professor of International Affairs in the Department of Politics and the Woodrow Wilson School of Public and International Affairs at Princeton University.

Walter Goldstein is Professor of International Relations at Rockefeller College at the State University of New York in Albany. He was the Ira Wade Professor of International Political Economy at the Johns Hopkins SAIS Bologna Center in Italy.

Marie Gottschalk is an associate editor of *World Policy Journal*.

Ivan L. Head, president of the International Development Research Centre, Canada, was formerly foreign policy adviser to Prime Minister Pierre Elliot Trudeau.

Louis Henkin is University Professor at Columbia University and co-director of the university's Center for the Study of Human Rights.

Stanley Hoffmann is chairman of the Center for European Studies and C. Douglas Dillon Professor of the Civilization of France at Harvard University.

Robert D. Hormats is vice chairman, Goldman Sachs International. He was Assistant Secretary of State for Economic and Business Affairs in 1981 and 1982.

Michael Howard, formerly Regius Professor of Modern History at Oxford, is now Robert A. Lovett Professor of Naval and Military History at Yale University. He is president of the International Institute for Strategic Studies.

Shireen T. Hunter is deputy director of Middle East Studies at the Center for Strategic and International Studies.

Chalmers Johnson is Rohr Professor of Public International Relations in the Graduate School of International Relations and Pacific Studies at the University of California, San Diego.

George F. Kennan, during his long diplomatic career, served many times in Moscow, including as Ambassador in 1952. In 1947, he devised the "containment" strategy that was to underlie postwar American policy toward the Soviet Union. He is now professor emeritus at the Institute of Advanced Study in Princeton, N.J.

Jeane J. Kirkpatrick is Leavy Professor of Government at Georgetown University and senior fellow at the American Enterprise Institute.

Charles Krauthammer is a contributing editor at the *New Republic.*

Rensselaer W. Lee III is president of Global Advisory Services, Inc. and an associate scholar of the Foreign Policy Research Institute.

Colin Legum has been analyzing political developments in Africa for nearly fifty years. He is consultant editor of the annual *Africa Contemporary Record* and editor of *Third World Reports.*

Frederick Lister served in the Secretariat of the United Nations from 1947 to 1981.

Scott B. MacDonald is an international economic adviser at the Comptroller of the Currency. The views expressed here do not express the views of the comptroller.

Jessica Tuchman Mathews is vice president of the World Resources Institute. She served on the National Security Council from 1977 to 1979 as Director of Global Issues.

Charles William Maynes is the editor of *Foreign Policy.*

Charles R. Morris is a principal at Devonshire Partners, a consulting firm specializing in mergers and acquisitions.

Joseph S. Nye, Jr., is Ford Foundation Professor of International Security at Harvard University.

Felix Rohatyn is senior partner in the investment firm of Lazard Freres & Co.

Jeffrey Sachs is professor of economics at Harvard University and an

adviser for the United Nations to several Latin American governments.

Steven L. Spiegel is professor of political science at the University of
California, Los Angeles, specializing in American foreign policy toward the Middle East.

Michael Vlahos is director of the Center for the Study of Foreign Affairs,
U.S. Department of State.

"Z" is a sometime observer of the Soviet scene.